STEEL POT: Volume 2

GOODNIGHT VIETNAM

A Vietnam Memoir

CURT STOCKER

Original Cover Art by: **Stacey Krull**

Olympus Story House

Dedicated to my wife: Michelle Luippold Stocker

Although she was never in the Army or went to Vietnam, for the past 28 years, she has lived daily with the twin legacies of the war; my PTSD and Agent orange-inflicted cancer. She is my forever Special Forces Soul Mate Trooper!

In Memory of:

John Imbach III
Frank Marion Streamer
Ken Lawlor
Michael R. Shapard
Colonel Willie O. Lawton, (USA Retired)
Captain William D. Robinson, Jr.
Thomas J. Roberts
Thomas Boyett
James Sweet
David E. Waterhouse.
&
(Since I do not know their real Vietnamese names)
Wally & the Beaver & the Girl Next Door

Prologue

STEEL POT Part 2: *"GOODNIGHT VIETNAM"*, is the second half of my 1968-69' Vietnam memoir.

Previously, in **STEEL POT**, after being drafted in 1967, I chose to take an extra year by enlisting for Armed Forces Radio, as the best way to still serve but avoid the infantry. That path would also allow me to continue in my chosen career of broadcasting. However, I soon discovered that reality in the Army had a way of changing and blindsiding one in unimaginable ways.

After completing the Defense Information Schools of Journalism and Broadcasting, I discovered that there were a couple of ways I could still end up in the Infantry and one way was to be assigned to the Army of the Republic of South Vietnam's (ARVN) Infantry, as a "Foreign Language Announcer" (FLA).

When I received those orders, I pointed out that I did not speak the Vietnamese language and thus, the Army would have to find someone else. But I was informed it was not necessary that I be fluent in Vietnamese, as I would just be "advising" the ARVNs, who would be making the actual "announcements." Still curious, I inquired; "what announcements are you talking about?" Turns out, the duties of an FLA were, when the infantry got the Viet Cong trapped in a tree line, or some such place, to get a close as possible and broadcast appeals for them to "Surrender or die!" That position had the same MOS (Military Occupation Specialty) number as the guy on the radio, who from the safety of Saigon, hollered, *"Good Morning Vietnam!"*

That unseen twist in my career path is what made me an embedded member of the ARVN 9th Infantry Division,14th Regiment, operating in the Mekong Delta of Vietnam. STEEL POT chronicles the majority of my experiences in the Vietnamese Infantry, although I am still attached to the ARVN Infantry, as *"GOODNIGHT VIETNAM"* begins here.

Obviously, nobody can remember everything, especially when the subject matter contains some events one would prefer to forget. The disclaimer you see in the preface of many books '...*this is a work of fiction and any resemblance of characters to real people or events,"* is not in play. This is a recollection about real people and real events. There is no fiction in this tale. I can affirm that I have made a genuinely sincere effort to insure this a true and accurate account of my Vietnam tour.

Within those bounds of accuracy, it sadly became true to me, with the passage of time, there were some exact names I could not recall. In those cases, I have bestowed nick names upon those individuals. Overall, there are no fictional situations or characters in the book and the nick names do represent real people involved in real events.

The only contrived portion of the book is the quoted dialogue. However, if you prefaced each quote with the caveat, *"...or words to that effect,"* their content is accurate to the events of each particular situation.

The names of Vietnamese individuals were even tougher for me to accurately recall. Most generally, I've defaulted to 'Nguyen', 'Kahn', or Thanh'. But in each case, anybody who is mentioned is a real person who was in the actual situation being detailed. It is my hope that our interpreter, Corporal Ba, and our ARVN Counterpart, Ti Ui Troung, survived the war and that one day I might see them again.

Along with the unavoidable violence of war, **STEEL POT** is a first-hand account of the GI marijuana subculture birthed by the Vietnam experience. The story of marijuana is so rife with false and contrived information, it has taken 80 years for the truth to begin winning out but eventually, it will!

I began smoking pot in October of 1966, over a year before I went to Vietnam, so I was not among uninitiated upon my arrival. In fact, I even brought some with me! But, I had no real concept of how much stronger Vietnamese weed was, compared to the Mexican strains we had available at the time. What a pleasant surprise it all was.

My mission is to demonstrate the truth to the people who have spent their lives demonizing marijuana; that they are completely wrong; scientifically, factually and morally. Their plan was to portray pot as the evil twin of heroin. Ironically, the DuPont Corporation became one of the main anti-marijuana proponents because they desired to stamp out the Hemp Industry. They're purpose and motivation was the immense profits they would reap by switching everybody over from hemp rope and canvas sails to their new inventions: *nylon rope and rayon fabrics.* The bald-face lies they invented about Hemp were totally off the scale, considering that industrial Hemp doesn't even get you high! Talk about irrational!

Even more interesting is the fact that once the laws were passed, they made it 99% impossible for anybody to conduct marijuana research! However, in our ever-changing atmosphere, the preponderance of new and accumulated marijuana research continues to disprove the *"Schedule One myth".*

Vietnam exposed such a preponderance of young Americans to marijuana, who otherwise would have never found it, that I firmly believe the war may be the single most important factor creating the conditions of today's looming legalization.

Chapter 1

Tedious. It had been that kind of day. Walking through the endless paddies and the tree lines created a tropical malaise of heat and exertion that was enough to bring anybody down. Then, a little bit of shooting would get everybody up on their toes only to have it followed by another long period of frightful anticipation, not knowing when it was going to start up again, although the Kid always knew it would. He was moribund with depression as he plodded along behind Lt. Wilson and Con, the skinny little rat faced RTO that Tu Ta Kim had given Wilson the morning of the Junk assault. Behind the Kid plodded Cpl. Ba, feeling clearly the same malaise as the Kid.

Upon his arrival back in Tra Vinh, the Kid had been greeted with a veritable tropical monsoon flood of very bad news. It first came from Wilson on the way back from the Tra Vinh airport. *"I've made some changes in the deployment of our resources,"* was the way he put it, *"I've called Boujold in from Tan An and sent him out to pull Bat mobile operations with Sweet in Cang Long. If you hate that place half as much as I do, you'll be happy to know we're out of there. Sweet even brought in your stuff. From now on, Stocker, you and me are joining up with Captain Metz and "D" Company... and our first tactical operation with the Battalion is tomorrow. Aren't you excited?"*

To death. I'm excited to fucking death, you maniac bastard! The Kid cursed him as he pulled his boots out of the mud of the paddies with every step. If looks could kill, Wilson's head, bobbing along in front of him, with his steel pot bouncing up and down with his uneven gait, would have long ago exploded.

At least I got that 1049 for the transfer and my agreement to extend done and sent off while I was in Can Tho. If I'd have waited to do it down here, it would take it an extra month to make it through channels. Shit. I just hope to God I live that long! My God, if anybody would have told me I'd be extending for another year here before last week, I'd have told them to go pick shit with the sparrows.

1

Once again, D Co. had been forced to abandon the easy walking along the tops of the dykes to struggle in the muddy waters of the paddies themselves, by the presence of numerous foot mines implanted in the dykes. It was 1600 hours and D Co. had suffered 10 casualties from the mines, 3 of them KIAs.

Up ahead, the Kid spies Captain *"what's his name?"*, raising up his M-16 rifle horizontally, in the classic 'halt' motion, while he is being handed the mic by his RTO. The officer was an archetypical big tall blond guy from Minnesota who was new in-country and to the regiment. The reason he was there was that Metz had developed a bad case of dysentery and had gotten medevac'd to Saigon and *"Minnesota"* volunteered to fill his slot. He was a man anxious to go out on his first operation, looking for some action, and he wasn't disappointed.

A few hours earlier he enjoyed his baptism of fire and his first time ever being shot with a fully automatic weapon all rolled up into one! And Charlie had come just a hair from taking him out on his first shot! 6 hours later *Minnesota* was still buzzed on the adrenalin from that!

The Kid stood still in the stifling heat and when Cpl. Ba got to where he was at, he stopped too. Sharing a drink from the Kid's canteen, they both obviously agreed they didn't want to be standing anywhere near the prime target the two officers and their RTOs presented, confabbing out in the middle of the paddies.

After a lot of head nodding and *yes-siring,* the captain returned the mic to the RTO and with the other, he signaled a directional change.

Shit! We are heading for the nearest tree line!

It never made any sense to the Kid, the way the battalion ran around in the paddies chasing the ghosts of the VC and how they figured to corner them and why they never did. There was no way he understood how to use the map to find coordinates as accurately as they did when they called in airstrikes and artillery. He had no use for any of that. And although he had now seen a Hoi Chanh, some prisoner VC and others dead, the Kid had still never seen a Charlie running free in the woods, a target to be shot at but that mattered not because the Kid had lost all desire to shoot anybody. *Captain Minnesota*, on the other hand, was going off the deep end. *Look at that, the captain has an M-16 and I'm carrying a pistol! What a scream! Yes, he's Wilson's kind of man! Really fucking in to this war. The two of them will probably become best buddies.*

As the ARVNs made their way up to the tree line, the scene remained calm; nobody disputed their entry. Upon breaching the palm and brush

2

thicket, the Kid imagined he was on one of Dante's lower levels of hell. Of course, there were no loud speakers and no Ti Ui Troung. In fact, since the security breakdown incident north of Vinh Long Bridge, Troung had refused to have anything to do with Wilson and the Lt. frankly didn't give a shit since he wasn't interested in PSYOPS anyway.

Picking their way through the underbrush, they soon realized this particular tree line was in a wild state. Tree lines situated near hamlets were groomed for ease movement and use of the soil but nobody apparently lived within or routinely passed through this neck of the woods and it was choked with foliage. *This fucking place is south of the boondocks! I can't see five feet in front of me!* ARVN pfcs hacked away with machetes as the command squad and its cover made their way slowly through the dense, fertile greenness of the delta, where water, sun and soil combined to make the plant life an entity with which to be reckoned.

The slow pace of the movement gave the Kid plenty of time to think. And foremost on his mind was the second flood of bad news waiting for the Kid at Tra Vinh. It came at him out of the immense stack of mail that had piled up for him in his absence. There were 8 letters from Flo but the second one he opened was the one that contained the bombshell.

Sept. 24, 1969

Dear Curt,

I don't know where to start. Do you remember when I told you to be careful what you write because I thought My Mom had been reading my mail? Well, it turns out I was right! She got a hold of the letter you wrote on Sept 17, where at the end you said you'd tap your heels like the Wizard of OZ and say you wanted to be at the Traveler's Motel? When she saw that, she got out the phone book, found out there was a Traveler's Motel and then she went there and saw that you were registered the day we went to Disneyland!

Needless to say, the shit really hit the fan and she was on my case like a rat on cheese. She said she knew the only reason we'd go to a motel is to do it! Then she accused of being a whore and it got really ugly. She said things about you that I'm surprised didn't burn your ears in Vietnam! You are the worst thing to walk the surface of the earth. All you wanted was my virginity and you don't really love me. She cried about losing her little girl and it was all that evil Curt's fault!

At first, I was really pissed off that she read my mail. Then I was mad at you for writing something like that, that could get us into this kind of trouble. But after I thought about it, I figured, my mom loves me and I'll

3

always love her because she's my mom, plain and simple. In her mind, I was going to be a virgin until the day I was married and then only have sex to have babies. One time for each baby would most likely suit her idea of how Lo and I and Jacquie should live our lives. Anyway, I got to thinking, I don't want her mad at me for the rest of the year, so I have decided to make the decision that we are no longer engaged.

She is right. We are too young. Oh, I will still write to you. I can't totally turn off what I feel for you, but for now, I think it is best that we consider ourselves un- engaged. You are free. That should make you happy.

I hope you understand, Curt. I'm still waiting for you to get back and every time I watch the news and see that GIs have been wounded or killed, I worry and worry about you. That was so sad when you wrote me that John Imbach was killed. I know how sad you must be. I pray everybody else is safe.

And even though we are no longer engaged, I have a feeling that...

I'll see you later!

Flo.

He had almost committed it to memory. *My 'Dear John' letter. That fat bastard of a first Sergeant back at group said I'd probably get it before a half year was up and he was right on the freaking money. And he said if I wanted to be at Armed Forces Radio, I could do it by extending and that's what I've fucking done. I think I'm going crazy. At least I made it to 21!*

Of course, Flo's letter was not signed "love." But she did sign it with their signature line, so to him, that meant there was still hope. Plus, when the Kid realized the letter had already been in the mail when he did it with Li, he experienced a complete absolution from the guilt he'd been experiencing for that act. *Yes, Flo, we are no longer engaged. But we'll have to see what happens when we finally see each other again. If we ever do see each other again. In a day or two, she'll have the letter about me taking an extra year for radio Saigon, but that won't mean squat to her now that we are no longer engaged. We certainly won't be married so we won't be getting together in Hawaii on the second tour for R & R. Her mom wants to kill me. Hmmm. She didn't say how her father felt about me. I always felt that A.J. liked me more than she did. Oooop! Incoming!*

Hitting the ground, the Kid looked around to locate Wilson, who was easy to find, at the base of the antenna that stuck up out of the foliage, from Con's back, like the stick and flag in a golf hole, because the little rat like

4

man was never far from him in the field. *Con's getting a little lazy with the antenna; he usually grabs the tip and bends it down.* Laying low in the bush, listening for more rounds, in the eerie quiet that followed the volley, the Kid noticed the soft patting sounds of raindrops on the palm fronds and realized that it was beginning to rain. Tomorrow would be Oct.1st; the monsoon still had a couple of weeks to go.

Radios crackled and the leaders of men from the officer's corps rose up and signaled, to any troopers who might happen to be able to see them through the foliage that it was time to move up. The ARVNs responded and the unit continued to move through the bush, brushing off the occasional AK-47 round as having the same nuisance quality as a mosquito. *Until you get bit.*

Making his way through the twisted foliage of the tree line, the Kid tried to envision his latest 1049 making its way up the chain of command, to Saigon and Sgt. Shamus and Lt. Colonel Armstrong, where they'd sign it and save him from this madness. *It must be in Saigon by now, maybe even to AFVN. Tomorrow is October. If they sign it, that means I'm almost halfway to being out of PSYOPS! Oh yes, living in this country would be a cakewalk if I didn't have to come out here and get shot at and I never had to see or do anything with Wilson again as long as I live! I could have Li as my kept woman, set her up in an apt. Show her I really care for her... Get laid all of the time and never have to visit a whore house! But if I'm paying her anything at all, doesn't that still make her a whore? She's really hot... do I want to marry her? No. Do I know what I want? No. Is being single a good thing or a bad thing? I don't know. I think I still want Flo more than anything on earth.*

The Kid could not hold that thought because the trees 30 meters in front of them exploded and the whole command element immediately hit the ground. The flash was followed by a huge rolling ball of black smoke and yelling and screaming but there were no additional explosions or small arms fire so it apparently wasn't a mortar attack or an all-out assault; *it must have just been another booby trap.*

This kind of pressure was sometimes harder to take than actually being shot at, walking along, dreading the taking of every next step, because of the fear that it would trigger the *Rube Goldberg cocktail of death,* as the Kid had christened it.

Advancing to the location of the incident, they discovered another 4 casualties: 2 of them KIAs. D Co. had now lost five dead and had 9 wounded to show for the day and still no body count. There was no way a medivac could come into the woods; they'd have to haul them to an edge. And the fact that they were attempting to advance through booby trapped and contested woods, astronomically reduced the chances the wounded would get the major medical attention they needed any time soon.

The two newly dead ARVNs were wrapped in ponchos and four soldiers prepared to carry them out of the woods, tied like dead deer hanging from poles. The unit medics had stretchers for the two wounded men so in all, with the casualties and the 14 men it took to haul the KIA's and the wounded that couldn't walk, the VC had taken 28 soldiers from the front line.

When the rain came harder and harder so did the VC, apparently encouraged by the knowledge that the ARVNs couldn't call on any air support. At least 3 automatic weapons opened up on the command unit and with the response, so much lead from both sides zinged through the foliage than all the Kid knew he could do was clutch the ground and hope they wouldn't throw in any mortars! Cpl. Ba, likewise hugging the ground near the Kid's boots had actually pulled out his rosary!

Suddenly, popping up out of the foliage about 10 meters off to their left, a M-79 grenadier caught the Kid's attention in his peripheral vision. Quick as the Kid had ever seen, he loaded and fired off four rounds, fanning them in an arc, sweeping across their front. It silenced the AK's and when it did, an entire squad up and charged off into the murky green, shooting their M-16s on fully automatic, trying and capitalize on the overall effect of the fuselage just laid down. Captain "Minnesota" was right behind them, and Wilson with Con followed hotly while the Kid and Ba brought up the rear. There were no VC bodies to be found.

The SOP of the Charlie element ranging in front of the ARVNs was to let them advance a little, then nailing them with rifle fire before taking off again.

I think I've got it figured out why we don't see them; it occurred to the Kid as he rose up for one advance, when they run, they know where we are and where they are going... and when we run, we chase them but don't know where they're going and then they always stop and we eventually come right to them!

He finally caught up to Wilson at a point where their advance was stopped at a break in the foliage. An opening of about 80 meters, or about a half dozen paddy dykes distance stood between them and the other tree line their maneuver map said they should enter at this point. If they didn't cross at this point, it was easy to see, the open distance was far greater further along. The VC were already on the other side and were not going to allow the ARVNs any sort of free passage.

6

While they huddled on the ground, behind some fairly stout fallen palm tree trunks, the Kid related his enlightened theory of why they never saw the Cong. "In a nutshell, they know where they're going and they know where we are, we don't know where they are or where we're going!" he smiled.

Now Con the RTO didn't understand a word that the Kid had said but when the Kid smiled when he stopped talking, Con smiled too, waiting for Wilson to answer.

"Stocker, there may be something to what you're saying," Wilson panted as he was catching his breath, "but sooner or later, we'll catch them or get them with an air strike... one way or another, we'll get those bastards!"

"And when we do," the Kid saw an opportunity to advance his agenda, "shall we cup our hands and pretend they are loudspeakers so that we can complete our mission of convincing them to surrender?"

The look on Wilson's face turned from neutral to anger in a matter of a couple of seconds. He disliked it immensely when the Kid got up the nerve to *question* what he was doing. He was in charge, and he was going to do whatever the fuck he wanted! And what Wilson wanted was to be in the thick of the fight and to finally collect his scalp. "Stocker, your problem is that you can't get with the program. You're still stuck on that PSYOPS thing when the Vietnamese Polwar man won't even show up at the dance. How we gonna do any PSYOPS? And I've told you before and I'll tell you again, Uncle Sam would want his soldiers in the field, fighting, not sitting around looking for a way to get out of work!"

Now the Kid showed a little bit of neck hackle, "Hey, am I here? Am I not laying in the same fucking mud, being bitten by the same bugs getting shot at with the same bullets you are? Sir? But if by 'get with the program', you mean get my M-16 and pretend I'm an ARVN private, I don't think that is in my official Army job description, not to mention I don't think our superiors back in Can Tho would appreciate hearing that some field team was completely ignoring the mission.

Escalation!

Wilson lay there, with bullets flying over their heads, contemplating this thinly veiled threat from his enlisted lackey. Giving the Kid a genuinely hard look, he said, "Don't you even for a second think that Captain Ronnie Smith, my good friend and buddy, isn't aware of, or supportive of all our activities here with the ARVN 14th Regiment." Now he was really pissed. "Going over my head in the chain of command *is not an option for you*, Specialist. You will not *accuse* me of dereliction of duty… I do *my job*!" now he was literally shouting, "Don't you *ever* fucking fuck with me, Stocker!"

At the first lull in the firing, half a dozen ARVNs jumped up almost in unison and with the riflemen putting out tons of cover, charged out to the first row of dykes and dove safely behind it. They recovered and prepared to fire and working smoothly like a real team, rocked over, laid their M16's on the top of the dyke for support and blazed away while the remainder of the squad moved out to join them. And with that, Wilson was up and off, running and dodging out into the opening hell bent for the dyke. The Kid, not quite through with the conversation, bolted after him, with Con dogging him step for step with the totally unarmed Ba bringing up the rear.

This is such bullshit. We are so off our mission, maybe your friend Capt. Ronnie will let you get away with this crap, but I'll bet Group might like to know about this. No wonder we don't get any Hoi Chanhs.

The PSYOPS element came to land up against the dyke in a cluster, something the manual advises against, clustering, but there they were, all but Con. *Where's Con?* The Kid craned his head back to see that Con was stopping to pick something up. *What the hell?* The little RTO plucked something from the water that the Kid couldn't quite identify, then wheeled and dashed for safety, coming to rest behind the dike, ten meters to their left.

No sooner had the PSYOPS team arrived at the dyke than half the ARVNs commenced to firing and half began running toward the tree line, doing their fair share of shooting as well and lo, they get in and keep going, except for a couple, that wave the rest of the men on.

Rising, Wilson, the Kid and Ba step up on top of the dyke and over to the other side and begin moving toward the trees. There is no shooting for the moment. Con walks over from where he'd ended up and taps the Kid on the shoulder. The Kid turns to see, and Con holds out his hand and in it is the Kid's .38! Mouth falling open, the Kid's hand flies to his holster and yes, it is empty. *It must have fallen out during the run to the dyke! Thank God Con saw that, or I'd be totally unarmed!*

"Wow!" the Kid took it from the smiling and nodding Con, "*cam on u lam bou coup!* thanks a lot, buddy! You saved my ass!"

Laughing punctuated their conversation; Wilson had seen the whole thing. "Guess you owe him big time... at least a carton, I'd say," he smirked.

"Yeah. A carton at least!" Flipping open the cylinder, the Kid looked to see how muddy the pistol had gotten from falling into the paddy water. *Not too bad,* he flipped it shut. *Gotta be more careful!*

By the time 1630 hours had rolled around, D Co's total number of casualties for the day still stood at 14; of which 5 were dead and 9 wounded and the VC body count was still zero. The realization that it was time to establish a perimeter for before dark was starting to sink in across the board when the radios started popping with word that the unit had managed to capture two VC; a man and a woman! The prisoners were now being held at a collection of huts not far from them, at the location of the proposed headquarters position for the night, at the center of a perimeter that was now being established.

"A perimeter! Now that's some good news!" the Kid nodded positively at Ba, they were both physically and mentally shot, "things will be better when we rest and get a bite. Even an hour's sleep tonight would be nice.

"Prisoners!" Lt. Wilson exclaimed, "this should be interesting!"

"Oh, you don't get a lot of prisoners?" *Minnesota* inquired, winded but still game in this newness of his status as a combat veteran.

"Uh, no," Wilson entails, "in fact, up until now, every operation we've been on, we've never seen any prisoners taken. Seen some body count, but no prisoners. We helped guard some prisoners on a work detail in Tra Vinh, once, but the VC down here have a 'fight it out' mentality, that's for sure!"

"This must be your lucky day, Sir," the Kid caught the big guy's attention, "go on your first operation, get shot at for the first time and now, you're going to get to see a real live Viet Cong all on day one! Did I leave anything out?"

"A clean kill," the big blond Capt. with the almost square jaw allowed himself a second to ponder. "Yep, a clean kill and it would have been like bowling 300!"

After hearing the clean kill declaration, the Kid was convinced that *Minnesota* was just like Wilson, really into the war and not one bit squeamish about what one must do.

The Kid, on the other hand, had recently become more squeamish about what was going on around him. His first reaction to the dead ARVNs today had been sort of *"ho hum, no big deal. Seen lots of dead guys, now. Dead people happen all the time. Then, a few minutes later, it was what am I thinking? Dead people and wounded people all around me and all I can do is live the next moment. Will I be dead or alive? I must be getting numbed out to the whole fucking scene here, if I take dead men as ho hum! I want to live, like Susan Heyward in that movie. Look at scared shitless little Ba. Every time he looks at me, I think he's thinking: Americans get to leave the war at the end of a year, but an ARVN is in for the duration! I can't imagine being sentenced to this forever... wait a minute, if I get killed out here, it was forever.*

It took them about 20 minutes of whacking through the bush to locate the coordinates on the map that had been selected as the headquarters position. It turned out to be the four abandon huts set in a small clearing around a typical rural fishpond. As the 2nd platoon command element approached, the work of establishing the perimeter was in progress. They were all very happy that it wasn't any darker, lest they be taken for the enemy. The ARVNs were busy digging rifle pits and setting claymores and establishing fields of fire and working like a colony of ants on speed trying to set up before it became pitch black.

Two of D Co's platoons had converged to set up the night's fortifications. In charge of everything, was Tu Ta Than, the ranking Vietnamese officer on the operation. The PSYOPS crew had operated with him on overnights before. The fiftyish, almost totally gray headed ARVN major nearly always had a pleasant little smile on his near oval face. Little because he had some of the thinnest lips the Kid had ever seen.

Than had been calling the shots all day, while maneuvering with the 1st platoon and he must have had this place in mind all the time because he seemed completely comfortable in it, compared to the beehive of hurried activity that surrounded them. He sat on a knee-high 3-legged round stool that had been brought out of one of the huts, by the edge of the fish pond and casually smoked a Salem. His steel pot sat on the ground at the tip of his *Dumai* stick, the top of which lay propped against his legs.

"Hey, Ba, look! It's Tu Ta Than! You know he sets a good, safe perimeter!" the Kid lavished praise on Than, in hopes of raising Ba's morale.

But then his eyes found them, off to his right; the two prisoners. They are back against the foliage, kneeling on the ground, bound with bamboo sticks stuck through their elbows behind their backs with their hands tied in front. *A man and a woman?* The Kid walks toward them and as he draws closer, he makes a frightening discovery. *Oh my God! This isn't a man and a woman... they are fucking teenagers! Neither one of them can be more than 16 or 17... They're freaking children!*

The Kid kneels down slowly to take a closer look at them. *They're both in distress, from running and getting caught. I wonder if these two were part of who's been fighting us all day.* The boy was wearing faded red shorts and if he'd had a shirt, it was either ripped or torn off and his brown skin over young muscles was scratched and bleeding several places, as if his escape route of last resort had been through a thorn thicket. His black hair was shaggy but not too long past his ears and his face was a little on the broad side but not square and his eyebrows were bushy. *Why, he looks a little bit like Tony Dow! Wally, in Leave it to Beaver! And she looks like.... oh no.... her face reminds me of Shauna McConnell, the girl next door!*

10

In fact, the girl prisoner, to the boy's left, looked so remarkably like Shauna, the girl who grew up next door to him on Bluebell Street, in Boulder, that it really shook the Kid up. *They are probably close to the same age.* She was 3 years younger than the Kid and behind him in school at the point where the Kid was always getting out of one school as she was coming in and thus, it was not acceptable for them to date. But that never stopped the Kid from thinking she was one of the cutest girls in all of Boulder. Sometimes after his paper route on Sunday morning, he sneaks over and wake her up by knocking quietly on her window and they would talk through the screen. They both had the hots for each other but knew they couldn't do anything about it.

And here was a girl VC, about her age, with slim build and black hair to match, cut shoulder length with shaggy bangs across the front. She was dressed in blue shorts and her torn and muddy muted green blouse was staying closed only by the grace of two remaining buttons. Shauna had brown eyes and she had brown eyes, but the main thing was the warrior girl's jaw line and chin; it was cut fine like Shauna's; not jutting, but well defined. In fact, the way Shauna looked had a lot to do with why the Kid went for the girls he did; dark-haired Donna and Flo both had a distant resemblance to her.

Three ARVN PFCs stood guard over them, their M-16s slung over their shoulders with the rifle barrels pointing at their heads as Capt. Nguyen, Than's XO, was questioning them, in as nasty a tone of voice.

Ba interpreted what the XO was saying for the Kid. "He is asking them how long they have been VC and if they are from this area. They were both caught armed and he is trying to get them to tell him where we might find other weapons or ammunition or other fighters, but they refuse to talk."

Here was a teenage girl whose life was not proms, dates and shopping at the new mall. She was a member of the VC 10th Battalion, packing an AK 47, going into combat and now, she had become a prisoner of war. Even though the anguish of capture was etched upon her mud splattered face, the Kid sensed in her a certain inner strength. She glanced at him but shied away from making full eye contact.

The boy was receiving most of the grief from Capt. Nguyen, who was now getting into his face, much deeper than any drill sergeant had ragged out the Kid. In him, too, the Kid could see a resolute acceptance of his circumstances, regardless of how dire. *I wonder what their relationship is; boyfriend-girlfriend? Brother and sister? Cousins?*

11

"Hey Stocker and Ba..." Wilson is hollering at them from back by where Tu Ta is sitting at the fishpond, "We got C rations, better come eat!"

Turned out that Wilson had one of the ARVNs packing enough MREs for PSYOPS team and he'd thrown in an extra for Minnesota. When the Kid bends over to pick out his MRE out of the pile, he doesn't even bother to look and see what he's got because he can't get over how much the girl looks like Shauna and the boy like Tony Dow.

Boxed army meal in hand, the Kid sits down on the ground by the edge of the fishpond, about 3 feet from Tu Ta Than. He smiles up at the major and the major, between bites of a leaf wrapped rice ball, smiles back at him.

Just as the Kid begins to rip open the box, the fleeting moment of relaxation is blown away when a bullet blisters the ground between him and Tu Ta. With a startled gasp, Than rolls off the stool and flattens himself on the ground as another half a dozen rounds crease the space he had just vacated!

"SNIPER!" Wilson screams.

At the first shot, the Kid, who was already sitting down, laid back along the ground and got as thin as humanly possible as shots continued to wildly spray around Tu Ta, with a couple coming real close to him! From where he was laying, the Kid saw a half dozen ARVNs on the far side of the pond, grabbing their weapons and darting into the brush.

30 seconds later, when the shooting stopped, the Kid and Tu Ta carefully picked themselves up off the ground and looked at each other and laughed; the first round couldn't have missed either one of them by more than a few inches!

Some yelling is heard amid the brush and emerging quite quickly from it, the ARVNs are back and in their grasp is the sniper! And if the Kid thought the first two VC prisoners were young, the Charlie held by the upper arms between two ARVNs, couldn't have been more than 10 or 11! The terrified barefoot boy was clad in once white mud-stained shorts and a dirty gray shirt. He was shaking like a leaf.

The soldiers brought their prisoner directly in front of Tu Ta, whom he had just nearly shot. The ARVN who carried his weapon placed the butt of the piece on the ground next to the boy's foot and everybody chuckled as the old Chinese Chicom rifle was a site taller than he was! *And five times as old*

"It's a fucking museum piece!" exclaimed Wilson, as he took the rifle from the ARVN and examined it's well-worn wooden stock and grip and super long barrel with an inverted 'V' aiming stand attached to the front beneath its site. "This is World War II shit!"

Tu Ta spoke to the overwhelmed child in Vietnamese and Ba translated for the Kid, Minnesota and Wilson; *"So this is the sniper who almost killed me! If this is all the bigger they are now growing them, perhaps we are winning the war after all!"*

The line drew big laughs. Then, with the wave of a hand, Than ordered the boy to be taken over and bound up with the other prisoners. Glancing over at them, the Kid noticed the prisoners were discussing the proceedings quite intently. A piece of bamboo was cut, a length of rope produced and in seconds, the youngster was trussed up in a similar style. But it wasn't until the guards took him and pushed him down on his knees next to the girl that the Kid made his earth shaking discovery: *Holy Jesus! The boy has the age, size, cowlicks and the looks of Beaver fucking Cleaver! My God: we've captured the VC equivalent of Wally and the Beaver... and the girl next door!*

As soon as he was down on his knees, next to the girl prisoner, the new capture looked up into her eyes, blurted out something and then really began to cry, with his head leaned over to rest against her left arm. Appearing to be far more distressed that she had been earlier, the girl tilted her head down and spoke some earnest words of comfort to the boy and they seemed to calm him.

Hmmm. I'll bet they are all related. And the little guy was trying to rescue them! Why else would an eleven-year-old try to take on an army with a single rifle.

The boy who looked like Wally Clever also leaned forward and spoke some words to the child who looked like the Beaver and again, he seemed to buck up and compose himself.

Imagine the real Beaver as an eleven-year-old prisoner of war! On your knees, Mathers! We have ways of making you talk! Except he'd be my age now. Well, hell; Tony Dow went to DINFOS; it could have been him here instead of me on this very assignment!

The Kid's head spinning as he walked back to his meal, which was lying on the ground where it had fallen when the miniature sniper opened up on them. The Kid picked up the partially opened box, sat down in the same spot he had been and proceeded to eat. About halfway through, Capt. Nguyen came over from his interrogation and squatted by the Major and gave him a report on what intelligence he was able to glean from the trio, which apparently was nothing.

13

Letting out a fairly heavy sign, Than motioned with his head towards the woods and spoke the word, *"...fini."*

When he said that, Ba, who was now sitting next to the Kid observed, "It looks like they are going to shoot them."

"What?" the Kid exclaimed. "Tu Ta, you're not going to shoot those prisoners, are you?" he asked, with an alarmed expression on his face.

"Why, yes, we are," he answered, quite matter of factly.

The Kid sprang to his feet "You can't do that! They are prisoners of war! That is against the Genève Convention! We must protect them and..."

"Yes, yes," the older man interrupted the younger, "...protect them and see that they are taken to a proper place for interrogation. *Ha Shi,*" he addressed the Kid in his Vietnamese rank, "they have already *been* interrogated. And they chose not to speak. There is no safe place to take them but, because our losses today are so heavy, we do not have enough men to guard them. And my men are very upset that we have no body count, so we shall shoot them and count 3 VC KIA. That is not what we are here to do? *An bic?*"

The Kid was in total disbelief and stood there, silently staring, mouth gaped opened and for one of the few times in his life, speechless.

"Is it not?" Than continued his rationalization, "just as they have been trying to shoot us! *That boy,*" he pointed to the culprit, "he *just missed* killing us both! You have a very short memory, Stocka. The three of them were all armed, there is *no question* they are VC. They will never change; they will always be *VC until they die...* So, why should it bother you that we shoot them?"

"Because it is wrong!" the Kid found his tongue, *"they're children! And they are prisoners of war!"*

"They are members of the Viet Cong and proud of it," Than countered, with resoluteness upon his leathery, weathered face. " They are soldiers of the enemy and it is our *duty* to kill them.

From his front left pants pocket, the Kid produces his wallet and pulls it out of the plastic bag he used to keep it dry on operations. Extracting the MAC-V card he was given at in-processing, entitled: *"The Enemy in Your Hands,"* he waved it in the major's face, pointed to the line and read: "It says right here, '... the captive in your hands must be disarmed, searched, secured and watched. But he must also be treated at all times as a human being. He must not be tortured, *killed,* mutilated or degraded, even if he refuses to talk. If the captive is a woman, treat her with all respect due her sex!'... So Tu Ta, you *can't* shoot them!"

14

Than did not respond verbally but gave the Kid a granite hard stare.

Turning to Minnesota, the ranking American on the scene, the Kid implored him, "Sir, stop this! You *can't* let them shoot these prisoners!

Although he was the ranking American, Minnesota was at a total loss of knowing what he should do. After all, he was new in-country, it was his first operation and, he had never before been confronted with a life and death situation quite like this.

"Sir!" the Kid implored him again when he didn't answer immediately, "You can't let them do this! It's fucking wrong and it's a violation of the Geneva Convention! You've got to stop them!"

A mildly panicky look pervaded his face, "Well, uh, you know, we are just advisors... and this strikes me as an ARVN issue," Then, confronting Tu Ta Than he asked, "... is this standard operating procedure? Is it really necessary to shoot these people?"

Than answered, "We have lost 14 men today, Dai Ui, and with no body count... my soldiers wish to even score. This *is* war."

"Lt. Wilson," the Kid frantically pleaded, looking for support wherever he could find it, "this isn't right and you know it. We must stop them!"

Without hesitation, Wilson agreed, "Yes, Stocker, I agree! This is not right men... uh... we can't..."

But no sooner did the words start coming out of his mouth than he was cut off by Minnesota. "Don't bother getting involved, Ross, this is not your call. All you are is an attached PSYOPS officer. And it's not mine, either. It's Tu Ta's. "But, if it'll make *you* feel any better," he pointed at the Kid, I'll put in a call to the TOC."

Minnesota signaled for his RTO, who was a scant two meters away. "Silver City One, Eldorado One, over..." he waited a couple of seconds for the reply.

"Eldorado One, this is Silver City One, can I help you, over?" It was the voice of the Boar Hog!

"Uh, Roger, City One, we got a situation here, involving a Vietnamese decision as to the disposition of some detainees... and I am asking if I have any type of jurisdiction in the chain of command for this matter, over..."

After a slight pause, the Hog's voice came back; "Eldorado one, if I copy your last transmission, you are asking if we have any say over what the Vietnamese do with their prisoners and the answer is negative. That is entirely an ARVN concern, over."

"I copy, Silver City One, out." He handed the mike back to his RTO "Well, there you have it; it's out of our hands."

Just like Pontius Pilate. Now the Kid was getting nervous. He would not be a party to the shooting of three children, *VC or not...* not if he could help it. "Wait a minute, Lt. Wilson, maybe we can get them to *Chu Hoi!*"

"Yeah! Great idea!" Wilson concurred.

"Tu Ta," the Kid approached the major, "if we can get them to Chu Hoi, can we have them?"

Than silently evaluated the Kid's request through squinted eyes. But, when Capt. Nguyen leaned over and whispered something in his ear, he immediately said, with a flourishing wave toward the prisoners, "Go ahead. Do your best."

First, the Kid went over and whispered to Ba, "Please! Help me. You've got to explain to them if they don't Chu Hoi, *they'll be shot.* We have only one chance to save them!"

"OK!"

The Kid lead Ba over to the prisoners, with Than, Wilson, Minnesota and Capt. Nguyen trailing after, all wanting to get a closer look at what was about to transpire. It was twilight and the light at the base of the palm trees was beginning to fade, but the Kid could still clearly make out their nervously inquisitive faces, there on the ground, surrounded by a semi-circle of six ARVNs who had been preparing to remove them. The officers stopped about three meters short as the Kid and Ba advanced to within a couple of feet of the trio.

Sinking down onto one knee and getting on their level, directly in front of them, the Kid began with the teen on his left, made eye contact with him, smiled nervously, then moved his gaze to the girl in the center, in whose brown eyes he almost emotionally lost it, and lastly, down to the now somewhat defiant little sniper, with his nose running because he'd been crying.

After engaging each of them with a reassuring smile, he took a deep breath. *This is my only chance.* There was no need for loudspeakers; they weren't trapped in a tree line and he was so close he could have whispered his message. With arms open and palms turned up in invitation, he said in a low, pleading, emotion choked voice: *"Chu Hoi, em... be Hoi Chanhs!"* No answer.

Then, twisting to look up at Ba over his shoulder behind him said, "Ba, tell them! The ARVNs want to shoot them and the only way we can save them is if they *Chu Hoi."*

With that, the Catholic youth from Saigon, with no love lost on any VC, launched into a speech and while Ba spoke, the Kid watched their faces as they assimilated what he was saying. When Ba finished, the three of them first shared a brief moment of silence and then put their heads together for a rapid-fire exchange of hushed comments and discussion that lasted about a minute.

Rising to his feet, the Kid waited for their decision.

"The older ones are trying to talk the younger one into it," Ba whispered to him, with his right ear cocked in the prisoner's direction. "Yes, that is what they are saying."

Finally, they had made their decision. It was the littlest one of all that delivered their message, loud and clear; *"CAM BAO YA!"* He screamed, and the way he said it made the two older ones smile with obvious pride.

The kid sniper has guts!

"Well, there is answer," Tu Ta stepped forward, *"Cam bao ya...never!* And I do not believe any of them will ever change their minds." He then stood directly in front of the Kid and challenged him; "if the tables were turned, *Ha shi,* would you Chu Hoi to the North Vietnamese?"

"Absolutely not!"

"Exactly. That is why I think PSYOPS is *dinki dao!*" the Vietnamese commander said contemptuously, "it *beaucoup* waste of time!"

And with that, Capt. Nguyen jumped out from behind Than, barked a command at the six guards and the prisoners were jerked to their feet and straight away removed into the foliage at their back, each one suspended between two ARVNs.

The Kid was beginning to seethe beneath the surface. *I've got to report this to somebody, but who?*

From behind him, he could hear the officers having a discussion about the situation and it sounded like Minnesota said, *"...just make sure he doesn't see anything..."*, then Tu Ta left them and followed after Capt. Nguyen.

Wilson and Minnesota approached the distraught Kid.

"We lost 14 men today all told, why don't you feel sorry for them?" Minnesota laid it on him.

"I do feel sorry for them, but this is different," he strongly responded, "those kids were captured in combat! They are prisoners of war and executing them is fucking murder! It's a *criminal offense* for God's sake!"

17

"It's not good, I agree," was the best Minnesota could offer, "but I see the collateral damage as being very minimal." He ticked off his points. "They are, without a doubt VC. They were offered a chance to live but chose death. Nobody has a problem with it but you, Stocker. Who are you to stand in the way?"

Shit! I don't believe this day I do not have a camera on me! Mother fucker! If I could get some pictures, they wouldn't do it. "I am an American soldier, duty bound to uphold the Geneva Convention. And so are *you,* Captain."

"Ah yes, but this is not a matter that is taking place within the American Army, Specialist," the captain reasoned, "we are just attached here, it is out of our jurisdiction."

"Is not the Republic of South Vietnam bound by the Geneva Convention?" The Kid, ever the debater, shot immediately back.

Then Wilson chimed in, "You're just going to have to find a way to get over it, Stocker. It really is none of our concern." he said, but he could see the Kid wasn't buying what he was selling so he switched tacks and laying a hand on his shoulder said, "Hey, we gave it our best shot. You and Ba tried to get them to Chu Hoi... I never thought for a second any of them ever would... but you tried. You did the job you were sent to the field to do, but you failed. Accept it. They're just 3 nameless gooks who almost killed us. Now we have no choice but to forget 'em and move on!"

The Kid stood in silence, but rage was building. *Nameless gooks? They do have names... Wally and the Beaver and Shauna McConnell, the Girl next door. And they are CHIDREN, you bastard! I didn't sign on in this fucking Army to shoot children! No, you can bet your sweet ass that I will NEVER forget this! CAM BAO Ya! Never!*

Chapter 2

It was the most restless night the Kid had ever spent in his life. Because he was mad at Wilson and Minnesota, he had chosen to sling his hammock in one of the other huts apart from them, down at the end of the group. He'd found a place where he could tie it low and when he climbed in, his ass was only swaying six inches off the ground. The lower it was, the safer it was, and that was his theory in case any stray stuff started flying around in the middle of the night. Ba joined him, throwing his poncho down along the dirt floor because a couple of the higher-ranking ARVN sergeants flopped on the sleeping platform.

A half dozen times during the hot, tepid, breezeless night, the Kid heard bursts of shots being fired for one reason or another, with none of it sounding like incoming. But each time, he imagined that the shooting was the execution of the children, especially the third time, when he thought he heard muffled screams, but he couldn't tell if his mind was playing tricks on him or not, cut loose and drifting as it was on alternating currents of fatigue and disgust.

Who can I tell? Who will help me prove it... if they do shoot them? Who's' going to believe me, if Wilson and Minnesota pretend it didn't happen or that the US Army has nothing to do with it? How did I come to be in this fucking place? I can't believe they'd do this! ARVNs shooting those three kids sure makes a lot of what we are supposedly fighting this war for total hypocritical bullshit! I fucking hate this war! It is wrong wrong wrong and shooting children, for ANY reason is flat ass despicable! Oh God I hope I live long enough to get out of PSYOPs and the field and all this madness and see Flo at least one more time. Screw the Army. If only I could find a way out. Any way out... other than getting shot.

Drifting in and out of consciousness at one point, the Kid experienced the sensation that his hands were tied behind his back and when he tried to pull them free in the semi-dream, he almost fell out of the hammock! *Whoa! Talk about a rush! Ah, ha! It's only 6 inches.*

The Kid was so glad when the horizon began to gray up and as soon as it was light enough that he could be reasonably sure he was not exposing their position to anybody outside the perimeter, he rose out of his hammock, stepped outside of the hut and after walking around it once, picked what he deemed was the safest spot and lit up a KOOL.

A majority of the ARVNs were already up but only now are they lighting small fires with which to heat water for tea. Sitting upon his steel pot, he caught sight of Wilson and Minnesota emerging from their hut and seeing the Kid, they made their way straight over to him.

"Morning' Stocker," Wilson greeted him as he lit up a cigarette, "sleep OK?"

"No, Sir."

"Ah, well, neither did we," he rocked on the heels of his jungle boots and stretched, arms spread wide, "at least we didn't get attacked last night, that's a bonus!"

"Stocker," Minnesota then squatted down next to him, "Tu Ta finally said last night that he decided not to shoot those kids, so you can stop worrying about that."

"Oh, really? And where are they?"

"Uh," the blond captain hesitated, "I'm not sure, they've got them under guard somewhere out of sight, but they'll be treated like prisoners of war, so... that's that," he attempted to completely quash the incident.

Yeah. Sure, the ARVNs changed their minds. "Can I see them?" the Kid asked.

"No, goddammit, Stocker, we don't have time to play your silly fucking games here", Wilson vehemently rejected his request, showing his increasing anger at the Kid, because he was not so willing to let the matter slide. "We gotta get ready to move out, we've got a damn site of a ways to go today to get out of this place, so get you get your ass ready."

The Kid stared back at him, through the dirty lenses of his grey framed army glasses, "I am ready, sir," he flatly intoned.

Rising up, Minnesota flipped away his first butt of the morning and said, "Well, hell, Ross, let's go see if Tu Ta's man has the tea or coffee, or whatever the hell he's makin', ready yet. Stocker? You want a cup?"

"Maybe, in a minute," the Kid replied, looking off to his right and seeing a group of 3 ARVNs emerging from the foliage over in the direction they had taken the 3 prisoners the night before. "I gotta take a leak, first."

And with that, the Kid ground the butt of his KOOL into the mud by his helmet, rose up and walked slowly toward those ARVNs, as they made their way over to where a pair of their comrades had started one of the cooking fires.

"Chao," he greeted them as he squatted down by the small blaze, over which they had a quart sized aluminum pan hanging by its wire handle above the orange flames from an improvised stick tripod. Reaching into his pocket, he pulled out his pack of KOOLs and offered each of the five a smoke, which they all took, with smiles on their faces. One extracted a burning stick from the fire and lit everybody up and nodded their approval and voiced their thanks.

After they had all taken a couple of puffs, the Kid casually inquired, "O dau em?" *Where are the children?*

One of the soldiers looked him in the face, "VC?" he questioned, then after checking visually with his buddies he answered with a quirky half smile, *"Em het roi,"* he made a shooting motion with his hands and arms, then they all laughed.

The Kid's knowledge of Vietnamese was sufficient for him to interpret without the help of Ba: *'The children are dead.'*

Leaving the ARVNs and walking back to where Wilson and Minnesota sat sipping their freshly brewed hot drinks with Tu Ta, the Kid stood in front of them. "You lied to me, Sir." he flatly stated to the big Swede. "I just asked those men over there where the VC prisoners were, and they said they were *Het Roi. An bic het roi, Dai Ui?* Het roi means 'dead', Captain."

"OK, Stocker," Wilson jumped up so fast that he almost spilled his tea "what if they are? You didn't see it. The prisoners are here, somewhere. And how do you know those men didn't misunderstand what it was you were asking?"

The Kid remained silent. *Let him talk.*

"Here's the bottom line, specialist," the fully steamed lieutenant laid into him, "things are tough enough out here, without somebody like you creating problems. We don't know for a fact that they shot them. If Tu Ta says the prisoners are being guarded, then they are being guarded. Do you want to call Tu Ta a liar to his face?"

The Kid glanced at the Stoney faced Tu Ta, who was pointedly ignoring them, but did not speak the accusation.

"O.K. then," Wilson spoke up, "you better drop this whole fucking thing because me and the Captain are getting pissed at you and we're backing Tu Ta on this one. If you report this, you had better have names, places and times... none of which you have. I will ask you one time: did you see them get shot?"

21

Silence.

"Answer me, specialist, that's an order!" Wilson forcefully demanded.

"No sir."

"Do you know their names?"

"No sir."

"Do you know, for a fact, that they are not being held as prisoners of war?"

"No sir."

Now Wilson was on a roll, determined to put an end to this problem before it got any bigger. "Do you even know where we are?"

"Somewhere in Cang Long Province?"

"Ha! No, Cang Long is not even a Province. See?" He turned to Tu Ta, "I told you he couldn't read a map!" then back at the kid; "So how are you going to report this? You don't know *who* they were, you don't know *where* we are, and you never *saw* them get shot. What would your report say? You got nothing. Now, listen and listen good, Stocker," he was reaching his point, "if you persist, nobody here will support your allegations. And your 1049 for getting transferred into Armed Forces Radio Saigon? You can damn well fucking forget it! I will personally see that the only thing it will ever be any good for is wiping your ass! Oh! One more thing," Wilson paused for dramatic effect, "if you don't like the way I'm operating our field team, you could always request to be reassigned, like, I hear there's an opening with the armored Cav... Robert's old slot. It never has been filled... how'd you like to fill it? I could put you there tomorrow."

The death sentence assignment! "You're going to punish me because I believe we should uphold the Geneva Convention?"

"No, Stocker," Wilson formed a twisted little half smile with his lips, "no assignment in this man's army is for punishment. It's all jobs that's gotta be done... by someone! You know as well as I do, this is a hardship tour!"

Lying sack of cow shit! I'm already being punished for being here with you. This has pushed me over the line; I am 100 % opposed to this war and everything that has to do with it. Oh, I won't break any regulations or refuse to do my duty... but I swear to all of the Gods who have ever existed; the days of blind cooperation and tolerance... are over!

Then, just as Wilson lifting his canteen cup to his lips, Charlie kicked off the day's festivities by dropping a pair of mortar rounds not 75 meters from the command element causing the Lt. to drop the cup and immediately fall upon it as he hit the ground. Automatic weapons fire simultaneously broke out on the north end of the perimeter.

Here we go again! The Kid made a fast, low dash back to the hut where he'd slept to get his steel pot. *It's gonna be a long fucking day.*

Chapter 3

It was Sunday, not that it was that much different from any other day in Nam, but most of the men were not working and there was no operation in progress that day and Sgt. Spencer almost always had a mail call on Sunday before lunch.

Mail call was an event that had become much less exciting now that his relationship with Flo was over... or at least drastically changed. The Kid mulled over his new situation as he waited in the large group of American officers and enlisted men congregated in the Tra Vinh mess hall in anticipation of the delivery.

At last, Sgt. Spencer could be seen coming down the walkway with the big canvas sack over his shoulder.

"Yaaaaayyyy, whooo hooooo! The collective cheer went up.

Maybe I'll get a letter and she'll say she's changed her mind, the Kid fantasized as Spencer began calling out the names. But he hadn't gotten a letter from her in over a week and didn't get one from her today. What he did get was a package from his dad. It was rectangular, longer than most but not that thick. Opening it up, he found it contained two items; one was a small box and the other was a new pool cue!

Oh wow! Hey! Look at this!" the Kid hollered to the group as he rose from the mess table where he'd opened the package and held up the two parts, one in each hand. "You'll fuckers will all be sorry shit now!" he exclaimed as he screwed the butt end into the tip end. "Look! a new cork tip AND it's straight!" he made an imaginary shot. It was the cheapest cue his father could find that still broke in half, but it actually had a tip!

"Partner partner!" Ernie waved his hand in the air from the other side of the room, while much of the pool shooting crowd let out a noise of alarm; the Kid already beat everybody too much.

"No way! He's my partner!" Lt. Wilson asserted his claim; the Kid had indeed been his partner most of the time when they had previously come to town from Cang Long.

24

"Not anymore," the Kid flatly declared. *I'm pissed at you. What I really mean is I will never be your partner again.* "Cam bao ya!" As he spoke the Vietnamese word *'never'*... He could hear an echo in his memory, of how the *Beaver,* the littlest of the ill-fated VC trio, had shouted it directly at him before he and his two companions were hauled off to be shot. In fact, that audio imprint was having as much impact on the Kid's psyche as the reoccurring mental visual of Captain Robinson's half missing body.

"What's in the little box?" Pete pointed to the small parcel that had been lost in the excitement over the new pool cue.

Picking it up, it immediately stuck the Kid as being the other thing he'd asked his father to send him for his 21st birthday and ripping open the package, he discovered a hard eyeglasses case that when flipped opened, revealed a pair of gold wire rim glasses with round lenses... *YES! Just like John Lennon's!*

"Far fucking out!" the Kid exclaimed as he unfolded the earpieces, removed his gray plastic framed army glasses and for the first time, placed the bright, shiny new glasses onto his face. *This old prescription still works well enough!*

As he gazed around the room to show off his new look, there were cat calls and laughter aplenty, but it was Sgt. Rammerman, the mid forties lifer infantry advisor who had been with them on a couple of operations, that decided to speak up.

"You look pretty funny in those!" the sergeant loudly put the Kid's new look down and as he said it, all eyes in the mess hall quickly gravitated to the Kid, to check out just how funny he did look and in that split second of silence, the Kid very matter of factly shot back.

"Not half as fuckin' funny as you look *THROUGH* them!"

The entire room fell down laughing. Sgt. Rammerman turned beet red. Any faint comeback he might have had died in a flustered stutter on his lifer lips.

"Cool!" was Pete's reaction to the Kid's new eyewear.

"OOO, let me see the cue!" Ernie made his way over to their table to examine the Kid's new lumber.

And as all of this was taking place, Sergeant First Class Earle Brooks, the tall *but not tall enough to play basketball* NCOIC of the Tra Vinh compound approached Lt. Wilson, as he sat reading a letter from the states and engaged him in a conversation that quickly caught the Kid's attention.

"Lt. Wilson," Brooks began.

"Yes, Sgt. Brooks, what is it?" Wilson looked up from the handwritten page.

"I'm gonna need you to start pulling officer of the day duty and your men to pull guard duty while you're in, being a little shorthanded, we need some help around here."

"Excuse me?" was the surprised lieutenant's first response.

"I said," Brooks looked perturbed that his words were not understood, "We are shorthanded and I need you to start pulling officer of the day duty and your men to start pulling guard duty when you come in from the field to help out around here."

"Well, I don't think so, First Sergeant," Wilson contentiously scoffed, "when we come in, it's after we've been way out in the field on operations and in combat and shit. We come here to relax. You guys who are here all the time, you're not out in it, so when we come in, you guys should guard us so we can get some rest, for Christ's sake!"

Brooks had a frown on his slightly jowly face; he hadn't expected the lieutenant to be too happy about the request, but he hadn't expected this somewhat rude refusal, either. "As long as you eat in my mess hall, you'll do what I say and you and your men are going to pull guard duty and you're pulling OD duty and helping out around here."

Wilson considers his reply for a few seconds before telling Brooks, "Well, I don't think so." Then, turning to the Kid, whom he knew was sitting behind him, he said, "I don't want you eating here in this mess hall anymore. There is no way *I'm* pulling OD duty and I don't think it's right for you guys to pull guard duty, either! So stop eating here in the mess hall. Just eat on the local economy and I'm going to check out moving us into the CIA compound and leaving this chicken shit outfit for good!"

"Oh yeah?" Brooks put both hands on his hips, "as if the spooks would have you!" And with that, he turned and walked out the screen door.

"Don't eat in the mess hall?" the Kid was shocked as he sought actual clarification. "Don't eat in the mess hall? Sir, you can't be serious!"

"That's an order, specialist," Wilson confirmed his intentions. "I don't want that fucker Brooks having anything to say about us or what we do or when we do it."

"But Sir, this is the only place we can get American food in the entire province! And you are saying I can't eat here? Because *you're* having a beef

26

with the first sergeant?" Ironically, it was nearly 1100 hours and the smell of lunch being prepared for service in half an hour was driving the Kid nuts.

"Well, I'm going to take this up with Major Gillmore, but until I tell you otherwise, I don't want you eating in this mess hall." Picking up his mail, Wilson stuffed it into his front lower right fatigue shirt pocket as he went in search of the major.

"Shit!" the Kid exclaimed.

"Man o man, he is some loon! Don't eat in the fucking mess hall?" Pete exclaimed, "we all pity you, Kid, ya know?"

"Yeah. Tell me about it." The Kid gathered his mail and made his way back to his bunk area to put it away.

Damn! I was looking forward to lunch. That bastard! The Kid sat down on his bunk and thought for a couple of seconds about what had just taken place. *When and where am I gonna get breakfast when we're in here? I gotta go out for every meal? Shit. That is not fair! Of all the pig-headed crap. Don't eat in the mess hall? So now I must find somebody to go eat with. I'll get Wilson. Yeah, since he'll be eating out too, and work on him, about how inconvenient and why, when all we eat is Vietnamese food in Cang Long and out on operations… God dammit, I want American food!*

After parking the new cue in his locker, the Kid sat down on his bunk and taking the new glasses off his face, he examined them closely. *Cool! I am so tired of black horn rims and plastic frames! These are really neat!*

Sitting on the edge of the bunk, the Kid succumbed to the overwhelming urge to flat flop back down on the mattress and close his eyes, holding his new glasses in his right hand. Life had not been easy since Wilson had pulled them out of Cang Long. It was the middle of October and already this month, they had been on four operations with another one scheduled for tomorrow. And Wilson was all excited because it was going to be a helicopter insertion.

At least I'm going to get a helicopter ride tomorrow. No sooner did he have the thought than he had to marvel at how little it took to make him happy these days. He was going to have a helicopter ride and be up where it was delectably cool, all right, for maybe 20 minutes, but the final destination was somewhere in the Mekong Delta where, sure as a diarrhea shit followed after a malaria tablet, Charlie would be waiting. Otherwise, we wouldn't be going there.

The mattress felt so good against his back that the Kid just laid there, his feet on the floor, his wire rimmed glasses clutched in his hand, and he let his mind fly. Two of the four operations they had just completed, had been overnights, where the Kid had slept in his hammock out in the boonies, fighting mosquitos fruitlessly all night with nothing but insect repellant, so any mattress time was something to be appreciated. *Oh God, does it feel good to just lie here! When I'm in Saigon, I'll have a mattress every night! Sheer Heaven. Rats. I wonder if I'll make it to Saigon. How long can my luck hold out? I should have reported what happened to those three kids out in the jungle. Why didn't I? What if I didn't do it so Wilson wouldn't kill my transfer to Armed Forces radio, and I end up getting killed instead? How Ironic would that be! Will I feel like a selfish coward at the end, when my life flashes before my eyes, or will I realize that there's nothing I could do to stop it and after it's done? What good would it do me to try and report it if they are going to call me a liar, anyway? It wouldn't give those three kids their lives back. I vow, if I live, I am going to do everything I can I do to help stop this fucking madness. Blowing people in half and shooting children for fucking body count is evil! Neither side is innocent, but we shouldn't be here. It is their business.*

"Kid... Kid... hey Kid!" the familiar voice of Pete brought him back to 'Nam, "Hey, Sweet just pulled in from Cang Long and he's looking' for you!" spoke the head that peered around the corner and into his lower bunk.

"Oh!" The kid sat up with a start, having been so quickly brought out of such a vivid dream, "OK, I'll be right out!"

Putting on his new glasses, the Kid emerged from the Servant's quarters in time to see Sweet coming out of the door to the mess hall. "Hey!" Jim hollered with a wave when he saw him. "Geeze, Kid, I haven't seen you since you went to Saigon!" He walked up to stand in front of him on the lawn by the volleyball court. "Whoa! Look at those new glasses! Man! Do those ever make you look different! I bet you didn't get those in Saigon!"

"Nope. My Dad sent them for my birthday!" the kid smiled, "how's Bouji doin' out there at Cang Long? Didn't he come in with you?" he looked behind Sweet, as if the former were concealing the latter.

"He didn't come in. Doesn't want to take the chance to drive the road unless he's got a really good reason, like he's leaving to go home." Sweet took off his sunglasses, "he just reads a lot and smokes some dope. You can bet your ass we aren't running too many operations, and nobody gives a shit."

"Never thought I'd hear myself say it," the Kid pensively set his jaw, "but, I wish I was back at Cang Long. That is so much safer than what we're doing right now. All kinds of shit has been happening..."

28

"Hey! Tell me over lunch!" Sweet pulled him toward the mess hall.

"Uh, I can't! Lt. Wilson just this morning, believe it or not, has given me an order not to eat in the mess hall."

"Say what?"

"Yep. Can't eat in the mess hall. He's having a fight with the first sergeant and Top said if we eat in his mess hall, he can tell Wilson what to do... so the fucker said we had to eat on the economy. He'll probably tell you the same thing as soon as he sees you."

"Well," Sweet said slowly, "don't that beat all shit, because I just went into the mess hall looking' for you and Wilson is in there, eating himself... right now!"

"Really?"

"Yeah. Go look!"

They walked over and looked through the mess hall screened windows and sure enough, there sat Wilson, chowing down. Now the Kid was somewhat perplexed; Wilson had ordered him not to eat there, yet he was still doing it himself. "He must not be serious about it. He must have realized how stupid of a thing it was of him to say," the Kid reasoned.

"Maybe. What the hell; there he is stuffing his face. You eating or not? If he's serious, when he sees us, he'll tell us!"

"OK. What the fuck. If he can, we can."

Small as the Tra Vinh mess hall was, the officers' and enlisted men's rooms were separated only by an imaginary line, defined by a wide-open decorative arch, not more than 6" thick, which split the room in half but divided nothing. Once a person advanced through the line and signed the log and paid money, like the Kid, if they too, were on RNA (rations not available), one would then go through the chow line and from there, into the officer's half to obtain silverware, condiments and drinks. In performing this feat, the Kid and Sweet walked right in front of Wilson, who sat alone at one table in the middle of the room, staring off into space and he chewed, acting oblivious to their presence, most likely absorbed in the hatching of some plot or another.

He can't be serious, or he wouldn't be here eating himself. I wonder if he talked to Gillmore? If he wanted to talk to me, he would get up and do it. Guess it doesn't really matter after all.

And with those thoughts, the Kid sat down with Sweet and enjoyed a sumptuous lunch of American food; hot meat loaf and gravy, buttered peas, fresh green salad, homemade bread and butter, lots of fruit and with nary a dog or a snake on a plate anywhere in site. About half way through their meal, Sweet and the Kid noticed Wilson rise up, walk past them to bus his dishes and then he left the room without so much as a glance at their direction.

The Kid dropped his fork and looked at Sweet. "I swear to God, Jim, there are days that I think I'd just kill him if I thought I could get away with it. I mean, that fucker is going to get me killed s*o it was like this, your honor,*" the Kid turned to an imaginary judge somewhere above his head, "it was self-defense. I had to do it because he was going to get it done to me!"

"Yeah," Sweet chuckled, "I didn't know the M-79 grenade launcher was loaded, your honor!"

"When you are going' back out?" the Kid inquired as to Jim's schedule.

"Tomorrow."

"Oh, good, you'll be around tonight when I clean everybody's plow with my brand spanking new pool cue with a cork real tip!" he beamed.

"Where'd that come from?"

"My Dad. Part of my birthday." The Kid took a long, deep drink of iced tea. "Dig this. A couple of weeks ago, on the first operation we went on when I got back from Saigon, we were out with A company and Tu Ta Than. They captured 3 VC, uh more like the local Junior Achievement chapter of the VC and the ARVNs shot them for body count. One was a girl and the other two were boys... 2 couldn't have been more than 16 or 17 and the other like 10 or 11. Pretty fucking sick!"

"No!"

"Yes."

"Did you see it?" Sweet had stopped eating.

"No. If I'd seen it, I'd be obligated to turn Tu Ta and all his fucking command in for violating the Genève Convention. They claimed in the morning that they didn't shoot them."

"Shit!"

"On the other hand, thank God I don't have images of that swimming around in my head with the top half of Robinson. After Than said they were going to do it, I tried to talk him out of it or get Wilson or this blond fuck of an asshole lieutenant from Minnesota to stop them. Wilson agreed with me and protested, too, but Tu Ta pretty much told him to butt out. I asked *Minnesota Fats* to call TOC and tell them what was happening and when he

30

did, Boar Hog was on duty and pretty fuckin' much told the ARVNs to go ahead and shoot them. So, I asked if we could try to make them Chu Hoi... Tu Ta Than said go ahead and ask… and we did. But they didn't. The next morning, I was talking to some of the ARVN privates and they said they shot them during the night."

"God no!"

"Yes! So, I told Wilson and that fuck brained lieutenant from Minnesota, whose name I can never remember, that I was going to turn Than in for violating the Geneva Convention and they said they'd call me a liar!"

"So you're saying Wilson wasn't for doin' it?" Jim wanted to know.

"No. I'll give him that. He stuck up for the Geneva Convention and I think he might have even seen the point that us getting a couple of Hoi chanhs, like we're supposed to be doing, would have been a good thing, but after it all came down, he was like, *we didn't have anything to do with it... forget the gooks and get on with your job Stocker.*"

"Damn!"

"And then, he threatened me. He said if I said anything, I'd end up in the armored cav in Robert's slot and that I could kiss my 1049 to Armed Forces Radio Saigon goodbye!"

"No!"

"Yes! He said I would be using my 1049 for toilet paper! But what the fuck difference does it all make, Jim? I mean, today is October 16th, I have to survive another 159 days of him dragging me everywhere to hell and gone all over the Delta before I get out of this hell hole. And, we are going on a fucking helicopter assault tomorrow!"

"Well. Never thought I'd say it," Jim mimicked the Kid's wording earlier, "but it sucks to be you... this week anyway."

Amen, brother.

They finished their meal mostly in silence and when they were through, they went outside and sat down on the bench in the shade of the servant's quarters and lit up, wondering where Wilson had gone in such a hurry without saying anything.

"Hey! My new pool cue... let's shoot some while nobody's on the table!"

Chapter 4

Flying along at about 2,000 feet, occupying the door seat, the Kid gazed down from the Huey chopper at the paddies, canals and tree lines below, that still cast a shadow across the rice fields. Then, lifting his eyes he looked right, across to one of the other choppers, bathed in the first rays of the sunrise, flying parallel to them, barely 30 feet away. He could see Lt. Wilson, sitting at the door next to the machine gun, looking back at him. The draft was buffeting his steel pot, but it was held on by its chin strap and with a broad smile on his face, he flashed the Kid the thumbs up. The Kid flashed it back, *even though I'm really not in a thumb's up kind of mood.*

The sun had just risen fully above the horizon's rim to the Kid's left and even at that altitude, its heat making capability was instantly felt. It illuminated the flight of 12 choppers, traveling in 3 groups of 4, carrying the 90-odd men that comprised A Company and their PSYOPS attachment to begin another two-day operation. Of course, there were no loudspeakers.

The choppers were crewed by Americans and were from the 9th Division out of My Tho. For some strange reason, the Regiment could not locate enough ARVN helicopters to perform this mission. That was an immediate bad sign to the Kid, who had seen for himself that ARVN chopper pilots did not like to fly into contested areas, and this led him to believe there might be some contesting upon their arrival at wherever it was they were headed.

Am I going to find out what it's like to land in a hot LZ? Whatever happens, I gotta admit, this is better than those fucking junks! That was the worst. Talk about feeling like a sitting duck, that slow moving boat thing does it. Of course, I could have jumped into the water off the boat... here, jumping would be a problem.

Sitting next to him, Cpl Ba rides along in his usual *'Please, Mr. Custer,'* *funk. Nothin' I can do about it, Ba; I don't want to be here either.* The Kid looks back across the open air at Wilson and Tu Ta Than, whose silhouette he can see leaning forward next to the lieutenant, studying his battle map. Wilson notices the Kid is looking and gives his fisted arm a pull like he's signaling a semi-truck driver to blow his horn. The Kid flashes him the peace sign, souring his expression. *Ha! He didn't like that! My, aren't we having fun now. What I'd like to do is kick your miserable ass out that door for volunteering us for these operations, and you too, Tu Ta, you murdering bastard!*

The Kid was wearing his prescription shades. The new wire rimmed glasses were safely locked up back with his new pool cue at Tra Vinh. He surveyed the faces of the other passengers on board. Lt. Wilson's RTO, the loveable and wiry rat faced Con was seated next to Ba, holding the PRC 25 between his legs. Capt. Wally's RTO sat next to him, holding his radio the same way. There were four additional ARVN troops squeezing in on the floor of the bird in front of those who were lucky enough to have an actual seat.

The American door gunner, a flight-helmeted black GI Spec. 4, with a microphone located about an inch out from his lips, sat facing the Kid with his back to the co-pilot, but all of his concentration was centered on the terrain below. The expression on his face, beneath his mirrored sunglasses, betrayed no feeling of impending doom or anything like it. *I wonder how much of his time he spends thinking about getting shot down. Ommmm please not a hot LZ, please not a hot LZ.*

Near as the Kid could tell, they had flown southeast out of the Tra Vinh airport, where the unit had loaded up in the pre-dawn. He knew it would be too early in the morning for the sniper to be at work and he was right. His only hope was that where they were bound, the VC there would also be late risers. *Fat chance.*

Wilson had invited the Kid to join him on his chopper with TuTa Than, but the Kid declined. Along with Wilson, he now hated Than and preferred not to ride with either one of them.

After about 20 minutes of flying, the three pods split up and as they descended, the Kid could see the other groups going to fairly wide dispersal points, on their left and right, so as to position the company's assets, which consisted of 3 maneuvering units of 30 men each, at their particular lines of departure for the operation.

Their flight began setting down, back from the nearest tree line by about ten paddy dykes' distance. The gunner is poised, ready, but holding his fire. The Kid eyed the tree line, looking for any indication that they were taking fire. *Is it gonna happen... is it gonna happen? Do I wish I was carrying an M-16? No. Still don't want to carry that piece of shit. Do I wish I was anywhere else on earth? Well, almost...* The gunner gave the Kid an encouraging smile as the bird settled its skids on an "x" formed by the intersection of two dyke lines. Immediately, the Kid clamored out and stepped down into the still somewhat cool water of the paddies. Once out, he extended an arm of support to Con, who balanced on the landing skid of the chopper while he brought the PRC-25 off the floor and smoothly around in one motion while inserting his arms to be affixed upon his back. He then stepped off the skid, like a man exiting a subway train, and dropped into the paddy with hardily a splash, and stood smiling and nodding next to the Kid.

Swiftly unloaded, the choppers did an immediate *didi mau*. The door gunner flashed the Kid the Peace sign as they lifted off, leaving the unit in the relative quiet of the countryside. Charlie had not sent a welcoming party. *Thank God.* Whether or not they would encounter opposition at the tree line was the next question. "Well, I'm sure glad they're not shooting at us...yet," the Kid said to Cpl. Ba, as he, Con and Wally's RTO slogged over from their drop point and join Wilson, Tu Ta Than, Dai Ui Nuygen and Captain Wally, who were dropped one paddy of their right.

Rising out of the mid-calf deep water, shoots of green rice plants prepared for another day of photosynthesis. The Kid had been observing their progress on all the operations they had recently completed. As they trampled the tender shoots, their boots made a sucking sloshy sound as they pulled their feet out of the mud with each step. Radio traffic was light, and it appeared that none of the 3 LZs had been hot. In fact, Charlie was making himself scarce. *"Very different,* thought the Kid, *I don't like that.*

Four point men advanced quickly on the tree line, moving up and dropping behind the second dyke row out, all spread out across the command elements' front. Tu Ta Than, and the entourage walked boldly forward but all of them, to a man, were ready to drop at the first shot.

As much on edge as they were about who might be waiting for them just inside the trees, there was a little relief as they watched their advanced guard enter the foliage curtain with still no reports of gunfire, rockets or anything else. Quickly, the rest of their 2 combat squads and the command element closed on and entered the tree line.

Pushing at a quick pace, they soon emerged into a clearing on some huts and quite to the surprise of the Kid, something else was very different: Vietnamese civilians were there, working the gardens by the fishpond. There were three women, a couple of toddlers and a teen aged boy. To see civilians, much less a man or boy of military age out in the villages, was a rarity. *Oh, he's missing his left leg from about the calf down! Guess that's the million-piaster wound out here, now he doesn't have to fight for either army. Different today. I wonder what the hell they have in store for us? Did these people not have time to run and hide, or are they pro Thieu?*

While the women stopped working and spoke to the ARVN soldiers who stood in front of them, the Kid realized that the boy had noticed him and was crutching over in their direction, obviously well-schooled in the use of his solo crutch, with a big grin on his face.

Approaching to within five feet of the Kid, the young boy stopped and greeted him, "Bonjour!"

French?

"Ah!" said Ba, "we are so far back into the Delta today, the people who live out here believe the French are still in power. If they see a white man, they believe he must be French!"

The Kid smiled, "Chao, Ong" he responded in Vietnamese, which made the boy smile back, "Toi khong Fransi, Toi Mai!" *I am not French; I am an American.*

The teen cocked his head in surprise. "Khong bic?" *I don't understand.*

Then Ba took over and explained to the boy that living in the backwaters of the Delta, he had been unaware that the French were gone for many years and that the 'South' Vietnamese were now allied by their American friends. The boy was still scratching his head as the unit moved on, deeper into the growth beyond the huts.

"Hey, Ba, where the fuck are we, do you have any idea?" the Kid inquired as they walked along, keeping a wary eye out for anything that looked booby trappy.

"I think we are somewhere in the middle of the Ca Mau Peninsula, but I don't know where, exactly. There are not many towns or even big villages out here."

They continued to encounter small hut and hamlet clusters at fairly regular distances as they moved through trees along great expanses of paddies. Walking wise, the going was fairly easy, but the longer time passed without any shots being fired, the greater the unit's anxiety became upon the prospect, that surly it must come. *It always does.* But it was another hour before it did, in the form of a booby trap.

Two ARVNs were wounded; one with a foot mangled so bad that it might leave him like the boy they had seen earlier, while the other one had been hit in the knee cap by a piece of debris from the small explosion.

That incident was followed by another long stretch of nothing happening on any of the three element's fronts. As they walked through the foliage, at one point, the Kid and Ba found themselves walking along next to Wilson and Con the RTO.

"Pretty quiet today, Sir, I wonder if this is a VC holiday or something?"

"Yes, it is quiet. What a disappointment this is turning out to be," the Lt. spoke without trying to make eye contact as they moved ahead. "Hell, at the briefing, intelligence said they had good sound information that this place was going to be crawling with *beau coup* VC, but there ain't shit here."

"What a pity," the Kid sarcastically intoned, causing Wilson to finally stop walking and turn to face him.

"Enjoy it while you can, Specialist," he said with a strange expression on his narrow face, "there's some changes coming down that are going to radically alter our lives... something really exciting, different and interesting, but I can't tell you yet, not until I hear that it's all set."

The Kid stared back at him. "Till *'what's'* all set?"

"I can't tell you 'what'... until it's set," now Wilson was amusing himself.

"So, are we going to stand here doing 'Who's on First,' or are you gonna tell me *what the fuck you are talking about?*

"No. Never mind. I shouldn't have said anything, I can see that now," Wilson began walking again, "don't worry, I'll know as soon as we get back from this operation if 'WHAT' is going to happen or not. And if it does or doesn't, I'll tell you then."

For the rest of the day, it ate at the Kid, not knowing what 'what' was. Wilson had him going with that little 'I've got a secret,' mechanism, only it wasn't a game but rather something that was going to alter the Kid's life. *It can't be good. If it's something that is making HIM happy, it can't be good. And getting shot at must be in there somewhere! I'm fucked.*

A cloudburst came and went, and their pace slowed somewhat, because it turned out, there were lots of people around the huts they encountered, women and children that was, and it was necessary to talk with many of them to get information. *Fat chance. Look at all the Kids... like these mommies are going to rat out the fathers of their children. Cam bao ya.*

When they stopped for lunch, the Kid ate in a daze. The hot air, humidity and sweat pasted his uniform to his body while his mind wanted to escape, to trip the light fantastic on any plane of the Universe, other than the one he found himself on that instant. *I've lost Flo. I'm in the middle of a war so endless that the fricking natives think we're French. We're going to spend the night out here where no amount of bug repellant will keep all the mosquitos away. I know those goddamned Charlies are cooking up something special for us because they never acted like this before. And look at Wilson, all smug with his precious little secret. Ain't life grand. What in the fuck did I do to get sent here?*

Following a round of cigarettes, the unit moved out and almost instantly, they took another 3 casualties on a foot mine. The Whiskey India Alpha's now totaled five for their element and 8 on the day for Company A. And the VC hadn't even fired a shot at them. *Some things never change. Charlie is putting the hurt on us and he doesn't even have to show up!*

At about 1500 hours, Capt. Wally and Tu Ta had a short discussion about rather or not to call in medivacs for the 8 wounded men or just wait until later in the day. Wait, was the decision.

Then, almost like magic, the Kid glanced down at his watch and saw that it was 1700 hours. *Wow! The day has really gone by pretty fast. They'll be talking perimeter here any minute!*

Breaking out of thick foliage, the command element came upon a particularly large structure on the edge of a tree line, looking out over a modest sized paddy area, surrounded by other tree lines that made it an open oval, about of about 300 meters wide by 500 meters long. If the oval were a clock, with the tight ends being 6 and 12, the big hut sat at the 7:00 position, with 6 being to the right. Sitting not more than 25 meters back from the paddies, the house was so big it seemed out of place, compared to all the other huts they'd seen that the day.

Once again, people were present and Tu Ta was speaking to a young woman who held a child on her hip while an old woman behind her was in the act of gathering up five more kids, none older than six or seven. Than was informing her that she was going to have guests tonight, while the old women, with a barely concealed sense of urgency, was rapidly herding the children inside.

The Kid began looking for a place he could sit down and have a cigarette. Smiling at Ba, he sensed they shared a happiness that it had been a day without any real contact. But almost immediately after the last child and the grandma had disappeared into the hut, they heard the first couple of distant 'pops.' *Was that gunfire?*

The sounds also caught the attention of the rest of the command element, which stood near the entrance to the hut, discussing establishment of the perimeter and the calling of a medivac in to pick up the day's wounded and 5 seconds following, sporadic bursts automatic weapons fire came from the 12 o'clock position in the oval and with the ensuing response, the unit then fully engaged! *Those sons of bitches! They waited until the 5 o'clock whistle to start today!*

37

Everybody hit the deck as AK-47 rounds began screaming into the position. From where he was laying, the Kid could see that one of the squads had been working down the middle of the paddies towards the 12 o'clock position, in order to establish the perimeter and it was at them that the fire was being directed.

"What the hell's going on? Over!" Wally screamed at Tu Ta, while kneeling behind a palm tree.

Than was attempting to establish communications with Capt. Nguyen, who was in charge of the squad out in the middle of the open. Ba translated for the Kid the response that came back.

He said, "...*We are taking fire from our front, more than 2 or 3 VC... maybe 5 or 6.*"

"Hey! Now we're cooking'" Wilson cracked, full of relish.

Everybody was still down on the ground in front of the door to the hut. From inside, the wailing terrified cries of the half dozen babies issued forth, as bullets continued to hit all around, with multiple rounds striking the hut itself. The rounds were not necessarily being aimed at them, but the hut was on nearly a direct line behind Nguyen's squad, out in the middle of the paddies, at whom the bullets were being shot. As soon as the ARVNs got their M-60 working from their right side, the command element caught a breather.

The Kid rose and looked inside the hut door, to see if any of the children or women had been hurt and was surprised at what he saw. *Well, I'll be dammed, look at that! They got their own built-in family bunker! Amazing! They all fit inside it!*

The mini bunker was built sunken into the ground about 3 feet deep while rising two feet above the earthen floor, with the top of it being another two feet thick and forming a platform table in the room. From the light of a candle the women had burning inside the small bunker, the Kid could see an area, easily five by six foot. There wasn't enough headroom for an adult to stand, although, with all of them huddled together as far from the door as possible, that wasn't an issue. When the Kid looked in, he noticed the women showed signs of anxiety, not knowing if the soldiers were coming to drag them out. The Kid reassuringly made a "stay there" gesture to them and when he emerged from the hut, found himself at the tail end of an important conversation.

"Yeah, but it's late in the day," Wally was saying, "We can't get too caught up in this right now, because we don't have a perimeter... "

"But Dai Ui Wally," Tu Ta took command, "we need to take the tree line in front of us, or they will threaten us from there all night! I am ordering Dai Ui Nguyen to assault the tree line!"

"And we can get some air support" Wally was into it, "this might be our big chance for a large body count on this operation!

"I want to go!" Wilson exclaimed, "I want to go be in on the assault!"

Than glanced at him and then over to the Kid before saying to the excited lieutenant, "If you want to go, that would be good to have another radio out there in case anything happens to Dai Ui's. Yes, go...and take Stocka… to get 'chu hois!' Then he laughed.

"But we don't have any loudspeakers," the Kid protested.

"Well, then Kid," Wally spoke up, "I guess you'll have to get really close and yell like hell!" Everybody, except the Kid and Ba laughed uproariously.

"The man's right!" the light went on in Wilson's brain, "thank you, Tu Ta! Come on, Stocker and Ba, and I don't even have to ask you, Con, I know you'll be right with me," Wilson slapped his faithful RTO on the shoulder. "We're going' right up front! Right now! Stick with me, all of you!" Con, of course, does but Ba and the Kid follow reluctantly a few meters back.

Wilson immediately led them toward the edge of the paddies where an additional 3 men from the 2nd squad were getting a pep talk from the senior ARVN NCO, who was preparing to take them out to join Dai Ui Nguyen's men for the assault. The older ARVN was a master sergeant who had a greying fu man chu style moustache. *I'll call him Sgt Fu in the book.* Ba translates for Wilson as Sgt. Fu explains his plan: *We're going to advance directly out, a dyke at a time, and join up on Dai Ui Nguyen's left. There was support coming, some Cobras, he didn't know when, but everybody had to hustle to get into position for when the air cover materialized.*

Sgt. Fu gave the wave, and the men began moving out into the paddies. With the PSYOPS four trailing the ARVNs and shading to their left, the eight men dashed the 20 meters to the first paddy dyke and knelt, to make sure everybody was ready for the next rush. *Charlies aren't paying any attention to us; I can see they're still putting some fire on Dai Ui... I guess the closer we get to them, the dicer it'll get.* As they rose and sloshed through the watery square of growing rice shoots to the next dyke, the Kid had cause to switch from his prescription shades to his clear lenses. *Getting darker. Don't like this.*

Suddenly, the movement of the reinforcing group was spotted by the VC who were engaged with Nguyen and they began firing at them, causing the advance to momentarily all drop into the rice. They were, however, quickly back up and moving forward. Wilson, with Con seemingly attached to his hip, also rose from his covering dyke and rush forward in a crouching run.

Feeling the heat of the rounds, the Kid and Ba make a silent agreement to stay down and low crawl to the next dyke and no sooner would they arrive at Wilson's position than he and Con would up and bolt on to the next one. *I'm still crawling, the Army spent a hell of a lot of time teaching me how to low crawl in basic training and I will get them their money's worth today! I can't believe douche bag Wilson wants to go up front for no good reason. We are not assault troops! And look at him! Got his Luger out... I will admit, he is somewhat inspiring to the ARVNs, I'll give him that! But I'm still crawling... Damn! The fucking volume of AK is serious. That's beau coup Charlies in there for sure!*

As he crawls most of the water in the paddies is about elbow deep but moving through one paddy, there is enough water that he is tempted to try and float in it while his hands and knees are propelling him through. Every few crawls, he checks for his .38. *Please don't make me need it please don't make me need it ooooommmmmm oooooommmmmmm.* He can see Wilson, laying behind the dyke ahead, looking back at him, angry eyes smoking beneath his steel pot, obviously upset that the Kid would not get up and run with him and the boys between dykes.

"God dam it! Stocker! Keep up!" he screamed and was up and off again!

More crawling. I will keep up, Sir. At this pace, sir. With the amount of lead that is flying, I look at this as protecting government property and you should too you terminal John Wayne fuck head!

In fairly steady fashion, they all arrive online with Dai Ui Nguyen's men in about 5 minutes and as they did, the PRC-25s crackled with exchanges. Tu Ta and Wally had secured a pair of Cobras to aid in the assault and they were coming around in 120 seconds.

From 9 or 10 paddy dykes out from the trees, which was about 200 meters, the 15 ARVNs and the VC continued to steadily trade fire. The ARVN goal was to achieve a position behind the first dyke out, an advance of 180 meters, from where the final assault would take place.

Wilson is on fire! He is in his element, waving his Luger at Dai Ui Nguyen, who is more than happy to have the American Lt. Volunteer to come up and help with the charge. Look at that fucker! I can't imagine whatever it is that possesses somebody to want to BE in this shit! Whatever it is he has in store for us couldn't be any worse than this! Man o man the volume is heavy! They are not going to let us in... Red Rover Red Rover, send nobody over! Holy shit! Is that the Cobras?

Looking back and locating them by the noise of their approaching rotors beating the tropical sky and sometimes pop-pop-popping like shots during a high G turn, the Kid picked up the Cobra gunship helicopters that had been called in to help. He spotted the first one as it came from his right onto to the 6 O'clock line of the oval, preparing to bring fire on the VC in the 12 o'clock position in front of the ARVNs. It is directly behind them, and the Kid marveled at how the design of the gunship, when going from side to frontal view, really did seem to make it disappear.

Suddenly, emerging from the circular rocket pods on either side of the thin nosed chopper, a pair of rockets flew over their heads, on a shallower than 45-degree angle, it made the hairs on the back of the Kid's neck stand up as he watched the smoke trails lead to explosions in the tree line in front of them with thundering flashes of orange.

"Come ON!" screamed Wilson at the top of his voice "now's the time to MOVE UP!" and he continued to run with the ARVNS amid the rockets flying overhead and the VC putting out automatic weapons fire from their concealed positions. First one and quickly another ARVN went down to the Kid's right and a medic immediately diverted off the advance to treat them.

Between looking back to see when the next rockets were being fired and reacting to the bullets that came close enough to attract his attention, the Kid and Ba almost simultaneously decided to run and try and catch up a little. Looking up, he could see the scrawl markings of the 4 rocket smoke trails hanging in the thick air, like fat strands of spider silk, ready to float down and ensnare them.

Arriving at the next dyke, the Kid dove behind it and peered over to see that the squad, Wilson and Con were already two dykes further up. Slithering over the mud barrier, he could feel and hear rounds passing over his head in such volume and at a height that made him fear if he got up, he would be shot and thus, continued low crawl. Ba was sticking with him and at the next dyke, as they caught a breath behind its protection, the Kid could see deep misery pour from his face along with his sweat. They both knew there was nothing they could do but continue to advance and rolling across the top of the mud wall, they began crawling through the next paddy as the pair of Cobras came around for their second pass.

This time, being even nearer to the tree line, the closeness of the rockets when they hissed overhead and the sound of the explosions when they

41

impacted in front of them were geometrically magnified and under the cover, all of the squad, save for the Kid and Ba, made it into position behind the first paddy dyke 20 meters out from the trees. It took another 3 minutes of crawling before the pair arrived next to Lt. Wilson and Con, who along with the surviving 12 ARVNS, were laying low behind the dyke while the VC holding the tree line pounded it with fire.

How did I come to be here? I could easily die today.

Wilson was on the radio to Wally and the Kid could see a few meters to his right that Dai Ui was also on the radio. *Orders are coming down. Wow, look the tracer rounds are starting to glow! Jeeze! AK 47 tracers are orange!*

They had ended up in the middle of the ARVN line, which was spread out at intervals of about 5 meters separation, for at least 50 or 60 meters, across the front of the trees. VC fire could be seen coming out of the trees in several places to both their left and right, to the extent of the ARVN presence. "Sir!" the Kid nudged Wilson as soon as he got off the radio, "look! Their tracers are orange!" They watched a dozen rounds bounce off the dyke and fly over it.

"That mean's it's really getting dark fast!" Wilson panted, wincing from some close rounds.

"VC shoot *low* today!" Dai Ui Nguyen hollered at Wilson, "no good! Numba 10 for sure!" The two Americans looked at each other and laughed.

"That's no shit...shootin' low is *numba* 10 thou!" Wilson yelled back, still chuckling!

The Kid was beginning to realize exactly how fucked up their situation was becoming. *This is a genuine FUBAR! I count at least a half dozen VC in there shooting at us from what must be well dug in positions and we're out here in the open, it's getting dark and don't have the perimeter set yet... and we gotta get in there and clear them out? With the VC "shooting to low today", I don't think it's going to happen. And where does that leave us? Deep in the Shit!*

"Are we going' in?" The Kid questioned the Lt. with an anguished expression on his young mustached face, blue eyes partially concealed through his mud splattered glasses. "You want me to yell *'Chu Hoi'* or anything, Sir?"

Wilson laughed again, laying prone in the mud and water of the paddy, steel pot sticking up above it by about two inches. "Stocker, I swear to fucking God, if anything happens to you today, I'll sure as hell miss you!"

"Hey! VC mutha fuckas! *Chi Hoi!* Right now, you bastards didi mau over here!" the Kid yelled and they broke out laughing again. *Why are we laughing? This ain't funny. I wonder how many shots have to hit in the same place to wear through this fricking paddy dyke. What difference does it make, in a few seconds, Dai Ui is gonna yell charge and these fuckers are gonna get up and shoot their way into the tree line and I'm gonna watch from here, because I sure as hell ain't going to rush into the trees with this frickin' pop gun. Damn. Do I wish I had my M-16? No. If I was shooting back, I'd be drawing fire. My job is not to draw fire. My job is to get them to surrender...if I need one, it will be there, on the ground, next to a dead ARVN. Hey, there's nobody's M-16 laying around... Gee, this is amazing that we haven't taken any more casualties than the two guys that got hit while we were moving up!*

Laying there, he was beginning to catch his breath from the incredible physical feat of crawling all the way up to the very front through the mud of the rice paddies in the heat of the Delta. Not once did it occur to him to think about snakes. He watched individual soldiers lay their M-16's on the top of the paddy dyke and while remaining low behind the mud barrier with all but their hands and forearms, fire at the tree line while not really seeing where the enemy fire was coming from and thusly, not successfully suppressing it. The tracers in the clips of the ARVNs were red. Red was going in and orange was coming out. From his angle, he could see the colors crisscrossing and mixing in the air. Mud was exploding off the front of the dyke, kicking a good five feet up into the air and sprinkling down on them.

My job is to convince the VC to surrender! Yeah, get them pinned down.... Gettem' trapped and get up there with a bullhorn. Who's got who pinned down NOW? Fat fucking chance! They are throwing out the fire! My God! I've never been in fire this heavy! Man o man, if the Cobras were shooting at these guys now, with us here? Mrs. Stocker, your son was killed by friendly fire, but he was doing his duty... No, I wasn't. I wasn't doing my duty. I've been misappropriated! Where's my speakers? Lying fucking bunch of Army Bastards! You're going to be in Armed Forces Radio, Curt... you're going to be a foreign language announcer, Curt... Why is it that the Army can't tell you the fucking truth? Why?

"They say on the radio, we might be falling back," Ba breathed to the Kid, in a fear filled tone of voice barely audible in the din of the automatic weapons fire.

"Say what?" the Kid was shocked.

"Yeah!" Wilson confirmed, "Tu Ta is calling it off and we're supposed to fall back!"

"You gotta be fucking kidding me!" the Kid exclaimed, "fall back?" *Oh no. We have to fall back in front of these fuckers who are blazing away at us?* The Kid closed his eyes and pictured his death, shot in the back while retreating from a place he never should have been in the first place. *How did I come to be here?*

When, just three of four seconds later, he opened his eyes and looked to his left, where Ba and Wilson had been, nobody was there! He turned his head to the right, where Dai Ui Nguyen had been; nobody was there! In fact, there was nobody to his right or left. *Say what?* And looking behind him, the Kid saw that everybody, *except him,* had gotten up and ran!

Holy fuckin' Batshit! I am alone at the front!

The adrenalin jolt was earth shaking. It was hard for him to tell if time was flying or stand still, laying there solo in the water and mud, 20 meters from the Viet Cong, who were at that instant, directing their fire over his head at his fleeing mates. Full retreat! Everyone on the ARVN side, save the Kid, was now over a full paddy dyke away and rapidly getting smaller.

Holy fucking shit! If I get up and run, I'll be an easy kill! If I stay here... I'll be captured! Or killed! Or captured! In that instant, *'fear of being captured'* trumped 'fear of being killed', and with that realization, the Kid jumped up and bolted from behind the paddy dyke and in 3 steps, hit full stride in the race of his life!

All the tracers were now orange and screamed by from behind, not only on his left and right, but over his head as well. Close one! Close one! Coming to the first paddy dyke, he hurtled it like he was Jesse Owens, and it was then he noticed a Huey chopper with Red Cross in a white circle painted on its nose, was settling to the ground back by the big hut. *The Medivac! They're picking up the wounded! Hope they don't need to wait for me! Should I zig zag? No! You stupid fuck! Just run! Run and don't look back!* He hurtled the second dyke and when he passed them, the Kid was moving so fast that he hardly noticed Lt. Wilson, Cpl. Ba and Con, plodding along at a speed that could only be described as pedestrian. The Kid didn't know where the finish line was, but he knew he hadn't gotten there yet. He might not have been capable of running on top of the water in those paddy dikes, but he was sure as hell running on top of the mud!

As he sprinted toward the chopper being loaded with dead and wounded ARVNs, the Kid determined that the volume of fire from the tree line now passing over his head was being directed at the chopper. *Why those fuckers are trying to shoot down the Red Cross chopper!* Multiple rounds were hitting short by a few meters, evidenced by staccato splashing water in the paddies in front of the chopper. More dykes, more hurtling and as he drew within 50 meters of the big hut, the chopper lifted off, peeled immediately back around in a 180-degree maneuver away from the incoming and was gone.

Slowing to a stop in front of Wally, the Kid gasped for breath. "Those fuckers left me up there at the front!" he exclaimed to the captain.

"Left you? Stocker, how can you say they left you when you're the first one back?" Wally looked at him with a crooked mouth showing below his brown eyes. "Tu Ta's the one who decided to call it off, soon as he got confirmation from the TOC that a Spooky could come cover us while we set up a perimeter."

"Spooky?"

"Yep, be here any second. You wouldn't want to be down where you were in a minute or so," Wally checked to his backside, "we're pretty secure behind the hut and over to the left and right, it's that tree line to the front I hope he hits right on the money, right where they're concentrated."

Just then, Lt. Wilson staggers up with Con right behind and Ba not far back. "I... swear... to God... Stocker...." he attempted to speak while being completely winded, "I never seen... anybody run that fast... in my entire life! You should be in the fucking... *Olympics!*"

Con, who didn't appear to be that winded, took a knee and swung the PRC 25 down off his back while Ba flat collapsed to the ground. The shooting remained sporadic.

"Yes, Sir," the Kid broadly smiled to Wilson, "I was fuckin' moving', wasn't I! When I looked around and saw you guys had all *didi maued*, it scared the living shit out of me! I was motivated, goddam right I was flyin'! I think what happened was, when the chopper came in, they stopped trying to shoot soldiers and tried to knock the bird down, otherwise they would have got us all!"

"I think you're right." the Lt weakly nodded up and down, still trying to catch his breath.

Within a minute, Spooky arrived on the scene and immediately went to work. The men watched as the C-47 with its 3 side mounted mini guns flew a loop around their position and hosed the jungle with a stream of red tracers that poured down while its macabre machine gun sounds floated on the hot, humid air above the sound of the airplane's engines: *Brrrrrrrrrrrrrrruppppp brrrrrrrrrrrrrrrrrrruppppppppp!* Spooky made three loops and the darker it got, the redder the tracers became. There was no tracer fire going up to take Spooky on; the VC had chosen to break it off.

All the while, standing there in front of the hut, the Kid couldn't help but notice the crying in the background, emanating from the hut; it was the children hiding in the bunker. *How afraid must they be? I mean shit, a major battle with air support being fought in their front yard. I can't imagine what it would be like to be shot at by Spooky! If we weren't here using their hut, they'd be in a free fire zone. I wonder how many huts like this one are just on the other side of or in those trees that Spooky is shooting' up? And it's probably their relatives we're trying to kill while they try to kill us!*

Once Spooky left, the battlefield momentarily fell silent, and it was quickly becoming night. The Kid was exhausted from the ordeal.

From the doorway of the hut, which was now covered by a green army poncho, Wilson called, "Yo, Stocker," motioning for him to come inside. When he did, the Kid found the interior lit by 3 candles that sat on top of the family bunker. Tu Ta, Captain Wally, their RTOs, Con, Ba and Sgt. Fu were already settling into various corners of the area and as big as the hut had appeared, it was now crowded with and smokey from the cigarettes of the men who were not going to spend the night in rifle pits on the perimeter.

"You can tie your hammock up over there," Wilson pointed to the two main supports posts in the middle of the hut.

Walking over to them, the Kid pulled his green nylon hammock from his right front cargo pants pocket and tied it up. He placed his steel pot on the dirt floor by the post where his head would go and eased into the hammock to try it out. He immediately discovered that from where he swung, he had a view to his right directly into the family bunker. The light of a single candle within revealed that a couple of the children were craning their necks to get a look at him; a girl of about 5 or 6 and a boy of maybe 3 or 4. At least two or more of them continued to make with some serious crying and the Kid was given pause to wonder how long it might last.

He lay there, swinging slightly back and forth, with his eyes shut tight. *My God! I thought I was dead meat! How did I ever get out of that? I don't think I've ever been more scared in my entire fucking life! Hot and humid. A pack of kick ass VC just waiting outside. Crying babies inside. Attack or not, I know there ain't gonna be no sleeping' in here tonight. I just hope we don't get attacked. I hope to God they won't risk their children and don't target this hut because of them. Hey, I bet that's why Tu Ta is staying here, that sly old bastard. Human shields! Yeah!*

"Hey, Stocker..." Wilson walked over to him, "hungry? We got some MRE's here."

46

"Maybe in a bit," he sat up, "laying down felt pretty good but I don't think we'll be getting any Zs with the babies crying, so might as well eat!"

"No fucking shit," the Lt. agreed but took it a step further, "if they keep it up, we might have to shoot'em!"

The Kid about fell out.

"Ha!" Wilson barked with a laugh, "relax, I was just joking!"

"Well, not so loud... you don't want to give Tu Ta any ideas!"

However, after they'd eaten their MRI's, about an hour later, the children still continued to cry, and the Kid imagined more than one person in the hut relished the thought of shooting them all.

The Kid's head was totally blown off the scale of controlled conciseness and behind his tightly closed eyes, a stream of thoughts and visions bombarded him, like shrapnel or the bullets hitting against the paddy dyke. A vision of Flo's face flew by so fast it made him think of the cyclone that swept away Dorothy in the *Wizard of Oz.*

I am spiraling out of control. Still not down from the rush of being left up there. What if those VC were friends with the 3 VC prisoners the ARVNs shot last week? I would rather be dead than captured... outright dead. I guess that's how those kids felt. Yeah. But that still doesn't make it right. My God! What a rush! I wish I could have got a better look at Wilson's face when I passed him! The Kid's body shuddered, as he tried mightily to stifle the nearly overwhelming urge to laugh as he recalled how totally shocked the Lt. had been in the peripheral image stored in his memory. *Shit. I must have used up my whole adrenalin allotment for the next six weeks! Talk about tripping' like acid!* Then in quick succession, the images of Captain Robinson's body, Li's face, his new pool cue, Flo's 'Dear John' letter, John Lennon in his round glasses, the Armed forces radio Saigon control room, Shauna McConnell's face *or was it's the VC girl's face?* Flashed past his third eye, like billboards on a highway. And still the children, who were no more than 8 feet from him, continued to heartily cry. He repeatedly relived the instant when his survival instinct kicked in and he jumped up from behind his shielding paddy dyke and sprang into motion, arms pumping, legs firing like pistons... *hurtling those dykes... Coach Swinsco would have been proud!* He recalled his high school track coach, who kicked him off the team when he was a senior, for smoking and skiing. *Never could have run that fast toting an M-16... and if I would have had one, would it have made any difference at the tree line? I don't think so, not with Tu Ta pulling the plug like that. How did I come to be here?*

Mercifully, right after 2100 hours the children began to run out of gas and the bawling degenerated into low sobbing and the Kid could hear the mother and the granny attempting to sooth them with hushed voices in the darkness of their shelter. *Will this night never end? What am I talking about? All I have to look forward to tomorrow is another day of this same fucking shit! At least we'll go back in tomorrow... if they don't hit us right at the end of the day like they did today! Clever little sons of bitches!*

The Kid rolled out of his hammock to land on all fours on the floor, from wince he stood up to go outside and take a piss. He had never bothered to take his glasses off so he could see in the dim light from the single candle set up by Tu Ta's radio man in the farthest corner. Easing out through the poncho cover, the Kid emerged into pitch blackness. A few stars were visible through an opening in the clouds of the late monsoon season, and he stumbled slightly, as if drunk, looking more up than for a good place to urinate. *Hell, this is good as any.* He stops and hauls it out and immediately let's go and as his fluids collided with the Delta mud, he had to wonder: *What the fuck is Wilson is up to? What the fuck is it that he's doing that's going to change our lives? What the fuck is 'What?'*

Chapter 5

It was the next day following the end of the last operation and after being gone all morning, Wilson finally materialized after lunch and found the Kid shooting practice racks in the empty Tra Vinh club and Ba sitting at a nearby table happily bored and smoking. He motioned for the Kid to come and sit at Ba's table.

"Yo, Mi!" he raised one arm to attract her attention, "three cokes, *see vous* play,"

"Well," he addressed the Kid and Ba, "I just came from the TOC where I was talking by phone with Capt. Ronnie Smith in Can Tho and everything is ready for our next assignment!" *Suspense.* "We are taking over an 'Armed Propaganda Team'!" Wilson spoke the words with a slow deliberateness and ended with a smile, as if he expected the Kid and Ba to be delighted with his announcement and show him due appreciation but they responded with blank looks.

The cokes hit the table and Wilson dug out the MPC to cover it.

"Everything is armed around here, Sir, you'll have to give us a little more specific information; what do you mean, *'armed propaganda team?'*" the Kid took a sip.

"Well," he began, "as you know, when PSYOPS gets a VC to defect, sometimes they are rehabilitated into Kit Carson Scouts, who go out with American units and tell them where the booby traps and tunnels are at... and shit like that there... but now, Captain Ronnie Smith came up with this new thing, to take a group of them and turn them into what is called, an *'Armed Propaganda Team '*. An 'APT' will consist of 24 ex Viet Cong and two American advisors... and an interpreter," he added, with a nod to Ba. "The team goes back at night, into the area from where they defected, and they'll point out the other VC and we'll either kidnap'em or kill'em!"

He must be joking. I hope to God you're joking! "You must be joking, Sir," the Kid nervously smiled back, always being one to appreciate a good joke.

"No."

"Go out with 24 guys who have already switched sides once?"

"Yes," Wilson said, deadpan serious.

Silence. The Kid digested the news. *He's not joking.* "Now, let me get this straight," he pushed his round wire glasses up higher on his nose, "we are going to go out with 24 guys who have already switched sides once, in the middle of the night, and we are going back to where they used to live to kidnap or kill other VC? Is that essentially it? Have I got it exactly right?"

"Exactly right. I always tell everybody what a smart boy you are, Stocker, I appreciate you not letting me down."

"I see," the Kid said as he glanced down at his coke, bubbling away in the grip of his left hand. "This sounds like commando shit to me. That would make it a volunteer situation. Is this a volunteer assignment, Sir?"

"Yes, it is."

He would have lied if he could. "Then count me out." the Kid unequivocally stated with a dismissing wave of his hand, punctuating by a smile to Ba. *Ball's in your court,* he reverted his attention back to the lieutenant.

"Stocker," Wilson shook his head slowly back and forth as he looked into the face of his spec. 4, "after all we've been through, and I thought you'd want to come with me on this assignment. This is the wave of the future for PSYOPS. Screw all that loudspeaker bull crap and MED-caps and the MSQ 85's. This is an incredible opportunity to really make a difference! I've already told Capt. Smith we'd do this. It is his very own special pet project!"

"Well, you should have spoken to me before you spoke *for* me, don't you think, Sir? Because my answer is *no*."

The Lt. paused and took a drink as he marshalled his argument to win the Kid over to the project. "Tell you one thing, if the APT works out, I promise you we'll only be going one operation a month, not the six or seven... or eight like we're doing' now." He was sure that would win him over, knowing how much the Kid hated operations.

The Kid and the lieutenant locked eyes as he formulated his answer. *You expect me to say to you, 'oh really? Only one operation a month? Such a deal! Oh golly, I will go with you on your ATP... but I say, "No. N. O, that's a big negatory-o, Sir."*

Wilson broke off the stare, fully comprehending the delicateness of his predicament, knowing it was within the Kid's right, to not volunteer for a volunteer mission, sensing that the Kid was digging in and looking for a conflict. If he couldn't get the Kid to join him as a willing partner on the APT project, he'd have to tell Ronnie Smith that he lied; Stocker hadn't volunteered after all. That could be a major problem in his life.

Now Ba was grinning at the exchange, not fully understanding how it was the Kid could even tell Wilson *'no'* without Wilson just giving him the order to do it. He would have to ask the Kid later how this was possible.

"Come on now," Wilson was going into his *'aw shucks'* routine, "I mean what the heck, you haven't even met'em yet. Will you keep an open mind about this thing until we can go out and you can meet them and see if you like'em or not?"

The Kid lit up a KOOL. "*You've* met them?"

"Yep," the Lt. lit a Winston, "this morning. Major Gillmore, the Hog and I went out to their compound so they could show me where it was, and the Major introduced me to their *Dai Ui* and we're going back out later this afternoon! Their compound is on the south edge of town, about a mile past the airport."

The more I hear the less I like.

"They pull their own security," the Lt. continued, "the ARVNs don't trust them and since they've been kicking the ARVN's butts for years, they don't trust the ARVNs to defend them... not to mention that their former associates *really* want them dead."

And you want to go hang with these fuckers? My common sense tells me to avoid these dudes like the plague!" He turned to the young interpreter at his right shoulder, "See Ba? Didn't I tell you? He's lost it. Off the fucking deep end!"

But when the lieutenant continued with what he had to reveal, the Kid began to truly realize just how far off the deep end he was.

"When we go out on operations, since the Hoi Chanhs aren't in the ARVN army and won't wear ARVN shit, we're going to get these really cool uniforms tailored made for us."

The Kid's mouth fell open. *We are going to operate out of uniform?*

"Don't worry, the Army is going to pay for them... it isn't going to cost you a paper dime. We're going' downtown from here, to the tailor next to Mi's dad's place, to get measured up for them. But Ba, since you are an ARVN, you can wear your uniform."

Now Ba's mouth is also open, like he wanted to ask questions, but the necessary English was escaping him. What little he was sure of, about what

51

Wilson was saying, meant big changes to his life and so far, he did not like it one bit! Any talk of doing anything with deserters scared the living piss right out of him.

"Now wait, you're going a little fast here, Sir," the Kid put up his hand like a traffic cop, "I thought I just heard you say we were going out on operations, and we weren't going to be wearing US Army uniforms? Uh, is that even legal? I mean, if we got captured, wouldn't we be considered spies? Or at the very least, non-official combatants? Oh," the Kid snapped his fingers, "that's right, I forgot, you don't particularly find it necessary for us to *entirely adhere* to the Geneva Convention."

Being fairly good at reading people, the Kid observed that his zinger truly hit home, causing a serious burn in the lieutenant's psyche. But, since it was necessary for Wilson to conceal his true feelings while trying to convince the Kid to do something that he really didn't want or must do, he flew by the verbal slight without batting an eye.

"No," he shook his head, "not like that at all. It's just that when we go out, we all must be dressed the same way so we can tell 'who's who', when the shit starts happening. It's a logistical thing... no big deal, Stocker, really! We're advisors and we can dress to best advise by putting ourselves in the same uniform as our team! Happens all the time! Plus, we're going to get M-1 Carbines, which is what they prefer, since we can't get any AK47's. How cool is that? I know you don't like the M-16."

The Kid stared at him and said nothing. What he was asking, was for the Kid to agree to a volunteer assignment and the Kid knew, since he held the rank of "specialist", he was not bound by Army regulations to do so, nor could he be ordered to perform a dangerous volunteer combat operation without his consent. So Wilson had to make it seem cool. "I swear," Wilson raised his right hand like he was testifying in court, "once you meet these guys, you'll feel differently about the whole thing."

"And we are meeting them *when?*" the Kid crooked his head.

"Right as soon as you finish that coke, we're going to the tailor's and after that, we're driving out to the Hoi Chanh's compound."

Once done with the cokes, Wilson gave the Kid only enough time to lock up his precious new pool cue. Then, leading the way through the courtyard he indicated the Kid and Ba should climb into a jeep he had borrowed for the run. Not a word was spoken on the drive until Wilson pulled up in front of the Waterfront Tailor Shop and they walked inside and the sharply dressed bespectacled proprietor, with a yellow pencil stuck over his right ear through black slicked back hair, rushed forth to meet them.

"Ba," Wilson called the interpreter to his side, "tell him that the two of us," he gestured to the Kid and himself, "want 3 sets of uniforms each, pants and shirts, made from a durable material that is of a dark, muted color... like this burgundy here!" He laid his hand on a bolt of cloth in the tailor's rack as he finish his sentence. "And that we want military epaulets on the shoulders."

Ba spouted his magic, and no sooner was he done than the tailor unsheathed his pencil, whipped out a measuring tape and began sizing up the lieutenant as he made a bunch of notes on a pad of paper. The Kid's measurement quickly joined the lieutenant's and he turned to Ba with his estimate.

"He say they be ready in two days," Ba translated for Wilson, cost you $40 MPC.

"Excellent!" The lieutenant gave the deal his stamp of approval by forking over a $20 MPC as a down payment. "Now, we need to go back to the compound, I have to pick up a couple of things we're taking out to 'the boys,' and Stocker, I want you to grab your M-16 and a bandolier, just in case we need some fire power on the ride back in tonight, because we'll probably be out there until sunset."

Oh great. The Kid said nothing. There was nothing to say. Wilson had what he considered to be a dream assignment and he was having trouble containing his excitement. He had an extra little 'bounce' in his step, as they made their way back to the jeep and shooed off the half dozen young Vietnamese children that were playing on it.

Back at the compound, the Kid fetched the M-16 from his locker to augment the presence of their pistols and all the while, his apprehension level was breaking the thermometer. *Ex VC. I don't believe it! How the fuck did I ever.... ever get into this situation? 'You'll LIKE'em,' he says... 'You'll think they're just the coolest guys you ever met!' he says...'Only one operation a month,' he says... Lying sack of shit I says... I still haven't said I volunteer, and I don't think just meeting these guys is going to change my mind about wanting to go out in the middle of the night. Fuck! I hate it when we stay out there overnight with OUR battalion... don't want to do that with anybody who was ever on their fucking side. Shit! It's scary enough being out there in a defensible position all night, inside a perimeter, not out sneaking' around looking for the trouble... you find it; it finds you... what a fucking loser deal this is! Comes with the job he says. It's not the job, I say. I do not want to do any commando crap... I didn't sign on for any fricking commando crap and looking to find some more VC in the dark? Surrounded by VC, with ex-VC, looking' for VC. Let me think of a worse situation...*

Hmmm. I can't. Total fucking bullshit! So why does Wilson think I'm going to change my mind to the point that he ordered those fricking uniforms?

It was a point the Kid continued to ponder on the drive out to the Hoi Chanh's compound, which was just past the big curve in the road, by the airport and a mile up Highway 4. It was on the absolute edge of what could be considered the town of Tra Vinh's defensive positions. *Wow. We're on our way to go meet a bunch of Viet Cong! Ops... ex-Viet Cong, I mean. This is going to be pretty fucking interesting, even if I don't ever volunteer for the assignment! I wonder what Wilson has in that sack that he put in the back?*

Chapter 6

When Wilson pulled off the pavement, the Kid could immediately see the compound. The brush and trees beyond it had been cleared back a good 100 meters. Rows of intermittently set concertina wire ringing the 50-meter square enclosures formidable shoulder high bunker like wall. It was topped with a sparkling new chain link fence, which was additionally crowned with 3 more rolls of concertina, strung out in a triangle of two on the bottom hanging down and one more running along the very top.

Glancing at his Seiko, the Kid noted it was 1430 hours. *2:30*, he translated it back into civilian time. The razor wire was pulled to the right side of the road to permit the passage of traffic and two men from inside the compound opened the gate at the approach of the jeep. Sentries were visible in bunkers located on the corners of the compound as Wilson drove through the gate and parked next to a fresh, new looking white plaster building in the center of the enclosure. It was large enough to indicate it was like a commons area and likely contained the unit's kitchen facility.

To the right, four smaller houses made of plaster appeared to be of family size and were obviously occupied as women watched them while children ran in and out the doors. The excitement of having American visitors was almost too much for them. On the other side of the whitewashed commons structure were four more houses in various stages of completion.

Three men emerged from the main building to meet them. The one in front, who most certainly appeared to be in charge, was about the Kid's size, 5'10' and sported a heavy black moustache and had a haircut like Moe Howard's. His jaw, however, was much stronger and squarer than the lead Stooge's and a very jagged four-inch-long scar decorated his right cheek on an angle from his mid-ear to his chin. It looked like a river with little tributaries. *I'll have to get the story on that.* He appeared to be in his early 40's and he was dressed in white cotton pants and wore a light tan button up short sleeve shirt that was fully open, displaying a muscular chest that was punctuated by about a half a dozen renegade black and gray hairs. The two younger men, who could have been anywhere from 18 to 25 years of age, stood behind him and smiled, obviously on duty.

"Men yoi, Dai Ui," Lt. Wilson saluted the man and then extended his hand to shake. "Dai Ui Kanh, this is Hashi Stocker and Hashi Ba, our interpreter." The Kid saluted him and offered his hand, discovering the man had a very firm grip.

"Chao Dai Ui," the Kid grinned.

"Chao Hashi," the Dai Ui returned the smile.

Ba did the same, "Chao Dai Ui Kanh," he said and bowed slightly as he shook the man's hand but did not salute. He quickly withdrew his from the Hoi Chanh leader's grip and looked like he thought it might be prudent to count his fingers.

By the time the introductions were concluded, all the children in the compound had gathered to the right side of the building, staying back a respectful distance, but assuredly captivated by the presences of the Americans. The Kid smiled broadly and lifting his prescription shades, he winked at them, causing a peel of laughter to erupt from the group. *I still got it!*

With a casual sweep on his arm, the ex-VC commander motioned toward the door and the group began to head inside out of the tropical sun.

"Oh! The goods!" Wilson snapped his fingers and returned to the back of the jeep to fetch the sack he'd brought.

Entering the building, they found themselves in a spacious room with a ceiling vaulted by support beams. It took up half of the structure and had two doorways leading off to other areas, one of which was clearly the compound's communal kitchen. The center of the room was dominated with the ever-present cable spool table, which was a good 6 feet in diameter. Around it were gathered an eclectic collection of wooden chairs, boxes and benches upon which ten people could easily sit.

Kahn moved directly to one of the chairs that had a back and sat down. The Kid sat to his right and Ba ended up on his left while Wilson selected a stool directly opposite them; one that made him look a little taller. Once the guests were seated, other members of the unit entered the room tentatively and took up the remaining half a dozen seats. *Here I am in a room with 9 ex Viet Cong! Un-fucking REAL!* All of them appeared to be young; in their early 20's, maybe even teens, except for one man, whose outward appearance made him to be the same age as Kanh or slightly younger.

Once they were all seated, Wilson immediately lifted two fifths of Cabin Still Bourbon out of the sack and sat them on the table along with a carton of Salems. "Ba, have Kanh bring in some glasses, we're gonna do some drinkin' and get to know these fine fellows," he beamed. Opening the carton, he took out a pack, broke the seal and tapping out the contents, tossed the pack in the middle of the table with a gesture inviting the men to help themselves, which they all did without hesitation.

As they passed the green pack around, the Kid rose and pulling his Zippo from his pocket, he lit up the cigarettes of all the men he could reach and each one thanked him as he did.

There were no fans in the room and the smoke hung heavy over the table as the 9 men all smoked. *I wonder if this place even has electricity.*

A woman came forth from the kitchen with a tray of odd shaped and sized glasses and cups and proceeded to place one in front of each man. Picking up a bottle and twisting off the cap, Wilson proceeded to fill his own glass, which was about the size of two shot glasses, and slid the bottle to the next man, pantomiming that he should fill his glass and pass it on. The bottle quickly went around the table and soon everybody, including the Kid, had a glass.

Rocking forward from his stool, Wilson raises his glass in a toast for Ba to translate; "Here's to our success as an Armed Propaganda Team!" he throws the drink down the hatch and the Hoi Chanhs followed suit.

God how I hate fucking bourbon! The Kid thought as he took a tiny sip.

Across the table, Wilson had already poured his next double shot.

"Another toast," he again rises with his glass hoisted, "here's to all the sewing machines and Hondas that we're going to liberate, and YOU can keep!"

Ba launches into some long-winded explanation of the toast and as he does, the Kid notices that the smile is gone from the Captain's face and that he takes a serious, appraising look at the lieutenant before drinking the toast.

The Kid hesitates, staring into the caramel brown liquid in the bottom of his glass, wishing only to leave it there.

"Dammit Stocker, drink! You don't want these guys to think you are some weak shit pussy, do you?" Wilson wastes no time getting after him.

Begrudgingly, the Kid followed the Lt's order and as soon as he did, he noticed that Kanh was now giving Wilson the eye, sizing him up and he senses that there is some potential friction developing between him and the lieutenant.

"Another toast," Wilson has the glasses filled again. This time, he does not stand to make it, "here's the best APT that is going to kill the most VC of any armed propaganda team in the history of the Delta!" He throws the shot down even before Ba finishes the translation.

"Drink that shot, Stocker," Wilson admonished him, "be a fucking man for once! Drink! That's an order!"

"Well, if you're going to put it that way," he took a sip.

"*ALL OF IT, NOW!* Specialist!"

"OK OK! Geeze!" the Kid downed it.

Wilson fills the glasses again. "Ba, have the Captain make a toast!"

After hearing the request, Kanh sat and contemplated his toast for a few seconds and then stood and spoke, with Ba making a quick translation:

"He says, '...we drink to the day we may all return to our homes in peace!'"

Well, who would have thought? Looks like I got myself an ally! "I'll sure as hell drink to that!" The Kid salutes and downs his 3rd shot without hesitation, much to Wilson's delight.

One of the younger Hoi Chanhs sitting next to Wilson asks to look at his Luger and as the lieutenant took it out and removed the clip to show him, the Kid started a conversation with Kahn through Ba. "Ask him how long ago he Chu Hoi?'"

"Almost one year ago," came the answer back.

"Did you bring these others with you?"

"No, they all came by themselves," Kanh answered through Ba.

Then, through Ba, Kanh asked the Kid a question. "You do not particularly like to drink whiskey, do you?"

"Cam bao ya!" the Kid shook his head no, which made Kanh laugh. Then he motioned Ba to come close so that he could tell him something to relay on to the Kid. Ba chuckled as he listened. *I can't wait to hear this!* When Kanh finished, Ba rose out of his chair and circled around to deliver his message to the Kid, making sure he was close enough that Wilson could not hear.

"Kanh says he likes you and hates the lieutenant because the lieutenant drinks too much. And that he makes toasts to looting and killing... Kanh says he thinks the lieutenant is ass hole number one!" at which point, the Kid broke into laughter and Kanh looked at him and the two of them laughed. Across the table, the Kid glanced at Wilson, who was totally pleased that the two of them had apparently found some common ground. *That's what you want; isn't it? For me and Kanh to become friends.* As for him, Wilson was still sucking down the whiskey at a heavy clip and keeping an eye on the Chu Hois who continued to pass around his luger.

"Di sao an Chu Hoi?" the Kid knew enough Vietnamese to ask the one question he really wanted Kanh to answer; *why did you defect?* But the answer took forever! As Ba assimilated Kanh's reply, the Kid watched Wilson for a few seconds. Now he was breaking the Luger down for one of the ex-Charlies and while he did it, he continued to drink. Wilson was obviously in a drinking mood and the VC were helping him, doing the old *'let me give you part of my drink and we toast again'* routine.

Hmmm, it looks like Wilson is actually getting a little bit drunk!

Finally, Ba signaled the Kid he was ready to tell Kanh's tale:

"This is what he say," Ba began, 'he was a member of the Viet Minh and he fought at Dien Bien Phu when he was 28. After their great victory he came home to the Mekong Delta. His family has a farm south of here, near the town of Mac Bac, on the Bassac River. All he wants is to grow rice, marry, have children, and see his grandchildren, live and die and be buried on the land of his ancestors. He was waiting for the election that was supposed to be held, agreed upon in Geneva, after the French were beaten. But Diem and the Americans did not allow the election because they feared Ho Chi Minh would win and because the French told the Americans Ho was a communist, they did not want him to win. Kanh said he did not wish to begin fighting again, as many of his friends said they would have to do. He chose to support the Diem government because it recognized his deed. But when Diem appointed a province chief who refused to recognize Kanh's deed... because the man wanted his land, that is when he joined the Viet Cong. This is about 1959.'"

Fascinating! The man is fighting solely for his land! Over on the other side of the table, Wilson has continued to drink and now, he's opening the second bottle! 5 of the Hoi Chanhs think this drunk American is pretty interesting. He's singing now and trying to get them to join in. *"I got uh... tiger by the tail its plain to see..."* The man was a sucker for an audience.

The Hoi Chanhs are trying to get him to drink more by proposing toasts. But instead of drinking, the Hoi Chanhs are emptying their glasses behind Wilson's back, into a tea pot on the floor. It is like there are two different meetings taking place in the room; Wilson is getting frat boy red neck drunk while the Kid and Ba continued to visit with Kanh.

Ba's translation picked up again: "So now, Kanh is a Viet Cong. He rises in rank and is such a good soldier, that he is sent to Moscow for one year of training in 1965. When he come back, he is made Dai Ui. Then, one day, a group of cadres arrive to teach his soldiers about the revolution. They tell him that when the North wins, all land will become communal property; there will be no private property and therefore, no need for his deed. This angered Kanh so much that he sought out representatives of the Thieu government and when they promised to recognize his deed, that is when he Chu Hoi!'"

"Dam!" the Kid exhales, "that's quite the story, Dai Ui." *All this poor guy wants is what's been in his family for hundreds of years! They beat the French and they never got their election.*

Armed with this information, the Kid was stunned by a wave of realization; *now I know how I came to BE in this place! They never held the election! If we'd have let them hold that democratic election, they'd have picked Ho and that would have been that! Instead, we are here allegedly fighting for democracy even if we had to stop an election to do it! Now the question remains... how do I get out of this fucking place? Look at Wilson over there, drunk on his ass. He sees me talking to Kanh. I bet he thinks we're becoming best friends! Well, I do like him. A little bit. But if you think I'm going out with him and them, Wilson, you finally are drunk out of your fuckin' mind!*

The woman who brought the glasses came back out of the kitchen and sat two giant plates of sliced pineapple on the table for everybody to share.

"This is Kahn's wife," Ba said, "and those two boys over there," he pointed to a pair of youngsters standing in the doorway who appeared to be about 5 or 6, "those are his sons. His only hope is that the war is over before they are old enough to fight for either side."

Before long, the sun was fading and even Wilson sensed it was time to return to Tra Vinh before it got completely dark, unless they wished to spend the night with the 24 ex Viet Cong.

"Let me drive, Sir," the Kid insisted as he and Ba helped Wilson get into the back seat of the jeep.

"OK. sssss fine with me," he didn't resist.

So with Ba riding white knuckle shotgun, holding the Kid's M-16 locked and loaded at the ready, and Wilson singing in the back, the Kid drove like a bootlegger on a run back to town. *How the fuck am I going to get out of this?*

Chapter 7

It was sturdy, well sewn and looked like it would last, he had to give it that. But, as the Kid looked at Lt. Wilson wearing one, his blood ran a touch chilly, as he tried to comprehend why it was, that this assignment precluded the wearing of the US Army uniform. Wilson had tried the uniform on immediately upon their presentation, half hiding from the view of the street behind a stack of cloth bolts, even though the tailor's shop did have a changing booth.

"What do you think?" he turned to the Kid as he finished tucking in his dark burgundy shirt tails into his equally wine-colored pants.

Like I give a shit what you look like in your new clothes... "Well, all right, Sir!" the Kid patronized him to the Nth degree.

"If the Hoi Chanhs like them, this is what we'll get. I mean, I'll tell the Hoi Chanhs this is what we're *going* to get!" He quickly corrected himself, not wanting to lose any of the control he had over the ex VC, with whom he wanted to cast their lot. "Hey, well, go ahead and try yours on! I'm not going to pay him if they don't fit you, too," he motioned for the Kid to delve into the stack of uniforms that had been presented to him.

Glancing over at Ba, who was most amused by the whole scene, the Kid shook his head and figured he, too, would try his on there behind the stack of cloth. *The shirts are good, the pants fit really nice. Too bad I must dis these threads, I kind of like them!* "They're OK, Sir, I guess," he shrugged, not wishing to convey any enthusiasm for any part of the operation. He hadn't asked for Wilson to get these made and in no way did he feel that the fact that the uniforms had been made, obligated him to accept the assignment.

"You look numba one!" Ba gave the Kid the thumbs up, "we must take your picture, send to ex-girlfriend!" the grinning Viet demonstrated that he'd been hanging out with the Kid too long and had adapted his dry sense of depreciating humor.

"Hey! At least I *had* a girlfriend!" the Kid shot back, slugging Ba's arm.

"OK! You might as well just leave those on," Wilson reached for his wallet, "we're going to meet the Hoi Chanhs at the firing range here in about a half an hour."

After transferring the contents of his pockets to his new threads *Oooppps, better leave the pot in the fatigue pants pocket...* the tailor gave each of them a polyester woven bag with plastic handles in which to cart off their new uniforms and the uniforms they had arrived wearing.

From his store two doors down, Win's father, Nguyen, observed them emerge from the tailor's shop and as the Kid started climbing into their jeep, he noticed the awkward look on his face. "Chao, Ohm," he waved and said, indicating his new clothing, "long story!"

"Kong bic?" Nguyen hollered back.

"Tell him *'long story,'* Ba," the Kid spoke over his shoulder to the interpreter, who was already seated on the back seat, which Ba obviously did, eliciting an understanding nod and a wave from the Win family patriarch. If the Kid was lucky, the day would end with a session at his house, smoking the bong and listening to Sgt. Pepper.

Straight away, they found themselves at the rifle range, located just past the Battalion's compound, the same one where Wilson and the Kid, earlier in their tour, had helped to guard the VC laborers who had built the open sided shelter in front of which they now waited. Looking at his watch quite frequently, Wilson appeared to be upset about something.

"What? Are they late?" the Kid interjected as Wilson checked it for the umpteenth time.

"Not them I'm worried about," he deposited his butt in the can provided by the edge of the shelter, "it's Sgt. Mixx, he was supposed to meet us here with our load of M-1 carbines, which I'm issuing today to you and the Hoi chanhs."

The Kid took a swig from his canteen. "You don't need to issue me one, Sir. Like I said, I'm still not going to volunteer to go on this little clambake."

Through his dark prescription shades, the Kid watched as Wilson measured his response and thought hard before finally saying, "Now there you go again, Stocker, I'm not going to ask you for your final decision yet. Let's give it until tomorrow, so we can see how it goes here at the range today, see how you like the M-1 carbine. I mean whatever you finally decide... let's just shoot the weapon and see what it and these guys can do and just have some fun... it's really a neat gun! OK? How about that?"

NO you fucking bastard... NO NO NO NO! I'm not going to change my mind! "OK, sure. Why not?" he nodded as Sgt. Mixx pulled up in Spencer's International and parked by the side of the shelter away from the firing line.

"'Bout fucking time," Wilson hollered at the black, bushy mustached E-6 as he swung the gun metal grey and slightly dented door of the International open and stepped out onto the red dirt.

"What do you mean, Sir," he stood in front of Wilson, "I don't see no Hoi Chanhs here yet, so what are you getting so upset about? I was doin' you a favor by bringing this shit out here, Sir, so I don't need you gettin' a case of the ass over it. Sir." he added as an afterthought as he flipped a smoking butt off toward the target range and walked over to the shelter and sat down on the waist high plaster wall to wait.

Wilson looked perturbed but he knew Mixx was right; the Sgt was doing him a favor so he put a sock on it. "Thanks, Sergeant," he finally begrudgingly said.

Less than a minute later, an ARVN duce and a half pulled into the range parking area and in the back, the Kid could see Kanh and ten of the Hoi Chanhs. Half were dressed predominantly in black while the others wore light colored shirts and mostly tan shorts. While they were climbing down from the high bed of the truck, Wilson motioned for him and Ba to come help remove the box of rifles from the International and once they were all out of the truck, the Hoi Chanhs gathered around the Lt. and his box of arms, without being told. Only Kanh wore a hat. The others were bare headed, if one didn't count the shock of thick black unruly hair each of them sported.

"Chao, Dai Ui," the Kid walked up to Kanh and smiled as he greeted him.

"Chao, Hashi," he smiled back, his grin distorting into the jagged scar on his right cheek, making it look like the wound had possibly opened his mouth up that wide when it happened. "Chunta de choi!" *we play!* He motioned to the rifles visible in the box in front of Wilson next to four green cans of ammo.

I must ask him how he got it.

OK, Ba," Wilson said to the interpreter who stood at his right hand, "tell'em we're gonna issue them all a M-1 Carbine and this is the weapon we'll all use on operations, so we only have to carry one caliber of ammo., so we're gonna do some training with it here today."

As Ba launched into his spiel, the Kid's mind pondered many things as he gazed at the faces of the armed propaganda team assembled before him.

63

Look at them. I wonder if there is one among them who has come this far, as an agent of the commies, to kill us all when the time is exactly right. I'll bet that's the mutha fucker right there. Oh yes, he looks like a tough one. I can sense his bad attitude and desire to be anywhere but here. Wouldn't want to get in a knife fight with him! Wonder what Flo is doing right now? If it's light here, its night there and she should be in bed. Or on the bed. Travelers Motel nude Flo blossoms in his mind as the Kid recalls making love to here for the 10 thousandth time. *The high point of my entire life. The best thing that ever happened to me... the hottest experience of my entire being. And look at me now. Rifle range, ex-VC, kill crazed lieutenant whose so stupid as to volunteer us for this and thinks it's fucking cool. But I gotta admit, Kanh is cool. I can see his men really like him.*

When Ba nodded to the Lt., that he had imparted his information and commands, the men began stepping up and pulling their M-1 Carbines out of the box and grabbing a couple of clips each and as they become armed, Kanh directs them to begin moving over to the range so that weapon familiarization can begin.

"Kid, here's yours," Wilson extended one of the compact, rather cool looking weapons toward him.

Hmmm. Escalation. He has never himself called me 'Kid' before right this fucking second! He's really pulling out all the stops, trying to score some points...

"Well, OK," the Kid stepped up and took it from the Lt.'s hand. Holding it with one hand gripping the wood encased barrel and the other hand gripping the trigger, he felt just like Vic Morrow's character, Sgt. Rock on *Combat* and operating the bolt to insure it was unloaded, he said, "But I'm telling you, Sir, it ain't gonna happen. I still ain't going. You give me this rifle, now I've got three guns and I'm in an MOS that requires NO guns. I will take target practice, but I will not be issued this weapon, Sir, because I won't be needing it."

"Then you can stop carrying your pistol, too," the Lt. shot back. Being faux friendly was one thing, but he wasn't going to lose command control of the situation as he saw it.

"OK, Sir, if that's what you say, Sir," the Kid cracked a wide grin, "Do you want me to take it off right now?" he made a motion to remove the shoulder holster. "I don't care. You think I'm going to change my mind and say I'll go, just so you'll let me carry this frickin' pistol again? That's pretty funny!"

It was not the reaction that Wilson wanted. He wanted the Kid to care enough about his pistol to want to do anything to keep the privilege of carrying it, but he obviously didn't. Wilson knew that the Kid thought *he* held the only card in the game that mattered, that being his free will ability to accept the volunteer assignment or not. The Lt. only hoped the Kid would not be too mad at him when he pulled the trick, he had up his sleeve! He would suffer through the Kid's rejections for the rest of the day before bringing it to a head tomorrow. But enough was enough, he was going to *make* him go.

Once over at the line, Wilson had Ba tell Kanh and the Hoi Chanhs to watch him and when he had their attention, he proceeded to field strips that M-1 carbine in about 30 seconds flat and when it was all laying in pieces in the ground in front of him, he looked up to see that he had the rapt attention of his class. They exchanged glances; *This Mai knows something!*

"Tell'em to do the same," Wilson instructed Ba, who relayed the command to Kanh who relayed it to the men and nodding and smiling, they all spread out and quite efficiently, broke the rifles down without so much as a 'how de doo', leaving only the Kid stand there with a rifle that was still in one piece.

"Pretty impressive," the Kid said, "Ba, tell them to put them together and do it again!"

He did. And they did! Wilson got a big chuckle out of it as the nine Hoi Chanhs seemingly raced each other see who could have his piece back in working order first to begin taking it apart again. In a flash, the ex-cong had demonstrated their expertise with the rifle, any rifle, since they came from an army whose main supply depot was what they could pick up off the battlefield.

They've seen some M-1 carbines before, the sly little bastards. I gotta admit, I like their attitude... but there ain't no way in hell I'm even going down to the corner with these guys after sunset.

"Numba One!" the Lt. gave his erstwhile commando unit the thumbs up, smiling at the Kid, watching him smile back, apparently having a good time for the moment.

Wilson had Ba send some of the Hoi Chanhs down the range to attach fresh target silhouettes to the stands in the distance so that target practice could commence. No point having a weapon if you aren't ready to use it and don't have any idea of what it'll do when you must kill somebody.

It seems to relax them, the Kid observed, as the Hoi Chanhs filled clips and shot them up, like a clay pigeon shoot back in Ogallala, openly engaging

65

in more friendly competition; most of them must have known each other for a while, it appeared, and the Kid detected, there was a definite pecking order. Kanh and a couple of the others seemed particularly concerned with the abilities of one of the skinniest among them.

"He is recovering from a bad case of dysentery," Ba confided on the health of the frail looking VC. *Ex VC gotta think they are all ex-VC.*

As they awaited their turns to fire again, the Kid stood next to Kanh in a relaxed moment, with Ba by his side. *I'll need Ba to really hear this story.* Pointing to the jagged, lightning bolt like scar down his right cheek, he asked with the only Vietnamese word he thought that he knew would

Why? I need to learn how to say how!

Kanh pointed to his scar and said, "This?" and launched into the tale for Ba to relay. The Kid watched the expressions on Ba's face as Kanh recalled the tearing of his flesh in the event that created his signature scar, complete with turning and ducking evasive maneuvers and hand gestures to show the angle the projectiles had come from to give him the wound... *I can't wait to hear this!*

"Ok,' Ba, caught his breath as he prepared to tell Kanh's tale, "this is what he say: it happened two years ago, in spring of 1966. He and half a dozen men were traveling up to area by the Cambodian border on the north side of the Mekong, near the Parrot's Beak, to retrieve supplies for his unit. They are to meet men with supplies brought down the Ho Chi Minh Trail. Some kind of American recon-nas-siance patrol found them right when they met up and after they pinned them down, they called in an air strike on them and when they realized that the jets were coming, they all ran for cover and to find shelter in any hole and he was still running when a bomb went off and a piece of shrapnel came flying by just as he looked away from where he'd turned his head to see what the jet was doing and as he turned his face away, it came flying by and just grazed his cheek and if he had turned to the other side when he turned to his left, it would have hit him square in the head. He had a hole all the way through his cheek about an inch and a medic put two big stitches in it to sew it up and he is lucky he did not lose any teeth or die from any infection. A very lucky man! he say." Ba wrapped up, smiling and gesturing with his hand to Kanh, indicating the story was his.

"Wow!" the Kid exclaimed," got it in an air strike. OK!" He got Kanh's attention and pointed to a little scar, not more than half an inch long across the inner part of his right arm three inches down from his elbow, "Dog bit me when I was five!" he said it was a big deal.

Ba snickered at the Kid's humor and when he finished translating, Kanh laughed and then, quite casually, took his new piece, flipped the selector to semi automatic and put three rounds into the head of a target sillohuette at the left side of the range.

"Steady as a rock," said Lt. Wilson, who had apparently been observing the whole scene and almost immediately, he put three rounds into the same target's head. "Het Roi!" he laughed.

Kanh looked at him approvingly and then back over to the Kid, who lifted his M-1 to his shoulder and rapidly firing 3 shots, hit the dirt right in front of the target, and when he quickly retracted his weapon and blew the smoke out of the barrel, both Wilson and the ex VC captain howled with laughter. *I still got it!*

Once M-1 carbine training was over, the Hoi chanhs got back in the truck to return to their compound and Wilson remarks to the Kid as they climb into the jeep, "Let's go over to the whore house and get laid, my treat!"

The Kid turned to look at him. *You think you're going to buy me off with a piece of ass?* "Uh, well, I'm really not interested in any of the whores there, Sir, and you don't have to go getting me laid because my answer will still be no, but if you want to go, I'll ride along, it's not like I've got anything better to do."

"You might change your mind when we get there. Who knows," he said, firing up the engine, "they might have some new talent you haven't ever seen before!"

"If I could make a suggestion, Sir, if we're going to the whore house, perhaps we should fire by the compound and drop off these clothes so we don't have to cart them around because we sure as hell can't lock up this jeep."

"Good thinking... Kid," the Lt pulled up to the edge of the road, "that's what I like about you, you know how to *think!*"

While at the compound, the Kid quickly changed clothes back into his uniform and grabbed his Polaroid camera. Emerging from the servant's quarters, he could see the look on Wilson's face, sad that the Kid did not wish to remain dressed in his new APT costume, but he let it slide.

Ba had been waiting in the jeep, parked in the shade of the tall trees by the gate and just as Wilson and the Kid climbed in and prepared to go, a mini convoy of 3 jeeps and a 3/4-ton truck pulled into the compound and who should be in the second jeep but Sweet!

"Hey! Jimbo!" the Kid hollered, "Howz it hangin'?"

"Low and to the left," he smirked, while brushing some of the road dust from his fatigues and ejected the clip from his M-16 and checked to see the chamber was empty by clicking the trigger with the barrel pointed to the lawn of the great house. "Chao Ba," he acknowledged the interpreter's presence.

"Chao, Sweet," he answered.

"Still no Boujold?" the Kid inquired to his erstwhile friend.

"Nope. He still doesn't plan on coming in till he's ready to DEROS, he's just gone under a hundred. Double digits to January!" Sweet gave them the update on the Bouji man.

"We're headed to the whore house," Wilson casually stated, "you can come along if you want."

"Ah, no thanks," he winced, thinking Wilson should know by now, after all of the times he said it, that he would do no whoring or cheating on Barbara while in the Nam. "What I want is a shower and a cold beer and to see if there's any mail here for me."

"Well, Sir, after we... I mean 'you' get done at the whore house, can Sweet and I go over to Win's for the rest of the afternoon?" *I know you're going to say yes, because you want me to say yes...*

"Sure, I guess. I don't see this taking more than an hour or so," he reckoned.

"Or three minutes," the Kid chided the Lt.

Wilson gave him a dirty look, but the Kid knew, as long as Wilson thought he could get him to say he'd go on the APT mission, that he could get away with verbal murder.

Chapter 8

Mama San's place in Tra Vinh was only about 5 blocks from Win's house on the west side of town. Her operation was concealed behind a white plaster wall that was high enough that one couldn't see inside from the street. Entering through a wooden gate, the trio of Wilson, Ba and the Kid found themselves in a small open courtyard that had numerous rooms off it, where the girls did their business.

At the far end of the courtyard was a table under a tin awning that extended out from the wavy red tiled roof, and situated around it were Mama San and two of her 'girls'. Although the term 'girls' was a bit misleading, for the two who sat with Mama San were the oldest looking whores the Kid had seen since his arrival in-country.

They'd have to be the last women on earth. "Ooooh," said the Kid in a low voice to Wilson as they approached the table and Mama San rose to greet them, "how are you every going to choose between those two beauties? I hear the one with no teeth gives a truly epic blow job!"

If looks could kill, the Kid would have been as dead as if he'd been shot in the back of the head by a VC with an RPG. But, the Lt. knew the Kid spoke the truth. One of them looked older than Mama San herself and the other one was just plain; not ugly, but just as ordinary looking as any fish monger's wife down at the Cholon market, albeit it dressed in sparkling white cotton pants and top, the only up-side was that she was much cleaner and better smelling.

"Chao, Mama San," Wilson greeted her and the Kid could tell from his expression, that he didn't think much of the sporting ladies, either, but since it was his idea, he had to act a little bit excited. "We're here for short time... no offense to the present company, but have you got any other girls around today?"

Her expression was one of perplexion that dissolved into irritation as she glanced from the Lt. to her working ladies and back again.

"Yes, Trung Ui," she put on a broad grin, "Quan working now, be done in maybe 15 minutes, you like her plenty!" the middle aged Madame pointed to one of the rooms off the courtyard where the door was closed.

This action caused the two older whores to engage in a discussion between themselves and respond to the Lt. with looks of major disgust. Then the plain one rose up and walked over to the Kid and put her arm through his and said, "You want short time? I numba one good time... you like beaucoup!"

Her face was thin and her hair was cut a couple of inches above her accentuated color bones and looking into her eyes, the Kid noticed that her eyes were kind of pretty, as they peered back at him, with thinly veiled pleading. "Cam on but no cam on," *thanks but no thanks*, the Kid shook his head, much to the amusement of Ba, and the woman retrieved her arm and sat down with a pouting look as her slightly too wide mouth turned down at the corners on her lightly wrinkled face.

"You want cold drink while you wait for Quan?" Mama San inquired, "Got cokes."

"Sure!" Wilson said, and the three men sat down at the shaded table as she departed to retrieve them.

"Ba?" the Kid got his attention, "you up for either of these babes?" he indicated the women.

"Oh you sick, Stocker!" he made a terrible face, "Cam bao ya!"

Chuckling, the Kid sat his Polaroid on the table and reached into his pocket for a KOOL.

"Camera..." the Plain One smiled, trying out her English, nodding for assurance she had the word right.

Pretty smile. "Right! Camera, but not just any camera, you take picture, you see right away! Ba," the Kid sought assistance, "tell her how this works and that I want to take her picture."

Ba explained but when it got to the 'take her picture' part, she seemed upset for some reason and said, "No... no take."

"Oh, well, Sir?" the Kid turned to Wilson, "why don't you get up and stand over there and I'll take your picture to show her how it works, plus, I want to get a shot of you in your new APT uniform," he opened the camera up to prepare it for use and indicated where he wanted his subject to stand.

"All right," Wilson chose to cooperate. Getting up off his chair, he moved a couple of steps over to his left, toward some clothes that were hanging on a line across the courtyard, he turned and said, "How's this?"

70

"OK!" the Kid framed it, taking him from mid chest up, "... and cue the cheese," he snapped it off and immediately, the camera spit out the blank picture.

Placing it in front of the Plain One he said, "Watch," as he used his hands to point from his eyes to the white square of paper that had been ejected by the camera. And as the Plain One looked on, the Lt., at first just lightly, came into view, all dressed in his new APT uniform, with his jungle hat that was starting to look a little raggy from being washed and getting wet. Reaching into his pocket, the Kid took the magic Polaroid chemical bar, tapped it out of the black tube and passed it over the picture a couple of times to stop the developing process and seal the image on the black and white film.

"Not bad," he appraised his work, "I've got a bunch of friends back home who wonder what you look like," he smiled at Wilson.

"Because I tell them what a nice guy you are," the Kid said it in a tone of voice that Wilson couldn't tell if it was the words or the way he was saying them that was most sarcastic.

"I only wish it was in color!" *So everyone could see that burgundy suit you got on.*

As Mama San reappeared with the cokes, Wilson wondered out loud, "I wonder who's in there doing her right now. Some guys, I wouldn't want to go after."

"Care to name any names?" the Kid went fishing.

"Uh, no, cause you'd probably run and tell'em."

Just then, the gate to the courtyard swung open and Ernie's head appeared. "Ah, there you are, Kid, uh, Lt. Wilson, we've got Sweet in the jeep, and we're here to get Stocker so we can go to Win's and listen to Sgt Pepper, is that OK?"

Wilson looked at Stocker and back to Ernie, "yeah, sure. Take him. He's a pain in the ass anyway."

"Uh, no offense, Sir, I hate to tell you," Ernie grinned, stepping all of the way into the courtyard, "but when you come here, you're supposed to fuck the whores, not let the Kid fuck you in the ass! Anyway, that's how we all do it."

The Kid had to laugh. Wilson did not enjoy being the butt, so to speak, of any joke but, considering how nicey-nicey he was being to the Kid, he could only fake laugh and say, "sure, go on ahead."

71

"All right! Thank you, Sir. See ya Ba, Chao Mama San, Chao Plain One!" and grabbing his camera and the picture he'd just taken of Wilson, the Kid followed Ernie out the gate with a smile on his face.

"Hey! Sweet! Hi Peety!" he hollered as he swung into the back seat behind Pete, who was riding shotgun. "Thanks for the rescue!"

"No sweat, GI!" said Pete, "all right a couple of hours off! Let's go get stoned!" and as he said it, all four of them sang the Dylan line from Rainy Day women, in unison; *"everybody must get stoned!"*

Pulling up at Win's, they found Mrs. Nguyen in the yard, speaking to her neighbor and as they piled out of the jeep, she ended her conversation and moved to meet them at the front door.

Chao, Gentlemen," she said with a smile, "how are you today?"

"Chao Mama San Nguyen," they all chortled as they entered and cached their weapons at the front door; the Kid even removed his shoulder holster and left it hanging on Sweet's M-16. As they entered the living room, Win came out of the kitchen and greeted them.

"Look! You found the Kid!" she grinned, "you no boom boom short time eh? I didn't think your Trung Ui would let you go."

"Well, he's being nice to me right now," the Kid began to explain, "he wants me to say I'll go on this top secret mission I can't tell you about, but it is volunteer and I'm not going... *cam bao ya!* So he numba one nice to me... for now."

"Let me put on record. You want *Sgt Pepper,* I know I know," she looked up at 8ft high ceiling as she said it, walking to the record player and turning it on: the record was already sitting on the turntable. "And now," as the Beatle's band tuned up in the beginning of the first cut, she said, "you all want fried potatoes? Yes?"

"Yes!" Ernie answered. "We are so totally predictable!"

"Yeah, we are!" exclaimed Pete, "Let's do something different, let's go into the kitchen and help Win and her mom make the potatoes before we get stoned and listen to *Sgt Pepper's.*"

They all though that was a good idea, including Win and her mother and together, the six of them went into the Nguyen family kitchen. It was a spacious, open arrangement, with ample wooden topped food Prep Island in the middle with pots and pans hanging from two of the tiled walls.

"Hey, I want to take a picture of your kitchen!" The Kid hurried back to the living room to get his Polaroid and upon returning, Sweet took it from him.

"Let me take a picture of the three of you," he said to the Kid, Pete and Ernie, "you guys are like the 3 Musketeers and you were nice enough to turn me on to this whole deal over here with this incredible family, you guys should have a picture of the three of you." And with that, Sweet climbed up on a chair on one side of the food prep island, where Win had all the potatoes washed and ready to cut up and said, "Here, you guys, move closer together so I can get you all in. Stocker, you gotta get a real camera, this Polaroid is a piece of shit! I can't believe a graduate of DINFOS would be running around here with a frickin' Polaroid! OK, say cheese! Opp! That was your last one," he said as the picture flew out of the boxy unit, preparing to develop.

Win and Ernie commenced to thin slicing the potatoes as Mrs. Nguyen filled a 12 inch wide bowl bottomed pan with cooking oil and when it was fully boiling over the gas stove, she dumped in the white slices.

"Look!" said the Kid, holding up the finished picture, "Sweet, this is a pretty good shot, if you like the camera or not."

When the fresh kettle fries were done, Mrs. Nguyen drained them in a cauldron and dumped them into her round, white serving dish and salted the golden brown beauties to taste. They looked delicious and all of them beamed at the enjoyment of life's little pleasures in a war zone as they settled into the living room and flipped the record over: pot, potato chips, beer and Sgt. Pepper playing on the Victrola.

Heaven. This is as close as it gets to it, in Tra Vinh. Oh shit... I know Wilson is going to bring this APT bullshit to a head soon. I wonder what that fucker has up his sleeve because he continues to put time in to having me train for this mission when there's no way I'm going. Even though I really like Kanh, I mean what makes more sense than fighting for your ancestor's land? Especially if you're an Oriental. What the fuck else is the guy supposed to do? Any way this war goes, Kanh is fucked. If he doesn't get killed. And if he gets killed, his wife and kids are really fucked! They'd be the wife and sons of a traitor to both sides. Nobody will have them. When all he really wanted was to provide for his family. This fucking war is FUCKED! Governments say do this do that and it is the little common bastards who get screwed and killed while the big corporations make money hand over fist! They don't care how many Wallys or Beavers or girls next door get killed. The corporation that makes the Spooky guns doesn't care who gets strafed. The men who make the bombs that fall out of the B-52 never see the blown-up hamlets and the chunks of flesh. Ask them and they'll say the war is the right thing to do. My country, right or wrong. Democracy! Then, why didn't we let them have that fucking election according to Geneva? Hmmm, I wonder who's going to win OUR election. I wonder where my absentee ballot is? It should have been here by now.

"Kid?" Sweet nudged him with the bong, "you looked lost. Hit or pass?"

"Another hit, fur sure!"

"... will you still need me, will you still feed me, when I'm 64...."

Chapter 9

Things were jumping in the Tra Vinh Club. It was 2100 hours on a Friday night, with no operations scheduled for the next couple of days and everybody was unwinding. The Kid and Sweet had been hot on the pool table and were taking a break while Pete and Ernie used the Kid's one good stick to beat up on Wilson and the Boar Hog.

Wilson was still wearing his new APT burgundy pants, smartly bloused, although he'd gone to a white t-shirt on top and he had his pack of smokes rolled up in the sleeve, like he was Marlon Brando or something and Boar Hog was wearing a black t-shirt with a big West Point written in block letters in gold across the front. The major was making a big deal out of chomping on a cigar his wife had sent him from Panama, wagging it around in his mouth like he was a maestro conducting an orchestra. But it didn't help him shoot pool any better.

"He was saying tomorrow," the Kid leaned forward so Sweet could hear him talk over the stereo blasting from behind the bar, "he wants a decision tomorrow. Still gonna tell him no. Don't know what he's going to do because he already told me that he told Ronnie Smith back in Can Tho that I said yes."

"Well, if he asks me, the answer will be no, too!" Sweet affirmed. "That would leave Boujold and he had his taste of combat and he doesn't want any more."

"Neither do *me,* "said the Kid," but when I say no, I'm sure that's going to mean that we'll be out on a bunch more operations just to get even with me."

"We're not doing shit in Cang Long," Jim exhaled and ashed his cigarette, "Me and Bouji go over to the office about ten or 11, give some candy to the Kids and buy a coffee at the shop. That's it!"

"You lucky mutha fucker!" the Kid cursed him. "Hard to believe I'm here thinking about Cang Long as the good old days!"

As much as everybody was distracted by having a good time and listening to the music, there was no doubt about it, when it went off, it was a gunshot and everybody heard it and there was immediate major concern in the club.

"Shit!" Boar Hog yelled, "what the hell was that?"

It had come from outside the mess hall club building, from across the courtyard and over in the maintenance building behind the volleyball court, the haunt of Mr. Kim, the Korean technician and contract laborer who kept the appliances running on the compound.

Rushing thru the door, the first men out encountered a dazed looking *Sgt. Hicks,* the black master sergeant, almost staggering as he walked out of Mr. Kim's quarters, an Army issue .45 in the grip of his right hand at the end of a limp arm, pointing toward the ground.

Making his way around *Hicks,* Sgt Spencer barged through the screen door of the small building and immediately screamed out, "O MY GOD! Christ! Oh God Oh God! He shot him! *Hicks* shot him in the head!"

As the words came out of his mouth, Boar Hog immediately drew his own pistol, which he was never without, and pointed it at *Hicks,* "drop it, *Arlen,*" he firmly commanded.

The sergeant let the piece clatter to the walkway and put up his hands, "The fucker said he wasn't going to pay me. He owes me $3,000 from poker and he was going home tomorrow and he wasn't gonna *pay* me!"

"So you shot him?" Boar Hog sought to confirm the confession as the crowd had now grown to include nearly everybody in the compound, most secretly happy it was just a shooting and not an attack.

"Yes, I shot him! I fuckin' shot him! He was gonna leave with my $3,000! God damn right I shot him! I need that money, oh Jesus, what have I done," he began to sob and say words nobody could understand, like he was talking to his wife or somebody who wasn't really there.

"Uh, you have the right to remain silent," Major Gillmore had now made his way downstairs from his quarters in the big house and had begun to exert his influence, "anything you say may and will be used against you, and words to that effect," he added as an afterthought. "Major Boarz," he turned to the West Pointer, "we'll need to gather evidence," he grimly shook his head. "Sgt. Spencer, find some way to restrain Hicks, he's under arrest for murder."

As the crowd began to melt away, Boar Hog spotted Wilson, "Ross! You want to take some pictures of this for evidence?" he asked, "and maybe help clean it up when we're done?"

"Stocker, do you have film and can we use your Polaroid?"

"Uh, sure..."

"OK, fine. Sweet," he looked at Jim, who stood by the Kid, "you're going to help me," and as he volunteered their services to Boar Hogs' legal task, Sweet's expression was awash in the immediate shock he was experiencing at getting roped into the mess. The Kid could clearly see he was thinking… *why me and not you? It's your camera!"*

The Kid retrieved his camera. *Oh yeah, I load my last role of film and a bunch of it is going to get wasted on this shit! Poor Sweet! He has to go see this... I bet Wilson picked him because he still thinks I'm going to change my mind. God! I can't believe Hicks just shot him like that! Over a gambling debt! Man does the value of life ever stink in this fucking place. Inside a nice, safe compound, then bam! Dead. Killed by one of your own.*

He pushed through the hangers around and handed the camera to Lt. Wilson and as he and Sweet headed for the door to the maintenance shack, Spencer was coming back from supply with a body bag and a shovel and a broom.

The Kid, along with Pete, Ernie and Vineola, retreated to Pete & Ernie's cubicle where they sat down on the floor a big plush cushion Pete had made downtown, and the bottom bunk, while Ernie put the copy of Sgt. Pepper, that they had brought back from Win's, on the battery operated record player, which was the only turntable in the compound. They'd heard Sgt Pepper already ten times that day but none of them could get enough.

"My God!" Vineola exclaimed, "What do you think is going to happen to Hicks? He can't get the death penalty... can he?"

"Theoretically, I guess it's possible," Ernie thought, "but highly unlikely. He killed while in an emotional state, so, hell, I guess a good lawyer could most likely get him off on manslaughter."

"I don't pity Sweet," the Kid shook his head from side to side, "I'm so glad that fucker Wilson didn't drag me in there. I've seen brains and it ain't pretty!"

"Boy, did that empty out the club or what?" Vineola tapped the Kid on the knee, "did you get your cue stick or is it still over there?"

"Wow! It's still there! Thanks for reminding me!" the Kid jumped up and ran straight over to the club and found it in the hands of Capt. Metz, who was playing the Boar Hog.

"Ah, Capt. Metz," the Kid stopped talking till Metz took his shot. " ... I've come for the cue but... well, if you promise to beat him, you can use it and when you finally lose, you bring it to me, deal?"

"Deal."

With that assurance, he returned to the group in the airmen's cubicle, only to find upon his arrival, that the turntable's batteries had worn down to the point where the Beatles were sounding a little slurred.

"Almost time to set it on 45 rpms," Ernie matter of factly said, because that's how they did it when there weren't any fresh batteries' they play it on 45 and at first, the 33 rpm would be fast. Then once, it would be perfect, the 33 at 45 wearing down. Then on the next play, it would be too slow. Well, since the player also had 78 rpm, they'd take it up and the first song would be like the chipmunks and then one song would be normal and one song would then be too slow and the batteries would die completely.

It was on the last throes of the 45 rpm segment that Sweet returned to the group.

"My God, it was horrible!" he began, "Hicks couldn't have been more than like 5 feet away when he shot him, I would imagine, right above the eyes in the middle of his forehead! Jesus! Brains were everywhere! It was fucking Sick! Stocker, you lucky bastard! He might have made you do it if he wasn't trying to get you to go on the APT. Even as much as said so, when we were cleaning it up. I only used five of your pictures. I don't know if I got it all, but I think I got enough. Fuck! I'm sure as hell glad I didn't owe Hicks any money!"

Chapter 10

Since the previous evening had been so unusual, Wilson hadn't given them any kind of an agenda for the day so Sweet and the Kid slept in before finally getting up to have lunch together prior to Sweet's departure with the afternoon convoy back to Cang Long.

Sweet was still pretty grossed out by the events of the previous night and the Kid sensed any topic other than Mr. Kim's demise would suffice at the table.

"So, who now, as the day approaches, do you think is going to win the election?" the Kid posed the question, as he buttered a piece of French bread. The date was getting close and being in the war zone, it was hard not to think or talk about it, since the war was the hot button topic within the campaign.

"Well, Nixon is looking like he's got an edge, I think." Sweet considered the question, "I mean, that's only because Hubert has shown us nothing, had to spend all his time running from the shadow of LBJ... but we all know it doesn't make a shit pile of beans difference to us who wins the frickin' election; we'll still be here in the 'Nam come the rest of 1968 and half of '69. Tricky Dick and his 'I've got a secret plan to end the war,' is his grab the anti-war vote. And this thing he's doing, called the 'southern strategy', you picked up on that yet? Where he's trying to get Republican shit over on the rednecks in southern states who've been Democrats since Lincoln and reconstruction. Only possible because LBJ passed the Civil Rights bill and pissed all the southern democrats off." Sweet put down his fork and picked up his iced tea, "It'll be freaky as hell with Nixon as president, but I think he's going to pull it off, much as I don't want him to. I want to see my man from Maine," he hoisted a toast with his iced tea, "Mr. Edmund Muskie, be our next VP!"

"Yeah," the Kid sighed, clicking his plastic glass, "even though it would mean President Humphrey. You know, it's hard to believe that I was for Nixon in '60, because my Mom is such a Republican, but when Kennedy got in, I was starting to think he was really cool and I liked him a lot. But after he got shot and Johnson got in, I actually liked Barry Goldwater over him... there's just something about Johnson I've never liked, even with the civil rights stuff and the war on poverty... and LBJ ended up doing what he said he wouldn't do; '...*send American boys to do what Asian boys should do for themselves*... '"*The* Kid delivered the line with a Texas twang." I have never understood where the war fit in... Other than making money for defense contractors... I guess it's left over from the French and since they said Ho Chi Minh was a communist, Johnson had to do it or be painted soft on communism."

"Wouldn't want that!" Sweet mockingly said.

"That's why Ike pulled the plug on the Geneva accords election. Shit, if that bastard hadn't of done that, we wouldn't be here," the Kid thought back to his conversation with ex-VC Capt. Kanh. "Then Eugene came along, and Bobby got hot and I started to think of myself more as a Democrat, for sure. I was so for Bobby... ah, I'd be willing to bet the same people who shot JFK shot Bobby... I've never believed that Lee Harvey Oswald shit from the moment Jack Ruby shot him to shut him up so he wouldn't be around to contest his innocence."

"I don't doubt it and I believe we haven't heard the end of that story, either!" Sweet concurred. "But back to the election, who are the independents going to vote for? Humphrey? Might as well be Johnson. Nixon? Maybe, if they buy his shtick about a secret plan to end the war. "

The Kid kept looking around for Wilson, but he didn't seem to be in for the midday meal. "Ya know, this whole secret plan to end the war, if the plan was really any good, don't you think he have it out there on the table and be talking about what the plan was, or even doing it? If that fucker could articulate an exit strategy from Vietnam, he be singing it from the roof tops! For some reason, I have the feeling that Nixon is a lying son of a bitch. There's just something about him that says, oh, I don't know... *lying son of a bitch!* I still haven't gotten my absentee ballot and if it's not here by now, it's most likely too late, even if it does show up in the next mail call."

"Well, I haven't got mine yet, either." Sweet stopped eating, 'wouldn't you know it, our first election, we're in a war zone and it looks like our votes won't be counted. What a total fucking bummer!"

After Sweet departed for Cang Long, the Kid kept expecting that Lt.Wilson would materialize any minute and there would be training or something with the APT. After all, it was Friday and technically, still a duty day. And he'd keep trying to get the Kid to change his mind and say he would join the project to which the Kid would say no. Same song, different verse.

He wrote some letters, read about the Colorado Buffaloes football team, playing Kansas over a week ago, in the Boulder Daily Camera newspaper from the subscription that his parents had gotten him, played a couple of racks of pool with Rick Vineola and had a beer with Pete and Ernie. In all, it was a very pleasant and relaxing afternoon.

About 1700 hours, right before the Kid was planning on heading into the mess hall for dinner, Cpl. Ba came over and found him in his cubical, dressed in fatigue pants, a green t-shirt and flip flops, sitting on his bunk in the direct path of the wind from the fan, sipping another beer and reading a book. He had easily sneaked enough hits from the slowly dwindling cache in his pants pocket to have a nice, pleasant buzz going.

"Chao Kid," Ba came into the area and sat down on the Kid's guest chair, which doubled as his footlocker, "you want work on Vietnamese and help me with English after dinner?"

"Sure, Ba, I got nothing better to do. Did you eat yet?"

"Yes, I ate at ARVN mess before I came over. I will wait here for you... OK?"

"OK, I won't be long."

Over at the mess hall, the Kid paid his money, got his chow and sat down, back to the door, across from Vineola and Sgt. Spencer in the rapidly filling mess hall. For a skinny guy, Vineola could sure as hell pack away the groceries and he had his mouth full when he spotted Wilson come through the door and informed the Kid.

"Yo, your lieutenant's still alive and kickin'," he said, gesturing with his forehead and dark arching eyebrows for the Kid to check behind his back as he shoveled in another fork full of mashed potatoes.

Twisting around, the Kid watched as the Lt. passed through the enlisted men's half of the room to enter the chow line. Wilson made eye contact and the Kid nodded a greeting but got no nod in return. *Like I care.*

Not wanting to keep Ba waiting too long, the Kid hurried and upon finishing, bussed his tray and headed immediately back to his cubicle, not bothering to even try and talk with Wilson. *He knows where to find me.*

And sure enough, not 15 minutes after the Kid had returned from dinner and began the language lesson with Ba, Wilson came into his cubicle in a very un-timid manner and stood before the Kid, who sat on his bunk looking up at him.

"Stocker," he said very deliberately, "do you know what Article 31 of the Uniform Code of Military Justice is?"

"No."

"That is where it says that you have to be advised of your right to remain silent, kind of like the civilian Miranda decision," he reeled off the purpose of the UCMJ's Article 31. "I am advising you of your rights." he stared at the Kid, his mouth straight without a hint of trickery or joking.

"Oh?"

"So, now that I've done that, I'm going to ask you a question," he paused for effect. "Did you or did you not eat in the mess hall tonight?"

Without so much as a second's hesitation, the Kid replied, "You know I did; you saw me in there when you came in to eat. Why do you even ask?"

Ignoring the Kid's question, Wilson continued, "and you've eaten in the mess hall any number of times in the last four days, haven't you?"

The Kid gave the Lt. a serious look as he paused to consider where the conversation was actually headed and almost instantly, it flooded back into his head: *the fight with First Sgt. Brooks and him telling me not to eat in the mess hall anymore. But he never stopped eating there... he never told Sweet not to eat there... it's got to be OK.*

"Of course, I've been eating in the mess hall, Sir, all of us have been eating in the mess hall, including you." the Kid answered.

"Well," Wilson drawled as a sly smile spread across his face, "that's beside the point. You were specifically instructed by a superior officer, *me*, not to eat there and you willfully disobeyed my order. Stocker, I'm going to have to give you an Article 15."

"I won't take it," the Kid flatly replied, engaging him eye to eye.

"Then I'll have you court-martialed for insubordination!" He firmly declared.

The Kid's jaw dropped. The Lt. was now threatening him with turning it into a felony violation of the UCMJ!

"Unless, Stocker," he prepared to offer a solution to both their problems, "*Unless...* you'd choose to reconsider your decision about volunteering for the Armed Propaganda Team. If you do that, I might drop the whole thing."

There. The cards were now on the table. The stare-down continued as Wilson waited tensely for the Kid's answer. A flurry of thoughts raced through the Kid's mind. *So that's your game. Why, you might have staged that fight with Brooks just to set this whole thing up. I have always wondered why you went ahead and brought those uniforms and had me do all that training... you son of a bitch, you had this planned from the start! Hmmm ... I think I can work with this. I think I've got a ton of really good material here and I like my chances! I like them a lot more than I like the thought of going out with you on that stupid fucking APT patrol in the middle of the fricking night!.*

Breaking the stare and looking over to Ba, the Kid sees he is completely baffled as to what, exactly, is taking place. His English and his grammar might not be totally up to snuff enough to follow the exchange, but 'court martial' is pretty universal army language for *big trouble.*

"Are you serious about this, Sir?" the Kid finally says, although he can readily tell from his demeanor this is not Wilson's idea of a joke.

"Yes. Very serious. Troops just can't go around disobeying orders from their superiors," he self-righteously pontificated.

"Two things strike me, Sir," the Kid began, "and I ask you: if this was truly about insubordination, and I was the kind of soldier you couldn't trust to carry out orders, why would you want me to go into a commando style combat operation with you?... and if you were serious about the charges, why are you giving me such an easy out... "

"I'm not giving you an easy out!"

"Oh, but you are!"

"I'm not! I'm not giving you an easy out! And I *will* court martial you!"

"Then go ahead and do it!" *I can so work with this! It's fucking Christmas!*

Wilson was shocked at the way the scene had played out and for just a split second, the Kid could see that he was checking the plan over in his mind, trying to figure out where it went wrong. "OK!" he fairly screamed, "consider yourself court martialed! You are relieved of duty pending the filing of charges first thing in the morning!" And on that note, the Lt. stormed out of the cubicle.

The Kid turned to his anguished companion. "Don't worry, Ba," he tried to calm him down, "it's not like they're going to take me out and put me in the tiger cage or shoot me first thing tomorrow. Maybe he'll cool off by then. But don't worry! He's just trying to get me to say I'll go on the APT, that's the real reason he's court martialing me, not because I ate in the frickin' mess hall! In fact, I'll bet he thinks I'm going to think about it and decide I want to head it all off at the pass and that if I'll go hunt him up right now, and tell him I'll do the APT, and he'll still drop the charges."

So I've got to make sure he doesn't. Going over to his footlocker, he made Ba get up and opening it, the Kid removed a pair of the burgundy Armed Propaganda Team uniform pants. Grabbing his shaving kit out of his wall locker, he carefully pulled out a double-edged razor blade and cut the legs off the hated pants, just above the knees, effectively turning them into Bermuda shorts.

Ba gaped as he destroyed the new uniform pants but the Kid laughed while he was doing it, imagining the look on Wilson's face when he saw what he'd done. *After all, he said the uniforms would belong to me, no matter what my decision was...* Putting them on, he turned to Ba. "Let's go over to the club and get a beer!"

It was Friday night and the club was just starting to fill up with off duty soldiers, USAID workers and CIA agents, but not so much so that Wilson couldn't plainly see across the pool room from where he was sitting with Metz, when the Kid walked in with Ba and stepped up to the bar to order them a drink. Ba was so freaked out by the Kid's openly hostile act that he nervously moved away from him a good five feet and checked to see if Wilson was going to come after the Kid flat out.

While waiting for his beers, the Kid turned slowly and casually to his side until he brought Wilson into his peripheral vision. *Well I'll be... smoke is coming out of his ears! This will seal the deal nicely, if I don't say so myself!*

"Yo, Kid... nice shorts!" Vineola walked into the bar, "where'd you get'em?"

"The Lt. bought them for me!" he indicated to Wilson, who was now breathing heavy gasps, muttering something to Metz, trying to hold his anger in check. Then, instead of doing anything, the Lt. rose up and huffed out of the club.

"Looks like Wilson has a case of the ass for you, Stocker. What did you do?"

"Other than cut the legs off these pants? Since I won't volunteer to go on the APT, he is saying he's going to court martial me for disobeying an order he gave me last week to *'not eat in the mess hall!'* Can you believe it?"

Rick was slightly taken aback, "Court martial you? For eating in the mess hall? No shit?"

"Apparently no shit," the Kid calmly smiled.

"And that doesn't bother you?' Rick inquired, a little uncertain whether or not the Kid had lost his marbles.

"Nope. Not any more than getting shot at does, that's for sure!"

Chapter 11

For the second day in a row, the Kid slept past 1000 hours. Following a leisurely cooling shower, it was nearing time for lunch and Lt. Wilson still had not shown up to take his bogus pressing of charges to the next level and the Kid pondered his situation.

Whatever happens, one thing I know for sure; I'm through working with Wilson. That's a given. If I can't work with this bullshit that he is court martialing me for disobeying that fucking goof ball order to not eat in the mess hall, then I deserve to go to jail because I must be too stupid to walk around. I mean, he never gave the order to Sweet or Boujold and he was eating in the mess hall, it went on for days. He was violating his own order! And he didn't say anything until he wants to pressure me into going on the APT. He smiled to himself. *I'm fuckin' airtight!*

Filled with a sense of confidence and dressed in his fatigue uniform, so he would be ready for any kind of formal action or return to duty that Wilson might have in mind, the Kid headed over to the mess hall for lunch. Upon entering, he was given to pause for a second. *Hmmm. Now, I wonder if this would be a violation. After all, he's claiming that the last thing he actually said about anything, before last night,' was don't eat here, eat on the local economy.' But, since I have now been relieved of duty and put on restriction, I can't. So, this has to be OK!*

Comfortable within his logical rationalization of the situation, the Kid entered the mess hall, paid his money, got his food, chose a seat at a table where his back was to the wall and he could keep an eye out for Wilson. Being a Saturday, the Tra Vinh mess hall was only about a quarter filled and sitting alone, the Kid had a sumptuous lunch. In fact, he had finished all but the last three bites of his meal when Lt. Wilson appeared, entering through the screen door right in front of the Kid's table.

It was almost like a melodrama or a rehearsal for a bad school play when he stopped, looked up to see the Kid and feigning big eyed surprise, said in a loud stage voice, as if he wanted to be sure everybody in the mess hall was a witness, "What are YOU doing eating here?"

"Sir," the Kid calmly responded, "I guess I like American food," and without a word in reply, Wilson spun on his heels and pushed through the screen door and made a left turn up the sidewalk toward the officer's digs.

The other 15 occupants of the mess hall, some of them who knew what was going on and some that didn't, exchanged perplexed and knowing looks among themselves and with the Kid. Finishing his last 3 bites with a flourish, he put down his fork and lit up a KOOL, pushed back from the table, took a long, deep puff and awaited the inevitable. And sure enough, before two minutes had passed, Wilson barged back into the mess hall and right up to his table.

"I've just made arrangements for you to be on the next Air America flight back to Can Tho, where you'll report to Captain Ronnie J. Smith, B company commander. Pack your gear immediately and wait for me on your bunk till I come to get you." And with that, he wheeled around and banged his way out the screened door.

Bingo! Standing up the Kid snuffed out his unfinished cigarette in the middle of his empty plate. "Gentlemen..." he said to the room with a broad grin, "I seem to suddenly be the shortest fucking person in Tra Vinh. So in the words of the immortal Buggs Bunny, *'so long, suckers!'*"

As he gathered his belongings and stuffed them into his duffle bag, Pete, Ernie and Vineola all materialized, one at a time, about 10 seconds apart, in that order.

"So he's really going through with it, huh?' Vineola looked more scared of the courts martial than the Kid and he wasn't even the one getting it.

"Fuckin' A, Kid," Pete exclaimed, "This is unreal! A court martial! God! What are your fans back home in the Music City gonna think?"

"Uh, can't say that I know. I just hope I don't end up Bobby Fuller when he fought the law..." the Kid continued to cram gear into his duffle bag. "Hey, Pete," he stopped and took from his pants pocket the less than half ounce of pot, all that was left from the score he'd made in Sadec, over three months ago, "maybe you better take this and the pipe, too. Since he's after me, they might take the time in Can Tho to search me for contraband, which would make their job of crushing me that much easier, if they could find any."

"OK. Thanks," he stuffed what couldn't have been more than 5 joints worth into his pocket.

"Yeah! This is the first time I'm not holding since some time back in July," the Kid stopped to think back on it. "Got a feeling I better go into this one clean as a whistle!" His three friends looked quite disappointed by the rapid developments. "Hey, don't worry, guys, if I didn't feel like I could make this situation work out, I wouldn't go down this road, but this is like major *'Catch 22'* material, getting courts martialed for eating in the mess hall... shit like this I couldn't make up. This is gonna look great in my book! Really! This excites me!"

It didn't take long for the Kid to assemble all his stuff and he was lucky in the circumstance that none of his clothing was currently in being laundered, so he even had all of his clothes, although half of them were soiled. He had it all in his duffle bag and one laundry sack. His pistol was unloaded and stored in his goodie box, which made the shape of the laundry bag quite square. It contained all the odds and ends he had left from the various food items people had sent him, assorted shake a pudding's, hard candy, some mini boxes of cereal, stuff like that. No way could anybody below E-6 get away with wearing a side arm back at battalion headquarters, *especially one being courts martialed...* His M-16 lay across the duff, along with the two halves of his pool cue.

"You know, there's a good chance I might not ever be back here to Tra Vinh again," the Kid paused, as the reality of what was taking place sank in; at the very least, he knew he would no longer be under Lt. Wilson, whatever the fuck was going to happen. "Win or lose a courts martial, you get a transfer, so shit! This *might* be it! This *might* be the last couple of minutes I ever spend in old Phu Vinh!" he used the pre-viet cong name for the place.

"Dang, Kid," Pete moaned, "you're not taking that stick, are you? You just said yourself that you don't know where you're going to end up... I mean, do they have a pool table in Can Tho? If you leave it, till you find out if your new address and if they even have a pool table... can we use it and then mail it to you? Just us 3?"

It made the Kid smile, "You're right, Pete, it can stay here 'cause here was where it was meant to be, so you guys can have it and say who gets to use it!" he handed it over.

"Wow!" Vineola exclaimed, "You'd do that for us? What a guy!

"Only one stipulation," the Kid sounded serious, "when it gets passed on, make sure it only goes to a genuine pot smoking anti-war head and never falls into the hands of a war mongering lifer drunk fuck ass or any officers!"

"Deal!" the three of them said in unison.

It did not take long for Lt. Wilson to come for him, with the keys to Sgt. Spencer's land rover in hand. "Come on, Stocker, let's go."

Hefting his duffle bag up onto his right shoulder and holding his M-16 in his left hand and with Ernie toting his laundry bag, they walked out of the servant's quarters into the courtyard, across what was left of the yard and the volleyball court, under the portico arch and to where Wilson had the Land Rover pointed toward the gate.

Ariv'oui, Tango Victor, he gazed up at the stately palms that grew in the front yard of the old ritzy French mansion. "Pete," he shook his hand, "thanks for being a fan! Ernie," he shook his hand, "thank you and both of you actually, for letting me join the *Sgt. Pepper at Mai's House Club...* tell her and Mama San, her little sister and her dad, good bye from me... and Rick... remember, shoot at the hole the table is tilted to... OK? That's *'Draino city'...* money in the bank!"

Wilson sat in the driver's seat, tapping his fingers on the steering wheel and looking impatient as they threw his gear into the back of the Land Rover and as soon as his butt hit the passenger's seat, the Lt. gunned it out the open gate. Over his shoulder, he waved to his buds and watched the compound vanish from sight.

Then, looking at Wilson, he could see that the Lt. was resolutely keeping his eyes on the road ahead as they drove through town and on to the Tra Vinh Airport.

I wonder if he's working today of all days? The Kid glanced at the section of trees from where most of them were convinced that the Airport Sniper operated. Once again, the ride had been without exchange of dialogue between them but as soon as Wilson parked the jeep beside the small terminal, he wasted no time in speaking his mind.

"Goddam it, Stocker, it didn't have to end like this! I hope you see this is all your fault and you are forcing me to do this."

"I'm forcing you?" the Kid almost spit out the words, "Sir, with all due respect, this is about you trying to *force me*. What you don't understand from your viewpoint, Sir, is that I owe it to myself and my family to say no to going on this commando APT bullshit. It is a volunteer position... Sir... I am not now, nor will I ever be commando material. I don't want to *kill anybody!* Shit, I mean, I've already been set up by the Army one time, from enlisting to be in Armed Forces Radio and ending up in this stinking fucking PSYOPS shit. And then you, Sir, in your command capacity, chose not to do anything that has to do with the reason I'm actually attached to the unit... you drag me along on all those search and destroy missions and you wonder why I don't bend over and let you get me involved in this commando thing? Where lots of people, possibly including us, will be killed? No thanks. Nothing personal, Sir, but no fucking way, no thanks!"

Wilson frowned and looked exacerbated "Shit, Stocker, I thought you had more guts than that!"

"More guts, Sir?" the Kid answered coolly, "It's not a question of guts. I got plenty enough guts and I know you know I do. I know you think you have shit to prove, but I don't feel that way. I am not looking for a way to show how brave or stupid I can be. I am more interested in surviving, doing my job and getting home in one piece, and if that is wrong in your book, I don't give a fucking shit! There is nothing you can say that will make me volunteer to go out on an APT mission and what I think that demonstrates is *more brains*.... Sir, and I'd like to keep them on the inside of my skull."

Deeply engaged in thought, the Lt. chewed on the inside of his lower lip. Finally he replied, "Well, OK, you've made your bed. Uh, before the plane gets here, why you don't get out those APT uniforms, I'll have to see if they fit Sweet."

Moving to comply, the Kid speculated with a slight smile, "That makes sense. I don't guess you'll try to get *Boujold* to fit into them." They were near the top of his gear and he quickly had them out, all except the pants he'd butchered, and as he laid them on the Land Rover's seat, he asked, "What makes you think Sweet is going to volunteer?"

"I don't. That is why I'm going to promote him to Sergeant, so he won't be a Specialist any more, and then he won't have a choice because I can just order him to do it. That's what I should have done with you," the Lt. revealed his crucial mistake and new plan in one breath.

"Wouldn't have worked. I wouldn't have given up my Specialist status for anything, just for that reason, Sir. So I guess this is what was meant to be. I don't reckon that I'll be managing your record career, now, all things considered... Sir."

From a distance, the report of airplane engines grew louder and before long, a twin engine aircraft, painted in the blue and white trim of Air America, turned onto final for landing at Tra Vinh. *Hmmm... the Sniper does have the day off!*

As the aircraft set down, a couple of ARVN officers and two civilians emerged from the terminal where they'd been waiting, obviously other passengers for the flight. They Kid had never seen a twin engine Air America plane before. All the previous ones he's seen and dropped leaflets from where the needle nosed single engine STOL craft. This one looked like it was straight out of *Sky King*.

Glancing at his watch, the Kid saw that it was 1330 hours. Soon as the plane stopped taxiing, he picked up his duffle bag and Wilson, in a show of efficacy, picked up his laundry bag to carry out to the waiting twin engine puddle jumper.

Standing beside the open cabin door behind the wing, the co-pilot took the Kid's gear and stowed it in the aft cargo port. Pointing to his M-16, he said, "Clear that weapon and carry it inside."

Pulling back the slide cartridge feed and pulling the trigger, the Kid demonstrated to him that it was unloaded. Then, turning to Wilson, he got in one last dig as over the roar of the idling engines he said, "Gee, I wonder if they're serving *food* on this flight and if they do, Sir, am I allowed to eat it?"

If it would have been worldly possible, the Kid got the feeling Wilson would have punched out his lights on the spot but instead, he ignored the loaded comment. "When you get in to Can Tho," he spoke loudly, "report directly to Company B HQ. Capt. Ronnie Smith will be waiting for you." And with that, he turned and walked back to the Land Rover as the Kid climbed into the fuselage, finding 3 of the 9 seats already occupied by 3 Vietnamese men dressed in civilian clothes. He took the seat on the right side of the plane, directly opposite the door. The 4 other Tra Vinh passengers climbed on board as their lite baggage was stowed and took their places in the two rows of single seats on the plane, leaving only one of the 9 seats empty.

Out the window, the Kid watched the Land Rover depart from the airport as the co-pilot climbed back into the craft and pulled the steps up, closing the door.

"How long to Can Tho?" the Kid inquired of the middle aged, grey on the temples pilot, dressed in the standard white shirt, black neck tie and dark grey slacks of the Air America fraternity.

"Well, hard to say, we've got two more stops to make before we go back to Can Tho... I don't know, maybe by 15 or 1600 hours, depends on some variables."

Once the co-pilot was seated, they wasted no time in turning the bird around and moving into position for takeoff at the far end of the runway. The Kid couldn't help but think about the day when Paul Heineman flew out and the Airport Sniper had put a round through the engine of the Air Vietnam Flight. *Not now dude, not now, please... please... ommmmmm ommmmm,* he silently chanted as the plane gained speed on a bumpy roll and lifted off, up into the Mekong Delta sky. *Cam on!*

As the twin engine craft circled Tra Vinh to head southeast, the Kid gazed down, picking out the American compound, the riverfront coffee shop, Mai's father's hardware store, the A Company compound down by the river and last but not least, Mai's house, all familiar landmarks he would never see again. As soon as a couple of the Vietnamese passengers up near the cockpit lit up, so did the Kid. Leaning back in his seat, inhaling the menthol smoke deep into his lungs, he closed his eyes and what came to him was the feelings and sensations of the time when he and Rick Willis had tried to ride inner tubes down Boulder Creek in June of 1965, the year of the flood. The water had been so high, the two of them thought they would get a great ride and not be scraping their asses on any rocks. But what happened was, as soon as they entered the water, the rushing, frothy spring runoff had seized them, ripped the inner tubes from their grips, tore the tennis shoes from their feet and washed them down the creek, through the middle of Boulder, like a couple of turds flushed down the toilet. The Kid thought they were going to die and they would have, if they hadn't caught a hold of some low hanging willow branches below the tiny falls at Sewell Hall, by which they able to pull themselves to shore.

Swept away! God I hope I'm doing the right thing. What am I saying? Of course I'm doing the right thing. Volunteering for the APT would have been the wrong thing... there's no doubt in my mind about that! Thank God I was on the debate team and not the football team. I'm going to need it all now. Still, I can't believe Wilson is even trying this, to courts martial me because I won't go with him on the APT. If I lose this one, I'll probably get busted down to E-2... maybe go to the Long Binh Jail and you can bet your sweet ass, Kid, you'll be kissing your Armed Forces Radio assignment good bye forever. Stop! Don't even THINK about losing... I'm NOT going to lose. I'm in the right. It's a totally bogus trumped up charge and just because he's a Lieutenant and I'm a Spec. 4 doesn't mean he can get away with this. But wait... I've been screwed by the Army before! Fuck. I hope I've done the right thing. I will find a way to beat this!

When Lt. Wilson had hatched his plot to get the Kid to cave in under the threat of courts martial and agree to become a part of the APT, he could have had no idea how much the Kid loved and thrived on exactly that type of situation.

Reaching into his shirt, the Kid found the lucky Canadian Beaver nickel that hung around his neck. Taking it out, he looked at the beaver. One of the things the nickel very frequently made him think of was Mrs. Beavers, his speech teacher at Boulder's Base Line Junior High School. She was the real reason he'd gotten so good at debate. She was beautiful, in that *Natalie Wood* sort of way that he truly loved. Her name at first had been Miss Summers, Dalene Summers. And from the first time he had walked into her classroom and laid eyes on her as a 7th grader, the Kid wanted so very much to please her, to make her notice him and like him more than any of her other students, that he had excelled at speech. She had such a body and face! It was easy to pay attention in class, looking at her with rapt concentration; she was so smoking hot, he couldn't help it. With his eyes closed, that one special day, late in the 8th grade, vividly replayed itself in the Kid's head. She had called the Kid and a couple of the other boys forward to get hall passes so they could go to the office and retrieve the film strip projector. She had been standing behind her desk and when she bent forward to write the passes, her spring dress had dropped away from her chest and from where he stood, the Kid could see her entire white lace bra and most of the incredibly enticing items it held, all the way down to the little pink bow that nestled in the cleavage of those two magnificent breasts. It had taken her almost 30 seconds to write the 3 passes and the Kid's knees nearly buckled while he saw literally everything but her nipples. Then, Dalene Summers had gotten married, to a man named John Beavers, who was extremely handsome and looked a lot like John Kennedy. But, much to the guffaws of all the boys in junior high, she had become *Mrs. Beavers.* After the marriage, it was nearly impossible to say her name and not think of her lingerie. 7 years later, it still made him breathless to recall the sight. Needless to say, the Kid pretty much worshipped the ground on which she walked. It was in her class that he had first experienced the art of formal debate and of course, he had kicked everybody's ass. The Kid always had a way with words to begin with, and Mrs. Beavers couldn't have possessed a more willing and pliable student.

Watching the endless rice paddies of the Delta spread out below him, he recalled how he had felt when, during the summer of '62, as he prepared to enter Boulder High School, Mrs. Beavers had called him at home and informed him that she had recommended him for honors speech class at Boulder High and that he was to become a member of the BHS debate team as a sophomore! He had demonstrated such a talent for debate, he was being placed in a class that one couldn't even take until junior or senior year and then it was still by invitation only, from Mr. Wally Schneider, debate coach extraordinaire. He was on the team for 3 years and in his senior year, with his partner, Larry Ryan, their record had been 27 wins and 6 losses. He eventually went on to the University of Colorado debate team... before dropping out of CU to go to Tennessee for Donna Nadeau.

Out of all the people Wilson could have picked to take on with a legal pickle, the Kid was determined to prove himself to be the worst possible choice. *I will rip Wilson a brand new asshole! The Buck Owens song came into his head... I got a tiger by the tail, it's plain to see...*

93

The first stop for the Air America flight was Soc Trang. There, three of the Vietnamese got off and 2 new ones got on. *All you guys are spies, aren't you!*

The second stop was at Bac Lieu, down near the coast of the South China Sea. There, two of the Vietnamese got off, but they sat there waiting for over an hour before the 2 men they were picking up arrived. The Kid ask permission to deplane and take a piss, which the captain granted. After all, even though he was technically a prisoner, where could he escape to in Bac Lieu?

When the Air America plane finally landed at Can Tho Field, it was 1730 hours. By the time he secured a ride to the B Company orderly room, to report to Captain Ronnie Smith, everybody had left for the day. The head clerk, Paul Hoch, was upstairs in the main Battalion HQ and after he signed the Kid into the unit, he took him to Eakin Compound for chow.

At the New Villa, First Sergeant Ozelle Jones assigned the Kid to a bunk in an interior room on the second floor, one of the hottest and stuffiest room in the entire old hotel; in fact, it was Boujold's old room. It was the same one he'd used while passing through on his way to Group in Saigon so he was familiar with the tiny battery powered fan that Bouji left out of pity for all who followed after him, and its regular occupant, one PFC George Gaugle.

The Kid also knew that Gaugle was a card short of a full deck and that, as Bouji put it, '...his elevator did not run all the way to the top floor', and 'he wasn't the sharpest tool in the box. The Kid had found, however, that Gaugle was basically a very nice and sincere person.

He enjoyed a shower but skipped the club's movie that night, some beach blanket bingo thing with Annette and Fabian. Made him think too much of Flo. He had a couple of beers before the fatigue of traveling most of the day set in and he retired early. He tripped the switch on Boujold's little yellow plastic electric fan. *Thank God it has batteries!*

Chapter 12

It was like he was in a tunnel and somebody was calling out to him. Am I dreaming? He could hear yelling and echos, but it didn't make any sense; it wasn't his name or any words he could understand. However, the one thing he did sense was, that it was getting closer. Whatever the disturbance was, from within the still, early morning dark of the interior room of the New Villa, as the Kid lay there, it roiled closer and closer to him. What the fuck is going on? I don't hear any shooting...

"All right all right! Everybody roll out and go immediately to the roof! Everybody report to the roof immediately right now *ON THE DOUBLE!*" the words finally sank in as the Kid gained consciousness. "Don't get dressed, don't do anything but go straight to the roof!" the unseen voices of sergeants and officers barked as they worked their way up the stairs of the New Villa, rousting all of the troops and literally herding them directly to the club on the roof to await further instructions.

"Don't bother getting dressed I said! Come on come on! Everybody report to the club NOW... Immediately... to the roof! *On the double!* fall out... fall out! Come on, let's go Let's Go! Move it move it gentlemen!"

As he and George Gaugle walked out of their room and into the hall and over to the stairs, all of the GIs from the ground floor were coming up the 6 ft wide tile staircase and as they made the landing on the third floor, the Kid, George and the others were joined with the troops that lived there and as they went up the final set of stairs and came out in the club, it was clear what was going on. *They're holding a surprise shakedown inspection!*

"All right, men, listen up! First Lt. Harry Regan bellowed, "I'm sure you've all figured it out be now, this is a shakedown inspection!"

A general groan rose from the rapidly growing group that would soon swell up to about 60, which is how many enlisted men were in A company of the 10th PSYOP Battalion, less the dozen or so who were at that moment, off on guard duty or working night shift on the printing presses.

"Here's the drill," Lt. Regan continued, "all the occupants of a room, will be taken back to your room by an officer, who will search your room for contraband or anything else it is against regulations for you to have. And until you are taken down to your room, you are all ordered to remain here and be ready to be called to go! You will not be permitted to return to your room before inspection *for any reason!*" He surveyed the bleary eyed men into whose life the intrusion was being made. "Do I make myself perfectly clear?"

No set response, just a lot of subterranean grousing, because the men knew there was nothing they could do about it. If anybody had been careless with their cache, they're just about to go down.

The Kid can only smirk as he pictures himself giving his last five joints to Pete and Ernie. *Clean as a fucking whistle*. He'd just happened to still be standing by the back stairwell, not more than five feet from it, when up from below and into the club came Capt. Ronnie Smith, Commander of Company B, the man to whom the Kid was instructed to report yesterday.

When Capt. Smith entered the club, he walked right by the Kid and stopped, barely two feet in front of him. As he surveyed the room full of milling, half dressed soldiers clad mainly in green boxer shorts, t-shirts, flip flops and not much else, and said to a 2nd Lt. who trailed him in and stood to his left, "I wonder which one is Stocker? I've only seen him once... I'm not sure I can even pick him out..." And like the sun rising in the east, as it was on that early Sunday morning, painting the clouds a magnificent pastel orange, it dawned on the Kid; *this shakedown could have been triggered by a reason to search me!*

Capt. Smith, of course, had no idea that Stocker was standing directly behind him when he spoke those words. But when the Kid stepped forward and at a distance of less than 6 inches from behind his right ear, loudly stage whispered in a very crisp but calm voice the words, "Right here, Sir!" the captain just about jumped out of his shorts while he spun around in mid air to land on his feet facing the Kid.

"Oh!" the dirty blond and crew cut flat topped officer from Kentucky had to visibly regain his composure since the Kid had so clearly gotten the drop on him. "Uh... Stocker... you were supposed to report to me yesterday!"

Geeze that haircut makes his head look square "Yes Sir, I know that, Sir, and I did go directly to Battalion headquarters last night, as soon as the plane got in, but you had left, Sir." the Kid plainly stated. "I signed in on the day log and spoke with Specialist Hoch, Sir, if you want to check it. The flight was delayed in Bac Lieu, Sir. Nothing I could do about it."

Ronnie Smith digested what the Kid had told him briefly. "Well, OK," he conceded there *wasn't* anything he could do about it, either, and turning

96

to the dark complexioned 2 Lt. in the baseball cap who was with him, said, "take him down, search his stuff and report back to me."

"You want me to go down now, too, Sir, we're in the same room," Gaugle interjected as they turned to go.

"Yeah, I guess, why not?" Smith sent him along with the wave of a hand.

And as the Kid followed the Lt. down the stairs, he grasped his lucky Beaver nickel in the fist of his right hand and gave it a squeeze. *Thank you Lucky Beaver nickel, thank you! Oh jeeze, if I was holding right now I be so fucked! I wonder if this whole charade is for me? Shit! If it is, I hope nobody else gets busted!*

Entering the room, the 2nd lieutenant, whose uniform looked like it was brand new off the rack and never ever been washed even once, surveyed what was there to search and pointing to the Kid asked, "Which of these lockers is yours?"

"That one, Sir," the Kid moved to pick his pants up off the floor and pulling out his key, unlocked the paddle lock and opened the door. "But there's nothing in it except the shirt I wore yesterday, my M-16 and my .38. Since I just came in from the field last night, I didn't bother to unpack because I want to see if there's anything else anywhere in another room... no offense George, the company's fine... but this room is pretty hot. So all my stuff's right there in that duffle and one laundry bag... Sir."

"Yeah, it is a little hot in here," he took off his baseball cap and tucked it into his pocket, revealing a fairly bushy head of black, unruly hair, "you got a .38 huh?" he questioned as he picked up the gun tucked into it's black shoulder holster and drew it out for inspection.

"Yep. It's unloaded, by the way, not that you thought to check it. Out in the field, they let enlisted men do anything they want with weapons. If a guy wants to carry a sawed off shotgun, nobody gives a shit and if you've got an extra gun, so much the better!"

"OK," he put the pistol away. Satisfied there was nothing in his shirt or the locker, the Lt. crossed over to the Kid's bunk and pushed the mosquito netting back so he could sit down while he went through the rest of his stuff. "I don't know how you guys manage to sleep in here!" he exclaimed as he pulled the bags over where he could get into them.

"And this is as good as it gets!" the Kid replied to the Lt., whose name tag name read Borilli. "Do you mind if we smoke, Sir?"

"Uh, no, go ahead," he had become occupied with the opening of the Kid's duffle bag.

Watching the dark haired and somewhat shaggy officer going through his gear and private effects allowed the Kid to get pissed off about the whole Army experience all over again as he went to get his cigarettes out of the pocket of his fatigue shirt in the locker and his Zippo from his pants.

Look at this. Stuck in the middle of an old hotel in a sauna for a room, under charges for disobeying an order with some schlep going through my stuff because they can do it if they want. Oh GOD how I hate the fucking Army and the way they own you and lie to you and treat you like shit and try to fuck you over like they are doing me. Borilli had to stop his search to mop the sweat from his brow and he looked up to see what the Kid and Gaugle were doing. The Kid flashed him a big, broad shit eating grin. *That's right, make sure you take the time to look in everything and maybe you should look twice, because you're not going to find jack squat, you lame ass! Because for the first time in month's I am clean! Squeaky fucking clean, you mutha fucka! You should have searched me 18 hours ago! Ha. If Wilson had searched me when he read me my rights! Luck of the Beaver! Score one for the Kid!*

"So, George," the Kid diverted his attention to his companion, "why is it that you've never gotten out of here?"

"Nobody wants me for a room mate," he nervously said, smiling in a tentative and shy way. "Sides, I like it in here good enough. In fact, it's like a private room until one of you field guys comes through and needs to use the bunk."

Now the Kid knew that Gaugle wasn't necessarily book or street smart, but the two times that he'd been through Can Tho, he had bunked in here with him and he'd developed something of a sympathetic attitude toward the light brown haired PFC with the slightly large nose and lightly pock marked face, who was outwardly a touch on the 'slow' side but tried as hard as anybody.

"Hey!" the Kid smiled reassuringly at him, "you're a great room mate, George! Don't let anybody tell you otherwise!" Then, turning his attention back to the Lt., he saw that he had come to his shaving kit. Unzipping it, Borilli rooted through it and suddenly, pulled out a small dark brown colored glass bottle. Setting the kit aside, he examined the little bottle further, by unscrewing the cap and dumping out some small dark colored pills into the palm of his hand. Looking down at them, he looked back up at the Kid and back down to the pills and stood up.

"Come on," he said, "Captain Smith said he wanted to talk to you as soon as I found anything."

The Kid gave him a stare and asked, "How long have you been in-country, Sir? Couple of days? I couldn't help but notice your uniform is a touch on the new side... or better yet, how long have you even been in the Army? Brand new ROTC officer, are we?"

The Lt. stopped in his tracks and assumed the kind of startled expression on his face that indicated he was about ready to pull rank because his authority was clearly being mocked.

"Those are *water purification* tablets, Sir," the Kid almost laughed as he spoke, "iodine tablets! Come on, let's do take those upstairs and show the Captain! He'll be real impressed! Yes sir, you got the goods on me... I'm *so* hung out to dry... let's go!"

Borilli showed a hint of uncertainty. "Uh... well... I'll just put them in my pocket for now and continue the search and then we'll go up," he backtracked.

Of course, the rest of the search yielded nothing but, still clutching the brown bottle of iodine tablets, Borilli dismissed Gaugle and took the Kid back to the roof only to discover that Captain Smith was not there; he had gone down to a room to conduct some of the shakedown searching himself. "You just stay right here with me, till he gets back and takes a look at this," he indicated the bottle with a nod.

"Sir," the Kid deadpanned, "you seem like a nice guy. Why don't you take that bottle and go over and see one of the officers or sergeants, whose uniforms are a bit more worn than yours, and ask him what those are... before you make a fool out of yourself in front of Capt. Smith."

With something of a dirty look, Borilli finally saw the wisdom of the Kid's suggestion and spying another Lt. with a faded uniform, walked over and showed him the confiscated bottle. Although the Kid could not hear what was being said, he could see the Lt. nodding his head with a smile, confirming that they were, indeed, iodine tabs and not speed or LSD. Walking back to the Kid, Broilli sheepishly said, "Thanks. But Capt. Smith still wants to see you now, even if I don't find anything."

Fine. "You can just keep'em, Sir," the Kid pointed to the bottle still tightly clutched in his hand," from my situation, no matter what happens, I don't think I'll be needing them." And with that, Borilli returned the pills, clearly perplexed as to if he had a right to be pissed at the Kid or not.

Ten minutes passed before Capt. Ronnie Smith finally returned to the roof and located Lt. Borilli and the Kid. As he walked up, he looked expectantly to Borilli, obviously hoping for some good news.

"Nothing to report, Sir," Borilli said when Ronnie stopped in front of them.

"Very well, thank you, Lt." he glanced at the Kid and back to him, "you can go help with some other searches now," Ronnie dismissed him. Then, turning to the Kid, he gave him a look of supreme irritation before he spoke. "This is the part of my job that I absolutely hate."

And I'm supposed to feel sorry for you?

"All the reports I heard from your field team, I thought things were going great guns out there and then... I get this call from Lt. Wilson and he tells me you've created a serious problem by disobeying his orders. First you're on the APT then you're not on the APT... And then some shit about unauthorized use of the mess hall... what the hell is that all about?"

"May I remind the Captain that there are two sides to every story?" The Kid knew this was not the time to call Wilson a liar but he did point out one fact; "I was never on the APT, for example, Sir." *Not to mention Wilson was forever telling me what close personal friends you are, Ronnie Smith. Everything I say can and will be used against me.*

"Well, sure," Smith had a cynical look, "I'll hear your side of it. If you want to make a written statement, you can. Lt. Wilson is sending me one and I told him to have it on my desk by Monday at noon. So Monday, tomorrow, you will report to B Company Headquarters at 0700, because I don't know what I'm going to do with you yet, and after lunch, at 1300 hours, if Wilson's report is in, we'll have an official meeting about these charges and their disposition. Is that clear?"

"Yes sir," the Kid replied.

"Very well, you are dismissed." With that, Ronnie turned and walked over to Lt. Regan to see what else he could do to assist in finishing the inspection and soon left the roof with another trio of GIs in tow, off to their room to paw through their belongings.

Knowing there was no way he could get back to sleep in the inferno that served as his and Gaugle's room, the Kid walked casually over to the walkway that went around the roof club and lit up a KOOL while he stared off into the distance, where he could see a Caribou lifting off from Can Tho Airfield, about 3 miles away. *I wish I was on that plane and it was going to Saigon.*

"So this is the man causing *all* the stir," a voice came from behind him. Turning around, he saw the voice belonged to Paul Hoch, 10th Battalion head clerk, the man who had signed him into the unit last night.

Lotta guys' named Paul in 'Nam.

"Next to somebody getting killed or wounded, a court martial is just about the most exciting thing that happens in a clerk's life," he got a nodding compliance from the three men who accompanied him. One of them was Lou Wimbish, the first person the Kid had ever met in Can Tho. "Stocker, you've met Lou, right? Hoch read his mind. "And this is Ken Willert, my room mate and one of our printers, and this is Ron Edwards, he a type setter, does a lot of work for the unit newspaper.

"Hey... hey... hey," the Kid shook hands with the three.

"Since we're already up, we figure to head on down to the USO to get a little breakfast. "Curfew's been over for half an hour, now," Hoch said, "probably not too crowded down there yet. Later on Sunday, it can really fill up at the grill and you can get in a bit of a line... you can join us if you want. I think we can tell you a thing or two about your situation."

"Ah! That would be very nice. Thank you," the Kid smiled, knowing that Paul Hoch was the head clerk of the entire unit and if anybody 'knew' anything about situations, it was Paul. "The USO, huh? Now there's a luxury we don't have out in the field!"

"Yeah, that's what we've heard," Edwards spoke with traces of a southern accent, "fucking hardship tour. Hey, weren't you the one with Boujold when he went out and finally got into some real shit?"

"Yes, I was. Saw the whole thing, beginning to end," the Kid caught their interest. "In fact, I spent two solid months almost entirely in Boujold's company."

"You poor man," Hoch grimaced, "you'll have to tell us the real story! Somebody was saying Boujold had ARVNs shot on either side of him... gotta be bullshit, right?"

"No. It's true. 100% NOT bullshit. I saw it fucking happen with my own eyes and when they went down, he went down, only he wasn't hit, but Wilson and I both thought he was dead... long story short, I'll tell you all about it at breakfast! It was freaking wild, man!"

The four men stood there for a split second, exchanging glances. "All right!" Wimbish exclaimed, "Let's get our weapons and meet at the front gate," and they all dispersed to their rooms.

Chapter 13

The Can Tho USO was located along the main drag, about half way between the New Villa and Battalion headquarters. It had a sign on the door which declared;

"US Personnel only! No Vietnamese allowed!"

No Vietnamese, that is, unless they were cooking or cleaning up. Hoch had been correct in his assumption that due to the early surprise inspection, they'd beat the morning rush.

The Kid was amazed to discover that you could custom order a bacon/ham or sausage and egg and cheese breakfast sandwich, on toast, with hash browns! And the place was air conditioned... *a regular slice of heaven!* Obtaining their food, the group sat down at a table in the main dining area and at first the Kid talked and the group ate. He gave them the short but fittingly graphic report of Boujold's only experience in major combat and his inglorious exit from the field. Then the Kid ate while Hoch gave him the inside scoop on his legal situation.

"The thing is, Stocker, the unit has lost the last two court martials they've tried and yesterday, when word came in that Wilson was sending you back to be charged, they were jumping through hoops and running around like the Keystone Cops to make sure they had their ducks lined up for you."

Not good news. They all ate while Hoch continued. "They're gonna try like hell to get you to take an article 15, because they don't want to have a trial, but there's a variable in this whole deal. The new Battalion commander, Lt. Colonel Willie O. Lawton, who just took over last week, nobody knows anything about what he's like right now. He's too new. Black guy. Came up through the ranks. He was like a private on Pork Chop Hill in Korea. From what I've seen, he's pretty sharp. Plus, we got a new XO, too, Major Gregory, just got here in September. Seems to be a fair guy, and if you do get court martialed, he'll most likely be the one to hear it. So there's two new guys, not in charge when the unit lost the last two, can't give you a real gut read on either one but early indications are they're better than what we had."

The Kid chewed slowly. It was a lot to digest and his thought patterns were interrupted by the arrival of two more GIs to the table. One of them, had a big black bushy moustache, a large nose and dark hair while the other one had brown hair, a slight moustache with narrow features and wore glasses.

"The 'B' team; Birnbaum and Boyett!" Wimbish exclaimed to the pair, 'glad you guys could make it! Stocker, Mark Birnbaum... and Tom Boyett, he introduced them, "we can make room."

"Wait till I tell you!" Birmbaum seemed overjoyed as he settled his plate and sat down, removing a Nikon 35mm single lens reflex camera from off his shoulder and hanging it on his chair, to be out of the way while he ate. "Ronnie ended up searching our room *himself* and he took the time to unscrew and look into all of the hundred or so little aluminum film cans that I have stacked on my shelf!"

"It's a hundred and fifty cans, if not 200!" Boyett enhanced the details of the story.

"Then," Birnbaum continued, "he opened my camera case and there were two more film cans nestled in the very center of my equipment foam cutout, surrounded by two Nikon bodies and two lenses and he says... 'Oh, well... I'll trust you for those two... I don't want to disturb your equipment...' *and that's where the dope was! The only two he didn't look in!"*

High fives and laughter abound, all the way around the table.

"I left what I had and my pipe in Tra Vinh!" the Kid laughed.

"Did anybody get busted for anything at all by the time you left?" Hoch asked the new arrivals.

"Hadn't happened to anybody yet," Boyett answered, "and they were almost done. I mean, what the hell? Who among us who smokes is stupid enough to keep it in our rooms? You *deserve* to go down if you're that dumb!"

"We keep it on top of the 3rd floor latrine," Wimbish said to the Kid, with a whisper.

"Yeah, I know, Boujold told me all about it," the Kid replied, pushing back his plate. "The thing I don't understand is why all you guys in here want to go out to the field where you get shot at?"

"After you've been here for a while, you'll know," McCauley knowingly nodded.

"Today's surprise shake down was just the tip of the iceberg," Willert picked ups the baton, "we have to pull guard duty; we have to guard the officer's billet at the Villa Cruz and also battalion headquarters and we fill a lot of sandbags, that's for sure! There's all kind of extra hassling shit they do to us... maintenance... leaflet drops... and worst of all, lots and lots of real bullshit training. It never ends."

"Well, I sure as hell don't know how long I'm going to be here. Hoch," the Kid turned to Paul, "don't I get a transfer after a court martial?"

"Yes, you are entitled to a transfer, win or lose after a court martial. But, like I told you, they're going to try and make you take an article 15 and have it over with. Then you don't get a transfer. Plus, if you lose the court martial, they are absolutely going to send your ass to LBJ for a month... minimum! Then you won't come back here... if you come out at all. We're hearing rumors about bad race riots happening up there!"

The Kid had heard them too.

"What are you actually going to be charged with, anyway," Wimbish inquired, "I mean, what it is really all about?"

The Kid gave them the Cliff's Notes version of Wilson having a fight with the first sergeant and telling him not to eat in the mess hall, then not telling anybody else and then eating in the mess hall himself and seeing the Kid in there with Sweet and still not saying anything to either one of them about it. Then, when it was time to try and force him to volunteer for the armed propaganda team, the Lt. ups and cracks his ass with charges.

"Hmmm," Hoch considered what the Kid was telling him. "Seems to me, they are going to say you disobeyed the order and since you didn't deny he told you that, you will be found guilty. The only defense is, if it is an illegal order and most of the time, they say you have to obey the order and file a complaint about it later."

"The way I see it," theorized the Kid, "he may have said what he said, but all of his actions between when he said it and when he charged me, cancelled it out."

"Now that makes sense to me," Wimbish commented, "but this is the ARMY we're talking about here, Stocker..."

"And you know it doesn't feel in any way compelled or obligated to make sense," Willert added.

104

He silently stared back. "You're right, I know you guys are right. But in my mind, I guess it made even less sense to volunteer for that APT and I was *way tired* of going out on all those operations with no loudspeakers... not that I ever *wanted* the loud speakers... but point being, Wilson didn't give a shit about PSYOPS. So either way, I was in a fucked situation down there in Tra Vinh and I think I can work with this. I mean hell, it's not like I disobeyed an order in combat or fell asleep on guard duty or got busted with pot *or anything like that,* this is totally contrived bullshit and I think I can point it out!" they all chuckled, *"I can fucking work with this!"* he pretended by be a boxer, pumping his fists in an abstract combination of air punches.

Chapter 14

The Kid half was reading an old copy of Life magazine, from August 23rd, which had a cover story about how they were planning handling security at the now infamous Democratic Convention, and half watching B Company clerk, David Hoffman, as he typed away dispatching the company's business.

It was almost lunch. "Hey, Dave," the Kid rose up from the chair he'd occupied, almost steadily, since 0700 hours and walked the four paces over to stand in front of his gun metal gray desk. "If I didn't go to Eakin Compound for lunch, could I use your typewriter to write some letters while you're gone?"

Coffman never stopped typing. "Sure, no problem," he said, throwing the carriage and the sound of the bell, "soon as I finish this, it'll be time to go, so yeah, have at it. There's paper in the bottom drawer right."

The 'this', that Coffman was finishing, was the charge sheet on the Kid. Wilson's written report on his brash violation of the Uniform Code of Military Justice had arrived promptly at 1000 hours, and by 1030 hours, Capt. Ronnie Smith had emerged from his office with a larger than life shit eating grin on his face and instructed Coffman to prepare an Article 15 for the Kid.

"Don't I get a chance to tell my side of the story?" the Kid had questioned the captain, who was rocking back and forth on the heels of his jungle boots with unconcealed glee.

"Of course, you can tell me your side," he stopped rocking, "we still have our appointment at 1300 hours. But after reading Wilson's report, I can see that this is basically an open and shut case. He gave you a pretty direct order and you pretty much disobeyed it... about a half a dozen times... Stocker. So you can tell me all the 'your side of it you want,' but I don't think it's going to change anything."

"Well, Sir," the Kid began in a cordial voice, "how nice it is... no let me say how refreshing it is... to know that when I finally tell you my side that
106

you'll listen with an open mind and that you haven't made pre conceived decisions in advance... *or anything like that.*" he icily finished.

Ronnie looked confused because, after all, wasn't that what he'd just done? But then, as the realization set in that perhaps it might be a touch fairer to at least hear the Kid's side, he tried to put a better spin on it. "Sure, we'll talk, but with my experience in these matters, I was just trying to save Specialist Coffman some time."

Right.

With the understanding that the Kid wished to stay and type some letters, Capt. Smith made a big show out of locking the door to his office and he and Coffman exited to catch the Eakin Compound chow trucks.

Pulling out a piece of bright white paper from the drawer, the Kid rolled it into the carriage of the Smith Corona and resting his fingertips on the keys, he prepared to write his best friend, Larry Ryan, back in the states.

October 25, 196

Armando,

You'll never believe this. Remember when I told you I was giving up wanting to be a lawyer because I'd be a disk jockey and in radio for the rest of my life? Well, I'm sort of back to being in lawyer mode... because, get this, I'm being court martialed! Yes, indeed, I am in legal hot water with Lt. Wilson!

Here's what happened in a nutshell. The goon wanted to get me to volunteer for a middle of the night commando thing with these 24 ex-VC and I told him no fuckin' way, Jose, so he cooks up this fake deal to court martial me over... having to do with him telling me not to eat in a particular mess hall, in order to force me into volunteering. Can you believe it? Yes, I'm being court martialed over eating in the mess hall! No fucking joke! This would be really funny if there wasn't a chance I'd go to the Long Binh Jail, fondly known by the troops as LBJ, after the commander and chief.

Some of the guys around here are suggesting that it might be better if I take the article 15, which is the difference between a misdemeanor and a felony, at least then, I won't go to jail but I'd get busted and lose some money and never get a chance to be on Armed Forces Radio so I'm kind of torn. I'm using the company clerk's typewriter while the clerk's at lunch. When he and the Captain come back, I've got a "hearing" (and I use the term loosely) with him and then, I have to make up my mind if I'm going to ask for a trial or bite the bullet and plead guilty. Not really in my nature to plead guilty, but the word is, out of all court martials, 98 percent end in conviction and this unit has lost the last two in a row, so my odds have been damaged by circumstances beyond my control. I'm in a jam, Stan. This is the fucking army and they could find me guilty for the hell of it.

At least I'm out of combat, for a while, that's the one good thing to come out of all this bullshit. If I take the article 15, there is a good chance I'll get sent back out to the same place I was, but more than likely attached to the armor unit, which is worse! That's where they send all the guys they want to fuck with, to the spot where they have the greatest chance of getting killed! I'm back in Can Tho and the head clerk of the unit is trying to help me, so I'm not without allies. The guys here have really cool reel to reel tape recorders with huge fucking speakers and all kinds of music, a lot of it stuff I haven't heard yet, because I was stuck way out in the boondocks, so that's kind of nice. This dude, Tom Boyett, has an incredible selection. We listened to music in his room yesterday for about 3 hours. (one stayed out of our indmays!) It was great! He had the Stones live on the Jumpin' Jack Flash Tour, a near complete sets of Dylan and the Beatles and a bunch of shit I've never heard of before. Being stuck out in the Delta has put me totally out of touch with the music. Boyett is from Oklahoma and he says he's played in bands and knows the guys who are in that band, the Disciples that we used to see at The Rock up in Estes Park!

Talk about being at the crossroads. Whatever happens, I won't be with Wilson any more. This could screw up my transfer to Armed Forces Radio. I could go to jail in a place where they are currently having race riots. No more Flo. I definitely want to go back to Nashville and WKDA but sitting here in the 102 degree heat and 88% humidity in late October, I know you are getting ready for ski season you lucky bastard and I'm really missing that. I could go for standing at the top of A.Basin right now this second!

Well, gotta go. Hope you don't have to send my mail to the Tia Long Binh Jail!

Take care,

Manuel

He continued on and wrote nearly identical one page letters to Dave and Patsy in Nashville and one to his brother at Army medic school, at Ft. Lewis, in Washington State. He decided to not write his parents until he had a better grasp of where he stood and what was going to happen. *No sense in making them worry, wouldn't change anything on this end.* As he pondered over writing Flo, Coffman returned from lunch.

Shortly on his heels came Capt. Ronnie Smith, sharing some joke with a couple of other officers, laughing it up in the hallway before entering the B Company orderly room. Still clad in sunglasses, he unlocked his office and said, "Come on, specialist, let's get this thing over with."

Taking a deep breath, the Kid pulled himself together mentally and, with a look and nod of support from Coffman, he entered the office of the Company commander and came to attention in front of Smith's desk, where he was settling in. "Specialist 4th Class Stocker reporting, Sir," he snapped off one of his most regulation salutes and held it, waiting for the return.

Holding back for a fractional beat, just enough to let the Kid know that he was in control, Capt. Ronnie Smith returned the salute and said, "At ease, specialist, you can take a seat or stand... your choice, I don't think this is going to take very long. The longer it takes, the more pissed I get."

The Kid chose to stand at parade rest, with his feet apart and his arms behind his back. "Pissed? Pissed about what, Sir? Pissed that I want to tell my side of the story? Am I not innocent until proven guilty?' You say you are pissed at me for taking up your time? I'm not very happy with this situation, either," *at least he seems to be paying attention,* "because I do not believe I've done anything wrong. The order he is accusing me of disobeying was never obeyed, *not by anybody,* including him, Sir. Not even once. In fact it was not an issue of any sort until my refusal about going on the APT. By the same token, Sir, I'm not stupid. I know the APTs are your pet project and Lt. Wilson is your personal friend and he tried to sell me on it real hard. He gave it his best shot, Sir, but, I'm not trained for any commando shit nor do I have a taste for it. So, Sir, I can only hope you realize I'm within my rights, according to army regulations, to decline the assignment and not to volunteer because it is a volunteer's only assignment. And that is being held against me, and I feel this whole issue is exactly that!" The Kid stopped talking and waited for some response from the captain, who seemed to be mulling over a number of issues in his head.

"What does Lt Wilson say in his report?" the Kid finally broke the impasse and pointed to the manila folder that sat on the center of Smith's gun metal gray desk, in front of a picture of his wife and two kids. "Can I read it? I have a right to know the accusations against me."

"Yes, that's right, you do." Ronnie said, as he opened the manila folder and picked up Wilson's typed statement and handed it to the Kid across the desk. "But it doesn't say anything about you refusing to go on the APT mission. The part I don't understand is why you think that has to do with that?

The Kid quickly scanned it; *'On or about the 16th of October, First Sgt Brooks of the 72nd advisory team, came and informed me that any PSYOPS men who were getting Rations Not Available (RNA) pay, could no longer eat in the mess hall. So I instructed Specialist 4 Curtis L. Stocker, that since he was receiving said RNA payments, he could no longer eat in the Tra Vinh compound mess hall. Subsequently, he did eat in the mess hall, several times, thereby violating Army regulations, pertaining to eating in a mess hall while drawing pay for RNA. He also disobeyed a lawful order from me, a superior officer, to wit: 'do not eat in the mess hall.'* The Kid stopped reading and looked up to see Smith was waiting for his reaction.

That lying son of a bitch! Brooks never said one word about RNA when he came up to Wilson in the mess hall. Wilson never said one word in his statement about Brooks telling him he was going to have to pull officer of the day duty if we kept eating in the mess hall and that was the reason he said not to... What is this bullshit about RNA?

"Sir, that's not how it happened at all." the Kid collected his thoughts, "RNA payments were not an issue because it was OK to eat in the mess hall on RNA, if you paid for your meals and I did. Sir, Lt. Wilson never told me not to eat there because of RNA payments. Check the mess hall pay records, we started getting RNA a couple of months before the 'don't eat in the mess hall' BS started." Smith stared back at him, straight faced as any professional poker player that ever lived and chose not to comment. "He told me not to eat there," the Kid continued, "because First Sgt Brooks was going to make him pull officer of the day duty and all us men guard duty when we were in from the field. Wilson said no, we weren't going to do it and Brooks said, *'as long as you eat in my mess hall, you do what I say,'* so Lt. Wilson said to me, 'Stocker, I don't want you to eat in the mess hall any more and we are going to move out to the CIA compound.' But then, Sir, Lt. Wilson went and had lunch in the mess hall, not more than an hour later. I know this because Specialist Sweet came in from the field and was going to lunch at the mess hall and asked me to join him and when I told him Lt. Wilson said we couldn't eat there any more, Sweet told me Wilson was in the mess hall... eating... and that Lt. Wilson had seen him and not given him any orders to not eat there..." Still Smith stonewalls with no reply.

"So what the hell?" the Kid threw up his hands, "Am I the only guy who doesn't get to eat in the mess hall over some ridiculous little power struggle between two grown men?"

The logically bold attack made Smith squirm slightly and as soon as he had readjusted and settled his butt cheeks, he finally spoke. "So, Stocker, from what you've said, you admit he told you not to eat in the mess hall, which is to say you admit you're guilty of the offense detailed on these papers. You've been warned under Article 31 that anything you say can and will be used against you." And with that, Capt. Smith pulled from the manila folder, the Kid's already prepared Article 15 papers and laid them in front of the Kid at the edge of his desk.

The Kid momentarily froze, *wow! The fucker is going for the quick close! Anything I say can and will be used against me. Still, I've never denied that. My defense is that the order was not given to others or obeyed by even Wilson himself!* "Yes Sir, it is not in dispute that at one point, Lt. Wilson did say, 'do not eat in the mess hall... for whatever reason' and, about 45 minutes later, he went and ate there himself!"

"Well, Specialist, that is beside the point," Smith now seemed very sure of himself, "the bottom line is, Lt. Wilson gave *you* a direct order to not eat in the mess hall and you went 'n did it. By your own admission, and that's enough for me. What I've had Coffman do, is prepare an Article 15, with one count of disobeying an order." He paused for dramatic effect, "I could have made it a lot worse. You apparently disobeyed orders *and directives* and I could get you with a count every time you did." The declaration was punctuated with a grin. "This will be your only chance and if you don't take this deal I'm offering you right now, I can assure you, you won't like the alternative, which will be a summary court martial on a lot of counts. It'll be a FUBAR train wreck and it won't be pretty."

Holy shit! This is more Catch 22 than Catch 22! And now Wilson is lying about why he told me not to eat there. I can't believe this. Multiple counts... yikes! Maybe the deck is stacked too deep against me. Maybe I better run a loss check. "OK, Sir, although there is a lot more to it than that, let's say for a minute, that I did disobey an order and I take the Article 15, what would my punishment be?"

Sensing victory was within his grasp, Smith lit up a cigarette and leaned back in his chair while he considered the Kids question. "I'll most likely bust you one grade, back to PFC, fine you $100 and restrict you to your unit for one week while you're off duty."

"And what will my duty assignment then be, assuming I take the Article 15?"

Another rye smile crossed his boxy face, "There is that opening with the 14th Regiment Armored Cav," he slowly began, "the one that's been there since Roberts left. You could go there. Or..." he tried to reel the Kid in by playing both parts in the 'good cop - bad cop' game, "there might be *something* beside the Cav, maybe down in Ca Mau, I'll have to look into that. So, Specialist, are you going to accept the Article 15 or do we take it to the next level?"

Am I screwed or what? Can I gamble on a trip to LBJ? Fuck. I hate to throw in the towel... I need to go to the JAG office and talk to somebody. "Well, all things considered, I must say I am *leaning* toward taking it. However, Sir, can I have a day to think about it? I might not need a day, but I just want to think about everything for at least a little bit before I sign it."

"OK," Smith seemed relieved, "that seems fair. I'll give you 24 hours... or less. Dismissed," He saluted, signaling the meeting was over.

"Yes Sir," the Kid returned the salute, "24 hours, or less." He executed an about face and left the room. Right outside the door, Dave Coffman was there to press a piece of paper into his hand.

"Directions to the IV Corps JAG's office," he indicated the paper with a nod, "you can walk from here. His name is Lt. Ellis, he's a Navy lieutenant, which is like a captain and he's there now, I just called to confirm it and I think you'll find out something very interesting if you go talk to him. He's over behind the USO.

The Kid smiled on his way out the door. "Why, thanks, Coffman! See you in a couple of hours, cause I'm gonna do lunch at the USO, too!"

Chapter 15

Walking down the wide main boulevard of Can Tho, from the big curve in the road where 10th Battalion headquarters were located, back toward the USO, gave the Kid time to analyze his plight. The broad street was packed with Hondas, jeeps, mini busses, mini taxis, bicycles, cyclos and pedicabs, all hustling civilians and military traffic along in both directions but the Kid didn't see any of it. All he could see was a stripped shirt and a room mate named *'Bubba'*, if he made the wrong decision here.

In short order, he arrived at the USO and by looking at Coffman's map, found his way down the small walkway to it's west and ended up back in a series of old French commercial buildings ringing a small courtyard that had been turned over to IV Corps for it's use. He spotted the sign: *Judge Advocate General IV Corps, MAC-V USARV.*

An Army E-6 manned the front desk and no sooner had the Kid switched from his prescription shades to his wire rimmed glasses when the sergeant usher him up to the threshold of one Lt. Donald P. Ellis, or so said the name plate next to the door.

"Specialist Curtis L. Stocker reporting, Sir," the Kid saluted the husky, slightly curly headed man in black horn rimmed glasses and a very strong jaw, who sat up quite straight behind the rather large and ornate wooden table with round legs that served as his desk.

"At ease, soldier," he snapped off a return salute, "so, you must be the guy who's in trouble for eating in the mess hall!"

"Yes sir, I am," the Kid went to parade rest.

"Well, pull up a seat and relax, Specialist Stocker, and tell me all the sordid details of your dastardly crime," he grinned as he indicated a chair for the Kid to take. "Just tell me one thing right off the bat," he gave the Kid a penetrating look, "this whole thing sounds more than a little bit weird and I'd bet it doesn't have anything to do with eating in the mess hall, does it?

I like this guy! "No sir, it doesn't have anything to do with eating in the mess hall, but now, from the statement that Lt. Wilson sent to Captain

Smith, my company commander, he's changing the reason why he said he gave me the order..."

Holding up his hand for the Kid to stop taking, he picked up the pen that lay atop his yellow legal pad and said, "Why don't you start at the beginning."

And so the Kid did, giving him far more detail than the Cliff's Notes version but much less than *War & Peace* version, as he recounted how the whole tale unfolded. He told of how Sgt Brooks and Wilson began feuding over officer of the day duty and guard duty before the order was given and then ignored, by everyone for days, until the armed propaganda team assignment. He encapsulated his persistent refusals to volunteer and Wilson's threat of an article 15 and court martial over based on Sgt. Brook's 'if you eat in my mess hall', comment. This brought him to the place where Wilson sent Smith his written statement that accused him of an entirely different crime, that of disobeying a directive to not eat in the mess hall while drawing rations not available... something they had all been doing all along, "...only you have to pay for your meals," the Kid finished to take a drink of the iced coke Ellis's assistant had placed on the desk for him while he spoke, "so, at first, I didn't think it was any big deal."

Ellis wrote furiously, his head occasionally nodded positively as he scribbled away and when the Kid concluded, the Navy officer looked up from his pad and said, "I think I can help you. In fact, I know I can. You go back there and tell Captain Smith you refuse the article 15. If it all happened like you say it did, I'm pretty sure I can get you off."

"Well, all right!" the Kid virtually jumped to his feet and stuck out his right to shake hands with the man who would be his salvation, much to Ellis' amusement, as if sealing a business deal. "Uh, when you say 'pretty sure', how sure are you?"

"I'm no miracle worker," the navy man smiled as the Kid sat back down, "but lucky for you, I think we can handle this one with something less than a bonified miracle, so I'd say 80-90% sure, Specialist," he said, "nothing in life is 100%, but 80-90% sure! This Lieutenant Wilson sounds like a real winner," Ellis surveyed his notes. "Since I'll be defending you, I tell you what: let's call your Captain Smith and have him send over a copy of Lt. Wilson's statement and the court martial papers as soon as they're drawn up," he picks up the phone. "Hello, Operator, do you have the number for the 10th PSYOP Battalion, Company B HQ, and would you ring it please?" Waiting to be connected, he said to the Kid, "I can't wait to tell my colleagues about this one! Ha! *And I got it!* What a scream... Hello!

Captain Ronnie Smith? This is Lt. Donald Ellis, that's Navy Lt. Ellis, by the way, calling from Four Corps JAG, how are you today, Captain? Uh huh, that's nice, I'm sure... Captain... the reason I'm calling is, your Specialist Stocker is presently in my office and as of now, he is my client as he has chosen to refuse your article 15 and I am taking his case."

The Kid could barely conceal his laughter at the expression on Ellis' face as right after he announced there would be no acceptance of the Article 15, he held the phone away from his ear. "Now Captain... settle down... you don't need to take that tone with me. Specialist Stocker is entitled to his day in court and I will be there every step of the way to make sure you do it according to the book. Yes, Captain. Yes, Captain. I imagine he and I will finish up here in about an hour... or maybe two..." he winked at the Kid, who was holding up two fingers. "Yes, Captain, I will tell him to return to your HQ immediately following. I'm sure you know where my office is, so when I can I expect to see a copy of this Lt. Wilson's statement? Well, I'm, sure he's a fine officer... yes... but I seriously question his judgment on this one. Say what? Oh, come now, Captain, if I told you that, I'd be doing your job! Don't worry, I'll be in touch," and he hung up.

The Kid felt totally energized. His mouthpiece was a 'go-getter'. *He seems pretty fucking cock sure of himself. I hope to hell he really knows what he's doing!*

"He's madder than a wet hen," Ellis chuckled, clearly entertained by the event's unfolding, "here's my card with the phone number for this office." he slid a white rectangular object across the desk for the Kid, "you can call me if you need to, like if he starts picking on you. Plus, as soon as he finalizes the charges, we can meet and plan our attack."

"Yes sir!" the Kid stood and saluted, "thank you Sir. I feel a lot better now." Then, a degree of doubt snuck into his skull, "you're sure we can win this, right?"

"Don't worry about that cracker Smith," Ellis said, "I already know he's the kind of guy who never has the time to read all the regulations, because if he knew what the hell Lt. Wilson has done here, *either way...* the way he tells it or the way you tell it... it doesn't matter, he'd have already *dropped* the charges!"

All through lunch at the USO and while on the walk back to 10th PYSOP Battalion HQ, the Kid thought about what Ellis had said. *'... If he knew what Wilson had done... either way? Hmmm, I wonder what the fuck he means. He seems pretty sure about winning this, I hope to hell this guy is not just some loon who is bored and is using this for a little excitement and deep down, he doesn't give a fuck about me or what happens... he's got nothing to lose.*

Arriving at Battalion HQ, he enters the gate in the masonry wall under the watchful eyes of the Vietnamese guard, and crosses the tiled courtyard to enter the building in the first floor foyer that leads into the B Company orderly room. Opening it like a teenager who is sneaking in after being out late past curfew, he catches Coffman's eye and the clerk flashes him an approving smile.

"He's here, Sir," Coffman called out over his shoulder, as soon as the Kid closed the door behind him.

"Send'em in!" Smith literally bellowed through the open door of his office, making Coffman wince in pantomime.

Tossing his baseball cap on a chair, the Kid strode into Captain Smith's office and coming to attention two paces from his desk, delivered the salute, "Specialist Stocker reporting, Sir!"

Through obviously gritted teeth, Smith quickly snapped off the return salute, "God dammit, Stocker... you told me you were going to take this Article 15!"

"No Sir. I never said I was going to take it. I said I was *leaning* that way, but wanted to think about it and you gave me 24 hours, or less, Sir, and this is less. And after thinking about it and talking to the JAG, I have decided, as you were informed, that I *refuse* the article 15, Sir," the Kid answered in a calm voice.

"Specialist... I don't think you understand the severity of your situation!" Smith looked at him, gaped mouthed as if in wonderment about how a person could be stupid enough to turn down this particular article 15. "This JAG bastard is blowing smoke up your asshole. All the while he's painting you a rosy picture and you think it all looks pretty good, but, if you make this into a court martial, the punishment for being found guilty of disobeying an order in a combat zone can be up to and including *death!*" he spit out the last word at double volume and waited to see what kind of reaction this news would have on the Kid.

Death? You gotta be kiddin' me! "Oh yeah, right. Like this is a death penalty case," the Kid sarcastically countered, "don't make me laugh. I can just see you trying to get the death penalty for somebody whose crime was eating in the mess hall! How much do you think the network press back home would love that? What a bullshit thing to say!"

Smith was mega pissed by the turn of events. "OK. You wanna play hardball? I'll play hardball! I will give you one more chance to take this Article 15," he pushed the paper across the desk toward the Kid, "or I will rip it up and when it goes to court martial, you will be facing 6 counts of disobeying an order *AND 6* counts of disobeying a directive and when you lose. You will be busted to E-1, fined $100 per count and you'll end up do up to 6 months in LBJ and your tour in Vietnam and your time in the Army will be extended by that same amount of days!" He heavily breathed, sweat running down his face from the afternoon heat. "Did you know all that? Did your smarty pants JAG lawyer tell you that? It's your choice, mister!"

The Kid stared back into the Captain's seething blue eyes for about 5 seconds, then calmly picking up the papers, he extended them to Smith and said, "I ain't taking your *stinkin'* Article 15, so go ahead... have at it, Sir... *Rip it up!*"

On the verge of boiling over, Smith snatched the Article 15 out of the Kid's hand and ripped it in half, wadded it up and slammed it into his waste basket on the right side of his desk. "OK, smart ass, that's it! I will have Coffman type up your charges for a summary court martial and I'll nail you with so many counts... you are going to jail, *Stocker,* mostly for being a stupid fucking pig headed son of a bitch because, as you'll realize while you're getting your asshole fucked in the stockade, *you could have done this the easy way!*"

"Well, Sir, your easy way doesn't work for me. So as soon as Coffman's done, I'll need a copy of the charges and Wilson's statement to take over to *my lawyer* so he can see how many *mistakes* you've made... and he's pretty sure you've made a *big one,* already."

"What mistake?" Smith sat up bolt straight.

"Like *I'd* tell you? Oh please, Sir, if I was that stupid, I'd be out on that APT patrol with Wilson right now! It's like *my lawyer* said, '...if he told you that, he'd be doing your job...'"

Smith shot him a fresh smoking hot dirty look and was now visibly grinding his teeth in anger.

"Is that all, Sir?" the Kid flippantly inquired and with the contemptible glare exuding from Smith's face, the Kid knew, *if looks could kill, I'd be so dead.*

"Dismissed," Smith hissed, in a very snake-like manner as he returned to the Kid what could only be described as a very *'curt'* salute.

Chapter 16

The Kid looked at his hole cards again; *6 of diamonds and 10 of clubs. No help.* Seven card stud was the furthest thing from his mind as he surveyed the table while Ron Edwards dealt the last face up cards of the hand and gave his running commentary.

"Jack of Hearts to the pair of fives, no apparent help... OOO, Seven of spades making a pair of sevens... 8 of clubs to go with the other two clubs, possible flush... big ace to the King-Queen, possible straight... 5 of spades to Stocker, not helping him, but really hurting the pair of 5's across the table... and the dealer gets a four, no help... pair of sevens bets!"

Lou Wimbish, who held the pair of sevens, hesitated and seeing no real power of the table said, "Check."

"Check," agreed Ken Willert to his left.

"Check," followed Paul Hoch to his left.

"Fold," the Kid flipped over his hand and pushed it away.

"The dealer checks," Edwards looked to Ling Foo on his left.

"Isn't this exciting," Harold deadpanned, holding the 5's, "I bet half a buck," and with that, he rips a blue MPC one dollar bill in half and drops one piece into the pot.

Edwards watched the pot get right from all the remaining players before dealing out the last face down card, with flicks of his right wrist sending each one to it's proper hand, "down and dirty gentlemen," he said with his soft Kentucky accent as he sat down the deck and checked his own final card, looking at it long and hard.

As the remaining players rechecked their own cards and stole glances, looking to see if anybody's face betrayed their luck or lack of it, the Kid lit up a KOOL and took a sip of his Budweiser and leaned back to watch. It was then he sensed somebody was standing to his left. Looking up, he saw that it was Dave Coffman who stared down at him, with a strange expression on his face.

"Hey Dave?" the Kid responded, "What's up?"

"We just got word from the field, Wilson's MSQ 85 got hit with a mortar shell earlier today," the poker game stopped. "He and Sweet had it out somewhere, not sure where from what I heard. It didn't get blown up totally; I guess they got tagged on the back rear right. Lucky neither of them were in it or standing by it when it happened."

"Fuckin' A! No shit?" the Kid exclaimed, "I picked a good one to miss!"

"Geeze, Stocker," said Hoch, "your luck may suck at cards, but it sounds like you lucked out not being there!"

"Yeah! It's the nickel," the Kid lifted it up off his bare chest and showed it around, "the lucky beaver nickel comes through again!"

"Whatever," Coffman wasn't through, "Captain Smith is flying down to Tra Vinh tomorrow to meet with Wilson and interview Sgt. Brooks as part of your pre-trial investigation, so he's going to see how badly damaged it's and maybe take a picture."

"Smith's going to Tra Vinh? I should get to go too! The defense reserves the right to investigate, too!" the Kid slammed his fist mockingly on the table. "

"Ask him tomorrow morning," Coffman suggested, "he might let you go... you never know. In all fairness, he should."

"Oh, well, then forget that, you wont' be going!" laughed Ling Fook, "Smith be fair?" he looked around the table to see total agreement, while indicating to the other players, they needed to finish the hand. "I see your buck and raise you a buck," Ling Fook responded to Wimbish's bet.

Lou stared back at him and said, "Well, Stocker had one of the fives, the chances of you having the other one are 1 out of 52, so I don't think you've got the full house or even 3 of a kind, so I see you dollar and raise you two!"

"Call," Ling Fook threw in the MPC paper coinage and waited for Lou to flip'em over.

"Two pair, Kings high," Lou revealed a king to go with one showing.

"Ha. Just so happens, I *do* have the other 5! Got it on the last card!" Ling Fook turned it over and raked in the very nice little pot. "Thank you thank you thank you very much!"

"Deal me out," said the Kid as he stood, grabbed his last buck and a half off the table and stuck it into the left pocket of his burgundy Bermuda's, retrieved his Budweiser and began walking thru the moderately busy Roof

Top club toward the nearest of the two stairwells, having decided to go on down to the 3rd floor balcony to refresh his high before the movie started at 2000 hours.

Making the landing on the third floor, the Kid glanced to his left, out the door leading to the "L" shaped balcony and there in the doorway, sitting on a bucket, casually leaning back against the rail, was Richard Zewe, whom the Kid knew, was actually on 'guard duty.'

"Hi, Zoo," the Kid nodded as he passed.

"How high?" Zewe shot back with a grin.

"Not currently high enough," the Kid continued on to where two shirtless figures, who turned out to be Benny Vargas and George Carillo, stood in the middle of the balcony with fore arms propped on the 6" wide white tile railing, passing a filter tipped joint between them.

"Evening, gentlemen," the Kid said, mirroring their pose at the rail and by doing so, automatically joined in the rotation.

"Hey!" said Benny.

"Hi," replied George and immediately offered him the joint. He drew the pungent Asian smoke deep inside his lungs and holding the hit in, passed the joint back to Benny, who took a hit and handed it back to George all the while the pair continued their conversation. They were pretty excited about some band, Kid picked up... they were talking about playing live music in a band somewhere.

When the joint came around again, before the Kid had even blown out the remains of the first hit, he had to admit, the boys of the 10th PSYOP Battalion had it pretty damned good at the New Villa. There was a movie, 6 out of every 7 nights, really new ones, a huge club, ping pong *But no pool table...* and all kinds of music and hot stereo equipment 3 or 4 different rooms where once they were stoned, they'd sit and listen to a wide variety of music!

Behind him, the doors of three rooms of the balcony's east facing side yawned opened; the prime real estate of the whole hotel. Unless you believed Lou Wimbish and Ling Fook, who lived around the corner, facing the whore house across the alley where total female nakedness was seen on many occasions, although the building blocked any other kind of view. The Kid liked the view from the west side, the smoking side, where one caught a nice breeze, if one was to be had, because the third floor was the first floor in the hotel not screened by chicken wire to keep someone from chucking a grenades into their rooms. The doors to three rooms were almost always open and the twelve men who occupied them, were considered the luckiest renters in town. It wasn't easy to get into one of these prized rooms; somebody had to DEROS for it to happen and then the room mates had veto power over who got to take his place and of course, he would only be replaced by another GI who smoked pot or at the very least, was 100% sympathetic to the pot smoking cause. In this way, the integrity of the balcony, often referred to as the *Embassy,* was kept in tact.

The plan for communal safety from being busted hinged on the 'one entry' fact of the situation. Since there was only one way on to the balcony, it was kept guarded by someone who was prepared to sound the alert. If a non-friendly headed for the location, the guard would greet them loudly, by their rank and name and hearing same, anybody who was smoking a joint at that time, would simply drop it over the rail, in the snake rich swamp below. The 50 foot long and 30 feet wide fish pond, which was surrounded on the side nearest the hotel by knee high grass, separated the New Villa from the Vietnamese dwellings that started right on the other side of the mini swamp and ran for some distance in a quilt of thatch and tin roofs, to the east.

There was a sidewalk that bordered the pond's west side, in front of the first row of clapboard and grass houses, but the side of the pond next to the hotel was tall, thick grass that nobody messed around in, ever, because it was a serpentine metropolis and the residents were packing poison. When a soldier stood smoking pot at the rail, with his fore arms resting upon it, there was virtually no way anybody could sneak up on him or catch what he dropped before it disappeared into the grass, because once visual contact was lost, there could be no chain of evidence that proved, beyond a shadow of a doubt, that whatever was picked up had been dropped by any one particular soldier.

What really amused the Kid was, there were lifers less than 10 feet away! Yes, right on the next floor up. While the men of the 10th smoked their weed, many a drunk lifer stood, staring out at the one red light on the tower at Bien Thuy Airfield. They were oblivious and incapable of discerning the sweet odor of the weed wafting up from below, because nobody had ever identified the smell to them and consequently, they had no idea what was going on one floor down, directly beneath their noses.

Oh, the lifers knew there was some pot smoking going on, somewhere... most likely away from the unit, by some troops... not many. But they had virtually no idea of how bold or brazen or how numerous the pot smokers had become. And of course, the whole fricking country smelled strange for the most part, so that factor wasn't a dead giveaway. Before the men figured out they could smoke right there and never be prosecuted, they kept it outside the hotel but now, they bothered only to keep it outside their actual rooms. And by only smoking in a position that allowed them to jettison the evidence, they became bust immune.

It took only 3 hits for the Kid to restore his high but just as he prepared to return to the roof, the rest of the poker table came down, all ready to toke up, so the Kid stayed for another joint. Laughing and smoking with his new friends, he arrived at a point where his thoughts wondered mostly back to his old friends, the ones out at Tra Vinh and Cang Long; Bouj, Sweet, Corporal Ba, Pete and Ernie... the ones from DINFOS, Dave Waterhouse, Al Viator, Tom Davies, Pete Erio, Alan P. and the Boy Scout... the late John Imbach. *Shit! I still can't believe he's dead!* And before that, Dave and Patsy Allen, Bill Langford and Sam Robinson in Nashville. *Crap. Now that I'm not engaged, I wish I hadn't written that letter to Donna!* And before that, Larry Ryan, Mike Barglow, Dave Wicks and Steve Meyers in Boulder. *I wonder if I'll even be around here long enough for any of these guys to become real friends. I wonder what the real skinny is on that mortar attack on the Bat Mobile. Nobody was hurt because they weren't near the truck? They were out alone? I smell something rotten like ' nouc maum' in the state of Denmark.*

Chapter 17

The Headquarters unit for the 10th PSYOP Battalion was housed on the second floor of an old colonial building. It sat back off a big sweeping curve, made by Can Tho's main boulevard, as it ran through the city. The curve, along with a side street, which angled off from it and ran straight in front of the PSYOPS building, created a triangular area that had been neatly landscaped into a small park.

Instead of walls and windows, PSYOPs HQ had screening that ran from floor to ceiling all across the entire front of the 50 foot long and 15 foot deep main room and through it, from where the Kid stood, he was looking out over the interior HQ compound wall and into the miniature park. He observed an outdoor barber shop, set up in the shade of high trees, where a thin middle aged man in a white armless T-shirt and kaki slacks used a pair of scissors and a comb to clip the hair of an ARVN customer. Meanwhile, 3 of his soldier buddies played dominoes as they waited their turns, 2 of them using the park's low bordering wall as both table and chairs, while the third squatted, gook style, between them.

It was just after breakfast and behind him, the Kid could hear Sp. 4 Hoch at his typewriter, attacking the massive pile of paperwork the head clerk faced for the day. The Kid plan to badger Captain Smith into taking him to Tra Vinh had been derailed quite unexpectedly, because he was now waiting to see the new unit commander, Lt. Col. Willie O. Lawton, who for some reason, had requested the meeting.

"Yo, Stocker, he's ready to see you," came the call from Hoch who gestured at the colonel's door with his head when the Kid turned around.

Giving Hoch a puzzling look, and accepting his shrugged shoulder for an answer, he approached the closed louvered door, took a really deep breath and knocked three times.

"Enter!" came the sharp reply.

Opening the door, the Kid stepped in, to see Lt. Colonel Lawton sitting behind his desk, smiling pleasantly back at him. Closing the door behind him, the Kid snapped to attention, "Specialist Four Stocker reporting, Sir!" he saluted.

"At ease, Specialist Stocker," Lawton returned the salute and the Kid assumed a modified parade rest stance.

He was a slim black man with closely cropped tightly curled hair, almost thin lips and very regular features, except that his ears stuck out just the slightest bit from his slightly narrow but well proportioned face. Rising up from his chair, he showed his 6 ft 2 inch tall and lanky frame as he gestured to a dark wood round table that sat off to the right of his desk in the very spacious office. "Why don't we sit down and have a little chat, specialist."

"Yes Sir, thank you Sir," the Kid replied, feeling a level of comfort he hadn't expected as he moved over to pull out one of the four wooden chairs at the table.

"You know, Specialist Stocker," he began as they were both seated, "I hadn't even been in this office for a full week when this court martial of yours came in the door and needless to say, I was somewhat surprised to hear what it was about." he smiled in a totally disarming way. "I have a hunch, about what a charge of this nature says on its face value."

Oh my God? This man smacks of intelligence! Thank you Lucky Beaver Nickel!

"To *'not to eat in a particular mess hall '*," the colonel continued, "is the kind of a problem a good officer would never let develop into something that needed summary court martial for resolution," he paused to look into the eyes of the Kid, who was leaning forward, locked in attention mode, anxious to hear what the 'Man' who basically controlled his life, was going to say next. "Having not yet met Lt. Wilson, I don't know if he is a good officer or a bad officer. But I also don't have to be told, in so many words, that this is about something other than mess halls and obeying orders."

"Yes Sir!" the Kid's face lit up, "it's not about that at all. What it's about is..."

Lawton lifted up the palm of his hand and stopped him from speaking, "I don't want to discuss the details of the case, Specialist. There is nothing I can do about it; I won't intercede nor will I be the officer who hears it. The only thing I can tell you is this: I will appoint the best officer I have in my command to conduct the trial and I will make sure you will receive the fairest possible hearing that can be had here in the 10th PSYOP Battalion."

"That is all I want, Sir!" he beamed, "a chance to present my case in front of somebody who will be impartial but fair and let the chips fall where they will."

124

"Well, good, because that's all I can do for you. You have a lawyer from JAG, right?"

"Yes Sir."

The man, who must have been in his mid to late 30's, had put the Kid completely at ease. "So, I understand you experienced a little bit of combat out there..." Lawton invited the Kid to share some experiences.

"Yes Sir, we actually got into *beau coup* shit, as a matter of fact," the Kid began, "we went on a lot of search and destroy operations with the ARVNs and we never took any loud speakers or loudspeaker teams with us, like we were supposed to... oh wait, I take that back, we had one guy, once, with a bullhorn come along, it was kind of small, though... like it might have been able to get Specialist Hoch's attention in the next room from here... if the door was open. But I never felt like I was ever doing the job my MOS as a foreign language announcer, is assigned to do, Sir, and we got shot at *beau coup!*"

"Yes, combat is no fun," he took a deep breath, "you ever see that *Gregory Peck movie, Pork Chop Hill?*"

"Yes Sir, I saw it once, on TV."

"Well, I fought in the real battle. And I saw some officers who truly knew how to lead and others who were only interested in covering their own miserable chicken shit asses and that is when I decided what kind of officer I was going to be... because I saw how important it was for the men to have officers that did the right thing. And being a black man, I also know a little something about what it's like not to be treated fairly..." he leaned forward in his chair toward the Kid, as if to make a point,"... *for purely arbitrary reasons...*" and he leaned back, "and that is something I absolutely will not tolerate."

I am so liking this man! "That's pretty wild, Sir. Was Pork Chop Hill anything like the movie?"

"A little. At least the movie was historically pretty accurate," Lawton briefly glanced down at the table and then back to the Kid, "but once you've seen heavy combat, you know that movies never really capture the genuine terror of a situation like that. Now, PSYOPS is another matter," Lawton changed the subject with a wave of his left arm, like it was a wand, "I volunteered to join PSYOPS because I believe that the only way to win a war of this nature is win over your enemy's *mind.*" he pointed to his closely cropped head with the index finger of his right hand, he arm held in much the position of a salute, "Otherwise, they'll just fight forever and there are

125

so many more of them than us that, if it boils down to a war of attrition, *we will lose.* Plain and simple. We in PSYOPS have a unique opportunity to do something really positive and I want to ask you some questions about your experiences in the field."

"OK."

"So there aren't any loud speakers out there, huh?" he casually asked for confirmation of what the Kid had mentioned earlier.

"No sir, there weren't and no efforts were made by us... read Lt. Wilson... or the ARVNs to obtain any."

"All right," he nodded in comprehension, "but for the rest of this conversation, you can omit any references to Lt. Wilson, but, if there were loud speakers and you could do the assigned mission, do you think that would make any difference?"

As he pondered the question, the Kid's mind swiftly arrived at the images of the three VC... Wally and the Beaver and the girl next door. The three young VC fighters they had taken prisoner and that he never saw again, after their refusal to Chui Hoi. His plea to them had not involved a loudspeaker. *This is not the time to get into that. If I did, Wilson would say I was making it up to get out of this court martial and Minnesota would back him. I have to take care of first things first.* "Well, sir, no I don't think it would," he finally said, "the dedicated VC all totally believe in their cause and getting up there in combat and hollering 'Chui Hoi' a couple of times through a loud speaker, in the heat of battle, is not a sufficiently persuasive enough argument to change any of their minds."

Lawton smiled at his comment "Yes that is an interesting take on the situation. Was there anything going on out there, that you felt was an activity where we were making progress?"

"Well, the one Chui Hoi we got like walked in off the street in Cang Long and told us a story that he was defecting because the other Charlies weren't 'nice' to him."

"What?"

"Yes Sir, no BS, Sir," the Kid grinned, "this Hoi Chanh said he walked 2 dozen mortar rounds down the Ho Chi Minh Trail all the way to the Delta, through air strikes and snakes and tigers and all kinds of bullshit and the VC he brought them to, took'em and shot'em off in like a couple of minutes and didn't say 'hello, thank you, offer him a cup of tea or a place to sleep, so he defected!"

"No! Really?" Lawton twisted his expression into one of disbelief.

"Yes! *True story!*" the Kid looked him right in the eye, nodding affirmatively.

"Ha! We'll make a new leaflet," the colonel envisioned, "ARVN… the polite Army!"

"There we go, that's a winner for sure, Sir." They both laughed and the Kid continued. "I will say that every time we went into a village and worked with the people on a MEDCAP or other Civil Action Program, I felt like we were making more progress than when we went out with the ARVN infantry and chased them all over to hell and gone shot at them all day long and they shot at us," the Kid said without hesitation, using up 95% of a breath. "Uh, Sir," the Kid made an effort to sit straight up, "there is one thing I would like to take this opportunity to request…if I may."

"Yes, Specialist, what is it?"

"Well, Sir, I've been sitting in the B Company orderly room now, on my ass, for a couple of days and I was wondering, if the colonel would permit me to volunteer to fly leaflet drops?"

The colonel immediately engaged his thought process, "Now let me see, technically, being under charges, you're supposed to be in the control of an authority at all times, and you aren't allowed to carry a weapon, but' he took a deep breath and exhaled, "considering the nature of your alleged crime, and the fact that we do need help with leaflet drops right now, and that I have your word nothing will happen from me granting you this permission that I, *personally,* will ever regret… then yes. I'll call down to Capt. Smith and have him release you to leaflet dropping duty beginning today!"

"Yes Sir! Thank you Sir! You have my word you won't regret it," the Kid had become genuinely excited about the chance of breaking free from the boredom of sitting around the orderly room. And the chance to get into an airplane and rise up above the heat was too much for the Kid not to take a crack at it. *Thank you Lucky Beaver Nickle.* "Thank you sir!"

Lawton glanced at his watch, "Oh, I've got to be someplace in a few minutes down at IV Corps HQ…" Lawton suddenly rose to his feet and the Kid quickly followed suit and in fact assumed the position of attention so that he could be dismissed.

"Yes, specialist, dismissed, but I will call Captain Smith before I go because you need to get out there to the warehouse," Lawton saluted.

The Kid returned it, executed a fairly strack 'about face' and was out the door, making sure to close it without slamming it behind him.

Downstairs, Capt. Smith was in the front part of the office, at Coffman's desk, putting a couple of items into a leather valise as he prepared to leave for the airport to catch his flight down to Tra Vinh to parlay with Wilson and check out the damaged MSQ-85. He couldn't fail to notice the smile that was painted on the Kid's face.

"I don't know what that fruity fuckin' grin is about, but you'll be crying out of the other side of your mouth when I come back with the evidence Wilson has for me that he says is going to hang your smart ass, Stocker!" he delivered a truly classic sneer as he stopped packing to check the Kid's reaction.

"Evidence?" the Kid repeated back the word to Smith, "evidence like what? The food I ate? Shit! That will be *impressive,*" he put in the dig. "Oh, by the way, if you give me a ride out to Can Tho Field, I could hitch on out to Ben Thuy where I'll be flying leaflet drops today."

This sentence stopped the captain cold. "What the fuck are you talking about?"

"I asked Lt. Colonel Lawton if it would be OK for me to volunteer for leaflet dropping duty and he said yes!"

"Well...uh, wait just a fucking second," the stunned captain replied, "I say no! You are going to sit right here and be bored as hell and not do anything outside this orderly room... the whole time up until your court martial!"

The phone on Coffman's desk rang. "Do you want to bet if that isn't the colonel calling to tell you the very thing I just told you?" the Kid smirked, "One dollar? Five? Make it $10, Sir."

Coffman picked up the phone, "Headquarters, Company B. Yes sir, he's right here, Sir," then extending the phone to Smith, "it's the colonel," he snuck a grin to the Kid as Smith snatched the receiver out of his hand.

"Yes Sir?" Smith rolled his eyes as he listened, "yes sir." he handed the phone back to the clerk but said nothing, just stared another one of those 'kill you with this look' stares at the Kid.

"Hey... Sir, if you don't want to give me a ride, I'll understand," the Kid acquiesced, as Smith's grip on the handle of his valise was turning his knuckles white.

"No," said Smith, "the colonel just instructed me to let my driver take you on to Ben Thuy Field," he said through gritted teeth, about as pissed as an army issue captain could get.

"Why, thank you, Sir," the Kid said with the lightest trace of southern accent, "that'll surly save the war effort some *valuable* time!"

Chapter 18

It was Tuesday, November 5th and being it was the first Tuesday after the first Monday in 1968, it was Election Day back in the United States.

Or *it will be when it gets to be that time there, because it's still November 4th in the states,* the Kid thought to himself, remembering how the international date line figured into *'Around the World in 80 Days,* starring David Niven, as he stared through the nylon strap-covered door of the C-47, at the endless rice paddies below. The empty bird was winging its way back to Ben Thuey Airfield completing yet another successful but boring leaflet drop mission. *Boring is good.*

Never did get my absentee ballot. Fuckers. You think they take care of the freaking troops! Bastard fuck Army. I hate it so much. Oh well, this is like a blessing disguise. Who the fuck would my first vote have been for? The Hump? He never struck me as presidential. Nixon? Hard to believe I was actually for him in 1960. Oh what the fuck... I was an 8th grader. And, like Sweet says all the time, 'It don't make a fuck of a shit load of difference to us who gets elected because we're still here.' Nixon leaves me so cold. What did I ever see in him? The influence of Mom, that's what it was. 'Secret Plan...' my ass' has a secret plan. If he had a plan, he'd be talking about it. If he wins, I can't wait to find out what it is... but I know it won't shorten my tour. Look at the paddies down there. Some soldiers are slopping through it right now, some where... getting shot at, stepping on booby traps...villages getting burnt and people dying. This ain't so bad! Flying along at 3,000 feet... just out of range of small arms fire... but what if the engine conked out and we had to ditch. Then we'd be right back into it... if we lived through the crash. Oh well, can't sweat the small stuff.

The Kid turned away from the door and looked back inside the aircraft, where a half dozen of his equally bare chested compatriots were lounging, drinking from canteens, and stretching out on the pile of broken down boxes which up until a few minute ago, had contained the leaflets they just littered all over to hell and gone along the border of Vietnam and the eastern part of Cambodia. It was his fourth day in the air, since Lt. Colonel Lawton had released him from the confines of the Company B orderly room.

The charges had been formally filed on Nov. 2nd. The Kid remembered when Captain Smith had returned from Tra Vinh, the Saturday before, he had with him the cash collection sheets from the now infamous Tra Vinh mess hall. The Kid was still replaying their exchange.

"You're history now, Stocker," the Kid recalled how Smith had scoffed at him when he gave him a copy of the charges and the evidence to take over and show Lt. Ellis. "Right here on these cash collection sheets, it shows, without a doubt, that you, repeatedly, did not pay enough for your meals while you were getting RNA. You were a dollar short every meal!"

"Say what? *Didn't pay enough?* What has *THAT* got to do with fucking anything? I paid exactly what I was instructed to pay, that is to say, what every swinging dick on RNA in the whole compound paid." the Kid countered matter of factly.

"Ah, well, haven't you ever heard, 'ignorance of the law is no excuse?' Smith's face lit up as he uttered the phrase, "you can't just say, *'I didn't know, your honor,'* and get off! I would think a smart ass, like yourself, would at least know *THAT* much!" he made an inch sign with the index finger and the thumb of his right hand. "See? That Navy JAG Ellis is going to get you run over by a freight train!"

"Hey? What's this?" the Kid pointed to a signature on one of the cash collection sheets, "isn't this Lt. Wilson's signature? Oh… look… doesn't it show he paid exactly the same amount for his meal that I did?" he wagged his own index finger between the two signatures and their identical amounts, a mere 12 lines apart on the page. "So, is he going to get hit by the same freight train? Or is his *ignorance of the law* somehow more *'special'* than mine?" the Kid made air quotes with both hands as he spoke the word, *special.*

"Let me see that!' the captain snatched it back from the Kid and took a look. Sure enough, Wilson's signature was on there in identical times matching that of the Kid's. He was obviously shocked he hadn't spotted this fly in the ointment earlier. "Well, it doesn't matter," Smith said with a sour look on his face, as he tossed the papers back down in front of the Kid, "he's an officer. Nobody gave *him* an order to not eat there! That's what this is all about. You just don't get that part of it, do you, Stocker? Or wait… is it that you can't accept that part… the part where you have to admit that you disobeyed his orders and are guilty and deserving of being busted!"

In the end, Captain Smith had to re-do the charge sheet and take out the money angle and go with the original version, that the Kid had been told not to eat in the mess hall while on RNA. The way he goosed up the ante was make it three counts of the same charge: *a violation of the Uniform Code of Military Justice, Article 90:*

Specification 1: In that specialist 4 Curtis L. Stocker, RA 12966317, B Company, 10th Psychological Operations Battalion, APO San Francisco 96215, having received a lawful command, to not eat in the Tra Vinh Field Ration Mess while receiving payment for Rations not Available, did on or about 16 October 1968, willfully disobey the same."

Specifications two and three were exactly the same, just the date was changed to October 17th and 18th. The Kid did have to admit, but only to himself, it was that kind of particular screwed up Army officer logic he feared was going to get him corn holed in the end, even though Ellis had continually assured him he had it aced. *But why won't he tell me what it is?* Still, he couldn't show any weakness in front of Smith. After all, the charge had gone from... 'He ate in the mess hall', to 'don't eat in the mess hall' while on rations not available, to the third version; you 'didn't pay *enough* to EAT in the mess hall' while drawing RNA, and finally back to the original.

The C-47 was dropping altitude as they approached Ben Thuy Field. This was the really dangerous part, when the plane was low enough that a sniper might get off some good shots from in hiding, somewhere just outside of the airfield perimeter. Sitting belted into their pull down canvas seats, they all felt relief as the wheels touched down. The crew anticipated the end of the work day and four of them had already made plans to hit the Scientific for the old steam and cream and Willert and Edwards were going to take him to a local Bien Xi Moi restaurant he hadn't tried yet.

After being in the field, Can Tho was like New York City, with restaurants, stores, a large American compound with a huge PX, a swimming pool and even a library of some size! *I kinda like this, but win or loose, I'm the fuck out of here! The Kid couldn't help but think on the coming of that day. Maybe it's like being out of Tra Vinh... in a flash... right after the trial. I wonder what the chances are, if I win, they'll send me to AFVN? If I loose, it's out of here and right into the Long Binh Jail! Can't think about that.*

The Kid stuck his M-16 in the locker, closed the door and secured it, along with his wallet, taking only a blue $10 MPC note, his ID and a pack of KOOLs. Ron and Will were waiting outside of Ozelle's orderly room door.

"We have to hit Taj's and change out some money first," Will said, as they waked down the stairs, through First Sgt. Ozelle's office and out the front of the New Villa.

A drove of Vietnamese kids played noisily in the alleyway between the New Villa and the whore house that faced it. The boys were now pretending their sticks were swords and hacked away at each other with great vigor. Whose children are those, the Kid wondered? Obviously the by-products of GI sex; a couple of them were clearly the children of black and Vietnamese parents. Then he spied an older girl, but not more than 15, with a lighter complexion and strikingly beautiful face who was standing back, sort of watching the younger kids to see that they didn't get into any real trouble.

"That's Sandy," Willert saw that the Kid had noticed her. "Her father was a French soldier and her mother will kill the first mutha fucka who tries to lay a hand on her."

"So would I, if she was my daughter," said the Kid, "but God fucking damn, is she ever going to be a heartbreaker when she grows up!" *The French again.*

"After the steam bath, let's eat at the Black Hole and fuck off Eakin tonight," Willert suggested.

"Hey, GI GI!" a bunch of the kids had dropped their sticks and decided to panhandle the soldiers and see what they could get. "GI GI you give chocolate, cigarette money OKOKOK!" they chorused as they ran around them begging. "GI, you numba one fo sur!"

The scale of ten was at its epoch. Everything was on a scale of ten. "Some nights, I just don't feel like getting back in that truck, Willert finished his thought."

"Sound OK to me," Ron said as he turned to the Kid, "watch your wallet when they get to packin' around you like that," he advised. "So, you wanna eat at the Black Hole?"

"What the fuck do I know, I'm with you guys," the Kid smiled.

As they got to the end of the alley, where it "T'd" on the main street of Bien Xi Moi, they made a right turn. Ahead, the Kid saw a somewhat tall but skinny black soldier with three cameras hanging off his neck, talking to Taj the Tailor in front of the billboard sign that pointed the way into his shop. The legs of the soldier photographer's jungle fatigues must have been tailored special because they were skin tight.

"Ling Fook! Doin' a little shootin?" Willert greeted the soldier.

"Yes, I went over beyond the bridge down past the MP compound and back into the neighborhood a couple of blocks to the west. Got some really great shots! Who's this? The wanted man up for trial from Tra Vinh?" He

133

lifted his camera and took the Kid's picture and then extended his hand. "Harold Ling-Fook at your service."

"Pleased to meet you, my grandfather on my mother's side and my uncle are both named Harold." The Kid eyed his three Nikons; Ling-Fook had nearly $2,000.00 worth of cameras dripping off him. "So, are you a combat Photographer?"

"Ha!" Ling-Fook laughed, "I wish! Actually, I tried to get into DINFOS to do just that, but I couldn't make it. What I do here is printing plate photography, for making leaflets and printing the unit newspaper. I'm just doing what I do in my spare time, trying to build a really bitchin' archive for when I get back to the states, I hope to put out a book some day."

"Groovey!" the Kid commented.

"Taj," Edwards addressed the tall and slim grey haired shop keeper, "we're on our way to the Scientific and we need to change out some MPC."

"Ah, yes, of course you may rest assured I will give you and your friends, especially your new friend here, the best of all exchange rates!"

As they walked through Taj's store, where the Kid had purchased his jungle hat, he was always amazed at his selection of goods. It was primarily clothing; after all, the sign on the outside said 'Taj the Tailor', but there was a lot more going on. A barber shop took up the back corner of his sizable shop. There was a ton of souvenir stuff, like black windbreakers with maps of Vietnam sewn on the back with embroidered tigers on them and lots of civilian clothes, suitcases, shoes, leather goods and there were also black velvet painting of tigers and jungle scenes and painting of Vietnamese women with coy expression on their faces all over the walls.

Arriving at his desk, Taj pulled a key on a chain out of his pocket and opened a locked drawer from which he pulled an envelope stuffed with cash. "What do you want to change, Edwards, 10 or 20?"

"What's the rate today?"

"The rate today is 26 Piasters to the dollar, so you give me ten, I give you 260 P, OK?"

"OK, yeah I can multiply by ten," Edwards laid the ten on his desk and Taj counted out 260 P in worn Vietnamese bank notes, mostly in 20 P denominations.

"What about you, Willert?"

"I'll change 20 MPC worth."

134

Taj counted it out and then turned to the Kid. "So, what's you name?"

"Curt."

"Kut?" he repeated. "You change money, too? Did I not sell you a hat in May?"

"Yeah, you did! What a memory, but I can't wear it here in town!" replied the Kid.

"You need change money, too?" Taj asked, with a wad of Piasters still in his hand.

"Yeah, is 10 enough?" he looked questioningly at Willert, who nodded in the affirmative.

"Well, I gotta go lock up my cameras," Ling-Fook said. "Tell you what, you going to the Black Hole? I'll meet you there in about an hour, OK?"

"Sure," Willert said as he waved to Ling-Fook, "come on men, we got work to do!"

The Scientific was almost directly across the street from Taj's place. Before the war, Can Tho had been nothing more than an agricultural supply town with a university and it still was not far removed from it. A farmer was driving a mother buffalo and her three calves up the dirt street as the three men crossed at a leisurely pace. Judging from the amount of buffalo dung on the street, it was not an isolated event. In front of the Scientific, a cyclo driver waited for a fare.

"Dong Hung", the Kid read the name on the shop next to the Scientific, "what do they do there, re-hang men who get their balls shot off?"

"You better hope you never find out!" Willert smirked. "I don't know what they do in there, never been in there."

"Me neither," said Edwards.

The buildings in Bien Xi Moi were right up against each other and each of the second floors had a porch area that was enclosed behind screens. Painted on the front of the porch was the real name of the establishment, the Phong Dinh, but a white sign, written in English in the lower left corner of the window said, "Scientific Steam Bath".

Inside the door, they were met by the hostess, a middle aged Vietnamese woman, dressed in a white top and black pajama bottoms who wore her black hair in a bun. "Minh Yoi, you all do steam bath and massage?" she handed each of them a medium sized white towel. The whole place exuded a humid, nearly mossy smell that sat moistly in their nostrils. Definitely not the cleanest place in the world.

"Minh Yoi, that's right, Momma San," Edwards said as he pealed off three 20 P notes and handed them to her. "60 P, it's on me today, the steam bath that is… you make you own deals with the masseuse for the grand finale after the massage."

"Sounds OK to me!" he said, looking around at the black and white tiled area with benches and hooks that was next to the door with a steamed up small window that had a crack running through it that was obviously the steam bath. The noise of fans whirred from up the stairs that lead from the steam area to the massage rooms. A GI who had just emerged from the steam bath showered under one of two shower heads further back in the room.

"Hi Ken, hi Ron," he grinned to Willert and Edwards.

"Hey, Larry, how's it hangin?" Edwards responded, "Oops, I guess we know the answer to that!"

The three of them stripped naked and hung up their clothes on hooks while Momma 'San clearly checked out their dicks with a grin on her wrinkled face. When they had wrapped the towels around their waists and were ready, she opened the heavy, meat locker like door to the steam chamber and the three walked into the hot mist.

"How ironic", said the Kid, "here we are in the tropics and we're going into a steam bath?" As their vision adjusted, they saw one other GI already sweating away in the corner of the six foot by ten chamber. Even hunched over, the Kid could tell from his size that the big guy had to be Manley.

"Manley, that you?" Willert said as he picked a spot to sit.

"Howdy, Gents. How was the leafleteering today?"

"Not bad. Didn't take any fire... that we were told about anyway," Edwards gave him a report. "We did the Ho Chi Minh - Parrot's Beak combo today, with an afternoon run down towards Soc Trang. We lifted 180 boxes. I'll admit, I feel it in my upper body, especially my arms!"

"Well, have a good one. I'm out of here and on to phase two and three," Manley stood and walked out the door.

After no more than five minutes of steaming, Edwards rose up and suggested to the Kid, "You'll want to grab your clothes when you go upstairs," Edwards said as he pulled his off the hook and took one of the dry towels Mama San was handing out at the bottom of the steps.

"Just take the first open room you find and lay down on the table, face down," Edwards said as they went up, "these girls are great with the massage, you'll love it!"

As they got to the second floor, the Kid could hear slapping and moaning coming from a couple of the rooms that were obscured by curtains pulled closed over the doorways. Finding an empty, he went in, hung up his fatigues and did exactly as Edwards had instructed, stretching out on the padded massage table and laying his head on the little pillow. Without his glasses, the whole room took on a fuzzy aura of soft edges thanks to his near sightedness. Almost immediately, a young Vietnamese woman entered the room.

"Hello," she said in a pleasantly musical voice, "how you today, GI?"

"Better now than I was," the Kid lifted his head to see if she was cute or not. Cute was the verdict.

"Undo towel, please," she said and the Kid lifted his body up enough to unknot his white towel and positioned the ends off the edge of the table.

Standing at his head, she began by rubbing his shoulders and neck. Then, moving to his left side, she worked her way down his back, digging and kneading with skilled fingers, all the way to his waist. Then, flipping the towel off his butt, she rubbed his left cheek and worked her way down the back of his left leg. The overhead fan evaporated the moisture still on his skin and left him feeling quite cool. Switching sides, she gave his right the same treatment. It was heaven. The war and the pain of separation from Flo momentarily melted away, leaving him in a state of genuine relaxation. Once she had made a round, she went back to his left side and with her hands together but her fingers spread, she did a pummeling thing up and down the meat of his back on either side of his spine. The slappy, clappy sound it made was what he had heard coming from the other rooms earlier.

"You turn over now, please," she quietly spoke. As he rolled over, she took the towel and covered his private parts and proceeded to massage his right arm and then his right thigh, down to and including his feet. Switching sides, she did the same to his left side. He lay there with his eyes shut, digging every second of it.

"There, all done, GI,"

"Ah, thank you."

"You want blow job?"

"Yes, I sure do!"

"OK," she said and left the room, slightly miffing the Kid.

Seconds later, a different girl entered, carrying a wash cloth. "Hello, GI, 60 P for blow job, you pay first, please."

As the Kid rose up off the table to get the money out of his pocket, he noticed that the new girl was not as cute as the masseuse but decided it really didn't matter. Fishing around in his pants, he came up with the piasters and paid her.

She took the money with a smile, stuck it into a pocket of her white pants, lifted the towel off his mid section and took his dick in her hand. She only had to play with it and his balls for a couple of seconds before the Kid went rock hard. Placing the washcloth on his stomach, she positioned herself with her back to his head and with one hand wrapped around the base of his penis, she stroked it a couple of time before lowered her mouth onto his anxious organ. The Kid had never had a real blow job before. The last thing he was going to do was ask virgin Flo for one. Needless to say, he'd always hoped he'd get one. His date to the senior prom, who he had dated for over a year, had once said she was going to do it, but when the head of his dick was barely in her mouth, she chickened out. There was no chickening out today, he gasped as she took his cock into her mouth and began gently sucking. But, after a couple of deep sucks, she elevated her mouth to the head of his dick and began using her hand to pump his cock up and down as she kept only the head inside her lips.

The Kid's game plan was to hold off as long as he could, but the reservoir was too backed up and in less than a couple of minutes, he stiffened his legs and gave in. Being the experienced pro that she was, the girl, with one hand strategically placed beneath his nuts, sensed he was about to come and pulled her head out of the way in a nick of time. It shot beyond where she had positioned the washcloth, way past the Kid's navel. She continued to pump him as he spasmodically ejaculated the content of his scrotum. And when he was done, she took the washcloth, wiped up the load in a most business like manner and without a word, was gone.

The Kid lay there, eyes closed, spent like the change from a broken piggy bank. He began composing a letter he would write later that night, to Larry Ryan, his best friend back in Colorado... *Dear Larry, you'll never guess what I did in the war today...*

Chapter 19

Later that night after dinner, when they had all settled in at the New Villa and were up in the Roof Club drinking beer and playing a game of Monopoly for real money, that being a penny equaling a play money dollar. *How ironic that MPC looks like monopoly money!*

The turn had barely gone around the table twice and nobody had passed GO when the Kid experienced an event of Deja vu. He felt the vibe of somebody standing off his left shoulder and looking up, the Kid once again discovered Dave Coffman standing... staring at him.

"Dave? What is it this time?' he asked, because Coffman stood there with a look on his face identical to that he had the night he told him of the mortar attack on the MSQ-85.

"We just got word... Lt. Wilson took the armed propaganda team out on a training mission where they were supposed to establish and hold a blocking position and elements of the VC 10th Battalion ran right through their position and killed half of them!"

The words were like a slap to the Kid's face; he had no immediate reply because he was actually waiting to see if there was any additional information but when it didn't come, he asked, "Is Sweet OK? Was he there?"

"From what we get, Sweet *wasn't* there," Coffman said, "but you lucky son of a bitch! If Wilson wasn't court martialing you... you would have been there! You are, without a doubt... one of the LUCKIEST mutha fuckers I've ever met in my LIFE!"

Glancing around the table, he noticed the other guys were staring at him, like he was in fact living some kind of charmed life and to tell the truth, the Kid was beginning to feel a wave of it, too, like he did that day back in Nashville, when he got the job at WKDA. Or the afternoon in Disneyland, while standing in the Matterhorn line when he leaned over and whispered to Flo, *let's get a room* and she breathlessly whispered back, OK!

"Geeze!" Hoch exclaimed, "I think that qualifies a genuinely dodging a bullet, Stocker! That means you buy us all a round! Right guys?" Isn't that the rule?"

"Is that how you do it up there in Seattle, Hoch? Make the rules up as you go along?" the Kid faked surprise. "Out in the field, it's the guy who does the dodging' who got drinks bought for him! But wait a minute... I'll buy the drinks... after all, I am the *lucky fucker!*" And with that, the Kid lifted some play monopoly money out of the box and twisting in his chair, he handed it to George Gaugle, who sat right behind him, on the corner of a table, watching the game over the Kid's shoulder. "George, go buy us a round and keep the change!"

With a half confused grin, George took the play money in his right hand and stood, as if were willingly prepared to do the Kid's bidding but clearly perplexed by the pastel script.

"You take that over to the bar and give it to RV Smith and tell him I'll give him the 'going exchange rate' for it later, after the movie," the Kid said, "tell him I want to run a tab, but be sure to use the words, 'the going rate' and see if he'll take it! Oh, and get yourself a beer and one for Coffman, too!" the Kid slapped him on the back and Goggle rushed off; he'd do anything to be a part of the group.

"The 'going rate'?" Hoch questioned.

"Right," the Kid pointed to the game, "a penny on the dollar! Six beers, I figure 4 bucks so four cents. I'll give him a nickel MPC and we'll call it even."

"You're gonna do that to RV?" Edwards chortled, because nobody in their group liked RV, "I gotta be there when you do!"

"Yeah," Coffman signaled that he had more APT news to tell, "it happened at dusk yesterday. I think they thought there might be a couple or three VC get flushed on this little operation there were running, but no, at least of dozen Charlies showed up and just fucking shot the crap out of'em as they ran right through their position!"

"My God! That's terrible!" the Kid exclaimed, as he recalled sitting at the table with the Hoi Chanhs, inside their concertina encircled compound on the edge of Tra Vinh, while they got Wilson drunk. *I wonder which one's got it? I wonder if Captain Kanh is OK?*

"And Wilson was the only American with them?" the Kid inquired.

"Yes," responded Dave, "him and his interpreter."

"Poor Ba!" moaned the Kid, "I really feel sorry for him." *But that's odd he didn't have Sweet with him, too. Why it is Lt. Wilson hasn't required the presence of Sweet? He said he was going to... but now, he apparently isn't making him do any APT stuff. What the fuck is up with that?*

"Shit, Stocker," Edwards exclaimed, "even though you're up on charges, things seem to be breaking your way! When is the trial?"

"November 14th. Make that lucky 14!" Hoch said to the group, "In fact, typed up the orders making Major Gregory the Trial Officer a couple of days ago. I still think that's a plus for you, Stocker. Even though he's only been here since September, Major Gregory is one of the fairest officers I've ever met. And Captain Ronnie is prosecuting you... so that's two strikes in your favor right there."

"Well, if they're in my favor, should they be *'balls?'* "The Kid joked." I mean, if I'm going to 'walk' on the charges... I need four balls, don't you think?

Chapter 20

November 12, 1968

Dear Flo,

It was good to hear from you. I understand, now that we are no longer engaged, you have a lot of other things to do and places to go, but I really appreciate that you are still taking the time to write. It is always exciting to get mail from a beautiful woman and your perfume is as sweet as ever.

To bring you up to date, the day after tomorrow is my big trial. All of the witnesses and accusers are supposed to arrive from Tra Vinh tomorrow. Lt. Wilson, Jim Sweet and Sgt. Brooks are all supposed to be here. Lt. Colonel Lawton is vacating his office to be set up as the court room. Nov. 14th. (Glad it's not on the 13th, even though I'm only superstitious about lucky beaver nickels... So as you read this, whatever is going to happen will have happened so the next letter you get from me will have a new address... it will be my new unit or (and I hope it isn't) the Long Binh Jail. Win or loose, I get a transfer, according to army regulations.

The final count is three charges, all for the same thing, eating in the mess hall, after being told not to, for three consecutive days. I still can't believe this is happening. My lawyer, Navy Lt. Ellis keeps telling me not to worry and when I ask him why, he only says, 'you'll see!' and he's got a big grin on his face. I hope he's not screwing with me. I don't think he is, but with the Army, you never know how the dice are going to fall.

So Nixon is the new president. Whoppptidoodledooooo!. Now that the election is over, he'll have to tell the world what his secret plan is... if he has one. Oh well, doesn't matter to me. I'll still be here next week, regardless of what happens at my trial. In fact, if I loose, I have to also serve the time I serve in jail to make it up! I'm still pissed that I didn't get to vote. War zone, 21 for the first time and no vote. No fair!

Today was the last day I'll be flying leaflet drops, unless I end up in another PSYOP unit. It's hotter than hell, loading them onto the plane, hauling them out of the huge metal boxes we store them in, but when we get up in the air, it's so cool that all the sweat is worth it, just to go for the flight because nobody has air conditioning, even here in Can Tho.

I'm writing this sitting in the Roof Club, waiting for the truck that is taking us out to the air base. The room I'm in is like hell, it's so hot. It's on the inside of the building and there is no ventilation. I'm so looking forward to being out of there. Up here on the roof, it's cool in the early morning, compared to my room.

If I win, and don't have to go to jail, I have no idea where I'm going to end up, because they can send me anywhere. Chances are, though, it won't be Armed Forces Radio Saigon, not now, anyway. If I win, I'll still have a chance that my 1049 will go through and I'll be extended and get assigned there, get a 60 day drop and be home in late March. After being out in the field in combat with the ARVNs, doing a year in Saigon will be a piece of cake!

I still spend a lot of time looking at your picture, Flo-retta, and I will, until I see you again. Then and only then, will we really have a chance to sort out our real feelings.

Win or lose, I'll write and let you know, but there won't be any point in you writing me back until I get my new address.

So, my Parnelli, know that some day, I'll See You Later. And Hi, Mrs. S. how are you dong these days? All ready for Thanksgiving?

Hugs and Kisses,

Curt

Chapter 21

From where he sat in the Eakin Compound mess hall, the Kid immediately spied Jim Sweet as he entered the room and stood in the olive drab dinner line. Rising, he waved and catching his eye, the Kid motioned for Sweet to join him and his buddies, seated about six rows deep within the hall. Sweet nodded a confirmation.

"Hey there, Jim! You don't have to thank me now for giving you this chance to visit the big city," the Kid greeted him as he arrived.

"Oh, right!" Sweet sat down his tray, loaded with dinner of roast beef, mashed potatoes and gravy, green beans, corn, salad, rolls and iced tea, and pulled back his chair, "this is a favor you're doing me, all right. Any reason that gets me out of Tra Vinh these days is OK... even your court martial!" he laughed as he sat down and everybody laughed along with him.

"We've got a lot to catch up on, James," the Kid had already finished his meal and was smoking, ashing his KOOL in the empty dessert compartment on his dinner tray, "what with Bat Mobile getting blown to shit and the crap getting shot out of the APT, I don't know which one I want to hear about first."

"I wasn't there for the APT thing," Sweet said, picking up his fork, "but it isn't fair that I should have to tell you about the other thing now, because I'm the only one here who hasn't eaten!" he shoveled in a mouth full of mashed spuds.

"That's fair," agreed the Kid, "we'll have plenty of time tonight to discuss all the particulars of what's happened down in Tango Victor since I *didi mau'd* and what the plan is for the trial tomorrow. So you and Wilson and Brooks all came up together?"

"Brooks didn't come," Sweet said quickly between bites.

"Say what?" the Kid sat up bolt straight, "Brooks didn't come? Hell, he was subpoenaed!"

"Yeah, that may be, but I was there when Wilson got the message he didn't have to come... from what I picked up on, it was the JAG that

144

cancelled him. But Cpl Ba is here and he really wants to see you!" Sweet informed the Kid and immediately started shoveling it in again.

"What the fuck? He never said anything about that to me!" He looked around the table at his new friends, who were surprised that he was surprised; up until now, he had been one cool customer, up on charges but totally in charge because the whole court martial thing wasn't half as scary as combat. But now, the night before the trial, there appeared a small chink in the armor, an unexpected turn of events. "Shit, it's too late to get a hold of Ellis now and even if I did, it's probably too late to get Brooks up here... I wonder what the fuck he's thinking." The Kid looked at Sweet, who was eating ravenously, but rather that chowing to slake his appetite, it seemed to the Kid like he was doing it to avoid conversing with or even looking at him.

"So too bad about Musky not getting to be VP. Did you get to vote?"

"Mmmm mmm," Sweet shook his head in the negative as he continued to concentrate on eating.

Something going on here. Strange fucking vibe. Strange. "Well, hey, Jim, we can talk back at the 'Villa," the Kid said, indicating he was leaving with his companions, who had just risen up, almost in unison, signaling their desire to go; they'd been ready go take showers when Sweet showed up but stayed because they knew the Kid wanted to talk to him.

"Sure enough," nodded Sweet as he washed down the remains of a bite with a sip of tea, "see ya back at the ranch!"

Strange vibe.

In the company of Hoch, Willert, Edwards, Boyett and Wimbish, and half a dozen others, the Kid caught the duce and a half back to the New Villa and once there, hurried to strip down, get his shaving kit and secure a place in the shower line on the 3rd floor, before it got too long.

Standing there wrapped in his towel, six men from the front, dangling his kit from his left hand, the Kid stared out at clouds painted by the sunset to the west. *What a weird feeling I was getting from Sweet. What's THAT all about? Fuck... I wonder why Ellis would tell Brooks not to show up. He's key. He has to tell the judge why Wilson told me not to eat in the mess hall that day. Why wouldn't Ellis tell me he was doing that? I hope it's not time to get nervous... he told me 90% sure he could get me off. This has to be a good sign, I have to believe it's a good sign that Ellis thinks we don't need Brooks. Got to look at it that way. Can't wait to find out what the fuck happened when the VC shot the mortar into the Bat Mobile. Hmmm. I wonder why Wilson didn't make him or try to make him go out on the APT mission?*

After his shower, the Kid gravitated to the Roof Club, got a Fosters and waited for Sweet to arrive, drinking and smoking with Edwards and Willert at the table nearest the front staircase.

After the longest time, Sweet showed up, showered and changed, and as soon as he entered the club, by the back staircase, the two guys in whose room he was bunking motioned for him to take the empty seat between them and join in a poker game. And much to the surprise of the Kid, he did.

Strange. He is actually trying to avoid me.

Walking over to him at the table, the Kid tapped him on the shoulder as he was getting him money out of his wallet, "Yo, Jim... we need to talk..."

"Oh, yeah... uh, I promised I'd get in this game, Curt," he was manufacturing an excuse, "if it's OK, can we talk later? You're not going anywhere, right?"

"Well, now that you mention it... no..." replied the Kid, "it's just that tomorrow is a pretty important day for me and you are a big part of it, that's all."

"Yeah, yeah, I know," he fiddled with his newly acquired stack of poker chips, "hey, I been out in the sticks, I just want to play a few hands and watch the movie so how's about we talk after that?"

"OK, you're right, we don't have to talk this second," the Kid said matter of factly; after all, where could he go? *And why do you not want to talk to me? What do you have to hide?* He returned to the table with Ken and Ron.

"Men... let's go smoke some rope," he said in passing as he picked up his beer, clearly on his way out if the others were coming or not.

The Kid had no desire to watch the movie that night, it was some stupid horror flick that hadn't been scary the first time he'd seen it. Instead, he smoked serial bowls in the company of numerous other soldiers getting stoned prior to the movie but for the moment, the Kid sat on the bench by himself. Covered with sweat and languishing in the heat of the night, he nursed another Fosters while smoking a KOOL for a change of pace. He wore his maroon APT shorts with no shirt and although he was liberally doused with insect repellent, he occasionally found it necessary to swat at a blood sucker or two.

From above, the sounds of soldiers laughing at the bad horror movie on the roof came down to him. Looking to his left, he noticed that nobody was on guard duty to keep the pot smokers safe, but since he was the only one there, he had to be his own guard and he was glad he was looking at the entry way to the balcony when somebody he at first didn't recognize, came around the corner and into view.

"Oh! Jim. It's you!" the Kid was relieved when he identified Sweet. "Didn't recognize you in the dark at first."

"Hey, Curt," he sat down next to him. He wore a light shirt, unbuttoned and from out of his right pocket, produced a pack of Winstons and lit up.

He sounds troubled. "Decided against watching that putrid movie, huh?"

'Yeah."

Wanna smoke some pot?" the Kid asked.

"Sure."

Standing and leaning forward, the Kid produced a pipe from the small ledge that ran around the outside of the top of the balcony's railing; the perfect place to keep it out of sight, easy to ditch. Checking to see it was still fully loaded, he sat back down and with his zippo, fired it off, inhaling a huge hit. And as he held the hit and passed the pipe to Sweet, he said, while trying not to lose any smoke, "I thought you were trying to avoid me!"

Not answering, Sweet took the pipe and sucked in his own giant hit and sat there, holding it, for what seemed an eternity before he exhaled. And after he did that, he inhaled a clean breath of air and only then did he begin to speak.

"I can't stand it. I can't fucking STAND it!" Sweet exclaimed, "I know something and if I tell you, Wilson swears he'll find thousands of opportunities to get me killed! He made me give him my word that I wouldn't tell you."

This sound pretty serious. "Then, you *have* been avoiding me and it's not me being paranoid?"

"Yes. He made me give *my word* that I wouldn't tell anybody...especially you!" Even in the low light of the night, the Kid could see the stress on Sweet's face, as he stared back at the Kid to gauge his reaction to his news.

Tell me what? "Well, shit, what the fuck, Sweet?" the Kid stood up in amazement, "tomorrow is my trial and you know something that might help me? And you won't tell me? How can you even consider that keeping your word to that asshole ... is more important than our friendship and helping me stay out of the fucking stockade? Jim..." the Kid looked him in the eye, "if you know something that will help me you gotta *TELL me,* Buddy. What is it?"

147

"OK. Ok. You're right. Really... fuck it... how could I even for a second think I could not tell you this, even though you know how much I value my word." Sweet took a second to compose himself. "You know the mortar that hit the MSQ-85?"

'Yeah..."

"It wasn't really a mortar... It was a claymore mine!"

"NO!"

"Yes! And Wilson is the one who strapped it on, to try that cockamamie scheme he was always jiving about, you know, the one where he'd cover the MSQ-85 with claymores so he could drive anywhere alone and if he got ambushed, he'd blow the claymores and drive on through? That one... He tested it and it didn't work! Then he filed a report that the damage he did to the truck was the result of a VC attack!"

Amazing. Fucking amazing! "More!"

"And then," Sweet quickly arrived at the point where confession became good for the soul and the story gushed out, "He made *me* fill out a report supporting him and he says if *HE* goes down, I"LL go down with him!"

"Why, that's fucking crazy! He forces you to fill out a false report and then says if you tell, you'll be charged with making a false report? He's one sick bastard. But now, we've got a pattern! He's the one who makes false statements and charges! I've fucking got him now!" the Kid was giddy with the power being presented to him.

"But Curt... if you can win without letting him know that I told you? If you could do that, then he couldn't come after me! If he finds out I sold him out, he swears to fucking God he will get even with me!"

The Kid looked at Sweet's pleading face. He knew how Wilson made good with his threats and considered the position Sweet was in; the man could do things and send you places where you could be more easily killed than not. The request was fair enough. "OK, Jim. I won't use it... unless I lose... then I'll jump up and start screaming about it from the rafters! But, if Ellis can pull it off, and he has kinda told me he has something up his sleeve, I won't use it. But, as part of the deal, you have to tell me all about it, from start to finish, I got time... start at the beginning, like what happened immediately after I left and end here on this bench."

"OK," Sweet took a drink of the beer he'd brought along, "I found out you'd been sent in when Wilson radioed out to Cang Long for me to come in on the next convoy and take your place! I'm goin' what the fuck? Over? So I get in there and come to find out what the deal is, that he's busting you

148

for eating in the mess hall and at first, I don't know what to think! I mean, we both have been eating in the mess hall since and still, by the way, but anyway, I'm thinking, he's going to try and get me to go on that APT thing! And sure enough, the first thing he does is says' he's going to get me on that assignment, but he's waiting for orders to come in, promoting me from Sp. 4 to Sergeant E-5, so I won't be able to refuse to volunteer, like you did, if you know what I mean. So while we were waiting for my promotion orders to be cut, he decides to bring in the MSQ 85 from Cang Long for the two of us to drive down to Ca Mau. Well, I asked who's going down there for us to take the Bat Mobile with, because it's not an APC, in case you haven't noticed... and he started talking shit about his wacky fuckin' claymore mine defense again and now I'm going nuts because I view that as suicide. But he's sure he can make it work. So he brings in the MSQ 85, leaves Boujold out there because he likes it now... he's down to about 50 days. Then he gets himself a claymore from the Boar Hog and we drive the Bat Mobile out of town by ourselves, to the south of town, out that real long and wide open stretch of paved road that branches off of Highway 4. We get a ways out, where there's nothing but paddies as far as the eye can see, with the trees way back from the road so nobody could sneak up on us. Wilson took the claymore and attached it to the back passenger's side of the truck, between the fender and the tailgate. We'd packed the area between the wall of the truck and the shell of the MSQ with sandbags to absorb the backwash from the claymore and he's ready to run the wires out into the paddies so we can stand back and blow the thing off and I said to him, 'Sir, this won't work. What is going to happen is, the claymore will blow a hole through the side of the truck bed and even with the sandbags, if it doesn't make a hole in the shell, the unit will be damaged anyway, it will blow a hole in the fender and it will make the rear tire flat. A claymore has a 15 meter backwash, I remind him. And he reminds me he is an artillery officer and he says, that's only because there's nothing behind it to stop it, if there was, there'd be less backwash and he was absolutely cock sure of it. So we string out the wires and get off about 50 meters in the paddies on the opposite side and Wilson gets ready to blow it off." Sweet stopped to light a fresh Winston. "And man o' man! When he touched that thing off, KABLOOIE! The truck rocked and rippled with the shock wave and smoke and everything I said would happen did... except the tire didn't go flat. It knocked the door open and the generator fell out on the road! You should have seen the look on his fucking face!"

"Oh, how I wish I could have!" said the Kid in a near daze at how good Sweet's story really was.

"But the worst part was, while we were looking down at the wiring right before Wilson set it off, we didn't see these two civilians ride up on a Honda, and they were just close enough when it went that one of them got his thumb ripped off by shrapnel!

Oh my God!

"If they'd been even a couple of yards closer, it would have killed them both! Right away, Wilson knows he's in BIG trouble. He gets out the first aid kit and does first aid on the guy, it's a miracle that their Honda was blown over but could still run, so Wilson stuffs $40 MPC into the guy's pocket and tells them to beat it.

"Then he turns to me and says, 'Sweet, we have to get our stories straight... we were driving along and got hit by Charlie...' Now wait a minute, sir, I stop him, are you asking me to perjure myself and cover up the fact that you just destroyed a bunch of Government property? Why, there's easily 3 or four thousand dollars worth of damage here and you want me to lie for you? 'Yes' he says, 'we're in this thing together!' I had to laugh at him. '...in this together? I say, what are you going to do if I don't go along... court martial me like you did Stocker? Oh man! He got hopping mad. He said 'this has nothing to do with Stocker but don't you forget for a second that I could court martial you!' Then, when we got back to Tra Vinh, he gets a couple of Combat Loss reports and fills one out and makes me fill one out to support it. Then he made me swear, on my word, that I'd never tell a soul... especially YOU!" So please, please don't let him know that I told you. If you have to use it, I know you will, but if you can possibly help it... then he won't know if I told you or not." He stopped and waited to see what the Kid would say.

"Holy fucking shit fire, Jim. That's incredible!" the Kid's head was swimming with his new found knowledge. "So, is that why you didn't go out on the APT thing? Now you've got the goods on *him*!"

"That's exactly right," Jim grinned, "I told him since my orders weren't in, and since I was having trouble with my memory from being so close to that 'mortar attack', that I felt I wouldn't be joining him on the operation that night. And God, am I glad I wasn't there! Half of them got killed! Wilson was more than a little bit shaken up, but in all the commotion, he made a kill! And boy... was he ever fucking happy that he finally got to shoot somebody! He was all about telling everybody how he did it. What a sick fuck."

"Half of them got killed?" the Kid sadly recalled the afternoon he met them and they'd all conspired to get Wilson drunk. It had only been 3 weeks

150

ago. *Now half of them are dead.* "Did he take you out to meet them or train with'em? Do you have any idea about which ones' got it? Like the Captain? Do you know?"

"No."

"Hmmm. I've just been wondering if the Captain made it. He was a cool guy. Fought at Dien Bin Phu. Has a wife and a couple of sons," the Kid paused, "I choose to imagine he's still alive until I hear otherwise."

"I'm sure Wilson will tell you all about it, if he's speaking to you, that is," Sweet laughed.

The Kid sat there, puffing a KOOL, as high on adrenalin as if he had just struck gold. He continued to digest the information, wondering how he could best use it to his advantage, especially if he were going to try and keep his new found knowledge of the falsified report unknown.

"Actually, not telling will be fun," a light came on in the Kid's head, "think about it, Sweet, even though he got you to give your word, Wilson is absolutely sure that you are going to tell me what happened. We are friends and he knows it. That means from the second he shows up for the trial tomorrow, he's going to be sweating bullets to see if I'm going to start spouting off about it! All I have to do is be calm and look smug!"

"Well, I'm sure you won't have any trouble looking smug, Kid... 'Smug' is pretty much your MO!" Sweet adjudged, "and how about this... we can be whispering and talking low to each other outside the courtroom and when Wilson comes into view we'll shut up and stare at him!"

"Oh yeah! It will be hilarious! After what you've told me, I am so looking forward to this, now *I can't wait* for tomorrow!" the Kid made a fist with his right hand in front of his chest, to signify his grip on the situation.

That night, even though he was trapped like a baked potato in an oven of a room in the center of the hotel in a war zone 10 degrees north of the equator, with no relief from the heat in sight, other than Bouji's two bit electric putt putt fan, the Kid slept very well. *Very well, indeed.*

Chapter 22

From where they stood, about ten feet beyond Hoch's desk, deep in the orderly room, the Kid and Sweet watched out through the screen as Captain Ronnie Smith and First Lieutenant Herschel Ross Wilson exited their jeep upon returning from lunch at the Eakin Compound officer's mess. It was the first time the Kid had seen Wilson since being put on the Air America plane the day he left Tra Vinh.

"Time to tee it up," said Sweet.

"Let the games begin!" smiled the Kid.

The pair watched the two officers walk across the court yard below them, chuckling about something clever one or the other had said, paying no attention to the two GI's who watched them from a floor above.

Over confident. The large plain clock on the wall behind them displayed 1230 hours and the trial was scheduled to begin in 30 minutes. "I wonder where my mouthpiece is?" the Kid craned his neck to see if he could see a jeep arriving from the direction of the USO. He had tried to get Ellis on the phone earlier in the day but had failed and it did serve to make the Kid just the slightest bit nervous, even in light of the sledgehammer information he now possessed.

"You're right, Curt," Sweet spoke with resolve as they waited for the two officers to reach the top of the stairs and enter the orderly room, "he's gotta know that I told you. But, if it doesn't come up, I'll deny it! And then I'll still have it on him."

"Sounds like a workable plan," the Kid agreed. "Hey, I heard someplace that all of the extras in movies, like in the background? When it looks like they're having a conversation, what they are really saying is, 'carrots and peas, carrots and peas...' so let practice that technique... cue to officers and roll'em! Carrots and peas, carrots and peas!" the Kid whispered in the direction of Sweet as Wilson and Smith entered the room.

"Carrots and peas, carrots and peas?" Sweet whispered back, "Are you sure? Carrots *and* peas?"

A tremor ran through Wilson's head as he did a double take when he first noticed the Kid and Sweet engaged in conversation, a little ways out of his earshot. Smith went straight over to Hoch's desk and began asking the clerk questions and pointing at the Colonel's office directly behind them. Seeing this, Wilson sauntered toward the two and they appeared to stop their conversation.

In a preplanned maneuver, Sweet wheeled around in a one-eighty and walked off, leaving the Kid standing there alone as his former commander stopped about two feet in front of him.

"Hello, Stocker," Herschel slowly drawled like the Texan he was, "it's good to see you... how have you been?"

Oh brother... like you fucking care how I've been, backstabber? "Hello, Sir, I've been OK."

"So, uh what were you and Sweet talking about there?" he got right to the point, and expecting the worst, he was just trying to draw it out.

"You wouldn't believe me if I told you," the Kid cracked the slightest smile. It's good to see you... too," *shit eating grin.* "I've been hearing that you're doing exciting things without me," the Kid cocked his head to one side and raised his eyebrows just ever so slightly.

"Oh, really? Like what?" Wilson shuffled on his feet, and moved his jungle cap from one hand to the other.

Shifty bastard. "Like you took the APT out and got taken to the woodshed by the VC 10th. Tell me one thing, Did Dai Ui Kahn make it?"

A sense of relief swept over Wilson's face as he realized the topic of conversation was not going to be the MSQ-85. "No. No, he didn't make it," he shook his head negatively. "Fatal head wound, he was dead in the field, pretty much instantly, and I think he didn't suffer at all."

And with that news, the light that was Kahn went out in the Kid's head. He had really liked the ex-VC captain and had appreciated being able to talk to him and hear from somebody who had seen it and done it all, who was the essence of what the hell was actually going on in Vietnam. "*Toi xin-loi.* How many Hoi Chanhs got it all together?"

"We lost 12, half of what we had in the field that night," Wilson lit a Winston and the Kid could sense he wanted to tell him the story. "But we got four of them for sure, maybe five or six, out of what could have been 12 or 15 very heavily armed VC. Whole lot more than anybody thought was out there... that's for damn sure. Almost like they knew we were coming."

153

The Lt. had drifted into the thousand meter stare as he recalled the fight. "Kahn's right hand man, the one other older dude? He got it, too."

"Oh, man. What a bummer," the Kid nodded dejectedly but then brightened up. "You recall at the Tra Vinh airport, you said I was stupid to let this court martial happen, but see? I think I was pretty smart for missing that cluster fuck! Go on, Sir, you can admit it." *Silence.* "And you, Sir, I hear in all of that you finally made your kill."

"Yes. Yes I did," Wilson said with a clear sense of pride, "I had it on full automatic only had time to shoot from the hip, when I came face to face with him... I hit him in the torso with about 3 or 4 rounds... nearly cut him in half!" He gestured, swinging his imaginary weapon in a rising arc, from right to left, to demonstrate his technique.

Sick. I hope I never have to kill anybody... ever! "Well, Sir, I got to say, I was glad I wasn't there. It's like Monty Hall… glad I didn't pick that curtain!"

Wilson stood, looking reflectively stoic, nodding his head in understanding when the Kid decided to make him squirm a little. *Let's see if you've got your lying jock on.* "But I also hear that you and Sweet were pretty fucking lucky when the Bat Mobile got clipped by that mortar!"

It took him back a slight and an expression of defensiveness quick enveloped his face, at the specter of having to talk about the "mortar" attack, but he stuck to character and started right in. "Oh, yeah! If it had hit us a second earlier, it would have been in the cab instead of on the tailgate and we'd been goners, for sure!"

"OH! So you were *driving along...* when we first heard about it up here, you were outside and away from the truck. But you were *driving?* And BAM? That must have rocked the old Bat Mobile!" the Kid chuckled.

Wilson chuckled nervously right along with him, "Yeah, we were driving… but when it happened, we stopped and got out immediately and moved away from the truck in case they shot another round at it."

"Damn, not like the day we lucked out at the Nuyet Hang Bridge, huh? Where we never got hit! You think there's a chance it could have been an RPG and not a mortar? That they lined you up like a duck in a shooting gallery? And not a mortar, which has more of an 'arc' trajectory? Where'd it happen, any way?" *Lie, fucker, lie, you son of a bitch. Let me hear something real creative!*

Now Wilson was beginning to fidget and rock back and forth on his boots, "uh, we were south of town... and I don't know for sure... it could

154

have been an RPG, and I've thought, thinking more and more, it could have been an M-79 grenade launcher that some VC took off the battlefield..."

"Uh huh..." the Kid nodded his head, indicating he was ready to listen some more prime crap and kept quiet so that Wilson would be forced to stumble on.

"I don't think it was an RPG, I think we would have taken a lot more damage, even getting hit on the tailgate, like we did, if it had been an RPG, that's why I'm thinkin' M-79, now."

"South of town?" the Kid got back to another point, "what was going on out there that you'd want to take the MSQ-85? There aren't any villages worth squat down that way, for frickin' miles! And Ba wasn't with you?"

"Uh, yeah... well, I'd done a tune up on the engine, and wanted to take it out there so we could really rev it up and see that it was fixed all the way, you know... a test drive... so I didn't see the need to take Ba," Wilson offered up.

"Ah, look," the Kid diverted Lt. Wilson's attention out the screen, "my lawyer has arrived. Hmmmm. I wonder who that guy with him is? I've never seen him before. And I was expecting Brooksie..."

"Well, uh, it was your lawyer who sent down word Sgt Brooks didn't need to come up," Wilson immediately responded.

"Yes. So I heard," the Kid gave him a sideways glance, "I still don't know why, but I guess I'm about to find out. But the way I see it, Sir, if my lawyer said he didn't have to come, that can't be good for YOUR side... because he was a big part of my case, or so I thought. Obviously, he's developed something new. I wonder what it could be."

Then, from just inside the Colonel's office, Captain Smith stuck his head out and hollered, while flashing a look of disgust, "Lt. Wilson... could I speak with you, now, please?"

"OOppp, gotta go," Herschel said to the Kid, almost apologetically, "uh, may the best man win!"

"No," replied the Kid, " may the most honest and truthful man win... oh wait, *THAT* would *be* the best man... yes sir, you are right... may the best man win!"

It caught him off guard. The sheer mention of the word "truth" had a most unsettling effect on Wilson as he unsteadily turned to walk over and join Smith.

Sweat, you bastard. I am fucking LOVING this! Now the Kid stood alone, watching his lawyer and some strange man entering the courtyard. Navy

Lieutenant Ellis carried his brief case in his right hand and the unknown man whose shoulders displayed a Chief Warrant Officer's rank, carried a bound volume of something that was undoubtedly army regulations. Neither of them was speaking. The Kid gravitated across the front of the orderly room, past Hoch's and the other three desks that were positioned there, over to where the stairs delivered visitors up at the end of the room and was waiting right there when Ellis and his companion emerged.

"Ah, Specialist Stocker," Ellis smiled broadly upon seeing him, "well, today's the big day... are you excited?"

"Words can't describe..." the Kid shook his hand.

"Specialist Stocker, this is Chief Warrant officer George Schweitzer, Chief Schweitzer, Specialist Stocker," Ellis introduced them and then, turning to the Warrant Officer, he said, "Specialist Stocker is the defendant... and Specialist Stocker, Warrant Officer Schwitzer is the officer in charge of all the mess halls in the Delta." The Kid sensed a smirk cross Donald Ellis's face, "he's here to testify in your behalf."

"All right. I like that. Does this have anything to do with the reason you said Sgt Brooks didn't have to come?"

"Yes," Ellis nodded in the affirmative, "everything."

"Then, please to meet you, Sir," the Kid shook Schwiterz's hand, "I can't wait to hear all about it."

"Ah, yes," Ellis nodded in deference to the Kid, "I should have told you more, when I figured out Sgt. Brooks had nothing to contribute, but you were off flying leaflet drops and communications so difficult, and I couldn't leave a message about it... because it's my surprise for Capt. Smith and your Lt. Wilson."

"And me, I'm surprised because I don't know what the surprise is... yet..." the Kid stood, anxiously, with a pleading look. *Tell me for fuck sake! What are you doing with my trial?*

"Chief Schweitzer is here to testify that the order you are charged with disobeying, is an illegal order."

"And that means?" the Kid needed a little additional explanation, coaxing with his hands in a 'give it to me motion.'

"You've won!" smiled Ellis.

"But the trial hasn't even started yet," the Kid couldn't accept victory before victory was in hand. "What do you mean 'I've won?'"

156

"OK," Ellis began and then stopped, to step out of the doorway landing and into the room, as some other officers, who turned out to be Lt. Colonel Willie O. in the company of the unit's Adjutant, First Lieutenant Harry Regan, and Major David Gregory came briskly up the steps.

So we'll quickly be started. The Kid and Warrant officer Schweitzer moved to clear the way and as soon as they had passed, while not making eye contact with any of them, Ellis picked up where he left off.

"In a trial in a civilian court, at the end of the testimony, the judge gives instructions to the jury, about the rules of law that apply to that particular case. Since here in a Summary Court Martial, the sole presiding officer is the judge and the jury, it's the Uniform Code of Military Justice itself that gives *him* a certain set of instruction by which he is bound. And according to those rules, Army regulations take president over lots of other things and with the regulation Chief Schweitzer is going to present and testify about here today, Major Gregory will have no choice but to rule in your favor."

"No. Really? No bullshit, Sir?"

Ellis had to laugh. "What? You don't believe me? You're upset because It's too frickin' easy? You want more suspense?" he stood there, opened mouthed like, how could the Kid be so rude?

"Well, it's just that this is the Army and I've been screwed so many times, I'm starting to feel like a whore in a Saigon cat house, you know, permanently bent over at the waist, panties around the ankles. I'm sure you can understand... what with one guy doing all of the deciding... why I have reason to be unsure." *Should I tell him about Wilson and the false reports? He seems to have a pretty good plan of attack. Maybe I'll just sit on it. This is looking pretty damn good!*

Seeing Sweet returning from the latrine, the Kid moved into position to introduce him to Ellis. "Sir, this is Sergeant James Sweet. This is one of the men who was never given the order I'm being tried for disobeying here today."

Sweet shook his hand, "Pleased to meet you. You think you can get him off, huh?"

"Nice to meet you, Sergeant Sweet. It's pretty much in the bag," Ellis emphasized 'in'. "However, I'm going to put you on the stand to briefly state your knowledge of what was going on in the mess hall down there with regard to everybody else for some background, like the fact you never got a similar order not to eat in the mess hall, nothing we even really need to rehearse. After all, you guys are obviously telling the truth, which makes it real easy!"

157

"OK!" Sweet looked to the Kid to get an indication of if he'd told Ellis the secret or not but the Kid just smiled his best smug smile.

Ellis took his eyes off Sweet to motion to a partially grey haired master sergeant that had just emerged at the top of the order room steps. "Over here," he waved, "court stenographer," he identified the new arrival, "one of JAG's main functions is to make sure we always get a record of any proceeding, if humanly possible. In case there's any need for an appeal."

Soon as the master sergeant entered Lawton's office, Major Gregory stuck his head out the door and called to them, "Gentlemen, if you'll join us, I believe we are finally ready!"

Upon entering the room, the Kid saw that the Colonel had removed all of his art objects and family pictures from his desk and the walls, leaving it very plain. His desk had been moved to the left end of the room and turned inward. The little round table, where the colonel enjoyed his tea, had been given over to the court steno and placed to Major Gregory's right. Two very plain wooden tables faced Major Gregory's desk, in front of him and to his left, each supplied with two chairs. Captain Smith and Wilson took the table on the left and the Kid and Lieutenant Ellis placed their materials on the one to the right. *'Me and Dreyfuss", yeah, that's what I'll call the book... no... Dreyfuss and Me... Yeah, that's it!*

A solitary chair had been placed half way between the tables and Major Gregory's desk, right in front of where the Kid sat, facing toward the stenographer. *The stand.* Another four folding chairs had been placed in what was now the back of the room, to the left of the door, where Sweet and Warrant Officer Schweitzer were directed to be seated.

Having no gavel, Major Gregory vocally brought the court into session, "Ok gentlemen, all rise," he instructed in a slightly shaky voice, "by order of the commanding officer, 10th PSYOP Battalion, City of Can Tho, Republic of Vietnam, this Summary Court Martial is now convened and called to order, please be seated."

The Kid took a deep breath and as Major Gregory continued to read some more mumbo jumbo verbiage from the UCMJ his mind was bombarded with a miss-mash of thoughts.

How in the fuck did I come to be here? OH yeah, Donna Nadeau. I went to Nashville to see Donna... got drafted... enlisted for DINFOS... met Flo... did basic training... went to Indy... got assigned to PSYOPS... went to California and made love with Flo... Arrived in-country... got assigned to Lieutenant 'dick breath'... became a combat vet... wouldn't do the APT or kiss his ass so now, here I am, being tried on a bullshit charge of eating in the mess hall! I can't fucking believe it! Yes. It all does makes perfect sense though. Like hell it does. Am I going to have to write the military version of 'Jailhouse Rock?' Or I could call the book ' Catch 23'. Ellis says I have it in the bag. I don't even have to play the 'Liar' card I've got in the hole! I don't' know whether to crap or be happy.

"Uh, Sergeant Sweet, Lt. Wilson and Warrant Officer Schweitzer?" Major Gregory got the trio's attention, "it is required that you all leave the room until you are called as witnesses but, it is my understanding, and correct me if I'm wrong, Lt. Ellis, that once a witness has testified, they can remain in the room and listen to the rest of the testimony, is that right?"

"Yes Sir, that is correct," Ellis nodded affirmatively and smiled, assuring the Major he was doing a good job.

As he rose up from the table, Wilson exchanged an uncertain glance with Captain Ronnie, and sort of shrugged his shoulders and took a deep breath.

He looks more like the accused than I do, marveled the Kid.

Once the door closed behind the trio, Gregory directed his gaze to Captain Smith. "Captain, I think we are ready for you to read the charges against the defendant."

"Yes Sir," Smith rose from his seat, cast a cursory scornful glance at the Kid and, obviously caught up in the pomp of the moment, cleared his throat and read from his copy of the charge sheet:

"The charges are, *a Violation of the Uniform Code of Military Justice, Article 90, Specification One: In that Specialist 4 Curtis L. Stocker, RA 12966317, B Company, 10th Psychological Operations Battalion, APO San Frisco 96215, having received a lawful command, to not eat in the Tra Vinh Field Ration Mess while receiving payment for Rations not Available, did on or about 16 October 1968, willfully disobey the same."*

Specifications two and three read exactly the same way, except the dates of the offense were changed to 17 October and 18 October 1968. All the while, the grey haired spectacle wearing master sergeant court steno stared right at Ronnie and banged away on his device, never once looking down at the keys.

After reading the charges, Major Gregory called on Captain Smith to introduce into record, for purposes of identification, any exhibits that he planned on using during the trial.

In response, Ronnie introduced Lt. Wilson's written statement, the Tra Vinh mess hall cash collection roster for Advisory Team 72 (sheets #

9,11,12,13 & 15), a copy of the Tra Vinh directive pertaining to paying for meals when on 'Rations Not Available and lastly, a copy of the Kid's orders, granting him RNA status.

"Lt. Ellis," Gregory addressed the JAG, "do you have any items to introduce for evidence?"

"No, your honor," Ellis rose to his feet quickly before he spoke and sat as quickly back down when finished, where he found the Kid giving him a hard, questioning look. "Regulations are not evidence," he whispered to the Kid, giving him a wink and a smile.

Well, I'm glad he's having fun.

"Very well," Gregory said to Smith, "Do you have some kind of opening statement or do you just want to call the first witness for the prosecution?"

"Well..." Captain Ronnie rose to his feet, "I don't really have an opening statement, this is a pretty simple case, Sir, so yes, I think we can just cut to the chase. I'd like to call the first witness, First Lieutenant Herschel Wilson," he went to the office door, opened it and hollered, "Lt. Wilson!"

In walked Herschel, shoulders drooped, hang dog look, almost shuffling like a condemned man as he moved over to the witness chair and stood in front of it, facing Major Gregory. *What? No combat commando bravado today? Ha. He can't imagine in his wildest dreams that I'm not going to drop the bomb on the MSQ-85 debacle; he's expecting the shit to hit the fan any second! This is great!*

"For the record, please state your full name and rank," Major Gregory intoned.

"Herschel Ross Wilson, First Lieutenant, United States Army."

This is going to be good! The Kid slid forward to the edge of his chair as Gregory continued.

"Raise your right hand," the major began to give him the oath, "do you, Herschel Ross Wilson, swear that the testimony you will give here today is the truth, the whole truth and nothing but the truth? So help you God?"

Hesitation, no eye contact ... he's looking at the ceiling! Wilson takes a deep breath, "I do."

Look at that! Perjury already!

"Please be seated," the Major said, as Wilson lowered his right arm.

Meanwhile, Captain Ronnie Smith had remained on his feet, looking all at once anxious, excited and awkward as he glanced around the room to see that everybody present was paying attention and once assured they were, he launched into his presentation. "Lieutenant Wilson," he began while taking dramatically slow and deliberate steps from behind the table out to stand in front of the witness chair, "would you please tell the court where you were assigned to duty in October 1968, and what your mission was there."

"Yes Sir," Wilson sucked in a deep breath and his head nervously swiveled as he clearly attempted to avoid making eye contact with anybody, "as a member of the 10th PSYOP Battalion, I was attached to the 72nd Advisory team, as a PSYOPS advisor, operating with the 14th Regiment of the 9th ARVN Division, out of Tra Vinh, Republic of South Vietnam. My mission was to conduct a number of PSYOP activities, including MSQ-85 civil action programs and MEDCAPs, train and lead an Armed Propaganda Team and conduct Chu Hoi loud speaker operations with the ARVN infantry."

"OK." Smith paused to collect his train of thought, "Now, was one certain Specialist Four Curtis L. Stocker assigned to your command during this time?"

"Yes Sir."

"All right. Uh, so tell us what happened to bring us to this trial here today," Smith gave Wilson the cue to launch his tale of blatant insubordination.

"Well, it's a pretty simple matter. Specialist Stocker and I were out in the field with various Vietnamese units for extended periods of time, making it necessary for us to file the paperwork to be put on Rations Not Available. And because we were receiving money to eat on the local economy, during the times we were in from the field, regulations required that we pay for our meals that we consumed at the Tra Vinh mess hall." He paused to gage his audience and he made the eye contact he sought to avoid when he found all of them intently staring at him. "Otherwise," he continued, "the Army would be giving him money to buy a meal and then feeding it to him... which is like getting paid for the same thing twice. So many soldiers were doing that on July 21st, Major Gillmore put out a directive, to make sure everybody in Tra Vinh, on RNA, knew they had to pay for their meals. Then, when the Navy Sea Bee construction teams arrived, the compound population nearly doubled and First Sgt. Brooks came to me and ask me if I could have all my guys pulling RNA eat on the local economy to take the pressure off the mess hall and of course, I said yes. *Perjury.* So I gave Specialist Stocker an order not to eat in the mess hall. I told him if he would prefer to drop his RNA, he could eat there again, but he said he didn't want to do that, since we were out in the boonies so much. You can imagine my surprise when a few days later, somebody came to me and informed me that Specialist Stocker had

161

continued eating in the mess hall, in direct violation of my order and that is why I have preferred the charges. I specifically told him not to do it and he disregarded my order and went and did it... more than once!"

Upon Wilson pausing briefly, Smith jumped right in, "And you felt it was your duty as an officer, to address these blatant acts of insubordination?"

"Absolutely! Officers can't have the men not obeying their orders. Doesn't matter how small or unimportant the enlisted man might consider the order to be, orders are orders and must be obeyed. I will not tolerate anything less than complete compliance from any of my subordinates, which is the standard expected of all soldiers, especially in a combat zone, and Specialist Stocker fell far short of that standard!" He punctuated his damming statement with a small but very 'final' nod.

"Uh, as Lt. Wilson stated," Smith picked up, once he realized the Lt. was finished with his twisted tale, "this is a very plain and simple case. Lt. Wilson gave Specialist Stocker a direct order and he disobeyed it... plain and simple as that!" Smith stopped talking and smiled nervously, like *who can't understand THIS?*

"Are you done, Captain? If you're through," Ellis said, quite casually, "I've got a couple of questions for the lieutenant."

"Yes, I'm through," Smith returned to his seat.

"Lieutenant Wilson," Ellis did not bother to get up out of his seat but rather, leaned forward propped on his elbows, "in your experiences with Specialist Stocker, prior to this incident, would you say he was a good soldier or a bad soldier and had he done anything, up to this point, with which you could find fault with him as a soldier?"

"Well, no. He was a good soldier and quite frankly, that's what surprised me about his unwillingness to obey that particular order."

"OK. Now, in your written statement, you say that on October 16th that *somebody* came and told you about Specialist Stocker eating in the mess hall, in violation of the directive pertaining to RNA's and that you then went to Specialist Stocker and issued him the order not to eat in the mess any more, is that right?

"Yes Sir."

"So in the charge read here today, you are charging him with disobeying your order not to eat in the mess hall after he finished his dinner?"

OOO, this is going to be tough to explain, Wilson... say it's a typo! The Lt. literally choked as he concocted his answer, "Well, what he was then,

162

was in violation of the directive... which he knew about way before that night, that was the problem," Wilson just kept going in deeper.

Letting his answer dangle, Ellis gave the Lt. a shot of un-distilled lawyer glare and disdainfully said, "I see. Let's move on. At that point in time, had you given any of the other soldiers in your command the same order to not eat in the mess hall?"

"No Sir."

"Why not?" Ellis asked in a sudden tone of seriousness, holding his stare on him.

"Well, mostly because they weren't around when I gave Stocker the order. They were all out with other field teams."

"All of them?" Ellis posed again, "even then specialist, now Sgt. Sweet?"

"Yes."

"And when you finally saw them, did you give them the order not to eat in the mess hall?"

The Kid just sat there and admired Ellis's style as Wilson twisted like a worm on a hook.

"No Sir."

"In fact, didn't you see Sgt Sweet later that very same day that you gave Specialist Stocker the order?"

"Uh, yes Sir, I guess I did," his acting skills were quite well advanced, the Kid had to admire in part, as Wilson pulled on his chin and appeared to recollect.

"But you didn't give him the order, later the same day that you gave it to Stocker, is that what you are saying, Lt.?"

"Yes."

What else can he say? Sweet is in the next room and all three of our signatures are on the chow list! This is the most fun I've had since I came to Nam... sept maybe for Li in Saigon... No, this is the most fun!

"Why not, Lieutenant Wilson?" Ellis stood two feet in front of him, looking down on him, making him look very, very small and thin.

"I guess it was because I had a lot of other stuff on my mind," Wilson finally stammered.

Ellis glanced over at Ronnie and back to Major Gregory, "No further questions for the witness but I reserve the right to recall him if necessary."

"OK," responded Major Gregory, "Captain Smith, do you have any questions you want to ask in rebuttal to anything at all?"

"No Sir."

"All right, Lieutenant, you are excused from the stand and you can take a chair in the back if you wish," Gregory pointed with his pen.

Standing, Wilson faced the Major and said, "Thank you Sir, but I prefer to wait outside," and with that, he exited the room, closing the door behind.

The second he was out of the room, Ellis spoke, "Major Gregory, according to the testimony of Lt. Wilson to the fact that he did not issue Specialist Stocker the order to not eat in the mess hall until after dinner on the 16th, I move that Specification One of the charges be dropped.

"Motion granted," Gregory quickly acted on the motion, " Specification one is dismissed.

Well what do you know! I have won one!

"Now just a dang minute there, Sir!" Smith jumped up from his chair, "you can't do that! Specialist Stocker ate in the mess hall that day so he was still in violation of the RNA directive dated 21 July '68, to pay for his meals!"

"Really?" smiled Ellis, "I don't believe that is what you charged him with, was it? Besides, Specialist Stocker clearly paid for his meal that day, so where is the violation?"

Ronnie was starting to see it slipping away, "Yes, he paid, but not enough! He only paid half of what he was supposed to, meaning he was still in violation of the directive!"

Shooting Ronnie a dirty look, Gregory said, "Let me see the directive again." Looking at the directive and at the cash sheet he matched up the amounts. "Says here that Stocker paid exactly the amount stated on the directive."

"But the directive was incorrect. It has since been discovered that Stocker was supposed to pay twice as much! Ignorance of the law is no excuse!"

"Captain Smith..." Gregory was starting to get steamed at the Company B commander, "Specialist Stocker was not in violation of the directive, and he paid exactly what was posted on it. He was in compliance on that point and he's not responsible for the ignorance of the clerk, typist or first sergeant or whoever got it wrong. Besides, you chose not to charge Specialist Stocker with disobeying the directive, you chose to charge him with disobeying an order. Therefore, Specification one and two are dismissed."

164

Ronnie's ears are turning red.

"OK. Fine." Smith attempted to cool off and not lose it completely. "Uh, the other count is still in effect, right, Sir?"

"Yes, Captain," the Major was not amused. "Lieutenant Ellis, are you ready to present the defense?"

"Yes, Sir, we are." Between scribbling on his legal pad, Ellis leaned over to the Kid and whispered, "You ready?"

"Hell yes!" he breathed back low.

"The defense would like to make a couple of opening remarks for the record," Ellis rose to his feet and pushed his black horn rimmed glasses up on his nose. "Esteemed members of the court, the case before us today, according to the prosecution, has to do with insubordination... specifically the disobeying of an order from one Lt. Herschel Wilson, given to the defendant, Specialist Stocker. The defense contends that the case here today is not about that, but rather about whether or not the order in question was a legal order! The fact that Specialist Stocker disobeyed the order in question is not in dispute. But think about a man who has a completely clean record in the military being accused of disobeying an order that has to do with eating in a particular mess hall. That should go far in establishing a basis for just how strange this whole trial is." Looking directly into Major Gregory's eyes, Ellis delivered his set up. "However, in the end, I think the court will find that under any circumstances, the order given by Lt. Herschel Ross Wilson, to Specialist Four Curtis L. Stocker, was, in fact, an illegal order, releasing Specialist Stocker, from any legal obligation to obey it.

"You may be asking yourself, 'what, then, is this trial really all about? And I will tell you; it is about a lieutenant who was trying to get an enlisted man to volunteer for an assignment that he did not chose to volunteer for... by engineering a situation wherein he could threaten the enlisted man with legal action, thereby forcing or coercing him to volunteer. However, the defendant, Specialist Stocker, it turned out, was not the kind of individual soldier who could be easily intimidated." He stopped and took a drink from his glass of water on the defense table. "For the first witness for the defense, I call Sergeant James Sweet to the stand."

Ronnie went to the door and fetched Jim. From the time he entered the room and while he stood in front of the chair taking the oath, he tried to catch the Kid's eye and see if he could get any kind of a read on how things were going, but the Kid continued to stare at his note pad. But, when he finally sat down, the Kid flashed him a big grin.

165

"Sergeant Sweet," Ellis began, "let's cut to the chase. Are you aware of the day in question that Lt. Wilson gave the alleged order to Specialist Stocker, to not eat in the mess hall?"

"Yes Sir."

"How was that?" Ellis queried.

"Well, Specialist Stocker told me about it when I arrived at the Tra Vinh compound that day."

"An on that day, did you personally happen to see or be around or speak to Lt. Wilson yourself that day?"

"Yes Sir, I did," said Sweet, pausing briefly before he realized that Ellis wished for him to relate the events to the court. "Uh, I had just come in from Cang Long and I went looking for Specialist Stocker, to see if he wanted to eat lunch. As a matter of fact, the first place I looked was in the mess hall, because it was lunch time and I thought, for sure, he'd be there. Lt. Wilson was there, but not Stocker. So, I went over to the enlisted barracks and found Stocker and said 'let's go eat' and he told me he couldn't because Lt. Wilson had given him an order not to. I then told him I'd just come from the mess hall and Wilson was in there eating that very second. So we went over and had our lunch, saw the Lt. and he saw us and said nothing to me about the order or to Stocker about disobeying it."

"Your testimony is that Lt. Wilson was *eating in the mess hall* when you first encountered him that day?' inquired Ellis, glancing quickly at Major Gregory, to insure he caught the significance of Sweet's testimony.

"Yes Sir," Jim said.

The Kid glanced over at Smith, to see he certainly did not like the particular line of questioning Ellis was taking with Sweet.

"And, at any time, before or after Specialist Stocker was charged and sent in from the field, did Lt. Wilson ever give you a similar order not to eat in the mess hall?"

"No. Never," Sweet firmly declared.

"And while you were in Tra Vinh, after Specialist Stocker was sent in from the field, did you and Lt. Wilson continue to eat in the mess hall?"

"Yes Sir, we both did."

Now, Ronnie was shaking his head 'no', like Sweet was lying or saying something he shouldn't. Or maybe it was that he was finally seeing what it was that Wilson had done.

166

"Let me ask you," Ellis continued, "did Lt. Wilson ever request that you volunteer for the advisory position on the Armed Propaganda Team?"

"Yes, he did, and I told him no," answered Sweet.

"And what did he do in response, court martial you for eating in the mess hall?"

"No," chuckled Sweet, "what he did was arrange for me to be promoted from specialist 4th class to sergeant E-5, so that I no longer could refuse the assignment because it was outside of my specialties."

"Oh, I see; his response was to promote you?" Ellis held a classic look of shock in his expression.

"Yes Sir."

"So, that's promote you… and court martial Stocker under the identical circumstances… No further questions, you're witness," Ellis glided back into his seat, confident in the fact that he'd just made Lt. Wilson look pretty damn bad.

Smith was up and in a flash, he was nearly in Sweet's face, "Sergeant Sweet, let me ask you one thing… who's on trial here? Lt. Wilson or Specialist Stocker?'

"Well," Sweet paused briefly, as if it might be a clever trick question, before answering the only way he could; "that's easy, Specialist Stocker."

"Thank you, Sergeant," Smith smugly implored Major Gregory, "I just asked that to remind the court that Lt. Wilson is not the one on trial here today and any testimony about him eating in the mess hall is irrelevant!"

Ellis awarded an acrid look of pity to Captain Smith, in clear ridicule of his one-question cross examination technique; shoddy work by any standard. "You can step down, Sergeant Sweet, and if you wish, you can observe the rest of the trial from the back row there."

"Yes Sir, thank you Sir, I'd like that very much!" he said, making his way to the folding chairs, exchanging smiles with the Kid on the way.

Ellis checked his notes and continued. "The defense now calls Specialist Curtis L. Stocker to the stand."

The Kid stood, with a slight grin on his face, accenting his feelings of confidence as he took the three or so steps from his seat to the witness chair and stood in front of it, facing Major Gregory.

"Please give you full name and rank for the court," Major Gregory actually smiled back. *Now there's a good sign!*

"Curtis L. Stocker, Specialist Fourth Class, United States Army," the Kid spoke strong and clear. How the trial had thus far gone was incredibly encouraging. Two charges were dismissed already and he hadn't even opened his mouth and the super secret warrant officer witness was still to testify!

"Raise your right hand," Gregory read him the oath, "do you swear the testimony you are about to give is the truth, the whole truth and nothing but the truth?"

"Yes Sir."

"Please be seated," instructed the Major.

Once he was settled, Lt. Ellis began. "Specialist Stocker, for the record, will you please relate to the court, where you were and what your duty assignment was, at the time of the incident in question here today."

"Yes Sir," he made a point of engaging Major Gregory in eye to eye contact as he began his story. *You're the only person who matters.* "As you have heard, Lt. Wilson and I were attached to the 72nd Advisory Group and in our activities, we were spending most of our time out with the ARVNs so we were getting RNA but we had always eaten in the Tra Vinh mess hall when we came in, because that was the only place in the province where we could get American food. It happened about once or twice a week and a couple of times, not for a couple of weeks. This was the routine from the time we first got our RNA orders, in June, and it was never a problem. Now, the conversation with First Sergeant Brooks that Lt. Wilson testified that he had did, in fact, take place. I was present for it. But it was not about what Lt. Wilson said it was; it had nothing to do with a crowded mess hall. Brooks came to him and told him he was going to have to pull Officer of the Day duty and we men were going to have to pull guard duty to help out. Wilson told him no, we came in to rest up from being out in combat and he wouldn't pull OD and wouldn't have his PSYOPS guys pulling any guard duty. To that, Sgt. Brooks replied, '…as long as you eat in my mess hall, you'll do what I say.', and walks off. Wilson turned to me and said, 'well, if that's how he's gonna be… Stocker, I don't want you eating in his mess hall any more…' and I said, you gotta be kidding, and he says 'no, if we don't eat in his mess hall, then he won't have any say over me… and' he also said, 'we're going to move out and live at the CIA compound.'" The Kid rose from his chair and slipped over to the defense table and picked up his glass of water and took a sip. He observed Gregory waiting for him to resume in a very respectful, attentive posture as he placed the glass back on the corner of the table. *Renew eye contact, smile.*

"This all started three or four days before October 16th. Lt. Wilson and I had been spending most of the previous couple of weeks primarily going out on search and destroy operations, not really doing any of the PSYOPS work we were assigned to do, but I guess that is not really important here today but I bring it up because the Lt. had left Sgt. Jim Sweet and Sp. Four John Boujold out in Cang Long with the MSQ-85 and on this particular day, that he gave me the order, Sgt. Sweet came in from Cang Long and found me in the compound. He says, 'let's go to lunch', I say I can't, Lt. Wilson is feuding with Sgt. Brooks and told me not to eat in 'Sgt. Brook's' mess hall any more and he's probably going to give you the same order as soon as he sees you. To which Sweet replied, 'well, I just saw Lt. Wilson, he was in the mess hall, eating himself and he looked right at me and didn't say anything.' So I say, 'well, he must be blowing smoke at Brooks and he doesn't really mean it… otherwise, why would HE be in there eating? OK Sweet, let's go eat! And we did."

Upon admitting this, he paused and looked over at Captain Ronnie, who was writing so furiously fast, that the Kid thought the lead in his pencil might burst into flames. When Smith realized the Kid had paused, he looked up from his pad to see the Kid looking back at him. It elicited one of Smith's patented *'I GOT YOU NOW'* nods. The Kid gave him back a slit eyed smirky sly smile that he knew would really piss Smith off. Before returning his focus to Major Gregory.

"So sure enough, Sweet and I went into the mess hall and *there was Lt. Wilson,* eating away, not a care in the world, he looked right at both of us, because we had to walk right in front of him to get our silverware, and didn't say a thing or even bat an eye. That was the point that I determined, in my mind, Lt. Wilson wasn't serious about any order not to eat in the mess hall. Shortly after that incident, I come to find out that Lt. Wilson has volunteered us for an Armed Propaganda Team. As soon as he told me, I told him that I don't volunteer and I won't volunteer. But he keeps trying to get me to change my mind and I won't. Part of his plan to get me to change my mind included promising me if I did the APT, we wouldn't do any more search and destroy but if I didn't, we'd do twice as much. I mean, we'd been out on all kinds of combat ops, performing no PSYOPS, with no loud speakers or anything that had to do with PSYOPS and he promised that would stop. He tried really hard to get me to change my mind but I'm not interested so finally, he comes to me and says he is going to read me my rights and tells me he is going to court martial me for disobeying his order not to eat in the mess hall… unless I change my mind about the APT. He said he would *drop the 'charges'* if I did, and I asked, if he was so serious about the insubordination, why was he willing to give me such an easy out and he said he wasn't so I said go ahead and court martial me… and here we are today," the Kid gestured palm open at the room in which they all sat.

"Thank you, Specialist. If there isn't anything else you wish to add at this time, I see no need for any further questions," Ellis wheeled and nodded to Captain Smith, "you're witness."

"Thank you." Ronnie for once exuded confidence as he rose and walked over to stand directly in front of the Kid, about two feet back. "Specialist Stocker, you testified here today, *under oath,* that Lt. Wilson did, in fact, issue you an order not to eat in the Tra Vinh mess hall, is that right?"

"Yes Sir."

"And you then testified, *under oath,* that you proceeded to disobey that order on a number of occasions, isn't that also right?'

"Yes Sir."

Glancing over to Major Gregory and back to the Kid, Smith resolutely said, pausing ever so briefly between each word, "There… it …is! *The order was given and the order was disobeyed!* The proof of the matter just came out of the defendant's own mouth! No further questions!" He then sat down, placed his pencil on his legal pad, crossed his arms and glared at Lt. Ellis with an expression that clearly said, *'top that!'*

"The defense now calls Chief Warrant Officer George Schweitzer

The puzzled look on Smith's face was something the Kid would remember long after the trial was over. The captain had no idea for what purpose the CWO was testifying at the trial but he had to know it wasn't to help him make his case. "Chief Schweitzer? He timidly hailed out the door and then, he stood back as the Chief, at least 45 years or so old, wearing a highly starched set of fatigues, entered the room. The CWO, whose somewhat narrow face was bracketed by greying temples, stepped toward the witness chair carrying his dark brown bound volume of Army regulations in the crook of his arm.

"Please state your name and rank for the record," Major Gregory said, showing more than casual interest in what he was about to hear.

"Chief Warrant Officer George Schweitzer, US Army."

"Raise your right hand… Do you swear that the testimony you are about to give will be the truth, the whole truth and nothing but the truth?" Gregory read the oath for the fourth time."

"I do," he said and didn't wait to be told to be seated.

170

"Chief Schweitzer," Ellis sat on the corner of defense table, left foot on the floor and let his right leg swing the slightest bit as he got down to business, "Would you please tell the court what your duty assignment is here in Can Tho."

"Yes Sir," Schweitzer nodded his understanding to Ellis and faced Gregory to deliver his answer. "I am in charge of all mess hall operations for IV Corps. My duties include helping set the menus, making sure the supplies are ordered and delivered to the right locations to feed the right number of troops and … uh… pretty much making sure all of the Army regulations pertaining to the operations of mess halls are followed. This includes health inspections and compliance across the board… that's pretty much it, Sir."

"Well, I must say, that sounds like quite a lot of work!" Now Ellis stood up and walked toward Major Gregory while kind of looking at the ceiling fan, "Chief, let's cut to the chase, I'm sure you have a thousand other things to do today, so, let me ask you this question:" he pivoted and pointed his two index fingers at Schweitzer, "is there any circumstance under which an officer could lawfully order an enlisted man not to eat in a particular mess hall?"

"Yes Sir, there is one, and only one, I might add. Even prisoners have full rights to be supplied three meals a day," the chief flipped open his regulation book to an already marked page, "it says in the regs, that the only circumstance under which an officer could give an order denying troops access to consume one of the three main daily meals, is if there is a shortage of rations and there exists an uncertainty of when re-supply might take place."

"I see," Ellis said, "and if such a set of circumstances should arise, how is the situation actually managed?

"Well, if there is a shortage of rations, Army regulations stipulate, in the next paragraph, that it is the officers who must first give up their rations, so that the enlisted men can maintain their strength so that they will be capable of carrying out the officer's orders."

"If there had been a shortage of rations in Tra Vinh, would you have been notified?"

"Yes, Sir."

"Were you, during the month of October, or at any time this year, notified of a shortage of rations in Tra Vinh?" Ellis pointedly inquired.

"No, Sir," came the two word answer.

171

"And even if there had been a shortage of any type, let the court note that on every cash collection sheet from the Tra Vinh mess hall that contains Specialist Stocker's signature, you also find that of Lt. Wilson." Ellis approached Gregory's desk and pointed to the evidence exhibits and the Major picked them up and perused them, nodding up and down as he did, in agreement that what Ellis said was a fact. "Therefore, in lieu of a shortage of rations, and because Lt. Wilson didn't give up his, according to Army regulations, you must find that any order given by Lt. Wilson, depriving Specialist Stocker of his right to eat in the mess hall, is on it's face, an illegal order. Your witness," the

Navy JAG literally gloated as he sat down, yielding the floor to Smith.

Ronnie just sat there, holding his forehead in his hand, eyes downcast upon his legal pad. Smith had nothing; not even a one-question cross examination. He had zilch, no way to attack the regulations or the credibility of CWO Schweitzer so he lifted up his face and said, "No questions, your Honor."

A warm, satisfying glow settled over the Kid. *I see no need to drop the MSQ-85 bomb shell.*

"Ok," said Major Gregory, "Lt. Ellis, don't you get to make the first closing statement?"

"Yes, I do," Ellis checked his legal pad for a couple of seconds and started his wrap up. "Your Honor, I feel you will concur that with all of the facts and pertinent regulations admitted into evidence and by the testimony given, the court has no choice but to declare the order given by Lt. Wilson to be illegal and therefore, a verdict of not guilty must be returned regarding the charges made against Specialist Stocker here today. Lt. Wilson's reason for giving the illegal order was even challenged and not refuted and there is no Army regulation pertaining to mess hall use that counters the regulations cited by Chief Schweitzer... therefore, the court has no option other than to render a verdict of not guilty." And with that, he sat down, yielding the floor to Captain Smith.

Clearly flustered and on the ropes, getting ready to go down for the count, Smith rose for his closing statement with the appearance of a fish fighting for breath out of the water. There was only one place he could go and he went directly to it. "Sir," he addressed Major Gregory. "The defendant has testified here today that Lt. Wilson gave him an order not to eat in the mess hall. Lt. Wilson had his reasons, based on the situation in the field, to issue that order. The defendant further testified that he disobeyed that order. Based on that testimony alone, you have *no alternative* other than to find Specialist Stocker *guilty* of the charge. Thank you." He punctuated his ending with a shrug of his shoulders and sat down.

Short, sweet and vapid. Didn't mention the regulations and why he thinks it was even a legal order.

"Are we done?" Gregory questioned as Ronnie sat down. Nods to the affirmative all around. "Very well, uh, so I think I'll have you all wait outside, except for you," he referred to the court reporter," and give me a few minutes to make my decision. When I have it, I'll call you all back in and announce it."

A few minutes? With that, everybody rose and exited Colonel Lawton's office and poured out into the Battalion headquarters. Smith immediately pulled Wilson off to the side and proceeded to clearly blister his ass. The defense group of Ellis, Sweet, Chief Schweitzer and the Kid lit up cigarettes and had smiles all around.

"I think that went rather well," Ellis beamed.

"Well, Sir," the Kid smiled back, "I must admit, I do have a good feeling about how this is going to turn out. That was your ace in the hole... the Army regs, huh? Very nice, but I won't be completely happy until I hear that I'm officially off the hook."

"Don't worry, Specialist," he exhaled, "Major Gregory looks like a sane person. He'd have to be loony as a March fucking Hare on heroin to come back with anything other than not guilty."

"I sure as hell hope you're right," Sweet said, and then, pulling the Kid aside, whispered, "you didn't tell, did you?"

The Kid shook his head 'no.' "But it looks like Captain Smith has a few things to tell the Lieutenant!" he said, as they both glanced over at rabid Ronnie chewing Wilson's ass and they laughed, loud enough that Smith and Wilson both looked up from the butt chewing in chagrin at the happy pair, before Smith renewed his furious verbal harangue on Wilson, who's head was hung in remorse.

Paul Hoch walked over from his desk to talk with Sweet and the Kid. "How did it go in there? Judging from that, pretty good, I guess," he motioned with his head to the sorry scene of Smith and Wilson.

"We should know in a few minutes, or so the Major said," the Kid took a puff, still wanting to have the verdict in hand before beginning to celebrate.

True to his word, in less than 15 minutes, the court reporter came to the door and summoned the parties to return to the court room.

Once assembled, with Ellis and the Kid at the defense table, Wilson and Smith to their left at the prosecution table and Sweet and Schweitzer seated in their chairs at the rear, Major Gregory picked up a piece of paper and began to give the verdict.

"Would the defendant please stand." The Kid stood and assumed the position of attention. "In the matter of the United States Army vs. Specialist Four Curtis L. Stocker, on count three of the indictment, that he did disobey a lawful order from a superior, as chief presiding officer of the summary court martial board, after hearing the evidence in the case, I find the defendant, *Not Guilty*." He gave the Kid a big smile, "This proceeding is dismissed."

The beaming Kid pumped Lt. Ellis' hand with a double grip, Sweet came up and pounded him on the back, Schweitzer looked nervously at his watch and the court reporter began packing up his machine.

Catching the Kid's attention, Captain Smith issued him a new order... "I want to see you in my office, right *NOW!*" he barked, exiting in a huff.

"You better go," Ellis gestured, "If he gives you any shit, let me know. This is exactly why you're entitled to a transfer, win or lose, in a court martial."

"OK!" the Kid was all smiles, "let's do lunch in the USO to celebrate, on me!"

"For sure. And Stocker... in the future, stay out of the freaking mess hall at Tra Vinh, OK?"

"Yes Sir!" the Kid snapped off a salute and trailed out the door to hustle down to Company B, a floor below. Coming through the door, Coffman sat at his desk in front of the open door to Smith's office.

"Congratulation," he shook the Kid's hand as he passed.

"Thank you," the Kid said as he arrived at Smith's office, to see him standing behind his desk. *Oh look, he's so pissed he can't sit down!*

"You haven't heard the end of this yet!" the captain frothed, "I'm going to get to the bottom of this!"

"What the fuck are you talking about, Sir? Get to the bottom of what? Don't you understand, Sir? You just lost! You CAN'T try me again because that's *double jeopardy!*" the Kid emphatically said. "Ignorance of double jeopardy is no excuse, Sir, not even for captains." The Kid was amazed, from the fact that Captain Smith was so hot, that his hair didn't spontaneously combust.

"You admitted he gave the order and you admitted you disobeyed it?" he huffed. And Major Gregory doesn't fucking *find you guilty?* I'm going to write up a situation report and appeal the decision.

"God. You really don't know legal squat, do you, Sir." The Kid was enjoying every second of it, "there IS no appeal for the prosecution… there's no do over… no mulligans, it's double jeopardy, Sir! You can't try me for the same thing twice. And I guess you acting like this is why the Army gives somebody like *me* a transfer out of the unit after a court martial… and I'm looking forward to it… Sir. And by the way, I want to put in a request to see the Inspector General to complain about the way I was treated." Silence from Ronnie. "Is that all, then, Sir?"

Glare. "Yes. Damn it. But, you are now officially returned to duty and since you like flying leaflet drops so much, you will be assigned to do exactly that for your duty day the rest of the time you're here in the unit," he sarcastically saluted.

Returning it, the Kid was out the door. *Ah yes… a free man!* And who should be coming in to B Company to see Ronnie, but Lt. Wilson. Standing directly in front of him and blocking his path into the Captain's office, the Kid said, "You called it, Sir, the best man won!" He beamed in the glory of his fresh victory and was doubly delighted as he saw Sweet and Cpl. Ba was following Wilson into the room. "Cpl. Ba! Chao! Hey Jim!"

"Chao, Stocker…" Ba stopped to talk to the Kid, grinning from ear to ear, as Wilson proceeded on into Ronnie's office. "You won! Very good!" he shook the Kid's hand.

"Yep. And now I get a transfer out of here and maybe even… and I'm not holding my breath… out of PSYOPS!"

"You happy, but him…" Ba pointed to the closed door office that contained Wilson, " he is going to be very mad… dinky dau…how you say… numba one pissed off… no telling what kind of crazy stuff he will try now!"

"You sure as hell got a point there, Cpl. Ba, but I think Sgt. Sweet will have the answer to that." The Kid lit up a cigarette, "Not to mention, I think Lieutenant *pit bull* is in getting fixed at the Vet right now!" the three men had to laugh at the high volume level of ass chewing that was emanating from the Captain's office.

"Well, I'm pretty sure me, Ba and Wilson are flying out to Tra Vinh this afternoon, that was always the plan," Sweet said. "If you're getting a transfer, I probably won't see you again, I don't imagine."

"Could be. I 'm not sure what the time frame is on all of this, but Ellis said I get a transfer, so I'm takin' it. Let's stay in touch. I'd be interested to hear how things go back there in Tra Vinh. Hope I don't get sent to a place any worse!"

"Hey, it's not that bad." Jim smiled, "we haven't broken the tip off of your pool cue yet!"

Chapter 23

When the last case of leaflets was loaded onto the C-47, the Kid retrieved his canteen and fatigue shirt from where he had set them, in the shade of the green ¾ ton truck by the front passenger's tire. The twin engine craft was now loaded for its fourth and final leaflet dissemination mission for the day.

The crew had done three drops before lunch and the Kid had hoped that Sgt. Johnson would release him for his scheduled meeting at 1430 hours with the Inspector General, but the sergeant had insisted that the Kid stay to help load the plane. Ok. Fine. Now that the boxes of leaflets were onboard, the Kid checked his watch. *1300 hours, an hour and a half before the meeting. Not time to go on this flight and make it...*

"Well, boys, have a nice flight... I got to get on back to Battalion for my meeting with the IG... see ya!" the Kid waved to his comrades as he turned to head up to the main road to catch a ride back in to Can Tho.

"Not so fast, Stocker" First Sgt Johnson stepped out of the truck, where he'd been sitting on the passenger's side, smoking a cigarette while watching the men work. "You got to fly this last mission before you're released from duty here today, Capt. Smith's orders."

"You got to be kidding me!" the Kid stopped in his track and wheeled around. "Sergeant, it is 1300 hours, my meeting is at 1430. If I go on this mission and it only took an hour... I wouldn't have time to find a ride and get back to Battalion before the IG leaves! You have to let me go now!"

"No I don't. It's only fair to your pals on the crew that you fly this mission and not make them do it shorthanded, kind of like when you wanted to duck out on the loading. This mission isn't far off, it's just over to the Iron Triangle so it isn't going to take more than 45 minutes and when you get back, and I'll get you a ride in to make it to your meeting. So, Stocker, get in the plane. That's an order... a *legal* order!" the slightly graying first shirt appeared quite serious.

Seeing the futility of arguing, the Kid complied and in a few minutes, the bird was airborne and there was hardily time to even sit down before the plane arrived over the drop zone and the PSYOPS men had to go to work.

Busting open the boxes and passing them in a chain to the chute man, the well oiled and sweaty team kept a steady flow of leaflets belching out of the door chute.

All the while the men worked amid the roar of the engines and the wind passing by outside the fuselage, the Kid happily thought about his pending meeting with the Inspector General, the man who heard the grievances of the troops, and how the IG could affect his transfer to something better than another PSYOPS unit.

It was Tuesday, November 19th. A pleasant feeling of accomplishment swept over the Kid are he realized he was two days from the half way point of his tour, a major Vietnam milestone.

On Thanksgiving, I'll have six months! And when the IG hears about how Wilson screwed me over and tried to send me to jail on a bullshit charge, he just might be sympathetic enough to fix up my transfer to AFVN Saigon, and then, if I get the 60 day drop… I'll only have 20 days to be under a hundred! I mean, since Radio Saigon said they want me and I already have the paperwork in for an extension and transfer there… Oh, God! Wouldn't that be sweet! Got to admit, things have been looking up since that court martial! He hefted the boxes with a smile on his face. *The IG could get me in to Radio Saigon. I could be hearing in an hour that I'm going to Saigon!*

Once the leaflets were out the door and the boxes were broken down, they all took a break and sat, exhausted, as the lifting and throwing was catching up with them.

"This is so fucking boring," RV Smith drawled, "I wish we'd get shot at or something exciting, for just once," he fairly moaned.

"You're a dumb shit, RV, the Kid immediately jumped him, "don't go saying things like that… that's what make them happen. And if you'd ever been shot at you sure as fuck wouldn't be wishing for it to happen again!"

All the other 4 guys nodded in agreement with the Kid, although he was the only one there who had actually been shot at, none of them wanted the likes of what RV Smith wishing for.

As the C-47 rolled to a stop, the Kid was at the door looking at his watch. *1355 hours… it's gonna be tight! Thank God the sergeant has a ride for me or I wouldn't make it.* But when he hit the ground and trotted over to where Sergeant Johnson sat at the wheel of the three quarter ton, he got a rude surprise.

"OK, let's go!" said the Kid as he opened the passenger's side door.

"Change of plans, they've put on one more drop, so we gotta use to truck to load the plane. Looks like you're going to have to hitch in."

The Kid offered an accusatory stare at the first sergeant, noting that he was trying poorly to conceal a smirk. "Sgt. Johnson, you knew they'd added another mission after lunch, didn't you… and you still told me you were going to give me a ride, didn't you!"

"No I didn't," he smiled, "I didn't get the word until after the plane took off. But that's all beside the point, if you're going to make it, you better get moving, don't you think?"

"Won't you at least give me a ride to the gate?" the Kid pleaded.

"Nope. We have to get this bird loaded and in the air right away," Johnson was in no way sympathetic to the Kid's cause. "Like I said, you better get a move on, if you want to see the IG."

"Aw, come on Sarge, fuckin' A, give him a ride!" Mc Cauley ribbed him, "we're talking all of ten minutes difference!"

"No. And get your asses in gear and start loading up. Here's the manifest," Johnson stuck a piece of paper into George's hand.

Seething with anger and sure he had been purposely shafted from seeing the IG, the Kid turned and put his fatigue shirt on as he walked quickly toward the nearest road on the air base that had any traffic headed for the front gate. The fact that it was the hottest part of the day wasn't going to make his task any easier and as he broke into a trot, his mind was nearly screaming out his complete and total distaste for anything that had to do with the Army… in any way shape or form.

Fuck- the… Ar-mee, fuck-the… Ar-mee, the Kid chose a cadence count as he doubletimed, up the hill, down the hill…. Fuck- the…. Ar-mee… Hitting the roadway, he stuck out his thumb and in less than 30 seconds, an Air Force sergeant stopped and inquired, "Where you headed?"

"Can Tho and I'm in a hurry!"

"I can take you to the front gate, hop in!"

Great! The Kid took a swig from his canteen as sweat gushed from half the pores on his body. The sergeant had him to the front gate of Ben Thuy in less than five minutes, a duce and a half roared up and the PFC riding shotgun said they were heading to IV Corps HQ, which was only two blocks past 10th PSYOP Battalion headquarters… *I just might make it.*

All the way there, the Kid wrestled in his mind about what, exactly he was going to say to, or ask of the IG. Generally, he had heard that what

179

you got out of the IG was the luck of the draw… which IG you got to hear your grievance and what kind of a mood he was in that day. *Beaver nickel, don't fail me now. The Army OWES me, after what Wilson did and all that shit. Maybe this would be a good time to tell the IG about the ARVNs shooting those three kid prisoners last month. But I didn't see it happen… so what can I tell him? What would it do to my chance of getting a good assignment? Fucking bastards. All the shit I've been through. I'm supposed to be in RADIO, God dammit! You can bet your ass I'm going to give the IG a freaking fucking ear full of something!*

Partly because it was the hottest part of the day, the traffic on the Can Tho road was not that heavy and as the duce and a half pulled into the driveway in front of the 10th PSYOP Battalion, the Kid though he had it made; his watch said 1440 hours, but the IG couldn't have gotten out of there that fast… he was only ten minutes late… *surely the man will give me a little bit of a cushion!*

Flying up the stairs, he went straight to the desk of the man who knew everything. "Am I too late?" he breathlessly implored Specialist Hoch.

The Kid could not interpret his expression; as he did not answer immediately.

"Yes. Way too late," Hoch said, to the Kid's complete chagrin. "In fact, the IG left about an hour ago. He was out of here right after lunch."

"Fucking God damn shit!" exclaimed the Kid, *Somebody screwed up my meeting with the IG on purpose!* "I want to see the Colonel!"

"Hmm, that's convenient, because the Colonel wants to see you!"

"What?"

"I said," Hoch repeated slowly, like the Kid was a person incapable of understanding, "the Colonel… wants- to -see -you… the minute you arrive."

"Oh, really?" Hoch nodded in the affirmative. "OK," the Kid's curiosity meter flew off the scale as the head clerk rose up and walked over to the Colonel's office. Knocking three times sharply, he opened the door announced that the Kid had arrived. *Go on in,* he gestured with his thumb through the opening.

Still thoroughly hacked off that he had missed his appointment with the IG, due to what looked like a totally premeditated fuck job, one part of the Kid's brain was spoiling for a fight and on the other hand, the Kid was now a little nervous as to why it was the Colonel wanted to see him. Entering the

180

room that had, four days previous, served as his court room, the Kid found Willie Lawton seated at his desk.

"Specialist Stocker reporting, Sir," he stood rigidly and delivered a crisp salute.

Saluting back, Lawton said, "At ease, Specialist Stocker." The Kid struck an attentively posed parade rest and waited to hear what the colonel had to say.

"Close the door. " The Kid did. "Please sit down, Specialist." The Kid did. "Now, you had an appointment with the IG today, didn't you?"

"Yes Sir."

Pushing back his chair, the unit commander made a confession. "Well, you've missed him and I guess you can pretty much say that was my fault because I wanted to talk to you first."

A questioning look swept across the Kid's face. *Why would he fuck with me like that? I thought the colonel was a pretty nice guy.*

"When we finish this conversation, if you still want to see the IG, I'll fly you up to Group in Saigon tomorrow and you can see one there. Now, I am very aware that you are entitled to a transfer after your court martial. But Stocker, dammit, you've got talent and I need men with talent in my unit and I want you to stay. Is there any job in the unit that I could offer you to that would make you agree to stay?"

The Kid couldn't decipher if he was more flattered or surprised.

"Any job at all, name your slot," the tone of the Colonel's voice was welcome and inviting, offering out the hope of sanctuary in a country gone mad.

Giving it some lightning fast thought, the Kid said, "Well, Sir, how about making me editor of the unit newspaper?"

"We already have an editor, with whom I'm quite happy. But, how about you being assistant editor and working with him as the main writer?" Lawton suggested, "then when he DEROSes, you can be editor. How's that?"

"Yes Sir! I'd like that. I accept."

"OK!" he smiled broadly, showing his white, perfectly straight teeth. "Consider it done. Now, do you still want to see the IG?"

"No sir."

"That's excellent!" Lawton said as he rose from his seat and extended his hand, "I'm glad we have a deal."

"Yes Sir! Thank you, Sir!" the Kid pumped his hand in gratitude and for the first time since he got sent out of Long Binh to join up with the 4th PSYOP Group, he felt like something good had happened to him.

"The newspaper staff operates out of the graphics room here at HQ. In fact," he pointed over his shoulder with his thumb like an umpire making an 'out' call, "they're right on the other side of this wall, come on, I'll introduce you."

Exiting his office with the Kid in tow, Lawton ushered him down to the end of the headquarters room, took a left and down a corridor that had a screen on one side and wall on the other, and entered a spacious room that was actually the same size as his office, since it was literally right on the opposite side of the back wall to his office. When Willie walked in, everybody in the place, which consisted of five men, jumped up and snapped to attention in front of their work stations, in fitting respect to the Battalion commander.

"At ease, men," the colonel immediately said, "allow me to introduce Specialist Stocker, whom I suppose, some of you might already know. And although he is entitled to a transfer after his recent court martial, he has agreed to stay on here in the 10th and I'm assigning him to the staff of the battalion newspaper as assistant editor. This is our editor, Specialist Reagan," Lawton gestured to a brown haired, bespectacled soldier obviously in his mid 20's, "you'll be working for him... have you two met yet?"

"Yes Sir, we have," said Specialist Regan, who took a couple of steps from his desk over to where the Kid stood to shake his hand. "Welcome aboard, Stocker!"

"It's great to be aboard... Chief," the Kid attempted to pay him an editorial compliment.

The Chief continued with the introductions, "This is Bob Weston, our art director and main layout man for the paper and most of the leaflets... this is Michael Imrem, our main feature writer... and Ron Edwards, *wink wink* our varitypist... and Tom Boyett, one of our artists." The Kid shook each of their hands; they were regulars at the third floor balcony pot smoking embassy and even though Reagan didn't smoke, the Kid had met him because he lived in the first room on the corner of the balcony

"I've got some special projects in mind that I want you to do," the colonel continued, "and I'm sure Specialist Reagan has some plans for you and of course, if you should happen to come up with any kind of ideas of your own for stories, I fully expect you'll be working your ass off, Specialist

182

Stocker, making this unit look good… *on paper, at least,*" he humorously smirked to everybody else in the room. "Have you got a desk back here for him?"

"Well," Everett looked quickly around the room, "he can have that artist's desk there in the corner," he pointed.

"Fine," said the colonel, "uh, tell you what, Specialist Stocker, I'm going to let you take the rest of today and tomorrow off and then, since its Thanksgiving, why don't you just plan on starting Friday… OK?"

"Yes Sir." the Kid enthusiastically replied, "more than OK… thank you very much, Sir!" As he came to attention and snapped off the most sincere salute he'd ever given any officer, from the day he had entered the military.

Chapter 24

November 21, 1968

Dear Flo,

Happy Thanksgiving. Yes, it's Turkey day in 'Nam. I recall a lot of snow and cold on Thanksgiving back in Colorado and some of that would be great right about now. But even here in the tropics, I do have a lot to be thankful for. Of course, being found not guilty at my court martial is number one on the hit parade. Being no longer connected to Lt. Wilson is number two. And now, coming in at number three (with a bullet, ha ha), I know where I'm going to be for the rest of my tour… right here in Can Tho!

After the trial, I was supposed to get a transfer, but it turns out that Colonel Lawton himself asked me to stay on and said if I would, I could pick my own job! So now, I'm the assistant editor for DIMESION, the unit newspaper, you know the little one I've been sending you. Now I'm going to write for it. Granted, it's not radio, but considering that they could have sent me as a foreign language announcer to the Central Highlands or the DMZ, this looked too good to pass up. Sort of how you looked the night we met at the movie premier in Nashville… way too good to pass up.

Happy Birthday, by the way. You should have this on or before Dec. 7th. The PX is out of cards and the Vietnamese don't really have any Hallmark stores… yet, so this will have to do for now.

You wouldn't believe how overboard they go here for Thanksgiving but really, it no different than any other day. We're still stuck in this f'ing place, what ever day it is… (Hi Mrs. Stuckey). Of course, we are just back from a big turkey dinner with all the trimmings at Eakin Compound. I'm as stuffed as the bird we ate! We stopped by the USO on the way back and they had already broken out all of the Christmas decorations and stuff. By 'we' I mean a group of about eight guys that I don't really know all that well yet. All I can say is, it's nice to finally be in a place where we don't get shot at every other day. However, I do feel sorry for the poor bastards that are out there still getting shot at right now.

In fact, life so changed for the better from almost the very second Wilson pressed those ridiculous charges. This is going to be fun working for the paper. (November issue enclosed.) On page 10, there's a picture of the Bat Mobile where Lt. Wilson blew it up and said it was the VC. I won't have any articles in there until the December issue. My first day at work is tomorrow! I've met most of the guys who do the paper and all the other graphics in the unit and I think it's going to be a big barrel of fun!

My only real problem, other than being 8,000 miles from you, is I'm still stuck in that oven of a room where I bake like I'm wrapped in tin foil all night every night.

Today is a special occasion; I'm exactly half way to being home! But, you know what is going to happen? As soon as I get back, they are going to send Scott. He's in medic school up in Washington right now and he and Nancy are still getting married at Christmas. Then, boom! Here he'll be in June or July. Ha. He didn't think could get drafted out of the Peace Corps. What a raw deal.

Even though we are no longer officially engaged, I'm still missing you, Parnelli, and I'm still hoping I get that transfer to AFVN in Saigon so I can come home early and then get out of the Army early. Then we'll have time to figure out how we really feel about each other... Until later... I'm still going to sign it

Love,

Curt.

PS: ISYL

Chapter 25

First day on a new job!

The Kid sat on a wooden stool with cup of coffee and a yellow legal pad in front of him, pen in hand, at the corner of the big glass topped layout table that acted like an island the middle of the PSYOPS Graphics department. In attendance at his first staff meeting as a permanent member of the DIMENSION team were the Chief, Bob Weston, Tom Boyett, Mark Birnbaum, Ron Edwards, Mike Imrem and Lou Wimbish.

"First order of business," the Chief began, pushing his glasses up onto the bridge of his sharp nose, "is to say good-bye to Lou as a member of the group. Now that Curt has been assigned as Assistant Editor, he will be writing 90% of the stories Lou has been covering and Lou is moving on, so to speak, but he will be writing *Battalion Happenings*" one last time.

The Kid frowned, "Uh, gee, Lou... it was not my intention to take your job..."

"Hey, no problem! In fact, I'd actually be leaving it right after New Year's anyway, since Paul is going to DEROS and I'm in line to become the new Head Clerk for the Battalion, so I won't have any spare time at all," he took a sip from his dark tan mug. "And I'll be sitting at Hoch's desk right outside, that is, if you need any pointers on grammar or punctuation or anything like that."

"Oh. Well then, congratulations!" the Kid smiled. "How nice!"

"Thanks. It's not like you're putting me out on the street!" said Lou, "Paul has a lot of stuff to show me before he goes and this was just something I was doing because I like to write."

"OK, now," the Chief consulted his notes, "Tom, you said you had a pretty good idea of what you're going to do for the Christmas cover, right?"

"Right."

"Then I won't worry about that," Everett checked it off his list. "All right, for stories, here's what I've got. We need one on the first anniversary

186

of the Battalion. December first is one year we've been in Can Tho… I'll probably write that one… And George and I are doing a two page spread on the Aid for Orphans and all that's happened off of that first article he wrote bout the Providence Orphanage. And I'm also assigning myself to do one on the Air Force Fifth Special Operations Squadron out at Binh Thuy. Mark…" he turned to Birnbaum, "how's your article on the Han-Giang going?"

"What's a 'Hang Eye anne?'" the Kid asked off the cuff.

"Hospital ship," said Mark, "got some really great pictures, the developing of which is about all I've got done so far. I'll have the first draft of the text done by Monday."

"Good. That's a two page spread as well," the Chief noted. "Moving right along, on the Company B stuff, I've got Lt. Soule doing an article on the delivery of leaflets by artillery rounds, for a half page, and Soule said he wanted to do something for Christmas, some kind of poem I think, that he is calling *'Home for Christmas.'* I haven't seen it yet, but Phil is pretty good, so I'm not worried about it. Plus, I'm putting that next to a piece I'm doing called 'Christmas in the 10th', so that'll take up two pages. Mike," Regan looked up to see if Imrem was paying attention, "your article on Lt. Powell is going to be two thirds of a page, OK?"

"OK," *Little Mike* made a note on his pad.

"Now, for new guy Curt… I'm thinking, along with the regular features, we're going to need a couple from you and one of them will have to be on Captain P. M. Smith being appointed as the new A Company Commander next week. Too bad we just did a story on him working in S-4, but what the hell, it isn't a good thing to ignore the new commander officer. I'm giving you two thirds of a page for that."

"OK," nodded the Kid, "sounds easy enough."

"Then, I want you to do a feature on Sgt. Curtis White", Regan continued, "he sings and plays the piano and he's just won one of the places in the AFVN talent search contest, that thing they're doing to find enough talent to have a TV series featuring GI's and I guess the winners are also going to tour the country and do shows for the troops, *ala Bob Hope.* Anyway, it's a good bio story."

"OK," the Kid said, writing *Curtis White,* on his pad.

"But Curtis *not white…* Curtis black," Tom, sitting next to the Kid, pointed at what he'd just written.

"Curtis White is black?" clarified the Kid.

"And who's on first!" added Birnbaum.

"He also speaks seven languages," the Chief regained control of the meeting, "he's just a real talented and real nice guy. You'll like him."

"Do you think you can remember his name...? Curtis?" grinned Tom.

"Yes. I think so. And where do I find him?"

"He's up in Saigon but he'll be back in a week or so," Regan continued, "at least in enough time for you to get the story done and for number three, you'll be writing the R & R Location Review for this month, on Singapore. I've got a whole folder full of travel brochures and guide books that you can use for that."

"OK. Piece of cake!"

"And Mark, you're doing the *Focal Point* this month, right?"

"Right, I'm this month and Ling-Fook is next month," Birnbaum confirmed, as he pulled out a Winston and lit up, causing a chain reaction around the table, of clicking Zippos and flaming butt ignitions. "Plus, a few of us are going on a shooting safari down by the waterfront after lunch; want to come along?" he turned to the Kid.

"Sure! That is, if I can find some film for the Polaroid at Eakin," said the Kid.

"Man o man," Birnbaum shook his head, "if you're going to work for this paper, we gotta get you something to shoot with other than a frickin' Polaroid. After all Polaroid is French for hemorrhoid, it being a piece of shit camera."

"But I like my Polaroid," the Kid insisted, "it's really good when there's not a lot of places around to get film developed. I figured that was a good way to go in the jungle."

"Yes, but that's not an issue here in Can Tho, there's a dozen places to get film developed. I'm getting a new Nikon and I'll sell you my Pentax SLR, if you're interested."

"Well, I don't know..."

"Curt... it's a great camera and I'll give you a great deal so you ought to at least take a look at it. You'll have a hundred dollars on payday, right? I'll give it to you now and you can pay me then," Birmbaum moved to close the deal. "With a Polaroid, you don't get a negative so there's very little you can do to edit a picture and we need flexibility here. The Pentax is really easy to operate and I'll show you how. You'll love it!"

"If it's so good, why are you getting rid of it?" the Kid questioned.

"Because I'm buying a Nikon," Mark smiled a mile wide.

"I can see radio guy has a lot to learn about photography! Buy the camera! You'll never regret it!" Boyett encouraged him.

"Well, that's all I have," Regan stood up and gathered his materials, "so shall we get some work done around here?"

As they all rose up from the table, the Kid tapped Mark on the shoulder, "OK, I'll buy the camera."

And Boyett was right. He never did regret it.

Chapter 26

It was sweat dripping hot inside the office of Captain Powell M. Smith, the 10th PSYOP Battalion's S-4 officer. The subject of the Kid's first story assignment had been hell to get an appointment with, what with him being the head of supply and the new Commanding Officer of A Company.

"Captain Smith is a real dynamo," the Kid pondered his editor's *prepatory comments, 'the story angle is his desire to do both jobs...'*

Another Captain Smith, the Kid thought as he observed PM examining the documents of a batch of newly arrived supplies. *I hope my experience with this one is smoother than the last one. Oh well, I will give him the benefit of the doubt until I see otherwise. One thing I do know... he's still the 'enemy' of all pot smoking enlisted men in this unit.*

PM's hair was black, uniformly cut to half an inch short and receding to high points around his oval face. His slight frame stood about 5'10 and the insignia on his left lapel revealed that he was commissioned as an artillery officer. *Hmmm, just like Wilson.*

"So you want to do an interview for the paper, huh?" Smith spoke what both of them knew very well to be the reason for his visit. "Well, I'm busy as hell, now that I'm going to still be head of S-4 for a while after I take over as A Company Commander... so if you want, you'll have to do it on the fly. I gotta drive over to the New Villa and then go out to Can Tho field so you can ride along as ask me anything you want."

"OK, Sir," the Kid smiled. He had purchased a small hardback notebook off the local economy, something intended to be a diary or some such and pulled it from his front lower cargo pocket, the same one that used to contain his marijuana cache in the field. "Just let me make a couple of notes before we go... so, your whole name is Powell M. Smith, right?"

"Yep."

"What's the "M" stand for?"

"Not telling."

*"OK."*And where are you from in the states, Sir?' the Kid's yellow pencil was poised, ready to begin scribbling down the details he needed to later write his story.

"I'm from Baton Rouge, Louisiana," he looked up and grinned, "you know, the home of LSU… Louisiana State University… which is where I attended college. It's also where Pistol Pete Marovich plays basketball… and incidentally, the Tigers have a good shot at winning the NCAA Tournament this year," he said as he picked up his keys and motioned for the Kid to head on out the door.

Outside the S-4 office, Smith's jeep was parked in a patch of shade to the right of the doorway and as they climbed in, the Kid switched from his regular glasses to his prescription shades while he continued to ask questions. "What year did you graduate, Sir?"

"1964."

"And what was it you got your degree in?" the Kid asked as Smith depressed the clutch, turned the key and brought the engine to life and put the gearshift into reverse to back out.

"I earned a Bachelor's degree in foreign languages," he was twisted in his seat to look behind in preparation to back out.

"Oh interesting… and what language was it you majored in?"

"I'm fluent in four languages, actually: Spanish, Italian, Portuguese and Romanian," he said as he took his foot off the clutch and lurched back, causing the Kid difficulty as he tried to write down his answer.

"Impressive!" *Impressive.*

"Well, sort of," Smith half chuckled as he pushed the gearshift into first and headed for the main highway, "Spanish, Portuguese, Romanian and Italian are all romance languages, based on Latin, and have a lot of similarities, so it wasn't as hard as it sounds."

As the pair drove toward the New Villa, through his answers to the Kid's questions, Smith revealed that he was 26, had a girlfriend back home he called his 'Cajun Queen,' named Jean Denechaud, he planned on attending the University of Wisconsin to get his master's degree and figured he would remain in the service and attend Army flight school and Officer's career school, pull his 20 years and be able to retire with a pension at the very young age of 43 and really begin to enjoy his life. *Long time to wait for enjoyment… 43 doesn't sound so young or seem so close when you're trying to live till tomorrow. 20 years of this bullshit? Cam fuckin' bao ya!*

191

They arrived at the New Villa and the Kid continued the interview as they walked past the Vietnamese guard and into the orderly room. "What do you identify as your top priority when you've assumed your new post as A company commander?" he asked.

Stopping right outside the hotel door, he didn't even ponder for a second before he blurted out, "My primary concern as the Commanding Officer of Headquarters Company is the personal welfare of the individuals in the company. I plan on having an 'open door policy' and I will be available every Tuesday, from 1600 through 1700 hours, to hear any suggestions or complaints that anybody might have."

Inside the moderately cramped office, they found First Sgt. Ozelle Jones, dressed in his customary shorts, army issue green T-shirt with his dog tags hanging out, sipping an iced tea from a tall pink plastic glass.

"And people like First Sgt. Jones here, will be required to wear their uniforms during duty hours," Smith laughed as Jones rose from his chair because an officer had entered the room.

"Good morning, Sir," Jones extended to him a reusable manila envelope closed by a figure eight tie clasp and pointed to a canvas bag sitting on the unoccupied clerk's desk, "There's the return movies in there all ready to go... do you know yet what the new one's are?"

"No, Sgt. Jones, I'll find out when you do because I'm not going to open the bag until I get back here," and turning to the Kid said, "hey, you could have a scoop, if you find out what the movies are and put it in the paper!"

"Uh," said the Kid, "we're a monthly, these movies will be long gone by the time we print for December."

"Say, Captain Smith," Ozelle picked up a hand fan and proceeded to augment the ceiling fan as the morning heat was beginning to collect in his office, "you're becoming a regular feature in that newspaper... wasn't there a story in there how you were runnin' supply just last month?"

"Yeah, I actually tried to discourage this one, but he insisted," PM shrugged toward the Kid.

"Yes, well, it wouldn't be right not to have a story since you are going to be both, head of supply and the new Company Commander, Sir. But I did read last month's story and I'd say it was actually more about supply itself and your men than you, Sir, " the Kid pushed his glasses back up his nose. So I'm kinda going for the human interest angle here, Sir, if you know what I mean, all the schooling, your girl friend and that you like basketball and stuff like that... and whatever else I find out."

"OK… but enough of this standing around, we gotta be there to meet the plane." Smith picked up the bag of movies that he would normally have had the enlisted man carry, but since the Kid was making notations in his notebook, the captain hoisted the load and lead the way.

Once back in the jeep, the Kid continued while Smith drove. "When were you commissioned, Sir?"

"In June of 1966," he talked loud enough to be heard over the din of the engine and the traffic moving around them, once they got out of the New Villa alley. "I did it through Artillery Officer's Candidate School. And OCS taught me I can do more things than I ever thought I could do,' he endorsed the experience like a salesman. "Like me still being in charge of supply when I take over at A Company. There was a time when either one of those two jobs would have intimidated me, but now, I know both of them have to be done so instead of worrying about if I can or can't , I just find a way to get it done."

As it turned out, the captain had acquired a ton of experience in the *getting it done* department, during his short military career. His first assignment had been with the Continental Intelligence Center at Ft. Bragg, NC, as an intelligence officer and company commander. After that, he went to the Panama Canal Zone as a member of the 8th Special Forces Group. It was an assignment he drove to so that he could visit all the countries of Central America on the way.

"In all," he summed up his travels and the jeep pulled into the parking area of Can Tho Airfield, 'I've been to 33 foreign countries and 39 states since entering the Army!"

After making the movie exchange and while driving back, the Kid further learned that while a member of the 8th Special Forces PM was both a PSYOPS officer and guerilla warfare trainer for soldiers from Guatemala, Bolivia and Ecuador.

He wrote two books in Spanish while in the Canal Zone, on propaganda and its applications, and also graduated from the Air Force Tropical Survival School, Jungle Operations School and Special Forces Para- SCUBA School.

Shit. Just listening to that laundry list and trying to write it down has made me tired! Let's see, that's all in addition to the PSYOPS Officer's course, Military Intelligence Officer's Course, Jump School and Jump Master School… I hope I don't leave any of them out! I'll say he's one well indoctrinated son of a bitch!

And when the Kid was being dropped off at Battalion HQ, he asked PM, as a humorous afterthought, what he like to do with his spare time?

193

"Golf, play Bridge, go diving in the sky or scuba… and I used to love riding my BMW motorcycle but I had to sell it when I came into the Army. There, have you got enough for a story, you think?"

"Considering that I could write a feature on the lead in this pencil OR just the part that sticks out… yes, I think I do," the Kid smiled, "Thank you very much, Sir, for working me into your busy schedule… I can see that, *'I don't have the time'*, is an excuse the men of A Company will have to strike from their repertory." He gave his new commanding officer a salute and after returning it, the Captain gunned his engine, popped the clutch and was gone.

Chapter 27

Diving off the side of the pool, the Kid's body sliced through the green hued water and he reveled in the coolness of being totally submerged in liquid. He let his body slowly rise to the surface and when it broke, he shook the water from his head and treaded, surveying the surroundings as best he could, without his glasses.

It was not large, by country club standards, maybe 30 by 60 feet and it had been made on the cheap, by dropping a heavy green rubber liner into a hole in the ground but the clever way in which the Sea Bees had surrounded it with some pretty nice cement decking, had transformed the Eakin Compound pool into an oasis. The shallow end was four feet deep and deep end was eight. Eight feet, that is, if the pool was filled.

At the head of the pool was a patio area in front of which sat four small round tables topped with faded cloth umbrellas. A barbecue grill made from a 55 gallon steel drum, cut in half the long way, sat at the ready and behind it, another half dozen picnic tables were situated beneath the corrugated tin roof that protected them from rain and the vicious tropical sun. There were no locker rooms; the men would just peel off their clothes and leave them laying on and around the tables. The Kid was wearing the shorts he'd made out of the APT uniform as his swim suit.

Reminders of the war still in progress were everywhere; at the far end of the pool, which was adjacent to the edge of the compound proper, a 7 foot tall wooden rail structure was hung and strung with multiple rolls of concertina barbed wire. It was accented by a 12 feet tall lookout tower manned by an ARVN guard with a machine gun. His back was to the pool as he vigilantly surveyed the perimeter.

This is so cool! Compared to hell with Wilson in the field, life here in Can Tho is bitchin' good! Steam bath and a job that requires not getting shot at and no heavy lifting. That court martial was a God send! He gripped the talisman hung around his neck with his fist. *Thank you, lucky Beaver nickel... and Captain Donald P. Ellis!*

The Kid gravitated to a spot where touching with his toes allowed him to be neck-deep in the water without the work of treading. *7th Heaven.*

"Incoming!" screamed Mc Caulley and Edwards as the pair in unison cannonballed off opposite sides, both landing not far from the Kid and their waves washed over him. A noon swim, the Kid had discovered, was part of the daily ritual for the crew of the graphics department, the staff of newspaper and most of the headquarters Battalion clerks.

The Kid was finally getting to know his comrades and the nature of life in the New Villa little better. Stewing in the chlorine like an ice cube in a drink, he observed the Tribe of which he had become a full fledged member. Considering the length of time it had taken for his trial to happen, technically he was the new kid but he felt like he'd been there forever! It was a highly educated group, much like the one he'd been in at DINFOS.

Paul Hoch was the recognized Tribe leader because being the head clerk of the unit, he actually possessed power. He could even change a duty roster. *When he leaves, Wimbish may get his plum job but what I want is to get his bunk. How do I get that bunk?*

The Kid chuckled as The Chief shoved Ernie back into the pool, preventing the much larger and well muscled soldier from climbing out of the shallow end. Although very unimposing in his white with black trim stretch boxer bathing suit, the spindly legged *"Chief"* had the total respect of his staff. And he associated with, roomed with and worked with pot smokers except he didn't smoke. He didn't care if somebody else did. He just didn't. Wouldn't turn somebody in for it and for reasons of intellectual association, he had found himself a member of the pot smoking sub culture.

Mark Birnbaum and Harold Ling Fook; the dueling photographers, were working together, trying to get a game of 'Marco-Polo going'.

"Marco", yelled Birnbaum.

"Polo", echoed Ling Fook.

How fitting; one of them is named Mark and one of them is half Chinese! "You guys ought to yell it 'MARKO- FOOK-O!"

With Ling Fook being from New York and Birnbaum from Baltimore, they argued about everything… **Yankees or Orioles … lobster or crab… Long Island Sound or Chesapeake Bay…** One point they totally agreed upon, however, was that the 'East Coast' had 'the take' on everything. Between Baltimore and Boston, they had it all. What Birnbaum really had was the ugliest plaid swimming suit the Kid had ever seen.

Then there was Boyett, who had been swimming laps doing a back float. He was the epitome of the quiet spoken, never flamboyant… always observant artist. Bob Weston was senior to Boyett, but even Weston knew who had the real talent. Tom's dark hair flattened wetly against the side of his head when he stopped swimming and stood up to check his waterproof watch. It was almost time to go back to work. The Kid was highly envious of Boyett's massive music collection, that he shared with the clan on his ultra Japanese and totally rad Teac reel to reel tape deck and he got regular new releases from a well placed friend in the states.

Richie Wells, a member of the printing crew, snuffed a cigarette in an ash tray on one of the round tables and took off his gold rimmed prescription sunglasses as he prepared to dive in for one last cooling splash before getting dressed. As a black man from Los Angeles, he was all about life on the cutting edge, especially when it came to music. His facial features were framed by thick and curly but short cropped black hair that framed a perfectly proportioned face of high cheek bones and a strong, very *European* chin, creating a distinctive kind of look that said surly, there has been a mixing of racial blood in this man. The Vietnamese maids, bar girls and hookers all went nuts over Richie. The Kid had met him in Boyett's room… *or did I meet Boyett in Richie's room? Or are Tom and Richie room mates? I still don't what the fuck is what here.*

The Kid could sense it was a strong group, smart and energetic with a bonding communal purpose; to live to make it home and see their loved ones again. And while waiting, and indeed, to ease the waiting, it was their *mission* to smoke as much of the best Asian cannabis as was humanly possible.

The combination of the Kid's combat experience, coupled with his refusal to allow himself to get roped into volunteering for APT and his victory at the court martial, along with his Nashville disk jockey experience, had catapulted the Kid instantly up to a level of high visibility, not only within the group, but throughout the whole unit.

And some of it was not good. Captain Ronnie Smith, for example, was the kind of redneck who cherished a good blood feud and the Kid knew he was still pissed that he'd been beaten like a rented mule at the court martial. If there was any way Smith could do him harm, he imagined he would do it.

At least I'm out of B Company. The Kid drew in a deep breath and made himself into a ball, floating knees to his chest with his hands wrapped around his legs, face down, surrounded by water with eyes closed tight but looking down at the point he always thought was the location of his third eye. Sound carried to him from other trooper's splash fighting in the shallow end of the pool and while bobbing like a float on the end of a fishing line, the Kid's mind cascaded through a series of thoughts.

Hoch's leaving right after New Year's… I gotta bet the room mates have a big say as to who moves in. Can't ask for it… that's the key to not getting it. Gotta be invited. Keep being friendly… telling jokes and stories… Ken Willert's the senior man; that's good… Ken and I are getting along. And Roger. Ramjet, he's funny. I wonder what his last name is. It would be fun to be his room mate. Might mention that and in the next breath how fucking hot it is down there night after night… If I got it, I could blow everybody's mind by giving it to George Gaugal! No… not a chance… oh God, how I want to get out of that room! I wonder why there are only three bunks in that room. Wonder if I'm up to 30 seconds yet… couldn't be 30 yet, I don't feel any burn. Next breath, I'll have to time it. This is like being back in the womb, floating suspended in a liquid universe… all totally unknowing of any outside world… a world full of good things… the Kid flashed on Flo's face. *And bad things,* he flashed on the three VC child-soldier prisoners… *Wally and the Beaver and the Girl Next Door,* bound and trussed and shoved to their knees in the paddies. *And good things!* He sees the interior of the Traveler's Motel and Flo, ready to receive him. *And bad things…* the image of the poncho blowing off Captain Robinson's decimated half of a body makes him break the ball and come up gasping for air while planting his feet firmly on the bottom of the pool.

Chapter 28

It was a typical night at the New Villa. Following their showers, the clan would attend mail call and then begin to congregating on the balcony of the third floor in front of Paul D, Ken and Roger's room and torch off joints and pipes full of enough cannabis to make a bonfire. *"Purple haze is in my brain...* "The voice and guitar licks of Jimmy Hendrix wailed from out of Richie Well's room, one door *south, as the super strong weed was passed among the group of a dozen GI smokers. Guys would come and go, but the total, this early in the evening, was* steady at about a dozen men toking away at any given moment, all under the protection of the Embassy gate keeper. If a lifer were to pass by, it might appear the keeper was merely waiting in line to use the john, or talking to somebody who lived in the first room but in practice, there was never a time when the pot smoker's backs were not covered. And within their sanctuary they were free to enjoy all of the el primo Asian weed they literally wished. It's relaxing, enveloping effects made it very popular. *There was so much pot floating around the unit, Thor Hyderdall could have built Kon Tiki Two out of it and had enough stuff left over to last him the entire voyage... yeah, that's what I'll say in my book,* the Kid thought, while holding a hit of Cambodian deep within his lungs.

"Some day I'd like to try LSD," Ron Edwards said, grooving out on the Hendrix, "I hear it's really different than smoking weed."

"It is," said the Kid, exhaling, "I'm up to about a dozen times. Hell, the first couple of times, it wasn't even illegal yet! And believe me, there's good and bad trips. That's what they call it, *'Tripping'.* What happens to you while you're high is like, your trip, your experience, *'a trip'.* One night I and some CU friends were high on acid and we ordered a pizza. And when it came, we opened it up and I looked at it and thought it was a road map and when I said that, the other guys started seeing shit like pepperoni towns and little lakes of grease and another guy said a green pepper looked like the outline of a bus and so we ended up tripping on the pizza! And God! Did it taste good? Senses are greatly heightened on LSD. Sex is fucking mind blowing!"

"Tripping you say," Edwards passed a joint to Willert, "conjugate; 'trip, trip and fall, trip and travel, take a trip, be tripped, be the tripped, tripper, or the trippee, tripping on a trip... or... tripping while tripping on a trip!"

"By jove, I think he's got it," the Kid says in his best Henry Higgins. "It's a different kind of experience, and yes, it's way fuckin' different than weed. It's really physical, you feel it through you whole body and then separately you go on a mind trip. On weed, you know if you want to lay down and go to sleep, no problem... however with acid, you want to lay down and go to sleep... *BIG problem!* You get these body rushes and you close your eyes and see things like fireworks as your heart pumps blood through your brain.

"But, I'll tell you one thing, the biggest rush I ever got off of anything in this life... so far... was off the adrenalin from the first time I got missed really close and felt heat off the bullet as it went right by my right cheek and ear and the rush that powered through my body, when I realized how close I'd come to being killed, was not one fraction short of a fucking amazing!"

"No!"

"Yes!" *Wilson, you bastard, one thing's for sure... I'll never have to make up a war story!*

As the Sun set on another day in-country, the view to the west of the Embassy was always the best. The balcony acted a lot like a coffee shop or student union with soldiers standing along its length, some with elbows resting on the tiled rail, and others using the rail as a table for their beers and other drinks. The only seating was on the one wooden bench that held three guys, beneath Hoch's window and a folding chair down at the corner.

The subjects of conversation ran the gamut from politics and sports to home, women and music and what each soldier's day had been like. But always, the conversation was just a few sentences away from turning into a slam fest of how much they all hated the Army and what they were going to do when they returned to civilian life back in the states.

FTA before the AF's U, was their motto; *Fuck the Army before the Army Fucks YOU!*

Once suitably high, the pot heads would gravitate up stairs to the Roof Club and entertain themselves by giving the *Lifer Drunks* a rough time while waiting for the evening movie to start. Within the contained environment, created out of the need to retire within a well fortified position, the two opposing Tribes played out the drama of their dynamically opposed life styles *every night.*

200

New Villa housed all of the 10th PSYOP Battalion's enlisted men from E-1 through E-9 so there were a few older, more experienced sergeants who were very professional and did not drink to excess so not all the Lifers were drunks. But a quick census confirmed that well over half of them *were.* The rest of their number could as easily have been red neck southern draftees or volunteers or hard nosed Iowa farm boys, not real Lifers, but *Lifers in sympathy,* at the very least.

An accurate ball park estimation would have been; three quarters of non-pot smoking portion of the population of the New Villa was totally smashed by 2000 hours on any given night. And drinking to pass out was much more of an *'MO'* than it was a style statement.

Suffice to say, the polarity between the two groups was nothing short of monumental. The Drunk Lifer camp was anti-marijuana, anti-hippie, anti-peace, pro gun, pro war, pro army, pro liquor, pro stock car racing, pro country music and pro their country... *right or wrong.*

The Pot Heads, on the other hand, were anti-war, anti-army, anti-military, pro marijuana, pro peace, pro civilian life, pro rock and roll, pro grand prix racing and known to drink beer. They were pro their country, without a doubt, but not *right or wrong.* If the country was doing something wrong, they were bloody fucking well going to stand up and say something about it!

The Lifers were at a terrible disadvantage because they were drunk. For some reason, people who drink think being stoned on pot is the same. But it's not. Simple fact of life: It is easy to tell when a drunk is drunk. But, a straight person *or an especially a drunk straight person,* is incapable of determining if a pot head is stoned or not. When you are drunk, you are worthless. *Admit it, all you drunks.* But, when high on pot, a pot head can still think and reason and their physical dexterity is not only uncompromised it is in many ways enhanced. For the Pot Heads, the *Drunk Lifers were sem sem easy pickins* and they proceeded to generally beat them in every form of contest from ping pong to Parcheesi, Monopoly to Stratego and dominos, darts and every other game that was supplied to the unit by the USO. *If this place only had a pool table, it would be next to perfect!*

One of the most interesting aspects of the polarity between the Pot Heads and Lifers was that the Pot Heads moved freely in the Lifer's world of the Roof Club while no Lifers or their sympathizers were allowed penetrate the Embassy when *the issue* was hot. In reality, most Lifers were never even aware it existed. It was as if the Embassy were in a parallel universe.

Up for a beer and waiting for service, the Kid gazed out among the dozen or so tables that filled much of the area between the bar and the large movie screen at club's north end. The 12 ft. tall and 15 ft. wide gecko-covered surface was said to be the largest movie screen in Can Tho. Throughout the club, soldiers were reading and writing letters, playing cards and of course, drinking while waiting for the movie to start.

A lectern, used by command to conduct meetings and deliver lessons in mandatory training classes, was pushed to one side in anticipation of the night's film, *Hello Dolly,* one the Kid really didn't care if he saw or not.

The corrugated tin and Plexiglas roof, from which the club took its name, did not cover the entire top of the old French hotel. Immediately outside of the bar area, at the south end of the club, was an area still exposed to the sun during the day and the stars at night. The main water cistern for the hotel took up much of the area's left side. From it, water pressure was created to run the showers on the floors below and the slanted roof was cleverly designed to drain water into it. This worked great during the wet season but a pump truck would arrive almost every day during the dry season to fill it so the members of the unit could maintain personal hygiene.

'Hey, Curt,' the Kid turned to see the Chief standing behind him with a black staff sergeant, still dressed in his fatigues. "This is Sergeant Curtis White, the winner of the Armed Forces Radio talent contest I was telling you about. Curtis, meet Curtis!" he said to his own thorough amusement. "Curtis is going to do a story on your experience in the talent contest for the unit newspaper, Curtis!"

"Hi Curtis, pleased to meet you!" the Kid shook his hand.

"And hi back at you… Curtis," Curtis White grinned.

"Buy you a beer?" the Kid offered as RV Smith stood in front of him, signifying it was his turn to order.

"OK, sure."

"Two beers de jure, please, RV," the Kid said as he put down a MPC fiver.

"Two dee jeers beers… say what?" questioned RV, with a screwed up look on his jowly face.

"That's French, for beer of the day," Sgt. White translated for him.

"Well, I don't know about that, you'll just have to take what we've got, which today is Budweiser," said RV as he opened two cans and made change.

"I'll leave you two to talk," Chief said bowing out and went over to sit at a table with Weston and Ling-Fook.

"Well, shit fire, we might as well just do the interview, if that's OK with you," the Kid suggested, handing White one of the beers.

"Fine by me," the slightly built sergeant took a sip of the Bud.

I'll be dammed if he doesn't look a little like Nat King Cole. "Great, here; if you'll take my beer over to that table, I'll run down to my room and grab a note pad and a pen and let's see if we can knock it out before the movie starts… we've got a half an hour, at least."

"OK," he smiled.

Back in a flash, the Kid sat down and began. "Now, some standard *peripherals*, what's your full name?"

"That would be Curtis E. White," he replied.

"E-6 Curtis E. White. How about that? You're 'Curtis E… and I'm Curtis *Lee!* Curtis is a pretty popular name for black guys, wouldn't you say?" the Kid paused, waiting for an answer as the sergeant pondered the question.

"In fact, it is," he finally agreed with the Kid after apparently figuring in his head how many he might know.

"And I'm named after one of them," the Kid smiled.

"Oh, really?" that caught White's interest, "how so?"

"Yeah, really. But not actually on purpose," began the Kid's explanation, "I was supposed to be a girl, for some reason, they were totally sure of it and my parents were going to name me *'Sandra Sue Stocker.'* So when I turned out to be a boy, they didn't have any boys' name picked out. They argued about it and couldn't agree and it went on for a couple of weeks. Finally, the hospital called and said, 'Mr. Stocker, you have to name that baby right now, because we have to send his birth certificate in to the state tomorrow!' So my Dad grabs the Omaha phone book, flips it open, closes his eyes and puts his finger on the name, 'Curtis, Lee'… the Guy's name was Lee Curtis, but in the book, with the last name first, it was Curtis Lee, so he says, 'name him Curtis Lee Stocker.' Then a couple of months later, he got curious and called the number to see who I was named after and he said 'a *Negro sounding man'*, answered the phone, so I'm named after a black man who lived in South Omaha!"

"Ha. That's pretty funny," White smiled, "did he talk to him?'

"I guess not, the way he tells the story, he says he got 'tongue-tied' and didn't know where to start so he just kind of blurted, 'oops, sorry, wrong number,' and hung up. And where did you grow up?" the Kid got back to business.

"Philly. Lived there all my life before joining the Army."

"Uh huh," the Kid wrote it down, "and being a staff sergeant, you've been in the Army for more than one hitch, I would conjecture…"

"Right, I've been in for eight years now and I've just started my third hitch.

"Uh huh," the Kid scribbled away, "and where did you go to school?"

"Well, I started out and Mansfield State Teacher's College in Philly and from there, I went to the Eastman School of Music, at the University Rochester and finally, to Temple in Philly."

"Oh yeah? Were you there when Bill Cosby was?"

"No." White cracked a broad grin, "*everybody* asks me that."

"I bet," the Kid stopped writing, "his bit about playing football for Temple is pretty fuckin' funny, looking' out the ear hole of the helmet! Ever heard that record, *'Why is there Air?'*"

"Hundreds of times… *To blow up basketballs, volleyballs and footballs, any PE major knows that…,*" White quoted the punch line to the comedy album's title question.

"Right… so, how old are you?"

"28."

"And when did you start playing the piano?"

"When I was five."

"Five, huh? Did you parents kinda push you into it?"

"No, not at all. I didn't need any coaxing," the sergeant responded, "while other kids were passing notes around in school, I was writing down melodies that were going through my mind. Ever since I can remember, the music has just been there. I guess you could say I had the knack. After I learned piano, I went on to learn all the string instruments and then some of the bigger horns, like the baritone and the tuba."

The Kid thought of his youthful musical experience as he took notes. When he was 12 and brother Scott was 14, their parents bought a Hammond Organ and pushed them both into taking lessons. He hated it at the time and made his parents let him quit after one year only to later become greatly disappointed in his inability to master an instrument. *I am so jealous of you!* "What styles of music are your favorites?"

"When I was young, we always had music in the house but there was not the kind of contemporary pop there is playing on the radio today. I've always loved classical piano because I heard a lot of it early on but I've played in all kinds of jazz bands, dance bands and combos for everything from proms to chamber quartets and been in and started dozens of bands. Say, you're a disc jockey, right? Isn't that what I heard?"

"Right."

"Well to give you an idea, back then, *'Mockingbird Hill'*, was a big popular hit on the radio and everybody used to listen to the Grand Ole Opry."

"I've always admired musical ability but alas, playing other people's music to other people looks about as close as I'm going to get." The Kid looked down to his notes, "and you say *'all the string instruments?'*"

"Yep. All of them," he ticked off on the finger of his left hand; "violin, cello, base, guitar, banjo, mandolin, you show me a string instrument, with a bow or something you strum or pick… and I can play it."

"Jesus…That's impressive!" exclaimed the Kid. "So you've pretty much made a living playing music, huh?"

"Pretty much. I've played in groups that performed all over the country, especially in the south and east. You'll be amused by this, I once played at a Governor's Luncheon for Governor Maddox, of Georgia."

"That's wild!" the Kid wrote it down, *I'll use that for sure.* "OK, now explain to me, Sergeant; you've got a music background and you've won a talent contest to play on armed forces TV, how is it you come to be stationed in a PSYOPS unit? How come you're not in the Army band or something like that?"

"Well, I was," White paused to take a drink of his beer, which was warming rapidly in the hot tropical evening air and to wipe a small bit of sweat from his brow. "For most of my eight years I was in the music branch of the Army as a member of the 3rd Army Band, in Atlanta, Georgia. This is the show band for the Army. Our standard issue consisted of two tuxedos, two dinner jackets, and white shirts, blazers of different colors, shoes and ties. We played all over the country for different types of events and occasions. Dinner parties at Officer's Clubs were always great!"

The Kid flipped to a new page in his ledger. "All right, that's half, now how did you end up in PSYOPS and what is your assignment in the 10th?"

205

"I guess it all started when I signed up for Army Language School. I was waiting to enter a course on Arabic when it came back through channels that the school I wanted was full for the next term and they gave me three choices: to forget it entirely, to wait for the next class to start in which I would have priority or to go and take what was available right then. So I went… and Vietnamese just happened to be available."

"No way. Imagine that! I follow you so far," the Kid injected as White paused for the pause that refreshes once again. "Now, I hear you speak a number of languages, which is really strange, because one of the other stories I'm doing for the next issue is about Captain PM Smith and he speaks four. How many do you speak?"

"Seven," he calmly said, "fluently."

"Wow. What are they?"

"Spanish, French, Italian, Russian, Portuguese, German and now, Vietnamese."

"I see," wrote the Kid, "and English is eight, Canadian is 9, Australian is 10 and New Zealand is 11… Latin or pig latin?" the Kid pointed his pen at White.

"No!" White laughed.

"OK, then I'll just put down *speaks* 11 languages… and you're on a field team, right now, aren't you?"

"Yes. MACV Team 71, in Soc Trang, filling a translator-Interpreter slot and I'm loving it! I never really felt like I was in the Army when I was playing in the band, but I sure as hell know it now! And after being out in the field for a few months, I had a real desire to get back into the entertainment side of the Army!"

"That's pretty funny!" the Kid rapidly drummed his pen on the table, "I felt the same way about getting into another field of work while I was stuck out in the boonies as a foreign language announcer with no loud speakers in Tra Vinh and Cang Long! So you heard about the AFVN contest, *"Operation Star Search,"* over the spots on Radio Saigon and then what happened?"

"I sent in my information and with all my experience and record in the Army show band and all, they arranged an audition right away."

"Cool. So you get out of the field and get a trip to Saigon to do music. I've got some friends at AFVN Radio, did you meet any of the radio staff?"

"Uh, no. This talent search thing is being done by the TV station and doesn't have anything to do with radio."

"Oh. OK. Then, this trip you just made up there was your tryout?"

"Yes," the Sgt. Nodded.

"And was it like a competition… did you meet any of the other competitors or did you have an appointment or how did they do it?"

"Well, it was more like an audition than anything. They said they wanted to get enough talent to make a few tapes and have a TV show run at least once a week and they also are planning to put together a tour of bases around the country. I played a bunch of stuff, a little of this and a little of that and they said they liked it a lot and invited me back up in January to make a tape!"

"Far out! And what about the tour?" the Kid looked up.

"I don't know yet. They didn't say," the Sergeant sighed, "but what the hell, I don't care. I get it or I don't. I figure when I'm up there making the tape they might discuss the touring thing. They said it also had to do if a soldier was critical in his position and could be spared or not and crap like that, so only time will tell."

"Yes, about so many things," *I'm done here. I'll bet with him being a musician, he smokes pot, but he's an E-6, so I can't even ask.* "Well, I think I've got enough to write the story. If I don't, I'll just make some shit up."

"That'll work."

"So you ought to enjoy the movie tonight, I hear it's a musical," the Kid said as he picked up his stuff and prepared to move to where most of the clan had settled and was waving him over. "You can join us if you want."

"Thanks, but I've got a bunch of letters to write to my wife and kids."

"OK, Curtis, Evertt said he had a picture of you at the piano that he took before you went to Saigon, so I guess we've got all we need," the Kid shook his hand, "I'll try to make sure and get you a couple extra copies of the paper to send home when you're in it because it'll be easy making you look good!"

"All right," White flashed a friendly smile, "I'm looking forward to reading it."

After the movie, the Pot Heads drifted back down to the Embassy and fired up the joints again to renew their buzzes. Then, as sure as a cloud of locusts descending on a crop of Egyptian wheat, the Tribe would experience the nightly attack of the *raging fuckin' bad munchies!*

Of course, as prisoners in the New Villa, and with the curfew in the streets of Can Tho, because you could still get shot out there, it wasn't like they could jump in their jeeps and drive downtown to McDonalds for a snack. Instead, munchies time success or failure quite frequently depended on what had arrived to the soldiers from home that evening at mail call.

Some nights, it reminded Kid of a passage by Thomas Wolf, in *Look Homeward Angel*. Other nights, it brought to mind the movie Tom Jones or a Roman Orgy and still other nights, when all of the goodies sent in care packages from home got broken out and the pot saturated clan tore into it, shared it and passed it around, it reminded him of a Loony Tunes cartoon where the Tasmanian Devil freaking eats everything in sight!

"Look at all these Twinkies!" John Tearman, a tall lanky troop from Indiana pulled up a half dozen packages of the twin sponge cakes with the white creamy filling. "Good things these Twinkie torpedoes don't need to be refrigerated. I think they're fucking bullet proof!

"Somebody get out a sterno and the rack, I got some more Jiffy Pop today!" called Barry Fisher as he left to go to his 2nd floor room to retrieve it for popping on the Embassy bench, suspended above the little fire on a wire coat hanger frame, custom made for just that purpose; we got a lot of Jiffy pop.

"Mary Janes, anyone?" Boyett held up a handful of the hard pink taffy suckers, making everybody laugh, "Or would you all rather just suck on some more Mary Jane?" *Laughs all around. Mary Jane suckers... Ha! Good line. Wish I'd thought of it.* "This is my friend Carl's idea of a joke."

The music played, the pot was smoked and the sugar was consumed as the clan passed the evening, sweating in the tropical heat, until slowly, one at a time, they vanished off the balcony to go to bed or write letters or gravitate back up to the roof to see what's going on and maybe get another beer before last call a night. *And in the hot, tropical heat of the Delta, another day melted away. Yeah, that's what I'll say in the book.*

Chapter 29

The gecko rested at eye level on the outside of the screen wall that made up one side of the hallway that connected the graphics room with the rest of battalion headquarters. This being the far side of the Headquarters building, the white wall of the neighboring structure was only six feet away. Kid spotted the diminutive lizard as he came out of the room, on his way up front to the ice water cooler to get a nice cold drink.

Reaching up, he tapped it to knock it off but much to his surprise, the screen acted like a trampoline and it shot the gecko across the span where it stuck to the white vertical surface of the other building, much like a cat landing on its feet, where it scurried off.

Far out! Seeing another one further down, he did the same thing; tapped it with enough force to send it shooting between the two buildings, doing flips, to where it also stuck to the wall. *Cool! A flying lizard circus!* Seeing a third gecko, he did the same thing with the same results.

Emerging in the main part of the HQ office, he peered down the row of four desks that were lined up, facing outward, each a station at which a clerk or officer occupant worked. It was 0945 hours and the Kid had been writing on his Sgt. White story when he realized he wanted a drink from the orange cylindrical Gott water cooler that sat on one end of the filing cabinets that made up an island running down the middle of the elongated front office area.

Every morning, Bud Miller, the unit mailman, would deliver the container filled with ice water to headquarters, where it was appreciated by all until it was empty, usually before lunch, so he'd always fill it again for the afternoon. A drink of ice water any time he wanted it was one luxury the Kid had never found anywhere in the field so this was one of life in Can Tho's best little 'perks'.

As he stood there, sipping his second refill from the small white conical paper cup, he chanced to overhear a comment from a discussion taking place between Paul Hoch and 1st Lt. Harry Regan, whose desks were behind him, right next to each other.

"Intelligence reports are coming in saying that the VC are planning an offensive, like Tet, for Christmas," said Lt. Regan, with a worried look etched into his face.

"Shit. And I don't get to go home until the first week in January! Fuck!" exclaimed Paul D, "this is going to greatly piss me off if this interferes with my DEROS!"

"How solid are those reports?" the Kid jumped into their conversation.

"Well," Regan said, "they look pretty real. Traffic and references to it have picked up in the last couple of weeks, which is what's making everybody so nervous.

"Fuckin' A... I wish there was some way I could get the hell out of Dodge and not be here for Christmas," Paul chagrined.

"Yeah!" responded the Kid, "me too!"

"You could," answered Paul to the surprise of the Kid, "you've been here for over six months, and you could always go on R & R."

"How would I do that? I have in for R & R to Australia but because it's so popular, I can't go until February and it's my understanding there's no way to hurry that up," lamented the Kid.

"Not if you go to Australia, but you could always switch it off to somewhere else where you could go with no notice," smiled Paul.

"There is such a place?"

"Yep. Kuala Lumpur," said Paul, "I could switch you off Australia and book you into Kuala Lumpur in a heart beat. It's wide open, there's no waiting list and you can go there just about at the drop of a hat, as soon as next week."

"Really?"

"Really, Stocker."

"OK," the Kid had a gut feeling on this one, "then do it!"

Opening a drawer and pulling out an R & R request form, Paul twisted the sheet into his typewriter and began banging away while asking questions, "Name... rank... serial number... Date arrived in-country... request for R & R to Kuala Lumpur for, let's see, you could go from December 22nd until December 29th, that would get you out of the country for Christmas, until right before New Years'... do it for sure?'

"Yes. Do it!"

210

"OK," said Paul, who had the request completed in no time. "I'll just get Captain PM Smith to sign this and you'll be all set! Fuck I wish I could go with you."

"Well, fuck… I wish I could go home with you on January 7th," responded the Kid, "so I guess we're even!"

Just then, a soldier emerged from the stairwell and stopped to look around the HQ area like he was lost. It took the Kid a couple of seconds to realize who it was and in that instant, the trooper also had a lucid memory about the Kid.

"Hey… *I know you!*"

It was Stoney, his Saigon driver from when he'd gone to Group to get new glasses. He had apparently finally achieved his goal of getting out into the field. "Stoney? Is that you?"

"Sure as shit is… how ya doin' Kid?"

"Well well, you finally got your wish to get out of Group!" the Kid went over and shook his hand, "… congratulations, welcome to the 10th!"

Stoney smiled. "I hoped I'd run into you right away."

The Kid knew why Stoney hoped that, but he wasn't about to enunciate it in a room full of officers and non-coms. True to his name, Stoney would be looking to get stoned, of course. "Cool enough, man. Ya'll can drop by my room… I'm on the third floor you can't miss it."

"Man o man!" Stoney seemed pretty excited, "I've finally made it to the field!"

Paul looked up from his paperwork and chuckled over the comment, "This may not be 4th Group in Saigon, but soldier, and you've still got a ways to go to get out into the *'field'*.

"Whatever," Stoney responded, "all I care about is getting out of Group!" he proclaimed with a broad smile on his lightly freckled Irishman's face, "I so fucking hate that place. I don't care what happens to me down here, it's gotta be more exciting than Group in Saigon. I'm psyched… I want to see some action! I've been to the war and I ain't seen no war yet. *I want to see some war.*"

On the way back to his desk in the Graphics room, the Kid found another three geckos on the screen and as he walked by, he tapped them all and made them summersault across to the other building and again, all of them hit with their feet and stuck to the wall. *Cool!*

"Hey, guys," the Kid walked into the room, "I know I've only been working here for less than three weeks, but I'm going on vacation!"

"Say what?" Boyett looked up from the piece of work he was laboring over.

"I was just up front getting a drink and I over head Lt. Regan and Paul talking about some Intelligence reports that there's going to be a VC offensive at Christmas and I found out I could be out of the country if I picked to go on R & R to Kuala Lumpur... so I did! I just dumped Australia in February and changed to Malaysia for the week of Christmas... so I'll be out of here that week!"

"All right," the Chief stood next to his desk, "just make sure you've got your work done before you leave."

"Or what?"

"There is no 'or what', just make sure you have all your stories in, OK?"

"Sure Chief. No problem. I'm a team player... I won't let you down!"

"But you don't want to be with the team if the VC go on the offensive, at Christmas, it that it?" Ron Edwards sarcastically questioned.

"Uh, no, I'm still a team player, but if I can find a way to miss some unpleasantness, I'm sure as hell going to do it! What's wrong with that?"

"Nothing, I guess," said Ron, "we're all going to be more than a bit jealous if Intelligence turns out to be right and we get attacked with you out of town!"

"Well... xin loi," said the Kid, "I've paid and repaid my combat action dues already! Hey... look what else I found out when I walked up front!" he motioned for Tom, Ron, Bob and the Chief to follow him into the hallway.

"See that gecko there?" the Kid pointed to one of four lizards that were now on the screen, "watch this!" he went up and tapped the reptile, sending it flying through space to the wall opposite where it stuck like a dart in a dartboard.

"Oh wow!" they all exclaimed together!

"That's too cool!" chortled Ron, "let me try one!" And he did. "Look! It's the gecko Air Force!"

Then Tom did one, too, followed by the Chief. It was quite a sight watching the flying lizards stick to the wall.

After that, anytime somebody from graphics walked up or down the hallway and saw a gecko, they'd bounced him across the way to the other building. And damned if it didn't seem like when we started doing that, the number of geckos hanging out on the screen wall dramatically increased... *as if they all actually like it! Pavlov only had to beat his lizard a couple of times... yeah, that's what I'll say in the book!*

Chapter 30

The 707 Jet was far less than half full. The reason the Kid, or any GI in Vietnam, could go to Kuala Lumpur at the drop of a helmet was that it was the least attractive of all the places an American soldier had to pick from for an R&R destination and there was always room at the inn for some more GIs in KL.

The married *and engaged* men all liked to take R&R in Hawaii, where their wives and girl friends could meet them without a passport, usually sans kids. Everyone else much preferred Bangkok, Tokyo, Hong Kong or… the Big One, *Australia,* where the women and the beaches were supposed to be the greatest of all.

That's why a soldier had to wait 9 months, almost until the end of his tour, if he wanted to take his five day's of R&R in Australia; the list was frickin' jammed packed and nobody ever cancelled.

Except the Kid. He'd gotten up at 0700 hours to catch his ride, from the 4th PSYOP Group HQ, out to Ton Son Nhut for a 0830 hours check in. He'd packed all the gear he figured to need in one bag, the black valise sort of a deal that he'd bought from Taj. Other than his shaving kit, it's contents and his Army issue green boxer shorts, everything in the bag; two civilian shirts, a pair of slacks, his pair of APT shorts, three pairs of socks, flip flops, and a pair of tennis shoes, he'd also purchased from Taj. *I can hardly wait to walk around in a town in civilian clothes and not see anybody in any kind of a uniform.*

The plane departed at 0900 hours and the flight, southeast across the Gulf of Thailand from Vietnam to Malaysia, was just a little short of an hour and a half long. Tilting back his seat, the Kid shut his eyes and his mind began to wander.

I gave up Australia to be out of the country for Christmas… I can't believe it. But still, I had that feeling. If I stayed and they did the offensive and I got killed… ha… and while I don't want them to have an offensive back in Vietnam while I'm gone… just so my premonition can be right… if those fucking little VC bastards let me down and don't so much as have even some kind of a little pop gun offensive, I'll be pissed! No. That's stupid thinking. I don't want anybody to be attacked! If I hadn't walked out when Paul and Lt. Regan were talking about the intelligence report saying there'd be a holiday offensive, I probably wouldn't even have heard about it at all. Never heard about it again. I wonder if this is their idea of a joke. But here I am on the plane to Malaysia of all freaking places. No changing it now. Oh God, my tour is exactly seven months done tomorrow. I'm getting close to going under 150 days! Plus being in Can Tho and working for the newspaper is almost as good as R & R every day! I sure don't miss that crazy shit with Wilson. This will be nice. No matter where it is. Now my 1049 might be approved when I get back from this! Damn, that would be some good news for the folks back home. If the transfer goes through and I get the drop, when I get back from R & R, I'll be under a hundred days! And I'll get back six months of my life! A year in Saigon will be a freaking walk in the park! Gee, I hope I can get a call through to Flo and talk to her. That will be my Christmas present to myself.

Eyes closed, his hand went to the breast pocket of his fatigues and he extracted her picture, held it in front of his face and then opened his eyes and for ten seconds, drank in her beauty. Closing them and put the picture back into his pocket, she *must be the one. Why would I feel this way if she wasn't? The way our paths crossed. Is it preordained? Or now that we aren't engaged, will we ever really be together again? It's incredible that her presences could have so quickly and totally derail the four year thing I had with Donna. Why do I get involved in all of these long distance relationships anyway? Seem like almost all my life I've only wanted the girl who was too far away to really have. Why is that?*

Scott and Nancy are getting married in a couple of days. Too bad I can't be there for that. There goes our deal to be the best man at each other's weddings. Another casualty of the war. Oh well, that's OK, Scott, a man's gotta do what a man's gotta do. Ooh! I could call WKDA and be put on the air from the other side of the world! Yeah! Wait a minute, I better find out how much international phone calls cost first.

"'Scuse me a second, specialist," the Kid's introspection was interrupted and opening his eyes, a staff sergeant stood in the aisle, a slightly skinny dirty blond haired fellow with slightly bucked teeth, whose name tag said Powers. "I got some paperwork stuff to discuss with ya…"

"OK Sarge."

"I don't know how much money you brought but you'll need to change it over into Malaysian money at the R&R center, at the Tropicana Hotel where we give you the arrival briefing, so here's a form to declare that.

215

You'll pay for your week of hotel with MPC however, at the R&R center, before you go check in. The Army handles all of that for you. And here's an information sheet on Malaysian drug laws, from the Malay government, that we give to all the troops... they're pretty strict about it here... in fact, they don't mess around at all and if you get caught by their police doing something you shouldn't, we won't be able to help you."

"All right, Sarge, that won't be a problem."

"That's good," he said, "and this here is a sheet that says you aren't bringing in any foreign fruits or animals or diseases or any of that shit. Just check no and sign this one. Uh you don't have any fruit... do you?"

"No, Sarge, no fruit."

"OK. Just checkin'. That's my job," the Sgt smiled, trying to be loose funny and friendly. "You're gonna like it here. Get a chance to relax, the girls here are real nice and they all speak English since this was a British colony and it was the official language up until last year. A girl will run you $15 a night and we recommend the girls who will be in the hotel bars because they're all health inspected and have to be clean or we don't let'em work. Each hotel has a mama san who runs the girls and you'll pay her for your girl's services."

"Now that is nice to know."

"Yeah, if you get one you like, you can keep her the whole five nights or you can do what I like to do, and that is try a different one every night. When we get in, we'll clear customs and we have busses to take you over to the Tropicana Hotel, where the R&R support office is. The arrival briefing takes about 20 minutes, it's on the local customs, the town and the hotels. Then you pick the one you want and pay for it, then we bus you over, you check in and you're on your own until time to go back and we pick you up at your hotel the morning of your flight!"

"Sound great!" the Kid smiled and dropped the tray down in front of him upon which to complete the forms. He'd set aside $250 for his trip. "Hey, Sarge, how much do phone calls to the US cost?"

"Uh, it runs about a dollar a minute... ten minutes, ten dollars. One hour, $60.00; you could have a girl yank your tool for four days and nights for the cost of a one hour call to the 'World'. Any more questions? I'm here to help!"

"No, thanks for the information, Sarge."

Probably won't call WKDA...and I'll have to keep the Flo call to under half an hour. That is, if I can get through to her at all.

Peering out the window, the Kid spied the coast of Malaysia. Most noticeable to him, as the jet descended upon its arrival over the land mass was that the terrain below looked a lot like Vietnam *except there are no craters from bombs being dropped.*

Leaning back in his seat and closing his eyes, the Kid recalled the visit he'd paid to Alan P. before his departure. He'd gone over to AFN to see how his 1049 was progressing. It hadn't been approved yet, so he was getting a little on the nervous side. Then Master Sergeant Shamus said he could speed things up and give it a more positive spin if he sent a letter over to 4th PSYOP Group, actually stating the Kid had passed their audition and requesting his transfer. *That little document is going to seal the* deal, the Kid was convinced.

On final approach, the Kid observed that the airport had no protective concertina wire and machine gun bunkered berm surrounding it and compared to the activity at Ton Son Nhut, the place was quasi deserted.

Passing through Malaysian customs was done in a flash. They hardily looked into anybody's luggage, which in and of itself, was sparse as most of the soldiers, like the Kid, possessed only a single carry-on bag.

The bus ride from the airport to the R&R Center at the Tropicana Hotel, in the middle of the city, took 15 minutes and soon, the 60 to 70 odd vacationing warriors were sitting down in an air conditioned room at white cloth covered tables and complimentary Foster's beers were being placed in front of them by burgundy jacketed waiters. *So far, so good!* The Kid took a swig and looked at his watch; it was almost exactly noon as a black and bald civilian-clad American walked up to the lectern and threw the switch, activating the mike.

"Welcome to Kuala Lumpur, Gentlemen," the well muscled man began with a broad smile, show his pearly white and perfect teeth, "My name is *Captain Arnold,* and I am one of your R&R Center liaisons, here to help you with anything you might need during your stay with us. I think you'll find your experience here will be very relaxing. Nobody is going to be shooting at you and you don't have to do anything while you're here but have a good time and I think we've got a set up conducive to just that. OK… first order of business… I'm pretty sure all of you got the message that the Malay government frowns on drugs of any kind in their society. Now, I know how loose things are over in the Nam and I strongly advise you that if you are carrying any weed, or heaven forbid you have any opium, you go to the john and flush it right now before you leave this building. And don't even think for a second about trying to score anything while you're here. The result could be a long jail term and when you get out, the Army will bust you for desertion and put you in jail all over again and then give you a dishonorable discharge. *I don't think I can make it any clearer than that.*" The Captain looked over his group to insure everybody got the message.

"Also," the Captain said rather loudly, "while you are here on R&R, you do not, under any circumstances, discuss your unit, your mission or your job or any of your war zone activities with anybody who is not a member of the US Armed Forces! Is that clear?" he called for an indication of comprehension.

"Yes Sir," the group lamely complied.

"That being said," he smiled, "we've only got a few things we need to discuss before you are bussed to your hotels and you can start doing what it is you GI's all like to do on R&R... and I can assure you, there are lots of really pretty girls here in KL to do it with or to, if you get my drift!"

"Rah rah yeah woo hoo!" an enthusiastic fervor ran through the group.

"Behind me on the screen, we are going to run through the five hotels you have to choose from for your stay." And with that, the Captain quickly conducted a color slide tour of the choices, all about the same in regard to amenities and quality of rooms and all similar in price: from $8.00 to $10 per night. "Make your choice, fill out the yellow card in front of you, with the hotel name, your name, rank and serial number and put your MPC on the card. We have change if you need it."

The Kid picked the Merlin, one of the $8 hotels. *The air conditioning and the pool sound magical,* he silently one-lined to himself, since he was not conversing with any of the other soldier in the group. As the men worked through the process, the Kid studied them; it looked like a few of them might possibly be in small groups of three or four or with one other buddy, but most were like him; obvious lone wolfs for purposes of this trip.

"One option you have here, is taking a bus trip down to Singapore. Although it is part of Malaysia, it is very interesting and almost like a world of its own. Also, if any of you are going to take advantage of the incredible tailors they have here, and order a custom made suit, which will only cost you about $40.00, I advise you to get your tailoring measurement done the first day, like today, or they might not finish your duds before it's time to leave. And you don't want them to try and mail you anything from here to your APO because you'll never get it." He gazed around the room, "any questions?"

No.

218

It was just past 1300 hours when the Kid stepped off the bus in front of the Merlin Hotel. The staff was ready and quickly processed in the dozen GIs who had chosen to stay there. When the bellhop opened the door to his room on the fifth floor and ushered him in, he was pleasantly surprised at how nice and cool it was. *A fucking slice of heaven!* He tipped the rather skinny smiling man with his hand out a Malaysian dollar and when he exited, the Kid was alone. He flopped down on the large double bed with an ornately carved headboard featuring plants and leaves. The light green bedspread woven from thick fabric strands, was folded back at the top and the sheets and pillows formed a white band across it. The medium sized round table, chairs and dressers were made of a dark wood and the beige carpet couldn't have been any plainer. There was no TV but there was a rather new looking clock- radio device, on the night stand next to a black phone.

Rising up and going over to the window, the Kid pulled back the curtain and looked out only to discover that the room did not offer much of a view. In fact, there was a hillside that rose up sharply behind the hotel and crested above its top floor. Planted upon it was tall black pole affixed with a towering sign that was topped by a cross with a sign below that declared, *"Jesus Saves". There must be a church at the base of the pole.*

After unpacking and hanging up his meager wardrobe, the Kid leisurely changed out of his fatigues into civilian clothing, selecting the blue short sleeved shirt and the kaki pants. Loading his pockets with his prescription sunglasses, wallet, cigarettes and his zippo lighter, he grabbed his room key and proceeded to take the elevator downstairs.

The Merlin Bar & Lounge was heavily forested with plants of all sizes, both hanging from the high ceiling and growing in big pots sitting on the floor around the room. To the left of the bar, which was at the back, a grand piano waited patiently for someone to come play it. The bar was staffed by two bartenders who were preparing drinks and two waitresses who were busily tending to some of the GIs who had arrived and already been claimed by some of the dozen brightly clad girls who populated the bar.

Time check; 1330 hours.

An older woman, clad in a black dress, smiled broadly and pushed out her chubby cheeks as she spoke with the men, taking care of the business side of the arrangement for the pedaling of the flesh that was surly taking place. *Damned if she doesn't look like 'Bloody Mary' from the movie version of South Pacific,* marveled the Kid.

The seven unoccupied girls immediately began checking out the Kid and flashing him their smiles as he took a seat on a stool at the far end of the bar and ordered a beer. *Hmmm, I don't see one that really appeals to me, the* Kid considered the looks and vibes of the various ladies as he lit up a KOOL.

Then she walked into the bar, stepping briskly, as if late for a social engagement or an appointment. She carried a rather large white purse suspended from the strap over her right shoulder and wore a floral print sundress of red, yellow, green and orange flowers that was a touch on the short side. *Nice legs!* Her black hair was just off her shoulders and permed into medium wavy curls and her face was more cast in European features, with a sharp nose and tapering chin that made her appear less Oriental.

As she surveyed the room, to see if she had missed the boat on this load of GIs, her eye caught the Kid looking straight at her from his place at the bar. At that moment, she stopped and sat down at an empty table and returned the Kid's gaze with a big, bright smile, obviously inviting him hither.

That's more like it! He got up immediately and strolled over to her location and holding his cigarette so that the smoke did not blow in her face said, "Hello."

"Hello," she smiled back, "welcome to Kuala Lumpur! My name is Judy Chong."

And a lovely Judy you are! "Hello, Judy, my name is Curt."

"Please sit down, Curt… unless you see another girl here you prefer better?" she asked with a question mark ending and a hand gesture to her co-workers.

He had to laugh, *talk about cutting to the chase!* "No, Judy, I don't. I would love to 'partner up with,' 'go out with,' 'date'… uh what is the term you use here while we're together?"

"We say, 'pair off', as in, *shall I pair off with you?*"

"Why, yes. I'd very much love it if you did!"

"And to think, I almost didn't come down here today," she said.

"I'll take that as a compliment, Judy. *I bet you say that to all the guys, but I'm very glad that you did come because now, I intend to…, too! Time check: 1340 hours.*

True to her calling, Mama San had picked up on the fact that an agreement had apparently been struck between the 'pair' and she materialized at the table to complete the transaction. *Man! She does not waste any time.*

"Hello GI, I can see in your face that you like Judy. You two are hitting it off, right?" she stood beside them, "you want her for the whole five days?"

Now the pressure was on; *she's cute…. that's for sure… I could do her for five days, but I think I need to be alone when I call Flo…and who knows if there's an even cuter one out there?* "Actually, Mama San, why don't we make it for two days," he looked over at Judy, "we'll see how it goes, you know… see how the pairing is… see if both parties are happy…"

"Ok, GI, whatever you want, is OK… OK? So you give me $90 Malaysian," she stuck out her pudgy hand and waited while the Kid fished out his wallet and pulled out the cash.

"$90 Malay dollars," he counted it into her hand. Mama San re-counted the money and rolling it up, stuffed it down into her cleavage, which was quite ample, to be sure. Smiling, she nodded to the Kid, "OK, later, if you want to keep Judy or get another different girl, you come see me."

"Sure thing," said the Kid, noting as he did, a slightly perplexed look on Judy's face. *She probably wondering why I didn't take her for the whole five days but hey… I don't have to explain anything to anybody. That's the beauty of this.*

"So," the Kid turned to Judy as Mama San went on to her next deal, "what do you like to do for fun?" *Like screw, maybe?*

"Bowling is fun. I like that, and I like movies… and there's the zoo and sight seeing at the Bantu Caves, there is lots to do here in Kuala Lumpur, Curt. What do you like?" her voice was ultra friendly.

You are so going to find out. "I like bowling and movies, and zoos," he snuffed out his KOOL. "Have you had lunch yet?"

"Yes, I have, but we can do what ever you want," Judy flipped her hair back with a slim hand, "what ever you want, we do. OK?"

Any thing I want? Wow. I want to take you upstairs and make love to you right now, this second, so I guess I will. "I'm glad you speak English," the Kid confided.

"Yes, we all speak English. The British were here for decades. If we go to the movies, you will hear in English but there are sub-titles on the screen for Malay and four Chinese dialects!

"Interesting." the Kid returned her smile, "bowling would be fun, I haven't done any bowling for gee, and it must be a year! I'll bet I could get a sandwich or something at the bowling alley, and kill two birds with one stone, don't you think?'

221

"Oh, yes, for sure," she said, "if that's what you want to do, I have a change of clothes with me… I'd rather not bowl in a dress."

"Great!" *that is a great idea,*" he finished off his beer and stood up, "let's go on up because there are a couple of things I need to get in the room, too!"

"OK," Judy rose up to follow and the two left the bar and proceeded to the elevators where the Kid hit the call button and one of the doors opened immediately. *Time check: 1350 hours.* Once inside, the Kid selected the fifth floor and as the elevator took off he commented on her purse. "That's one big hand bag, if I don't say so myself!"

"Hmm, yes," she nodded, "I have lots of things with me, since we will be staying in your room. And I have appropriate clothes, depending on where you want to go."

"I see," the Kid said, as they exited the elevator and walked the ten paces to his door and inserting the key, he opened it and let them in. From the way she looked over the room the Kid surmised that she'd likely been in quite a few of them, even this one, a time or two before.

She placed her purse on a chair and he sat the key down on the dresser before he turned to her with a smile on his face and a boner in his pants, but Judy was looking away and didn't notice. Placing a hand on her shoulder, the Kid rotated her slightly, looked into her dark brown eyes, drew her to him and she was quite cooperative as he leaned over and gently kissed her on the lips.

"Uh, Judy, since you're going to take off your dress, you might as well just take the rest of you clothes off, too," he said as took a step back, " because what I really want is you naked, on the bed, with all your clothes *off.*"

The small degree of surprise on her face at what he said dissolved almost immediately into a smile and she showed him her back. "OK. Unbutton me."

Judy didn't have to ask twice. The Kid undid the three buttons on the back of her dress and at once, she drew it up over her head and tossed it on top of her purse over on the chair and stood before him in her white bra and bikini panties. He drank the sight in, running his gaze from her feet to her face. Kicking off his tennis shoes, quickly raced through his buttons, undid his belt, open his zipper and dropped his pants on the floor where they were brutally kicked to the side. Clearly, the Kid's dick was busy pitching a tent in his boxers as he bent over and turned down the covers to expose the pure white sheets.

Judy reached behind her back, unsnapped her bra and dropped it straight to the floor, revealing a primo set of small but nicely sculpted and very pert breasts. With a swift downward motion, her white bikini panties were laying on the floor and she stood there for a split second, observing his eyes examine her exquisitely tan skinned body before she lay down, face up, in the center of the queen sized bed. "Like this?"

Jackpot! He left his glasses on. Off came the boxers and the Kid lay down beside her. Propped up on his right elbow, his left hand caressed up her arm, over to her breast and down her flat stomach, coming to rest cupped upon the top of her fuzzy little mound. "Can I ask you a question?"

"Yes."

"How long have you been doing this?"

"About a year, now."

"Do you enjoy it? The having sex part?"

"Oh yes, very much!" Judy answered without hesitation, before quickly adding, "most of the time, anyway. I did find out early that some GIs are better at it than others but, almost any GI is better at sex than a man from China or Malaysia. I don't know why."

"Really?" the Kid laughed, "that's funny! And you have to see the doctor each week?"

"Uh huh. We work one week and take one week off. We get tested and if OK, work again."

"I see." *We'll be forgetting the condom here!* The Kid kissed her again, this time slipping her a little bit of tongue and finding a ready tongue in response. While continuing the kiss, he let his middle finger track down from the top of her muff to delve deeper into the secrets hidden within and as he did, she parted her thighs to give him easy access. The Kid was delighted to discover that she was showing the sign of anticipation for the coming act of penetration when he detected her natural lubrication beginning to surface from within.

That was all it took. He couldn't stand it any longer and he rose up and positioned himself between her legs and settling down upon her, he earnestly probed a couple of times until the tip of his throbbing penis found her groove and tracking down, the head engaged the delicate opening and then, discovering she was indeed wet enough, with one inch motion inward with each mini thrust, the Kid was straight away inserted it all the way in to the hilt! Judy let out a low moan, wrapped her arms around his back and pushed her pelvic bone up hard against his. He happened to notice the time on the nightstand clock: 1359 hours... *Amazing! I've known this girl for less than 30 minutes!*

The Kid began to take strokes, pulling his member almost all the way out and putting it all the way back in. He hadn't actually been laid since September, with Li, on his trip to Saigon for glasses. Instead, he had satisfied his desire to orgasm by imbibing in the old *Steam & Cream,* a couple of times a week, at the Scientific Steam Bath. But none of the girls there would really put a penis all the way into their mouths so it was more of a hand job than a nob job. But as far as the Kid was concerned, for just getting one's rocks off, it work quite nicely. However, now that he was back in the saddle, he had to admit, as he looked at Judy's face and slowly plumbed the interior of her hot pocket, *any way you slice it, nothing beats a good old fashioned fuck!*

Her hands were now affixed to his butt cheeks and she telegraphed it when she wanted him thrusting harder or if she wanted him to stay in deep so she could grind against his root. *Oh wow! I can feel her little clit boner against my shaft! Yankees! Yankees! Pull out, pull out!* He had almost lost it. After a few seconds to let his overheated meat cool off, he put it back in, much to the approval of Judy. *She's either 100% into it, or Audrey fricking Hepburn!*

The clock happen to come into his view as switch from having his right cheek against her's to the left side. Hey! I've managed to last five minutes! But he didn't make six as his pent up desires came to a head, a half a dozen strokes later, in a hotly ejaculated explosion. Feeling his orgasm, she either sensed that was an excellent time to fake it or she really did cum too. I'll never know for certain.

"Thanks, I needed that," he said, still deep inside her and hard but instead of going for the double, he realized he'd better pace himself and after a couple more playful strokes, rolled off . He lay there next to her for a few moments, the hum of the air conditioner droning lightly in his ears, *Close as you can get to heaven in the orient without getting shot.* "Cigarette?" he offered, as he began retrieving his KOOLS out of the pocket of his shirt on the floor and the Zippo from his pants.

"No thank you, I don't smoke. They frown on women smoking in Malaysia," Judy said, remaining on her back. "OK, now you 'got' it, do you still want to go bowling?"

He lit up and reclined against the headboard and taking a drag on his KOOL, "You bet!" At that, Judy got up and headed for the bathroom.

The Kid smoked his cigarette and relaxed in the sexual afterglow while he listened to the water run in the sink and the toilet flush. *Here I am, on the big R&R and what am I going to do second? Go bowling. Oh well, there's going to be plenty of sex. Nothing says R&R like a lot of really good, hot and frequent sex.*

Ten minutes later, Judy emerged and fetching her bra and panties from the floor by her side of the bed and put them on. She took her sun dress and hung it up in the Kid's closet and from her extra large purse, produced a neatly rolled up pair of dark tan Bermuda shorts and a pink sleeveless top. She was dressed in a flash. "Ready for bowling!" she announced, finishing up the last two buttons.

"You look very cute," the Kid complimented her, "what else have you got in there?"

"I have this and my toothbrush and a fresh bra and panties for tomorrow and a very skimpy bathing suit. The pool here is quite nice."

"Good idea. Hey, I need to buy a new swim suit while I'm here… as a matter of fact. So let's go bowl and on the way back, can you take me to a place where I can buy one?"

"Yes, I know a store, not far from here," she said.

On the way over in the taxi cab, as the Kid watched the civilian scene pass by, with no soldiers or remnants of explosions or bullet hole riddled buildings, he realized two things: that he was out of the war zone and it was now just about 24 hours since he's smoked any pot. *Thank God it's not a problem.*

Chapter 31

The bowling alley was immense and well lit. It had 50 lanes and when they entered, the Kid saw that a number of now civilian clad GIs from the plane were there, some with girls and some not, rolling away, drinking beer and acting like they didn't have a care in the world.

Almost immediately after they obtained their shoes, found two balls and located their lane, a waitress came by with a menu and at one glance, the Kid quickly decided on the cheeseburger and French fries with a beer. "Anything, Judy?"

"Yes, a Coke, please."

The best part of bowling, the Kid soon discovered, was looking at Judy's extremely cute ass as she lined up her shot. *I am definitely fucking her from behind later tonight.* But the entertaining little dance she did when she got a good result was the best. It consisted of rising up on her tip toes as the ball approached and when it struck the pins, she'd hop up in the air and sink on her knees into a semi-squat position and swing her arms out to try and make the pins fall down. And then, while still low, she'd spin around to see if the Kid was watching her when she made a strike.

The Alley cheeseburger was magnificent. *Totally deluxe. I bet this bowling alley is owned by a bunch of old geezer lifer sergeants who know a gold mine when they see one. It's too Americanized not to be!*

After the third game, in which Judy bowled a 145 and the Kid 117, he decided he was tired of the bowling scene and suggested they go purchase his new swim suit and head on back to the Merlin for a swim and of course, that was fine with Judy.

At the rather large store where she took the Kid to acquire his new suit, she knew exactly in what department and where that particular item was. "I worked here before I switched professions," Judy smiled. She pulled out three suits of different styles and colors and suggested those be the ones he try on. Viewing such activity as a waste of time, he held each one up and reckoned the dark blue one would fit just fine and paid the clerk the $7 Malaysian.

Back in the room, when they hit the stark naked state while changing into their swimming suits, the Kid had a serious decision to make; *Now or later? Before or after swimming? Hmmm. After… yes, definitely after… when she's all squeaky clean.* Judy modeled her canary yellow bikini for the Kid.

"Very nice," he said, "so nice that if we don't go right now, I'll have to remove it. "

"If that is what you want," Judy gestured to the bed.

"Well, I do… but let's go. There will be plenty of time for *that*," the Kid matter of factly said.

When they arrived at the indoor pool, he was shocked to discover that it wasn't all that much larger than the one at Eakin Compound. It did have a one meter diving board but not a high dive. Only three other soldier/local girl couples were using the facility, two of which were frolicking in the water while one pair reclined in chaise lounges and sipped big fancy colorful drinks complete with paper umbrellas.

They draped their towels over two lounges, kicked off their flip flops and after carefully laying his gold rimmed round glasses on a small adjoining table, the Kid dove in. Judy, on the other hand, chose to carefully lower herself into the pool, further up in the shallow end, apparently trying not to get her hair wet. Spying her location, the Kid swam up to her underwater and playfully grabbed her with both hands wrapped around her left thigh and she let out an equally playful scream.

Surfacing, he swept her off her feet and began to carry her around in the water, bouncing off the bottom with his feet, as she wrapped one arm around his neck, putting their faces in close approximation. "When I was in high school, my girlfriend and I did it in a lake once," he said.

"It?" she questioned.

"Yeah, *'It'*, we did it… made love… *in* the lake," the Kid explained, noting from the look on her face, that she might be wondering if that is what the he had in mind.

"How did you do that?" she asked.

"Well, I slipped my suit down a little, she wrapped her legs around my waist like this," he took his arms from underneath her and maneuvered her into the position, with a hand on either butt cheek, "and then I pulled the crotch of her suit to one side, like this," he reached around her left leg with his right hand and demonstrated, "then I just slipped it in her."

"Oh!" she exclaimed, as his fingers played with her privates, "was it fun?"

"Yes and no. It was OK if I left it in, but when I tried to do strokes, the water would wash the slick stuff and it didn't work so well. So I don't think we'll try that here today. Not when we can go back to the room and really do it up right." Just thinking about made the Kid pop a huge boner and from her position with her legs wrapped around him, Judy detected it.

"I think I can say, we will be going upstairs before too long," she said, as a mischievous grin painted her face.

"Most likely... but I can't get out of the pool until this thing goes down a little!" the Kid whispered with a laugh at the though of parading around the deck with a gigantic hard on. With that, he let Judy float free and he began to swim. By the fourth lap, the blood in his dick had returned to other parts of his body and once at the shallow end, he climbed out and Judy followed.

Without so much as a word, they collected their towels, flip flops and his glasses and walked toward the elevators. Once in the elevator, the Kid pinned Judy against the back wall and gave her tonsils a thorough examination with his tongue and as she dug her fingernails into his back while she returned his kiss, the fuse of the rocket in his pants was instantly relit.

Inside the room, wet suits were frantically peeled off and locked in a naked embrace, they fell upon the mattress, madly, frantically kissing. The Kid pulled back to look at her nude physique and then began, by kissing both nipples first, to work his way down to her body, pausing to lick and tenderly kiss her naval on the way across her stomach, to the top of her mound. Switching his position to between her legs, he first took a real long look at her beaver and then he licked the inside of her thighs, about an inch from the top on either side and she gasped as he succumbed to the desire to taste her there, at the focal point of her most sensitive anatomy.

"Oh, my! You are the first man to ever do this to me! I have often wondered what it would be like!"

"Wonder no more!" the Kid said, looking up at her from his place between her legs.

"And I hope this is not the last!"

"It won't be," he prophetically forecasted. Judy didn't last long; in less than a minute, she entered the throes of something the Kid was sure she couldn't possibly faking.

Dis-engaging and getting up he instructed her, "Come over here to the edge of the bed and turn around on all fours." She quickly complied and standing behind her, he only momentarily admired her incredibly cute little ass before straight away making good on the promise he'd pledged to himself while watching her bowl. Holding a shapely hip in either hand, he couldn't imagine it was humanly possible to have any more fun than this in Australia.

When he finally experienced his own orgasm, they separated and fell gasping on top of the bedspread, feeling the cooling effects of the air conditioning blow across their sweating skins. Rolling over onto his back, The Kid fell into a deep sleep and did not dream.

Chapter 32

The restaurant Judy picked for their dinner that night was authentic Chinese. So authentic in fact, the only name on the outside was written in Chinese and the Kid never did find out what it was called, but the food was fantastic.

The place was not at all crowded because he had slept a long time and it was well past the dinner hour when they finally sat down to order. *Time check 2130 hours.* Over dinner and seated side by side, on the side of the table away from the aisle, they were able to engage in quiet conversation and through it, the Kid discovered that Judy had a serious, political side.

"We had a war here, much like the one you are fighting in Vietnam, between the British and the local native guerillas," she said, "it went on for years but finally ended 5 years ago when the British said we could at last become an independent nation. Which we did, in September of 1963."

"Yeah! I saw a William Holden movie about that war once, a few years back when I was in high school, it was called *"The 7th Dawn"*. I was thinking about that on the flight over here today. Did you ever see it?

"Yes, we saw it here. That movie was big news in Kuala Lumpur because the war had barely been over for a year when it was made. The funny thing about that war, if anything can be funny about war, that movie said the rebels were communists and the British kept trying to say that the Malay guerillas were communists. But they weren't. You see here for yourself that we do not have a communist government. Oh, some wanted communism, that is true, but most Malaysians say no to communism! We have very nice theatres here, as you'll see if we go to a movie. Everybody wants to be rich like the Americans. We Malaysians are proud of our country and extremely happy the British have gone home. Just like the Vietnamese will be happy when you Americans go home."

The Kid chewed on that and the food while he looked at the serious expression on her face, "You could be right. I met a Viet Cong captain, who had defected, and he said very much the same thing. Ho Chi Minh has engaged America in what is called a war of attrition? Do you understand 'attrition'?"

"Yes… who's people can die the longest will win."

"Exactly!" the Kid said, totally impressed with her grasp of the language. *That's amazing! But then again, she grew up with it. I really like that she has the slightest British accent!* "Americans are getting sick of this war already. How long can we go? Hard to say. I'm sure our politicians and generals think they can turn Vietnam into a situation to mirror Korea. But what it strikes me is that sooner or later, it comes down to civil war between the Vietnamese political factions. And North and South Vietnam aside, there was almost a civil war in South Vietnam itself, when the Diem Brothers were killed in the coup of 1963.. Nixon says he has a secret plan to end the war… and we all say, what is he waiting for? When he gets sworn in, early next month, we'll see then what the hell he's got, but I'm pretty sure it won't change anything in MY life."

"Have you been in much fighting?" she asked in a shy, almost reluctant way, knowing the question was close to the forbidden subject.

"Some. Much less so in the last couple of months," he pushed back from the table and lit up a KOOL. He liked the fact that there weren't any other GIs seated there at any of the dozen or so tables of the cozy room, which was mostly empty because it was long after the regular dinner hour. *Real local. Actually relaxing; I love it.* "Of course, I can't talk about my job, I suppose it would be OK to say I write stories for a newspaper. And, when I stop and think about it," He took a drink from his Fosters can, "I guess you might say I'm also writing a book, right now… writing a book about my year in Vietnam. And some day, maybe years from now… when I publish this book about *the year I spent in Vietnam,* this day will be in the book and you will read it and say, *"Hey… that's me!"*

"Really? I don't believe you. What are you going to call your book?"

"Uh, I don't know yet. I've thought of a bunch of different things, but it hasn't come to me yet. I'm going to try and do it, anyway, but first, I have to finish the year. I can't write about my year if I don't finish it. Then, if I do finish I have to write it and then if I write it, YOU also have to live long enough to read it… so who knows? But I do know I'm going to try!"

"Hmmm," Judy seemed to ponder for a second, "writing a book is too much to think about!" Then her face lit up as she picked up one of the fortune cookies that had arrived with the bill, "tell you what, here is your fortune cookie, Curt, do you want to see what it says? It's never bad."

"Never bad? Really? Then how can I say no?" the Kid took the crispy yellow twisted bow tie pastry from her, cracked it open and being careful not to tear the little paper that stretched between the two halves, he extracted the prediction of his future. Reading it, he jerked his head, and acted as if it was necessary to adjust his glasses and read it again, to make sure what it said. "You're right… this is very…very good!"

"What does it say?" Judy was truly curious after his reaction, "what is it? Tell me!"

The Kid looked at her and motioned she should lean close as they both sat on the same side of the table and said in her ear, in a whisper, "it says, *'you are going to make love tonight with a beautiful woman in a flowered sun dress!'*"

"No!" she hit him on the shoulder, "It doesn't say that! Let me see!" she tried to snatch it out of his hand but wasn't quick enough and he held it out of her reach in his right hand.

"Really!" the Kid had it between the index and middle fingers, "It does, I'll read it again…" he leaned back and began reading in a loud voice, *"your life will be enriched in many ways."* Made her laugh!

Chapter 33

The next day, Judy escorted the Kid on a sight seeing tour of Kuala Lumpur, with the first stop being at her apartment where she changed clothes and refreshed the contents of the bottomless white handbag.

The second stop was at one of Kuala Lumpur's most noted tourist attractions, the Batu Caves, on the outskirts of the city. There, from beneath the backdrop of a tropically forested a park, paths lead up to a rather large gaping hole, which granted entrance to the interior of the hillside. They stopped to marvel at the Cave's most famous side attraction, Asia's only five legged cow. The extra leg protruded from its back and hung off its right side; the Kid took a picture with his Pentax.

The closer they got to the entrance to the cave, the less enthusiastic Judy appeared to be and when the Kid asked her if she really wanted to tour the cave. For the umpteenth time... she didn't hesitate to say no.

"If you don't mind, Curt, I'd rather go to the Zoo."

"Fine by me," agreed the Kid. But, when they arrived at the Zoo and began to stroll among the haunts of the exotic animals, it only served to remind him of the visit he and Flo had made to the San Diego Zoo in those scant days prior to his departure for the 'Nam. Suddenly, he became distraught that they were no longer engaged. Granted, he'd had as much sex in the last 24 hours and he'd ever had in one day and Judy was hot, to be sure, however, it all only served to make him think how good it had been to make love to the one he *did* love.

They bought a couple of iced lemon drinks and located a nice shady spot with a patch of grass, where they could sit down and cool off, in view of the tiger exhibit. The big jungle cats were of the same frame of mind and languished in the shade of the tall trees that marked the left edge of their enclosure.

"Do you want to see a movie tonight, maybe?" Judy inquired, breaking the silence between them, apparently sensing the distance created by his pre occupied his mind at that moment.

"Sure, why not?" he snapped out of it. "What's playing?

"Well, I'm not sure, but on the way back to freshen up for dinner, we can drive by the theatres and see what is on the playbills and find the starting times."

The Kid appreciated the fact that Judy was well prepared and as practical as she was. And when the taxi did stop at the theatres, the Kid was surprised to see that of the pictures playing, titled, *"The Fox"*, starred Kuer Duella, the actor who had played *'Dave,'* in *"2001 a Space Odyssey,* "This made him immediately want to see it. He then spent the rest of the afternoon and dinner trying to explain *2001*, to Judy, all about Hal the Computer and how it trapped Dave outside the ship. He acted both parts; *Open the pod bay door, Hal... I can't do that, Dave...* and the monkeys learning how to make a thigh bone into a club and throwing it up into the air where it turned into a space ship and the black monolith and going to Jupiter. Judy was amused by his attempt and prolonged it by asking silly questions.

That night at the movie, he marveled at the way Malaysian theatre owners dealt with the five language factor. As Judy had mentioned the previous day, there were the four sub-titles that let all the non English speakers follow along. Extra help in English wouldn't have hurt, either, because it turned out that *"The Fox"* was a supremely confusing film. It was about an extremely handsome wandering loner who ends up in Canada or Maine and comes upon a farmstead that is the home of two women, one young and beautiful, the other a shade older and controlling. He dug the younger chick, but it was rather apparent he was interfering in their lesbian relationship. They wanted him to stay for the specific purpose of killing a fox that was raiding their hen house and devouring their chickens. Now I see it! The Kid experienced an epiphany, the *handsome wanderer is the fox in the older lesbians' hen house!*

It all started to make sense until the end where the older lesbian had the wanderer chop down a huge old dead tree on the property and it ended up falling on the younger chick and killing her. Walking out afterwards, the Kid's mind was reeling with possible messages from the film. *Accident? I think not. The older lesbian figure out the younger chick slept with the dude and fixed it so the tree would get her... Or, was it that the younger chick just found love only to have life snatched away from her? Did the guy really bang the chick or not? They're too vague. They ought to let you know somehow... Was it about the loner who finally found love yet somehow was the instrument in its destruction? Ha. How in the holy fuck did I come to be in this situation? How did I get to be here? I so hope I get to talk to Flo tomorrow.*

"So, what did you think?" Judy inquisitively asked, "Wasn't it sad the young girl got killed by the falling tree?"

"Yes, it was sad but when you stop to think about it, none of them were ever too happy anywhere in that whole movie. I mean, why was he a drifter? We never found out what he was running from. And why were two women all alone in the middle of the north woods? Definitely not a comedy," he shrugged his shoulders. "Why don't we go back to the hotel and act out our own love scene?"

"Why am I not surprised you would suggest such a thing?" she smiled.

Later that night, after making love, they lay in bed, Judy sleeping and the Kid nearly wide awake, thinking about tomorrow being Christmas Eve and the call he was going to make to Flo the United States. *How did I come to be in this place?*

Chapter 34

"Is this where I can set up some telephone calls to the United States?" the Kid asked a man behind the desk to which he had been directed. The gentleman had a haircut and a jaw set that made his head look square and it immediately began to bob up and down in the affirmative manner.

"Yes, sir, this is the place, and I can assist you," he smiled accommodatingly and continued with the nodding, "I need your room number and the telephone numbers you wish to call and if you have any that are reversal of charges. Sometimes one gets right through. Another time will have to wait. I don't know why, but this is a good time to call, in the States, It is yesterday evening."

"OK," the Kid attempted to mimic his nodding rate as he slid a prepared piece of paper across the surface to him, having already decided that he was only going to attempt two calls. "The first one is a collect call to my parents in Colorado, which is an hour earlier than the second one, and this number is my girlfriend in California, and I'll be paying for that call."

"I will do my best, Mr. Stocker," the nodding finally stopped, "there are not more than a half dozen calls in front of yours and we have four international lines so I would estimate you should be waiting in your room in no more than 20 minutes, . When we succeed in obtaining the party, I will call you and we can make the connection."

"Thank you." The Kid checked his watch; 1000 hours, it was his understanding that the time difference between Kuala Lumpur and the States was 11 hours to Colorado and 12 to California, making it 9:00 pm in the mountains and 8:00 pm on the coast. *She should be home. But its Christmas vacation so there's no telling.*

He had just finished having breakfast with Judy in Merlin's restaurant and she had gotten the slightest bit testy before she finally departed, due to the fact that the Kid would not commit to seeing her for another night or two later in his stay. It was something about not being able to work again for a week, if she'd been with one GI, because of the testing requirements. She compared it to a taxi driver waiting at the airport for a good fare and then ending up with a fare that was but across the street! *That's pretty good, I'll have to steal that, the Kid chuckled, but damn it, I want some novelty on my R&R! Judy was nice, I had a great time. However, I feel no obligation to her. What the fuck? I want a new and different girl tomorrow. One of those Indian girls I've seen around. Yeah, they are way hot looking. And a Hindu girl won't be upset about having to work on Christmas!*

The headlines of the free morning English newspaper beckoned to him, and he picked one up out of the rack by the elevators; *something something Apollo 8 flies around the moon… something about the coming of Nixon… nothing about any kind of a VC offensive back in Vietnam. But then, again, that is a good thing. This will give me something to do while I'm waiting for the phone calls to go through,* the Kid thought, tucking it under his arm, knowing he would be reading the paper on the can taking a dump, inside of two minutes.

Once in the room, he hurried to take care of coffee and breakfast inspired business quickly and then only lingered for about ten minutes, reading about Apollo 8 in the *Malay English Rag,* in order that he not be trapped on the john for his first call. But he finished the paper and laid down on the as yet un-made-up bed briefly to relax and all of the sudden, it was a half hour later and he was awakened by the ringing phone.

"Hello?" he swept up the hand piece and answered while simultaneously springing into the sitting position on the edge of the bed.

"Mr. Stocker, I have the Colorado telephone number on the line," the unmistakable voice of the square headed desk captain enthusiastically announced, "and they have accepted the charges, please go ahead."

Immediately wide awake. "Hello! Mom? Dad?"

"Hello? Curt? Can you hear me?"

"Dad! Yes! I can hear you really well!"

"Merry Christmas, Ho Ho Ho," Dwain, spoke in the fake Santa voice he liked to use every year when he passed out presents to the family from around the tree, before switching to his regular, "I can hear you pretty good, too! What a wonderful present, getting to talk with you at the holidays!" he paused, having heard the instructions, to give the person on the far end a chance to answer back.

"Geeze, Dad, my first Christmas away from the family and I figure there's no way I could get any further away than I am right now, without getting closer! So tell me first off, how was the wedding?"

237

"It came off pretty good. Scott and Nancy are married. Yep, the wedding was yesterday, the 22nd, and even though you weren't here, they had it announced that you were the best man, and Herb Goodrich stood in for you. Scott said he knew you were there in spirit, and we all said a prayer for you and the rest of the soldiers."

"Aw, that's nice. And where did they go on their honeymoon?"

"Hot Springs…" he said, and they both laughed.

"Did Mom cry? *Dumb question.*

"Did she cry? Hell! She's *still* crying!" his dad exclaimed, "but I think part of it might be you're on the phone and tomorrow is Christmas eve and all… here, Curt, she can't wait to talk to you!"

"…Hello, Curt?" His mother's tiny voice came to him, out of the black handset, from over 10,000 miles away.

"Hi Mom!" he answered, "It's already Christmas eve here in Malaysia! I love you guys and wish we could be together, but I'm past halfway done with my tour now!"

"Oh, that's great! Merry Christmas, Honey," she was sniffling a little, "it's so good to hear your voice… now you've got me going like a faucet!" she broke out in full-fledged sobbing.

"Now, Mom Mom Mom, pull yourself together. Dad is paying good money for us to talk, not cry, and so stop it… stop it now… mothers aren't supposed to act like babies! Babies are supposed to act like babies!"

"I'm sorry," she sniffled, "I'll try to control myself, just let me blow my nose." He could hear her giving it a really good honk in the background. "There, I'm better," big sigh. "The wedding was beautiful, and Nancy was a beautiful bride… it was just too bad you were the only thing missing."

"Well, the only thing that would be missing from my wedding right now would be Flo…" the Kid half laughed.

"I had a feeling that might happen when you went over there," his mom quickly shot back. "Honey, it might be for the best. Why get married so young? You're going to have a lot of living to do when you get back and you might not want to settle down right away."

"You could very well be right, Mom. But I know I'm going to see her first thing when I get back… so I don't know where that might lead. In fact, I have a call in to her and I'll most likely be talking with her right after we hang up… so I don't know. Uh… I actually had a dream about Donna Nadeau the other night though… how about that?"

238

"Funny you should say; we had dinner with Frank and Lucy Nadeau a couple of weeks ago and they were still sad that you and Donna broke up. They thought you were going to be their grandson in law for sure when you went to Nashville... they said they could hear wedding bells."

"I know, I know... but when I met Flo, she did something to me, I don't know what, I was totally blown away and I'm still not sure it's really over between us yet."

"Well, whoever you finally end up married to, we'll love her like a daughter. Scott and Nancy seem real happy, that's all anybody can ever ask for... and we really like her parents... except their *Democrats!*"

"Oh, come on, Mom, remember, I'm almost a Democrat myself now. Only bad thing about the party is LBJ."

Not wanting to debate with him about politics, she quickly changed the subject. "Did you get all of our Christmas boxes? I think we ended up sending four of them."

"I don't know, Mom, and since I'm not there now, I won't know until I get back. I got one of them, if what I got was one, before I left a couple of days ago. It had a big can of Almond Rocha candy in it, was that one?"

"Yes, I believe it was. And there was a bathing suit in one box, since you said you were getting to swim a lot at your new town."

"Oh, I didn't get that one for sure because I bought a new swim suit here yesterday."

"Your father and I can't tell you now thrilled we were when we found out you were transferred and assigned to the newspaper!"

It's still plenty dangerous. "You guys and me both! What I'm doing now at Battalion Headquarters is pretty safe, all things considered."

"But what is this talk about you going back for another tour? To go do radio in Saigon?" she let out a big sigh.

"Uh, yes, Mom, but... it isn't a done deal yet. I'm waiting for word from AFVN Saigon. I went up there and interviewed and it *looks* like a sure thing, but you know the Army, they're so slow with everything and you never know how it's going to turn out. I hope to hear first thing when I get back from R& R. In fact, when I'm in Saigon on my way back, I hope to heck I can find out then."

"I wish you wouldn't do that. I wish you'd do your tour and come home," she flatly stated.

"But Mom, if I get this transfer, I'll be home in March instead of May! In like 90 days! That's only 3 months and this could do wonders for my career. It's what I *do*, Mom… If I get this job and have a show over here, there won't be any place in the country I could go and not already be known! Don't you see? This could be one incredible springboard to my future! Plus, I'll get out of the frickin' Army six months early and it might keep Scott out of here, since they can only have one of us here at a time!"

"Or just delay the inevitable. He's a medic… you and he both know they are going to eventually want him there."

"Maybe, but you never know… it could end by then… especially if your new man in the White House, old *Ski Jump Nose* really does have a secret plan to end the war," the Kid countered her argument, *although I don't believe it.*

"OK, Honey, your dad wants to talk to you some more, so you be good… and you be careful! We love you, Curt! Bye bye… Merry Christmas!"

"Bye Mom… I love you too!"

He could hear his Dad clear his throat as he took the phone back from Irma.

"Curt… Your Mom and I were talking, and we were glad we didn't know you were getting a *court martial* until it was over and you won! We were pretty shocked when we read that! You never cease to both scare and amaze us!"

"Yes, sorry about that, Dad, But I figured it would be easier for Mom to take that way, but too bad *you* couldn't see it! I cleaned Lt. Wilson's plow! If it had been any shinier, it would have blinded his mule! He didn't fuckin' know what hit him. The whole thing against me was so much fabricated bullshit, it was truly unbelievable. Remember when I said I was going to write a book about my year here? This is some great stuff, Dad. He wanted me to volunteer for some commando shit I wasn't going to volunteer for, plain and simple and when I wouldn't, he went after me like nobody's business. *And* I didn't even have to play all my cards. Wally and Mrs. Beavers would have been proud, and will be, if they ever hear about it!"

"Well, you know that I always thought it was a good thing you were on the debate team. Except when you decided you wanted to argue with me and wouldn't quit!" Dwain laughed.

"What can I say? Am I a chip off the old *blockhead* or what? Speaking of which, I really like getting the Boulder Daily Camera, but I wish they had *Peanuts* in the comics."

"Do you want the Rocky Mountain News?" he asked, the tone of offer in his voice saying, *there isn't anything I wouldn't do for you.*

"No, that's OK, because if I get this transfer, I'll be home in 90 days! So the *Camera* is plenty. But hey, Dad, thanks for sending that pool cue for my birthday! That was great! I really kicked some ass with that stick! There's no table where I am now, so I left it with some friends down in Tra Vinh, where they really need it."

"Well, OK, I guess. Anyway, I don't know what this is costing, so we better think about cutting it off." The Kid could hear him call out off the mouth piece, "Irma, do you want to say anything else? No?" *I think I can hear her crying...* "No, she just says that she loves you, so do I and all our friends send the love, too. Merry Christmas, Son, and need I tell you to be careful."

"Merry Christmas to you, too, Dad. Give my best to Scott and Nancy when you see them and ... I love you... goody bye." He hung up.

Letting out a pensive sigh, he reached for his KOOLs and lit up. Standing, the Kid walked over to the window, where he'd already pulled back the blinds and cracked it open. He gazed at the cross above the Jesus Saves sign as he blew the smoke through the screen. *That's good, they don't think I'm in a lot of danger. That was great, getting a chance to talk with them on Christmas Eve. Hmmm, square head is most likely placing the Flo call right now. I hope. Oh jeeze, just to hear her voice! What am I going to say? Hell... what is SHE going to say? I don't think she'd say anything to upsetting on Christmas Eve, so maybe she won't be playing straight with me... something to consider. What am I thinking? No matter what either of us says, what happens when we actually see each other again is what I think is going to tip the scale one way or the other.*

He went to the bathroom and ran himself a glass of water and dropped in a few ice cubes from the plastic insulated bucket that presently sat atop the tank of the toilet. He walked back over to the bed and took a long drink. *Ahhh, the luxury of ice water!* Then, the silence of the room was pierced by the thunderous ring of the telephone's archaic sounding bell. *This is it.*

Lifting up the receiver he said, "Hello?"

"Hello, Mr. Stocker, we have your call to California, go ahead, please..."

"Hello... Flo?" he said in a rather shaky voice.

"Hello? Curt?"

"Flo? Is it really you? I'm actually hearing your voice? It's actually my Parnelli?"

241

"Merry Christmas, Yes, it's me. How are you? Uh, I guess that's a silly thing to ask," her tone sounded apologetic.

"No, it's not… I'm OK, really. In fact, this week, what with being on R & R and all, it's actually quite relaxing to be out of the country and some place totally safe."

"That's nice!"

"So, wow, this is really a good connection. uh, what time is it there?"

"It's just now 9:30 at night."

"Here, it's 11:30 in the morning, on Christmas Eve, that means I'm calling you from tomorrow!"

"That's pretty cool!" she responded.

"So where are you? Are you parents or Lo there, or can you really talk?"

"I'm alone, on the phone in our room. Lo's out on a date with John and my parents are across the street at a party our neighbors have every year."

"Good. You know, I gotta say, I wish that we'd have eloped to Las Vegas the day we went and picked up my car from the Victorville VW dealership, then we wouldn't have broken up and we'd be having R & R together in Hawaii right now!"

"That's funny, that day when we came back from getting your car, my dad told me he was surprised we'd *hadn't* eloped to Las Vegas, he was sure that was our plan."

"Well, he must have thought it would be OK because he gave you permission to cut school and come with me."

"Make no mistake about it… my Dad loves you… my Mom hates you. End of story."

"But alas, we didn't elope and here I am in Kuala Lumpur, all alone by myself, instead of with you," the Kid took a puff on his KOOL

"Oh yeah, right," she shot right back, "like the Curt Stocker I know is going to go on R & R and not get laid?"

"Well, OK… we're not engaged any more, so there's no reason to not talk about it," he matter of factly admitted, "just like I said to you before I left, if you wanted to sleep with another guy, I'd have no problem with that. I mean, you knew you weren't *my first* and I really don't expect to be your one and only for all of time. *Awkward silence.* "I mean I don't believe in the double standard." *More silence.*

"The memory of us making love in the Traveler's Motel is the one thing that's keeping me sane."

242

"Too bad *Mom* had to find out. Who'd have ever thought that she'd like go so totally Perry Mason on me after she read what you wrote in that *one letter?*"

"Uh, sorry about that. You know the last thing I wanted to do was piss your mom off. But she was young once and your dad went to war. She had to know I didn't want to leave without making love to you."

"I'm sure she did. That's why she read your letters. But anyway, let's not talk about that," he waited to see what she wanted to talk about. "I'll have your record collection ready for you to pick up when you get back… several people have parts of it right now, but none of the original acetates."

"Oh, thanks. But I'd rather have you back than all those records."

"That may or may not be, Curt, I've got to be honest with you," she made a long pause but he didn't jump in. "I mean, I still think a lot about you, Curt, I do, and I have dreams about you and what's happened between us. But I just don't know how I *feel* any more. Don't take it wrong, I'm glad you called, and I want to talk with you and even *see* you but I just don't know about the rest of my life. Like, I might not want to leave California and live in Tennessee and you've said you are for sure going back to Nashville."

"True, I did say that. But that doesn't mean I want to live there for the rest of my life. I'm not opposed to living in California… if I could live there with you."

"Lo said to say 'hi,' she chose not to comment on the Kid's declaration.

"Tell her 'Hi' back." Pause. "When I get back in country from R&R, I should find out if I'm going to get my assignment to Armed Forces Radio Saigon. I hope to get a hold of Alan P. before I go back to Can Tho to find out. And if I do, I'll be home in March, and not May. Then I'll have a month leave and when I come back, I'll only have a year left in the fucking Army, and not a year and a half."

"I hope you get it, then, since that's what you want."

"What I want is you." *Silence.* "What I want is you and for it to be like it was inside my VW bug the night we saw *'Gone With the Wind'* at the Oceanside Drive In," the time and place he had proposed. *Silence*

"I'm not saying I don't still have feeling for you, Curt, I just haven't sorted them out yet," she firmly communicated.

'Fair enough. Let's leave it at that," he knew it would do no good to press the issue over the phone from the other side of the world. "When I find out if I got the assignment, I'll know when I'm coming home and I'll let you know, because I'm still going to come see you first thing."

"Ok, Curt, *I want you to know,* I want to see you, too. Hey, speaking of seeing people, have you seen Waterhouse or Tom Davies or any of your other DINFOS friends besides Alan P. and Georgie yet?"

"No."

"That was so sad, when you wrote me about John Imbach, Curt, I cried for him... Some nights, I can hardly watch TV because I'm afraid I'm going to see something absolutely horrible about the war and it makes me think bad thoughts about things that could happen to you... and I know you tell me you've got that stupid lucky beaver nickel, but I just can't help but worry about you."

"Now you're starting to sound more like my mother than my girlfriend. I talked to my parents just before this call to you, as a matter of fact. Scott and Nancy are all married off."

"That's nice. I'll have to send them a card. I have so much on my mind I forgot they were getting married this week."

"Yeah. My Dad said my Mom cried and is still crying. She was a mess when we spoke on the phone. They don't want me to do this extension for Saigon thing."

"I don't imagine that they do. I'm not sure how I feel about it... even though we are no longer engaged."

"You keep saying that phrase, *even though we are no longer engaged...*" *he* immediately responded, "I've got that. Lots of guys get the old 'Dear John' over here, so I don't have a horse named Silver, and I am over that part of it, but if I get it, Saigon is pretty safe."

"Unless they have another Tet Offensive or something like that."

"Well," he slowly said, "to tell you the truth, they were supposed to... we had intelligence that's what they were planning for Christmas, that's why I switched off Australia for R&R and came here this week. If it's going to happen, it'll probably be tonight." *Silence.* "I hate this fucking war."

"Me too. Just think of all the people who'd still be alive if it hadn't happened."

"I often do. Well, Flo, I don't know what this has cost so far, but to be on the safe side, I'd probably better sign off. So, Merry Christmas my Parnelli... and I'll see you later... OK?"

"OK! I'll give you that... Merry Christmas, Curt...I'll see you later," she said their signature phrase back and hung up.

He placed the handset back on its cradle and sat there on the bed, looking at her picture with her voice still ringing in his ears; *I'll see you later. You didn't say I love you, but you did say 'I'll see you later…*He stood up and sighed heavily. *It's Christmas Eve. What am I going to do?* Eying his Pentax sitting on top of the dresser, he decided to go for a walk around town and take some pictures.

As he emerged from the front doors of the Merlin, the bell captain motioned to the cab at the front of the quay to move forward but the Kid held up his right palm and waved him off. He stood there on the steps for a few seconds contemplating his direction and finally chose to begin his walk to the left, which led up the front side of hill behind the hotel.

It was a little past noon, but for some reason, it did not seem as hot as it was in the jungles of Vietnam at midday and with the Pentax slung over his shoulder, he set a fast pace. He quickly noticed that he was out of the commercial area and into a residential section of town. The sidewalks were clean and broad with garden squares on either side of entrances to the three and four story buildings that were the neighborhood norm. Near the top of the hill, he could see only the cross on top of the Jesus Saves sign, but the road apparently did not go in that direction.

While he walked, the conversation with Flo replayed repeatedly in his head. *I'll see you later…* Then, from behind, a flurry of sudden and loud sharp reports cracked out in rapid succession! *My God… gunshots!* Bang bang bang bang bang! Immediately in survival mode, the Kid in a flash jumped down behind the front of a Volkswagen parked on the street, in time to hear the boys who had set off the string of firecrackers laughing at him from some concealed position to his rear.

Bastard kids! I bet they do that to all the GIs. At the top of the hill, the Kid took a right and headed back down toward the commercial area of KL and was soon walking past shops that offered all manner of art and consumer goods. He stopped in front of one store that had a display of birds in a cage out front. There were so many predominately green birds with trim of red and yellow in the three-by-three foot cage that he was compelled to stop and take a color slide. The birds filled the whole frame and with some hanging upside down from the top and others clinging to the side, he reckoned it would be impossible to tell which way the slide was up!

At one point, he realized that it had now been a total of four days since he'd had a puff of reefer but that was the only thought he gave it as he became engrossed in the shops that lined the street. Kuala Lumpur was very different from Saigon; the stamp of the British Empire was all over it as much as the stamp of France was all over the Vietnamese capital. The stores here were closed front, with doors and windows whereas most shops in Saigon were open fronted, with no doors or windows, but rather were locked up with sliding metal gates that came down like garage doors from the top.

Rounding one corner, the Kid came upon a bright white building with an extremely high peaked and sloping red tiled roof that was set back from the street and surrounded by flower gardens. Curiously approaching it, he could see in through a large open entry way where his eyes fell upon an ebony black and golden statue of a life-sized sitting Buddha, perched high on a dais, beneath an Indian arch of filigreed gold. It was stunningly beautiful, easily the most remarkable depiction of Buddha he had ever seen. *Oh wow! I've got to have a picture of this! I wonder what kind of polished stone that is! And look at his robes of gold. There's got to be hundreds of thousands of dollars worth of gold here!*

The shrine was devoid of any other people. Reverently removing his shoes at the door, he tip-toed in and surveyed the high vaulted chamber of the 30 by 30-foot room, becoming enveloped by the quietness of the place. An ornately woven carpet of flowers upon a white background, surrounded by a green scrolled border, stretched out in front of the altar which rose up in graduated steps of gold until at the top, it was only as wide as the statue itself.

Standing beneath it, he looked up at the shining black face of the Buddha and marveled at the calmness of its' expression; *not actually smiling, but clearly at peace.* Urns filled with gray sand held joss sticks of incense, a couple of which were still smoldering with trails of smoke, denoting that other had recently been here, to engage in meditative prayer or to seek divine intervention. He stepped back to the point where he figured he could get the whole altar, including the arch, in the shot. Lifting the Pentax to his eye, he looked through the finder and activated the light meter. Open doors on either side of the altar made it difficult for him to get a good reading for the exposure as the Buddha's location between them was much darker. Finally splitting the difference, he advanced his film, composed his shot and took the picture. *I hope it turns out... glad I'm shooting color slides!* The Kid enjoyed looking at the Buddha for a few more minutes, before he returned to the front door and put on his shoes to continue his walk.

Not far from the shrine, he came upon a confectioner's shop and went in to buy some delicious looking candies to eat in his room later that night, in a private celebration of Christmas. *As much of a Christmas celebration as a Buddhist can have, anyway.*

246

Eventually, he tired of walking and realizing he didn't know exactly where he was, he hailed a cab and once in the back simply said, "Merlin Hotel, please," and in less than ten minutes, he was dropped at the front door.

Immediately upon entering his room, the Kid changed into his new trunks and proceeded down to the hotel pool where he took a nice long swim with plenty of laps. After that, he went straight back up to the room and stretched out on the bed and took a nap.

When he awoke, the clock showed 6:30; 1830 hours. The Kid smoked a KOOL, took a hot shower, shaved, dressed and went down to the hotel restaurant. He dinned alone that evening on a T-bone steak with a baked potato and a tossed green salad, with vanilla ice cream for dessert. *I wonder how the boys are doing in the embassy tonight. Hope to hell the offensive rumors are bullshit. But if they aren't, I don't feel bad about not being there… I've pulled my share of combat. None of them had to put up with Wilson's bullshit, so fair is fair!*

Following dinner, he returned to his room and turned on the radio to the classical music station and smoked another KOOL. At one point, he went over to the window and looked out into the pitch-dark night. Since it was at the back of the hotel, there were no street lights or traffic. In fact, the only thing lit up was the neon Jesus Saves sign, the cross in bright white was suspended above Jesus' name in red and 'saves' below that, also in white. Looking at the cross did not give him the soothing feeling he'd felt from gazing upon the face of Buddha. Lifting up his camera, he set the shutter speed at 1/30, focused on the cross and snapped off a frame.

Thinking what it was that a Buddhist should do alone on Christmas Eve, he turned off the radio, arranged himself on the floor at the foot of the bed, in a close approximation of the Buddha's lotus position, closed his eyes and prepared to meditate.

Ommmmmmmmmmmmmmmmmmmmmmmmmmmmmmmmmm…. Deep breath. *Ommmmmmmmmmmmmmmmmmmmmm*

Got to clear my mind. Got to calm my inner soul. I'll see you later… he heard the voice of Flo, clear as a bell from earlier in the day. That made him think of her and his thoughts went back to the night they had met in Nashville, the first time he had laid eyes on her, at the movie premier, when he said, out of the blue upon coming face to face with her in the crush of the crowd…him on one side of the rope and her on the other… *I'll see you later. But will I ever see you again? I've made it this far and even though I'm in much less danger, am I going to make it? Yes. Yes, I will make it. I cannot think of it any other way than making it through this hell and going home. But... I'm going to come back. Is that the right thing to do? Is Mom right? Am I being a fool? Am I fucking myself? Should just do my tour and get the hell out of here? No. I want that radio gig in Saigon. And I sure as hell want the six-month drop that goes with it. Oh Jesus, I cannot wait to be out of this fucking army! My mind does not seem to be calming down at all.*

In the quest to clear his mind of worldly thoughts, the Kid wasn't having much success. In fact, as he sat there on the hotel room floor, his specific thought meter was registering quite the opposite. *How can you have a thought and it not be a thought of something connected to the world? If only I hadn't gotten drafted. What a fuck up. Wait... maybe it wasn't a fuck up... this apparently is my destiny, to come to Vietnam and experience the things that I have... and will... and then to do something with it... or about it. The war is just plain gross! The Army so sucks! I still can't believe they shot those 3 kids. The image of them trussed up on their knees materialized in his head. He could see them clear as day. He heard the youngest one yell his refusal to defect at him; Cam bao ya! Why didn't I report it? I did everything I could. Is it because I didn't really see them do it and they all said they'd call me a liar? And claim it didn't happen? Them all saying they were just another three VC that deserved to be dead, and they were more 'useful' to us as body count? How could I possibly overcome that? My word against all of them. I swear to God... or Buddha, when I get home to the states, I will find a way to oppose this war! Dai Ui Khanh was right; this is not a war for Americans. This is something the Vietnamese must settle between themselves and nothing America does or can do will change that. Am I happier about not being shot at or not being hit when I am being shot at? Why do I have so many dreams about guillotines? Could it all be related to that one book I read about the Sanson family when I was in 7th grade? I mean, why? Whoa... maybe I WAS a Sanson? That would explain why I've seen the scaffold so many times. No. It can't be. Wouldn't that have been horrible? To realize you were the son of the hereditary executioner of Paris? He worked for his dad and couldn't quit... wait a minute... I worked for Dad and couldn't quit! Still, Buddhists say all suffering takes place in this world. Man's inhumanity to man...no question there has always been suffering with plenty to go around. Just like that night we didn't have a perimeter set up and Spooky came and hosed the jungle with the mini cannons. No telling how many little home bunkers full of crying children they shot up that night, just on the other side of the paddies. I mean, those hamlet houses are all over the place out there. Spooky never knows how many VC he kills, let alone innocent people... women and children... cripples... water buffalos, pigs, chickens. If Spooky is flyin', something or someone is dyin'. You get in the way of the US Army… tough shit little fuckers. Ha. That's what Wilson tried to do to me… I got in the way of his Army… tough shit little fucker. Hmmm. I still got a bad feeling about Ronnie Smith. He's not the kind of man to forget about how bad Ellis made him look in that trial. Maybe I should have made Sweet bust Wilson's ass for lying about the MSQ-85 attack, to destroy his credibility… that would have been fun! A year ago, after Christmas dinner, is when I set out from Boulder to drive my bug to see Flo in California. My God… all the stuff that's happened in 1968. My mind is genuinely blown! And now it's almost 1969. Now there's a funny year! Talk about a gold mine of ideas for radio. Man and woman of the year for 69'. The American Restaurant association ought to run a campaign; 'everything is fine when you eat out in 69!" Catchy. Wow. This is the first Christmas Eve I have ever spent away from my family. Ever. In my entire life! But, in my book, I won't have a "Christmas in Vietnam" chapter until next year when I do Christmas in Saigon. And you can bet your sweet ass I will be doing R&R in Australia on my second tour!*

Then, stealing into his thoughts with all the subtly of a gang of machine gun wielding bank robbers, a memory from the not-too-distant past shook the Kid out of any pretense he was maintaining about meditation… *the poncho blowing off what remains of Captain Robinson's body.*

The Kid opened his eyes and rose to his feet. *God… I wish I'd never seen that.*

Chapter 35

He aimed very carefully. Finally confident in the bead he had drawn, he pulled the trigger and sent the cue ball with firm, but not overbearing speed, across the pristine green felt, where it converged on the red three ball that rested almost snug against the rail, two inches to the right of the side pocket. Upon contact, the three snapped off the rail and rolled back across the table and fell dead center into the side pocket where the Kid stood. Chalking his cue, he prepared to deliver the *coup de-grass* to his fifth straight opponent. All that was left was to sink the 8 ball, which sat barely two inches out from the corner pocket, about an inch off the rail. With the softest of rolls, he made it drop out of sight, leaving the cue ball in its previously occupied position.

"Next," he said, stepping back to lighting up a KOOL and take a sip of his beer. *I think I could get used to shooting pool here in the Saigon USO; these are great tables, that's for damn sure!* Checking his watch, the Kid noted it was still a couple of hours before he had to catch a ride out to Ton Son Nhut for his flight back to Can Tho. It was the afternoon of New Year's Eve, and he was looking forward to being 'home' from his R&R trip and blowing some serious dubage out on the Embassy balcony.

The Kid had arrived back from Kuala Lumpur on the afternoon of the 28th and from there, had managed to cajole the 4th PSYOP Group first sergeant out of three more days in Saigon, *taking care of this… shopping for that…* Not only had he succeeded in locating Alan P., he and Georgie had taken the Kid to a real American Embassy holiday party, being held at one of the consulate's buildings. He had found it very interesting, seeing how the 'other half' lived in Saigon, day in and day out. It was very cush; pulling *another ten months in Saigon is a sacrifice I'm willing to make.*

His new opponent had finished racking up the 8-ball set but, as the Kid settled into position for the break, a familiar figure walked into his field of vision, just beyond the triangle of painted ivory balls. *Tom Davies!* Instead of shooting, the Kid stood up and inquired of the GIs seated nearby, waiting to play, "Hey, who ever is next… an old school friend I haven't seen in 7 months just walked in and I'll let you play this guy if I can come back and play the winner. Deal?"

"You bet!" a totally shaved bald GI stepped forward to claim his stick.

"Curt!"

"Tom!" they clasped hands and patted each other vigorously on their backs, "What a surprise to see you! How have you been? Or should I say, 'where have you been?'"

"Yeah, where works… I've been to R&R in Hawaii with Kate!" he smiled, from ear to ear, "just got back and I don't even get to spend a night here before I have to fly out to Tay Ninh. Could have just stayed at the fucking airport but nooooo… I had to go sign back in country at the unit and then turn right around and go back out to fly out, but somebody mentioned you were here shooting pool and I detoured, so here I am, and I've got about 15-20 minutes tops, before I have to run."

While talking, they had gravitated to an empty table, not too far from the pool action, and sat down. "Man, you've heard about Imbach, I imagine."

"Yes, heard about it," he sadly nodded, "poor unlucky fucker. Did you ever hear any details… how it happened or anything like that?" Davies lit up a Winston.

"No, I tried to write to Waterhouse, but I don't know if he never got it, or I never got his answer… it had to be one or the other."

"How ever it happened, I guess it doesn't matter much now," Tom theorized, "dead is dead. On the other hand, Specialist Stocker, word is that *you* were in on a little action… both in the field and in the court room! You dog! You got your ass court martialed, and you won! *Fuckin' A!* When we heard that and we all laughed our asses off! And let me get this straight… it had something to do with *eating in the mess hall?* Is that right… really?"

"Yes, it is, and I did!"

"Can't deny that infamous luck," Tom laughed, "you and that frickin' Beaver nickel of yours!"

"No doubt about it!" the Kid pulled it out of his fatigue shirt and dangled it in front of him, "hasn't let me down yet and I've been in some pretty tight fucking jams," he put it away. "What about you? Been anywhere that made you soil your drawers?"

"Seen my share… had my close calls and tell you one thing: there's no loud speakers where I'm at. Foreign language announcer my ass!"

"Ha! Me either!" The Kid and Tom both shook their heads in disgust, exchanging a knowing look. "But now, after the court martial, I'm assistant editor of the unit newspaper and things are going pretty well. Turns out the Lt. Colonel, who commands our unit, is a fan."

"What do you mean? He heard you in Nashville?" Tom questioned.

"No. He likes me. He came into the unit right when my court martial started and he kind of figured it out right away that I was getting screwed all along. He's black and apparently, he's been screwed by the system a couple of times himself, but he's really cool and there isn't anything I wouldn't do for him," the Kid affirmed. "Lt. Colonel Willie O. Lawton, is his name."

"Well, that sounds like a pretty fuckin' groovy *fan club member* to have!"

"Doesn't it drive you mad to hear Alan P. on the radio? Been out to see him? I've been out to see him and Georgie at AFVN a couple of times. They introduced me to the OIC and NCOIC. I played my air tape and my Sgt. Pepper's Family Band and Hit Parade Show intro for them. They loved it and told me they were going to approve my extension for Radio Saigon!"

"You're extending?" Tom had a surprised, questioning look on his face.

"Yep. They said it was a done deal. And I'll get a 60 day drop to set it up so that when I finish my tour in Saigon, I'll get a 6 month early out! I'm so excited I can hardily fuckin' *stand it!* I should find out if the 1049 has gone through within a few days of when I get back to Can Tho."

"Cool. But… I don't know if *I'd* extend… Kate would kill me herself!"

"Yeah, well, I don't have that problem with Flo, anymore," the Kid lamented, "got the old *Dear John* back in August."

"Ouch! Too bad."

"Maybe. Maybe not," the Kid snuffed out his KOOL. "Have to see what happens when I see her in March… that's when I go home, if I get the extension package, meaning I'm under 90 days! Double figures!"

"Wow. Hard to believe. I was feeling good about being under 150," Tom said, "I'm going to try and get an early out for college when I get back. All I want is out."

"I hear you there, bro. Oh! Yesterday, Alan P. and Georgie took me to an Embassy holiday party, real swank deal. It was class A uniforms only I didn't have one with me, so Alan P. loaned me a set of Kakis, but I didn't have any dress shoes. So I went to this store and found out the shoes would cost me $8, just to wear one time… then I saw that an Airborne badge cost

50 cents, so I bought the badge, bloused my combat boot, wore those and went as an Airborne guy! Saved myself $7.50!"

"Gutsy, Kid… Lucky for you no Airborne guys were there!"

"Oh, there was one, all right, but he was so drunk, he couldn't tell the difference between shit and el shinola. Who the fuck cares if I wore an Airborne badge to a party? I mean hell, I bet we both have seen enough combat to earn a Combat Infantry Badge, but we have the wrong MSO, which means we can't ever get one, so FTA!"

"Yeah! You're right. I was pissed when I found *that* out!" Tom agreed. "And where did you go on R&R?"

"Kuala Lumpur," the Kid sounded a little dejected. "I heard there might be an offensive at Christmas, so I dropped Australia, which I would have had to wait until February to go on anyway and took KL to get out of the country for Christmas, then no offensive. Oh well. I'm doing Australia on my extension R&R, for sure!"

"Well, it was sure great seeing Kate!" Tom exclaimed, "we never spent more than half an hour on the beach… it was sheet time all the way!"

"You're a lucky man, Tom. Kate is a beautiful woman!"

"Well, looks like I should hit it and get on out to Ton Son Nhut," Tom glanced at his watch. "If you get that extension, that means we won't be flying home together, so if I don't see you again, good luck! I hope it works out for you."

"Yeah. Good luck to you, too. Say hello to the boys for me… and Happy New Year!"

"I will, and the same to you." On that note, they shook hands and Tom walked out the door, just as word came from the pool table that the Kid was up.

Chapter 36

Hoch had dispatched a jeep, driven by Moyssiadas, to Can Tho Field to pick the Kid up. "Are we going straight to Eakin for Chow?" the Kid asked, checking his watch to see if it was after 1730 hours as he tossed his black leather travel bag into the back seat of the topless vehicle.

"Nope, we're going straight back to the New Villa, the unit is having a New Year's party up in the Roof Club and they're grilling steaks and got a whole bunch of beers on ice and other food up there. Been going on all afternoon!"

"Wow. Far out!"

"And you'll for sure have the munchies when we get there," Moisiadias handed the Kid a joint.

"What service!" exclaimed the Kid as he whipped out his Zippo and torched it off.

"Yeah! This should be really good tonight; we hired a Vietnamese rock and roll band to play and some of the guys have heard them and say they're pretty good!"

The Kid was flying quite high as the jeep neared Bien Xi Moi and the New Villa and it only served to accentuate the *homecoming* feeling he was experiencing. He'd been away for less than two weeks and while he certainly didn't miss his Dutch oven room, he had missed the fellowship of the tribe and the nights on the balcony smoking that ass kicking pot. *I wonder what everybody got for Christmas.*

The light was on in his room, but George Gaugle wasn't home. A note was stuck to his mosquito netting with a safety pin: *"Come on up to our room... we have your mail. Paul, Ken & Roger.* He was so relaxed from R&R and the joint he had just finished that he had to think for a few seconds to remember the combination to his locker. Once unpacked, he changed into his APT shorts and flip flops before hustling up to the third floor.

"The Prodigal Son returns!" exclaimed the voice of Mike Imrem, who was posted on Embassy guard duty, as the Kid emerged onto the balcony,

"Welcome back, Curt!" He shook his hand and a dozen men all smoking there along the balcony rail welcomed him amid handshakes and slaps on the back.

"Ah... it's good to be back!" the Kid worked his way down to Hoch's door.

"Is that the Kid Stocker?" Hoch's voice came out of the room, "Hey, dude, welcome back! I got your mail in here, come on in!" Entering the room, the Kid found Paul, Ken, Ramjet, Birnbaum, and Wimbish sitting on the beds and the floor, all wearing shorts and flip flops but no shirts and all with a Fosters in their grip. "It's in that sack there," Paul pointed with a joint.

"Smoking in the room?" the Kid was a bit surprised.

"Aw hell, we got the guard up and the lifers are so drunk already, they last thing any of'em are interested in doing on New Year's Eve is leaving the bar! So, we're getting more than a little loose tonight! Good fucking bye 1968, you rotten assed year and *hello 1969! The year we all go home! WHOOOOOO!"* Paul hollered; the Kid could tell he'd had a few himself.

It was a huge bundle of mail and packages that Bud the mailman had accumulated for the Kid while he was gone and when he hefted the bag it was like somebody had mugged Santa and given him the loot!

'Far fuckin' out," he declared as he sat down on the floor and undid the knotted ropes and opened the green canvas bag and while smoking the circulating joints, he casually looked the haul over. There were five brown paper wrapped packages of varied sizes, almost two weeks' worth of Boulder Daily Camera newspapers, a copy of Billboard Magazine, and a rubber banded stack of at least two dozen letters. He thumbed through them, seeing ones from his parents, Grandpa and Esther Stocker in Omaha, his 'unofficial-official' fan club president, Pat Bowen, another from Dave and Patsy Allen, along with a bunch of other Christmas card looking envelopes from Nashville... *must all be fan mail... one from D.J. Dan... one from Larry Ryan... and Flo. Yahoo! A letter from Flo!*

"You know..." he looked up at the guys, "I can smell the steaks grilling, and I'm hungry as hell... bet you guys already ate but, is anybody beside me hungry? I'll open these boxes after dinner and sponsor *Monster Munchies* for dessert, but I'm smelling those steaks and it's getting to me."

"Sure, what the hell," Hoch stood up and stretched, "we were actually kind of waiting on you. Yeah, let's go nail some of those steaks! I need to practice for the steak I'm going to eat in the Returnee's Steak House, *in ten days!"*

"That's right, you bastard," said Ken, "keep reminding us you're going under ten days tonight... we won't be sorry to see your ass go!" Then he called out to Roger, "Hey, Ramjet, have you made up your mind who you're going to vote for to be our new room mate yet to replace Paul?"

Ramjet cracked a smile, "Yes, I have. Have you?"

"Yep," Willert smiled back at Ramjet and then looked at the Kid, whose attention the exchange had obviously gotten, and back to the Jet, "let's hope we can avoid another embarrassing series of five *one to one ties.*"

The first person the Kid ran into when he topped the stairs and entered the Roof club was Sergeant Major Lamareaux, the highest-ranking enlisted man in the unit. The sergeant major was a big, well-built mid westerner with a close crop of red hair and a few freckles sprinkled across his not yet plump face. *I like the sergeant major. Out of all the NCO's I've ever dealt with in the whole freaking Army, he's one of the fairest men I ever met. There are few Lifers I like, but the sergeant major is one of them...*

When he saw the Kid, his face lit up, "Well, hey! If it isn't the man who beats Court Martials! Happy New Year's. Specialist Stocker!" he stuck out his hand to shake.

"Hey, Sergeant Major, thank you very much and back at you with the Happy New Year!" the Kid shook the big paw, struggling hard not to let the top shirt's grip break him down.

"How was your R&R?" he asked, taking a sip of beer immediately after.

"It was pretty good, Sgt. Major," the Kid's left hand accepted a beer that Ron Edwards was passing him while he pretended to flex the knuckles of his right. "Got to talk on the phone to my parents and my girlfriend, or ex girlfriend as the case may be... it was good, although I gotta say, I wish I'd kept the Australia trip, but I'd have had to wait another two months to go there."

"Better get a steak while there's some left," he pointed over his shoulder, before his attentions were demanded by Sergeant Johnson, who had just walked up with an apparent pressing need to ask about something.

There were four grills set up in the open area to the left of the covered club and the smoke from the charcoal searing the fat off the steaks sent pungent columns of light amber almost straight up into the humid Asian sky. For some reason, it made the Kid think of burning huts as the smoke curled up toward the clouds that towered over Can Tho, offering the sunset something to paint.

256

Acting grill masters, Barry Fisher and "*Tall* John" Tearman, were handling two grills each that were loaded up with what must have been 40 or more steaks, some of which were at all the various stages of the cooking process, from rare to ultra well done.

"Hey! Curt! Welcome back!" called out Barry, his face sweating beneath his dark and tightly curled hair as he plied his heated task. "What looks good to you? You like Medium? I got a nice medium for you right here!" He picked up a double thick paper plate and plopped a giant T-bone upon it.

"Wow! Thanks!" the Kid looked down at it, "I've been saying 'wow' a lot since I got back! This steak looks great! And I though the Sgt. Major said you were running low."

"Well, yeah, but we just got orders to throw on these 25, because the officers are all coming over here to party from Villa Cruz. Ain't nothing going on there, so they're crashing our party," scoffed Barry.

"I see," said the Kid. Picking up a fork and steak knife, he found the table with the other food items on it and sat down his beer and cow so he could fill another whole plate with baked beans, corn on the cob and watermelon. Then he and Wimbish located a couple of empty tables for the group, to the right side of the room up near the front. The tables were a little more crowded together than usual because an area had been cleared for the Vietnamese band, which was just beginning to set up its equipment.

"Never in all the time I've been here, have I seen a Vietnamese band not play *House of the Rising Sun,* as one of the first three songs," Lou commented, "did that make any sense? Anyway, I'll bet you five dollars these guys play it no later than the third song."

I don't think I'll take that bet," chuckled the Kid, knowing that musical fact was true of his experience as well. "The way I figure is, the ones who only know it, play it first and then the others warm up first before they play it."

"You know, it's difficult to cut a steak at this table while sitting in a butterfly chair! It's just a little low for the angle!" Lou said as Paul, Roger and Ken walked up with their full plates.

"Pick it up and eat it like a corn dog," Ramjet suggested to Wimbish, "it's a fucking hardship tour, go ahead, and eat your meat like the animal you are! Or look! Sgt. Pepper is cutting his with a bayonet!"

Sure enough, the diminutive Sgt. Pepper was going at his porterhouse with his bayonet.

"Hey, look!" Ramjet pointed with his fork, "Sgt. Zazulack is going to sit with him! I swear to God, Sgt Z is twice the size of Sgt. Pepper! That's so fuckin' funny that they like to hang out! We ought to get a picture of 'em together, with Pepper standing on a chair, then he'd only be about six inches shorter than Z!"

"That would be a scream! Now I live to see that photo! We'll have to work on getting that shot!" said the Kid. *If ever there was a man who looked like Elmer Fudd, Sgt Pepper is him.* "Zazulack reminds me of Herman Munster."

"By God, I never thought about it, but he does!" Paul's tone of amazed realization had a theatrical quality to it, "I'll remember that when I'm back home in the States… in 9.5 days… oh, have they told you you're getting my bunk yet?"

"Dammit!" screamed Ramjet, slamming the table with the palm of his left hand, "Hoch… what the fuck are you doing? We were going to string him out! Have some fun, extort some groceries, you knew that!"

"Oh, you think you're so short we can't find a way to get even with you for this in nine and a half days?" Willert questioned.

This all left the Kid sitting with his eyes wide open, glancing from face to face to face, and hoping that what he was hearing wasn't some cruel short timer's joke. *I'm getting out of the furnace room? I can't believe it! I get to move into the best fricking room in the New Villa? For real?*

Finally the trio quit jawing each other and looked at the still silent, gaped mouthed Kid. "Believe it," Roger nodded, "but until numb nuts here blew it, we were going to have some fun and tell you it was up for grabs and find out what it was worth to you.

"Wow. And WOW again!" the Kid shook his head as if in a daze, "the *Embassy Suite!* I can't believe it! And why aren't you *still* extorting me? Like you know I'd pay *something* to get Paul's bunk!"

"Because, truth be told, it was between you and RV Smith, not that we didn't always want you anyway… in fact everybody knew it, but RV was the only one who actually asked. And we, ourselves, would pay not to be roommates with RV, so even though your final victory was by default… welcome to the room, man," Ken shook his hand. "Can you believe it? RV not only had the balls to ask, he thought he should be entitled to move into the room! We told him, *'Hell will never freeze over in Nam so consequently, you'll never be our roommate, '!'*"

"All of the sudden, Paul, you can't be short enough!" groused the Kid, "perhaps I can help you pack?"

"Well, hey, nobody who doesn't smoke weed can be in our room, we all know that. Besides, they love your jokes!" Paul said, "So it was basically a no brainer."

Not long after the sun set, the Vietnamese band was tuned up and ready to go and sure enough, their opening number was *'House of the Rising Sun.'* About halfway through the song, or so the Kid imagined, he happened to notice that Tom Boyett, Benny Vargas, George Cabrillo, and Don Hartman had entered the club and they were standing back by the bar, talking amongst themselves and pointing at the stage area. A handful of GIs were dancing with some of the whores who were attending the fest, from Sgt. Jone's whorehouse across the street, and the Kid couldn't tell if the group was pointing at them or something else.

"The officers are on their way over," said Paul, "they weren't smart enough or sober enough or cool enough to plan their own party, so they gotta glom on to ours. Hey, even your buddy Wilson is in town and he's probably going to be here."

"Oh. Really?" *Won't that be fun?*

"Yeah. And because there's no place for them to sleep over here, they've made arrangements with the ARVN MPs on duty to escort them back at about 0100 hours. How funny would it be if their drunk asses got ambushed on the way back? There was a captain here, whose brother was also here in Nam on TDY and came to see him. They went to a bar and got drunk, and he had a jeep wreck that killed his brother!"

"No!"

"Yes! But I forget his name," Paul lit up because he'd finished eating, "talk about a bummer! So, tell us about your R&R… how were the women?"

"Well, the first two nights, I had this Malaysian chick, Judy, who was smokin' hot. She gave me a blow job that was out of this fucking world! I'm going to have to try and describe it to the girls over at the Scientific! I know when she was doing it, I thought it was indescribable, but I'm sure as hell going to try! For Christmas Eve, I took a break, talked to my parents and Flo…"

"She on or off?" Wimbish encapsulated the question.

"Sorta off sounding, if you know what I mean," the Kid said, not really knowing in all honesty. "Then I did some sightseeing, had a big restaurant dinner and got some sleep. On Christmas, I got hooked up with this Indian woman,"

"What tribe?" Edwards cut in.

"Bombay Taj Mahal Cleveland Indians," the Kid said without missing a beat, "Ashanti, was her name, which I though was more than fucking perfect... I called her 'Ahsanti-claus' and she'd look at me funny, like she didn't get it. Ashanti wasn't as cute as Judy and she wasn't as good in bed, either she wasn't really into it at all. She might as well been chewing gum and watching TV or reading a magazine while we did it, for all she cared. Then, for my last night, the Mama San got me this Chinese chick, Jeni, who was kind of skinny... wait a minute; did I say 'kind of skinny...'' what I mean to say was, she looked like frickin' Twiggy!" *Big laugh...* "You shoulda seen the gap between her thighs! But she had a pretty face and she liked to get on top and go for it."

The band finished the *House of the Rising and Son* and launched into *"Hang on Sloopy."*

"Sounds like you had a good time!" said Paul, but not half as good as I'm going to have in 9.39 days!"

"Shut the fuck up you ass wipe!" hollered Ramjet, "we don't care how short your dick or you are!"

"And I don't care you don't care I'm so fucking short!" Paul crowed like Peter Pan.

Just then, Boyett, Ben, George and Don walked over to their area and sat down at an adjacent table.

"Hey, men," Ron greeted them, *"Que pass-o low?"*

"What's *que 'passo',* is, when those gents take a break, we are going to commandeer their instruments and play a couple of songs," Tom informed the group. "Me and the boys, we've been practicing down in my room with the acoustic guitars and Don here's been drumming on a footlocker, so this is our big chance to *'go electric'!"* like Bob Dylan. Soon as they take a break."

"Oh. Cool," nodded Edwards, turning his head to scratch his neck, "hey, look, the officers have arrived!"

And sure enough, up out of the stairs came a stream of the unit's brass, with the two company commanders, the Captain *Smith Brothers,* Ronnie and PM, leading the way. Up behind them were Lt. Regan, Lt. Culp, Lt. Kazmarskyj, Lt. Sitzer, Lt. Powell, and on and on, until at least 20 of them were in the Roof Club, the last of them being *Lt. Wilson!*

"What a raw deal for Birnbaum and Wells," said Lou as they watched the officer's emerge from the stairwell, "almost all of the officer's all come over here to the party and those guys still have to be on guard duty back at the Villa Cruz."

The brass were all dressed in civis; not one of them was in uniform, which meant they were there to party. Lots of Hawaiian shirts, cut-offs, T-shirts and open buttoned and flip flops were the order of the evening. The fact that most of them were carrying M-16's looks a little strange.

"They're armed pretty well," said Paul, as they checked their weapons with the two bar tenders, where the pair could keep an eye on them.

"Party crashers!" accused Ling Fook, "this means we'll have to be a little bit more careful down in the Embassy."

Now the Vietnamese band was playing chords that indicated their next song might be Gloria… and it was. And right after they butchered *"Wipe Out"*, they were ready for their break, Tom, Benny, George and Don approached them and with gestures, indicated they wanted to borrow the instruments and play a bit while offering them cigarettes.

Sure, no problem, the native band indicated by hand gestures and smiles, taking the smokes which, they immediately lit up with their own Zippos as they walked off to get something to drink.

Don sat down on the drummer's stool and began appraising the set. Boyett strapped on the lead guitar while Benny took rhythm and George the base. After a quick check of the tuning, the four huddled, obviously coming to an agreement of which song they were going to attempt, and with that, they took their places and Boyett stepped up to the microphone.

"Hello ya'all… "He said and then waited for a couple of seconds as the crowd focused on them. "We been practicing some, but that doesn't mean we're any good… yet. Anyway, this opportunity to play some electric is too much to pass up, so bear with us… We'd like to extend a Happy New Year's hello to our esteemed guests," he gestured to a large pool of officers standing off to his right side, "and know that we're all here to have fun, and if you're not, screw ya' all and Happy New Years anyway! A one and a two and uh *three four five…*"

On Boyett's count, they began to play and issuing fourth out of the speakers was something of a rhythm and blues sound that wasn't half bad, indicative of the fact there had, indeed, been practice. Soon, it developed into a noticeable Bo Diddley number. *"Hey Bo Diddley…* "Tom sang and George and Benny answered back…*"Hey Bo Diddley… and Tom sang it again and this time, the crowd answered back. Hey Bo Diddley… yeah! This will be great in the book! Holy crap! They're drowning in potential!*

261

They got it going'! The Kid lit up a KOOL and smiled in enjoyment to the members of the Tribe, who were all bopping along to the sounds, certainly impressed with the impromptu rock band togetherness of this kick ass music.

They ended up playing three songs, each one getting a rousing shock of applause from the assembled troops of the 10th. They sounded like they played together for years!

Absolutely great! I must be stoned out of my mind or they're incredible… or both!

The Vietnamese band, standing off the side, appeared to be into them as well, observing their technique closely and pointing and talking excitedly amongst themselves. Before starting the next song, Tom nodded in their direction, "And finally, this last song, we'd like to dedicate to this fine Vietnamese Band here, who so kindly lent us their instruments," Boyett said, in a sweeping gesture to them "round of applause for the boys," he egged on the soldiers, who responded eagerly, "and we hope you fellers like it. And you, yeah you… the drummer! Watch this man right here," he pointed to Don sitting in the percussionist's chair, "because… *THIS* is how you play *Wipe Out!*

On that cue and with flailing arms, Don broke out with the classic Wipe Out drum rip and when Tom cut in the guitar, the two of them were playing the song dead on and when Benny and George started jamming on it, musical magic happened and there wasn't a single person sitting down in the whole joint. When Don got to the final drum solo, with all three guitarists laying in the punctuating signature lick, the entire focus of the crowd present was on him and the way he was punishing the drums. And when they drew out the ending with more jamming, when they at last wrapped it up with a big final finishing note, the applause and warrior male roaring was nothing short of remarkable. *They brought the house down! Yeah in the book I'll have to say the brought the fucking house down!"*

"Jeezus! That was great!" the Kid screamed at Paul, Ken, Roger and Lou, "bet you the officers are glad they brought their brass asses over here tonight! They should have to pay a cover to get entertainment like that!"

The Kid circled around to the back of the stage area while he watched the soldiers mob the group and compliment them and slap them on the back in an open demonstration of their amazement at the performance. He had already thought Tom Boyett was talented, but from what he'd seen now, from the way Tom played guitar, to the way he fronted for the group and was the obvious de facto musical director, he was… *Damned impressive!*

I hope someday I can get my act as tight as Boyett's. The man is fucking gifted! Graphic design, photography, and now music! Fuck-n-a! Has he has got it going on or what?

The Americans unstrapped the guitars and stood them in their metal stands and Don laid down the sticks and as they all began to vacate the stage, the Kid caught Lt. Wilson, in his peripheral vision, emerging from the crowd on the left. He was walking slowly forward, toward the instruments, with his eyes glassed over and locked in a stare at the red Fender Boyett had been playing. The Kid flashed on all the times he'd seen Wilson commander guitars and start performing when they were out in the boonies and seeing clearly that was where this was headed, he made it a point to be standing behind the guitar when the Lt. came to stand in front of it. Looking up, Wilson was surprised as he suddenly realized it was the Kid.

Although he spoke no words, the expression on the Kid's face and the way he negatively shook his head from side to side said, plain as day, *"You think your weak shit can follow that act?,"* to which Wilson's response was to sense the reality and he turned and walked away with shoulders slumped.

Ha! Look at that!

The Kid caught up with the band down on the balcony where they were toking up: "Hey! You guys were great! No fucking shit!"

"Thanks! Glad you liked it," Boyett wiped some sweat from his brow with the back of his hand that held the beer, "we could get really good if we had those electric guitars all of the time."

"And a better set of drums," Don Hartman quickly added.

"Gawd!" exclaimed the Kid, "you guys played *Wipe Out* like you'd been together as a band for *frickin'* years!"

"Well," said Don, "if you've ever been a drummer in any band, in the last five years, you've played *Wipe Out* at least a thousand times! Hell, it's probably the reason you *became* a drummer!"

"Yeah," said Benny, that's the one song we've all played the most, for sure. That was easy up there."

"With what I heard upstairs, I say if you guys had a chance to practice and maybe write a couple of your own songs, how's about I be your agent after the war and we go to Nashville and we get you a recording contract! You'll be famous! We need a good name, though," the Kid pondered, as the members of the band seized on the idea around him.

"Yeah! Just like Jimi Hendrix; he was in Nam when he got his act together!" recent history was cited by Benny.

263

"Wouldn't *that* be a fucking hoot!" George conjectured."

"So you *really* know people in Nashville?" Tom questioned the Kid.

The Kid nodded in the affirmative, "Oh yeah, really. Lots of them. You know, I've been to a few sessions, and you play every bit as good as most of those guys who back up the headliners."

"Thank you for the compliment... I think. I do have some friends who've taught me well," he replied, before taking a big hit on a hot smoking pipe that had just been placed in his hand.

"Yeah, in the music business, I've met a bunch of musicians, record label guys, producers, and the works. They were all by the station at one time or another and they all wanted to be friends with the DJs, hoping it will result in more air play for their songs or artists," The Kid took the pipe from Tom, who held his hit. "Really. A bunch of them. Can't you see the PR angle?" The Kid motioned with the pipe, to an imaginary headline somewhere off the balcony in the air that was filled with marijuana smoke. "New band rises from fires in Vietnam! Something like, 'fighting to keep up morale! It would be a *fuckin' scream' PR man's wet dream!* But the band needs a really great name... like 'Phoenix" it rose from fire!"

"Been to Phoenix, didn't like it," flatly stated Benny.

"Yeah! We need a really bitchin' name! Too bad the Grateful Dead is already taken, "Don cut in, "that would be a perfect name for a band from a war zone!"

"Wait till you hear us with Richie singing," Boyett was getting excited. "Richie's on guard duty tonight."

"I wish I could sing... I can't play anything and I'd love to be in the band," lamented the Kid, "it's not to be. Guess that's why I'm a DJ, but the band needs a manager! And a name... it'll come to me."

'Oh, look," Ling Fook said, tapping at his watch, "it's 2030 hours. Wow, time is flying tonight, only 3 and a half hours left in 1968, and it's goodbye to a truly fucked year, if I don't say so myself," the lanky photographer-philosopher asserted.

The Kid took another hit and stared off into the distance at the red light that was a communications tower at Bin Thuy Airbase. *A year ago New Year's, I was with Flo... we went out to that bonfire beach party and made out like crazy because It was our last night together and I had to leave to drive back to Indiana at two in the morning. God was that a crazy drive. Some of the dreams I had, like the one outside of Las Vegas where I woke up three times before I finally actually woke up! Ha, that was the spirit telling me to 'wake UP!' Well, that's all water under the bridge. Now it's going to be 1969. If I get the 60-day drop, I'm fucking down to 90 days!* And just as the Kid was starting to feel a little bit short for the first time in his whole tour, Hoch, let him know what 'short' really was.

"At midnight, I'll officially be down to single digits!" Paul fairly screamed.

"Ohhhh!' exclaimed the Kid, "that means I'm that close to getting out of the Oven! I think I'm just going to go ahead and move up here and sleep on this bench," he gestured to the wooden structure below the window of his soon to be room."

"The mosquitoes would suck you dry," Edwards emphatically said, "in about a New York fucking second."

"Oh. Yeah, I forgot about them. But this marijuana smoke keeps'em away nicely, doesn't it?" The Kid took another hit on a passing pipe.

"I think I just saw one," Wimbish pointed up, like he was tracking one's flight, "somebody better light another half a dozen Joints." And more than half a dozen somebodies did, all racing to be first, amid the grinding of Zippo flints, a roiling cloud of cannabis smoke and to the howling laughter of the Tribe.

"I got a question for the group…" the Kid stood holding a joint in an elevated position over his head, "do mosquitos get more stoned by sucking out our pot laden blood, or from flying through the smoke that surrounds us in the air?"

After the slightest silence, Edwards jumped all over it. "Seems to me it's a moot point, Curt, since they're doing both, making it scientifically undeterminable!"

"Well, that's just like asking, which gets you higher, smoking it or eating it?" Hoch continued down the path, "I've heard eating it will get you as high, but just not as fast as smoking it. You guys should try it … after I'm gone, of course, because I'm 3 hours from single digits, baby!"

Upstairs, the Lifer-red necks were getting plastered like the ceiling of the Sistine chapel. The officers were normally a hard drinking lot on a workday but on the drinking holiday second only to St. Patrick's Day with the next day off, they were getting so sloshed, it was a foregone conclusion they'd be finding it necessary to recruit a few of the 'sober' enlisted pot smokers to drive them home to the Villa Cruz.

The Vietnamese band had been inspired by the performance of the Americans and they were making a gallant effort not to totally embarrass themselves. But after the second time through House of the Rising Sun, at about 30 minutes before midnight, the crowd got restless and started yelling for Boyett, Vargas, Hartman and Cabrillo to do an encore.

Of course, the boys were more than ready to oblige and the Vietnamese band, which had apparently run out of gas, was more than willing to turn over the instruments.

They got ready in a flash and busted out with a stirring rendition of 'Twist and Shout that quickly set the 10th Battalion party into motion. As all the drunk sergeants and officers tried to out-do each other with gyrating alcohol inspired dance moves to the Chubby Checker classic. A couple of them fell over.

It looks like they're dancing with each other! I should get some good black mail pictures!

Next, the boys tried their hand at *Louie Louie,* which they played pretty good on the instrumental part of it and since nobody really knew what the actual words to the song were, whatever came out of Boyett's mouth worked quite well. After that, a bunch of the guys started yelling, *"play Wipe Out again! Play Wipe Out again!* So they did and when they finished, Sgt. Major Lamaroux walked up to Boyett's mike and made an announcement.

"Gentlemen, in just one minute, according to my watch, It will be midnight and 1969!"

"Whoopee, Yay! Yahoo! Yee-HAWWW" the intoxicated and stoned off the charts crowd stomped, hollered and wailed.

"Do you guys know Olde Laing Sine?" He turned to Boyett.

Shrugging his shoulders, Tom took a quick visual survey of the group, "Well, I sort of can play anything…guys, do you want to give it a try?"

"Shit yeah! We'll give it a hell of a fuckin' try!" promised Benny.

"30 seconds!' bellowed the Sgt. Major.

And as he prepared for the count down, the Kid took a deep breath and recalled where he'd been exactly one year ago. *I was getting ready to kiss Flo. I wonder if she's kissing anybody tonight. Which is actually tomorrow for her, because of the International Date Line. Like she would have told me if I'd asked. Oh well, can't blame her if she is but I know I'm not!*

"Ok! Here we go!" Lamaroux lead the count, "Ten, nine, eight, seven…"

"Six… five… four…" the enlisted men of the 10th and the guest officers all joined in…"three… two… one…"

Happy New Year! 1969! I'm lucky to be alive! The Kid shook hands and exchanged hugs and slaps on the back with his compatriots in the Tribe as all the men in the Roof Club did the same, whooping and hollering it up to the somewhat awkward but totally identifiable refrains of *Auld Lang Sine,* courtesy of the spontaneous GI band.

From around the New Villa, a smattering of celebratory gunshots could clearly be heard. And from several locations, some close and some farther away, red tracer bullets cut glowing hot arcs across the Delta night sky. *Oh, look, tracers... dumb fucks shooting into the sky... like the bullets aren't ever going to come down some place! Wait a minute, the volume of fire out there is increasing! Holy shit? Look at the shooting out at Binh Thuy! Are the VC launching an offensive?*

As it turned out, the Kid wasn't the only American to have that identical thought at the same moment. The volume of gunfire did get heavier at such a rate that it attracted the immediate attention of nearly every swinging dick on the roof and instantly inoculated them with a sobering hit of adrenalin.

"You don't think…" a voice loudly speculated.

"Are we under attack?" another anxious voice raised the frightful question.

Then, somebody, be it an officer or a senior NCO screamed out at the top of his lungs, "Everybody get your weapons and man your posts!" And with that, a full-blown madhouse cluster fuck of a Chinese fire drill ensued. Men were running in every which direction. The officers all mobbed the bar area, where their M-16s had been checked, the enlisted men jammed into the two stairwells that would take them to the lower floors, where their weapons were stored in their rooms, along with extra ammunition, steel pots and flak jackets.

Damn! "*I should have stayed for Christmas and taken R&R at New Years! Shit; drunk men with loaded guns… this could get hairier than a monkey's ass at the San Diego Zoo!* thought the Kid as he found himself crammed at the back of the mob trying to get down the stairwell closest to the bar.

The only people on the roof who weren't running around like a pack of freshly decapitated slaughterhouse chickens, it turned out, was *the band.* In fact, amid the spreading mayhem of the drunk and panicked men and against the backdrop of gunfire, that now seemed to completely ring the New Villa, they actually started to play.

Is this like the band on the Titanic? The Kid stopped in his tracks and turned in amazement to listen to the heavy blues rift that issued forth as Boyett stepped up to the microphone and began to sing:

267

We were playin' a gig at a party...

In the shack around to the back...

And just as we were laying down tracks,

The VC decided to launch an attack!

And we got the blues...

.

Yeah Yeah... George and Benny vocally refrained back as a just a few of the men seemed to notice but the Kid was completely mesmerized by the surreal spontaneity of the performance.

We got a major major major case of the blues...

When Charlie comes at you with his AK 47

And shoots in a mortar round or two,

You know what you've got

Is a big whoppin' ass case of those

Nasty old Ground Attack Blues....

From having been in dozens of actual fights, the Kid comprehended that the New Villa wasn't taking any fire yet but as recollections of his combat experience kicked in, he realized something... *Hmmm, better get my gun.* The jam at the stairs suddenly opened up and, in a flash, he was down to his 2nd floor interior room where he found George Gaugle standing like a statue, already into his gear and holding his M-14 clutched in his white knuckled hands...

"I'm scared!" he declared to the Kid.

His knees are shaking!

"George... don't panic," the Kid tried to calm him down, as he grabbed his steel pot off the top of his locker and plopped it on his head, "I don't think we've taken any fire yet... there's a really good chance this *isn't* an attack or if it is, we aren't the objective!" He pulled on his flak jacket and grabbed his M-16 out of his locker along with his bandolier and jacked a clip into the magazine port but didn't chamber a round.

"I'm still scared, Curt!"

The Kid laid a hand on his shoulder, "come on, stick with me, we can get through this, whatever happens! Uh, where is our assignment? I don't think anybody ever told me…"

"We're supposed to go to the second-floor balcony," Gaugle informed the Kid of the plan for the defense of the New Villa in case of an attack. "Everybody's supposed to man the balcony on the floor where they live!"

"OK then, let's go!"

When they emerged on the balcony, the pair found the walkway already manned by close to ten soldiers, kneeling behind the double row of sandbags that lined the balcony rail, with rifles at the ready, some of which were actually stuck right through the chicken wire covering that protected the rooms of that low floor from thrown grenades. The PSYOP warriors of the second floor, 95% of which had never seen any combat, were frothing at the bit ready to open up on anything that moved.

"Go down to the far end!" Lt. Regan shouted an order to them. He was the officer who had come down to command on the second floor, "and hold your fire… hold you fire everybody… we are not taking any, so don't anybody go shooting their weapon and attracting attention to us! Plus, there civilians in those shacks right across from us…"

"Come on you fuckin' Gooks!" The Kid heard one soldier challenge the still phantom foe, if indeed, any of the tracers had been fired by the enemy; thus far, he'd only seen red ones, no AK 47 orange. As he and Gaugle quickly made their way down the line to their assigned positions, he appraised his fox hole companions. *Hmmm, guess the second floor does have all the red necks… I gotta admit, I don't know half of these guys! Man o man, am I ever stoked about moving up to the third floor! Hey! I can still hear the band!* The Kid knelt on the checkered marble floor and sure enough, from two floors above, he could hear the band was still at it! *The Ground Attack Blues mixed in with rifle fire! It could be a hit! Like Country Joe and the Fish! This is fucking wild! That band could be a fricking national fucking hit!*

Settling into their assigned position, the Kid tried to calm Gaugle. "George, I really don't think this is going to be an attack... You can hear the firing is finally dying down," he insisted to his petrified companion, but he could see in his face that George wasn't yet ready to buy any of it. But after a couple of minutes the tracers creasing the sky and the clatter of automatic weapons significantly subsided and he began to see that what the Kid said was true.

"In a way, I want to see some action and, in another way, I don't…" Gaugle released a baited breath.

"That's normal, George, but I can tell you this. After having seen action, I'd rather not see any more action. But if it happens… it happens and you'll deal with it. Thank God, it looks like it's *not* happening here tonight!"

The consensus they could stand down came five minutes later and as the second-floor squad congratulated themselves on a job well done, the Kid, still carrying his weapon, made his way straight up to the Roof Club to find the band.

They were sitting at the table closest to where the instruments were and they were all drinking beers, smoking cigarettes and laughing it up with the Vietnamese band members, acting like nothing ever happened, *which it didn't.*

"Hey, guys!" the Kid greeted them as he walked up, "I think I've got a really bitchin' far out name for the band!" silence ensued while they waited for him to deliver. Tapping his helmet with the barrel of his M-16 he said, "Steel Pot!"

"Steel Pot?" Boyett repeated with a questioned look on his face.

"Yeah. Like *Iron Butterfly*…only it's *'Steel Pot!'* You got your helmet for soldiers and war… but the word *'Pot'* is a double intender! When I thought of it, I got this picture in my brain of a helmet turned upside down with a pot plant growing up out of it!"

"A pot plant made of steel?" George mused. *Not bad!*

"Steel Pot?" Benny looked at the Kid askance, "I always thought that *Iron Butterfly* was stupid, but 'Steel Pot?' I don't know, maybe we should go downstairs and smoke on it."

"Steel Pot…" Boyett said it real slow, "… have to sleep on it. ... Maybe come up with a list. But for sure, Steel Pot on the list!" and he quickly added, "actually, right now, it *IS* the list!"

"All right! Boyett, Dude… can you remember the lyrics to that song you were singing when the shooting started?"

"That song? We were just making it up as we went along," he pondered for a couple of seconds, "I think we're going to call it *'ground attack blues!'*"

A little later, when the Kid finally went to the oven to turn in, he discovered Gauggle was not in the room. Walking out to the second-floor balcony latrine to take a leak before retiring, he saw George, still vigilantly on guard at his position down on the rail.

Chapter 37

A platoon of combat booted feet pounded out the cadence... 'Yo left, you lef, yo left right left... yo left, yo left...yo left right left...' The sun was not yet up, but the early morning air of Ft. Campbell, Kentucky, still had the taste of yesterday's heat and humidity about it as the Kid inhaled and exhaled deeply, running quite easily in his first formation exercise in boot camp. They had spent the first day learning how to get into formation and March. Now, on the second morning, the drill sergeant fell them out and commenced to run the whole platoon on a morning eye opener. Since the only high school sports team the Kid had ever made was the track team and because he took the time to work out in advance of going in to boot camp, at what he imagined was a quarter mile, he wasn't even breathing hard yet. But some of the pudgier guys who obviously hadn't run a city block in five years, were screaming bloody murder... Hmmm, it's so early, if I was at WKDA doing my air shift, I wouldn't even get off work for another half an hour! This is exactly like being in jail... don't want to be here, don't want to lose three years out of my life... it cannot be avoided... must do my time to get out or never get out... yo left, yo left, yo left right left... stupid drill sergeants yelling... 'Come on you pussies! We're only doing a half a mile before breakfast you pack of bawling crybaby candy ass momma's boys! Why in fucking blazes are they all wearing Halloween costumes?' How did I come to be in this place? He snapped out of the dream. Ah... the reality is worse.

The tiny fan purred above his feet at the far end of his lower bunk, moving just enough air to make it possible to spend a whole night in 'the oven'. Looking at his watch, he sleepily determined it was 0700 hours. The humidity he'd been tasting in the dream about boot camp had a distinct similarity to that of his and George Gaugle's room. Then it struck him, what today was... *Oh boy! Today is the day I move out!*

It was January 7th, and Paul D. Hoch, the acknowledged leader of the Clan, was leaving this very day, to return to Saigon and two days hence, on not only to the United States, but back to civilian life as well. *Lucky bastard.* The Kid had the slightest touch of a hangover because the clan had partied long and hard the night before, going as much for the booze as the pot. There were many an emotional toast, all very necessary, to properly sendoff of a comrade who was much loved and appreciated.

As usual, George had already gotten up and left earlier to make breakfast at Eakin Compound, which the Kid always skipped, wanting the extra few good moments of sleep the early morning promised. He hadn't gotten much sleep at all, since moving into the oven, nearly two months ago. And now, his long nightmare was at an end!

Lifting the mosquito net, the Kid rose to sit on the edge of his bunk and touched his feet to the always warm tile floor. The only light in the room came from the high walls, opened at the top two feet all the way around the room, designed to permit some ventilation to penetrate and move through the interior of the old French hotel. Additionally, a light bulb in the hall outside the closed louvered door shone a pattern on the floor.

Pulling a cigarette out of the pack of KOOLs that lay on the corner of his foot locker next to the head of his bunk, he flipped open the Zippo and lit up the first butt of the day. The dream he'd just awakened from played over again in his head as he exhaled and felt the nicotine rush wash over him. *This is a good day, as good as days get in Nam… I'm out of this fucking room tonight! I'm going to miss Paul, but oh God! Tonight I sleep by a window!*

After a few puffs, he stuffed the burning cig into the empty Victoria Bitters can sitting on the floor by his feet and rose to turn on the light and find his canteen to facilitate the brushing of his teeth. Spitting the residue into the sink, the Kid turned on the spigot and splashed his face with some non-potable tap water, lathered up and quickly shaved. He put on his glasses and proceeded to get dressed in a clean set of fatigues.

Each day pretty much began the same way and it was like the dream he had; the only thing he could do was keep running and some days, it felt as if the ordeal would never end. Still, today had something to look forward to and with that little bit of sunshine in his head, once dressed, he made his way down to the street to catch a pedi-cab to Battalion headquarters.

Standing on the corner of the intersection of Bien Xi Moi Road and the main drag into town, the Kid was waiting to flag down a civilian Vietnamese vehicle of public transportation when an American jeep pulled over and the PFC passenger indicated by jerking his thumb over his shoulder that he could hop into the empty back.

"Thanks!" he hollered over the din of the early morning rush hour as the jeep pulled back into the flow of the traffic. "You can drop me at PSYOPS, on the big turn by the dry fountain," he spoke into the driver's ear. The corporal nodded that he understood where it was, and the Kid didn't say another word until the jeep stopped by the side of the road at the fountain and he hopped out. "Much oblige!" he waved, and the pair was off, most likely to Eakin Compound.

Checking his Seiko, he noted it was 0728 hours, a couple of minutes before the appointed time for beginning the work day and right on schedule, one of the duce and a half chow trucks had just unloaded at least 20 fellow PSYOP warriors returning from breakfast and the Kid stood at the end of a throng, all of them queing for the single narrow staircase that was the only route to the second floor. The sun was just high enough to light the walled courtyard through the high trees as the Kid took the opportunity to light up another KOOL as he waited to enter the building.

At last, emerging from the staircase into the main HQ area, the Kid noticed that Paul and Lou, were already in, apparently going over some of the responsibilities Wimbish would officially inherit when he became 'the man', the second Paul walked out the door.

"Hey!" Paul was grinning literally from ear to ear, "Curt... come ride out to the airport with us? My flight is at 0830 but we're leaving in a couple minutes!"

"Uh... sure, why not? Oh wait, I gotta ask the Chief if it's OK... let me run right back there!" The Kid wheeled to head for graphics. *Lots of geckos today* the Kid bounced at least half a dozen off the screen, left right left right, the lizards gyrated through the air sticking their landings onto their white wall LZ.

Upon entering the graphics room, he noticed it was already a beehive of activity. With the morning show on AFVN playing in the background, Boyett and Weston were both bent over their glass tables while the Chief was holding court with Edwards, Imrem and Birnbach, who stood surrounding his desk.

With his cigarette curling up smoke out of the ashtray to his right and steam coming off the coffee in his cup to the left, Tom was framed by goal posts of white smoke as he poured over some piece of art in front of him on the glass table.

"Mornin' Tom," the Kid said as he stopped to take a look at what he was working on, "geeze, what is that?"

"Oh, I'm working on a new masthead for DIMENSION, the one we're using is kind of tired and I've got an idea to spruce is up and make it a little bit … how shall we say… more modern… 'Psychedelic even. See? The wrap around letters will say DIMENSION, I know now all its says is 'dime', but I'll have the rest of it done by lunch."

"Oh, yeah, now I see it!" the Kid smiled, "groovy!"

"It's time for changes," Tom took a puff on his Marlboro, "new masthead… Paul's going home… new room for you, Curt, and I got some new music from my buddy Carl! I can't wait till you hear The Band!"

"What band?" the Kid asked.

"The *Band*," Boyett said with what could only be described as special emphasis on the word, 'band.'

"Well, you'll have to tell me the name of the band later, I gotta ask Chief if he'll let me ride to the airport with Paul, and with that, the Kid stepped over to the group of four men.

"What, Stocker?" the Chief immediately asked.

"Hey guys… pardon the interruption, but chief, can I ride out to Can Tho field with Paul?"

"Is your story on R & R in Hong Kong done yet?" He looked real serious, tapping his pen with an expectant rhythm upon a list, written on a yellow legal pad that sat upon his rather scarred and beat up gray metal desk.

"No."

"Then, no, you can't go," Reagan said with a totally straight face, much to the chagrin of the Kid. "Only kidding!" he countered, as soon as he got a reaction,

"Of course you can go! You know I don't give a shit if you go to the airport or not, I know you'll have it done today before 1600 hours. That's your double drop-dead deadline, so go, go now…we're working on some stuff."

"Stuff? What stuff?"

"Actually, we're arguing about the sacrificial pig for the AFL in the pro football championship next week," Birnbaum began rocking back and forth on his heels in a subtle but clearly apparent act of arrogance. Being from Baltimore, the Colts were a lock to win it all over the lowly New York Jets, in his mind at least. "This year, they decided to name the game 'the Super

Bowl' I read, after a super ball of all things, and Imrem here thinks the Jets are going to be *super* and actually win the game!"

"Namath *can* win it!" Imrem goaded him, "if he gets drunk the night before and has a good day."

"In your fucking wet dream on the dark side of Mars is the only place where the Jets or any team from the AFL beats the true NFL champion within, I say, the next five years... or more!" Mark knew the Kid had grown up in Boulder and was a Denver Bronco fan and never failed to miss a chance to let him know how bad they were. After all, they'd never ever even had a winning season, let alone been to the playoffs.

"OK, whatever you say," the Kid smiled at Birnbaum, "I'll gladly discuss this with you when I get back... hey, he's leaving right now, you know everybody's gonna get up front and do him a huge frickin' cat call!"

"Hell yes," Weston stood up," I don't want to miss this one!"

As everyone from the back entered the front area of Battalion HQ, they discovered the goodbye was reaching a crescendo. Kid caught Paul's farewell handshakes with Colonel Lawton and the rest of the HQ command staff; Sgt Major Lamaroux... Lt. Harry Ragen... Major Gregory... the Smith Brother Captains, P.M. and Ronnie... and Dave Coffman, from Company B... Lt. Powell, and a couple of others that had him surrounded. They then commenced patting him on the back, just short of actually beating him up.

"And wherever you got, in the years to come, we'll remember you and you remember us," Wille O. summed it up to a cheer from the group.

"Thank you," Paul was trying hard not to go all emotional, his baseball cap tightly crumpled in his left hand, "this is an incredible outfit, and Lt. Colonel Lawton, Sir," Paul snapped off one more salute, which was promptly returned, "It has been a privilege being on your staff for these past 3 months."

"Thank you, Paul," Lawton smiled in his winning way, "you are one of the hardest working clerks that I've ever known in my nearly 20 years in this man's Army!"

Paul looked at the doorway to the stair well to his left and finally got a little teary eyed. "God. Now that I'm ready to walk out that door, it feels like I just got here! Where did the year go? Don't anybody answer that!" And everybody howled with laughter! "Ramjet... is my jeep ready?

"Jeep is ready!" Roger pumped his right fist.

"Then, let's go... uh wait, now who's going... finally... Ah! Stocker... you're going, right?"

276

"Right"

"OK, then, its Ramjet driving, you, me riding shotgun and Willet is supposed to meet us here but I don't see him! Fuck it! Let's roll! See ya 10th… love ya, 10th" Paul waved with his right hand vigorously over his head as he ducked into the stairwell for one final time.

As Paul emerged into the courtyard below, there was a solid wall of men lining the front overlooking screen of the second-floor office, from one end to the other, clapping and hooting and waving.

Willert, it turned out, was already waiting at the jeep. He took Paul's one bag and placed it in the back. "You ready?" he flipped a lit butt out into the street.

"Soooo *fucking* ready!" Paul leaped into the shotgun position as Ramjet climbed into the driver's seat and Ken and the Kid piled into the back on either side of his bag. "To the airport, James!"

During the drive, the Kid kept thinking about the last time he went to an airport with a friend named Paul, who was going home to get out… at Tra Vinh, on his birthday, when a bullet from the airport sniper ignited the fire in the engine of the Air Vietnam DC3. *Tra Vinh, Cang Long… Tan An. fuck, it was like I was never there. Here I am living in town with a PX, movies… restaurants… steam baths and blow jobs… shit, I haven't been in any combat now for over three months! And tonight, I'll sleep next to a window and I'm down to 79 days… life is good! Oh, wait,* he looked at the back of Paul's head, *but the day I leave is as good as it will get… yeah… that will be the day!*

While the Kid and Ramjet refrained, Ken and Paul both lit up joints as soon as the jeep pulled out onto the main drag, heading west to Can Tho Field. "I'm sure as fuck going to miss this!" Paul held up his marijuana loaded filter tipped Winston, "Ain't no $5 bucks a pound back in the world! I wish I'd had the guts to put a pound or two into my hold baggage."

"Better safe than sorry," the Kid conjectured, "you wouldn't want to get out of the Army only to be arrested when you hold baggage came in and go to jail."

"Yeah," said Ken, "they can't look into all the hold baggage from every GI coming back, but what bum luck if they happened to pick yours to really check over."

"Oh well, what the hell! I don't care! *I'm going home!*" Paul sucked in another huge hit, "I won't need a plane to fly to Saigon," he spoke while holding in the hit.

Once at Can Tho Field, Paul checks in at the flight desk to insure he was on the manifest and then the foursome stood off to the side and quietly talked while waiting for his flight to be called.

"Curt," Paul turned to him, "in addition to my bunk, I've left you another present."

"A present? What?"

"Can't tell you," Paul smirked, "then it wouldn't be a present anymore. No need to thank me when you figure out what it is."

"Figure it out... not find it?" the Kid questioned.

Paul only grinned his trademark smile, "yeah, *'figure out'*, and would be more accurate."

"How will I know?" now the Kid's curiosity was really piqued.

"You'll know. When you finally 'get it,' which will likely be the day you lose it... which means you already *have it*... I know you love good riddles. I actually just figured it out myself yesterday when I was cleaning up some unfinished shit on my desk... enough said. So, Roger and Ken," Paul switched the subject, "you think you can live with this stiff?"

"Yeah, I think so," said Ramjet, "if we can't, we'll just heave his miserable ass off the balcony and feed him to the snakes!"

"If you recall, we did have a choice," Ken reminded them, "it was him or RV Smith..."

"Too late to change your minds now!" laughed the Kid, "but the day you want to trade me for RV, I'm sure hell will be frozen solid!"

"Really *Roger* the hell out of THAT!" Ramjet concurred.

Soon, the terminal loudspeaker came to life; "All personnel with seats on the 0830 to Saigon, we are now loading through door #3. Be sure to clear all weapons... have a nice flight!"

"This is it!" Paul took a deep breath and exchanged hugs with the trio. "Guys, be safe and take it easy!"

"Hope to see you again someday, you lucky fucker!" Ken shook his hand.

"You left Stocker a present and you didn't leave one for me?" Ramjet questioned.

"Couldn't. Nothing personal, or *personnel,* you might say, see ya, Ramjet!"

278

"Pack leader," Paul spoke to the Kid, "the bunk is now officially yours!"

"Leader of the pack? What do you mean?"

"Well, you're a combat vet, you beat a fucking court martial, the Colonel loves your ass, you tell the best jokes and now, you own the best bunk in the New Villa... I'd say that makes you the defacto leader of the pack!"

"Oh, well, then cue the fuckin' Shangri-la's and give me the black leather jacket!" chortled the Kid.

Then, with a fruity expression on his face Paul delivered a half salute and turned and walked out the door, into the wavering heat rising off the corrugated tarmac and up to the Caribou loading for Saigon, where he stopped and waved to his buds, and was gone.

"74 days and that's *me!*" exclaimed the Kid as the trio turned to leave.

"He left you a present?" questioned Ramjet. "What the hell is that all about?"

"I sure as hell don't know," puzzled the Kid, "I know I like presents but half the fun is knowing what it is!"

Chapter 38

That night, after they all returned from dinner at Eakin Compound, the move didn't take more than two minutes. Ken and Ramjet carried his footlocker, Edwards carried his laundry bag and the Kid grabbed all of the clean uniforms and the shoulder holstered .38 snub nose hanging in his locker along with his M-16 and it was done in one trip.

Stepping through the door of his new quarters, the Kid had to just stand there in the middle of the room, right under the fan, holding his stuff, and take it all in for just a handful of seconds, *Wow! It's amazing how different it feels, now that I live here!*

"One minor change, Stocker," Ramjet lit up a Winston and used it as a pointer, "you get the upper bunk and I'm taking Paul's lower… I mean, if that's *OK* with you?"

"Shit yeah! Are you kidding? Nice of you to ask, Ramjet… but like I care what fucking bed I sleep in next to the window? I mean, this is my room only thanks to you guys! So upper lower, they're both right next to the freaking window!"

I'm out of the oven! Life is good!

Once his uniforms were hung up, the Kid sat down on his footlocker and unlaced his boots, "I'll have to leave these to get polished tomorrow," he said, setting them aside. Rising up, he took off his uniform shirt and pants and opening the footlocker, he pulled out a laundry bag, into which the soiled garments were thrown. He then selected the maroon APT cut offs to wear for the evening, with no shirt, and giving his gold glasses a good shove back up to the bridge of his sweaty nose, he was ready to party.

Right outside the door, the evening smoke out was already rolling full tilt, with easily a dozen other bare-chested or t-shirt clad dudes wearing cut offs and flip flops, strung out along the rail. Just about everybody was smoking their own refilled filter-tipped cigarette joint but a couple of pipes were also making the rounds with newly acquired stuff the boys were test smoking.

Wimbish and Edwards were sitting on the well-worn wooden bench that occupied the space right outside the screen covered window of his new room. "Between you and me, Curt," Wimbish began, "we pretty much picked old Paul's carcass clean… I got his job and you got his room, which is really the only stuff he had worth shit."

"Amen, brother," the Kid nodded his head as a newly lit bowl found its way into his grip and he took a deep hit and held it as he thought about what Lou was saying. Feeling the smoke permeate his blood stream and as it did, the increasingly rosy glow of the sunset seemed to explode inside his brain. *What's this 'present' he left me?* "Hey, Lou, he didn't say anything to you about a 'present' he left me, did he?"

Just then, *Tall* John Tearman came around the corner and out on to the balcony and called out, "Hey, the duty roster is posted, if anybody wants to go take a look, to see who's going to be on guard duty with me tonight for the late shift at Villa Cruz!"

"Aw shit," Edwards lamented, "I guess we should go take a look and see who are the unlucky dozen for tonight."

And with that, half the tribe began meandering down to the first floor, to the bulletin board where First Sgt. Jones posted the daily duty roster, consisting mainly of men who were assigned to keep an eye on things over night at the Villa Cruz printing plant and for the officers who lived there. The duty was broken up into three four-man shifts of three hours each so over the course of a night, 12 EMs would take turns guarding the quarters of the Battalion's officer corps.

The first shift was not so bad because you went on duty at 1800 hours and were done at 2200 hours. And the last shift caused you to be awakened at 0130 hours to get trucked over with an MP jeep guard at 0200 but at least you got some sleep before hand and when you were done, you got the rest of the morning off!

The unit bulletin board was located on the first floor of the New Villa, in the hallway right outside of Ozelle's office. It was the official posting site for all sorts of pertinent company information. In addition to guard duty rosters, there were sandbag detail rosters, leaflet drop rosters, company training schedules and anything else the Officers and NCOs wanted the troops to know.

But of primary importance was the nightly guard duty roster for Villa Cruz. Crowding into the tight space, the men craned to read the names typed on the list and cries of 'rats' and joy indicated who was and was not on that night.

All right!" Wimbish enthused, "I'm *not* on and I thought for sure it would be my turn again by tonight. Somebody tell Dunichek he's on first turn, he's up on the roof kicking ass in a poker game… oh he's gonna hate that he must take off in an hour!"

"Shit fire, I'm on tonight," cursed Edwards, "2nd turn. I don't mind 2nd, it's not that bad. Come back, get a little sleep in the cool time."

My name's not on it again!

"All right, I'm not on it!" Boyett was standing by the Kid, "hey, you gotta come hear my new tape of The Band, Curt, a couple of us are going to listen to it right now in my room."

"All right, let's go!" said the Kid, "what's the band's name again?"

"The Band."

"Right," the Kid looked askance, "OK. What are we going to listen to?"

"Music from Big Pink."

After a quick interlude to gather beer and munchies, a contingent of Birnbaum, Wimbish, Edwards, Richie Wells, Benny, George, Don, Ken and the Kid arrived at Tom's room where they found places, squeezing in like clowns in a circus car, shoehorned in to the upper and lower bunks, the footlockers and the floor. It was still hot enough in the day that the additional heat of that many men being packed into such a small room was unnoticeable.

"A couple of guys, you said," the Kid laughed at Boyett.

Clouds of cigarette smoke curled up off the butts half of them were smoking, while sharing strategically placed coke cans as ash trays. To the rhythmic squeaking of the antique overhead fan turning forever too slowly, Tom threaded his space age looking Akai reel to reel recorder. His sound system held a position of envy in the unit and possessed an alter like presence in the room. The stainless steel machine sat on the back half of a very steady, specially reinforced wooden table and wires ran from its posterior to the twin speakers sitting on wall locker tops in the corners to either side. The quality of his equipment, especially in a war zone, just reinforced the Kid's appreciation for how good they all had it in Can Tho.

"This is courtesy of my friend, Carl, to whom we all owe the endless vote of thanks for keeping us musically as current as possible. Ok, Curt, there's a song on here that was written by your buddy's mother," Tom prepared to hit the play button.

"What the fuck? One of my buddy's mothers?"

"Ronny of Ronny and the Daytonas is from Nashville, right? And his last name is Wilken, isn't it?"

"John Buck Wilkin. Yeah, it is."

"Then it's his mom, Mary John Wilkin, who wrote a song The Band covers on this tape... if you don't know, and obviously, you don't, I'll tell you when it starts to play." With the touch of his right index finger, he set the machine in motion.

"So what's this band's name again?"

"The Band."

"Yeah, right... the band... what's the name?" and as the Kid sat perched on the far edge of the bottom bunk, trying to figure out why Boyett wasn't giving him a straight answer, the first crisp and clean tones of the albums opening song, *Tears of Rage,* sprang from the speakers and washed down and over him. *Wow! Some kind of combination of horns and piano? 'She carried you in her arms...* on independence day...' the words were understandable and clear, not subjugated to over instrumentation and word slurring, like a lot of the new material that groups were putting out right before the Kid had left the continent.

"Oh, hey," Benny suddenly snapped to life as the first song came to an end, "next week, when we go up to Group, we're going to try real hard to buy some instruments so we can practice on a regular basis!"

Since New Year's Eve, the GI band, in concept and reality, along with music in general, pre-occupied almost all of the Tribe's waking hours. If they weren't over in Tom or Richie's room listening to tapes, they were listening to the band practice with what instruments they had.

As Boyett's new tape played on, the Kid absolutely fell in love with the songs that he was hearing for the first time. "Wow... these guys are going to be huge!" he said, taking long sip of beer.

"Going to be? Going to be?" Boyett repeated twice. "Curt... they already ARE huge! This is Bob Dylan's back up band!"

"Oh, really? What's their name again?"

"The Band."

"Yeah, the band... what's the band called?"

"The Band." Tom replied, a little perplexed that his message wasn't getting through to the Kid.

"I mean, what we are listening to?" the Kid tried for clarification.

"Music From Big Pink", Tom said, slowly.

"Big Pink…that's an interesting name for a band," the Kid mused.

Boyett just shook his head.

"We are in for a treat," Wimbish said in a matter of fact way, "next week, Boujold will be back in from the field to process out to go home. I can't believe how short he is… he's down under 15 days… and he got here right before Tet."

"Ha! I got out of his old room just in time for him to end up back in there for the duration," the Kid laughed.

"Oh, well, it'll give him something to complain about," Edwards commented, "that man has to have something to complain and whine about or he's not happy…Stocker, you spent more than a couple of months with him out there, is that so or not?"

The Kid thought about it for a second and right as he got ready to speak, out of Boyett's recorder came the lyric… *"… We can talk about it now… it the same old riddle only start in from the middle…"*

"You know, it was the case. Of course, he always used to complain and whine about not getting to go to the field. But, when he finally came out there to replace Roberts, his thing was crying about not getting to go out on the search and destroy missions where the shooting' was, so he could mix it up with the Cong. However, after his one time out there, he NEVER whined or complained about that or hardly anything again. He was a changed man… and when I say change, I'm talking underwear!" the Kid howled before he stopped and got serious.

"Actually, it's no bullshit, he's lucky to be alive. I saw it with my own eyes! I thought they'd fuckin' gotten him for sure when he went down because two ARVNs on either side of him *DID* get it."

But did you ever milk a cow? I had a chance one day but I was all dressed up for Sunday…

"Wow," Ramjet breathed, "fucker got his wish to be a combat vet. He used to say he hoped he wouldn't have to go home and make shit up. Sometime I think I want to see a little action… but a couple of hits on the old bong and it passes."

The talk stopped while the men seriously listened to the music for a good while. And at last, Boyett said, "OK, Stocker, here's the song I was talking about. It's called *'The Long Black Veil.'*" Check out the words.

Ten years ago on a cold dark night,

some one was killed beneath the town hall lights...

there were few at the scene, but they all did agree

that the man who ran looked a lot like me...

The judge said son, what is your alibi?

If you were somewhere else, then you won't have to die.

I spoke not a word though it meant my life...

I had been in the arms of my best friends' wife...

The Kid listened raptly, and his thoughts went back to a late evening before his midnight shift on WKDA in Nashville, when he had encountered 'Bucky/Ronny' at the Shoney's Big Boy on 4th Street, right across the street from Printer's Alley. *"Let's go up to my mother's office and I'll get you stoned before your show, I got some new stuff,"* he invited the Kid to join him. They drove in Ronny's Corvett out to her office on Music Row. You'd think Ronnie would have a fricking GTO, but not the case. When they entered, the Kid took note of the gold record on the wall, but since it was country and western, he didn't pay much attention to the title. That must have been for this song, he realized.

She walks these hills in a long black veil

and visits my grave where the night winds wail...

nobody knows and nobody sees...

nobody knows but me.....

The scaffold was high and eternity near...

she stood in the crowd and shed not a tear.

But some times at night when the cold winds moans...

she visit my grave and cries over my bones...

285

"Gee, what a dark theme," the Kid pondered. *I smoked dope in her office!*

"Yeah, The Band chooses some interesting material among the songs they don't write themselves, "Boyett nodded.

"What's their name again?"

"The Band," said Boyett.

"Yeah… what is it? Oh, yeah… *Big Pink!"*

"If you say so," Boyett smiled and slowly shook his head.

Chapter 39

The prodigal son coming home in the Bible had absolutely nothing on John Boujold coming in from the field. His previous reputation, that of being a man who was all talk and no action, had been replaced by an aura of *"... I've seen just enough fucking action that* everybody *who hasn't seen any can kiss my ass!"* Indeed, Bouji was now given the benefit of the doubt.

"Lookie here!" Ron Edwards exclaimed, when Bouji walked on to the balcony at the Embassy as the sun was setting to the west, "the mighty warrior returns in triumph!"

"At least he's not being carried on his shield…" Willert laughed, "Christ that would give us all hernias!"

Bouji gave Ken the evil eye stare. His fatigue shirt was unbuttoned and he held a cigarette in one hand and a red paper cup that surly contained Drambuie in the other. "That's right, start with the fat jokes, but let me say this," and flipping the cigarette off the balcony, he pulled open his shirt, "I may still be short but you bastards can't call me fat anymore! I lost 40 fucking pounds out there in the field! Check it out," he struck a classic comic book Charles Atlas pose, with the paper cup hanging down, his fingers clutching it crane like from the bent wrist of his curled up right arm. Then he sucked what belly he had left up into his rib cage and if his ribs had stuck out any farther, he'd have resembled a holocaust picture. "And yes, I am short, make that short *short*… in fact, the shortest fucking bastard on the balcony, let me *remind* you! So have at it. Take you best shots at the *Boogie*… because six days from today, *I'll* be in the World and you fucks will be right here!" He pointed down to the white and blue trimmed tile of the Embassy floor.

There was no disputing the Bouji was right. Looking around the circle, you could almost see everyone making their own end of the day calculation, as to how many days they had left. *69 days and that's me!*

"If you lost all that weight, how'd your ass stay so big?" Richie remarked.

287

"Thank you, thank you, ladies and germs... but I must say in all, I'd really rather be in Philadelphia!" Boujold gave it his best WC Fields and he took the pipe from him and promptly sucked a gimongus hit down into his lungs and held it without coughing.

"So, Bouji," Ramjet lifted the pipe from his hand, "word has it your baptism of fire included a belly flop in a rice paddy and a brown out in your shorts!"

He exhaled the hit, "Oh yeah! God, I thought I was a goner when all those rounds were flying and ARVNs dropping like pigeon shit! Only I wouldn't really call it my baptism of fire... we did take a few rounds right here at the New Villa during Tet, when I'd just arrived last year. I was here for barely over two weeks when that Tet shit hit the fan. Talk about an eye opener, *God almighty!* There was a body that laid out there where the alley meets the street, we could see it for 3 days before somebody moved it. But, yeah... that first operation that Wilson took me on... no, up until then, I hadn't seen any company sized maneuver action close up like that, gotta say."

"And tell them about the part where you broke a nail we had to medi-vac you!" The Kid smirked, causing Bouji to give him an inquisitive look that clearly questioned what it was the Kid might have told all they guys about that day.

"Ya didn't kill anybody, did you?" Richie asked.

"Uh no. Didn't even get a shot off, to tell the truth," He said.

"Oh, well, we don't want the fuckin' truth to wreck any of the stories," Edwards cut in, "don't you go damaging your reputation by telling us the fuckin' truth about anything! So how many VC are you gonna tell everybody back home you killed?"

"Just a couple," Bouji smiled, "but they were really BIG!" he stretched out his arms like a fisherman bullshitting about his catch and everybody laughed.

"Oh, God, I can't wait to wrap my teeth around that steak in the returnees Steak House," he said with his eyes closed, as if he were picturing the piece of T-Bone beef that he would rip asunder. "Two more days to Saigon and five more days to Ohio!

"With tomorrow being your last night in Can Tho-ho... we'll have to have a major party down, so you'll be 'Still-High-O" when you get to O-hio!" Edwards joked.

"And I get a day back crossing the International Date Line!" Bouji savored the nectar of his situation.

"So, all you have to do is survive spending two nights down in the oven..." the Kid brought up the unpleasant circumstances of where the *no longer* fat one was bunking that night. "I got out of there just in time for your return! Don't worry, I installed a fresh set of batteries in your little fan... I figured it was the least I could do, to thank you for leaving it."

"Ah. Thanks, Curt. But I will tell you this, I don't fucking care where I'm sleeping for the next two nights, because I'm fucking out of here!" His smile exploded beneath his black and rather bushy moustache. "Ah shit! It's finally here! I'm going home!"

"Well don't go all weepie eyed cry like a baby candy ass on us," Tearman cut in, "we don't want to hear about how fucking short you are. You short guys never get it. Rub it in... rub and rub and rub... all you do. Jesus... I can't wait to be *short!*" the *tall one* exclaimed while squatting down. Everybody laughed, and Bouji, laughed most of all.

"You want to be short? Just keep going all the way down on your knees, John," Bouji shot back, as he pantomimed unzipping his pants.

Bouji was very much in demand that night and he circulated from the Embassy up to the club, where everybody was buying him drinks, to down to Boyett's room where Tom wow'd him with a bunch of brand-new music. Out on the balcony, he was never without a pipe or joint continually stuck in his face and without fail, he was always attended by the red Dixie Cup full of Drambuie. It wasn't too far into the evening when everybody began to realize that Bouji was shit faced as a cow's hoof in a feed lot.

"Hey..." Wimbish attracted Bouji's attention, "Boujold, here comes your replacement! *Stoney!* Here he is, your ticket to the field has finally arrived," he hollered as Stoney had just turned the corner and arrived in the Embassy for the first time that night.

"OOOOh," responded the Kid, "allow me to introduce you... Stoney, this is John Boujold, once fat now thin, once a combat cherry and now well broken in... once long and now shorter than your fucking dick... Bouji, meet Stoney, the man who by default for some reason nobody in the whole unit comprehends, is your replacement in the field!"

The two soldiers shook hands. "Yo," said Stoney, in a rather cordial way, like he was worried if Boujold didn't like him, he wouldn't get to replace him. They shook hands.

"Where are you from?" inquired Bouji.

"New York."

"He was my driver when I was up at Group getting new glasses! He was crying about getting out of Saigon into the field back then and that was 4 months ago! He drove me all over to hell and gone, out to AFVN and the PX and Ton Son Nhut... we had a great time, didn't we, Stoney!"

"Oh yeah. And so far, driving a truck is all I've done here. I can't wait to get out in the field and have some real fun!"

The Kid looked perplexed. "Well, Stoney, having been out there and in here, I can fucking for certain tell you that as far a Nam goes... I keep trying' to tell you all, duty in Can Tho does not suck like it does in the *uber-boonies!* I say... *Viva Can Tho!*" The Kid thrust his beer into the air, only to find there was no popular support for his sentiments. "Bouji," the Kid looked for another opinion, "what do you say... in *here* or out there?"

"Out there. But mostly because Ozelle would have eventually killed me if I'd stayed in here."

"See? Ha!" Stoney pointed at Boujold who was clearly supporting his position.

"Bouji... who are you for in the Super Bowl day after tomorrow? The Colts are gong to kill the Jets," Birnbaum confidently predicted. " Fucking A... I wish I could see that game live! The Jets don't have a Frenchman's chance at Dien Bin Phu! We're going to stay up tomorrow night and listen to it over the radio. Wait... Stoney... you're from New York and you don't like the Jets?"

"No. Fuck the stupid Jets... I'm a Giants' fan!" Stoney flashed his Irish grin.

Boujold turn a blurry eye to Mark and slurred something to the effect of "... I don't give a shit because I'm a Cleveland Browns fan... when you live in Ohio... you don't have any other choice."

"You mean you don't know that Cincinnati got a team this year?" Birnbaum looked at him like Bouji must be *smoking something* a cut above everybody else...

"Really? In the NFL? Nobody told me. I'll be damned. God, I am just starting to realize how far out in the fucking boonies I've been. Son of a bitch; I was out there for six months!"

"Well, actually, in the *AFL*, now known as the AFC." Mark scoffed, "but with the merger agreement, all the teams in the AFL and the NFL are now playing each other in the regular season.

"Jeezus, I'm afraid to hear the rest of the stuff that went on in society while I was out there," Bouji stood, mouth agape.

"You might have to go to a half way house to re-enter society, *Boojie my Boy,*" the Kid stole his WC Fields from him for a line.

"But… always a Cleveland and Jim Brown and 'Lou the Toe' fan" Bouji resolutely affirmed.

"I'm still looking to get some money on this game," Birnbaum waved a hand in the air, "that's 13 points I'm giving… any takers? Anybody? 14?"

No takers.

"14?" Mark looks around the room, "and still no takers?"

Later that night, the Kid found Boujold hanging over the rail outside of Ling Fook's room and couldn't tell if he was setting up to puke or trying to get a look into the Sgt. Ozelle's whore house across the alley.

"So, Bouji," the Kid lit up a KOOL, "I take it Wilson didn't give you any more shit out there after I left."

"Nope. Not a bit," Bouji indicated with a gesture that he'd like to bum a cigarette off the Kid, who complied and immediately lit it with his zippo. "After he came back from your trial, he was a different man. He kept me out at Tan An for a while. Then Cang Long. He basically fucking forgot I existed, which of course, was fine with me."

"No action out at the Vinh Long Bridge?"

"Very little action of any kind. I fucking loved it. The food was good, hauling water for the shower was a bummer, but I read a lot of books and smoked a ton of weed and did fucking nothing for two whole months!"

"Did you see Sweet at all?"

"Couple of times, in to Tra Vinh, but you can bet your ass I avoided that ride as much as possible. Why take a chance?" he ashed his cig off the balcony, and they both watched the ash fall toward the guard's post right below them inside the chicken wire anti grenade façade.

"And Wilson?"

"Well, both times I saw Sweet, Wilson wasn't in with him. The first time I saw him, he said he'd been in for over a week, just relaxing and shooting pool, hanging out at Wen's house, eating her mom's homemade potato chips and reading Perry Mason books. I sort of got the impression that Sweet was pretty much doing whatever it was he wanted and Wilson wasn't giving him any shit at all."

"Small wonder," the Kid grinned.

"What do you mean?"

"You're going home in a couple of days, I guess I can tell you now what happened, if Sweet didn't already."

"Already tell me what?" he stood back from the rail, wondering what kind of revelation was coming forth.

"So, Sweet didn't tell you that the mortar strike that fucked up the MSQ-85 back in October was a self-inflicted wound, put there by Wilson as he tested out his freaking insane claymore mine on the truck as an ambush preventive weapon theory?"

Bouji's mouth fell open, in what appeared to be mock surprise before it dissolved into a wide grin. "Yes, he told me. Said he wanted to be sure somebody was getting some good out of the information, if anything ever happened to him!"

"Yep! Can you believe it? He blew up the fucking Bat Mobile and falsified the report and made Sweet do one too. So Sweet can pull the plug on Wilson's whole career at the drop of a dime! Talk about having somebody by the fucking nuts!"

"So at your trial, you knew that... but didn't use it? Doesn't sound a bit like you."

"Didn't have to. What a fucking screaming bag of monkey nuts fun that was! Court martialed for eating in the mess hall. The more stuff that happens like that, the more my book will have to be a memoir than a novel."

"Either way, I hope it has a happy ending," Bouji smiled a crooked Drambuie induced grin. "And are you really extending here another year for Armed Forces Radio?"

"Yes. I should be hearing any day now that it's all gone through. Then I get the 60 day drop and, in the end, I'll get out six month early out from the whole fucking Army. Getting a half year back will be the best part of it... that and going home in 69... make that almost 68 days."

"Well, good luck on that. I don't think I'd take another year here no matter how much of a drop I was going to get. I can't fucking wait to never see this place again in my whole fucking life!" Bouji's voiced his opinion on extensions. "What about Flo? What does she think about the extension thing? Are you still friendly, even though you're officially not engaged anymore?"

"We barely write to each other anymore," the Kid sighed, "so it doesn't matter much what she thinks about it. I'm going to do it. I just wish the paperwork would come back from Saigon. It's way overdue."

Just then, Ron Edwards walked up to the pair. "Hey, Bouji, let's you and me play ping pong for money!" he slapped him on the back.

"Uh, I don't think so," he shook his head and for a split second, both Ron and the Kid thought he might topple but just then, 3 more of his friends showed up, stuck a pipe in his mouth and with a big toke, Boujold rallied on what was possibly his third wind.

Amid all the small talk and smoking and drinking, the Kid finally drifted out of the herd at about 2330 hours and after brushing his teeth, fell into bed, in the top bunk next to the window in the best room of the whole New Villa. After carefully tucking in his mosquito netting, he laid down on his back and closed his eyes. He found it easy to ignore the low conversations of the 4 or 5 men still smoking at the Embassy rail, who had the courtesy to move down the balcony toward the alley when they noticed the Kid retire.

No matter what anybody else here thinks about duty in Can Tho, I'm loving it! Fuck the field and all the hardship, not to mention guns and bullets. In succession, like pulses from the strobing light of a slide projector, the Kid saw in his mind's eye, the orange tracers from the VC rifles bouncing off the paddy dyke in front of him the day he'd gotten left alone at the front… the poncho blowing off the body of Captain Robinson… and the three VC soldier/ children captives, kneeling on the ground, with their arms staved back, hooked around bamboo rods with their hands tied in front as a semi-circle of ARVNs stood behind them, with the barrels of their guns casually pointed at the backs of their heads. A shudder ran through his body as he shook the last image off. *No matter what anybody says, Can Tho is a relief after that! I can live without all that shit and worse. I'm glad that Sweet has the goods on Wilson. Jeezus, what a deal Sweet must have out there right now… telling Wilson what he will and won't do. Well, Herschel's got nobody to blame but himself. And here I am, in a bed by a window where it is possible to actually feel a breeze and get a little high-quality sleep!*

And on that note, along with a fleeting image of Flo's face smiling at him from an earlier, happier time, he drifted off. But no sooner had he gotten to sleep than somebody was shaking his bunk and frantically whispering his name.

"Stocker! Stocker! Wake up!" It was Edwards, *"Boujold's been busted!* Ozelle found a bag of pot in his locker! They're down in the orderly room right now!"

The Kid was instantly wide awake. *"Oh fuck! No way!"*

"Yes, *fucking A way... he's screwed!"* Ron breathed out low, trying hard not to wake Ramjet and Willert, who had gone to bed long before the Kid.

Climbing down out of his bunk, the Kid slipped into his flip flops and clad only in his green boxer shorts, he and Edwards headed for the stairs. Upon hitting the first floor, they could hear a heated exchange was taking place in the orderly room between Boujold and Ozelle so they held back to listen.

"...but I'm supposed to go *HOME* the day after tomorrow!" Bouji exasperated, "you can't do this to me, Sarge!"

"You should have thought of that before you put that bag of pot in your locker," Ozelle calmly said.

"For the 20th time... *IT"S NOT MINE!"* Bouji nearly screamed, "I did not put it there! Why the fuck would I take a chance like that?"

"Right. It was just in your locker...you should have thought about that, Boujold. How stupid of you not to keep you nose clean right before your DEROS." Ozelle chided.

"Jesus H. Christ all mighty... I *WAS* keeping my nose clean! If you dust that bag for fingerprints... mine won't be on it!"

"Sure. Whatever you say," Ozelle responded after a slight pause, "like that's going' to happen. "Talks cheap. You'll have your chance to tell Captain Ronnie Smith your side of the story tomorrow. For now, Boujold, I'm restricting you to the unit until this gets settled, one way or another."

Silence.

"Don't do this to me, Sergeant..." Bouji said in an even, measured tone, "I know we had our differences and on occasion, I kind of gave you a rough time or two... but Sarge, *I'm begging you...* don't do this to me! *PLEASE!* Just let me DEROS and I'll be out of your hair forever!"

"Not my call now, Specialist," came the sarcastic reply, "come sunup tomorrow, you're just going to have to face the music. Now, get the fuck out of my office!"

"You fucking cocksucker!" Boujold screamed.

"Whoa! Careful there, Specialist," Ozelle slammed his open palm against the surface of his desk, "calling me a cocksucker? Really? You're walking way over the *fucking line mister!* Cross it one more time and I'll charge you with disrespect of a non-commissioned officer. But since you've got enough trouble for one man, I'll let it slide... for right now... *BUT!* I *strongly* suggest you return to your God dammed room and stay *the fuck out of my sight!*" he dismissively finished the conversation.

The Kid and Ron were still hanging back unseen in the hallway as Boujold came barging by them and pounded up the staircase, *"FUCK FUCK FUCK!"* he screamed through his clinched teeth, punctuating as each foot stomp that carried him past them toward the second floor. The pair followed in his wake.

"Bouji!" the Kid called out to him as they hit the second-floor landing. "Bouji… wait!" but he did not stop and actually gained speed until he had made it to the third floor and out on to the Embassy where he finally stood at the far corner of the balcony and moaned what amounted to a two word prayer, *"Oh God!"* As he buried his face in his hands.

The Kid came up and standing next to him, couldn't think of what to say.

"I swear to God I will get a weapon and shoot every single mother fucking one of them!" Boujold slammed his fist down on the white tiled railing. *"God damned sons of asshole fucking bitches!"* the profanities rolled from his mouth like water from a fire hose. He was fast losing it and outside the fact that he still had his own weapon, there were 3 or 4 fully loaded M-16's and M-14's conveniently laying around in every single room of the New Villa, a fact not lost on the Kid as he remembered the Tra Vinh incident when *Sgt. Hicks* shot Mr. Kim over a gambling debt.

"Shit fire, Bouji…for Christ sake, don't go doing anything like THAT!" The Kid reacted, "don't even fucking *say* that shit! There's gotta be something we can do. First off, tell me what exactly happened? Is that your pot? I can't believe you'd really put it in your locker!"

"Yes. Shit. I was going to take it up to Saigon so I'd have something to smoke for the last couple of days until I left for Long Binh… *FUCKING SHIT SHIT SHIT!*" he screamed out into the hot humid tropical night.

His admission made the Kid lift his head and look above them to see if any lifers were hanging over the rail from the club above, listening. There weren't, although Ozelle's whores across the street weren't having any trouble hearing.

"Well, how'd did anybody find out about it? Why did they go look in your locker in the first place?" the Kid questioned the circumstances.

"I don't fucking know," he shook his head, "maybe somebody overheard me mention that I had it and went and told Ozelle." He snapped his fingers as if to punctuate a revelation, "I'll bet it was fucking RV Smith who did it, he was hanging around me almost all night. I'd bet anything he's the fucker who turned me in. He always had it in for me."

"Possible. He's still a little pissed at all of us Embassy regulars because we never let him get into a room up here," the Kid speculated.

"I swear to God... *I will shoot them all!*" Bouji had now worked himself into a major league froth.

"Bouji... seriously, don't go saying shit like that. You know it's not worth it... I mean what's the worst that can happen? You miss you DEROS by a week or two and they fine you $100 in pay... that's not worth throwing your life away for! Now, tell me you'll calm down and go get some rest and we can see what's to be done about this tomorrow...OK?" the Kid laid a comforting arm around his shoulder and started to walk him toward the stairway and like a steer resigned to his fate, Bouji allowed himself to be lead off the Embassy, slipping into a near trance like state as the Kid lead him down the stairs and put him to bed in the oven.

Chapter 40

The Kid encountered First Sgt Ozelle Jones sitting at his desk the first thing the next morning at 0630. A hot cup of coffee steamed within easy reach of his right hand.

"Good morning, First Sergeant," he got his attention, "Hey, I hear that Boujold got busted for pot last night… is there any truth to that rumor?"

Ozelle looked up from the paperwork that lay before him on his desk and suspiciously appraised the soldier who was asking before he ventured an answer. "It's not a rumor, Stocker, and it's none of your business so my suggestion to you is you just go on to work like a good soldier."

"Uh, you can say it's none of my business, but last night, after it happened, Bouji was out on the balcony and I got woke up by his raging moaning, crying' and carrying on and suffice to say, he's in a terrible state and saying things that he'd regret if I repeated them… which I won't. But let me tell you, Sarge, he's in a fragile state, thinking that his DEROS is getting fucked with and if this bust goes through, who's going to be responsible if he flies off the handle and does something really stupid that hurts a lot of people?"

"And just what the fuck do you mean by that, Specialist?" Ozelle turned in his chair to give the Kid his full attention, with a serious expression painted across fine nearly chiseled features and his ruddy complexion, all accented by his well trimmed black eyebrows pressed together in a concerning arch.

"Well," the Kid thought for a moment about his reply, "let's just say a war zone is not the best place in the world to seriously fuck with somebody whose condition is in a hair trigger frame of mind. Common sense."

Ozelle continued to stare at the Kid as he digested what it was the Kid was trying to say without actually saying anything at all. "And you point is?"

"This is flip out stuff, First Sergeant, fucking with a man's DEROS over a nickel bag of pot. Now look at this for a second; you say you found a bag of pot in Boujold's locker. For openers, except for Gaugle, you know as

297

well as I do that's a transit room. So a lot of different dudes have recently bunked there. I was even in that room and used that locker up until a few days ago. How do you know for certain that pot was Boujold's? For that matter, how do you know it's wasn't Gaugle's? That'd be a clever place for George to hide his cache...in the transit locker..."

"Oh! Now it was yours or Gaugle's?" a smile spread quickly about his face. "Now I know you're plain fucking loony because you used Gaugle and clever in the same sentence."

"Sarge, I'm just saying' you never know! The question is: *how do you know its Boujold's?* Was his lock on that locker? Did you have a witness when you opened it and found the stuff or did a 'certain somebody' tell you it was there? What if perhaps the 'certain somebody' was the only person who knew there was a bag of pot in that locker?

Ozelle's brains were burning as he analyzed what the Kid might really know or where he was going with all of this. "Hmmm, Stocker, for somebody who opened the conversation asking if Boujold got busted or not, you seem to know quite a bit about it."

"I don't know shit, Sarge. All I'm doing is speculating. *Fishing.* But, it seems to me the Army doesn't have an air tight case against Boujold because of the transit thing and because of the fact his lock was not yet on the locker, you don't have shit to pin on him. In fact, who was it that came to you and said Bouji was holding?"

"Can't tell you that," Ozelle shook his head, "doesn't really matter who dropped the dime on him, we found the pot in his locker and how do you know he didn't have a lock on that locker?"

The Kid didn't know; he was just flipping stuff out there, so he ignored the question. "If you court martial him, that person is going to have to come forward as your probable cause. Even under the UCMJ, a person has the right to confront their accuser. And what if that person just happens to have a history of being a Boujold hater and planted that bag... *which is why he even knew it was there*... just to get even with Bouji for all the real or imaginary things he had against him by fucking with his ticket home? What if some other GIs might be able to say they heard this stoolie plotting just such an act of revenge? How do you think the Colonel is going to feel if the unit loses another court martial? Gee, that would be four in a row the unit lost, wouldn't it?"

Ozelle remained silent for a contemplative five seconds. "Well, for someone who's only had one court martial, you're turning into quite the shithouse lawyer, Stocker. If you end up giving Boujold some bad advice, you might regret it for the rest of your life."

"I think the best thing that could possibly happen, First Sergeant, for the unit and the men's overall morale... and of course, for Boujold, would be if that alleged evidence got lost."

Ozelle gave the Kid a disgusting sort of look and then just shook he head slowly back and forth, "Aren't you a piece of work, to come in here and actually suggest that. Jesus H, just get the fuck out of here, Stocker," he'd finally run out of patience and dismissed him.

Exhaling a deep breath, the Kid turned and walked out the door and as he did, he pulled out KOOL and lit up. Other than laying down a large barrage of probable doubt, in the long run, he knew there wasn't much that he could do to help Boujold out. *What a stupid thing to do Bouji ... putting that bag in your locker. You spent way too much time out in the Boonies. You lost touch with the reality of this place.*

Climbing on board a cyclo, the Kid headed toward work but decided, as he approached the USO, to stop in buy an egg and bacon sandwich to go, which he ate on the ride in another cyclo to Battalion HQ. He wondered what the buzz was going to be about Boujold's bust as he walked up the narrow stairs and emerged in the HQ room.

The first thing he saw was Wimbish and Lt. Regan engaged in a discussion.

They seemed engrossed with a document that Lou held in his hand and when the pair noticed him, they immediately motioned for him to come over.

"Yo, gentlemen, what's up?" the Kid greeted them with a smile but did not get smiles back. "So, Lou; is that about Boujold getting busted?" he motioned at the paper Lou held.

"Uh, no, he nervously replied, "this is the answer to your 1049 request for an extension and assignment to AFN Saigon."

"Finally!" the Kid's face lit up, "all right! This is my lucky day!"

Lou held it forth for the Kid to take and as he read the first line, the light and the smile vanished from his face. *Your request for an extension and assignment to AFN Saigon is denied.*

'WHAT THE FUCK?" the Kid fairly screamed, *"denied?"* He looked at the bad news in front of him and read further down into the text. "It's been denied, and they say it's for no slot in your grade."

"Denied for no slot?" the Kid's brow wrinkled as fought the urge to crumble the bad news into a little ball. " But… the commanding officer at AFN said it was a *done deal! I had a letter of acceptance from the fucking program director!"*

"That's a shame, Stocker," Lt. Regan sympathized, "uh, looks like you'll be with us a little longer than you anticipated."

"I don't fucking believe it!" the Kid groaned, as the reality washed over him. "This is a joke, right?"

"Oh, it's not a joke," Lou chagrined, "although it would have been a really good one… huh? And I seriously doubt that it would do you any good to resubmit it because they didn't give you a 'good' reason for the denial, which if they did, it might be something you could address and mitigate, otherwise, forget it. Denied. Het roi. Kaput. Not worth a clerk's time."

"Fuckin' fuck fuck fuck!" the Kid beat the paper against his thigh. "Lt Regan, could this have anything to do with the court martial? *Even though I won?"*

"You tell me," the Lt. looked him in the eye, "this is the Army. Don't you know by now?"

"God damn it!" The Kid moaned, as the reality of the situation well up inside him; he knew there was nothing he could do. "I just got back 60 days. Shit fucking fire! I'm back up over 100!"

"Yeah, what a bummer," said Lou.

"Auugggggg!," the Kid screamed like Charlie Brown in the comics as he half crumpled the cursed document in his right hand and headed back for his desk in the back room.

Upon entering, he found Tom already working at his graphics table and the Chief at his desk, poring over somebody's copy. "Look at this shit! he declared, straightening the paper back out, "my 1049 to extend and be assigned to AFN Saigon has been denied! *Son of a fucking bitch!* I just went from 68 to 128 days!"

Boyett looked up from his project with a sympathetically abject expression on his face. "Stocker, you are a troublemaker and everybody's got you figured out." he took a puff on his Marlboro. "Last thing they want is you on the radio in Saigon, poisoning the attitude of the whole fucking Army. And you're surprised?" he sarcastically inquired.

"Well, yeah. In a way," the Kid paused to consider, 'I mean, we had a deal, me and the First Sergeant and the CO at AFN… *we shook on it!* I'll bet Ronnie Smith had something to do with this!"

Ron Edwards walked in just as the Kid spoke; he must have already heard. "Let me punch your Chaplin card, Curt," he stuck out his hand like a conductor looking for a ticket, before pulling his hand back, "oh wait! *You* don't get a Chaplin card punch, at least you'll have a great room to live in for your extra 60 days… and you're not busted, like Boujold! Look at it that way. You have no choice but to get over it."

The Kid scowled at Edwards; he knew he was right, but he was so incredibly far from over it. The wound was too open and fresh. He sat down at his desk and stared down at the notes he had in front of him from one of the stories he was working for the next issue. Staring blankly, his mind was way beyond the words on the page. *AHHHHHH! Another 60 days! I'm back up to four fucking months! I had counted those days gone and now I've got them back. Goddamned fucking Army. Can't treat you straight no matter what you do! Gonna fuck you over. Period. That's what the Army does. Someday… some way… I'm going to make the Army pay! It owes me for all the fucking lies it's told me about being in radio. It owes me for the courts-martial and now it owes me for the drop.* "It's Wilson and Ronnie Smith that did this to me… they finally found a way to get me. I hate those fuckers… I hate the Army and I hate this war. It's all pure, unmitigated mother *fucking bullshit!"*

But Edwards ignored his anguish, "I wonder what's going to happen to Boujold?"

Chapter 41

That evening, the tribe, just short of a dozen strong, waited on the balcony in suspense for Boujold's arrival. He'd been summoned from the New Villa to Battalion HQ late in the day, by Colonel Lawton, and everybody was already gone to Eakin Compound for dinner before the meeting ended.

"My bet is that Willie offers to give him an Article 15," Barry Fischer speculated, "that way, they can nail him and not have to hold him back for a trial and he's getting out when he gets back stateside anyway, so who really gives a shit if he gets busted to buck private and has to pay a fine? If it's anything else, I'll be fucking shocked."

The fact that Bouji was being busted for pot had not dampened the desire of the tribe to light up as several pipes and joints passed from hand to hand.

"You know," J.C. Compton spoke up, "I really don't understand what it is that you guys see in that stuff, why you smoke it and take the chances that ya'll do, when you know, it can lead to the kind of trouble that Boujold is in right now."

JC, a Texan by birth, was a unique member of the tribe in that he didn't smoke pot at all. Having come over to Vietnam on the PYSOPS packet ship, he'd been a tight member of the Tribe from the very start. And although he'd never ever even taken one puff, he was an accepted and welcome member because of his general intelligence and dry sense of humor. Essentially it was by default, because JC wasn't drunk lifer material, and he personally couldn't rationalize hanging with the unit's beer and whisky sponges.

"Well, JC," the Kid took the lead, "one of these days, you just might have to take a puff and find out why it is we do smoke the weed."

"I don't know," he pondered, "If I never try it, I reckon I'll never miss it."

"True enough," the Kid nodded, "or you could say, you'll never know what you're missing. You know, I've got to tell you, the first time I smoke pot back in Boulder, and I did it with the intention of demonstrating it could be smoked only once."

302

"And we all see how well that went," Edwards blurted out and the whole group laughed heartily. "Did you get high the first time you smoked?" he asked the Kid.

"Yeah. I did. But you're right, I've seen a lot of people smoke and not get high the first time, that's for sure."

"But I don't think that would be a problem around here," Willert asserted, "JC if you try this stuff you'll get off, no doubt about it!"

Nodding, the Kid said, "For sure, I'd pretty much bet on that, too. This is the best fucking stuff in the world! Of all the bad things about Vietnam, JC, this is one of the best benefits in the whole fucking war! If you don't smoke pot here, and you finally do smoke it after you go back and you realize… you were here in Pot fucking heaven… and didn't smoke, you'll shoot yourself. Plain and simple."

The tribe pretty much nodded and puffed away in agreement, waiting for a response from JC but he just stood there, contemplating the whole situation.

"Anyway," the Kid continued, "it is enlightening but the reason we smoke it is for the way it makes us feel… like *really good and relaxed.* The high is so superior to being drunk, there's no valid comparison. You aren't stumbling around incoherent; you still have all your balance and faculties of logic…. You don't slur your speech. That is why a pot head can beat an Alkie at just about anything… ping pong, pool, board games and persuasion. Plus music sounds so cool when you're stoned… it's like you're hearing songs you head a thousand times for the first time. If you really want to know why we smoke it, you'll have to try it one of these nights."

Just then, Bouji emerged from the stairwell and walked out onto the Embassy balcony. All their heads turned, and everybody looked at him in silence, waiting for him to speak. A wide grin slowly broke like sunrise across his round face.

"I'm off the hook!" he said, palms open and turned up in front of him. The Tribe waited with bated breath for details. "The colonel said they broke the chain of custody of evidence or lost it or some fucking other legal beagle bullshit like that. *Oh hell! I don't know and I don't fucking care!* Because as soon as I walked in and reported, the first words out of his mouth were, '… Boujold… you're off the hook!'" I really didn't even listen to what he had to say after that because I was so relieved, I got weak in the knees, and I thought I was going to faint dead on the floor! I swear to God, if he wasn't a man and my commanding officer and black… I woulda kissed him on the spot!" Bouji laughed.

"All right! Yay! Wha-hooooo!' the group yelled as the closest of them, Tall John, Edwards, Mike Imrem, and Barry Fisher, all slapped him on the back.

"What's 'black' got to do with it?" Richie was quick to respond to Boujold's statement with a smile.

"Yeah!" Ling Fook joined in, "what's black got to do with it?"

"OK...let me rephrase... if he wasn't a man, a man or a man in *command,*" Bouji went for the bottom-line common denominator. 'swear to God I would have kissed him..."

"Give that man the pipe!" Willert hollered, and Bouji didn't hesitate to take it.

Now there was real reason to celebrate Boujold's last night in Can Tho; the man was skating like Dick Button and tomorrow, he'd be driven out to Can Tho field where he'd climb aboard that Caribou and fly up to Saigon to process out to go home. This was Bouji's finest hour.

"Out of all the bullets I dodged here in 'Nam," Bouji began to wax poetic, "this is the best... uh except for the real ones that didn't kill me! Ah, now I can really enjoy my last night in Can Tho!"

"Needless to say, we're pretty happy for you," Richie Wells raised his can of Budweiser in a toast. "To Bouji, DEROS, ETS and the World! If Boujold can make it then, by God, *ALL of us can make it!*"

"Hear hear!" the Tribe heartily drank and laughed it up.

"And here's to having Stocker around for an extra 60 days!" Edwards quickly made a second toast.

"Hear hear!" the tribe drank again, all except the Kid.

"You look more than a *little bitter*, Curt," Willert stated the obvious.

Without speaking, ala Jack Benny, the Kid looked over the smiling crowd. His anger was still simmering just under the surface with the reality that his plan to transfer to Armed Forces Radio Saigon was now nothing more than twisted wreckage at the end of the runway.

"Oh yes. Know that I am super pissed," he ashed the filter tipped joint he was smoking off the rail. "And, since I no longer need to maintain a low profile, from now on, my only mission remaining with my time in service is to *FUCK THE ARMY!* FTA!" he held up his beer in his own toast, "before the Army fucks me... *AGAIN!*"

"FTA FTA FTA!" the group raucously responded.

"Yeah! Fuck the 'Army before the Army fucks YOU!" the Kid fumed, "words to fucking live by, that's for fucking sure. From now on, I am in attack mode. I am so pissed at the fucking *fuck around* and *fuck over* the Army has given me…that my asshole is so sore I can't fucking stand it anymore but I can't sit down… *Philip Upchurch combo… part two…*"

The mental picture and the moldy oldie reference drew a pretty big tribal laugh, and the Kid could really do nothing but laugh along. But as the minutes passed, the boiling rage within his mind bubbled and festered until he finally unlashed a primordial scream that really demonstrated the dept of his rage.

"AUUUUUGGGGGGGGG!"

"Whoa!" Boyett exasperated, "careful you don't bust a gut!"

"Here's something you'll all love," Wimbish spoke up, "I just today got the training schedule for February."

"Puke… crap… shit," was the general reaction within the group. Training was generally a massive waste of time and it was something everybody constantly schemed and angled to dodge.

"And you'll all be so happy to know that the day before Valentine's Day, we have a training class scheduled… on the evils of… *Mary-huana!*"

"NO!" Edwards gasp.

"Yes!" Lou affirmed.

"That's another one I'll be looking to miss," Tall John said what most of the men were thinking as a *'me too'* murmur traveled through the group.

"Not me," the Kid coldly said, turning heads in his direction. "I'm going to go to that training class and I'm going to tear the instructor a brand new fucking asshole! I'm going to go to the library and do research and hit him like I would any opponent in a format debate… with references and information, quotes and trap questions that will make him look stupid! What the fuck, like I said, now that I'm not going to Armed Forces Radio, I got nothin' to lose, so *I can't fucking WAIT!*"

"Well now, I gotta say, I changed my mind… count me in that!" Richie exclaimed and as he did, a new murmur went through the tribe as plans were immediately changed in favor of attendance because the Kid, they knew, was not one to make an idle boast of that nature. If he said he was going to tear the instructor a new asshole, they immediately expected that the instructor better go to the PX and stock up on toilet paper.

"Ho boy!" Edwards said, "This is exciting! When is this training, Lou? I need to mark it on my calendar."

"February 13th Day before valentine's," he said.

"I got a couple of things to do," the Kid flipped his joint off the balcony and wheeling around, went into his room to get his paper and pen to write a letter to Larry Ryan.

Walking up to the Roof Club, the Kid spied an empty table under a light to the far side of the movie projector cabinet and set up there. Spreading out his paper and envelopes, beer, pack of KOOLs and an ashtray, the Kid sat down in a green and white plastic butterfly chair, lit up a fresh KOOL and began to write. The movie of the night wasn't schedule to start for another 45 minutes. *Plenty of time.*

January 18, 1969

Dear Larry,

Well, Armando, you better shelve the plans for my Homecoming party in March, because I just found out today that my request to extend and transfer to Radio Saigon has been denied! No real explanation from the fucking Army, thank you very much. I had a deal with the commander and NCOIC (sorry...that's non commissioned officer in charge) of the station and still didn't get it. Needless to say, I am fucking pissed to the nth degree! Talk about getting ewescraed, taking an extra year for radio and having all of this happen.

I'm pretty sure it was Capt. Ronnie Smith, Lt. Wilson's dear friend, who pulled the plug on me. But now, its water under the bridge and my new arrival date is the now the old date... May 20th. Well May 20th back to the states but since I'll be on the west coast, I'm still going down to Vista first to see Flo first, so now I should be arriving in Boulder about May 25th, give or take a couple of days. One never knows until it all happens in the fucking Army.

Got a special request for you, something I'm going to need before Valentine's Day. Turns out we're going to have a training class on the evils of Marijuana and I am taking it upon myself to go to said class and tear the fucking officer who is teaching it... into little pieces... my goal is to make him cry like a Catholic school girl from Mt. Saint Gertrude's Academy.

There is a library here at Eakin Compound and I'm going there tomorrow to see if I can find any books or magazine articles on marijuana but I'll bet they ain't got shit and since there's not much chance I'm going to find anything of historical value, a favor I would ask is for you to go to the CU

306

library and see if you can find me anything I can use. What I'm thinking, is any research that was done in the 1920's or 30's to establish marijuana was dangerous back before the law was passed, is flawed. Their scientific practices back then had to have some holes in it so if you could find me a study or something that I can show was all fucked up in its methodology or results that would be great!

Other than the cabash on my plans to be home early, things are going OK here for now. Nice being out of the South Vietnamese Army and in a big city where it is fairly safe overall. You still never know when they're going to flip a grenade in your jeep or try to blow up your truck, but for the most part, not much happens war like here in Can Tho. And of course, we've got the scientific steam bath and blow job parlor across the street, so I can't complain.

So, are you dating anybody other than your right hand these days? Any new word on your draft status? Like are you going to Canada any time soon? If I had it to do over, I'd take a more serious look at the Canadian option. The fucking war so sucks like a Hoover! Don't tell Rick I said that...

Oh. And Happy Birthday! I forgot to send you a card on New Years... I'm sure you'll forgive me. Wish I could mail you some of what I wish I could mail you but can't take any chances like that... Ha ha. Just know as you read this you can bet your ass that... even though I'm in the Delta, chances are my elevation is Boulder High!

Take it easy!

Curt

As he addressed the envelope to Larry, the Kid was deciding who he needed to write next with his quasi-tragic news; his parents and brother, Dave and Patsy Allen in Nashville or Flo, when he noticed that RV Smith was standing next to his table. The Kid was always amazed at the shape of RV's head, kind of oval but larger on top and tapering down to a slightly pointy chin. It was very much like a football flattened on one end and when you looked at his crop of naturally curly brown hair above his radar ears. *One look and you can tell RV hasn't had an easy life.* "Hey, RV... what's up?"

"Hey, Stocker, not much," RV shifted nervously on his feet, as if he had a lot on his mind and didn't know where to start.

307

"So, RV. Did you want to talk to me about something? Need somebody to help you with your homework? What?"

"Uh, no… I don't have any homework," he smiled and chuckled nervously, momentarily looking away before getting to his intended topic. "What do you think is going to happen to Boujold?" he spoke in a slow drawl that the Kid had a rough time placing. It was like half southern, half mid-west like Missouri maybe and the bottom line was the Kid could have cared less to know anything about RV's personal data, like where he was from or rather or not he was a stock car racing fan.

"Why should you care? When were you ever a friend of his?"

"Just curious, I guess. Heard he got busted for marijuana and I figured if anybody would know what happened, it would be you."

"Oh. That's funny, I heard that a couple of guys *say you* know a little bit about it." That the Kid would speak these words seemed to touch a nerve in RV.

"What do you mean that I'd know anything?"

"What I mean is the word is that somebody dropped a dime on Bouji about there being something in his locker… know anything about that?" the Kid put the ball in RV's court.

RV's eyes fluttered and he took a noticeable breath. "Uh, no, not me. I surely don't know anything about that, except what I've heard people talking about it around, you know?

The Kid didn't answer right away, just looked on as RV visibly became more stressed. "Well, then, RV, you'll be happy to know that the Colonel said Bouji was off the hook, and he'll be leaving as scheduled tomorrow morning to go home."

"Oh! Great" He seemed relieved.

"Yeah, we just heard. Bouji said it was something about the chain of evidence being fucked up or some such shit, so it's pretty much turned into a non-event."

"Well, that's good!" RV said with a sigh, "that would have been a major bummer if he'd gotten his DEROS set back."

"No shit. You really think so? Anything else? I got some letters to write."

"Uh. No." he looked at his watch, "as a matter of fact, I've got to get ready for guard duty in about an hour. Uh, you on duty tonight?'

"Hmmm. No, I don't think so, I didn't go look at the duty roster myself, but nobody came and told me that I was, so I'm thinking that I don't." *When was the last time I had duty? Hmmmm.*

"All right then, Stocker, I'll see ya later!"

"Right. See you later, RV," the Kid said as he turned and walked off.

What the fuck was THAT all about?

Just then, Mark Birmbaum and Mike Imrem appeared with a ton of supplies between them including a radio, some beers and a bunch of other stuff and started moving in on the table next to the Kid's.

"Hey, Curt! Mark sat down his gigantic radio and began setting up for the football game between the Baltimore Colts and the New York Jets, which was going to broadcast beginning at 0100 hours, with just a 3 or 4 minute delay through telephones and microwaves or some such technical wizardry. Mark could hardily wait for Joe Namath's Waterloo. Mike was only hoping the Jets would cover the 13 point spread, as he had earlier finally given in to Mark's incessant begging and wagered $5 MPC on the outcome.

"Mark, Mike," the Kid began to lose the urge to write letters. "Ready for the big game huh?"

"Yes sir ree!" Birnbaum exclaimed, "If I was home, I'd be at the big fucking party my family is having to watch the Colts trample the poor little Jets. God I wish it was going to be on TV here!"

"Don't you know it?" Imrem chimed in, "it's going to be historic… anyway, that's my bet."

The Kid looked over their supplies for the game, "Why are you guys setting up so early?"

"Just antsy, I guess, you know, pre-game butterflies, sorta," Mark shrugged, as Ron Edwards walked up to the Kid's table.

"Hey, the band is getting ready to practice in Richie's room, if you want to listen," he informed the Kid.

"Yes, I do! I'll be right down," he said, pulling out an envelope to finish off addressing Larry's letter so I would go out in the morning. Everybody else could wait a day for his news, but he needed Larry to get started right away on his proxy research, if he was going to have any chance finding the goods and sending him the information for his attack on the officer, whomever it turned out to be, teaching the marijuana training class.

As he hit the top step in the stairwell going down from the Roof Club to the third floor, he heard the band tuning up in Richie's room and he was a little surprised when a series of practice riffs were so hot that even in the heat of the tropics, it gave him chills. *That has to be Boyett. That man has more talent in his toe than I have in my whole leg.*

But then, he felt a whole other kind of chill hit him as echoing voices collided around him coming from the club upstairs and out of the halls of the old hotel below.

"Mandatory company formation! Everybody report ASAP to the roof club... All hands report immediately to the roof club for a mandatory company formation!"

The Kid stops on the steps and does an about face as traffic was now coming from below and was heading, enmass, up the steps to the roof to see what this suddenly called mandatory company formation was all about.

Emerging back into the club, he catches the eye of Birnbaum and cocked his head in a questioning *what the fuck is this all about manner* to which Marc's response was a shoulder shrug with his palms up in a classical *I surly don't know myself pose.*

As the PSYOP warriors entered the club, they naturally gravitated into their comfort zones of association; tonight, the alkies were on the east side and the pot heads on the west side, over where Birnbaum and Imrem had been setting up their Super Bowl listening party.

The band, Richie Wells, Tom, Bennie, George and Don all approached their area in a group, with equally questioning looks on their faces.

"Do you think this could be another shake down?" Richie spoke the thought that was now arriving in the brains of all the heads present.

"Could be," speculated Birnbaum, "but everybody's clean in their rooms, wouldn't you think? And the officers' aren't here... if it was a shakedown, they have a bunch of brass here to help conduct it."

As Ozelle made his way to the front of the club, moving through the parting crowd, RV Smith was rapidly talking into his right ear while trailing him like a pet puppy dog. The first sergeant's hands held no papers, like he'd have if there were something official coming down from higher up that he was announcing. *Strange.*

Standing next to the ping pong table, Ozelle surveyed the group to see if the necessary personnel had assembled yet and when he was sure they had, be began.

"OK, men, OK...OK... listen up... this will only take a minute." The crowd settled and he spoke. "It has been brought to my attention, gentlemen, that there is a soldier here among us, who does not pull duty… one of our number who never takes a turn on guard duty or whose name never graces any duty roster… what do you all think of that?"

Out of the assembled members of A company, there emanated a throaty grumbling noise that was mostly accentuated with the words … *"BOOOO HISSS HISSS BOOOOO….."*

"…That's right, there is a soldier here among us who does not contribute to the unit as we all do…" Ozelle paused for dramatic effect, and you could see the crowd anxious and eager to discover who the slacker might be, and the First Shirt did not keep them waiting any longer. *"Specialist Stocker,* It appears that for the entire time since you transferred from B Company to A Company, in early November, the transfer was not made on paper and consequently, Specialist Stocker, your name was never added to the duty roster and you have not pulled one shift of duty since the conclusion of your courts martial… and since you didn't pull any duty before it, for the entire time you have been assigned to this company, you haven't pulled duty once!"

The Kid gasped in surprise. *By God… Hoch's gift!* That's what he was talking about!

The company gasped at the revelation and then, almost immediately, the lifer drunks exploded in a chorus of boos, epitaphs, and name calling while the Tribe howled with laughter, cheers and beefy calls of " *KID… KID… KID…" all while shoving him around like a pinball.*

"Specialist Stocker…" Ozelle nailed him with a razor sharp glare, "front and center…"

As he was bounced and shoved out from his location within the Tribe and pratt stumbled toward the front of the club where Ozelle stood next to the ping pong table, he smiled broadly at the lifer drunks; their boos are like nectar of the Gods to him, all the while the unit's pot smoking faction wildly cheered him on. Arriving at the table he executed a 180 degree turn on his heels, faced the assembled unit and when he did, he accented it with gripped fists above his head in a boxer's victorious salute, in reaction to which the gathering, both pro Kid and con Kid, went freaking nuts.

"Settle down settle down, now people!" Ozelle locked him in eye contact, as the *brew ha ha* died down, "Specialist Stocker, what *do* you have to say for yourself?"

Looking from the First Shirt's eyes out over the crowd, which had grown immediately quiet waiting for his reply and most likely an apology, the Kid said,

"Nothin'."

For a split second, the crowd was in silent disbelief before an unbelieving moan arose like a wave, they would not excuse him, of all people, to say nothing so he quickly continued, ..."OK, OK... I admit, *I'm one lucky mother fucker! So sue me!*" and with that, he stuck both arm up in the air in the classic Churchill "V" for Victory pose before reaching down and with his right hand and holding up his lucky Beaver Nickel and jangling it in front of the crowd.

The totally predictable reaction rolled all over him; more ruckus and boos from the drunks clashing against the cheers from his compatriots and when the noise died down a little, he hollered, "Go ahead and admit it... *you all wish you were me!*"

Well, he might as well have thrown kerosene on the lifers' fire but the pot smokers belly laughed for a full 30 seconds.

When the pandemonium died down a little bit, Ozelle stepped back in. "You can thank you good friend RV Smith for spotting the fact your name never showed up on the duty roster, Stocker."

The Kid turned and gazed over at a proudly smirking RV, sending him a first class *if looks could kill you'd be dead evil eye special,* as he theatrically pushed his round gold glasses up on his nose with his bird finger.

"Don't you want to apologize to your fellow soldiers, Stocker? Don't you feel it wasn't fair that some of them should be pulling your duty?"

"Hell no, First Sergeant. I got nothing to apologize *for*... I'm not the one who fills out the duty roster... in fact I've never filled out a duty roster in my entire fucking life and seriously doubt that I ever will! I mean, after the way I've been fucked around in this man's army... I reckon I flat got exactly what was coming to me!"

Pandemonium again seized the room.

"OK OK, settle down," Ozelle waived a hand over the crowd, "Stocker, since the roster is already set for tonight, we won't be changing it. But you can bet your *self proclaimed allegedly lucky ass,* that you will find yourself on guard duty tomorrow night! Dismissed!" he ended the meeting and turning to the Kid he said in a low voice, "...come with me, Stocker. I want to have a *word* with you."

Following him down the 6 flights of stairs and into his office, the Kid sat down in the chair that was to the left of Ozelle's desk.

Sitting down, the first shirt pulled out a cigarette from the open pack of Marlboros laying on his desk and lit up. Exhaling, he gave the Kid an appraising dirty look. "So, Stocker, how long did you think you could get away with this?"

"Get away with what, First Sergeant… I haven't done *anything!*"

"Yes you have. You *had to know* you weren't on the duty roster."

"Sarge, I gotta tell you, seriously, I literally never gave it a second thought. When I didn't come up on the duty roster that was the end of any attention I ever paid it. Why the hell should I?"

That line obviously struck a nerve and Ozelle was seething. The Kid could see he was trying to keep his cool as he pointedly remarked, "Just because you beat one court martial, Specialist, don't go thinking you can fuck with me. I could charge you under the UCMJ because there's a legal word for what you were doing… it's called *"malingering…"* and Specialist… *I can make my… shit… stick!"*

There was what can only be described as a 9 months' pregnant pause between each of Ozelle's last three words.

"Understood, First Sergeant. Are we through here, First Sergeant?" the Kid asked in a cautious and very non-patronizing manner and with a dismissive nod and a waive of a hand from the top shirt, he got up and left.

I can make my shit stick… True enough, as he headed for the stairs, the Kid knew with those words ringing in his ears, that Ozelle was the one NCO in the entire unit that he would prefer not to have on his case.

Chapter 42

Just shoot him. That's what one of his Ft. Campbell drill sergeants had said about what you do if you catch one of your mates sleeping on guard duty. *Just shoot him because him sleeping on guard duty could cost the life of everybody in the unit.* The words came back to him as he sat on the folding chair behind the sandbags that defined the third floor guard post, which looked out over the canal that flowed past the Villa Cruz. The placid water below gave it the air of a ship's bow.

A bead of sweat ran down his forehead and into his left eye, causing him to clinch it tightly to expel the astringent bug repellant that was part of the sweat mix. *Remember if you rub it... you make it worse.* The sky was muted with clouds that only permitted the plethora of stars to shine through small windows, as if each were a framed picture of some constellation or another. The canal was as black coffee and there were but two small reflections to break the monotony, coming from the single streetlight that illuminated each end of the bridge on the main drag, about 2 city blocks to his right. There was as yet no hint of the sunrise that would signal the end of his shift.

With his right hand resting on the M-16 that lay in front of him on the bags, he Looked at the Seiko on his left wrist and noted the time: *0400 hours.*

Two down, two to go. Sliding off the chair, he sat briefly on the floor as he pulled a KOOL out of his fatigue shirt pocket and lit it up. Reassuming his seat, he kept the lit ember of the cigarette between his legs and would bend over below the sandbag lined alcove to take a puff so that no light was visible to any snipers who might be out there below... somewhere... looking to draw a bead on the red glowing tip. It was Ok to smoke cigarettes on guard duty, so long as it was done in such a way as to conceal the ember being visible from the street below. He recalled the nervous smokes he'd taken while out in the jungle on patrol in the middle of the night. *This is nothing compared to that.*

Sure is quiet... too quiet... he silently chuckled at his private joke because most of the time, a night at Villa Cruz was anything but quiet. From his post 30 feet above the street, when he first began his shift, he could hear the three giant printing presses rhythmically humming away but now the 3rd shift print crew was apparently taking a break or a press broke, or they were installing new plates and possibly loading paper. The massive presses were the real reason the Villa Cruz existed; in addition to being the officer's billet, it was home to the battalion's entirely massive printing operations.

The trio of presses, which bore the names *the Good, the Bad and the Ugly,* spit out more than a million leaflets a month as three shifts kept the presses running constantly. There might be a lull or two for maintenance, but in reality, the presses ran relentlessly. A very large number of the unit's enlisted men were printers, including both of the Kid's room mates and 4/5th of the band.

Gee. I was not on the duty roster for two and a half months! Ha ha. Let's see… the average duty is twice a week, so in 10 weeks, I've missed pulling 20 shifts. And Ozelle has the nerve to tell me I should feel bad about it…because I'm a malingerer… and my mates were doing my work? Fat fucking chance of that. I so don't feel bad. Why should I? Thanks, Paul, wherever you might be now. That was a great gift! He spotted all that time, I was still on the B Company roster!

"Psssst…. Stocker…." it was Birnbaum, who was manning the other top floor guard post at the rear of the building, "… you awake?" he half whispered.

"Hey Mark… yeah… I'm awake," the Kid replied in a quiet voice, "so don't shoot me. But, uh, abandoning you post is a hanging offense, don't you know?"

"Only if you get caught!" he chuckled. "All of these fucking brass were so drunk when they passed out, none of them are going to be up before revile." He paused briefly before slathering on the lament. "Shit I still can't believe the Colts lost to the Jets! Mutha Fuck! I don't even care about the $5 I lost to Mike, but God… the utterly endless amount of bullshit I gotta take over the next week or so is way over my head!"

"Yeah… that Namath is something," the Kid exhaled, "My cousin, Sharon, is married to this guy Phil from Alabama and he would pretty much suck Namath's dick if he'd let him. Namath Namath Namath… that's all the guy talks about and now it's going to fucking be worse!"

"Well, I knew there was definitely a chance that they'd cover that 13 point spread… but to win the fucking game… I'd have bet my life against that."

"Good thing you didn't. Oh wait, we bet our lives everyday we spend in the Nam?" the Kid theorized.

"Speaking of which… I really wanted that Armed Propaganda Team gig that the Chief gave to Ling Fook on that story you're doing with Sweet. I just haven't gotten out into the field enough to satisfy me. I hate this fucking place."

"Well, I tell you what; the Chief has me working on doing a big story about all the 10th PSYOPS team activity, working with the American 9th Division, over in Dong Tam. One of my best friends and roommates from DINFOS is with the 9th so it will be a blast… let's set it up for you to shoot that, it's most likely going to happen the first week in March. "

"Well, OK, now you're talking! I could dig a little action! Get some combat shots!" he enthused.

The Kid tamped out his KOOL and tried to flick to butt all the way to the canal but came up just short. "I for one hope *NOT*. I'll skip the action. Action is over rated. Give me good old boredom. Didn't I tell you that when Boujold and I were on troop indoctrination at the main Cang Long base for three weeks, we never once went on an operation and we didn't work a lick at fucking anything and the only bad thing was that we saw the same film over and over again every night for two of those fucking weeks? *"Once before I die,"* the only redeeming feature was it had Ursula Andress in it. After the first week of it, Bouji made the comment… "… If I see this flick once more… *I will die!*" But I fucking loved it because Wilson wasn't hauling my butt all over to hell and gone and there was no action!

Birnbaum laughed. "Yeah… old fuckin' Bouji is flying home today," and with a jealous tone added, "he finally saw some action, the lucky bastard."

"You sure as hell got the lucky part right! Almost got *killed!*" the Kid had to laugh and they were almost making too much noise.

In a suppressed tone, Birnbaum said, "Boy did he luck fucking out on that marijuana charge. Speaking of lucking out… how are you liking guard duty, now that you're run is over, Mr. lucky beaver?"

"Aaaahhh, I keep telling you guys, even with having to pull guard duty a couple of times a week, this is a far *FAR* better deal than the field. Hey, speaking of guard duty, don't you think you'd better get back to your post?"

"In a minute. It's not like the sappers are scaling the walls to get in here." After a pause, Mark added, "Sure is quiet… too quiet…" and a split second after he said it, the printing presses below them roared to life, making them both laugh.

Chapter 43

"Stoney goes to the field." That'll be the headline," the Kid said as he looked off at some imaginary broadsheet and spread out his hands to signify where the bold type front was written in the air. "Stoney goes to the field… right as Nixon declares… *Peace!*"

Stoney frowned and the Kid had to laugh. At long last, Stoney was finally going to get his wish; he was scheduled to catch a chopper to Sadec at 0800 hours. He was one state north of giddy as they sat on the bench outside of the Kid's window and smoked pot late into the night.

"Don't tell me you're afraid of a little *peace?* The Kid kidded.

"The *piece* I can handle, it's the missing the war part I won't be able to handle. I will not come to the war and miss it! No fucking way. Hey… Stocker… you know about as much Vietnamese as any American here, right?"

"Well, yeah, for somebody who's not actually Vietnamese," he wondered where this was going.

"So, uh, what's the Vietnamese word for Coca Cola? Like I wanted to ask a gook for a Coke?" Stoney inquired.

"Oh, there's not really a Vietnamese language word for it, they just use our own word, 'coke'."

"Coke," he repeated back. "OK, and what's the Vietnamese word for cane, like a walking cane," he demonstrated ala charades a man walking with a stick.

"That one I don't know," the Kid slowly spoke as he digested what Stoney was up to. "Say… you're not planning on asking a Vietnamese person for Cocaine, are you?"

"Well, yeah! Why not?"

The Kid took a puff on his joint and smiled at Stoney, not the sharpest knife in the drawer. "Two things, Stoney. First, a Vietnamese person would have to speak *English* to understand what it was you were trying to say that way. If you found out what the Vietnamese word for cane was and you ask somebody for a Coke and a cane… you would get a soft drink and a walking stick. Second and most importantly, there is no cocaine in Asia. The coca plant is native to South America and as far as I know, that is the only place it grows."

The smile floated off Stoney's face as he realized he would have no cocaine in Vietnam. "Rats."

"There is, however, tons of opium out there and I highly suggest you stay away from it. That shit's bad!"

"Yeah, I could go for some good opium. All the opium in the city is bullshit. Is *Sadec* a good place to be?" Stoney continued his quest for information.

"Sadec is ok. They sure as fuck got opium there but, you won't be staying. Sadec is ARVN 9th Division headquarters and you'll get sent out from there to some place to hell and gone down in the Delta. Ca Mau, Bac Lieu, Soc Trang, Go Cong, Tra Vinh, Vinh Long, those are some of the places you could end up at and they are all the luck of the fuckin' draw."

A silence ensued as they leaned against the white wall, as each man continued to smoke his own joint like it was a cigarette. "Which one of those towns would most likely get me in the action?" Stony finally broke it.

"A better question would be which one wouldn't be likely to get you into the action? God I keep telling you fucks that action is way over rated!"

"I know. But I gotta find out for myself."

Chapter 44

The Kid's attention was attracted to Ernie Wilson, who was standing on a chair next to the wall, his hands grabbing at the framed picture that was hung there, up high. "What ya doin' Ernie?"

"Taking down LBJ! We got the new Richard Nixon to put up and today is Inauguration Day, so we got a new commander n chief to lord over us; he's in that tube on my desk. Here, Ron, let me hand you this," he pivoted and passed the dark, inch-wide wooden framed picture into Edwards waiting grip.

Holding it flat and waist high with both hands, Ron stared into the color picture of LBJ staring back at him, deadpan no smile expression and all. "Kinda makes me want to hock a really big fucking loogie in his face," he smiled.

"Better wait," the 10th's own chief, Everett Regan cut in, "he's still the commander 'n chief, remember the international dateline? Nixon won't be president until its January 21st here, so that would be an act of total disrespect for the commander and chief... until about this time tomorrow!"

"Yeah!" Mike Imrem exclaimed, "Then we can go at him with the darts, exacto knives, chop sticks and everything up to and including the kitchen sink!"

It was funny, but the Kid was not yet in the mood for laughing.

"Yep, here's the new sheriff," Ernie pulled the picture of Nixon out of the tube and flattened it as best he could on his light table, while securing it with a touch of tape on each of the corners.

"Hmmm, you know, Nixon looks an awful lot like LBJ... the only real difference is the ski jump nose and the five O'clock shadow," the Kid observed. "No wait... Bob Hope! ... Either way, too scary!"

"And the size of the ear lobes... LBJ's are monstrous but Nixon's aren't a hell of a lot smaller," Mike compared the two pictures. "As scary as Nixon may be, at least he can't send any of us to Vietnam!"

"Amen to that shit, brother!" Ron pumped a fist in the air

Wilson finished framing Nixon's picture and stepping up on the chair, he hung it from the same hook LBJ had just vacated. "There. I wonder how fast his secret plan to end the war is going to work."

"Don't let's hold our breath," the Kid sarcastically grabbed his nose as he continued to speak, "I'm betting there ain't no plan. If he had a real plan, he'd be so tickled pink, he'd tell the world! The world has heard nothing… so I'll bet that's what his plan is… nada zippo zilch!"

"Speaking of plans," Ron cut in, "the plan for tonight is to get JC Stoned for the first time!"

"Really?" the Kid turned with a look of surprise, "he say he finally wants to try it?"

"Yep. Today at breakfast, he said he was going to go for it tonight!" Ron informed the Kid. "This is going to be fun! I don't think we have to worry about him not getting off the first time, what with all the freaking kick ass stuff we've got right now."

Something out of the ordinary would be fun tonight and JC Compton was going to be it! What with Boyett and Benny and George gone to Saigon to see if they could wrangle some better band instruments, the initiation of JC officially into the Pot Tribe would be a hoot!

As he prepared to sit down at his desk and begin work on the story presently on his front burner, the Kid decided to first return to the front of Battalion HQ to fill his coffee cup with ice water. Walking through the screen enclosed hallway, he casually flipped a couple of geckos over to the next wall without looking to see where they landed. Then, as he entered the main room and approached the big orange water cooler, he heard a voice speak his name from behind, and a seriously surprised voice it was.

"Curt Stocker!"

The Kid turned to see who it was and got one of the biggest surprises of his Vietnam tour. Standing in front of him was Gary Reed, a boyhood friend and fellow classmate from Boulder High School, whose family held membership in Trinity Lutheran, the same church the Kid's family attended so they had not only gone to public school together, they had been in the same confirmation class!

"Well I'll be go to Hell! I come to Vietnam and who do I find? Amazing!"

The Kid looked at him, mouth gaping in complete surprise and it took him a couple of seconds to speak his name. "Gary Reed! *Jesus H confirmation class!* I don't believe it!

320

"Wow… really!" Gary's surprise clearly exceeded the Kid's. "What are the chances you and I would end up in the *same Army,* let alone the same unit? I can't believe it; I get stuck in PSYOPS, come halfway around the world… and here is Curt *Freaking Stocker!*"

They shook hands, "Welcome to Can Tho!" the Kid emphatically said.

"So… last I heard of you, you were in Nashville, people were talking that you landed a gig on some radio station bigger than KIMN! You'll have to tell me how that happen." Gary was still grinning from ear to ear.

"Long story. Hey, Jeeze, funny you should show up! Some of the guys just started a band here, round about New Years Eve… Obviously you aren't still in the Showmen, *what with you here and all,* so shit fire, I can't wait for you to check them out!"

Having been lead guitar in The Showmen, had been one of Boulder High's most popular student bands in the mid-sixties, the Kid was immediately given to wonder if Gary might want to get involved in the tribe's band.

"Those days are over, but it was good while it lasted,' Reed opined. "So, the unit has a band! Interesting! I will have to check that action out."

"Ahem…" it was Wimbish interrupting, "if you don't mind, Stocker, I was in processing Specialist Reed, so let me suggest you and he can play catch up later because I've another guy waiting to process as well and so why don't you two continue this love fest later tonight…OK?"

"Sure, Lou, obviously we didn't plan this to piss you off or anything!" the Kid finished filling his cup, "Gary, I'll see you tonight up in the Roof Club!"

"All right!" he refocused his attention back to the paperwork that Wimbish was hammering on him.

It was then that the kid also noticed the other new man waiting to be processed, a young black man, a slight bit on the skinny side, with a well defined moustache that circled his upper lip and hung down on the sides just about a half inch below the corners of his mouth. It made his face look like simultaneously sad and mad.

Hmmm. That man has a case of the ass against someone!

Chapter 45

All through dinner at the Eakin Compound mess hall, JC Compton has this strange and almost goofy look on his face. Tonight was going to be special, that much he knew, but he didn't know what really to expect or how it was all going to come down.

A few different tribe members had attempted to describe to him what the feeling was like, to take the smoke into your lungs and the sensations that would be unveiled as it permeated through his body and into his brain. It must really be good, though, he thought, otherwise, why would anybody put up with the risk that came with smoking it?

As Barry Fischer, the last member of the group of 6 that occupied the table finished his meal, they all rose up in unison, grabbed their trays and headed for the bussing station to deliver them to the Vietnamese civilian women who handled that part of KP.

Everyone to the man, in a flurry of Zippos, lit up cigarettes as they exited the mess hall and walked by the rows of officer's billets, heading for one of the 10th PSYOP duce and a half trucks waiting to take them back to the New Villa. The traffic of officers on their way to the mess hall required them to periodically offer up a salute.

"I'm kind of nervous," JC half chuckled as they sat down in the back of the truck already occupied with another half dozen men who were waiting for the load to fill up for departure. Since some of the men in the truck were not members of the Tribe, nobody gave any response to JC's comment. One of them, in the person of RV Smith, specifically, caught the comment and the Kid could see he was curiously waiting for an explanation that wasn't going to be forthcoming.

"Hey…Robespierre…" the Kid called to RV with the nickname he had given him off the 'R' in R.V, which stood for Robert, "word on the street is that you're calling me the biggest of all bull shitters that ever walked earth."

Surprised that the Kid was even speaking to him, RV suspiciously eyed him. "Yeah. Pretty much everything out of your mouth is BS, Stocker. You're the BS'er who never shuts up."

"Well, RV," the Kid began coolly, "one of the new guys, Specialist Reed, is from Boulder, Colorado, my hometown. He has known me for more than 10 years. Feel free to ask him anything you want and see if you can find out my past reputation for bullshit… *or not!"*

"Thanks. I'll make a point to do that," he slowly replied. "Hey, Stocker… speaking of bullshit… I see you're already on guard duty for the last shift again to night!" RV laughed and winked at his two buddies, *Frank* and *Al,* who joined in his mirth.

"So why do you keep such a close track of my activities, RV? Is it that you don't have any life of your own?" Just then, three more GIs piled into the truck and the load was big enough that Moysiadias, who was driving, hollered back that they were departing.

Belching diesel smoke, the big truck engine came to life and soon they were rolling down Can Tho's main drag on their way back to Ben Xe Moi. The sun had gone down a half hour earlier so the breeze from the drive had a nice cooling effect as it evaporated the soldiers' sweat. There was not much conversation as the group all took responsibility to watch the civilian traffic that buzzed around them, trying to get where they all needed to be before curfew. A show of vigilance was good protection against the stray grenade that could easily be tossed into such an inviting target offered by a truck load of Americans. There weren't many dangerous threats inside the city of Can Tho, but that was one of the ever present variety.

Once back at the New Villa, the consensus was pretty much showers first and changing out of their uniforms before they assembled on the balcony in front of the Kid, Willert and Ramjet's room for JC's baptism of smoke and fire.

Ken, Ramjet and Ron had a **Stars and Stripes** Newspaper laid out on top of Ramjet's foot locker, dragged into the middle of the room for the occasion. The antique overhead fan cranked away, slowly as ever and certainly not fast enough to blow around the array of marijuana that the three had laid out.

"OK," said Ramjet, "we got the Vietnamese, the Cambodian and somebody told me this stuff was from Thailand, but who the hell knows and who the fuck cares… it's pretty fucking good shit is what it is!"

"I say we just flat steam roll him with the Cambodian," Edwards advanced his game plan, suggesting they start JC out on what everybody currently agreed was the top of the line stuff. Near black in color, the *Cambode* grass was in peak condition, more than ready to smoke but still a little on the moist side with all the resin it contained. It was strictly pipe material, virtually impossible to roll into a joint.

"Hey… let's let him pick!" suggested John Tearman, who had just entered the room in time to catch on to what was being discussed.

"No," cut in Ken, "only because he's never smoke before, he wouldn't know what the fuck he was picking. No, he's counting on us to lead the way! My suggestion is to start with the regular Vietnamese stuff and see what that does to him, then as he moves up in quality, he'll appreciate the difference!'

"Brilliant," said the Kid, "Makes perfect sense… like, if we got him drunk on whiskey and then gave him a beer, he couldn't possible even feel the beer."

"And where *is* the guest of honor?" Ron began looking around for JC.

"Speak of the Devil!" said Tall John, as he spotted JC on the balcony in the company of Richie Wells and Don Hartmann.

"Here he is," Richie good naturedly shoved JC into the room, "we were playing him some music and when we get him stoned, we're going to take him back and play the same song again so he can see the difference!"

"Got the sweaty palms," JC made a comment, "the only part of me that didn't previously sweat in this country. Might have to start putting Right Guard on my palms… so that's the shit, huh?" he pointed and the three piles sitting on the foot locker.

"Three kinds, it's sorta like wine," the Kid began, "and they are all four or five times better than the stuff we get back in the states from Mexico. In fact, *JC, My boy*" the Kid switched to *WC Fields* (and Boujold), "this shit, in whiskey terms, is Wild Turkey and grain alcohol mixed *together!*"

Producing a dark wood straight stemmed Marcham pipe out of his pocket, Ron bent down and took a big pinch of the Vietnamese pot and stuffed it into the bowl. "OK, JC, let's take this out to the rail and you can have at it!"

"Well, all right!" he beamed in his Texas drawl, "let's get high! Right? High is what you call it right?

"Right…" all the friends in the room responded in unison.

Once on the balcony, Ron flipped open his Zippo and fired up the bowl. He took in a couple of puffs to get a good ember cooking before he passed it to JC. With everybody watching him, like he was on display in a department store window, the lean and shirtless Texan lifted the pipe to his lips and with a perplexed look of anticipation, took his very first hit.

"OK, now, hold it in," Ron coached him, "you gotta let it get into your blood…it's not like tobacco, where you draw it in and blow it right out…"

At that point, the smoke exploded from JC's mouth, exhaled in a fit of coughing. Being a cigarette smoker, nobody in the tribe expected him to have any trouble with the smoking part of the operation but the way the marijuana smoke expanded in his lungs with his initial toke certainly caught him by surprise.

"Maybe take smaller hits until you get the hang of it," Ron suggested, as Tearman took the pipe from JC's hand, hit it himself and passed it on to Don, who hit it and passed it to Richie, who hit it and passed it back to JC.

Now the pipe was really cooking and when JC gently hit it for the second time, drawing the hot, pungent smoke deep down into his lungs, he succeeded in holding it in for about ten seconds before he exhaled without coughing. "Hmmm, I do like the taste," he commented, affirmatively nodding his head.

"And that's not the best part," the Kid smiled as he took the pipe from JC and had a big hit.

In addition to Ron's pipe, there were all of the sudden a number of filter tipped joints being passed back and forth between the growing group, which now numbered at about a dozen GI's and included Terry Stage, Birnbaum, Barry Fischer and Mike Imrem among others who came and went after a couple of hits.

"So, when am I going to feel something?" JC asked the Kid after another hit.

"Well, I reckon it won't be too long until you feel some effects," the Kid speculated, "after all, this is the best fucking stuff in the entire world, so I'd imagine you should be getting off in a couple more hits…this is the kind of stuff that only take a couple of hits to do the job for most of us."

Nodding his head in understanding, JC took one of the filter-tipped joints that was floating by and hit that. Next Ken placed his brass bong in the dark-haired Texan's hands, which was loaded with the Cambode and he took a big freaking hit off that. "Oh! This tastes a little different," he analyzed the newly introduced stuff. "But I still don't feel anything."

"Nothing at all?" Richie inquired, "Not even a little light headedness?"

"Nope."

"Don't worry," said the Kid, "while it is true that a lot of people don't get stoned the first time they try it, this stuff should put you some place way north of higher than a kite! I mean, *we are all flyin' right now!*"

"Amen, brother," Ken said, "sometimes it creeps up on you, like a fucking Indian... and then, boom! You know you're high!"

It wasn't five minutes later when Richie was asking JC if he had yet achieved liftoff. "Feeling anything?"

"Nope," he shook his head and took another toke of a joint.

"Give it some time," Fisher clinically advised, "the high is very subtle. I remember it took me till the second time to get high when I started smoking."

"I'll be shocked as hell if you don't get off," the Kid reaffirmed the group's faith in the quality of their smoke, "just wait for it a little, don't need to worry about it, that's for sure! Oh! Hey!" the Kid was suddenly struck with the recollection of what had happened earlier in the day, "one of my boyhood friends that I grew up with got assigned to the unit today! Gary Reed! He's a guitar player and was in one of the best bands at Boulder High."

"Really?" Richie said, "We'll have to give him an audition!"

"As a matter of fact," the Kid recalled, "I said I'd meet him on the roof for a beer. Didn't have time to determine if he was a head or not so I thought I'd try to find out before he comes down here. Just because he was in a band doesn't mean he's smoking pot and he was always sort of a straight arrow, but I might as well go find out...save my place!" he said as he headed up on the roof.

With the New Villa at night being a closed, locked and guarded environment, it was not in the least difficult to locate Gary Reed, who even more conveniently was standing right there at the bar ordering a beer when the Kid emerged from the stairwell.

"Yo, Gary!"

"Hey Curt! Let me buy you a beer!"

"OK. Thanks. I still can't get over the shock that you're here. It reminds me of my life two life's ago! Wait until I write this to Larry Ryan! Nobody back home is going to believe that we've ended up in the same unit!"

"No shit! I was next to struck dumbfounded when I saw you walk up to the water cooler!"

"You knew this guy when you were kids, you were saying?" Sgt Johnson sought to continue a conversation he was having with Reed when the Kid walked up.

"Uh, yeah."

"Did he wear those ugly round glasses back then?" Sgt Johnson looked at the Kid sporting a sly grin as he said it.

"No. Those I gotta say, are new," Gary said as he clearly appraised the Kid's John Lennon look.

"That the best you can do, Sarge? My glasses are offended! Come on Gary, let's drink at the other bar. "

"There's another bar?"

"No." the Kid took his Hamms and motioned for Gary to follow, "there's no other bar, *this is a hardship tour,* but the view is nicer over here," he lead him to a place where they stood in the middle of the rail on the west edge of the Roof Club, standing at a spot that put them directly over the action on the third floor balcony, which was a scant 8 feet below.

Off in the distance, the red beacon at Binh Thuy Field now visible, a glowing dot, kind of like the embers on the ends of some joints being passed from hand to hand directly beneath their feet. The Kid could smell the burning herb as smoke roiled up from below and after taking a good whiff, he turned to see if Gary picked up on his theatrical action or the aroma and waited to see if he'd make a comment. But that is not the subject when Gary spoke.

"Gotta tell ya," Reed began, "as soon as word got out I was your boyhood friend, people started telling me crazy shit you've done and said I had to ask you about the court martial." The Kid just smiled. "Apparently the war hasn't changed you… it's the same old Curt."

"Yes and no. This war has changed me and my experience with the Army has most *assuredly* changed me… although I must admit this Vietnam thing has had its good moments, too. What about you? How'd you end up in the Army?"

"Probably the same as you, got my draft notice and enlisted to stay out of the infantry," he lamented. My MOS is military intelligence. How long have you been here?"

"I arrived in country in late May and I've been here since June one, except that I wasn't here in Can Tho for the first five months but way out in the field with the ARVN 9th Division, 14th Regiment, down in Tra Vinh, which is east of here."

"See any combat?" Gary took a sip of his Hamms.

"Oh fuck yeah! A ton. I was with this lieutenant who was of the headhunter persuasion and he got us involved in dozens of search and destroy operations. But I signed up for armed forces radio and got sent here as a foreign language announcer and I never once saw any loudspeakers…

327

like I took an extra year to get lied to about what the fuck I was going to be doing so to answer your question, yeah. I saw a lot of action."

Finally, Gary took a sniff of the air and seemed to acknowledge what was taking place right below them as he turned to the Kid with a knowing look. "Is that what I think it is?"

"If you're thinking pot, yes. My room is right below us and we've got this situation where there is only one way out on to our balcony, so we have an early warning system where we can jettison the contraband into the swamp there, if the need should arise. Do you smoke?"

"Well, I haven't been smoking in the Army. I've tried it a couple of times. But, what you are saying is, if I hang with you, I'll be tagged with guilt by association, is that about right?"

"Wouldn't deny it," the Kid had to agree with his theory. Then, calling down below with a cupped hand, he tried to get Ramjet's attention. "Hey... Ramjet... RAMJET!"

Roger looked up to see who was calling his name and saw it was the Kid from above. "What?"

"Any launch information on our newbie yet?" the Kid inquired.

Ramjet turned to JC, who was standing next to him and watched him shrug his shoulders. "Nope... nothing so far. Can you *believe* it?"

"Hey... JC!" the Kid waved to him, "How's it going?"

"Great! I guess. But nothing's happening Stocker, I don't get it. What gives?"

"It's different with everybody, JC, just wait, it'll happen!" Then to Gary, "That's JC and he's getting stoned for the first time tonight, I thought for sure he'd have no problem getting off, but it hasn't happened yet. So, where are you going to be working?"

"Well, from what I've been told, I'm gloing to be flying a lot of leaflet drops."

Just then, RV Smith walked up and butted into their conversation. "Hey, Stocker, I got a bet with Edwards that you can't beat *Frank* in *Stratego*."

"Go away, RV, can't you see I'm busy."

"Oh. You're not *afraid* to play him, are you?" RV put extra special emphasis on *afraid*.

The Kid knew what this was all about. It had started out as a just another of wartime's diversions, the playing of *Stratego* with the drunks, who for some reason, thought they owned the game. And although the Kid had no interest in any serious pursuit, over the past couple of weeks, he had began playing the board game and after a few games, perfected a new attack style that was killing all comers and the previous champ, *Frank*... wanted a rematch and he was sending his challenge through RV.

"Am I afraid? What do you fucking think? It's a board game, for Christ sake. God! All you "Smiths" are microscopic mental midgets... Ronnie, PM, and now you, I'm getting smitten by smiths!" The Kid waited for a reaction or a comeback, but RV just kind of stood there and took a puff on his cigarette but did not speak.

"Tell you what, RV, I'm kind of busy tonight, but tomorrow night, you tell Frankie boy that I'll be more than happy to kick his ass in two out of three, OK?"

"OK, Stocker, I'll tell him. Tomorrow after dinner before the movie, say around 1900 hours? I can't wait to see him make you look sick!" Mission competed, RV walked off in the direction of *Frank,* whom, the Kid could see from where he and Gary stood, was at that very moment engaged in a *Stratego* match against Moiziadis.

Gary stood there for a couple of moments, mulling over the encounter he'd just witnesses and said, "Hmmm. Just like Boulder High... either they love you or they hate you."

"Pretty much. RV most assuredly is my top hater," the Kid confirmed.

"Uh, where did you pick up *'the Kid'*? I've heard you called that today as much as *Stocker.*"

"That was my air knick name in Nashville. Yes, I freely admit I high jacked it from Larry but what the hell, Ryan can be the Kid in Boulder and I'm the Kid in Nashville and Nam. *No harm, no foul.* He came and visited me in Nashville, on his way to Europe, and you can imagine the size of the ration of shit he gave me when he listened to my show and figured it out."

"I'll bet!" Gary laughed.

"Hey, if you want, you can come on down to the Embassy, which is what we call the balcony, and have a puff... or not... come on, I want you to meet my room mates and a couple of the guys in the band. The other half of the band is in Saigon trying to scare up some more and better instruments."

The Kid could see that Gary was mulling it over in his mind before he said, "Uh, I'll take a pass on that right now, until I find out how the land lays here."

"OK, I gotta go back down and see how JC's doing. But seriously, Gary, come on down any time. Nobody's going to arrest you just because you happen to be on the balcony and if you're worried about 'guilt by association', you most assuredly stood convicted of that the second you showed up here."

"Gee, thanks a lot… 'Kid'!"

"Don't' mention it!" he said as turned to walk off. On the way to the stairs, he took a slight detour and stopped by the 'Stratego' table, where *Frank* and Moiziadis were locked in quazi mortal combat across the Napoleon era styled game board. It appeared, from the number of pieces left on the board, that *Frank's* red was kicking Moiziadias' blue troops' butts.

"Hey, *Franklin,*" the Kid interrupted him as he was slowly moving his right hand to pick up a game piece to complete a turn, "you and me, here, tomorrow and no crying like a frickin baby when I eat your lunch!"

"I can't wait! You'll be the one crying, Stocker," *Frank* confidently said.

"Now let me get this straight; I'm playing you but its RV and Edwards who are betting on us and we aren't betting at all, is that right?"

"Pretty much." *Frank* said, reaching for a cigarette out of his Salem pack that lay by his left hand. "I'm in it just to beat you, Stocker."

"How much is the bet?" the Kid asked RV.

"$5.00," he smugly said.

"You and your high rolling buddy are toast, *Frankie*, so be glad it's not your money," the Kid scoffed as he walked away.

Back down on the balcony, the Kid approached Edwards, who was leaning with both elbows on the tile railing, saying something to JC.

"Yo… Ronald, I just came down from the club and RV tells me you and he have a bet for me to play against *Frank* in Stratego and you're betting him $5.00 I'll beat Frank… and when were you going to tell me about this?"

"Like right now? Yeah, that's about the size of it," Ron smiled, "they got all excited tonight for some reason, I meant to mention it but what with all the excitement and your friend from Boulder and all… They wanted me to come down and get you right away, acting all pushy and weird. Kinda like makes me think they're trying to cook something up, you know? Shall I go ahead and set it up?"

"Already done and done. RV caught me on the roof like he's *Frank's* agent or something. Tomorrow night, 1900 hours."

"Well all right. Bitchin" fuckin' A!" Ron grinned, "It will be fun to figure out what their scam is… they've got something going for sure."

Turning to JC, the Kid gave him a quizzical look that said it all: "Anything yet, JC?"

"Nope," he shook his head.

Strange. I can't believe it. Smoking this shit and NOT getting OFF? "Oh well, tomorrow night *for sure,* JC!" the Kid assured him.

Chapter 46

The Kid sat on his footlocker reading the latest book he'd found of interest in the bin down at the USO, Harold Robbins' *"The Adventurers,"* as he waited for JC and the boys to finish their showers and change out of their uniforms. Willert and Ramjet were working the night printing shift so he was alone in the room.

Tonight, for sure, he was positive that JC's second pot smoking experiment would render a positive result. From a break in the fading sunlight that poured into his west facing door, he sensed somebody had just entered the room and he looked up to see it was the new black GI who had processed into the unit with Gary.

"Hey!" he greeted the man as closed his book.

"Hey," the rather serious looking GI gave him an appraising look as he answered back, holding a beer in his left hand, standing there wearing a dark red and black paisley patterned smoking jacket, loosely tied at the waist. "From all the shit I've heard since I got here, like listening to your buddy, Gary, talkin' to the battalion clerk when I was processing in… and a bunch of other GI's talking shit about you, I've got the impression that you are *the man* in this fucking hole."

"Well, uh, I don't know… what kind of *'the man'* do you mean?" the Kid rose up to stand in front of him.

"I mean, the man who beats court Martials, ducks duty and pretty much runs this place… the man who sets the pace, makes the moves and don't take *no shit* from *nobody.*"

"Wow. You figured all of that from just hearing people talk?"

"Pretty much," he pulled a cigarette out of his right breast pocket and lit up. "I was more than a little bit surprised by the reaction everybody had when they found out that Gary new guy actually knew you back in the hood and he was telling everybody that you've been a trouble makin' kinda son of a bitch since forever…"

"OK. Guilty, I guess. My name's Curt," he extended his hand to shake, and you are…"

"The name's Little… Harold Little. And I may be skinny, but I'm not necessarily *'little'*," he firmly shook the Kid's hand.

"Harold? Ling Fook's first name is Harold… two black guys in the unit named Harold… what are the fucking odds? My grandpa on my mother's side is named Harold," marveled the Kid.

"I came up here to find out how legitimate you are," Little said with a hard edge as he eyed the Kid, "how do you feel about the war?"

"I hate it," the Kid immediately responded as he motioned that Little could take a seat on the foot locker while he moved over to Ramjet's bunk while flipping his paperback up on to his own bunk.

Little sat down and continued his fact finding mission. "How do you feel about the draft and how unfair it is?"

"Its fucking shit," the Kid pulled out a KOOL from his fatigue pocket and lit up." I will admit, when I got drafted, I signed up and took another year to get Armed Forces Radio and all I really got to show for it was *fucked in the ass* repeatedly, so therein lies the source of my *pissed-offed-ness.*

Little gave him a sideways look as he weighed his comment. "Well, I'm not sure you know what *fucked in the ass* really is, until you live life as a black man in a white man's society."

The Kid had to smile. "Maybe not. But I did read *"Black like Me,"* by John Howard Griffin." And I did live in and work in Nashville, where I took some shit from my fellow DJ's at the radio station, because I had a black friend who scored all my grass… that I invited up to the announcer lounge one day and I took *el crapola* for that for *fucking weeks!*"

"Interesting," Little said with a token of a grin, "that's a small taste to be sure, but the kind of *'fucked in the ass"* I'm talking about is that blacks make up less than 20% of this man's army and we take over 80% of all the casualties. Did you know that?"

"No. I didn't."

"More than a little out of balance when it comes to 'fair', don't you think? And compared to whites, how many blacks have the money or the background to get into college and take advantage of student deferments? Kind of reminds you of the draft riots in New York City, during the Civil War… you could pay money for a replacement to take your place in the draft, so the rich boys never had to go. The college deferment is like almost its' carbon copy."

"Hasn't it been the truth since the dawn of time," the Kid slowly shook his head.

"True that. Point being, the draft is so fuckin' unfair to the lower classes, we are fighting and dying and the white men who own Hughes Helicopter, Colt Firearms and Dow Chemical are making all the jack and what we get is a ride home in an aluminum box that some white guy makes a lot of money manufacturing."

"Really," the Kid agreed, knowing in his mind that Little was exactly 100% right on the money with that observation.

A small silence existed between the two GIs as they both took puffs of their cigarettes and then Little continued. "When I got drafted, I took a whole bunch of placement tests and I did pretty well, but I was still sure I'd end up in the infantry. As it is, I was totally surprised that I lucked out and got made a clerk. In fact, I'm the new A company clerk, working for Sgt Ozelle. At least I'm working for a black man, but what I want to ask you, is how do you get away with all the shit you apparently get away with?"

The Kid thought about it for a couple of seconds. "Well, the first thing is, you gotta do your job better than anybody expects you to. You gotta strive to make yourself indispensable. Then you can carve out yourself some breathing room."

Little continued to stare at the Kid when he quit speaking. "Tell me this, Stocker, the real word is that you got some kind of special relationship with Colonel Lawton. Is that true?"

The Kid was basically surprised by this revelation that talk in the unit was that he in some way, had some magical pull on Willie O. He didn't really, but he had to admit, "Yeah, well, I guess he likes me more than a little bit."

"When I head that, and him being black and all, that's when I figured I was going to come up here and find out what you got going on. Because whatever it is, you are shaking up a lot of people, dude and if a black lieutenant colonel is cutting a white boy slack, he must have some powerful smack."

"I try to do my part. Want to smoke a joint?"

"Shit yeah!" Little finally broke out in a no holds barred grin, "I thought you'd never ask!"

Walking out the door, the Kid went directly to the latrine and standing up on the commode, reached up into the large black plastic bag and found one baggie that had his pipe in it, which he packed. Little was waiting for him at the rail and he fired it up on his approach and handed it to him. Little held the bowl under his nose to smell the smoke briefly before putting it between his lips and taking a huge hit, which he held in with his cheeks theatrically puffed out.

"Ahhhhh… thank you," he said amid the exhale and he examined the pipe, "this does go a long ways to making this place palatable!" Little took another hit before passing it back to the Kid. "So how is it you know I'm not a narc?"

The Kid thought about it for a couple of seconds. "Tone of voice. Plus you got the fire in your eyes when you talk about your causes. That and I'm a fairly good judge of character."

"Apparently."

"Here, you'll find this story amusing," the Kid began, "when I was on the air in Nashville summer before last, H. Rap Brown and Stokley Carmichael came to town and held a rally. Right afterwards, a big riot broke out in the predominately black part of town, so the radio station called all the staff in to discuss how we were going to cover it and how we'd talk about it on the air, and like that. So, the head of our news department, Gary Nolan, says he's scared to death to go into the black part of town to cover it and since we had no blacks on our staff, what are we gonna do? Well, Doc Holliday, one of the older DJs who gave me the most shit about bringing Jimmy up into the announcer's lounge says, '…*let's send Curt in… he's their friend!*' He meant it as an insult, everybody laughed, but I considered it a high compliment!"

Just then, a large group of GIs, JC Compton included, rounded the corner and came out on to the balcony. They were in a jovial mood. Walking right up to Little, JC held out his hand for the pipe, which Little promptly gave him. He took a freaking huge hit, held it and when he exhaled, said, "Who are you?"

The Kid cut in, "Allow me to introduce Specialist Little, who is in fact, gentlemen, the new clerk of company A… so we better get used to treating him like… *the man!*" Because he is the man."

"Hey Little… welcome aboard," the group, which included Ron and Don, Richie, Tearman, Fischer, and Tim Dunnichek all shook his hand in succession and as the line passed, and in a flash, more pipes and joints were unlimbered and fired up all along the rail and when Little stepped back and took a look, his jaw flat dropped. The scope and level of openness within the embassy was staggering to someone observing it from within for the first time. In the light of greeting and smiles all around, it easy to see that Little was outwardly relieved that the Kid was sponsoring his acceptance into the Tribe.

"All right!" JC howled, "Let's get fucking *down,* you muthas!"

"Whoa! That's the spirit!" the Kid enthused.

Little continued to be overwhelmed as more soldiers seemingly materialized out of nowhere and turning to JC said, "Fuckin' God dam! You were right! These sons of bitches *do* know how to *get down!"*

JC, by this time according to the Kids' unofficial count out of the corner of his eye, was up to at least three hits. Considering that everybody in the Embassy knew it was one hit stuff, the agreement was tonight *nobody* would ask JC if he was high yet.

But predictably, after another ten minutes, it was the Kid who couldn't stand it any longer and broke the deal, "So, JC, feel anything yet? Anything at all?"

"Nope," the dark haired Texan resolutely said, 'not a damn thing… wait… is that what I supposed to feel?"

"Uh, no, it's not like nothing. But like I said, you'll know it when it happens and you don't know until it happens. It'll happen," the Kid said but he was completely at odds to understand how any living creature crawling on God's green earth could resist the pungent invitation to *strawberry fields* sent forth in the powerful herb they were smoking.

"Jezzz sus! I am stoned out of my mother fucking mind!" Little exclaimed.

But still, there was nothing from JC so they just kept at it, smoking joint after joint, and pipe after pipe, mostly because it was there and they could; it's not like they had to save any for tomorrow. They watched the Vietnamese civilians passing on the walkway beneath the balcony, on the other side of the pond. One of the grass matt houses over near the middle of the pond was like a neighborhood store, that sold cigarettes, drinks, snacks and such and every so often a group of Vietnamese would congregate over there and smoke and talk while staring up at the American GIs, who were smoking and talking and staring back at them.

I wonder if they know we're smoking pot?

Chapter 47

As the clock neared 1900 hours, the Kid noticed Ron approaching from a scouting mission up to the roof. He was anxious to hear the report.

OK, Stocker, are you ready?" Edwards grinned, "They're up there right now waiting and I know Frank's good and loose because I bought him a couple of shots. He asked if you were down here getting stoned and I said what the fuck do you think and he said *this will be easy...*so there you go, he thinks you being stoned is to his advantage! The pigeon is on the perch, waiting for its plucking."

"Thank you," said the Kid as he flipped his joint out into the swamp. "Time to kick some *Lifer Alkie butt!*"

The Kid could almost hear the bullfighter's *Corrido* playing, to announce the entrance of the matador, as he entered the Roof Club with Ron trailing off his left shoulder.

Poised in his seat at the un-official *Stratego* table, where the mock battle board was left open and set up ready for play 24/7, *Frank* awaited the arrival of the Kid. He was backed by two of his friends, *Al* and *Bob,* who were apparently there to observe the mano-e-mano contest between members of the unit's two quasi warring factions. Having selected the red, Frank's pieces were already set up while the blues waited in a pile to be deployed by the Kid.

RV was standing at the back of the group, nervously smoking a cigarette, "You're late, Stocker, I thought for sure you either chickened out or were so stoned you couldn't find your way to the roof."

"You wish," the Kid slid into his chair and began sorting the 40 pieces that made up each army. "I'm surprised you didn't set my pieces up for me, *Frank.* Then you might have a chance."

For the pot heads, who never failed to find a way to work a needle under the ultra sensitive Alkies' skins, whatever the game or contest was, it harkened to shooting the proverbial fish in the barrel. This was basically due to the gross amounts of booze the Alkies threw down beginning the second their duty day ended. They were always well on their way to *Plastered Ville* by 1900 hours and, of course, *some of them* got an early start.

The most amusing part of the equation was that the Alkies thought smoking pot was a handicap. But in reality, the lifer drunks were easy pickings in whatever they wanted to challenge at, be it ping pong, Monopoly, chess, Yahtzee, backgammon, Tiddlywinks, Crazy 8's, Go Fish or their current hot game, Stratego. By no means was it just the dominance of the game playing skills of the Kid; most pot heads regularly beat most Alkies at everything.

Oh God how I wish this club had a pool table!

The one game the pot smokers avoided playing the Alkies at was poker. There was no question that the lifer sergeants of the unit, no matter how drunk they might be… or appear to be… owned that game and the pot smokers were smart enough to only play amongst themselves, after losing a couple of C notes.

As the Kid made his battle plan, Edwards placed a Victoria Bitters beer at his right hand and set an ashtray next to it. Then, laying a brown MPC $5 bill on the table to the Kid's left, he said while pointing to it, "OK, RV, put up or shut up!" to which RV put up and laid his bill on top of Ron's.

The object of the game was to capture the opposing army's flag so consequently, most players placed it in the back row and surrounded it with bombs. Each piece had a value, from #1 Field Marshall, to #9 Scout. The thinking was that a back row placement would force the opponent to take much longer to find it and thus, capture it. The Kid, however, had changed that accepted approach and had started placing his flag more forward in the ranks and protecting it with a layer of #7's between it and the bombs. That way, when a #8 miner took out a bomb, the Kid could immediately kill it with the #7 and then guard the #7 with a higher ranked piece nearby, when his opponent sent something in to kill the #7. But, since Frank was aware of the Kid's new proclivity to forward placement, tonight, he chose to put it in the back left of center, a position he had vocally proclaimed, at many games, that nobody in their right mind would ever use again.

The Kid's other basic innovation on the style of play had to do with the use of the #9 scout piece, which was the only piece that could move forward any number of spaces. Most players had them up front to scout but the result was scouts taking out scouts so the Kid moved them back to use when the board opened up and they could be sent for long reconnoiters.

"All set?" Frank inquired as the Kid leaned back to give his deployment a final check.

"Yep. You can go first." *Hmmm,* thought the Kid as he watched RV pacing around like an expectant father in the waiting room, *RV is looking extra spooky tonight. I think Ron is right, they got something tricky cooked up.*

Frank chose to start his attack with a center piece, moving it forward one square. "Feel the pressure yet, Stocker?" he joked.

"Oh yeah. its sooo unbearable," the Kid rolled his eyes as he made his first move. The game always started out slow by design, *"You'll* feel the pressure like the Nazi's at Stalingrad... *Frankie...* there is no retreat," he placed his move and thus engaged the enemy. A couple of turn later, one of them actually took a piece, as *Frank* jumped his 4 on to the piece advanced by the Kid, only to find out it was his 3.

"Damn!' said *Frank,* feeling the sting, "that's not typical, wasn't expecting that. I was thinking you usually go there with a 5 or 6."

"My plan, exactly," said the Kid as he moved his 3 ahead, with the intent of reeking havoc, maybe clear out some scouts and miners and draw out *Frank's* 2 or 1.

It was along about the sixth move that the Kid heard RV excuse himself to go to the bar by asking Frank if he wanted anything.

"No thanks, I'm good," *Frank* replied, his hand resting on a piece that he was apparently pondering to move , when all the sudden he switches his hand to another piece and then another one like he's completely torn and can't make up his mind.

Meanwhile, *Al,* one of the soldiers sitting behind *Frank* starts to engage the Kid in printing crew small talk, 'Hey, Stocker, you guys got the January issue all set, laid out and ready to shoot plates on Tuesday?"

"Sure nuff."

"Your friend, the new guy from Colorado... Gary, sez you've been a prick your whole life" *Al* snickered.

"You say he said I had my prick in the girls all my life?"

"No, he didn't say that" *Al* shook his head, "but, he did say if you said you were going to destroy the instructor, who ever it turns out to be, at that training class on marijuana, that we might want to attend... said he wouldn't fucking miss it for anything."

"High praise, indeed," the Kid looked up, "so are you gentlemen attending?"

Frank made his move.

"You can bet your ass we'll be there!" *Bob* jumped in, "we already can't believe you pot heads are getting away with the shit you're getting away with."

"What do you mean?" interceded Ron, "getting away with what?"

"All that pot you guys smoke down on third floor," *Bob* matter of factly says.

"What pot is that?" the Kid asked, looking puzzled.

"Yeah, right…" *Al* says in a low tone, "how far are you going to push it?"

Al's question was coincidentally very much in line with the Kid's thought process earlier in the evening at mail call, where he been in the front row, hoping that something was coming in finally from Ryan on the cannabis research he'd long distance ordered. "Depends. I won't know until I see what kind of material my old debate partner scares up. I'm thinking if he could find a study…any study… chances are it has a flawed premise or technique because the science couldn't have been too good back then. And regardless of what ever my buddy sends, one of my main arguments has always been: if they needed a constitutional amendment to make alcohol illegal, then why didn't they need one for pot? What bullshit. And I will stand up and call it fucking bullshit and welcome a *lively* debate with anybody about it."

"I'm gonna be there." *Al* smiled, "cause, you know, Stocker, you're not a complete ass like a lot of people say, you're just sorta half assed but, we all know for a fact that you are one fucking bad ass trouble maker and this marijuana thing ought to be bitchin' good. I can't wait!"

"And *Al,* I may be half assed but you have a face that looks like an ass, but we all know it's not your real ass because it's not *half fat* enough," the Kid returned the original fire but now he had been distracted from the game and thoughts diverted to thinking about a lot of developments taking place in the unit *and what's with the sudden interest of the Alkies in what's happening in the Embassy?*

"Come on, Stocker" Frank kibitzed, "quit fucking squawking like a hen and make a move!"

"OK. How's this?" the Kid tapped one of *Frank's* reds and took a #5 with his #3.

Frank answered by abandoning his center thrust interest and advancing a piece on his right, opening a new attack on the side of the board where the Kid had placed his flag. Their duel soon revealed Frank had some power on that side of the board but what really caught the Kid off guard was when he started bringing pieces through the middle and turning them to support his push on the left. *Damn! He's all over me! It's like he knows where my flag is…*

"All right, *Frankie,*" RV leered over his shoulder after he removed another of the Kid's pieces from the board, 'way to fucking go, you're kicking his ass! You need anything from the bar?"

"Nope." *Frank* said, without looking up at RV, his hand resting on a piece while he pondered a move. But again, every few seconds, he appeared to change his mind by moving his hand from one piece to another, each time looking off as if in deep thought of reconsideration, then shaking his head no.

What struck the Kid strange about this was that some of the pieces Frank touched were not in a position to *be* moved.

All of the sudden, Edwards jumped up and banged his fist on the table so hard that some of the playing pieces on both side fell over! "Ah ha! I knew it I knew it… *you mutha fuckers are CHEATING!*" he fairly screamed. "I just saw what you're doing! RV is standing behind Stocker and when Frank touches a piece, RV signals him what the value of Stocker's piece is in that location, by touching himself somewhere on his shoulder or face with so many fingers up! You cheating' fucking bastards! *You lose!*" And with that, Ron grab the two $5 mph notes, stuffed them his pocket and stomped off!

The Kid was blown away and sat there with his mouth gaping, staring at *Frank,* who continued to sit there with a sheepish look of resignation on his face as a blustering RV finally yelled in Ron's wake, "*Bullshit!* We did not cheat!"

The Kid gave RV a dirty look and slowly shook his head back and forth, "RV, didn't your momma teach you that cheaters never prosper?"

"We told them it would never work," *Al* chuckled as he and *Bob* got up to leave, "we were supposed to distract you while they did it," he admitted to being part of the conspiracy, now that the scam was over.

"You fucking low-Lifers!" the Kid said to *Frank* as he rose up from his seat, I don't believe I'll ever play *Stratego* with you ever again!"

"It was all RV's idea. I only agreed to it because I wasn't taking your money," Frank fessed up with a rationalization as to why it was all OK to cheat like that.

The Kid fixed RV with a stare. "RV, you asshole dickhead bastard of a mother fucking douche bag. I will get even with you for this. In fact, RV, this has earned you... *The Rats Revenge"!*

RV caught a breath as the smugness drained from his face. "The *'Rats Revenge?'* What the fuck is that?"

"What a simpleton you are, RV, like I'm going to tell you what's in the *Rats Revenge* is before I visit it upon you? No way. You will find out when it *happens* to you and when it does, it will be too late for you to do anything about it. Rats Revenge for you and are you ever gonna be fucking sorry!"

The Kid could see that RV didn't quite know how to take it. Of course, RV had no way of knowing that the Rats Revenge, an invention of the Kid's Dad, was psychological and never happened. It was designed to make the object of the Rat's Revenge, the *Revengee,* so to speak, punish himself by fearing something bad was about to befall him, over an extended period of time. From the mild panic that was spreading across RV's face, the Kid could see it was working. RV was already nervously contemplating... *when will it happen... where will it happen... what do I have to watch out for? Now all I have to do is mention it to anybody within earshot of him.*

The essence of the Rat's Revenge entailed the dispensing of constant reminders, thereby forcing the target to always be on guard...waiting and watching, convinced something bad was eminently coming... but it never would. The Kid would now and then mention *"Rat's Revenge"* every so often and have other people occasionally warn RV that the Kid was almost ready to do it so that he would never be able to stop thinking about it.

"Revenge is a dish best served cold, ass wipe, and nothing on Earth is colder than the *Rat's Revenge!"* The Kid admonished RV as he turned and left the club.

As he hit the third floor, the Kid could hear from the sounds coming out of Boyett's room, that the band was warming up and getting ready to practice with their new instruments, just brought back from Saigon. Down the rail, he could see Barry Fischer and Too Tall Tearman sharing a pipe with JC.

"Anything?" the Kid questioned JC as he walked up, to see if his maiden voyage blastoff had finally been achieved.

"Nope. Nothin'," JC shook his head and took another hit.

Fucking amazing!

"Jesus H Christ! The NERVE of those guys!" Edwards exclaimed, "What a bunch of douche bag muthas! I always said RV was a fuck head, but *Frank,* I'm surprised at that!"

"Nothing surprises me in this place," said the Kid.

Chapter 48

Five pounds, give or take a few ounces. That's what the brass figured it was, when they discovered and confiscated the Tribe's cache, secreted on top of the third floor louver. And with that event, February 1969 in The 10th PSYOP Battalion got off to a rollicking hot start.

It happened when the officers were conducting a shakedown of the New Villa during an attempt to find a case of stolen C-rations.

"I'd love to have seen the look on their faces when they found it," opined Terry Stage, as the Tribe smoked later that same evening on the balcony. "Can you believe that *Lt. Bronx* told them all that much pot was worth $500,000... in New York and all of the other officers accepted it as gospel?"

"You should have seen them running their finger through it and smelling it, like they'd found a sack of Lephercan's gold!" exclaimed Wimbish, who had actually been present at Battalion HQ when the booty of their monumentally horrifying discovery was brought in and laid it out on Lt. Regan's desk. "What a frickin' mind blow, a gaggle of captains, majors and Lt's were staggering around in a daze, when Willie O. comes out of his office, takes one look at the pile, one look at the officers and he just shook his head... and went back to his office without *saying a word.*"

"Well, *Bronx* is half right," said Birnbaum, "if you took that five pounds of prime pot and rolled it into pinners and sold them in Time Square, you could absolutely get five bucks a joint, 24/7, so you could clear a million, easy!"

"How long do you think it will take them to figure out that here in Nam, that much pot only costs twenty five bucks?" Richie wondered.

"I bet never," Barry Fischer was quick to comment, "Like who's going to tell them? However. The big question is, what do you think they're going to do about it? No doubt they're a little stunned. All of the sudden, the unit has a fuckin' *Godzilla* sized 'pot problem'."

The soldiers smoked in silence for a minute in contemplation of their situation. Naturally, Terry Stage, who was currently the Embassy gate guard, was on high alert.

"Lucky there weren't any repacked filter tipped cigarettes in there. If they'd seen those, they'd be on to us and we'd have to get them all out of our lockers," said the Kid as he passed one on to Tall John.

"Good thing we've got these or we'd have to be straight until tomorrow!" Tearman laughed before taking a huge hit. "If they'd found every one of our cartons, they'd have to say it was a *million dollar bust!*" he made his eyes look huge as he said it.

"I'll tell you one thing," Wimbish continued, "the way they were talking, they're really hot to hold that marijuana training class on the 13th. Now, Stocker…in light of what just happened, are you still planning on ripping the instructor?"

"You know it."

"So if they start cracking down on us, we'll have you to blame?" Lou suggests.

Fair question. "If they crack down on us, blame the five pounds of pot they found. I mean, what are they going to do? Shake us down some more? They just shook the place down, unannounced, with nobody here… and nobody gets busted. Actually, who the fuck knows if it was for stolen c rats or if that was just an excuse? Point being, if we don't keep it in our rooms or have it on us where we can't get rid of it, we'll be OK. Shit, there's always the possibility they'll crack down on us… if I have some fun or not, so why not have some fucking fun in this fucking Army in this fucking war? Have they figured out who it's going to teach it yet?"

"Looks like it going to be Captain Grimes," Wimbish said, naming the new battalion head of Propaganda Development Department.

"Oh. Too bad," the Kid frowned, "I kinda like him. I was hoping for either of the Captain Smiths; Ronnie more than PM, but either one of them and I'd be on'em like a raccoon with rabies! I just wish I'd hear from my old debate partner and God I hope he has some hot stuff. Hey, can you get me the training guide materials?"

Just then, something else happened on the balcony that was a watershed event.

"Guys…. Guys…" JC spoke up as he held one of the joints in his hand, a wide smile breaking across his face, "*I think… I must be stoned!* Oh my God! I am finally *stoned!* I can't believe it!"

"No fucking shit? Wait a minute, let me take a picture!" Ling Fook hollered as he dashed around the corner to get his Nikon.

"Halleluiah chorus!" exclaimed Ron, slapping JC on the back, "welcome to the club brother!"

"Wow! JC! That's great," the Kid gave him the around the thumb tribal shake with the right hand, "now, after about a week of toking up without feeling a freaking fucking thing, how is it that you know you're stoned right now?"

"Well," he paused, "I guess it was the band warming up, when they stopped tuning and started playing that one song… *Mona*… like the music went straight into my brain and drained down my back! *In fucking credible!* Let's go listen some more!"

"So JC," Edwards smiled, "now you know why we smoke it! Isn't this far superior to being drunk?"

"Yeah. *Way beyond fucking superior!*"

Chapter 49

January 31, 1969

Dear Curt,

It won't do you any good to be mad at me, you being over there and me here... but, try as I might, I could not locate any information on any scientific studies that were done regarding the harmful effects of marijuana before it was made illegal. Shit! It was legal up until December of 1937.

I did find out, however, that it wasn't made illegal by a constitutional amendment, like the 19th, that established the prohibition against alcohol. It was done by having it taxed in a really strange way and declared a Schedule One narcotic, which allows the gvt. to control it. Get this! The tax on pot is $100 per ounce, so nobody can afford to pay the tax which means anybody who has it on them for sure, hasn't paid the tax! That allows the cops to go all Al Capone on them. From what I can see, some guy named Harry Anslinger was behind it and strangely enough, it happened right around the time that booze was made legal again. Sorry I can't put the bullets in your gun. You'll think of something, you always do. And I'm sure you've got some bullets.

Ran into Hawkins at Crossroads Mall last week, she is probably going to marry Dave Davis. I told her you and I wrote sorta regular and she said to say Hi. So there you have it. Hi from the Hawk. The little bitch is looking better than ever.

Still haven't gotten the Greeting from Uncle Sam yet. There is talk now of the draft becoming some kind of lottery, using birthdays to pick who goes and who does not. That is supposed to do away with the rich boy college deferment, like I care. There is no way I'm ever going to Nam. I will go to Canada first you can bet your ass on that.

So let me know what happens. Oh... I heard that Gary Reed is being sent to Nam. If you see him, say Hi. Ha ha. Like what are the odds of that?

Looks like Crick Streamer might be getting drafted, too. Will let you know on that one.

Take it easy. Keep low.

Larry.

The Kid gritted his teeth. *Not what I wanted to hear.* But he suspected as much when he saw it was just a typical letter and the envelope wasn't fat enough to contain any pertinent information on the history of the marijuana prohibition.

What am I gonna do? I'll have to give this one some thought. I got nothing.

Rising up from the table where he'd immediately sat down to read the letter at mail call, he ambled over to the bar and purchased a beer and continued on down the stairwell to the Embassy.

Among the half dozen smokers there already getting stoned for the evening, he stopped next to Stage when Terry offered him a hit on his pipe. "So, we all take it that your long awaited letter from your debate partner from Boulder?" he gestured to the contents of the Kid's left hand.

"Yeah," he sighed before taking a hit. "But he couldn't find me anything I can use. It seems if there is any record of any medical or scientific tests or studies being done on it, they must be relatively obscure, which I find very strange. Very strange indeed."

"So now what?" Stage retrieved his pipe, "nobody would think the less of you if you called the whole thing off."

Don't know. But it suddenly struck him. "Hey… if I've got nothing and I had somebody search a university class library to find me something… *anything*… then chances are whoever is teaching the class cannot possibly have real shit either! All I gotta do is beat him to the punch and call him out for not having shit first! Then, anything that comes out of his mouth, I just have to stand there and ask him for a source that substantiates it and jump all over his ass when he doesn't have one! And once I own the '…you got nothin' position, I'll hit him with the constitutional amendment argument. Then he'll be on the defensive and never have a chance to ask me squat!"

Stage took a deep hit and stared off into space as he contemplated the Kid's plan. "That might work, but Captain Grimes is nobody's fool so it'll be interesting."

348

"Grimes is playing basketball for the officers tomorrow in our death match," Mike Imrem had been taking in the conversation. "He's a pretty good guy… for somebody from Kentucky! The game should make a good story in DIMENSION. I'd rather write sports than anything and this is going to be one of the few stories we can get in that don't have to do with military crapola."

Even though it was Capt. PM Smith's idea to play the game; since he was so batty nuts about Pistol Pete Marovich, the tiger from LSU, the enlisted men had seized on the idea with a vengeance and had assembled a pretty good team and they bothered to practice. All had played high school varsity and there was even a little college experience mixed in, between Lou Wimbish, Ernie Wilson, and John Walling, and the Detroit boys Tim Dunatchik and John Brnadic.

"Maybe somebody could give Grimes an elbow in the throat or something so he couldn't talk and they have to put up one of the Smiths to do the marijuana training," suggested the Kid. I want to slaughter a Smith… and I don't care which one!"

"And now we see the evil side of the Good Guy known as Curt the Kid…" Edwards smirked, "how bad *would* we have to hurt the poor Grimey one for him to be out for 10 days?"

Chapter 50

Given the generally high level of education among the men who usually got selected as PSYOPS warriors, evenings on the balcony at the New Villa often turned into discussions and debates on a wide variety of subjects, many quite academic in nature.

It often made the Kid imagine how things must have been back in the *olden days,* before the invention of radio and eventually TV, when at the dinner table, families had to talk to each other rather than all focus on a tube's slick imaginations. Or even way further back, he visualized the time when Socrates and Plato must have sparked philosophical *free for all's,* posing questions to the members of their circle at the Academy. *But they were into math... they would have laughed at me.*

Given the war zone surrounding them, the topics frequently involved religion and the hereafter; what it's like to get killed, heaven and hell, life after death, and of course, politics. Naturally, being the old school debater he was, the Kid relished these discussions and frequently set their direction.

"The way I see it," Terry Stage began on one early February evening, "the only way it can be is a fifty fifty deal; either there IS something after this life or there is not. Kind of like a binary number, it is *one or not one.*" But whatever it is... or isn't... everyone feel free to speculate, but when we go to bed tonight, it will still be only 50 - 50 certifiable in any direction."

"Ah," said the Kid, "that's leads to an argument I've heard from a lot of Christians who've tired to convince me to be a Christian by saying; '... *if there's a fifty fifty chance that God, heaven and hell do exist, then you should be a Christian just to hedge your bet, because you'll be a lot better off by betting there was a God and being wrong rather that betting there WASN'T a God and being wrong.*"

Smoking and silent contemplation takes place as opinions and arguments are formed.

"Well, I for one, feel we are still obligated to seek the truth rather than take the cop out route and cow tow to the possibility of believing something is so, simply out of fear," said Edwards. "I mean, how intellectually dishonest is it to settle on one theory over another based simply on fear?"

"Gotta agree," said JC Compton.

"Me too," agreed Ken.

"Third that," added Ramjet.

"So you can ALL burn in fucking Hell!" laughed Richie, "… or not… what the hell, who knows for sure?"

"Buddhists say that's what life is all about," the Kid jumped in, "seeking the knowledge to know what the meaning of what life really is. Then once you become enlighten, you don't have to come back and suffer in the material world, like being in an army, any more."

"Well, when they found the Dead Sea Scrolls that really made me think," Tall John entered the discussion. "They went a long ways in making the case for authentication of the Bible because they very accurately supported the Bible as it is today."

"Given me hedonism every time!" laughed Ramjet.

"My Dad says that he thinks when we die is when we can travel the immense distances between other galaxies and that there is one form of life or another in all of them and we all live our next lives a long ways away from Earth," the Kid said.

"Shit fire! That sound a lot like the *Urantia Book*," Edwards took a hit. "Anybody else ever heard of it?" Nobody jumped out with a positive response. "Yeah, it's a hefty book, talks about all these places in the universe, different levels and how everybody is trying to get to a place known as *Paradise*."

"Well there you go," said Boyett, "they've all got something like paradise or heaven or Valhalla…"

"Or the Greek's Elysian Fields," added the Kid, "and who could forget the Happy Hunting Grounds?"

"Actually, *Al* downstairs has a copy of the Urantia Book. I've looked at it a little and I've been meaning to borrow it, so now I will!" declared Ron.

At some point, during the discussion and the smoking of joints and bowls, Willert left the rail and went in their room to the desk where the Kid's transistor radio sat and flipped it on. It was almost 1900 hours and time for the AFN rock and roll show and the Tribe always wanted to see if they could catch any new music. But, when the last few seconds of news ended, there was a notable second of dead air that caught the Kid's attention and then, when the music started, the Kid got one of the rudest shocks of the entire war that came with the force of a mortar to the brain life!

The music that came out of the radio was the opening notes to the Beatles' *Sergeant Pepper's Lonely Hearts Club Band album*. And just as the vocal was supposed to start, it was podded down and replaced the voice of the announcer: *"Hello out there to everybody from the Delta to the DMZ! This is Scott Manning, coming to you from Saigon, and tonight, I have the distinct honor of welcoming you to the debut of the All New "Sergeant Pepper Show!"* and he timed it so that he stopped talking as the Beatles sang *"...Sgt. Peppers Lonely Hearts Club Band... you're such a lovely audience we'd like to take you home with us we'd like to take you home!"*.

What the fuck? "WHAT THE FUCK!!!" The Kid screamed in complete and total disbelief. *"My God! That bastard has swiped my idea! That dirty mother fucking son of a bitch of a douche bag asshole has hijacked MY fucking radio show!* Scott Manning had been there in September, in the room, when I played them my opening for the *"Sgt. Pepper Family band and hit Parade Show!"*

The Tribe was taken off guard by the Kid's outburst but in the immediate aftermath, they all stopped and paid attention to the radio. Many times, almost to ad nausea, *some would say,* he'd described to them how his show, that he'd actually conceived on the day he was confirmed to have a slot at DINFOS, would be. His Sgt. Pepper show would have debuted in 3 months, when he'd return from his early drop. He had attempted to relate to the Tribe what a cool opening the *Wild Child, Bill* Berlin, had made for him as a going away present from WKDA, but it was recorded at 15 IPS and there weren't any 15 IPS tape recording machines anywhere in the Delta. Except at Armed Forces Radio in Saigon.

Yes, there had been one at AFN and he had played the opening for *Sgt. Shamus,* Gary W. Gears, *Alan P.* and, of course, Scott Manning! And now that his transfer was off, all the sudden, here's Scott Manning flat stealing *HIS* Sgt. Pepper idea!

"I don't fucking BELIEVE it!" the Kid literally screamed. "He must have started putting this together the second he heard my transfer got killed!"

Boyett gave the Kid a sympathetic look. "What a bummer. At least you now have proof that it was a good idea…"

"Yeah. Thanks a lot!" the Kid grimaced back. "I ought to fly up to Saigon and frag his ass!"

"Did you say 'fag' his ass?" joked Branadic. Everybody got it but the Kid, who had worked himself into such an emotional tempest that he temporarily lost touch with reality.

"God damned son of a bitch dirty bastard asshole!" the Kid went off like he had a terminal case of Therets. *"Lie to me and rip me off!"*

"This is the all new Sgt Pepper show, coming to you from Saigon!" came Manning's over hyped voice; he was going for it in spades. The Kid had to admit his timing was crisp.

"Curt, forget it, come on down to Richie's room, we're going to practice," offered Boyett, "we're working on some new material!"

Chapter 51

All thorough the Kid's life, music, had been the great elixir. And never was it more so than in Vietnam and especially in the 10th PSYOP Battalion, all because of the band.

First, when the *10th Psychological Breakdown,* as the band had chosen to name themselves, acquired some greatly improved instrumentation up in Saigon, the quality of their sound went through the corrugated tin roof! Then, *without* the help of their erstwhile manager, they landed their own gig, on two afternoons each weekend, playing at The Hollywood Bar, a Vietnamese club across the street from the Ben Xe Moi MP compound, a quarter of a block down from the New Villa.

They were now in their second week of playing the gig and the word that something big was happening at the Hollywood got around Bien Xi Moi fast. The Kid could only marvel and the rapidity of their success, as he and Edwards, Ramjet and Willert walked across the dusty street toward the new hot spot.

The Hollywood and the band were so tropical Mekong Delta hot that the Chief had immediately, upon seeing packed wall to wall with dancing GIs, that the phenomena would be a fine story in the February issue... and so many people wanted to write it and photograph it, that it became a collective effort.

The Kid had selected the best shot of what he thought was a picture of each of the band's 5 members. The layout would be two pages and have 5 tall vertical shots covering the top two thirds of the page. The Kid had selected the best shot of each, from a deep pool of material that resulted from lots of GIs taking shots of the scene, simply because it *was a happening!* At that point in time and space, there was nothing cooler on the face of the earth.

The Hollywood Bar sat behind a shoulder high cinder block and plaster trimmed wall, which was topped not with broken glass but with woven wire of squares of barbwire, about 6 inches square; it would have kept a man out but certainly not a grenade. Since the band had begun to play, the Hollywood had overnight gone from an empty dive of a second rate whore house with very little business to a place that was a main gathering point for a whole lot of GIs. So many, in fact, the diminutive little middle aged dragon lady who owned the place had deemed it only prudent to hire armed security because her place was now a damned tempting target for a VC bombing attempt.

Thus it was that two serious looking square jawed ARVN regulars, moonlighting for some extra bucks on weekends, stood warily alert for anything out of the ordinary. One of them was always outside the door, kind of across from the entrance, watching all who entered the courtyard like area, his right hand resting on the pistol grip of his M-16 which was at the ready, dangling casually from the strap over his right shoulder. The other guard, also armed with an American issue M-16, patrolled just inside the door. He suspiciously eyed all who entered the establishment from off to one side. Of course they weren't checking IDs.

Because the entry faced west, afternoon sunlight poured in the double glass iron decorated doors and spacious windows on either side. The first chamber of Mama San's money making machine offered an ample room with a massively big wooden bar at the far end but no tables. All the action here took place standing on the hoof. GIs and Vietnamese bar girls milled around until a GI decided which one he'd like to approach and ask to dance or sit at a table in the big room and parlay over a Saigon Tea. This was a popular area for the striking of bargains that would later result in sexual consummation in one of Mama San's room upstairs over the club.

There was Mama San herself, sitting next to the bar, watching the liquor flow out and the money flow in! Such a tough grizzled old bird, or at least that's how she acted, and wanted everybody to think of her. Knowing that it was the kiss of death to show any weakness in the war zone, she kept control with sharp eyes and a shrill lash of a voice that she was not shy to use. The only thing she was shy about was letting anybody take her picture. Try and she would get upset and threaten to kick you out.

A double wide opening offered a snapshot glimpse of what was waiting on the other side. Gyrating bodies, a mix of soldiers and their "dates", bobbed and weaved and rubbed together in rhythmic dance, driven by a pounding drumbeat and guitar rifts of a definite bluesy nature.

Inside the Hollywood's dance emporium, one found the venue was made to look much larger than it was by a big high ceiling that floated 12 feet above the 30 by 30 foot floor area. Without air conditioning, the atmosphere would have been inescapably hot if not for the hard work of six low hung black ceiling fans, all cranking on high, pretending to evaporate sweat from above the floor.

The Kid would never forget the feeling that washed over him the first time he stepped through that doorway and witnessed the chrysalis of the boys going from a basement... *or in this case a balcony* band to a literally electric on the stage blowing the audience away performance talent! *This could be the Cavern and they could be the Beatles!*

The music had an edge and a bite, they had jelled as a band like moonshine; distilled quick by necessity in a hot climate and there to be savored right now. Their evolution had certainly been white lightning fast. And for sure, the GIs found them intoxicating.

Half the room was a dance floor, running right up in front of the band, who performed on a narrow stage that was raised barely a foot higher than the dance floor. Some moderately tattered posters of recent rock stars decorated the wall behind them, a scant 4 feet back. The other half of the room held the tables that held the drinks of the thirsty dancers, which made a lot of the money that was making Mama San a very rich woman by anybody's standards. And the gasoline that stoked the engine of her souped up money making machine was the band.

Upon wrapping up a Bo Diddlie number, the band members all modestly accepted the enthusiastic praise from the dancers and the non dancers alike, all cheering, stomping and whistling their appreciation. Being in here was, for a few precious moments, like not being in Vietnam.

Tom stepped to the mike and graciously thanked the crowd for the applause and segued right into the next number. "Here's a little piece of new music we've almost got figured out... it's not perfect, so bear with us... ready boys? *And a one and a two...* they commenced to get down.

Then Richie Wells' voice floated invitingly above it all as he belted out the lyrics,

"Get your motor runnin'...

head out on the highway...

looking for adventure...

and whatever comes my way..."

The crowd loved it and with renewed enthusiasm, took dancing to the upbeat tune to a new level. *Surprisingly good,* was all the Kid could think as he stood there, listening, nodding in time to the music, tapping his right foot,

356

not even looking for a place to sit down. And very listenable the band's music was, that combination of instrumentation that the boys had discovered; it was like they'd been together for years! The Kid easily identified the song… *the new material they're working on.* It was Steppenwolf, *Born to be Wild.* Boyett had found it among a bunch of new stuff on a tape recently sent over by his stateside buddy and music source, Carl. The Kid himself had heard the song for the first time about a week ago and was totally amazed at how quickly the band was able to cover it.

Sweat rolled off Richie's forehead and he rhythmically banged his tambourine, gyrated and sang to powerful, tight and harmonically sweet guitar licks of Tom, Benny, and George while Dan brought it all together with a drum beat that would make a KIA want to get up and dance.

"…Shoot all of your guns at once and explode into space…" they all sang together before they launched into an incredible jam!

This is fucking magic!

There were as many girls dancing with girls as there were dancing with GIs. When GIs tried to cut in on the dancing girl pairs, they found rejection as often as acceptance. The girls in the Hollywood bar could be very picky; after all, they were outnumbered better than five to one.

"Oooh, I really like THAT one!" Edwards pointed to a beauty, dressed in purple Ao dai, noticeable not only for her amazing face but for the fact that she was one of the few girls in the room who chose to dress traditional Vietnamese; the fashion trend for the rest of the Hollywood flock was anything that looked the slightest bit western.

More than any other bar the Kid had patronized in Vietnam, the girls of the Hollywood chose to shun dresses in favor of shorts and slacks. Pin stripped tops with matching pants was suddenly *haughty couture.* One particular femme fatal was outwardly proud of her matching leopard shorts and sleeveless top ensemble and literally held her nose in the air as she dismissed one GI after another who were lined up asking her to dance. They had no choice but to settle for less but lately at the Hollywood, there had been increasing choice and leopard pants would also make her choice shortly.

No doubt about it, the joint is hoppin! Just then, Willert waved to the Kid that he and Ramjet had found a table where a party of GI was just then leaving. Shoving their empty glasses and bottles to the center, the trio plopped down and looked to see where Ron had gone off to. The totally *out of this war zone* party scene gyrated and grinded to the driving beat of the GI band on the stage before them.

The Kid leaned back and took it all in, marveling that the dancers were so into it that he could see sweat beads being flicked off of hands and arms, maybe even foreheads, and landing on other dancers as the completely captivated mass was all but ready to go tribal, spurred on by the driving music bursting forth from the five Americans spread across the stage before them. The Kid watch and listen and could only marvel...*They are freaking amazing! They could be as big...or bigger than any band to come out of the war.*

Chapter 52

The basketball game was not so much a game as it was a schooling. The enlisted men slaughtered the officers by a score of 24-6. Capt. PM Smith didn't even suit up so his Pistol Pete impression pretty much entailed shooting himself in the foot.

The Kid missed the game because of a work assignment but he was just walking by Mike Imrem's desk the morning of Feb. 13th, as Mike was putting the finishing touches on the basketball story for the February issue of Dimension. "I need a catchy headline," Mike looked up at the Kid. "Any ideas?"

"Hmmm. How about... *'EM Police Up Brass on Court!*" the Kid lightning quick suggested.

"Fucking love it!" Imrem wrote it across the top of his galley as he smiled his approval. "So..." he segued, "are you ready to kick some more officer ass today?"

"I have been so waiting for this day," the Kid resolutely struck his right fist into his open left hand, in anticipation of the beat down he planned on delivering today at the marijuana training class scheduled for 1300 hours, right after lunch.

"So are we all!" said Mike. "People who never go to training are going."

And that was pretty much the truth of the matter. Speculative talk was hot as the day approached. Even the Alkies liked a good show and so they were more than casually interested in rumors about what kind of outrageous crap the Kid might trot out. The least anybody expected were some really good belly laughs... at the expense of the Brass.

As he ate lunch, the Kid was mentally rehearsing his attack. *Sir... do you have anything to tell us that resembles an actual fact? In fact, I KNOW you have no facts and since you assuredly have no practical experience, how does it feel to be making your presentation from an island of ignorance? How come there was a constitutional amendment to institute the prohibition on alcohol, but not marijuana? Why is it so easy to tell when a drunk is drunk but you can't tell when a stoner is stoned? How many fingers am I holding up? Trick question... one is a thumb.*

The truck ride back to New Villa was ruckus as the Tribe was feeling its oats. Today they would invade the wetlands and take it over. How liberating it would be to bust up off the third floor, out of the Embassy, brashly into the open air of the Roof Club, looking to throw down with the drunks. Only at this time of day, they'd mostly be sober.

"Hey!" excitedly yelled Ron Edwards, "I got it, since this is a marijuana training class, let's take some stuff up to the instructor and ask him if it's any good!"

Everybody thought that was a grand idea.

The faster flowing scooter traffic cascaded by their open duce and half, passing it on either side, making the Kid feel like they were riding on a rock in a river. *We will never get there as this rate... can't get there fast enough!*

The ironic nature of his feeling anxious to get to training class was not lost on the Kid. After all, what EM in the whole world did not hate *Training? "Training Class"* was army code for *Morals Education.* Training was a monumental waste of time but the Amy insisted, *just for the enlisted men,* of course, that a schedule of classes be conducted service wide every year and so it was done. A lot of the topics were the same from year to year, such as marriage and the family... how to stay out of debt... why you shouldn't patronize prostitutes or marry nationals on overseas assignment and what to do if you get VD... Why you shouldn't drink and drive; and of course, the evils of drugs, *especially marijuana.*

Being somebody who was into public speaking and *show business,* even though it was only radio... the Kid had always viewed training as if he were a judge at a speech meet. Did the presenter do his job? Was the information solid? Was the presentation smooth... did the speaker handle the close and how did he do in the question and answer portion of the event?

Most of the sergeants, lieutenants, majors, colonels and civilians sucked at training presentations, so the Kid viewed them as an opportunity for verbal mayhem and almost always, when he was forced to attend training, he'd do a little low level heckling or ask a question. The hardest one he could possibly construct. *Grimes will be fun. He's got some game.*

The Kid's attitude toward training had been set in concrete in basic training at Ft. Campbell, KY. His very first Army training class had been on *"Marriage and the Family."* And who do you think taught it? Why, it was the Catholic Chaplin, of course! Who else would the Army send other than the only Chaplin who had never been or ever would get or be married!

His opening: *"I'm sure a lot of you are wondering why the Catholic Chaplin is teaching this course on marriage and the family...well, uh, although rumors that I've never been married are true... that yes, I am an unwed Father... (wait for the laugh) ha ha..., but my parents were married, I know a lot of married people... and I've read a lot of books!"*

How nice. He read some books. And today it will be the same thing...' I've never smoked pot and there isn't anything real or scientific available to read about it, but I know its BAD BAD BAD because somebody told me so...' this is going to be so much fucking fun!

"Hey, Tearman" the Kid get's Tall John's attention right as the truck pulls up at the New Villa, "one time today, when you happen to be near ear shot to RV, let him hear the words *"Rats Revenge...'* say it like you're telling it to somebody else and see if he picks up on it and if he does, look surprised that he overheard you...OK?"

"Sure. But why?"

"I'm giving ole RV the Rats Revenge for cheating in the Stragego game," explained the Kid, "only what he doesn't know is the Rats Revenge consists of the victim being occupied with thinking about what bad thing is going to happen to him and when but in reality, something never happens. He just has to expect it for a long, long time, thereby administering his own punishment."

"Ah. Nefarious. OK!"

Along with his room mates, Tearman made about seven co conspirators the Kid currently had dropping the *rat* and *revenge* words and laughing about it around and near RV. *Talk about PSYOPS!*

Climbing down from the duce and a half, in the dust, diesel exhaust and the mid day heat of the Ben Xe Moi side alleyway that was the driveway of the New Villa, the Kid couldn't help but recall his boyhood military idol... *Sgt. Bilko.* The Phil Silvers show, *"You'll Never Get Rich",* was a family favorite and when he used to watch it, he imagined that was what the army must really be like. And for the whole day, while thinking about what he was planning to do, he savored a strong taste of the *Bilko* flavor to it all. The other feeling he had was that he was about to take the leap into uncharted territory.

A trademark of Master Sgt. Ernie Bilko had always been that he was one jump ahead of the brass and never suffered any repercussions for any of the madcap crazy shit he ever did. However, the difference between high jinks in the stateside army of TV land in the 1950's was a far cry from screwing around in an actual war zone so the Kid was given to ponder the ramifications and fall out his actions might generate.

By the very fact he was willing to make it a public statement and if lucky, a spectacle, the Kid knew retribution was always a possibility. But, at this point in his life, after combat and the court martial, the killing of his transfer to Armed Forces Radio and now the crowning blow of Scott Manning swiping Sgt. Pepper, the Army no longer had any leverage over him. There was finally nothing left the Army could to do to quash his bent for a little old fashioned confrontation. *All I'm going to do is argue about pot. What was the worst that could happen? They can't bust me for my opinion. Are we not here fighting for free fucking speech? So I piss off some officers... like I've NEVER done that before. I still owe them a big one for ever putting me in fucking PSYOPS. Oh hell yes I will so mind fuck with them here today.*

The men passed by their rooms and dropped off their hats and picked up Ken and Ramjet, who were waiting there, being off in the middle of the day as they were currently working the printer's night shift.

The Kid had only his pocket journal and his Pentax on him as they walked up the two flights of steps leading to the roof, he felt confident and ready... until he stepped out into the of club and saw the place was *jam packed to the fricking rafters!* Then he was juiced beyond ready.

"Shit! I do believe this might be a record for the most men who ever came to training," the Kid chanced to hear Ozelle say to Little, who stood next to him with a cigarette in one hand and a coke in the other. "Oh, and lookie here," the first shirt spotted the Kid, "it's the man with the plan himself! Specialist Stocker, our favorite shithouse lawyer! So... *how are you today, Shit House?"*

"Fine, Sarge. Feelin' fine! And feisty!"

"I'll bet," he grinned, clearly amused at the proceedings. "Well, I gotta hand it to ya, you sure as hell got everybody curious enough".

"Yeah! I keep waiting for the colonel to show up," Little glanced past them, down the stairwell, like he really was looking for Willie O. Then shot the Kid a smirk as Ozelle turned to look for himself!

"So you *really think* that this is the most men ever to attend a training class in the 10th PSYOP Battalion?" the Kid looked at Top with a squint.

"Ha! By fucking double, Stocker. But, shit that don't prove nothing but how fuckin' totally boring this hole is. That this," he gestured to the crowd in front of them, "could possibly be somebody's idea of a good time, coming here to see some wise ass shoot his mouth off... it's beyond me!"

362

"A wise ass? Shooting?" said the Kid, with his head looking from side to side, "a wise ass is on the schedule to shoot? What? Where? How many rounds?"

Ozelle looked at the Kid and for a second, and Little laughed a tiny, stifled *very little* Little laugh.

The mood in the Roof Club was festive and any casual observer would have agreed; *morale was up.* The standing room only crowd had noted his arrival and a murmur that ran through it, a regular mix of a few encouraging whistles, taunts, a few laughs and a couple *'fuck you Stocker's* to boot.

And I haven't even said anything yet.

Business was brisk at the bar and easily half of the orders were for beer. *You'd think this was a party and not training at all!*

A pair of Captains were milling about, confabbing by the lectern that was set up at the front of the club by the movie screen where it was normally placed for company meetings but neither one of them was Captain Grimes. It was Ronnie Smith and Captain Noel McLaughlin, the new head of supply. An easel with a large white tablet sat to the lectern's left and on it was the agenda for the meeting.

"Looks like Captain Grimes is not here," Ken took note of the personnel at the front of the room. "I wonder why?"

The Kid wondered, too, as he looked over the room. He had brought his camera along, with the plan to take a picture of the crowd from up front, right before he began his presentation. As Captain McLaughlin called the training class to order, the Kid snapped a picture of him from the back of the room, where he stood, looking out over the backs of skulls in the packed club, just another one of the standing room only crowd. *I might get a shot at Smith? Smith wants a shot at me for the court martial fiasco?*

Showtime!

"All right, Gentlemen," Captain McLaughlin began, "let's settle down and take care of business. Now, first we need to discuss a couple of administrative items.

Number one; there will be another couple of details put together to finish the Headquarters bunker. We still need at least 200 sandbags to complete the work. The names will be posted for that duty tomorrow. Number two; there's a rumor going around that a bunch of you are no longer taking your malaria pills every Thursday. That's gotta stop. You MUST take your pill. That's a standing order, Gentlemen. What if you get sent to the central Highlands after you haven't been taking the pill? You could very well get malaria because it takes a couple of weeks to build up your immunity… and you'd have it for the rest of your fucking life! Uh, so even though they make you shit and give you diarrhea, for God's sake, people, take the fucking pills. OK?"

Grumbling disrespect waffled through the assembled GIs, certifying their almost universal hate of the pink/orange malaria pill. "Only fitting that item was number two on the agenda," Edwards hollered out and got the crowd to laugh.

"And on the 16th, battalion has got a little fun and games lined up; we are all going to the range to shoot our weapons and stay qualified… in case the need should ever arise. This is mandatory for every swinging dick in the place, so the detailed instructions will be posted on the company bulletin board as soon as training is over.

"Number three or is it four," McLaughlin looked around the club to see if he had everybody's attention before gesturing to his right, "Captain Smith will be leaving us in a couple of days. He's shipping out early because of his hernia problem and is going to Japan for an operation, from winch he will be shipping out to go home, rather than return to us since his tour will be over before his recovery. So all of you can say good bye and wish Captain Ronnie Smith good luck, you can say hello to the new Company B CO, Captain Rostyslaw Smyk."

Good riddance! That announcement did not totally catch the Kid by surprise. Ronnie had hurt himself while assisting with the building of the Headquarters bunker, since he figured someday he just might need to use it. The hernia came from his showboating that he could carry a sandbag in each hand! Or so the story went.

But the next announcement absolutely caught the Kid and every other GI in the room totally off guard.

"OK, gentlemen," McLaughlin looked out over the crowd as he paused, "the rest of today's training class has been cancelled."

He slipped it in there so quickly, the announcement was initially met with stunned silence and disbelief. *A joke?*

What? A couple of startled voices rose from the crowd.

"I said, the rest of today's training class has been cancelled. You can all return to duty now. Thank you very much."

As he spoke the words for the second time, the reality of what he was announcing sunk in to the group; *there would be no showdown debate over marijuana held here today.*

364

A veritable explosion of BOOOOOs, catcalls and declarations poured forth from the company; lots of *buc buc buc* chicken clucking! The troops, lifer drunks and stoners alike, were major league pissed at being deprived of what they had explicitly come to see.

The Kid was stunned! He had been working himself into attack mode for the last month, not to mention the last hour, *and the brass calls it off?* While the ruckus and vocal dissatisfaction rose to a crescendo, the Kid moved out of the crowd, over to the side of the room and standing there, he clasped his hands, fingers intertwined, and shook them over his head in the classic boxer's victory pose.

Wild cheers and applause exploded from the Tribe and their sympathizers, easily 4 dozen strong, as they gave him a standing ovation. After all, he had essentially and single-handedly caused a training class to be cancelled!

Without looking, he could feel it and then, turning his head toward where Capt. Ronnie Smith stood, he confirmed it. *If looks could kill... I'd be so fucking dead... yet again!* The burning rivets of Ronnie Smith's eyes drilled him, awash with homicidal animosity and spite. In return, while locking his stare, he gave Ronnie a big sarcastic smile. *Ha. You're leaving town you bastard. I know you killed my transfer and I hope that hernia hurts like hell!* Ronnie looked away.

"Shit!" said Stage, "That has to set some kind of record for the shortest fucking training session I've ever been to since I joined this man's Army! My sincere thanks for that, Curt, if for nothing else."

"Well, then it's the daily double," popped up Boyett, "the most people and the shortest training meeting ever! *A combination I doubt we'll ever see again.*"

"That may be," agreed Ken, "but I'd be willing to bet two month's pay we haven't seen or heard the end of this."

Chapter 53

Staring at the framed picture of Commander and Chief Richard Nixon on the wall, next to the calendar, the Kid sat in his chair on the other side of the room, contemplating the incredible lie the long nosed man had told in the last election and gotten away with. *Had he not declared that he had a secret plan to end the war, wouldn't tell you what it was, but if elected, by the grace of God, he would implement his alleged secret plan and end the war. Peace with honor, that is what America would get if only they elected Richard Millhouse Nixon. What bullshit.*

"Don't you think he's taken long enough?" the Kid exasperatedly said as he rose and crossed in front of Tom's light table to stand beneath Tricky Dick's picture.

"Who?" asked Tom, without looking up from his drawing, "Wimbish?"

The band was playing at 1600 so they had planned on only working until about 1500 hours, when Wimbish was going to bring the company jeep for them.

The Kid pointed first to Nixon, then to the calendar. It was Sunday, February 22, 1969. "No, not Lou… *Nixon.* Don't you think that one month in office is sufficient time for him to implement his secret plan and get us the fuck out of here? I mean, he said it was ready to go, all we had to was elect him. Not only hasn't he told us what the fucking plan is, but one whole fucking month since his coronation, I mean inauguration, and what did we see, hear or get? Nothing. Hell, I thought by today we'd all be the fuck out of this fucking fuck hole," he smiled broadly.

"Jesus." Tom looked up from his work, "now tell us how you *really* feel."

"OK, here's how I really feel, its one week to March, this page gets ripped off and we show March of 1969. On that day, I will be down to 79 days. Breaking 80 for the second time, I might add, and if they hadn't shot down my radio Saigon transfer, I'd be at *19 fucking days,* less than 3 weeks!

We'd be talking fingers and toes here, but, a real 79 is kinda exciting, to be sure, but for now, real excitement looms on the horizon because on March 2nd, Mark and I are going to Dong Tam!"

To say the Kid had a major league itch to get out of town would have been an understatement in itself, but he was going to get to see his best friend and roommate from DINFOS, David Waterhouse. And for that, he was beyond excited because they had so much to talk about. It surely promised a major good time. Good enough to make him not think about going back out into the field after being out of combat for so long. It had now been almost four months since he'd been shot at.

Shrugging, he turned and returned to his desk to snuff his KOOL out in his ash tray. *Just because I'm going out in the field doesn't mean I'm going to be shot at.* His desk occupied the back corner of the graphics room, over out of the way from the tables where the real work of graphics was done, although today, he and Tom were only two people in the room working.

It was Sunday and they were among a skeleton crew of 6 that had been dropped off there from lunch at Eakin, to complete some work. Tom had a drawing for a leaflet he needed to detail and the Kid was working on story ideas for the upcoming excursion and reunion with Waterhouse.

Admittedly, the Kid had never heard back from his attempt to communicate with him by letter so he didn't know if Dave was still actually in Dong Tam, but since he hadn't heard he wasn't, he had to assume he was.

I'm finally going to hear how the Boy Scout died.

Just then, what could only be described as an audible commotion came rolling down the hallway from the front of Battalion HQ and four profusely sweating, frustrated looking men emerged into the graphics room. *Odd,* both the Kid and Tom thought as they first looked at each other, then at Ron Edwards, Ramjet and Willert entering the room in front of Wimbish, the only man they had actually expected to see, but here he was an hour earlier and with a group?

Looking serious as a heart attack and without hardily taking a breath, Ron walked over to the Kid and got right to the point. "Curt. After lunch, PM Smith all of the sudden calls a full company formation. And when everybody was assembled, he declared that it had come to his attention that the marijuana problem in the unit has gotten totally out of hand and it was high time that he did something about it. He then proceeded to whip out a piece of paper and read a list of ten names. All of us, but Wimbish, were on it. Us, Birnbaum, Tall John and the rest of the band, too. He said we were the worst offenders and then he named *you* as the ringleader! "

The Kids mouth fell open in shock. *Ringleader? Sheeeeiiitttt! You could get shot for that in the civil war, and right up to and including World War I! That tag is usually reserved for mutiny!*

"Told ya so!" Willert stepped forward and wagged a finger at the Kid. "Now what the fuck are we going to do?" The Kid could sense his desperation but more than anything, he knew that Ken wanted to jump up on a chair and scream at the top of his voice… *"I TOLD YOU SO!"*

"I wonder why the fuck he didn't name me?" Wimbish was clearly flushed, either over the whole incident, or from the fact that he, personally, didn't rate being included with the rest of what was obviously the "in" group.

"He didn't name any company or battalion clerks because he might need them when he presses charges," Ramjet speculated, "I mean, don't ya think *Little* should be on the list?"

"He read a list? I'm the ringleader?" The Kid incredulously asked of what he'd just heard, reading the genuine concern on the faces of his comrades.

"Yeah," said Wimbish, "and then after he read it he looked out over the group, real threatening like and said, *'we know there are a lot more of you out there occasionally smoking pot than just these 10 who smoke it all the time… and I'm here right now to tell you… that is not OK… it's going to stop and you won't get away with it! Or words to that effect, real fucking close to something just like that.'*

"Plus we're pretty sure the only reason he called the meeting when he just did was because he knew you were over here!" said Ken, looking at the Kid who was silent. "So, uh, what's the plan, Einstein?"

"That chicken shit." the Kid exclaimed at the same moment the reality of the situation washed like a wave over him. *Fuck. Have I gone too far? Have I really done it this time; screwed the fucking pooch and taken a bunch of guys down with me? Am I alone responsible for this happening? What is happening? Could I be heading for court martial number two? Shit. Wait a fucking minute. Smith can't do that! He's got no evidence!*

Then a smile broke out across the Kid's face. "He can't do that," he calmly stated.

At that, the four, who were all jabbering among themselves, all cocked their heads to the Kid like Labradors just spotting a tennis ball.

"Well fucking shit fire you say, but he *already did do just exactly that!*" Ken exclaimed.

"Yeah. Right. But he can't and he shouldn't have because…" the Kid declared definitively, "he doesn't have ANY fucking evidence! And if he doesn't have any evidence and he accuses us of it in public, that is a false accusation on its face and slander and you can't do that under the UCMJ! Captain Smith broke the fucking law and we got witnesses! Whooo Hoooo!" the Kid up and started jumping around like he'd sunk a winning basket with time off the clock. "Just because a couple of drunk fuck heads go up and tell him we smoke pot isn't good enough!"

Then, stopping in his tracks, the Kid realized by the complete silence that engulfed the quartet in front of him, that they were captured enough by the soundness of his argument that they continued to rationalize in their minds that the Kid could possibly be right but they hadn't yet bought it completely.

"Fuckin' A dudes!" he appealed palms up, "that son of a bitch can't publically accuse us of breaking the UCMJ in front of the whole god dammed company without seed one for evidence! That's cart before the horse jumping the gun fucking bull shit! The way I see it, we've been slandered, plain and simple. Falsely accused of a crime that he can't prove we've committed. You can't do that and I firmly fucking believe we can have him charged under the UCMJ for making false and slanderous statements! Who knows? We might even be able to get his ass busted! The whole fucking company witnesses his crime and he doesn't have any evidence or witness one to testify against us! Puts him in a really bad bind!"

The Kid wheeled to put a hand on Wimbish's shoulder, "Lou, we need to set up a meeting with the colonel. In light of the fact that our conflict is with our immediate commanding officer and we are in a war zone, we can't go through the chain of command. Just tell him that the ten of us want to meet with him about being slandered and see what he says. Willie's said on many occasions, that his door is always open and we all know he means it."

"OK." Said Lou, I'll make the request tomorrow morning.

Chapter 54

Later that afternoon over at the Hollywood, the mood of the Tribe was markedly tenuous. The normal good time had by all when the band played on Sunday afternoon had been bitch slapped with a wet blanket. Considering that the entire 10th Nervous Breakdown had been labeled as a band of miscreant lawbreakers, it didn't do much for their timing or party frame of mind. They collectively turned in a notably weak performance; that is to say they sucked. The Kid could see that Boyett was pissed but he couldn't really tell if it was about that or being on the pot list.

At curfew, when the Hollywood closed for the night and everybody returned to the New Villa for security lockdown, it wasn't long before the ten who had been named and a number of their closest friends were gathered in the Embassy Suite. The room held about a dozen GIs and another half dozen listened in through the window and doors.

Notoriety on this level was not something any of them had wanted. Not even the Kid. Although his desire to turn the marijuana training class into a debate match was in fact, getting most of the blame for it. He could hear the talk. *Gone too far… reckless… playing with fucking fire… tit in the wringer… hell, balls in the wringer! Ringleader!*

Still, he wasn't too worried about it. "OK!" The Kid casually called the group to order. Mark Birnbaum reached over and turned down the radio. "First off, just let me open by saying, Ken… yes… you told me so. Yes you did, *not before the class,* but you did say we hadn't heard the last of the marijuana training class fiasco and apparently, we have not. Could you get up and tell me again, here in front of the group? I am only offering you this your one last chance to throw it in my face like a really big pie, " he looked at Willert and smiled, "because then we gotta talk about what we're going to do about it. *And action!*"

Ken glanced around the room to see that everybody was looking at him so he did rise up off his bunk, where he sat between Ramjet and Little, took a little half bow and turning to the Kid and in a voice so calm and with a twinge of English accent, pointed two index fingers at him and said, "*I* fucking *told you SO!*" Everybody laughed and The Kid could see from the heads nodding around the room that agreement with Ken's opinion was in the majority.

Tough crowd. "Thank you Ken, can I have another… Remember, the cache bust was before the training class. It was most likely only a matter of time before something like this was going to happen anyway. Let's us not forget, that was 5 pounds of pot they took off this floor right before the training class, so me doing what I did cannot surly shoulder the whole blame. Hell, at the training class, I didn't even open my mouth! I said nothing! So it sure as hell wasn't anything I *said,* since I didn't get to say anything at all." A pause. "Bottom line, all I was really going to do was argue that pot is better than booze. I mean, I wasn't going to advocate the open and free use of marijuana in the unit, although… ya'll got to admit, we have been getting pretty fucking high profile here on the balcony as of late." A lot more head nodding in the group; they were willing to see where the Kid's thought process was going to take them. "It was probably only a matter of time before some of the drunks got tired of us always trashing them in everything from ping pong to Parcheesi, but the way I see it, we've got the son of a bitchin' company commander right where we want him! This is not some fucking Perry Mason parlor game of Clue we are playing here, this is the UCMJ. He accused us in front of a company formation. The UCMJ is all about written rules, so it's official. We are accused. Well, he has no fucking evidence. I gotta tell ya, *from my experience,* Mr. UCMJ likes to see some evidence. You accuse me with no evidence… I'm jumping straight into your shit with both feet, mister! Show us you're fucking evidence Captain Smith! A CO shouldn't fuck up like that. We, on the other hand, are running almost zero risk here. The five pounds belonged to nobody. Nobody's got it in their room, nobody carries it around on us… well, except for these filter jobbies…" *they all laughed.* As he waved one around.

'Well, I'm thinking maybe until this thing blows over," began Ron Edwards, "we should even get rid of them."

"Wait a minute," Little got up, "the Kid's right. Don't let's go off the deep end! We don't have to change a damn thing we're doing. What we got here is fool proof and why should we back down? What's going to change? The Army was chasing us before today and they'll be chasing us after tomorrow. I know I'm going to keep doing what I'm doing. Fuck The Army! If some of you guys want to stop smoking here on the balcony… well, shit, that's your business. But not me. I'll be right here, getting stoned at night and kissing off this fucking war zone with a sweet little high!" and with that, he pulled out a filter tipped joint and stepped outside the door and lit it. Then, exhaling his hit, he turned back to address the room while being framed by the door.

"And I tell you what" Little pointed at the Kid with the joint, "we all happen to know for a fact, even though *he* can't admit it, that for some stupid reason that only fucking God knows for sure, the colonel loves this honky bastard and cuts him slack he cuts for nobody else! I wish PM would have put my name on the list because then I'd have a reason to be in Willie's office tomorrow and see this all comes down!"

The Kid was actually a little embarrassed as the Tribe cheered Little's speech. "OK, so now you ARE putting me up for *'official'* ringleader?" he said to the skinny clerk who might as well have been Knute freaking Rockne psyching up the fighting Irish! And although he didn't know for an absolute fact that Little was totally right about the company commander's opinion of him, the Kid did know that when he was entitled to transfer, Willie O had personally invited him to remain in the unit. *That has to count for something.*

"All right!" he said, "now, who's coming with me tomorrow to meet with the colonel? I know Wimbish is running interference for us, but what I think is the best approach is for us to just drop in on him right after breakfast, before the day gets rolling, we get slipped on to the agenda, and take care of it first thing. Before Smith has a chance to do or say anything."

"Count me in," Willert was the first, "wouldn't miss it."

"I'm going," said Birnbaum.

"I'm there," said Richie Wells.

"Is more than five too many?" ask Benny as he turned to Boyett, "I think ten is certainly too much. Tom? You want to go? If you want to go, I won't."

Tom looked at him and took a couple of seconds to ponder his response before he said, "Benny if you want to go, please do. I'd rather just not think about it."

"It's hard to believe charging an officer with a court martial is what we're really talking about… if it is, I'll be telling my kids about this one… that is, if we don't get court martialed ourselves and I ever get married and have kids… hell yes! I'm going!" declared Tall John.

As the evening wore on, it appeared that Captain Smith's edict from earlier in the day had no effect on business as usual at the Embassy rail. Plus everybody knew that the Tribe's pro pot sentry was on extra double special code red early warning alert so in reality, they were likely safer than usual.

After all, what was the worst they could do? *Send us to Vietnam?* And when you looked at the turnout of GIs who were highly interested in what was transpiring in their closed society, who were prepared to visibly support the pot faction in the unit, even when it was under attack… it was easy to see why the brass was getting nervous.

The *lifers be damned* smoke cloud rose up thick with defiance, rolling toward the drunks directly above the Embassy, riding on the roof club rail,. To them it must have been like the smoke from the forest fire that killed Bambi's mother, evil and poisonous, challenging their world and all who would attempt to extinguish it.

The Tribe considered it a smoke signal, sent upward with a boldness born from the fact that our war party knows your war party doesn't have any paint and won't be getting it any time soon.

The Kid happened to look up and there, hanging over the rail and staring down at them from about eight feet above, were RV and his twin side kicks, *Frank* and *Al*. All three had struck almost the exact same pose, cigarette in one hand, beer in the other, leaning on their elbows, with matching smug leers painted across their faces.

"So, the word has it around the unit that you guys are through with your little deal down there on the third floor," RV openly took a great deal of personal satisfaction as he delivered that line while looking the Kid right in the eye, something he didn't normally do.

Everyone else on the balcony immediately stopped their own conversation.

"What little deal are you talking about, RV? You'll have to be more specific, we have so many?" the Kid answered back with a question.

RV smirked and chuckled and glanced from side to side, sharing his mirth with *Frank* and *Al* before speaking, "The little deal where ya'll think you can get away with smoking all the pot you want down there and nobody is going to do anything about it deal. *That one,* Stocker!" he punctuated his remark with one sharp affirmative shake of his head.

The Kid released what could only be called a *guffaw.* And after a slight pause, the rest of the tribe echoed that with a laugh as they viewed the surprised and perplexed looks on the Roof Club trio's faces. It was beyond the Wet clan's military comprehension that here was a bunch of men that had just been, for all practical purposes, indicted publically by their company commander for *felonies,* and they were laughing about it.

"Oh *Robespierre,* my boy," the Kid ashed his joint as he held eye contact, "it's hard for us down here to understand how you up there, can believe you are so allegedly smart yet you are historically stupid at the same time. You talk about all the pot smoking going on down here and yet, you don't actually know what marijuana even looks like... or for that matter, *smells like*."

"Bull fucking shit, Stocker," it smells just like all that crap you're smoking right now!"

"*Just* like it?" the Kid held up his filter tipped joint and examined it, "then this isn't it, just something that smells like it and you obviously wouldn't know either way *rats revenge*", his last exclaim hacked out like a cough at the end, to the amusement of the Tribe. "Can you believe it? RV thinks when we bought this stuff, *we got ripped off We'll have to talk to the PX about this tomorrow first thing!*" More laughing.

"So now RV's nose is an official scientific instrument? Edwards questioned, "that can tell pot from stuff that's *just* like it?" small pause, "look at the size of that fucking thing!" he pointed, I wonder if it has any moving parts?"

"Laugh all you want, Stocker," RV sneered, "we'll see how many of you hippies are fucking laughing down there tomorrow night!"

"Yes, RV, we will. We will... oh hey, by the way, we got some new ground rules for ya'all... from now on, when you talk about any of us down here and pot in the same breath, or go to the brass like the pusillanimous little weasel snitch bastard fuck you really are, and accuse us of being pot smokers, I would highly suggest that you have some actual pot with you for evidence when you do it. Otherwise, we will be laughing and you will be crying, *soon to be private E-1- Smith.*"

Silence from above. Laughter from below. And the three were gone.

"*Rats Revenge,* you fucker!" the Kid yelled up as loud as he could in their wake and then the laughing really started. *"Guys! Wait wait! We're laughing so loud and hard, somebody might think were all smoking pot!"*

Chapter 55

The Eakin compound mess hall buzzed around them with its cacophony of sounds made by hundreds of men eating; knives on plates, glass clinking glass, silverware being dumped in a tub by a Vietnamese bussing girl. It was a typical breakfast except the seven, who were preparing to meet with Lieutenant Colonel Willie O. Lawton. Generally the conversation was lively but today, each chewed silently while wrestling with his private demons.

A Maxwell Smart like cone of silence cloaked them. They all had to know when they started smoking pot, if you can't do the time, don't do the crime but the whole point of choosing to do the crime was to not get caught. As to what their liability was in their present situation, they had all come to the point where they agreed with and wanted to believe in the Kid: They hadn't been caught yet. The Kid wrote into the novel in his head. Still, what could be said at this meeting in defense of their actions? Was there some magic elixir that would diffuse the situation to the satisfaction of everyone? Well, not everyone. Either we seven are going to be unhappy or Captain Smith is going to experience unhappiness on a scale he ain't never seen. There's going to be a loser here today. That is, if we even got a meeting.

It wasn't a sure deal, but after talking far into the night, the consensus was that an immediate strike was their only course of action. The protocol was shaky but they felt they well within their rights to request the meeting directly, considering that due process, if not the chain of command itself, had been violated by PM's act.

Once the colonel arrived and was in his office, Wimbish would walk in, first thing, as he always did with the dispatches, and make the request that the colonel should see the 7 who would be at that second, waiting outside, petitioning him on his open door policy.

The possible results were many. Willie would see them or make them go through the chain of command to be seen later in the day. Or the request could be met with a delay if the colonel decided he needed more time to look into the matter, if he needed a fact-finding period to form an opinion.

The worst thing that could happen would be if Willie O called them in and revealed that Captain Smith getting up there and doing what he did was at *his direction. Talk about the kiss of death!* But somehow, the Kid just didn't think the colonel was that stupid. If he had decided there was a marijuana problem in the unit and he needed to do something about it, his opening salvo would not be fired from the mouth a loose cannon.

Riding back to battalion headquarters from Eakin, Ron gave voice to a concern that more than one of them had been thinking. "What if he asks us if we are smoking pot or not? What do we say?"

"We don't deny it but we don't admit it," the Kid had already worked that one out in his mind. "After all, that is exactly the point. We don't have to testify against ourselves. We dance around it like Mohammed Ali, If we do or don't', it really doesn't matter. Either way, the burden of proof is on the captain and we cannot be required to incriminate ourselves."

Sounds good, looks good on paper.

Being the only one there with any real court martial experience and four years of formal debate, the Kid was sure to be the mouthpiece. Not to mention that he knew most of the Tribe still agreed; he was the one who mostly responsible for this whole mess in the first place not to mention he had already been fingered as the ringleader.

In addition to Willert and Ramjet, *El Ringleader* was accompanied by Ron Edwards, John Tearman, Richie Wells and Mark Birnbaum.

As the group of 7 emerged from the stairwell into battalion HQ, their presence was immediately noticed; it was no secret what was going on. Certainly what had transpired at the company formation on the Roof Club the previous day had been the prime topic of discussion among the officers last night. The Kid noticed Lt's. Regan and Powell whispering while staring right at them but as soon as they noticed the Kid notice them, they turned their backs.

Like I can read lips.

The 7 had timed their arrival for 0755 hours, about five minutes before the quite punctual Willie O would emerge like clockwork from the stairwell and greet everybody with his electric smile on the way to his office, the door of which was in the middle of the front foyer of HQ.

As he entered the room, Wimbish called out the standard "Tin hut!" to announce the commander's presence and everybody there rose from their seat and or snapped to attention.

"At ease, carry on," he said as he removed the standard issue baseball from his head and ran his hand through his extremely close cropped hair to fight back some sweat before he stopped dead in his tracks as his eyes fell upon the waiting group of soldiers, who remained at attention.

After a pause of about two seconds, he turned to Lou. "Specialist Wimbish, is there anything on my docket this morning that would supersede my ability to meet with these soldiers?"

"No, Sir."

We haven't even yet asked for a meeting!

"Very well, then," he walked over to stand in front of his head clerk's desk, "then bring me the dispatches, give me five minutes and show them in." Turning, he looked at the 7 and locked eyes ever so briefly with the Kid, who was doing his best not to crack a smile.

Serious business. Hmmm, He knows why we're here. If he was going to diss us, he'd have kicked our asses back through the chain of command!

Suddenly the Kid had a pretty good feeling, not unlike the good feeling he'd gotten from not being shot while he ran through that hail of bullets fired all around him the day he got left at the front, But *pretty good, like the day of my court martial. And look... it's even going to be in the same room!*

Striding by the desks of the HQ staff, the colonel was followed into his office by Wimbish, who held the dispatches and additional paperwork in his right hand and closed the door behind him with his left.

"Well, I guess we don't have to worry about any old chain of command snafu," Ramjet nervously lit up a cigarette, "fuckin' a, he's going to see us right now! Shit, we could be walking into the biggest ass reaming since the dawn of fucking reaming!"

"Not getting scared, are you?" Willert chided his resolve.

"Uh. No!" Ramjet stammered, "But I am getting a little jumpy, sort of. Can you blame me?"

"Don't worry, Ramjet," Richie clamped a hand on his shoulder, "that's a brother we're going in to see. If anybody on earth would give us an even shake, it's a brother, *brother!*"

Couple of seconds later, Wimbish emerged from the door and proceeded to round up two extra chairs from around HQ and dragged them back to augment the ones they could hear the colonel moving around, scraping on the tile floor. After a minute, Lou emerged.

"Three minutes," he said with a grin, returning to his desk.

"I got to tell you," Birnbaum began, while looking for a place to ash his cigarette, "If this was Willie's predecessor, Major Kimberlin, I wouldn't be too fucking sure this was a good idea. He was an ex Green Beret and huge case of strack up the ass and he would have at least made us go through the chain for fucking positive."

Way before 3 minutes was up the colonel stuck his head outside the door and indicated to Lou with a hand gesture that he was ready, causing a flurry of cigarette snuffing in a lot of different creative places.

"OK, everybody, what I suggest is that you knock on the door and when he calls you in, you form a line behind where we set up the chairs and just one of you report, so make your pick out here."

"Him," Ramjet pointed at the Kid, "he'll report."

"Oh yeah! Make me look like the ringleader," the Kid spat out in jest, "this isn't just all about me."

"Curt," Richie clapped him on *both* shoulder, "it is about you. We are counting on you to get us the fuck out of this mess. No pressure, Jackson, but God damn it, we're looking for ole *Silver Tongue* here today. Kapish? He's your buddy or we'll kick your ass!"

Everybody laughed.

No pressure here. "Ok, gentlemen, let's go."

Sounds simple enough but as the 7 approached the door, their military formation was more of a scrum than a rank and file. That straightened out, however, when after the instructed knock on the door and the summons in, from a voice that dripped command, they could only go through the opening one by one. With a freelance curl around the chairs, the men stopped, spaced themselves the slightest bit and all snapped to attention and saluted.

The Kid spoke, "Sir, our group reports!" while all held the salute in place.

Willie O. very pointedly looked the lineup over, from one end to the other before he presented his own answering salute and said, "At ease, gentlemen," and while rising from behind his desk and moving around it, gestured with his right hand, "let's all have a seat."

The chairs were set up in an oval, occupying the center of his spacious office. Willie took the chair right in front of his desk, at 12 o'clock. The Kid decided to take 9 o'clock because he thought it would make it look less like he was butting heads with him. *This will demote me one rung down from ringleader…*

Without hesitation Richie did take the 6 o'clock, Ken sat directly across from the Kid, Tall John settled in on the Kid's left and Ron to his right. Mark was at about 4 o'clock and Ramjet sat at the 2 o'clock, next to the colonel's left shoulder and was staring at his rank.

"Alright, gentlemen," the Colonel surveyed the group and settling his eye contact upon the Kid he said, "would *somebody* like to begin?"

As they looked each other in the eye, the Kid did not feel threatened. What he felt from the tone was an open invitation to make the best of was fast becoming a very sticky situation for everybody involved. Obviously, the 7 could all go to the stockade for a few weeks on major marijuana charges. But Willie, on the other hand, could be looking at a preponderance of unwanted negative factors in his performance rating and on his permanent record if his unit was proved to be rife and out of control with a drug problem, as was being indicated here.

Not to mention that if all the pot smokers decided to turn themselves in, there wouldn't be enough men left to do the work and what were the odds of something like that making the papers back in the states? Yes. That will be my fallback position.

The colonel was a man whose mission was to find solutions. There was a war going on and any extraneous bullshit that screwed up his ability to excel at his job pissed him off. He would complete his mission. The one thing the Kid knew, without a doubt, was that Colonel Lawton was a fair man. He was sitting there more than willing to hear what his men had to say. And so the Kid dove in.

"Well, Sir," he cleared his throat, "we'd like to begin by pointing out that the country of Vietnam is literally awash in marijuana. From one end to the other. It is a fact that the stuff is everywhere. Just look at all the pot that they found in that shakedown earlier this month. There is, *no joke,* Sir, more pot in this country than you can shake a stick at. So, the obvious fact that there are some GIs in the unit smoking pot is beside the point. That the chain of command is going to attempt to seek out and penalize those involved with said pot is also a foregone conclusion.

"However, Sir, I think you'll agree, that in the pursuit of justice, for it to be *real justice,* there must be due process. And due process is not to slander people in front of a full company formation, based on the gossip of drunk soldiers, without one speck of evidence! For Captain Smith to openly accuse us of anything in front of a full and official company formation, I believe that would require him to be in possession of some legal evidence or otherwise, he is making false and slanderous statements. That is conduct unbecoming to an officer and I believe you'll find it to be a court martial offense under the UCMJ. I looked it up last night."

The Kid stopped to gage the effectiveness of his attack. It was factually correct and irrefutable. He had set the stage, defined the terms, discarded their liability, defended their position and smashed his opponent with a greater, provable liability of his own. None of the other six were chomping at the bit to jump in so Colonel Lawton spoke up directly.

"Well, I have my feelings about marijuana. I'm sure we all have our feelings about marijuana." He paused, as if he were thinking about telling us what his feelings about marijuana might be before he said, "But, regardless of what those feelings are, Captain Powell screwed up. Plain and simple, ya'll are right. He should have kept his mouth shut tight while he conducted his investigation and yes, he did slander the hell out of you." Willie paused and looked around the room before he said, "So. What do you want to do with him?"

The Kid's jaw must have fallen open because all the jaws on the other six had. *The colonel had just capitulated to our position. There was no argument, there was no speculation of what the degree of foul had been. There was no fight, no rebuttal, no give and take, it was a simple statement: "what do you want to do with him?" Shit. I can't believe it was that easy.*

Birnbaum was right there with the Tribe's olive branch. "Well, Sir, we're not looking to ruin his career. But what we are looking for is a little peaceful coexistence. He backs off. No more shakedowns, he doesn't take the word of the drunks as gospel, stuff like that."

"And in return," Ken offered, "we guarantee our performance will be off the charts. We will do our jobs better than anybody has a right to expect, not that we don't already… and" he added almost as an afterthought, "we'll make sure nobody is smoking on duty!"

"Plus we'll even keep an eye on the drunks to make sure they don't drink on duty or otherwise fuck us all up," Ramjet quickly added.

Now, what commanding officer could say no to an offer like that?

Willie O smiled, broadly. "I'll have a word with the Captain. Clearly, you're being rather generous with him, in light of everything."

"Yeah! It's not every day you actually get an officer by the balls!" Tearman couldn't resist injecting with an accompanying gesture, "maybe we should squeeze'em just a little longer!"

The group laughter was so explosive and loud that the Kid knew there was no way the room could have contained it. *I seriously wonder what the officers and noncoms listening outside are thinking right now? He really must be working us over!*

"For all the fun that would be, I think we can all agree it is best this matter is put to rest here today." Richie neatly summed it all up and as he did, Willie nodded to the affirmative, rose from his chair, signaling that the meeting was over, making the seven spring to their feet and assume the position of attention.

"If you gentlemen are satisfied, we shall speak of it no further. Dismissed," Willie crisply said and with that, the seven saluted, he returned it and they exited his domain, smiling enough that nobody in the front offices had any doubt as to their success, but not jovial enough to break the decorum.

The collective smirk could not be wiped off the Tribe's face! That's what I'll say in the book.

Chapter 56

Wimbish had waited until everybody was there before telling the story so he wouldn't have to tell it 20 times. It was the report of how Captain Powell M Smith came to his meeting with Ltc. Lawton later that same morning and how long it lasted and the condition of his face and volume of steam exiting his ears when he left.

"When he got there, he had this kinda goofy look on his face, and he sez… *'The colonel wants to see me?'* Like *surprise*… what could he possibly want? Yes Sir, I told him, and he got this little smile going on, thinking for all he knew that the colonel was going to tell him *well done* on sniffing out those pot smokers. So he goes in and I wanted to stand by the door and try to listen, but Regan and everybody was looking, obviously speculating on what was going on in there. I'll tell you one thing, there wasn't any laughing coming out, like when ya'll went in, so I figure he getting it good, based on what you guys told me came down in there. The meeting didn't last very long at all and when PM left the colonel's office, he didn't really walk out, he stormed out. I would fucking love to know what Willie told him!

"Now," Edwards rubbed his hands together before pointing up at the roof club, "time for a little revenge!"

"No, wait!" said Stage, "that's exactly what they are expecting. Instead, let's go up there and be real fucking nice to them!" The group wasn't immediately buying it; after all, a bunch of them had just tried to rat them out. "Really!" Stage was into it. "It will fuck with their heads like nothing else we can do! Think about it: they turned us in, we crushed them because they were stupid amateurs and then we go up there and we are all nice to them like nothing happened! They won't know what to think!"

"Yeah!" Little lit up a filter joint, "but let's be real cool about it, not all rush up there at once, but a few at a time, go up and buy a beer, get in a card game, just actin' like nothing happened… we don't say nothing about what we said and what Willie said."

"Carry on like nothing ever happened!" the Kid slowly repeated, "I fucking love it! Let me be the first, I'm going to go buy RV a beer!" and with that, he headed straight for the roof.

Almost as soon as he emerged from the stairwell, he spied RV, *Frank* and *Al* sitting over near the ping pong table. Stopping at the bar, he bought three beers and casually walked over to their table and placed one in front of each of them. The look on their faces was priceless. *Stocker was buying them beer? Must be poison or he spit in them.*

"Hey boys, you look thirsty!" the Kid smiled as he punctuated it loud enough for RV to hear but not move his lips; *"rats revenge."*

The trio spoke not a word so the Kid said, "Enjoy! Oh by the way, the word from downstairs is…. "Ha," he said in a flat tone of voice.

They looked back and forth at one another, trying to figure it out. Finally, Frank says back "Ha?"

"Yes. Ha. As in ha ha, it's tomorrow and we are still laughing."

Chapter 57

The 10th Battalion motor pool was allocated two duce and-a-halves, which is Army speak for a 2.5 ton truck. *A Duce & a half,* quite often in Army phonics, a *duce.* More were needed from time to time, to move large quantities of paper, both pre and post printing, but generally, the task of transporting the men to work in the morning and to Eakin Compound for chow and back to the New Villa at night, was done with the duces.

The unwritten code was that everybody, riding in the back of a duce and a half in Vietnam, was on guard against any kind of attack. Obviously, the gathering of that many GIs in one place was an open invitation. There wasn't much worry about road mines or command detonated mines on the streets of Can Tho because of the high volume of ARVN traffic and surveillance, day and night. It was the grenade thrower and the sniper that the men had to take vigilance against. It could come from the roadside or one of their favorite MOs, a passenger on a motor scooter. To guard against it, the men thought like Roman soldiers in a "turtle' formation; all vigilance being exercised to shield the group. The men of the 10th did not normally take their weapons to work with them in the city of Can Tho because the rest of town was an armed camp. But all the same, one man occasionally rode shotgun and when in transport, the shared feeling of alertness was a strong bonding mechanism. *Who among us does not want to keep grenades and the like out of the truck? Just as I thought.*

However, once the truck arrived at Bien Xi Moi, the protective nature of the group immediately dissolved. It was every man for himself as they chose to take care of their various needs. In any particular smaller group, it was entirely possible that *nobody* was paying attention. One group of soldiers might feel the urge for a little Scientific Steam bath action while others might only need the services of Taj the Taylor. And almost all troopers found it necessary at some point to visit the Vietnamese pharmacy. That was where GIs, who had late night guard duty, purchased "Obesotol", a French diet elixir that was in reality, straight liquid amphetamine.

Some of the men accidently discovered this substance was available locally and god was it cheap! Buck and a half for a bottle that would get you through two watches, guaranteed to keep you *bright and bushy tailed numba one GI!* The label featured the silhouette of a man at a pool table, very fat, with thinner 'hims' inside of each one until the dark outline at the center was a slim guy! Speed kills the appetite and of course you'll lose weight. But it will also keep you UP!

Little, the Kid, Edwards, Boyett and Willert had just come out of Taj the Taylor's and were standing on the street all lighting cigarettes when they heard a distinct *BAM!*

"Holy shit! What the fuck was that?" in different combinations was exclaimed by the group. *Had to be an explosion and everybody down the street was scattering in reaction!* A smoke cloud rose up about a block away on the left side of the street.

Terror attack!

Suddenly, Edwards threw up his arm and pointed at a motor scooter that was emitting a big puff of smoke as it accelerated, just turning on to the main drag! "Look! I'll bet they threw it!" he yelled, pointing at two men hunched over and riding it like tandem jockeys!

Then the calls frantically came, *"MEDIC MEDIC!"* From multiple voices down the street.

Because they had a sentry box watching the street, the MPs made a lightning response, literally swarming out of their compound. One jeep with 3 MPs screamed off after the motor scooter and an ambulance came out right behind it!

Now GIs were running around with some scant information, "Four men, 4 men down!" one man reported to anybody listening.

"I wonder who it is!" Little exclaimed, "Should we go try to help or get out of the fucking way?"

Since the MPs were there and surly medics came with the ambulance, it was the group's inclination to get out of the fucking way, so they retreated down the New Villa alley to the billet. As GIs materialized in the Roof Club, speculation ran rampant on who it was that got hit. Finally, definite identifications of the men involved in the attack were known.

The attackers had apparently been waiting, astride a running motor scooter, looking for a target of opportunity. When JC Compton, Mike Imrem, Paul Johnson and Mike Gyuriseck were walking together, less than a block away from the New Villa alley, in the vicinity of the Pharmacy, the assailants rode by in the opposite direction and pitched the bomb right behind them. But, possibly because of the scooter's momentum in the opposite direction from that of the GI's, the grenade or homemade bomb had continued to roll away from them before it went off!

The reports that followed were encouraging. The MP medics quickly determined the men's injuries were not life threatening and bundled them up for transport to Eakin Compound. From there, they would be medevac'd tonight to Saigon. The wounds they sustained were primarily on their backsides, mostly below the knees.

Everyone drank that night in the Roof Club, knowing how easily it could have been them on that chopper to Saigon. *After all, a totally random act of violence is one of this war's favorite MOs.* It is a strange oxymoron to watch a bunch of men assimilate a sobering event by getting drunk.

Any one of us could have been killed or wounded tonight and only by the grace of... pick your God or random chance... we weren't! Not tonight anyway. But there was always tomorrow night and that's why we'll have another drink and go down to the Embassy and blow some weed and try not to go freaking nuts.

Mike Imrem was a DIMENSION staffer, so the Chief, the Kid, Boyett, Tim Gellbach, Bob Weston, Ron, Harold Ling Fook, Birnbaum, Tim Dunaceck and Billy Smith were particularly distraught.

And JC, who had to smoke that Vietnamese dank shit for a week before he got off the first time, was now going to smoke it wearing a Purple Heart. If you don't count the time between when he got up and finished work before he lit his first bowl, he hadn't really come down since he went up. *Well, he won't be smoking any tonight, but they might give him some morphine! That's what I'll say in the book.*

Chapter 58

The Caribou's powerful twin engines quickly propelled the high tailed craft up off the corrugated metal runway and into the morning Delta sky. They would be climbing to about 3,000 feel on their way to Dong Tam and the Kid was very much looking forward to enjoying the 25 minutes of being bathed in the ultra cool air. He and Mark exchanged smiles in recognition they would also savor their liberation from the confines of Battalion Headquarters and the New Villa.

The pair was flying out of the Can Tho Airport on the daily 0800 milk run to the 9th Division base camp at Dong Tam, 75 miles up country to the north east. There they would be met by a member of the 10th Battalion's Detachment 4, the field team that was the subject of their story assignment.

The flight was only half full, the typical delta mixture of Americans and ARVNs in uniform and a couple of civilian types from both nationalities. Taking advantage of the extra room, Mark had began repacking his one main equipment bag and now had photographic do-hickeys spread out all over the place. Light meters, filters, lens cases, lens cleaners, both liquid and fabric; *all the trappings of a pro's pro.* As he arranged it all, the two Nikon Fs hung around his neck swayed to and fro, jangling on cue from the light turbulence and his movements. One had a short lens and the other's was telephoto long and Mark apparently had concluded that the only safe place for them on this flight was around his neck.

The story was going to be a marquee piece for the March issue of Dimension on PSYOPS in the 9th Division, the only American unit operating in the Delta that was fully engaged in combat and not advising an ARVN unit. They currently held the distinction of having the highest body count of any unit in Vietnam and provinces wherein they operated also had the highest Hoi Chan rates of any in the Delta, leaving the natural question to be examined; *is there a correlation?*

It was the *fully engaged in combat and the high body count* part of the equation that made the Kid just a touch nervous about the whole mission. 4 months had elapsed since the last time he'd seen any combat and he could

387

only hope the string would continue unbroken. But, if there was ever a point where the string might get a little twang, this was likely it.

It was March 3rd. The Kid had just gone under 75 days and the M-16 that lay across his rucksack seemed to be calling to him. *Hi Kid. Remember me? I'm here for a reason. Me too, said Mr. Steel Pot.*

Birnbaum, along with his neck candy cameras, was also slinging an M-16 and they had stopped by the armory on their way to the airport where each was issued an bandoleer of a dozen pre loaded 18 round ammo clips.

There had been no sense in bringing the .38 because the Kid knew no enlisted man was authorized to carry a sidearm in a shoulder holster like that on a US military base, and that's what the 9th Division at Dong Tam was. It was the base where his two room mates from DINFOS had been assigned to do basic public information work and where one of them had died in action.

He hadn't heard that Waterhouse was gone, so he was 90% assuming he'd be seeing David, his favorite old DINFOS roomie, in just a couple of hours. It had been almost 9 months since they'd parted at Long Binh and five months since the Kid had read John Imbach's name in the Stars and Stripes and four months since he'd written but never heard back but what the hell, that was the time period when he was all over the Delta.

And so it was the Kid had been left to wonder, more than occasionally, how it was that John became the first, *and so far only,* member of their class to die on tour.

The paddies of the Delta with their intersecting tree lines spread out below them and the Kid couldn't look down without thinking of how many times he'd almost bought the farm himself, stuck in the mud with Wilson. They would be passing over the many mouths of the Mekong on the flight path between Can Tho and My Tho, *one of them is where we made the Junk assault. God that seems like an eternity ago.*

In the present, he was relieved the focus of their main story did not call on them to participate in any search and destroy missions with loudspeaker teams. On the other hand, he was equally depressed to discover that the Chief wanted a sidebar story specifically that required *a night outside the wire.*

The Kid and Mark were going to document the 9th Division's MILCAPs, which stands for *Military Civic Action Programs.* Among the different types of MILCAPS, were ICAP, for Intelligence Civic Action Program, MEDCAP for Medical Civic Action Program and last but not least, there was the NITECAP for Night Civic Action Program. It was the NITECAP that had the Kid's attention because the sidebar assignment was to accompany a team to a tiny outpost hamlet and experience the essence of what *NITECAP-ing* was all about.

Your basic NITCAP begins just like a MEDCAP, but after the doctoring is done, the team sets up a screen and with a generator, shows propaganda films while handing out propaganda leaflets, just like a Batmobile operation back at Cang Long. But, the kicker is you stay in the hamlet overnight to show the Villagers that the brave Americans are not afraid of the VC. *Like freaking fucking hell!*

With that and the recent street bombing to think about, any fretting over the weed situation back at the New Villa took a back seat. It had been a little over a week since their meeting with the colonel and even though it was business as usual in the Embassy, the Kid figured PM was not done by a long shot. However, when you're worried about getting shot, that takes precedence over getting busted any day.

Taking a clue from Birnbaum, the Kid began loading a role of black and white 35mm Fuji film into the Pentax around his own neck. It was the SLR Mark had sold him for $100 after he got his Nikons. It was Mark who ushered him into the modern age of 35mm and taught him 40% of everything he knew. Boyett and Ling Fook each taught him 30% but Mark had photographically taken the Kid under his wing from the day he'd sold him that camera.

The Kid now shot the pics for most of his stories but any pictures he took on this trip, however, were just for him. This was Mark's shoot for the articles. Of course the Kid would be paying special attention to his technique. *They were a well oiled team, that's what I'll say in the book.*

The Kid certainly did not want to show up in Dong Tam to see Waterhouse not holding so he had brought one unopened pack of filter tipped joints. He would keep it sealed until he found out how safe it was or wasn't.

The pilot lit the smoking lamp and everybody, just about to a man, lit up. As he puffed his nicotine, the Kid again turned his eyes to the window and the flat green landscape below and his thoughts gravitated to Imbach. The big guy had been his and David's room mate for almost 6 months. John and Ken Smith occupied the bunk across from them in the four man room. John was such an odd duck. That's partly how he got the handle, *Baby Huey,* from most of the guys. That and he was built physically like the duck, Baby Huey, in the comics; large assed and smaller upper body, very oval head with short cropped reddish blond hair; *it was a good thing his*

389

ears didn't stick out too far. He had been the brunt of more than a couple of the Kid's comic barbs and he wasn't the type of person to barb back. Often he didn't know he was the object of the joke. To the Kid, he was *The Boy Scout.* The way he frequently cited his experiences from the Boy Scouts was just the tip of the iceberg of wholesomeness contained within. The man did not have an evil bone in his body. He was one of the good spirits. *Often, he was just "Scout..."* And now some of the things he'd said and done, just because John was an easy target and didn't like the Beatles, he kind of regretted. Still, the Kid's verbal sporting had been predominately good natured. The only reason they even knew each other in the first place was that fate had made them comrades in arms and the Kid knew because of that fact alone, he could never forget him. He recalled the evening he'd taxied John to the airport in his green bug, when *Scout* flew home to California for Christmas leave in '67. A Beatles song came on the radio *"She Loves You"* and of course he played it way loud. Then they attended Possible Overseas Replacement (POR) training at Ft. Leavenworth together before leave, since both of their homes were west of Kansas. *Roommates again.*

The Kid barely snuffed out his KOOL when the smoking lamp went out and the loadmaster, an Air Force E-5, made the rounds to check that all personnel were in compliance, belted and secured, along with the various loads of cargo. In minutes, they'd be landing in Dong Tam.

The air became increasingly warm as they began dropping altitude. The cool bath was over. The strip used by the 9th Division was located west of the city of My Tho, not far from the sprawling base occupied by the 9th Division at a spot that was once the tiny little village known locally as Dong Tam.

Now the base that covered it, full of American soldiers, was the central hub of commerce in this neck of the woods.

Leveling off out of his steep approach, the pilot smartly placed the Caribou on the runway and in no time, taxed down to the end where he swung the back of the craft around in a 180-degree turn. The loadmaster had the ramp cracked in a flash and the opening framed a number of trucks and jeeps parked waiting for the flight... One of the jeeps was surely a member of the PSYOPS team there with the express purpose of picking them up.

Beyond them, back about 200 meters on a plateau level that was easily 20 feet above the runway, the Kid spotted one of the largest, most massive bunkers he'd yet seen in Vietnam. What made it most impressive was that it appeared to be made out of bundles of corrugated runway sections, stacked up like a fort. *Gotta have a picture of that! I wonder if Dong Tam has an airport sniper?*

Feathering of the props signaled unloading and soon, the pair was standing on the runway looking toward a jeep slowly and deliberately inching toward them with but a single GI onboard. It stopped about 30 feet back, just off to the left of any prop wash and a soldier immediately stepped out. The Kid and Mark quickly recognized the tall lankiness and Irish complexion of Gerald Megenity. The Spec. 4, sent to pick them up wore a regulation baseball hat and was smoking a cigarette. There was none of the uniform freelancing here that the Kid had enjoyed with the ARVNS.

"Yo! Stocker and Birnbaum! Welcome to the field!" he walked directly to Birnbaum's equipment bag and hefted it up to rest the strap on his shoulder while the travelers collected the remainder of their gear and their M-16's.

"What's the best way to carry this?" Mark held up his steel pot.

"Like this," replied the Kid as he plopped his upon his head over his baseball cap.

"But then my jungle hat won't look cool!" frowned Mark.

"Mark Mark Mark… nothing is more uncool than a cloth jungle hat in a firefight," joshed the Kid as he pulled the finger grip slide loader of his clipless weapon for theatrical effect as he turned and headed for the jeep.

Megenity, their chauffer, was a member of the Tribe. Although he did not spend any considerable time in Can Tho, because he was in the field, when he did make back he was most welcome in the embassy.

Knowing of his assignment to write the 9th Division story, the last time Gerry had been in three weeks ago, the Kid had asked him to try and find out if Waterhouse was still in the Division PIO. As they got to the jeep, Gerry did not keep him waiting.

"Your friend Waterhouse is still here," he said, without the Kid asking, "I didn't tell him you were coming."

"Oh, wow! Thanks, Gerry! That's great fucking news!"

"Plus, I even checked on the way over and he's at the PIO connex offices right now and Captain Mitchell is at some stupid briefing or another and won't be back until after lunch which means we can go see your friend as soon as you get in."

Birnbaum climbed in the back seat with his gear and gave the Kid shotgun uncontested.

Gear stowed, they took off on the road that led past the massive bunker and away from the flight line. Not long after they had traveled down a corridor of Vietnamese businesses that preyed on the GI's, they came to the front gate of the 9th Division. The two MPs checking the flow of vehicles waved them through as soon as they saw the jeep contained nothing but Americans.

As they rolled by the imposing machine gun armed and double manned sandbag bunkers on either side of the gate, it was almost like being back on just about any Army post in the states. The rows of uniform barracks with tin roofs, marching units of GIs on the way to or from God only knew where, officers and men rushing around, trying to look busy, lest somebody see they weren't and draft them for casual labor, it all spoke of the military the Kid hated the most.

But it did serve to give the Kid a new appreciation for way he'd seen the war, up to that point; first with the Vietnamese and now as a journalist in a unit that was out of the military mainstream, to say the least. The view of a dozen GIs bent over policing up cigarette butts quickly convinced him, indeed, he had dodged the proverbial bullet.

"No sense dragging your stuff around," Megenity said as the jeep pulled to a stop in front of a complex of connex styled office looking structures, with antennas and shit sticking up off the roof. "First, go up there to that door and make sure he's still here and if he is, you guys can stay and I'll take your stuff over to our hooch and meet you back at our place after lunch. I'm pretty sure your friend will know where the PSYOPS hooch is. Then we can figure out where you all are going to bunk and see if the Captain has your agenda."

"Uh, Curt," said Mark, "if your friend is here, I think I'll go on back with our gear to the PSYOPs hooch and chill and you two can visit. I'll stow your weapon."

"OK. Thanks."

With that, the Kid turned and stepped onto the plank walkway that made up the front entrance of the connected connex chambers that apparently comprised the 9th Division PIO office. There was an aluminum trailer like door, with a threshold a foot above the planks. It contained no windows nor were there any windows in the flat green painted walls on either side. He tried the handle and found it locked. Turning, he smiled back at Birnbaum, who stood besides the jeep watching.

He knocked loudly three times and stepped back a pace, since the door opened outward and waited. There was silence for a few seconds and then heavy footsteps before the door fairly burst open and there with one hand on the door frame and one on the handle, stood Waterhouse.

392

It took less than a quarter second for it to sink in who was in front of him and when it did, he loudly blurted out in total surprise, *"KID!"* as he launched himself off the threshold and slammed into the Kid, locking him in a bone crushing bear hug, pinning both his arms at his sides. Using his 6ft 2 inches for leverage, he lifted the Kid up of his feet and shook him up and down, *"What are you fucking doing here?"*

"Oh, well, hell," Birnbaum laughed, "I didn't know it was going to be *this kind* of reunion!" making Megenity laugh as well.

"Dave!" the Kid struggled to break his grip and get put back down, "good to see you too!" He made a fist and gave him a shot in the arm. "We're here to do a story on 9th Division PSYOPS for our unit newspaper, and this is my photog, Mark Birnbaum, Mark, David Waterhouse, one of my room mates from DINFOS. He's a Texan and a Cowboys fan, but we forgive him. And this is Gerry, one of our field team attached here."

"Gentlemen," Waterhouse waved his hand before he quickly turned and closed the door behind him, "don't want to let the cold out," he smiled.

"So, uh, Waterhouse, if you take Stocker to the mess hall for lunch, you need to deliver him to the PSYOPS hooch, over off the football field, directly opposite the water tower, by about 1300 hours, OK?"

"Got it, will do!" responded Dave and to the Kid, "come on, Kid, let's get in out of the heat!"

"Air conditioning?" gasped the Kid as he stepped up and through the door, "I thought this was supposed to be a hardship tour!" He switched from sunglasses to his round gold frames.

"Oh it has been," Dave said, pulling the door shut behind him, sealing off the well lit nearly 20 by 30 foot office that housed half a dozen desks, "Whoa! Check those out!"

"A present from my Dad."

"And a moustache, too!" Dave appraised, "it's like you got an Inspector Clouseau disguise kit for Christmas!"

A mimeograph table and two light box layout tables, exactly like theirs in graphics back in Can Tho. Three of the desks and one of the light tables were occupied by warm bodies.

"Hey! Everybody!" Waterhouse had the Kid by the arm, "I want to introduce to you to one of John and I's room mates from DINFOS, the infamous and always entertaining one of a kind *almost* a man with the plan from the Music City... let's hear it for the *KID!* Real name Curt Stocker."

Waterhouse led the applause and whistled through his teeth while everybody else snickered but nobody joined in as the Kid took off his steel pot and weakly waved, feigning embarrassment at the garish intro.

"How'd you put up with him for so fucking long?" a blond-haired buzz cut GI at one of the light tables lifted his head to direct a question at the Kid, a cigarette hanging out of his mouth.

"Cotton in my ears, mostly," the Kid responded, while visually checking the place out. "Wow, so this is your office and that's your desk and you have air fucking conditioning! You lucky bastard!" He smiled at Waterhouse. A black and white framed picture of Tina sat in one corner.

Waterhouse grinned back, his white teeth a contrast to his black horn rimmed glasses, reminding the Kid of Buddy Holly, "There you go calling me *lucky bastard* when you, the lucky bastard *of all time,* are off beating a fucking court martial! If you want to talk Lucky Bastards, you gotta tell me that story first!"

"Oh. You heard about that."

"Yeah, third hand through Erio and Paul Green from Davies," Dave pulled a Winston out of the pack that sat on his desk and simultaneously lit it with a Zippo while sitting down on his low backed roller chair. "But it was hard to understand… uh you ate in a mess hall when you weren't supposed to eat in or ate twice or ate and got RNA or some such shit? Sounded like a set up. We all agreed *YOU* set it up!"

There was another office chair to the left side of Dave's desk and the Kid took it. "Long story. But you gotta tell me something first, *how did they get John?* Were you with him when it happened?"

The smile that had been on Dave's face since he first saw the Kid evaporated. "No. I wasn't." He took a really deep breath of composure followed by a long pause, "He volunteered to walk point on a search and destroy mission to write a story about it. From what a medic said who was there, John got hit multiple times, and any one of them alone would have been fatal… and the guy hit his heart with his fist when he said it, so I'm thinking that's where he got at least one."

Silence as the Kid digested the long-awaited information. *The Boy Scout was shot through the heart.* "He volunteered to walk point to get a story?" the Kid slowly reiterated. "Shit. What a bummer. I'm here to go on a NITECAP to get a story."

Another long pause.

"Oh! Hey, on a brighter note," Waterhouse switched gears, "we here at the 9th Division were fortunate enough to have the *Bob Hope Show* grace us with a performance right before Christmas!" His right hand pulled open the top drawer on the right side of his desk and he pulled out an 11X8" photograph and holding it so that the Kid couldn't see what it was, he continued. "He's got this chorus line of about a dozen stone cold babes they call *The American Cuties* and they open the show by coming out and doing this really hot *gogo* dance and when they finish up, they bow to the audience. "*Jones,* over there," Dave pointed and *Jones,* who without looking up from his work, waved his right hand in acknowledgment that he was *Jones,* "he was backstage and when they took their bow, he shot this!"

Dave laid the picture on his desk, the Kid took one look and his eyeballs almost literally popped out of his head! When the *Cuties* bowed at the waist to the audience, their ultra short shirts came up in the back to a point where every single one of them was showing the full glory of their beautiful panties. As his eyes feasted on the row of a dozen elegantly long pairs of American legs, running all the way from the floor to their cotton crotches, framed by an exquisite collection of butt cheeks, the Kid just about popped a boner! *The Holy Grail of American poontang!* "Jesus H. Christ!" was all he could say as his eyes ran down the row of alluring derrieres. "Imagine this *without* panties!"

"We do, on a regular basis!" Waterhouse laughed as he took the pic back and restored it to the drawer. "And no, you can't borrow this later tonight!" They both laughed.

"Shit, Dude!" the Kid exclaimed, "We are under 75 fucking days! But some days, it seems like it'll never end. The last time I saw you and John at Long Binh was an ice age ago."

"God how I know it!" Another pause. "So, uh, you're not engaged to Flo any more, I also hear tell."

"Nope. She sent me the Dear John in August. You and Tina still engaged?"

"Yep. We did R&R in Hawaii in January, not long after New Years. That was sweet! You must have done R&R by now."

"Uh huh. Went to Kuala Lumpur. I was signed up for Australia but heard there was going to be a Tet style offensive at Christmas so I took anything I could to get the hell out of Dodge," the Kid frowned. If I'd kept the Aussie R&R I'd be there today and not fucking here!"

"Well boo fucking hoo!" was all the sympathy Waterhouse could muster. "Hey, we got a little over an hour before lunch, we can take the long way to the mess hall and I can show you around the place a little. Just let me take care of a couple of things I need to send out today and we'll hit it," he reached for a small stack of documents sitting conspicuously in his In box.

After about twenty minutes of filling in squares and signing stuff, he was ready to go. He stood and grabbed his baseball hat and gestured at the Kid's helmet sitting on the corner of his desk. "You probably won't need that."

"But is this on the way to PSYOPS after lunch? You gotta take me to the PSYOPs hooch, remember."

"Right, better wear it."

Stepping back out the door and into the heat, the Kid switched his eyewear to shades and Waterhouse did the same. "That way," Dave pointed, and he squared his hat up on his head, "We'll see the important stuff first, that is to say the USO, and we'll finish up there just in time to get over to the mess hall before the big line forms."

They both lit up cigarettes as they began walking down the unpaved street whose rising dust bespoke of the late days of the dry season.

"You'll love the court martial story, Dave," the Kid began, I'll tell you that at lunch but if you want to talk lucky bastarding, I just about wore this fucking thing out," he pulled his beaver nickel from his fatigues and jangled it. "During the five months I spent with the ARVN 14th, in the clutches of this kill crazed lieutenant, he volunteered us for every crazy fucking operation that came down the pike!"

"Like what?"

"Well, there's this thing in PSYOPS called an armed propaganda team, heard of that yet?"

"No."

"You know what a Kit Carson Scout is, right?"

"Yeah, an ex-VC who goes out with the units."

"Right," said the Kid, "so an armed propaganda team is the reverse. Two American Advisors go out in the middle of the night with 24 ex VC, back to where they defected, and they point out the other VC which you then either capture or kill. Lt. Wilson, was his name, he volunteers us for one of those and I say no way and the whole court martial thing was over him trying to make me say yes and me calling his bluff! I didn't set it up, but it couldn't have been any sweeter if I *had* written the fucking script!"

"Uh, isn't it standard practice to get a transfer after a court martial? So why are you still there?" asked Dave.

"Well," the Kid began, "yes it is. But, the CO of our unit, this black colonel named Willie O. Lawton, personally requested that I stay. Offered me whatever position I wanted. Believe it or not. Kind of hard to say no to that and take a flyer on ending up in some unpredictable place, like, oh I don't know… here?"

"Yes, I see your point," Dave nodded.

"Yeah. He became CO right when the whole thing started. I think he could see on the face of the charges that there was more to it than just me being a miscreant... or in this case, a *mess* creant. So, Price, got any weed?"

"Ha!" Waterhouse smirked, "have I got any weed? Around here, the question is *how much* weed have you got?"

"Oh, good, then I didn't have to bring what I brought."

'Nope. Your weeds' no good here, soldier," Waterhouse said with a John Wayne accent before he cleared his throat and spat a loogie in front of him which he kicked dirt over as they passed. "Kid, I mean, can you seriously believe the weed in this fucking country?"

They silently recalled the day when the pair couldn't score a dime bag to save their lives in Indianapolis.

The Kid extracted the unopened pack of Winston joints from his pocket. "I suppose you guys are into this by now, the Vietnamese repack and seal."

"Oh yeah."

"In answer to your question, yes," resounded the Kid, "I believe the weed in this country is its only redeeming feature!" They both laughed.

"Almost makes you want to extend!" guffawed Waterhouse.

"Jeezus! I tried to extend! Wait till you hear this one. I went to Saigon in September because I lost my glasses down a well I and hooked up with *Alan P.*

And he introduced me to the PD and the OIC and I played them my Sgt Pepper tape and they *wanted* me. We had a deal. I submitted the paperwork and would have had a drop putting me on the jet in about 14 fucking days from today! And after my court martial, even though I won, they killed it! Fucking bastards, I could have had the slot! And look what happened! Scott Manning ripped off my whole act!"

"Yeah! The second I heard him come on as Sgt Pepper, the first thing I thought about was you and your Sgt Pepper Hit Parade and Family Band Show tape!

"He was fucking there when I played it for them. Nothing I can do about it now. He came out with it the week after my extension was denied. But what the hell. It was a good idea and he knew I wasn't ever going to do it, so he did. I guess I can't blame the fucking bastard, but I'm still *furiously fucking pissed!*"

Before long they came to a butt can and both deposited their spent filter tips. Looking at his Seiko, the Kid noted it was 1020 hours and it was getting hot, especially walking in the direct sunlight but the USO was right there.

Compared to the one in Can Tho, the 9th Division USO was five times the size and if it had been any fancier, it would have been classified as a shopping center. The pair got coffee and each a slice of fresh baked apple pie and found a table away from others and sat down.

"Man o man," said the Kid between bites, "some of our guys formed a band and are they ever fucking GOOD! The lead guitar player, Tom Boyett, also has this friend back in the states who sends him tapes of all the latest new music. It is so fucking far out! There's this one band, *Big Pink*, they are absolutely amazing. You'll have to check them out. Plus the friend sent him the new Beatles double album at the end of January. Have you heard any of it yet?"

"No!"

"It's pretty *fab and gear*..." the Kid intoned in a British accent, mimicking Ringo, "I mean really *fooking* good! After all, it's the *Beatles,* but some of the tracks are a little weird, both in subject matter and music. There's this one song, called, *'Happiness is a warm gun...'* more than a little bit strange."

"Well, I haven't heard it yet but...we've got TV here!" responded Dave, "as a matter of fact, *Laugh In* is on tomorrow night! It's really good without commercials, but they are censoring a whole bunch of stuff off it now, they must be getting a lot heavier into the political anti-war stuff."

Like a lot of the post, the USO was air conditioned, so it was easy for them to sit and talk and let the time slip by as they compared notes of their tours and waited to go to lunch.

Finally, Dave brought up the Boy Scout again. "Yeah shit. What a bummer, John barely made it to under 200 days. When he came up with the idea, I told him not to do it; he didn't have to prove anything to anybody. But he was determined to do this story about *walking point* and that morning, he was so fucking excited. He'd spent most of the night cleaning his M-16. I couldn't fucking believe it when I heard he was KIA."

"He had a stubborn streak, that's for sure," the Kid appraised his personality, "who'd have thought that out of all of us, Baby Huey would be the one to get it."

"Let us hope, indeed, he turns out to be *only* one of us," Dave spoke the unsaid thought.

They exchanged information on what they knew about their other DINFOS friends, and the time flew by as they finished their pie and chain smoked another couple of cigarette before rising to go to lunch.

Chapter 59

While they waited in the chow line, Birnbaum and Meginity arrived and joined them. There was a discussion about who was going to bunk where and it turned out that Waterhouse's cubicle mate was on R&R, so the Kid was going to take his bunk while Mark was going to quarter in the PSYOPS hooch.

During lunch, the Kid and Mark told the tale of Captain PM Smith calling them out, *in absentia,* at the company formation and how they crushed him in the colonel's office.

"Someday, Kid," Dave shook his head at the story's conclusion, "you're gonna play with fire one *too many times* and get the fuck burned out of you!"

"Yeah, well… since there's a thousand ways to get burned in this country, figuratively and literally, so what the fuck?"

"There's the attitude guaranteed to make these last 75 days exciting!"

After lunch, while walking over to the PSYOPS hooch, the visitors commented on the copious numbers and placements of bunkers. "Think of all the sweat in those sandbags," said Mark.

"You know it! Hell" Waterhouse pointed across the road, "there's at least 5 pounds of my sweat in that one *right there.*"

"So how often does the place get mortared?" inquired the Kid.

"About every other day, on average, "Dave cocked his head as he figured, "I mean, shit; is this place an easy target or what? But it usually doesn't happen during the day, it's at night that they get the tubes cookin'. Your chances of getting mortared here in the space of 4 days are about 100%."

"That's one thing I really like about the New Villa, Mark interjected, and "it's never been attacked in the whole time I've been there. And I don't think, from what I heard anybody say, including Boujold and Roberts, that it actually took any rounds at Tet, either."

"Good point to make with all the bozos that want to get out of there and into the field," smiled the Kid. "I keep telling them the field is overrated and far more dangerous but they're all dying to get out here. *Bad choice of words.*"

"However," Mark raised a single digit to the sky, "we are going to have a fucking ball being away from Can Tho on this assignment!"

When they arrived at PSYOPS, Dave met more of the team; Spec 5 Richard Rios, and Spec 4 Bill Sutton. He then wrote down the designation that served as the address of his billet and handed it to Meginity. "Here, this wouldn't mean anything to Stocker, so just bring him over here when you're done with him," and turning to the Kid he said, "Kid, see ya tonight!"

"You make me sound like laundry," sniped the Kid as Waterhouse went out the door and did not retort.

Not ten seconds later, Captain Richard S. Mitchell, CO of Detachment 4, entered the same door that Waterhouse had exited and Megenity called the office to attention. The captain flipped his baseball cap onto his desk, sat down his clipboard and barked, "At ease," before looking up to discover who was present and to the Kid and Birnbaum said, "Oh, good, I see you made it!"

"Captain Mitchell, Sir, good to see you," the Kid stepped forward and offered a salute that Mitchell ignored. "Mark and I have been looking forward to this assignment for a couple of weeks now, Sir!"

"Well, I gotta say, we appreciate any recognition we get. Sometimes it's like we're out her busting our balls everyday and nobody gives a flying fuck at a rolling donut about anything we do."

"Obviously, Sir, you must be doing something right because you've got the highest Hoi Chanh count in all of IV Corps," the Kid approvingly beamed at him, "I think that's one of the best storylines we can promote." He took his small notebook from his right cargo pants pocket and drew a ballpoint pen from his shirt pocket and prepared to take notes. "So, do you have a plan for our visit?"

"Uh, yeah," he fumbled in his shirt pocket for a cigarette, "sort of," he lit up. "Tomorrow, we're going to do a MEDCAP over at Long Dinh, a village complex about 5 clicks down the road, not far and close to totally secure… for all practical purposes." Standing, he motioned the Kid to follow him over to the map on the wall of IV Corps. It was chest high to his 6 ft frame and he ran the hand holding the cigarette up to a spot, "Long Dinh is here… well, while we're here, I can show you real quick." Switching to point with the index finger of his non smoking paw, he indicated their destinations, "Tomorrow Long Dinh, then on Wednesday, the two of you and Specialist Sutton and I are going to drive through Go Cong Province and you're going to see just how pacified it is... and then, of course, the NITECAP will be at Binh Trung, there."

The Kid bent in to take a closer look. "Hmmm, Go Cong? Shouldn't they change that to *No Go Cong?*" I mean once you go Cong, you can never go back, right?"

Birnbaum and Sutton smirked but Mitchell stared at the Kid with a deadpan expression on his slightly sunburned face before he burst into loud laughter which he abruptly stopped and said to the Kid in an unmistakably authoritative tone, "you are here to do a serious story, right?"

The Kid paused and edited the first line that came into his head; *as serious as a heart attack in a napalm strike, Sir! Snappy salute shuffle off to buffalo and said,* "Sir, I can assure you that there will be nothing funny about anything I write on this assignment."

"Good. I believe you. In fact, I like some of your stuff when you do the personnel sketches and battalion happenings, but you do have a *reputation* for the irreverent, if I may put it mildly. That's why I had to find out if you were here to work or goof off."

"Work, Sir. Plain and simple, plus I am spending some time with one of my classmates from DINFOS, bunking in his billet in fact, Megenity has it written down. That was him you almost bumped into on your way in his way out. I had another classmate here at the PIO, but he got KIA'd in September."

"Hmmm. Sorry to hear it," Mitchell intoned.

The Kid put on his reporter's hat and with pen in hand, began to question the Captain. "So, Sir, what would you say was your biggest problem here performing PSYOPS for the 9th Division?"

Blowing out a big puff of smoke, the Captain ashed his cigarette, looked at the ceiling before speaking. "I've actually got two major problems. Number one is the lack of US Army elements for security for the field teams because we just have so much shit going on. Nothing really bad has happened yet, but it's a ticking time bomb. The second one, related to the first, is that our continuous use of equipment makes it very difficult to keep it all on line. We frequently have teams doing two assignments a day. Sometimes we must go to My Tho and scrounge equipment from Vietnamese to keep the teams going. That and getting shot at on a regular basis are the main problems we face."

Writing furiously in his unique shorthand, the Kid inquired, "So, Captain, how many field teams do you have out there at any one time?"

"We have seven sub teams of different types. There are three "E" teams, audio-visual, and there are three "B" teams (loudspeaker humpers) and one Division Support team. You'll be going out tomorrow with the Division Support team on your MEDICAP story and you'll be working with one of the AV teams in conjunction with the NITECAP story."

The Kid paused in his writing and had to ask, "Uh, Sir, referring to the comment about the lack of US security on your operations, I gotta ask, what the security situation is going to be on that NITECAP story?"

"Well," Mitchell's eyes fluttered as he looked over at Sergeant Rios and then back to the Kid, "Sergeant, we've got two platoon of US infantry on call for the NITECAP, don't we?"

"Yes Sir, two platoons," came Rios deadpan reply, which did much too immediately relax the Kid.

"So what do you see us doing for the rest of today, Sir?"

"Well, you might as well take it off. All the teams are long out today, and we don't have any easy way of getting you to a spot where you could join up with any of them. And I've got a bunch of stuff to do."

"That's fine with us," Mark cut in with a smile, "is it OK if we hang at the USO then?"

"Sure. Why not?" Mitchell dismissed us with a wave of his left hand. "See you after breakfast, say 0730 hours for MEDCAP departure. That's about as early as they get the road mine sweeps done."

Chapter 60

It was 0800 when the PSYOPs contingent parked their Army green ambulance truck over to the far side of the Long Dinh bus stop. The broad, open area was bordered at the back by six plaster and tin buildings, which served the village complex as a combination gas station, transportation and food cart hub. No buses had yet arrived for the day so even before their engine was turned off, they were spotted by the growing crowd that was gathering in anticipation.

Out of the MEDCAP ambulance emerged the team; Specialists Bill Sutton, Gerry Megenity, three ARVNs, one of whom was the doctor and the other two Polwar sergeants. Birnbaum and the Kid brought the total to seven. The short ride out had been a little bit too far on the clown car side of reality. They had to sit on boxes of bar soap, medical supplies and leaflets. For the present, they left their weapons stowed away with Megenity specifically acting as truck guard.

The two journalists stepped aside and watch the team go to work. Pulling a box of bar soaps out of the back door, one ARVN hustled it to the front and climbed up on the vehicle's flat hood and straddled the box. Smiling broadly, he barked something that sounded like, *"du hoa!"* at the crowd, pulled out a sample and stuck it straight up in the air while the other ARVN produced a bullhorn and began an amplified explanation of what the team was there to do.

Birnbaum framed a shot of the queue and snapped 3 quick ones.

With their own hands in the air, it appeared that the mass cared not what the man with the bullhorn was saying, so long as they got a free bar of soap. The giveaway was designed to draw the crowd that had grown to at least 40, away from the back where the doc and Sutton were busy setting up the MEDCAP. Extracting a folding table, they set it into place about five feet out from the truck and by it put 2 metal folding chairs, one directly behind the table and the other slightly to its right. Pulling two boxes of medical supplies over to perch on the end of the truck, the doctor sat down behind the table, clearly indicating he was "in". A line of at least a dozen had already formed.

The Vietnamese doctor was a little older than the one the Kid had worked with eight months ago at the fortified hamlet of Tan An. He had strong beginning traces of grey in his temples. "Mein yoi, Bauxi," the Kid had addressed him when they first met earlier that morning, unlimbering some of the Vietnamese he had acquired during his 6 months with the ARVN 14th. After being away from it day to day, he was already getting a little rusty. Of course the doctor's name was *Nguyen. Dr. Nu, I'll call him in the book.*

For the next half hour, *Dr. Nu* furiously worked his way through the line of instant patients, dealing with what little he had to face whatever a villager might throw at him. The patient would take the seat across, speak their peace and point; mostly to rashes, ear problems, sore limbs and joints. Most consultations featured liberal amounts of pantomime. Occasionally a parent would place a child in the seat and start spouting. Dr. Nu would quickly examine them, feeling and probing with the effectiveness of a quick frisk. He would then grab a tube, carton or bottle out of one of his boxes and hand it to them as a dismissal. The man was a machine, a wonder to observe. He had to be, because this was only the team's first stop of three planned for the morning.

Standing there watching, the Kid was taken by how much empathy Dr. Nu actually managed to show each of his lightning round patients. And he also couldn't help but notice when he smiled, his dark moustache did this strange little dip down of its ends, forming a miniature *fu Manchu.* Some complaints he could clearly help, others perplexed him a little and about every fifth patient, he might make a note on his pad at the table. Hard as he worked, the line never got any shorter but still, Megenity had to call for the shutdown at the end of half an hour or otherwise fall too far behind schedule.

On a signal from the lanky specialist, one of the ARVN Polwar assistants to Dr. Nu moved in and announced that the MEDCAP had concluded, for that location, at any rate.

Before the table was stowed, Dr. Nu went through his supplies and filled up two ruck sacks with various remedies; one to be carried by each of the Polwars. Of the four Americans, three were going. The Kid and Sutton pulled their M-16s out of the truck along with their ammo bandoliers and each inserted a clip in preparation of moving away from the bus stop.

Mark would not encumber his ability to shoot pictures by being prepared to shoot otherwise and thus left his weapon with Megenity, who was going to guard the truck. Gerry looked quite content, with a lit up a cigarette between his lips, as he tuned on his transistor radio which sat on passenger's seat, propped up against his and Mark's weapons. The driver side door was open and the passenger's window rolled down and Gerry sat on the driver's seat with his feet on the running board. He was prepared to stand his watch.

Other than Sutton and the Kid, there was no American security detail and, the Kid quickly noticed, there wasn't any ARVN security around, *either.*

"Uh, I guess the prevailing opinion is that this must be pretty safe territory, like Mitchell says then, Bill, if they aren't even giving us some local militia?" the Kid questioned as they began to walk. "I'm sure he'll be shootin' more of that, "he pointed to Mark's camera with his left hand, "than we'll be shooting of this," he gestured with his M-16.

Sutton peered out from behind his sunglasses and the shade of his baseball cap, "Well, I ain't sweatin' it, been a while since anything happened in the middle of the day this close to Dong Tam."

Fair enough. But the Kid could not relax.

Dr. Nu seemed to have a good idea of where he was headed, so the Americans had no input other than to follow along. It was now pushing 0900 hours and the day was predictably heating up. Good thing the pair of journalists had chosen to leave their steel pots back at the barracks since nobody else was wearing one. The Kid had a full canteen attached to his pistol belt and he now pulled it out and took a drink while continuing to walk. The perspiration was already saturating his uniform.

From the distance of about 100 meters, the flock of a dozen white paper kites sparkled like *Lucy in the Sky with diamonds.* They darted and fluttered, catching the sun, as they rode between 40 or 50 feet above the ground. Their strings traced downward, not only to the dozen adolescent boys who flew them but to their gallery of admirers, who raptly watched the exhibition. That is until they saw the Americans!

The MEDCAP team got the clue they were spotted when the kites began to jerk rapidly downward through a pleasant morning breeze, the first early harbinger that the Mekong Delta's dry season was soon to end.

"Here comes the stampede!' the Kid intoned, reaching into his pocket for a handful of the hard Jolly Rancher candies from the bag in his left cargo pants pocket. "God knows I didn't bring enough. Hey, watch your pockets; they will try to get a hand in there, especially if you have both hands on your camera and can't protect yourself…oh, wait…*that's why I'm here!"*

Then they were surrounded and the customary Vietnamese junior mob scene ensued. "GI GI give me gum! Give me candy! Give me *pi!"* It was hard to tell which one said what or how many times.

The Kid hollered, *"Men yoi, Em Toi mun ancom!"* and held up his left hand, displaying the candy, drawing the wave's focus and turning it on him right before he tossed the sugar lures about 10 feet away, causing what could only be described as a rugby scrum after the half dozen wrapped pieces of brightly colored candy.

Four of the boys who had been flying kites held them up and posed for Mark with smiles on their faces, white teeth flashing. Dr. Nu and the Pol War ARVNs all got big laughs out of the whole process, pointing at the children fighting over the candy and punching each other in the arm like a couple of frat boys.

"Sure happy we didn't get mortared last night," said the Kid as he watched Mark photograph the children collecting the bounty.

"You can say that again," concurred Mark, while checking his light readings through the lens as he changed his angle before snapping off a couple more shots. "So, is your friends pot any better than ours?"

"No."

A couple more shots and Mark sighed, "We didn't smoke last night, the sarge was around so it wasn't possible. You're right, we've got a pretty sweet deal back in Can Tho."

"Yes, indeed." the Kid pulled out a KOOL and lit up. Sutton, the Dr. and the ARVNs were getting ahead of them. "To smoke here, ya gotta go walk around and try and avoid people. Waterhouse said there's like a couple of the hooches more notorious than others, where it's a regular smoke out situation, but theirs isn't one of'em, which is OK with me."

Mark shot a couple more pics of the kite flyers, "OK OK, that's it," he said dropping the camera to hang from his neck and shooing them away, "I'll send you all copies!"

The rest of their party was now about 50 meters down the road, which paralleled a 12-foot-wide canal, paddies to their right and on the left, a *solid wall of bush.* "We better keep moving, Mark," the Kid said after clearing his throat.

"Picking off stragglers is a prime Charlie M.O.," the Kid raised and pointed the barrel of his M-16 at the dense foliage on the far side of the canal. "I know that Mitchell said this place was pretty fucking safe, but no need to go tempting the devil or making it easy for them."

The two hastened to catch up, their new entourage trailing them like boat wake.

Shortly after they did, the group arrived at their next location. It was the hamlet complex school building, a large palm swayed over the log construction affair that was easily 20 X 40 feet. It opens on all four sides with a main beam that was possible more than 12 feet above the dirt floor. It was set back off the path about 20 meters and to one side, had a small soccer field showing real innovative home made goals. Under its shade, it appeared school was not presently in session and not more than a couple dozen people were waiting, clustered up at one end. But as Dr. Nu gave his salutation, two boys sprinted off from the group in different directions.

"The crowd will be here in a couple of minutes, Sutton predicted, "those boys are off to give the good Dr.'s 10-4. We've done this hamlet a couple of times and he's got a couple of places he likes to set up but he likes to keep a certain element of unpredictability out there, too."

"Interesting," mused the Kid, "one minute, nobody is worried about Charlie, the next minute, everybody is worried about Charlie. But, sounds like a good idea to me to keep'em guessing. Yeah. In fact, keep it as unpredictable as the presence of American security!" *As if the VC don't know exactly where we are…*

Sutton smiled, "Yep, you got it. This is how we live down here. "

Walking under the building's eve, the Kid stepped into the shade and found some small relief from the sun. Pulling out a KOOL, he lit up and in doing, brushed his hand over the pack of joints in his top left fatigue shirt pocket to make sure they were still there. It would be an easy matter to separate himself from the group a little bit, walk over to the nearest grass dwelling huts, open the pack of smokes and take some hits but he dismissed the idea as soon as it formulated. *We did promise the colonel no smoking on duty.*

Taking off his shades, he put on his gold rims and surveyed the scene. Dr. Nu was setting up where the teacher usually gave the lessons. The three by six-foot folding table and two folding chairs, situated in front of a green chalkboard that was attached precariously to a makeshift metal tripod, was his new branch office. There were no desks meaning the students must sit on the floor during lessons.

Mark didn't appear interested in any of the lean photo opportunities presented by the Spartan facility and its dim light. This particular stop would not be a big part of the story.

Sutton, who had just lit up his own cigarette came over and stood by the Kid as the locals began gravitating toward the makeshift medical operation, coming down paths from opposite directions. "Lucky we didn't have to haul any pigs out here today that only makes an operation a bigger cluster fuck than you can imagine.

"Pigs?" asked the Kid.

"Yeah. Pigs and chickens. We get them from the Dong Tam Civic Action Farm, it's like a permanent PSYOPS and MEDCAP operation set up like a farm. It's on a piece of ground just outside the 9th Division front gate, where the chances of it being attacked are like zero. They have a breeding program going on there where animals are raised to give to the locals, so they can breed even more. When we do it, we always give away a breeding pair and they are always just fucking squealing hell to move around. The farmer has to promise he'll give away the first litter in pairs, to other families and then any more litters belonged to him."

No wonder this place is so placated; we give them medicine and livestock here. What VC would want to mess that up? I wonder how many of the pigs end up in Charlie mess halls? How much of this medicine is passed on to the enemy?

An hour later, the party was again on the move, going deeper into the Long Dinh complex, to the third and last location of the day's mission. The entourage of children had thinned a little, figuring the Kid had exhausted his candy supply but an attentive little group of half a dozen boys continued to dog their every step. They were near the edge of the hamlets, marked by a log construction watchtower that rose up like a lone sentry.

Their location destination was at the base of the watchtower that topped an archaic looking outpost, made of mud and bamboo. As it offered a perfect vantage point to snare a couple of different views of the hamlet area, Mark trotted ahead to climb it. The Kid, not desiring of a climb, paused by the door of a hut where an aging mama san squatted by a basket of freshly picked mung bean sprouts and was rinsing them, a handful at a time, in a pan of water. A group of younger toddlers peered out from the doorway behind her.

"Chow, Mama San," the Kid bowed and smiled.

She smiled back, showing that beetle nut was indeed on the local menu. "Chow, Om," she replied, with a slight air of amusement, that the American was taking any interest in her at all, let alone that he was trying in Vietnamese.

"Chow Em!" the Kid pointed and waved at the children, eliciting instant squeals as they abandoned their post, all to his amusement. He gestured at where the Mama San was placing the washed sprouts and pantomimed eating some and she nodded *OK*. Now the 4 toddlers appeared over the hut windowsill, holding onto it with their little hands as they rose up to show the tops of their heads from the eyes up. The Kid reached down and picked up a pinch of the green topped white tuber sprouts, placed them in his mouth and chewed for about five seconds and swallowed. Looking behind, he saw the juvenile escort was still standing there, watching him because there wasn't anything more interesting to do.

The Kid had told them his candy supply was *fini- het roi,* but in fact, he knew he had 4 more pieces. Snaking his left hand down to the cargo pocket, he wrapped his fingers around them. Then, in a single move, he pulled his hand from the pocket and flipped the candies through the window, over the toddler's heads and said, *"BOO"!*

The squeals were ear splitting and Mama San laughed, displaying here red, rotted teeth. *Beetle Nut. What a curse.* He could see one of the older boys telling some of the other boys what had to be, *see? He had more candy ALL ALONG! But now it's gone! And so are we!*

Chapter 61

Later that night, the Kid would remember and recount to Waterhouse the fun he had scaring those kids and laughing with the Mama San and how bad her teeth were. But he would not remember the source of his lower intestinal distress… that innocuous small mouthful of mung bean sprouts, washed off, in non-potable water that tasted so fresh when he ate them.

The distress began after chow, while they were watching *Laugh In.* The Kid had been in anticipation all day, that there in Dave's barracks was a TV pulling in the Saigon AFN signal and *Laugh In* was on! All the troops, including the Kid, were in their casual wear, mostly consisting of cut offs, with civilian style T-shirts or bare-chested and flip flops.

At first, there was the minor distress, a slight rumble in his belly, sort of like it could have been gas on the move or something, but he had a sneaking suspicion that he shouldn't attempt a fart. It was not necessarily a problem out of the ordinary, nothing that would even indicate the need for Pepto Bizmo. After all, diarreaiha and loose bowels were a way of life in Nam. But as Goldy, Artie Shaw, Henry Gibson and Dick and Dan spun their magic, the feeling began to gain momentum until the Kid was thinking that *Laugh In* or not, he was going to have to hit the Latrine.

It was slightly after 1900 hours and not really all the way dark yet but night was getting close. The Kid had risen to his feet to visit to the facility when he heard three muffled *thuds,* from a distance, in quick succession. *Unmistakable what that sound was.*

"IN COMING! Incoming!" the screams echoed from a multitude of throats in near unison and the shells, acting like a starter's pistol, sent the men instantly into motion and the race to the bunker was on! Luckily, the Kid was already up and consequently, in front of the Herd. Charging through the screen door, he didn't bother to hold it for his companions because they were hot on his tail. Another round dropped and another as the throng performed a rapid and well-ordered split, circling through the bunker's two sandbag lined entrances that fed into the channel which emptied into the

411

safe room. The shells were hitting at least half way to the other side of the camp and none seemed all that close, but it was likely just the beginning.

"See Kid? I told you that you'd get mortared while you were here, proving once again I'm a man of my word," grinned Waterhouse, breathing a little heavy from the sudden adrenalin inspired exertion.

The 9th Division bunkers were actually quite spacious. Dug about 2 feet down into the red dirt, the sandbagged sides went up to a ceiling that was a good 8 feet at the edges and 10 feet tall down the middle. The easily 20X 40ft space was well lit and had been equipped with benches and boxes of books and magazines.

"I'm surprised you guys haven't' hooked a TV up in here, we're missing *Laugh In!*" the Kid exclaimed and in the next breath, "is there a latrine in here?"

"NO" came the many voiced reply.

"Why?" asked Dave, "you gotta go? If it's really freaking bad, you can piss outside the door, but no pissing in here, that's for sure!"

"Yeah, right. Like I wish it was number one."

"Oh. You mean you gotta *go.*"

"Right, Dave, I was just getting up to do exactly that and now, that I've jumped up and ran around, the attack is here," he pointed at his lower intestine, *"I really, really gotta go!"*

Another 3 rounds land and a couple of these are noticeably closer.

"You're just gonna have to hold it, Kid," Dave shook his head, "some times these attacks don't last but about ten or 15 minutes, you really should wait for the 'all clear'."

Somebody in the back turned on a radio; at least they'd been savvy enough to figure that one out. Then the 30 or so men, all of whom had been busy doing other things like watching TV, writing letters home, cleaning weapons, playing cards or listening to music, were now thrown together to do one thing: wait.

That suited everyone just fine, except for the Kid. Pressure was growing, he was almost to the point where he'd have to start doing the dance to help him hold it. Jumping round, the tenseness of moving his legs helped him keep his sphincter shut. *This is more serious than I thought!*

Another round, farther away, followed by the closest one to them yet demonstrated the randomness of the mortaring; the VC didn't care what they hit inside the base, as long as it was *inside the base.*

Ten minutes then passed and nothing had fallen. "Dave… uh, do you think I could make it to the latrine now?"

"Jeeze, I gotta tell you, it's better to wait for all clear. They very often throw in some late rounds after they think we've given the all clear, they want to get you coming out of your hole, it's a pattern."

"Well, it *will* be coming out my hole and I don't think it will make a very pretty pattern, but fucking A, if I don't make it to the latrine really soon, I think I am, and consequently… all of you," The Kid gestured by spreading his arms, "are going to be in big trouble!"

"Bigger trouble than a fucking mortar attack?" Dave asked incredulously.

"Stinkier and messier, that will be a fucking scientific fact!" the Kid wanted to laugh but didn't, "the only thing that could possibly be worse would be if the mortar hit ME right now… then we'd *all* be in a world of shit!"

"Oh well, then, good thing we're in a bunker!" Water house smiled at the Kid.

"Back to my original *problemmmmm.*"

Another minute passed and when it hit 12 since the last round, the Kid couldn't stand it any longer. "I'm going for it," he announced, "you'll all thank me later, I'm serious, and I gotta take a chance *right now!*"

Nobody tried to stop him as he left the bunker and started running toward the latrine, which was over dirt about 50 meters away. He was wearing flip flops so he wasn't really shod for speed but he was high stepping and gripping his sphincter tighter than a crab's asshole in hopes of holding back the brown typhoon. The latrine entrance was on the opposite side of his approach. Running around the corner, he flew into the head while unbuttoning his APT shorts and pulling down his green boxers. Not surprised that nobody else was in there, his ass was already bare when he went to sit down on the first opening closest to the door and as he hit the white oval, shit sprayed out his butt like water out of a garden hose in July.

AAAAhhhh. Thank God! After holding it for so long, the near liquid crap was more than ready to exit his body but as it continued to flow in an uninterrupted stream of exquisite relief until he heard it; *THUMP BOOM THUMP BOOM!*

Holy shit! More rounds! Fuck it. I am finishing this. If my fate is to get killed crapping my brains out on a commode in Dong Tam, at least I won't shit myself when I die!

Maybe it was only 10 seconds, or possibly 20 at the most, but it felt like an eternity before he got to the first place where his body was not expelling fecal material. Right then, the Kid jumped to his feet and pulling up his boxers and shorts and bolted for the door. At first, he tried to button his shorts as he ran but another round makes him just hold them up with his right hand as he concentrated instead on running. Then he heard somebody shouting.

"RUN KID, RUN!

In the fading light, he could see Waterhouse in his white shirt, standing at the bunker entrance, jumping up and down, waving his arm toward the bunker, imploring him, begging him to kick it into high gear as rounds continued to fall. He had come out and endangered himself because he was worried about the Kid.

In a double high step move, the Kid kicked off both his flip flops, turned on the juice and sprinted the last 25 yards barefooted. He was moving *so fast* near the end, he almost didn't slow down in time but Waterhouse withdrew inside away from the entrance, allowing him an unobstructed landing zone. Hitting the opening, he slowed himself with his arms on the sandbags and in the process, dropped the grip on his shorts which promptly slid down and nearly tripped him.

When he emerged inside the bunker, gasping with his pants down around his ankles, the entire population of the bunker took one look at him and after a silent second, fell down howling and laughing.

The Kid, stood like a statue there in the door, except his chest was heaving and he was panting, and when the mirth subsided, he said in the calmest Jack Benny deadpan he could muster, "Oh, Shit," *pant pant,* "I forgot to wipe!"

Waterhouse looked at him and said, "Kid! You fucking Neanderthal! I'm just glad you're alive!"

"Well, once I got down there, no way I was bringing that shit back up here! But, if I hadn't been crapin' when the first one came in, *I would have commenced to be crappin right fucking then!* I need a smoke" he said with a hand out; his were in the barracks, and was quickly supplied with a Winston and a light. He blew out the first puff and then he started shaking like he had malaria. *"Fuckin' A,* I say, a little too close for comfort!"

"I swear to God, Kid, you are the luckiest son of a bitch I ever met!" declared Waterhouse, then quickly with a stage whisper *"You can pull up your pants now."*

The attack continued sporadically for another 45 minutes and when the all clear finally came, *Laugh in* was over. As the group exited the bunker to return to the barracks, the Kid went and found his flip flops and headed back to the latrine to finish his paperwork.

Chapter 62

It was 20 miles from Dong Tam to the town of Go Cong. 40 miles round trip driving in one truck, armed with only four M-16s and a couple of grenades in the hands of Captain Mitchell, Bill Sutton, Mark and the Kid. It was farther than the one truck convoy he had done with Lt. Wilson and Boujold, coming back to Sadec from Vinh Long. It was almost three times the distance of the drive from Tra Vinh out to Cang Long.

All kinds of time for something to go wrong.

Captain Mitchell wasn't given to any wild Lt. Wilson-like delusions; that their truck could be protected by a brace of Claymore mines strapped around it. His delusion was far simpler; they needed nothing at all to be relatively safe. The whole purpose of the trip, he excitedly explained, was to show the pair of journalists just how pacified Go Cong Province had become. They were going to drive out to the town of Go Cong, drop in on Lt. Laurence Sauers and his team, have a bite of lunch and drive back.

Simple.

The captain was driving and Sutton riding shotgun while Mark and the Kid rode standing up in the back of the ¾ ton truck, leaning their upper bodies on the cab roof, feet spread for stability. The canvas cover had been taken off and the overhead frames removed and it was actually a good way to ride. Nice view, your ass wasn't being pounded by the irregular road surface and it offered a great breeze! It was an excellent position from which Mark could shoot 360 degrees. Today, the Kid had also brought his own camera.

As they motored along, the only thing that took the Kid's mind off the mortaring they'd received last night was visions of the Cang Long Road. *The only time I've fired my weapon. One truck convoy, very little fire power, nuts officer in charge. No options for support. Similarities? Check check check and check.*

The Kid looked at Birnbaum, who was bareheaded because his bush hat flapped behind his back as it strained against the chinstrap that kept it from flying away. The Kid had stuff his baseball cap in his back pocket.

Their sunglasses were their windshields and as the wind blew in their faces, they were like a couple of black labs in the back of a pickup. The captain had suggested it was OK to leave their steel pots at home but the Kid was quick to note that Mitchell's suggesting did not include M-16s.

"They must have gotten tired of mining this road," Sutton commented earlier while they were climbing into the truck, after word came the morning sweep had turned up nothing. "I think it's been over two weeks since they found one!"

How encouraging.

It was a gloriously beautiful Delta morning that blossomed before them as they fairly flew down the paved two-lane road. On the map between My Tho and Go Cong, Vietnam Highway 10 ran a straight course. Once away from Dong Tam, its straightness, in the wide-open paddies, made the ribbon of asphalt in front of them made the infinity disappearance.

But the most amazing thing the two journalists noticed was the wide expanses of complete dryness. The paddies were brown as a Nebraska cornfield in November!

"Wow," the Kid gestured to Mark, "it didn't look this dry from the air!"

"End of the Dry season, yeah, but there still an overpowering amount of green out there," Mark shouted back over the wind.

They had departed from the base as soon as the highway opened, so there was virtually no traffic out in front of them. Captain Mitchell had been saying how pacified, slowed down and plain boring life had become in the province, but he didn't say it was *this* deserted.

But the solitude didn't last for long. Ahead of them, they were coming to a section of the highway where the tree line was fairly close to the road on their right side. As they approached it, they noticed a stopped vehicle and activity on the road. Must be military or it couldn't have gotten out to where it was so quickly. Captain Mitchell slowed the ¾ ton as it came upon the jeep partially blocking the road, because there was naught for a shoulder. Standing at its front was a party of 4 men. Two were dressed in military style clothing, green but not necessarily ARVN uniforms, and two were in civilian attire.

They had been engaged in a conversation which ceased at the arrival of the PSYOPs truck. The two men in casual uniforms carried rifles and one of the civilians wore a side arm.

"I wonder what that's all about," the Kid tried to make out what they were doing. Nobody really thought for a second they might be VC because VC didn't drive jeeps.

Sutton hollered back to the pair, "That's *Kahn,* hamlet chief from Cho Gao, just up the road a couple miles."

Mitchell pulled past the jeep and moved the truck as much to the side of the road as he could and climbed out. *Kahn* was walking to meet him.

"Chow, Kahn!" the Captain waved, "what brings you out here?"

"Chow Dai ui," *Kahn* smiled broadly, his teeth not as bright as the aviator shaped reflective sunglasses he wore, "we have man come say he find VC tunnel so we see!"

"Really?" Mitchell put his hands on his hips, "a tunnel? Where?"

"Over here, back from the road," Kahn motioned to a location about 20 meters off the road at the same time indicating Mitchell should follow him. At that cue, Mark and the Kid climbed down and Sutton got out to accompany them.

"*Kahn* speaks pretty good English," Sutton said as they walked to the location, "it's a good thing since we didn't bring an interpreter."

Understatement. I wonder how Corporal Ba is doing?

When they finally arrived on the scene, they see an opening in the ground. Could be a VC tunnel, but was possibly just a hole in the ground, a sniper hiding place. The Kid found it easy to imagine it was the gateway to some gigantic complex, like ones they'd been finding up to the north and west of Saigon. Or it could be anywhere in between.

The slender 3'X2' opening was shored up on one edge by a piece of bamboo partly obscured by foliage, evidence in itself that this was, indeed, more likely a portal than some random hole in the ground. It was too narrow an opening and too dark inside to see how far it went in and the question under discussion was, who among them would enter and check it out? That in fact, was the point the men were debating when the PSYOP boys rolled up.

"What do we actually need to know?" Sutton spoke up.

"How far it goes…" *Kahn* expressed the obvious, "somebody has to go in, at least a little way, take a look. They all say no!" he pointed at his men and emphasized the NO.

The Kid didn't know how much English the other Vietnamese spoke but he could tell *Kahn's* companions knew he was dissing their cowardly ways to the Americans, but they apparently couldn't have cared less.

No way will it be me. "Birnbaum," the Kid looked at Mark, "ever want to photograph the inside of a VC tunnel? Could be the chance of a lifetime!"

"You mean the chance to end a lifetime. No thanks. How about you, Stocker? You're a shrimp."

"Sorry. Total claustrophobic. *Nevah happen, GI.*"

"What the fuck," said Sutton with a measured bravado, "I'd take a look, if I had a pistol to take with me."

No sooner did the words leave his mouth than *Kahn* whipped out his own piece, a US Army issue .45, and extended it to him by the barrel. Nobody had to translate the look on Bill's face, the realization that he had gotten himself into something akin to a shit pickle, as he took the grip, inspecting the piece, "round in the chamber?" in inquired apprehensively.

"No," Kahn shook his head.

"Here," Bill handed it to the Kid by the grip, "hold it while I take off my shirt."

"No! You're not really going in there?" the Kid gasped, taking the piece and pointing it at the ground. .

"Sure! What the fuck?" Bill squinted into the morning sun as he unbuttoned and whipped off his fatigue shirt, folding it once before dropping it on the ground and holding out his right hand for the gun. "Sides, I don't' have to go all that far, in fact, I'll get down there and take a really good look before I go all the way in."

"Take a good look with what?" Mark spoke up, I don't see anybody offering you a flashlight."

"Good point." Sutton paused to consider his lunacy. "Well, I've got my Zippo and it's got plenty of fluid, I'll use that!"

"Wow." The Kid said with a measure of wonder, "Sutton… you really are hot to do this, aren't you?"

Sutton took a deep breath. "Yeah. Shit yeah, this is the most boring fucking place on earth, *no offense, Sir,* and yes, I'm looking for a little excitement. And with my size, I figured I'd end up doing this here at least once, sooner or later. So what the fuck? Here goes!"

"Nobody is ordering you to do this, you know," Mitchell made sure it was clear on his end; this was strictly volunteer work.

A smile broke across his oval face beneath a shock of brunet hair; he'd have never gotten away with that much hair back in Can Tho. "Yes Sir, I want to give it a shot!" Clean shaven, he was one of the few men in the unit who didn't have or wasn't trying to grow a moustache.

The baby faced tunnel rodent, that's what I'll call him in the book. Must be about 5'5".

Sutton pulled back the action on the .45 and chambered a round. Turning, he looked down at the hole and then, dropping to his knees in front of it, he reached into his left front pocket and pulled out the Zippo. After flicking it to check the lighting capacity, he took the pistol off safety. Looking up at the group, he took a deep breath and gave the old thumbs up with his left hand, the one that held the lighter. "Wish me luck!" he said as he bent over from his knees to touch both elbows in front of the dark hole. Inching forward, he edged past the opening and into the abyss, Zippo hand first, followed by the gun hand before he lowered his head inside the hole. "Dark in here," he chuckled.

"Well, light the fucking Zippo!" Mitchell hollered down at him.

"Not yet, I'm trying to see if I can get my eyes to adjust," came the muffled reply as Sutton continued to inch in deeper to his waist, looking for all the world like he was being swallowed by a giant snake.

And there could be thousands of snakes down in that hole and even one VC would be too many! Shit, I can't believe he's doing this! The Kid shivered, surrendering to his own private feelings of claustrophobia, which at time could be intense. *Still, nothing has happened yet. In fact, nothing has happened in the field on this whole trip which is what leads me to believe this isn't going to end well. Law of averages.*

Feeling the weight of the Pentax around his neck, the Kid sensed there might be a photo opportunity. He wasn't quite sure what it was going to be, but for some reason, he lifted the camera up and took off the lens cap. Activating the light meter, he brought it to his eye and dialed up a shutter speed that centered the needle. Through the lens, he could see that Sutton had gotten to the point of descent down into the hole that the only thing left visible were the waffle soles of his jungle boots.

The Kid snapped off the frame. *Looking for light at the end of the tunnel!*

About that time, Sutton hollered back, "OK! I'm lighting the zippo! OK, I've lit the zippo! I see a dirt wall about 5 feet ahead of me!"

This caused excited discussion among the Vietnamese and after an exchange where all of them spoke at once, *Kahn* called to Sutton, "It look more like hole or tunnel?"

After a very pregnant silence, the Kid couldn't resist, "You do know what a hole looks like, Right Bill?" *got a laugh out of all the Americans.*

Sutton echoed, "Aw shit, I can't really tell," which made everybody laugh even harder, "but I ain't going any further because there's no room in here to turn around and I'm starting to feel like I might get stuck… I'm coming out!" With that, he began scrambling backwards, moving his body like a caterpillar in reverse, pushing with what had to be his elbows, actually moving pretty damned fast.

"*Fucking A!* I'm not ever going to volunteer to do that again!" Bill declared as he rose to his feet, handed the pistol back to Kahn and commenced to brush the dirt off his chest and the front of his pants.

Kanh ejected the round from the chamber, picked it up and put it in his shirt pocket ala *Barney Fife.*

Mitchell smiled at him, "That was pretty damn gutsy, Bill, but I don't think it rates any kind of medal!"

Bill was taking the opportunity to light up a cigarette just as soon as he picked his fatigue shirt up off the ground and got the pack out of his pocket. The Zippo was still in his slightly shaking left hand.

"We bring more soldiers back and some shovels, take a closer look later today," Kahn declared their mission of discovery at an end.

The group turned to walk back to the highway just as the first bus of the day coming out of Go Cong shot past on the road heading for My Tho, the occupants of the roof craning to see what the soldiers were doing by the side of the road.

"Good luck with that," Mitchell waved a salute at Kahn as the American boarded their truck to continue their journey.

"Well, that was a bit of nothing," Mark scoffed as the pair climbed up into the back, "I thought we were going to see some excitement!"

"Be glad," replied the Kid as the truck lurched into motion. He was again amazed at the desire of GIs to see action, almost of any kind.

They slowed down to drive through the hamlet of Cho Gao, a collection of mostly grass sided houses and huts, set only slightly back from the pavement on both side of the road. There was one white plaster walled building square in the middle of it all, with an enlarged parking area, obviously Kahn's headquarters.

"Where is everybody?" Mark commented to the Kid, gesturing to the lack of locals in general, "they can't all be out picking rice because it's out of season!"

Good question.

Once clear of the hamlet, Mitchell opened the throttle and again they were rolling down the highway at about 45 miles per. However, at 0930 hours, the breeze came hotter with the climbing sun. More traffic began passing headed in the opposite direction, mostly Hondas but with an occasional vintage automobile as part of the mix. The little bit of military traffic was ironically limited to them.

The hamlet of Hoa Dong, was but a blur and before they knew it, the ¾ ton was pulling into the town of Go Cong, the government and provincial headquarters for the province. The Kid found the place a lot like Tra Vinh, the island out in the sticks where the farmers came to buy supplies, half way between the rice and the nowhere that was 360 degrees wrapped around.

There was a core of the village, noticeably built up and Mitchell pulled the truck in to park next to a jeep in front of a somewhat decorative wall consisting of pounded metal strips cleverly hung between 7 ft tall plaster pillars. The Kid surmised this must be the PSYOPS unit's base of operation. The fence, which sat in front of a tan French style plaster building with a tin roof, featured a tall swinging gate with pickets. Each side had graduated slats, spaced four inches apart, demoting down in size from 7 ft tall next to the pillars, to where at the middle, they were still 6ft tall. But totally in line with the level of security exhibited on the trip thus far, half the gate was swung back and open. Not that it would have mattered; the fence wouldn't have stopped many rounds or deterred an attack of any kind, be it sapper or regular VC, but the building behind it looked substantial.

"Hard to believe we're less than 10 miles from the coast and there's some nice beaches down there!" Sutton grinned as the men climbed down from the back. "And another 30 miles across the bay puts you in Vung Tau! But somehow, I don't think the Captain has that on the schedule today."

"Shit, Sutton," Mark said, "you just tell the captain that you need a little in country R&R, after your harrowing experience as a tunnel rat and see what he says!"

"Are you trying to lead my specialist astray?" smirked Mitchell, who was standing right next to them.

"Oh no, Sir, I think it's entirely within the parameters of command to award such a feat of daring with some beach time. *Show me the downside, Sir!*" barked Mark, going for the operatic comic relief.

Mitchell just slowly shook his head in disbelief.

The group entered the building and Inside Lt. Lawrence B. Sauers, Sp. 5s Andy Simko and Jere Stansell and two uniformed ARVN officers await them. The main room is open and airy, with tactical radios sitting on a bench at the far end and an elongated table running down the middle, obviously already set up for lunch, complete with plates sitting on a white table cloth.

"Hello, Dick," Sauers stepped forward and shook Mitchell's hand, dispensing with the military protocol, "welcome to Go Cong! Stocker, Birnbaum," he spoke their names and he shook their hands, "glad you all could make it!

"Thank you, Sir," the Kid grinned back, "glad to be here!"

"Allow me to introduce you to Dai Ui Triem, my ARVN counterpart and head of S-5," the Kid and Mark saluted and shook hands with him. "And Lieutenant Ngoc, Chieu Hoi Chief of Go Cong Province," who smiled from ear to ear while saluting twice and shaking both their hands.

"We've got a little lunch being prepared in the back and we'll be serving it up in about half an hour. So why don't we sit down over here," he motioned to a older, worn looking leather couch and a group of folding chairs set up around a home made wooden plank coffee table that was easily 8 feet long but not more than 3 feet wide. "We have time for a little confab before we eat. You all like a cold drink? We've got some ice this time of day. *Ma!*" he hollered and a middle-aged Vietnamese woman, dressed in white linen, appeared at what must be the door to the kitchen. "Coca and *nouc da* all around," he made a circling gesture with his right hand, showing her who and where to serve.

"OK!" Ma nodded and vanished back through the door to fulfill the order.

The American and Vietnamese officers all landed on the couch while the four enlisted men pulled up the folding chairs on the opposite side of the coffee table. It's a good thing that four ashtrays sat upon the table because every single one of them lit up.

"I was telling Stocker," Mitchell began, "that here in Go Cong, your team increased the Hoi Chanh rate from just 220 in the first half of 1968 to a grand total of over 1,170 in the second six months of the year… an increase of over 400 percent!"

"That is really remarkable," the Kid pulled the notebook out of his cargo pants pocket while extracting a ball point from his left breast pocket began taking notes, "I'm surprised there are any still left to win over!"

Sauer looked to Mitchell and back to the Kid, "Well, that's not all that far from the truth. In fact, VC activity in Go Cong had dwindled to next to fucking nothing because most of the locals have bought into our programs and its working for them."

"That's great!" interjected the Kid, "What are you going to do for an encore?"

There was a pause as Sauer considered his answer. "Encore? For our encore, we're leaving town! Next month the plan is we turn everything we do here over to POLWAR and the local civilian Vietnamese," Sauer motioned to his Vietnamese counterparts, "Lt. Colonel Lawton informed me the last time I was in that he thought it was time to deploy our team somewhere else."

The Kid could see that the two ARVNs understood exactly what the lieutenant said because they immediately responded with affirmative nodding and a whole lot of showing their teeth in broad smiles.

"That's too cool," the Kid was struck with a bolt from the blue, "So, you guys have literally worked yourselves out of a job! Ha. If we did THAT same thing, everywhere, put a Vietnamese in each American position, *we could all go home!*"

Sauer sprouted a half smile, "If it were only that simple. But now that you mention it, I never thought of it that way!"

Since the key phrase, 'going home' had been uttered, there was a pause while each of the Americans at the table contemplated their departure from that Asian country. Then Ma emerged from the back room with the cokes on a tray and set it at the middle of the table so they could all help themselves and the moment was forgotten.

Lunch was soon served and from the beginning, the Kid knew that his discomfort from the previous night was not entirely passed but some of the dishes were too appetizing to pass up. Plus the small talk got even more intense.

"So," Birnbaum began, "I take it you guys don't get too many, if any movies or stuff like that down here in the boonies." Turning to the enlisted men specifically he informed them, "week after next, up in Can Tho, we're supposed to get *"HELP"*. That'll be a gas!"

"No kidding?" gasped the Kid, "where'd you hear that?"

"From Bud Miller," Mark referenced the unit mail man, "he just got the schedule for the month of March right before we left and HELP is supposed to be in the week of St. Patrick's Day!"

"Hot dam!" exclaimed the Kid, "I can't fucking wait! If I was you guys, I'd find an excuse to come in to Can Tho."

"Not gonna happen," Sauer immediately quashed the idea, "we got too much to do to get our asses out of here for any of my men to be gone any time up until we bug out for good."

The discussion then moved to the NCAA Men's basketball tournament, where the consensus was that UCLA was pretty much unbeatable at the *Big Dance* and that Captain PM Smith almost committed suicide when LSU didn't get in. The Kid had a good time picturing the methods that PM might employ to achieve that end.

As everybody was pulling out their after-lunch cigarettes and lighting up, the Kid surmised that the visit to Go Cong was not going to be a major part of his 9th division story.

"So, Sir," Birnbaum turned to Mitchell, "no chance on the beach thing, huh?"

Mitchell's mouth dropped open in mock disgust as he turned to Sauer, shaking his head, "Like a dog with a bone, you are, Birnbaum."

"Dog with a bone?" now it was Birnbaum's mouth open in surprise, "Dog with a bone? This is only the second time I've brought it up, Sir! Jeeeeesus! *Dog with a bone!* My God!"

It amused the Kid to hear a Jew invoking the name of Jesus for swearing purposes.

"No beach. The only thing we're doing this afternoon is driving back to Dong Tam," Mitchell lazily stated.

"Wow, Sir," the Kid cut in, "you weren't joking when you said we were driving down here for lunch, were you?"

"Nope. Ma's a great cook! We're all going to miss her cooking when Sauer and the boys bug out next month and we don't have a reason to come down. Cam on, Ma!" the captain waved to the cook, whose head had popped out the kitchen door at the mention of her name.

She stepped just outside the kitchen door, in her white pajama bottoms and once white kitchen soiled top to accept the compliment with a smile, a bow and a nervous laugh, showing her slightly bucked teeth.

Back in the truck, once Mitchell got out of town and they were rolling down the highway, the Kid tapped Birnbaum on the shoulder and lifted the as yet unopened pack of joints out of his pocket and broke the seal. Handing one to Mark he said, "I guess we are officially off duty!"

They laughed as each pulled out his Zippo and crouched down behind the cab, back to the window and lit up. Soon they were flying. If for any reason, Mitchell should happen to stop the truck before they finished, they knew they could just flip the joints off the back and they'd be OK.

It had been an ultra easy day for being in the war zone. It was like they went for a drive in the countryside and met friends at a roadhouse café for lunch. But as he inhaled the sweet pungent weed, the high Kid was achieving did little to purge the demon that had presently taken up residence in his brain.

And its name is NITECAP. Everything has been too fucking easy on this trip to the field. Something has to go wrong. When things are going easy, that's when it happens. Never fails. The VC haven't given up and gone home. Oh, wait a minute… this is their home! They go home every night.

Chapter 63

"Two American platoons, I told you, they're there right now." Captain Mitchell again reiterated to the Kid that yes, there was going to be American security present on the NITECAP.

The Kid was not totally buying it. "Would that be the same 2 platoons that were supposed to be around on the MEDCAP? Don't recall seeing them."

"That's because they're *so good* at what they do! Keeping you safe and you don't even know they're there!" Now Mitchell was smiling like the Chesser Cat.

The Kid was starting to figure it out. The light came on in his head when he recalled the Captain had said one of his two main problems was finding enough American security to cover all of his operations, yet, he never failed to say there were 2 platoons on the job every time the question came up.

"There really aren't two platoons, are there, Sir. That's just your stock answer." The Kid spoke it more as a statement than a question and then quickly added, "I perceive they're more like *Catch Twenty*-'two' *Platoon*," he put air quotes around the *'two'*.

Mitchell took a sip of coffee from the mug in his hand and thoughtfully sat it down on his desk and said, "I loved that book! Didn't you?" and without waiting for an answer continued, "OK, fair enough, Stocker, you can either go with that… *Major Major. ORRRR* you can choose to believe me, that there ARE two platoons of US security setting up to ring that village right now… *orrr there's not.* I guarantee you one or the other is, in fact, the exact situation. Whatever you choose to believe is what it is. I say go with what makes you feel good!"

The Captain was a pretty funny guy, the Kid had to admit, with an extremely wry sense of humor and quite ironic as well. *And that double literary reference to boot! I could choose to believe him and feel comforted, or go fucking nuts, knowing what most likely going on here is going to happen, no matter what I think or he says about any of this shit.* "Well, OK,

Sir, you've got a point. And such an honest face. I'm sure you're my friend *as well as my captain,* so, uh, OK, I'll go with the boots on the ground."

Now Mitchell was nothing but smiles, "All right, Stocker, I knew you'd see the light and get with the program. Now, doesn't that make you feel better about tonight?"

The Kid did not verbalize an answer but in a strange way, it did make him feel better to envision the Captain's assurance as he and Birnbaum prepared to head out for Binh Trung Village.

"Do you think two platoons will be enough?" Birnbaum intoned to the Kid under his breath.

Departure was set for 1530 hours. Since it was only 1000 hours, they had some time to kill. They'd held a weapons cleaning party the night before in Waterhouse's billet. Mark brought over his piece and the three of them sat around and kibitzed while making sure their Mattel specials were in prime working order. Turns out Waterhouse hadn't cleaned his in over a month so he welcomed the reason to break his fast. The Kid's was almost as dirty because all his M-16 had done lately was sit around their room gathering dust.

The pair chose to hit the 9th Division PX before lunch. They bought a bunch of items tribe members had requested they try to find. Mostly it was double AA batteries, Playboy Magazines, razor blades and extraneous grooming items to the tune of two shopping bags full.

When Megenity locked the merchandise up he said, "I'll be here with the key, so when you get back tomorrow, you can grab it on our way to the airfield when you go home. You're booked on the 1400 hours flight."

He referred to Can Tho as 'home'… if we get to go home.

The trio met up with Waterhouse in time to beat the big chow rush and after lunch, Mark went back with Gerry to the unit and the Kid went with Dave to his office.

"I won't be here when you get back tomorrow," Dave lit a fresh cigarette as he sat down at his desk, "got my own field trip scheduled, leaving in the morning to go out to a firebase… for a story."

"Interesting," said the Kid. "Look at us, we're almost under 70 days! Day after tomorrow we'll be in the sixties! Two months from the real world! And we both gotta go to the field and do stories."

Waterhouse ashed his cigarette and pushed his black framed glasses up on his nose, "Beats the fucking shit out of being a grunt!" They both laughed.

Opening a drawer, Dave took out the American Cuties Picture and slapped it on the desk in front of the Kid, "Here, something for you to dream about on bivouac tonight, you and your rifle... out under the stars!"

Picking it up, the Kid sighed. *No doubt about it, I'm getting kind of horney.*"Just what I need!" He lifted it up in front of his eyes. "We should get a shot of their faces and see if we can match the ass to the face when I get back!"

"You always were an idea man, Kid, I'll say that for you," Dave took the picture back and put it away.

"So, uh, what exactly are you going to do at the firebase?" the Kid inquired of the newly mentioned assignment.

"Just take some pictures of GIs doing their duty with their shirts off to send to hometown newspapers across America. And I gotta write a few lines for the paper here, too."

Strained silence.

"Sure glad we didn't get mortared last night," the Kid finally broke it.

"Means for sure, tonight," grimaced Dave.

"And I won't be here."

Around 1330 hours, Dave walked the Kid back to PSYOPS, where preparations for the night's activities were well under way. Around 1400 hours, all the personnel had checked in and gear assembly was near completion.

The mission team consisted of 13 men. They would be split traveling in two vehicles; the ambulance they'd taken to Long Dinh and the PSYOPs truck they'd driven to Go Cong.

Staff Sergeant Calvin D. Baker, would drive the PSYOPS wagon and riding shotgun was the operation's OIC, 1st Lieutenant Mark Mishkin, of the First Battalion, 11th Infantry. Team member Spec. 4 Don Workman, Birnbaum, the Kid, and a pair of 9th Division infantrymen completed the load.

One ground pounder came equipped an M-60 machine gun and 4 cans of ammo. The second soldier had slung his M-16 and was toting a huge bag of gear *that contained God only knew what,* all while humping around with a PRC-25 radio strapped to his back. Not only did the pair not ask for help, but they pointedly engaged in their own private conversation that precluded their truck mates.

In addition to their absorbed exchange, the Kid found it strange; both men wore flak jackets but neither had their steel pot. On the whole team, outside of Mark and the Kid, only Lt. Mishkin had brought the hard hat.

Better to have and not need than to need and not have.

Sergeant Rich Hamilton was driving the ambulance. *Dr. Nu,* his two assistants and a pair of interpreters filled out the operation. They were just finishing loading a generator and projector on to the ambulance for the showing of that night's propaganda films when Captain Mitchell came out survey the preparations.

"Looks good," the captain declared.

The Kid stepped inside the PSYOP billet and finished his prep. Sighing, he filled his canteen, made sure he had insect repellant, plenty of cigarettes and his ammo bandolier. He then sat down at a table and loaded his Pentax with Kodak color slide film for the excursion. *I'm ready! Although I feel more like a man waiting for the jailer to come hang him than a soldier on his way to a battle. Oh yeah.* Once he plopped on the steel pot, he felt more like a soldier and less like a convict.

Looking out the screened door at the men around the trucks, the Kid had the same old thought: *Are there any among us who are not coming back?*

When the clock hit 1500 hours, the party was ready to roll. First there was a necessary stop at the 9th division medical dispensary to pick up some last minute supplies. The troops there were busy unloading crates of stretchers when the ambulance pulled up. The Kid snapped a pic. *Hope none of those have my name on it.*

The NITECAP supplies were set aside and ready to load making it 1530 hours when the two-vehicle convoy pulled out of the Dong Tam compound's front gate. From what the Kid could recall on the map, Binh Trung Village was roughly 5 to 6 miles west and north of Dong Tam.

Their progress was immediately slowed as they came up behind a unit of 6 APCs driving in front of them on the road. *How nice. An escort!* The armored tracs were on their way to set up a night position for some tactical reason, out in the direction the PSYOPs men were headed. As they ate some of their dust, the Kid lifted his Pentax and took a shot of the crew perched atop the tail end Charlie of the armored beast convoy. Thinking of the tale Roberts had told him about his experience with the armored cav getting their asses kicked last June, down by Vinh Long, made the Kid wonder if he'd be better off with them or where he was?

Half way to the Long Dinh hamlet bus stop, the line of tracs and the two PYSOPs trucks took a right off of Highway 10 and headed north on

Highway 4, the main road up to Saigon. Not far after that, the tracs turned left off the highway and proceeded to make their way across a section of dry paddies.

In line with his new positive attitude, the Kid hoped the armored cav would be close enough to later lend a hand, should the need arise. But that feeling faded with the tracs in the rear-view mirror. Wherever it was they were headed, it was away from Binh Trung.

Hey, what me worry? There are two platoons of security waiting for us at the village!

Before long, they arrived at another hamlet that was divided by a canal, easily 40 to 50 meters wide. There was once a bridge here, but because of war, no more. Waiting to transport them across was an improvised ferry made up of 7 elongated, low sided metal boats that were each about 30 feet long. Strapped together and connected by two broad tire ramps, they made a floating platform vehicles could drive on to and then straight off on the other side. Since it was big enough to accommodate a Vietnamese civilian bus, the contraption was capable of transporting both the ambulance and ¾ truck on one trip. Or a whole lot of Hondas, jeeps and bicycles with ducks and chickens.

Once the trucks were on board, the ARVN operators pulled the contraption across the canal with ropes. It was actually more of a portable bridge than it was a ferry but it got the job done and in about five minutes from the time they began loading, they were on the other side of the canal, waiting to unload.

The Kid jumped down from the truck and trotted up on the bank to get a picture of the convoy still on the simple but very functional temporary boat bridge.

Barely another two miles down the road from the canal crossing, above the noise of the truck engine, the Kid detected the air disturbance of rotarblades helicopter and sure enough, his eye was drawn to a Huey dropping down to their front, until it was not more than 30 feet off the deck. Then it veered slightly off to the Kid's left and as it passed, he raised his Pentax and took a shot, not really having time to check his meter or focus. *I hope that one comes out!* From the passenger's side of the cab in front of them, he notices an arm of Lt. Mishkin waving madly.

"Ho!" Mishkin hollered, "that's my buddy, *Warrant Officer Bob,* he said he'd make sure we got here OK! All right *Bobby my pal!"*

"Got here?" Birnbaum hollered down, "got here *where?"*

"Binh Trung!" hollered back Mishkin, "we're here!" he waved his hand and pointed finger forward, "right here!"

What the captain pointed at was a roughly constructed bunker mini fortress that from all outward appearances, looked like it might have been slapped together by Pete Pan and the Lost Boys! *This is what guarded the southern approach to the village?*

The yellow and red stripped South Vietnamese flag flew proudly on a white pole that sprouted from the center of the little fort's driveway. *A pack of neighborhood tough kids could take this with dirt clods!* The tallest watchtower was technically on the third floor, counting that it sat on the roof of the main chamber.

Fifty meters ahead, on the opposite side of the road, a thick growth of palms and other foliage sprouted up among a now visible group of huts that was the roadside presence of Binh Trung Village. At first glance, it appeared surrounded by nothing but wide sweeping rice paddies, but upon closer examination, he could see huts and little clusters of huts spread out all over. One dominate tree line split the pool table flat panorama, running west of Route 4, tailing back into wavering disappearance.

Easing off the road, the NITECAP team found sufficient room to pull the vehicles a few meters away from any potential traffic. They parked up against about half a dozen motor scooters of varied Japanese manufacturers that were strung out along the plaster wall of what was assuredly, the main hamlet structure.

Standing in the back of the truck, the Kid did a quick survey. *And where are those pesky platoons hiding? I don't see them there… or over there or when we came into town? All I see is a bunch of Ruff Puffs running around.* So slowly he turns to the infantrymen who snobbishly have not spoken to any of them on the drive out and says, "So, uh, are you guys with the two platoons that are here… or will be here tonight?"

The two soldiers looked at each other and then back to the Kid and one of them, whose name tag he couldn't read because he was wearing a flak jacket finally spoke to him, "Uh, kind of but not exactly."

Oh a wise guy.

"OK. What does that mean? What do I get first? The 'kind of,' or the 'not exactly'?"

Then the M-60 machine gunner spoke up, "Wait a minute, don't tell me, let me guess," he pointed at the Kid, "Did that *Captain Mitchell* tell you there'd be two platoons of security here tonight?"

"Yes, he did."

"Yeah, he told us you might bring that up at some point," the machine gunner, whose name was also obscured by his flak jacket paused for effect, "what the Captain meant to say was, *'there will be two men, possibly from different platoons, pulling security here tonight'*. And we are it, Jack!" and the pair laughed. *They were in on it.*

"Seriously?" asked suddenly very interested Birnbaum, "you guys are all the security?"

"Fucking A, totally serious. 2 fucking platoons of security for this operation? Never happen GI, but relax, we do these all the time and Charlie don't give a shit!" said the gunner as he stacked his ammo cans on the ground at the end of the truck.

"There a problem here?" Lt. Mishkin spotted the exchange as he climbed down from the cab.

"The specialists here are lamenting the absence of American security, Sir," the gunner casually replied, sharp on the *'sir'*.

"Well, hell, Stocker and Birnbaum," Mishkin looked at their name tags to refresh himself as he spoke their names, "shouldn't be a problem, we got a machine gun, all the Ruff Puffs you could ever ask for, 3 armed PSYOPs guys, Dr. Nu and his boys… *and* the two of you! We're almost a platoon! We'll be OK."

With a sour look on his face, the Kid accepted the situation. *I fucking knew there wouldn't be two platoons of US here tonight! I just knew it!*

"OK, here's the deal," Mishkin fleshed it out, "they got the Alamo guarding the south end of town so we'll set up the M-60 on the north, the Ruff Puffs will take the east and you PSYOPS boys will cover the west and there you go, *instant perimeter.*"

The Kid looked at him suddenly and even through his shades the Lieutenant caught it.

"What?"

"You're not from Texas, are you, Lieutenant," the Kid flatly stated.

"No. Why?"

Because you just said *"Alamo"*, the Kid pointed to the mud hut fort, "and anybody from Texas would know that the Alamo *fell* on March 6. *Today is March 6th.*"

The captain's mouth formed into an "O".

433

"Really?" exclaimed Birnbaum, "how do you remember obscure shit like that?"

"I don't know. Read it a couple of times. I was real bummed as a kid when Davy Crockett died at the Alamo in the Walt Disney movie, so made it a point to read up on it. March the 6th, after a 13-day siege."

In the end, the Kid and Mark exchanged disappointed looks as they accepted the reality for what was. Stowing their weapons on the passenger's seat in the cab of the PSYOPs truck and both went into journalism mode. Mark began seeking subjects with his Nikons and the Kid, with notebook and pen in hand, began confirming the spelling of everybody's names. *Except the infantry stiffs; I'm leaving them nameless. Gunner and radioman, that's who they'll be in the book.*

Dr. Nu and his aids were quickly immersed in their work. The crowd assembling was naturally rural in its composition. Primarily dressed in white tops for the cooling effect, almost all of the would-be patients wore hats of some sort, the traditional conical hat and white pithy looking lids being most in vogue.

Of course, the phalanx of children had assembled and was proving more interested in the Americans than the Vietnamese medical team. The Kid had neglected to bring any candy but he was able, through hand gestures, to get bunches of them to pose for him.

Over near the end of the ambulance, the Kid noticed a little girl standing with her head framed by the very bottom of the Red Cross on its doors and above her was the shadow of a gun barrel. The Kid quickly snapped off the shot. Although the Ruff Puff holding the gun was looking away from her, the shadow of the M-1 carbine barrel looked like it was pointed right at her head. *How illustrative; hey little girl, we're here to help you or kill you... could be either or both, we don't know which yet!*

Then the Kid passed out a few cigarettes and got some more Ruff Puffs to pose for him. One in particular was interested in showing off his M-1 Carbine with the banana clip. He was wearing a jungle hat that had turned up sides ala an American cowboy hat. "Numba one!' he indicated of the carbine, holding it out to show the Kid and proudly shaking it.

The Kid was taken by the classic look of another young pair of Ruff Puffs' black pajamas. He had to have a shot of that, disproving the popular cliché that only the VC wore black PJs. All sorts of Vietnamese, even on our side, wore black pajamas. Yeah! *Wait a minute... are you guys VC? Come on, tell the truth!*

Another picture the Kid snapped off was a close up of the back of *Gunner's* jungle hat, one time when he walked past. It sported a dandy hand drawn peace symbol the size of a baseball with yellow glowing from inside the dark blue circle and lines.

A movement caught the Kid's eye on the ground. *It was a chicken and it crossed the road!* Following it, he at last focused in on the smallest, scrawniest chicken he had ever seen in his life! It looked like it had mange. Moving quickly, because *Chicken Little* was on the run, he managed to get a little ahead of it and snap a shot of it in full stride. Ironically, he noticed, for such a scrawny bird, it had huge drumsticks! *How weird!*

On the opposite side of the road from the hamlet, in the direction the chicken had taken him, the Kid now noticed a man thrashing rice in a bamboo enclosure. Around him lay bundles of rice husks ready for the process. The rice thrasher was set up in a paddy of just completed rice and a few of the adjoining paddies also contained finished rice. Obviously, the hamlet kept a few paddies in production through the dry season and this was their harvest. The man's arms rose and fell in a rhythm, drawing the bundle of husks over his head and slamming it down in the catcher. He paid no attention to the Kid or any of the hamlet's visitors. He sure wasn't taking time off to join the MEDCAP. *Imagine doing that for your whole life.*

Beyond the thrasher, the backdrop of the countryside was far more populated with random clusters of huts than he had first realized but his attention was drawn to the tree line. *Too far away and open for anybody to sneak up on us from that way; the Puffs in the Alamo would see them. Hmmm, all except that one section of tree line over there!*

His eyes had been attracted to a vegetative wall consisting of bushes concealing the bases of the palm trees that rose out of them. It was less than 100 meters back from the highway and was about 50 meters wide but it stretched back in a long line for some distance. *That gives me the creeps! The VC could use that tree line to move right up here!*

Turning back and looking across the road, the Kid observed that the MEDCAP portion of the operation was going smoothly. *Dr. Nu* and his assistants were working through the patients and since they were going to be here all night, there was no rush, unlike accompanied MEDCAPS run during the day when the unit knew it had to move on in an hour or less.

Hearing the blaring warning sound of a vehicular horn, the Kid looked south and saw an approaching bus barreling in their direction. Since it was now getting on toward 1700 hours, it was no surprise that the bus was not slowing down for the hamlet; there was a serious need for it to reach its destination before nightfall. It was jammed full and as it sped by, the Kid noticed a passenger hanging off half of the open back door and a boy riding on the roof waved to him as he lifted the Pentax for a shot of the north bound bucket of bolts. Within the perspective of the bus, it amazed him at how small, narrow and rural the paved road known as High 4 really was in this neck of the paddies.

At the back of the ambulance, he could see Baker, Hamilton and Workman extracting the generator and projector. He crossed over and walked with them as they trucked the equipment into the community building, a plaster structure dating back to the French. It was capable of holding a gathering of a hundred people quite nicely and was one of the main reasons they had selected this particular hamlet for the operation.

The two sergeants, Baker and Hamilton, humped the generator out the far side door and set it down. Running the cord from it back in, they commenced to setting up the projector on a pre-arranged table while Workman returned to the ambulance to bring in the screen and the films. The Kid said, "I'd offer to help but I can see ya'll are a well-oiled machine and I'd just get in the way."

He paced the room's white tile floor. A blue frame border ran around the room a couple feet out from the wall. Its side windows were open air, and they had no screens. The roof was vaulted and thatched, typical of nearly all the other community buildings the Kid had seen doing such work.

Meanwhile, Mishkin and his men were taking advantage of the time of day to fit in their supper as they dined on MREs, using the bed of the PSYOPs truck as their table. They appeared to be in a jovial mood, like the possibility of anything happening tonight was at best remote. Feeling his own hunger pangs, the Kid walked over and selected one of the remaining MREs and joined them. Mark noticed and stopped his incessant photographing to pick out his own MRE.

Between bites, Mishkin discussed the evening's security plan. We were in radio contact with the 9th Division TOC and they knew our exact coordinates. Even though we didn't have two platoons of US infantry for security, ha ha, we had gunships, Spooky and artillery available and any one of those *alone* should be enough to handle any kind of attack that might materialize. We also had a half dozen claymores.

With twilight coming upon the Hamlet, Mishkin, Radioman and Gunner swung into action. They moved the machine gun, ammo, claymores, the Starlite sniper scope and PRC 25 radio 50 meters up the road and began to deploy. The Kid observed one of the men wiring claymores off to the road's right, another setting them up to the left and the third, with dirt flying off an entrenching tool, prepared the M-60 position immediately to the left side of the road.

While this was going on, the MEDCAP portion of the evening concluded and Dr. Nu and the boys commenced cleaning up their equipment and certainly preparing to have some dinner themselves. The PSYOPs boys were in the Community building, threading the first film and preparing the printed handouts.

Conspicuous by their absence was nearly every single Ruff Puff that had been hanging around. The Kid hadn't noticed any mass exodus to the Alamo, or seen them digging in anywhere, but one thing was for certain, *they were all gone! Oh wait a minute, are they inside to watch the movies?*

Seeing the action was moving indoors, the populace, and especially the youngsters, had long ago begun filling the room and claiming the prime spots for watching the films, which as always, was an incredible treat to the locals.

Mark was in his equipment bag, fishing out a flash device while the Kid smoked a KOOL by the side of the truck. "So far, so good," he impinged. But, there were few times in his life he had felt more vulnerable.

"Yeah," Mark agreed as he attached the flash to one of his Nikons, "let's just hope this holds. We knew the easy part was the part with the sun up."

"And so it was."

"I guess all we can do is keep our fingers crossed!" Mark checked how much film he had left on each of his roles. "That was two platoons worth of smoke Mitchell blew up our asses."

"Wasn't even GOOD smoke. But, what did you expect? Those 9th division fucks were in on it. All the way out there were just waiting for us to ask!" the Kid scoffed. "They all think it's pretty fucking funny that we're freaking out."

At a point deemed to be 'dark enough', by Staff Sergeant Baker, he fired off the generator and the projector lit up the room to the *ahhhaas* of the crowd and a few seconds later, the first film began to play; it was the old *baby on the bayonet* number, the oriental operetta where the VC dance with babies affixed on their bayonets while wearing ugly masks. Cue the handsome ARVNs to sweep in to save the day!

"Seen it, know how it ends," mocked the Kid, watching casually through the window.

"Oh well, once more into the breach," said Mark, as he prepared to plunge in to try and find some decent shots.

Taking a deep breath, the Kid pulled out KOOL and lit it up. It was still too early for nighttime field smoking rules, *thank god,* so other than the Surgeon General's report, he didn't feel any danger was involved. Lifting his Pentax, he rubbed the back of his neck where the strap rode. He walked over by the community building and listened to the crescendos and laughter from the crowd as the villans got their comeuppance.

The first movie ended without a hitch. The projector and generator ran fine and the night was proceeding splendidly. With darkness at last upon them, the second movie, about the Thieu Government and what massive amounts of good it did the Vietnamese people, was being threaded by Workman.

As it began, the Kid turned from the community house, walked out into the middle of Highway 4 and gazed up at the emerging stars and tried to compose a lead for what he was going to write about the NITECAP. *Nothing. I got nada.*

That's when the story stopped being his to write. The Kid's eye picked up light movement in his peripheral vision and when it drew his head north for a more direct look, the scene in front of him exploded in an array of streaking tracer bullets, all heading from east to west, all orange as any AK-47 tracer rounds the Kid had ever seen!

Jesus H. Christ! That's gotta be a dozen men shooting and its goddamned close!

In the time it took to have that thought, sounds of the blossoming firefight arrived at the Hamlet with an intensity sufficient to shut the movie right down. Nobody could mistake what that sound was all about. Instantly the people madly scrambled for the exits.

At first the Kid was entranced by the action, but he quickly snapped to and ran for the truck. He and Birnbaum got there about the same time. They roughly placed their cameras into the passenger's side foot well and grabbed their M-16s and ammo bandoliers off the seat. Mark removed the jungle hat he'd switched to and quickly slammed on his steel pot. Each went for a clip to insert into their weapons and so occupied, when they both accomplished their goal, they bumped into each other twice while trying to move out.

Seeing this, Lt. Mishkin, who had minutes earlier just come back from the forward position to see how things were going, hollered at them, *"Tourists!*

Get over there on the left side of the road!" an order they immediately obeyed!

From where they landed, the Kid and Mark had a clear view of the action growing up the road. The defenders of the Binh Trung District Outpost hadn't been all that quick to respond but now, red tracers spewed from west to east in massive volume! The return fire created such a ballistic madness of red and orange tracer crisscrossing and ricocheting off *who knew what,* that it made the Kid ponder why everybody in the fight hadn't already killed each other on both sides!

Radioman, armed with his M-16, accompanied Mishkin and stood by him at the back of the PSYOPs truck. From where they huddled in the ditch, the Kid and Mark could hear the radio traffic being generated from the contact.

"Saber 1, The VC are attacking the Binh Trung Outpost...." OK, *we kind of know that. It's less than a half mile down the road from us!* "Support incoming."

"Saber 1, I copy."

Not 60 seconds later, the air began vibrating from the beat of unseen chopper blades and in an instant, the sky lit up with a bright red tracer stream pouring down from a helicopter gunship. Rounds bounced off the ground and redirected skyward and the VC answered with numerous orange tracers wildly arcing upward toward places where they obviously hoped to get lucky.

From his position, the Kid made an observation; *a half a mile mistake could be made flying in the middle of the night in the middle of a firefight and if that happened, the gunship would have us in the middle of it all!*

In spite of the initial returned fire, the gunship's desired effect was achieved and in less than a minute, the assault stopped. They could hear the gunship maneuvering around for a few minutes, but then it suddenly departed and the radio delivered the reason why.

"Saber 1, the radio coughed up some new news: *"The VC are mortaring Dong Tam... their 10/40 appears to be between you and Dong Tam, Saber 1, do you read?"*

"Saber 1, roger that!"

"We're putting in some arty, so If they run, Saber 1, they'll be coming right at you."

"Saber 1, Roger that I got it," Mishkin spat back. "That'd be why the gunship got out of here!"

Hearing that, the Kid had to think of Dave and all the men in the 9th headed for the bunkers, where they'd be waiting it out; one only had to survive the first shells that set off the alarm to beat the risk. *Out here, there ain't no fucking bunker! The VC mortar team is between us and Dong Tam?*

Dong Tam was about 6 highway miles away but as the crow and mortar shell flew, because of the turn north, it was more like 4 miles. Meaning the VC doing the mortaring tonight were likely just a couple of miles off Binh Trung's east side.

The box is growing tighter. The VC were attacking the outpost less than a half mile to the front, they were mortaring Dong Tam from 2 miles to the east. And when the boys from Ft. Sill opened up 15 seconds later, sending a trio of 155 mm shells whistling straight over their heads to silence the VC mortar squad, the Village of Binh Trung was nearly encased by action!

To make matters worse, the Kid had no idea where Baker, Hamilton and Workman were. Maybe they'd taken up positions on the east side of the village, just in case the Ruff Puffs didn't hear the direction from which the VC mortar teams might flee.

More artillery over their heads! More echoing reports were heard from the east, but action to the front had ceased.

Other than sweating bullets over the volatility of their situation, there was not much the Kid or Birnbaum could do but hunker down in their ditch and hope nothing came at them from out of that close section of tree line paralleling Highway 4.

Suddenly, a shrill human whistle splits the air, coming from the M-60 emplacement and at that signal, Mishkin and Radioman take off forward and as the Lt runs past he hollers down, *"Stocker Birnbaum come with me now!"*

Sucking in their breath at the surprise order, the pair jumps up and follows tight behind Mishkin and Radioman, the antenna bobbing wildly above his head. They quickly cover the short distance to the machine gun position and crouch low behind Gunner, who is working the Starlite sniper scope.

"What you got!" Mishkin demands.

"I count nine armed men coming down the road toward us," Gunner announces, here, take a look!' he passed the Starlite sniper scope to Mishkin.

Kneeling down next to Gunner, Mishkin took the scope and raised it to his eye. "Holy shit! Yes siree! I count 9, too," and turning to Radioman, "hand me the mike."

Depressing the button, he contacted the TOC. "Command, Saber 1, I am looking at an armed party on Highway 4, north of us and south of the Binh Trung Outpost; did the Outpost send out a patrol? Over."

A silence ensued for a few seconds before the answer came back, "Saber 1 that would be a negative, the Binh Trung Outpost does not have a patrol outside of their wire, so those you see would be enemy, and do you copy? Over."

"Command, I copy, out." He took a really deep breath before urgently speaking. "OK, men, we got company. Here's what we're gonna do; everybody step up here and take a look through the scope to get a feel for where they are and what your field of fire is going to be. Once everybody gets a look, I want Stocker and Birnbaum on the left, we'll take the right. Gunner, let loose straight down the middle and you two spray the left side of the road and we'll cover the right, because when we open up, they'll bail for the ditches. We need to take out at least a couple of'em and keep them as far back from us as possible!"

With that, Birnbaum stepped forward and took the scope from his hand and peered through it. "Oh shit! I can't believe how clearly I can see them! Fucking amazing!" He handed it off to the Kid.

Before tonight, the Kid had never even seen a starlight sniper scope, let alone looked through one. The ARVN 14 Regiment hadn't been so equipped. Hefting it and feeling the weight, he raised it up to his right eye and closed his left. It was quite remarkable. It was a single tube, about 3 times the size of a *View Master,* and a lot heavier. The scope concentrated all available light and bounced it off the objects in front of it. There in the distance, appearing as tiny glowing green silhouettes, the Kid sharply saw the squad of soldiers, spread out and walking right up the road, half on either side. *I also count nine.* They held their rifles in front of them in port/ready positions, as they took cautious, deliberate steps. Obviously, they had no night vision gear of their own.

It was not lost on the Kid that never before this second, on any of his previous operations, had he ever seen a live uncaptured VC, active in the field, coming to engage him.

Oh my god! I'm going to have to kill somebody!

Radioman swung the PRC-25 off his back and set it down by Mishkin. Taking the scope from the Kid, he took his own establishing look at the menace headed toward them and proclaimed himself, *"...ready!"*

'All right," Mishkin's tone was tense, "everybody lock and load. Now it is important that we all open up at once and don't tip them off so no

441

one shoots first and lets them drop and cover. Assume your positions and prepare to fire, everybody on full automatic, at my command!"

Chambering a round, the Kid chose a kneeling position to deliver his fire. The night air was quite warm and his palms were sweating, along with most of his body, but as he flipped off his safety and made sure, this time, that it was on full automatic, he felt a chill run up his back. It would be the second time in the war he shot his weapon, the significant difference being this time, *Oh shit! I am going to have to kill somebody!*

"Steady... steady..." Mishkin prepared to give the command to fire.

Suddenly the radio burst to life with a frantically off the charts appeal!

"*Saber 1, Saber 1... HOLD YOUR FIRE,* I repeat, hold your fire, those are friendlies in front of you! Do you copy?

The call had been loud enough that all the men heard it.

Collective GASP! Click click; the safeties went back on.

"Command, Saber 1... I copy, over," Mishkin reported.

The Kid, who from tension was holding his breath in preparation to shoot, just about passed out as all the air escaped his body. The adrenalin rush was massive but the release from the closeness of what they'd almost done... *but didn't...* was nearly overwhelming.

I almost shot our own guys!

"Holy fucking bat shit!" breathed Mark, "we just about shot up 9 of our own guys!"

Whoa! Jesus! Was *THAT* ever close!" Mishkin was now visibly shaken.

Those men on the other end will never know how fucking close that was, the Kid was thinking when he spoke, "So I don't suppose that's one of our phantom platoons..."

"Uh, no. Gotta be Ruff Puffs," Mishkin confirmed with a nervous chuckle, "that's all they got at the Outpost. I keep telling you there aren't any other Americans out here, Stocker."

"At least we wouldn't have been shooting Americans," Gunner added a pertinent afterthought.

"Oh, well, that would have made us all feel better!" the Kid sarcastically replied.

"Probably would have," Radioman promptly shot back, "guess they don't know how lucky they are!"

A split second after those words were spoken, the patrol's luck ran out as the VC opened up on them again from the right. Their response was immediate, relighting the panorama of a full fledged nighttime fire fight right in front of them!

"We should help!" Gunner urgently petitions Mishkin; his trigger finger must have been itching on that 60.

"No! *Fucking no!*" the Lt. instantly commanded, "*Jesus!* We're not in play right now! With the weak as shit perimeter we've got, we don't need to attract any attention! Shit! That would be like inviting them over! Shooting straight down the road when we didn't have a choice is one thing, but I doubt with them spread out and covered, even with that 60, you'd be effective enough from this distance to make it worth taking a chance!"

The Kid liked the way the Lt. was thinking.

It was way beyond watching an episode of *Combat* on a movie screen, the group looked on in awe at the exchanges that pulsed in front of them. Bursts from one side were answered by the other, little lulls were followed by violent, ejaculated opposing streams of rounds by multiple shooters, the volume impressive from the fact that only every fifth round was likely a tracer and it sounded like everybody was using full automatic. It was difficult if not impossible to determine who was gaining the upper hand until the gunship's reappearance was announced by a stream of red glowing death on the origination area of the orange rounds *and they ceased immediately.*

The chopper only stayed for about 10 minutes and once it cleared the area, the quiet of night in the Mekong Delta settled upon them like a cloak. But the possibility of it all starting up again, any second, created pressure without noise.

Then, from the distance, faint traces of reports of new action began to carry to them from other place all around the Dong Tam area. Way off in the distance, to the north of the Outpost, flares were being deployed by somebody looking to expose or discourage attackers… reports from automatic weapons fire drifted in from the west. *I wonder if this is how it sounded when Tet was starting?*

"OK, here's what we need to do," Mishkin issued his commands, "the little fuckers are active tonight so we gotta shore things up the best we can with what we got. "Give me the radio," he indicated to Radioman, "and you stay here with the M-60. Stocker and Birnbaum, you two take the left side of the road back here and cover that one close section of woods, that's the only thing that worries me on the left. I'll go check with the NITECAP crew, see they've got the east and make sure the Ruff Puffs are home at fort *'I don't care what the fuck you call it'!* Then I'll locate with the radio in the community building to call in support and be the reaction force for anybody who might get hit. Everybody got it? OK! Let's go!"

The Kid and Mark returned approximately to the spot they had ended up in when the action first began; across from the community building, in the shallow ditch by the side of Highway 4. They decided to move about 15 meters apart; close enough to whisper talk back and forth, but not right next to each other, so as not to both be taken out with one burst.

The Kid's field of fire was directly in front and to the right in an arc to the highway, keeping in mind, he wouldn't want to shoot in the vicinity of the M-60 position. Mark's field of fire was directly in front and to the left, keeping in mind he did not want to exchange fire with the Alamo. They were at the midpoint of the tree line stand that loomed up at them; the sky was dark but the foliage below forbiddingly darker.

Checking the time on his fluorescent faced Seiko, the Kid saw it was only 2030 hours. Barely an hour and a half had elapsed since the sun went down and they'd started showing the movies. The action had just started about 45 minutes ago now they were looking at being the only 2 men guarding their entire left side until the sun came up... an event that was easily 9 or 10 hours distant. He hadn't slept well for the past two nights and now, they were on guard duty less than half a mile down the road from live action that could come to them at any second.

And there will be no relief! Not much of a hole to hide in, either, and no entrenching tool to make it deeper. Fuck. How did I get into this spot? Not too worried about falling asleep with all the adrenalin running thru my blood right now, that's for damn sure. I can't believe how little security we've got! Please don't attack us please don't attack us!

They hear some rounds being fired from the direction of the Outpost but don't see any tracers. Red tracers answer back; it's still going on over there but between volleys, it is eerily quite. *The Ruff Puffs must have gone back inside.*

Somebody could be sneaking up on us right now! It's so hard to see! I wish we had that scope. Shit a VC could sneak up here and do us both. Fuck. I don't want to die! Jesus, I just turned 21! I wonder what everybody is going to think if I get killed? It will be too much for Flo. Even though we are not engaged any more, me getting killed will kill her. Mom and Dad will be so freaking devastated. Scott will be sad, goes without saying, but at least he won't have to come here if I get it. What will all my 'fans' in Nashville

444

think? Donna Nadeau will be relieved she got off this train. I wonder if WKDA will have a memorial for me? Dave and all the Good Guys will have to talk about it on the air. They won't be able to pretend it didn't happen. Ha! I bet they'll even have to mention it on WMAK! Poor little Pat Bowen will probably take it worse than anybody… because she's so sure if I die I'm going straight to Hell because I don't believe in Jesus. Guess that will make her my fan club president for life! Imagine! Me getting killed where Imbach got killed! What will the neighbors think? Shauna McConnell… I'll never get to tell her how much that VC prisoner looked like her! And all my parents' friends and everybody in the neighborhood will feel so bad for them.

How was I not smart enough to stay out of a situation where I'm laying on my belly in a ditch in the middle of the Mekong fucking Delta, with an M-16 in my hands hoping and praying I don't have to use it? Praying that we can hold this side of a paper-thin perimeter when the reality could be that VC sappers are crawling up here right now to cut our fucking throats!

"Mark!" he loudly whispered, "did you hear that?"

"Hear what?" Mark anxiously whisper replied back.

"Listen!" the Kid breathed the word. Silence.

"No. I don't hear anything," Mark finally responds. They lapse into a more prolonged silence. "Nothing! What do you think you heard?"

"Sounded like bushes rustling!" "They both listen intently again. "Now I'm not hearing it…"

As the night grew longer, the Kid's mind started tripping like he was on LSD. He heard real and imagined sounds, but some were real enough that they caught Mark's attention, too. Pyrotechnics abounded, both distant in the sky and closer on the ground. A position to the west of them popped a flare. *Could be at the firebase. Every half hour it seems like they do something around us… they haven't given the outpost any rest but they haven't touched the Alamo? Wonder why?*

About 2300 hours, Mark got up and retrieved their canteens from the truck.

The Kid couldn't believe how thirsty he was, but after all, he hadn't even thought of taking a drink since the attack started. He took a long drink and then sat, with his left hand on the canteen and the right still wrapped around the pistol grip of his M-16.

And I wonder what all of my Boulder High classmates will think when I'm dead? Especially Larry Ryan; he'll give a good speech at my funeral.

And Wally Schneider, my coach, and the kids from all the speech clubs that I ever debated. And Dalene Beavers. God was she hot! Will anything I ever did matter? Stocker's gone. He was fun while he lasted. Loved to party.

And all the girls I ever dated, made love to, or tried to date and make love to. At least Flo won't have to worry about figuring out if it will work between us. She'll talk herself into believing it would have been great and our kids would have been cute and smart. And Nadeau. It could have been Nadeau. If she'd just slept with me once, I would have stopped looking. But then, what real man could have said no to Debbie Jean Jones?

A flurry of rounds exchanged between the Outpost and their harassers broke the macabre spell of the Kid dwelling on his own possible death and brought him back to the black hole that was his actual reality. After each burst, he'd listen intently into the darkness, an act that if the silence continued too long, developed into the old *'it's quiet... yeah, too quiet'* gambit and sure enough, another burst from one side or the other would scare the *bejezus* out of him! Compound that with a lack of sleep from the two previous nights and it was no surprise that the Kid was hallucinating. The pink elephants were courtesy of Walt Disney's *Dumbo.* It came from the spot in the movie where Dumbo got drunk. That's when the pink and plaid elephants appeared, marching out of the darkness, in a cadenced dance, multiplying and marching, lines of them, from every which direction! *That's how the VC will come pouring out of the tree line! I'm fucked! Check the Seiko; 0100 hours, only 5 more hours to sunrise! God what I wouldn't give to light up a cigarette! Or a joint! Oh shit!* He slapped at a mosquito biting his neck and immediately regretted making such a loud noise!

"Mark" he softly called, trying not to betray any hint of panic.

"What?" came the reply.

"Just checking to see if you're still awake…"

"Oh yeah? Well, Kid, if I had been asleep, all your noise would have woke me."

"Don't talk to me, I'm sleep talking and it's dangerous to wake me!"

"Well shut the fuck up yourself then!" came Mark's retort in mock irritation.

At 0130 hours, Mishkin showed up to check on them. He kind of hacked a cough, like clearing his throat, knowing that nobody likes to be sneaked up on in a war zone in the middle of the night.

"How you guys doin'?" he breathed low, like he didn't want any VC just a few yards away to hear.

"OK, Sir," they both replied, very much in muffled unison.

"Another four and a half hours and we'll have it licked!" he chuckled, "hang in there, gentlemen! Everybody's doing great!" and he was off to bolster the others.

The air had cooled a little but it was still far hotter than anything the Kid considered comfortable. He pushed his glasses up on the bridge of his nose, for the 50th time that night. The dry season was actually making the mosquito problem the least of his worries. *If I could just time travel to sunrise!*

When the night glow Seiko Watch hands hit 0300 hours, the Kid had to take a wicked piss. Releasing the death grip he'd kept on his M-16, he stood, walked 5 paces to his right, unzipped his pants and let it drain. *If I was back in Nashville, I'd be in the middle of my show right now.* No sooner had he finished when he heard Mark doing the very same thing. At least I hope it's *Mark.*

As the night bore on, he couldn't help but relive the near shooting of their own men over and over again, their pale green Starlite sniper scope images dancing in his head. *My God that would have been fucking horrible to finally have to shoot somebody and it turns out to be our own men! They're just Vietnamese, the guy says. They're just humans, I sezs. Hmmm, since they're on our side, I've still never seen a live running free VC in the field that I could take a shot at although I know a bunch of them have taken shots at me. Please not tonight. Ommmm no shooting here tonight!*

Sporadic action continued the entire night. The tension of expecting the VC to come rushing out of the tree line never abated. But finally, the horizon began to lighten ever so slightly. Through his dirty glasses, the Kid watched the details of individual plants become discernable, in effect, melting away the forbidding black wall that had confronted them all night long.

Although they had not caught his attention the afternoon before, the Kid now noticed a collection of 3 or 4 huts not far from the trees. They were spaced back about 300 meters off to the left of Highway 4, in the open, not more than 100 meters out from where the tree line curved south. The reason he hadn't noticed them prior was that their drab brown color blended them almost seamlessly into the dry season paddies. But now, his eyes were attracted to a flash of color fluttering above their rooflines.

Holy mother of fucking pearl… that's a Viet Cong flag!

During the night, the VC had advanced to within 300 meters of their position and left their red and blue gold starred flag tied to a bamboo pole!

And due to a rather cooperative breeze, it now whipped and snapped at them in full display!

"Mark!" the Kid called and pointed with his M-16, "Take a look at that! A fucking VC flag! That's how close they came last night! Oh my god I don't believe it!" the Kid stammered.

Mark stiffly rose to his feet and slowly walked over to the Kid stood and peered out to see the VC colors wavering in the morning breeze. It was barely a little more than 3 football fields length from where they had lain all night, waiting for an attack that thankfully never came.

Hearing some movement, the Kid turned to see Mishkin emerging from the Community Center. "Hey! Sir! Come check this out!" he motioned for the lieutenant to join them.

"Wow!" Mishkin marveled, "I think they are letting us know they could have come in here last night if they wanted to."

"I think you're right," said Sgt Barker, who along with Workman and Hamilton accompanied the lieutenant.

Soon, a number of the Ruff Puffs joined the cluster of men to stare at the colors of the enemy and letting out a few low *choi duc oi's!*

"Let's go out and take it down!" Mishkin showed his command chops and the Ruff Puffs were immediately excited to do exactly that. The Kid stowed his M-16 and got his camera. If he hadn't needed the gun last night in the dark, he wouldn't need it now.

In the company of a half dozen well armed Ruff Puffs, the Kid, Mark and Mishkin walked at a deliberate pace to the huts. No people came out to greet them. That could mean the VC were lying in ambush, or they snuck in so quiet that the people were still asleep, or the VC did them in and their bodies were lying all bloody inside. Or, of course, the hut owners were VC and decided not to be home when the Thieu faction came to investigate the flag.

The Ruff Puffs took the initiative to move ahead and quickly checked the huts. As the American arrived, they were already out and standing in the center of the small compound, looking up the fresh cut 9 foot bamboo pole to which the NLF flag was tied. The Kid stepped up and stood below it. Lifting his Pentax to frame it and focus, he was most appreciative of how the wind did show it flying. *Much better than a limp rag!*

Almost the second he snapped the picture, one of the Ruff Puffs pulled the pole from the ground and dipped it to another who untied the flag. Holding one corner of the flag, he offered the other to Birnbaum and through sign language, encouraged him to help hold it up while the Kid snapped their picture. Then the Ruff Puff took the flag and handed it to the Kid.

"Nice souvenir!" Mark grinned.

"Of a night never to be forgotten."

Chapter 64

It was the classic Army *hurry up and wait.* They had finally made it in from the field following the NITECAP at 1230 hours. Their flight was due to depart for Can Tho at 1400 hours so Captain Mitchell hurried them through lunch and packing to insure Megenity could have them out to the Dong Tam strip not later than 1345 hours.

Checking his watch and seeing they'd arrived in plenty of time, Megenity said adios and left. Their arrival was in far more plenty of time because, it turned out, by 1500 hours, and the Caribou was still AWOL.

The Kid and Mark at first didn't think much about it, since they were only going to have a 15-minute wait, but Dong Tam Field was nothing like Can Tho Field. The main thing was the lack of an actual terminal. There was a tower, but it was isolated back behind the massive metal bunker, a long way off from where they waited and obviously a tough walk to get any information and what if the plane should come while one was halfway there or back? There were three other vehicles waiting, on the other side of the field, to drop off or pick up and for which flight was anybody's guess.

The spot where Megenity had left them was next to a strange looking ¾ ton truck that had no doors. At first glance, it was difficult to tell if it was abandoned or just a beater left there in anticipation of hauling some eventual cargo. It was not in good repair from a couple of recent incidents. The windshield was all shot up but strangely, the 3 bullet impacts had not penetrated or totally wrecked it. That and the fact it had no doors made it a puzzle but Mark didn't care. He hiked himself up into the driver's seat and promptly dozed off, his arms wrapped around the steering wheel serving as his pillow.

Standing in front of the truck, the Kid spied a picture that was too good to pass up. Getting as close as he could to the front of the windshield, he took a shot of Mark through the bullet riddled glass, *asleep at the wheel. Classic! I wish I could get some sleep. Shit. It's been 3 nights since I got any sleep. Let's see, the night of the mortar attack I didn't sleep, the night before the NITECAP I didn't sleep. Last night I for sure didn't fucking sleep, so I've been pretty much up for the past 72 hours! It's catching up with me. OOO I think I'm trancing!*

At last, the tell tale sound of an approaching aircraft snapped him out of it. From the whine, he easily picks out the Caribou on its elevator style approach to the Dong Tam Field.

"Mark!" the Kid rousted his photog, "our ride's here!"

"Bout fucking time!" he unpacked himself from the truck and began to collect his gear.

They watched the plane taxi in front of them and both had to laugh when they saw its name: "DAY TRIPPER". The Kid fired off a shot, focusing sharp on the name. *Love it!*

Day Tripper was the plane the other trucks were waiting for, but even with the 6 men who were walking over to load, the *Tripper* would be virtually empty. The loadmaster was out on the corrugated metal motioning for everybody to hurry the fuck up! Small wonder; they were an hour late.

It took no time at all for the loadmaster to square away the small manifest and their gear, working with the urgency of a game show contestant. From where they'd ended up sitting, the Kid and Birnbaum were far forward, just below the cockpit. Looking up, the Kid watched the pilot in the right seat run through his check list. *Good picture of Captain Day Tripper,* the Kid said to himself as he framed and shot it.

Taxi and takeoff happened in a flash, and they were airborne, climbing out.

Once in the air, the Kid looked out his window. From his forward position, he was right below the engine on the left wing and what caught his eye was a loose piece of metal, hanging off of it! *Let me get a picture of that!* After he took the shot, he motioned for Mark to take a look and how in need of repair their craft needed. He just shrugged his shoulders and leaned back in his seat, crossed his arms over his chest and closed his eyes.

Watching Mark conk out only made the Kid think one thing: *That looks like a great idea!* Loosening his seat beat the slightest bit to accommodate stretching out like Mark, he leaned back and closed his eyes.

It was like the album cover of Sergeant Pepper's Lonely Heart Band exploded in his head. The Kid couldn't actually tell if he was asleep and dreaming or awake and hallucinating. Faces of people he knew and famous people he'd never met gyrated, all swirling around and trying to tell him something but amid the noise of them all talking at once, he couldn't understand what any of them were saying. *It's the engines. No matter how tired I am, I won't be able to sleep with them wailing 10 feet away. And if I did, I'd just have to wake up in 20 minutes and I'd be worse off than I am now. If I can just relax a little. Yeah, that's it. We almost shot our own men, but we didn't do it! Thank fucking God I don't have to carry that baggage around with me for the rest of my life! Hey Buffalo Bill, who did ya kill? No thanks. All those people are flying in to see me? On jet planes? Flo will be here? And my parents? And every single one of the faces I see? I wonder if this is what the group Small Faces is all about? Why would everybody want to see me? Am I dead? Is what's left of me just what's left in all their heads? And when it's gone, I'm gone? When and where did they get me? Ah yes, it had to be when I fucked up the jump and ended up in the canal. I can see someone jumping over me... or is that me falling?* The Kid startles himself awake by throwing out his arms to catch himself in the fall. *"Whoa!"*

"What the fuck was that!" Birnbaum hollers over the engine noise, himself startled awake by the Kid being audibly startled.

"Ah, Jeez, the old *I'm falling* dream. Thought I was falling into a ditch!" The Kid tries to literally shake it off.

Mark falls immediately back to sleep.

The Kid closes his eyes but again, he can't find true sleep. *Nothing makes a difference except if you live or die. Or does it? Imbach was alive in my world until weeks later when I found out he was dead. I wonder if people can be kept alive by being alive in somebody's memory. I could be alive in lots of people's memories even though I'm dead. Wait a minute, is that what all those faces are? People trying to keep me alive? Or people I'm trying to keep alive? If I was dead, I couldn't keep anybody alive. Let me see that ditch thing again. I run... I jump... but I don't land...And again. Did I get shot? And again, I don't make it... and I can't breathe! My chest hurts! Did I get shot in the chest? Oh no! I hit my chest on the bank! That's what it was. What a relief. I'm not dead. It's a good thing I'm alive because all of those people are coming to see me. They're flying on jets, so they'll have to go to Saigon first. Maybe I should go meet them all there? Oh, yeah, they aren't coming unless I really am dead! Who do I want to talk to first? Scott, maybe, since he won't have to come. But he's coming to see me! How can he come and not come? Or maybe Flo! I can hardly wait to see her. When we see each other, we'll be engaged again. Unless I'm dead. But we won't be able to be together, unless I got stationed in San Diego and what are the chances of that? Wait a minute, if she's coming, that means I'm dead. Well, you never hear the one that get's you and I sure as fuck didn't hear it. Oh, shit! I remember hearing rounds hit in the water! So when I fall, I'm not dead! I can't breath! There goes that guy jumping over me again! Who IS that guy? Sure as hell isn't Captain Robinson; he ain't jumping over anything.*

But there he was in the Kid's brain, vivid as life, *on the stretcher with his poncho blown off.* The appearance of the captain from Cang Long didn't come as a surprise. The Kid had recently found the half soldier creeping more frequently into his thoughts, predominately in the waking state. Sleep was where he'd go to try and escape it but since today, he couldn't figure out if he was awake or asleep, there was no escaping it.

And here comes Wally, the Beaver and the Girl Next door. Who's more deserving to come to this party? I can't see their legs either, kneeling in the grass like that, hands bound with elbows hooked around poles. I wonder if they shot them in the front or the back?

The Caribou's wheels spinning to life rolling on corrugated metal woke the Kid up. *If, indeed, he had been asleep.* But, when he opened his eyes, it did feel like he was waking up. Mark slept through the landing. The loadmaster kicked his foot to roust him.

When they enter the terminal, the clock on the wall says 1630 hours. No ride is waiting for them so Brinbaum uses the phone and upon his return, said Gelbach was coming to get them in about 20 minutes. 40 minutes later Gelbach shows up.

"Sorry for the delay, guys, they had me going in 3 different directions," Thomas sprang from the seat to assist them, with their gear and their bags of loot from the big 9th Division PX. "You want to drop this stuff off at New Villa and go on to Eakin for Chow? Everybody dede mau'd cause it's Friday, HQ was deserted when I left. The only people there are Sergeant Valenti on CQ and Lt. Culp as the OD."

"Just take us to the New Villa and leave us!" exclaimed the Kid, "fuck chow, the only thing I want to eat right now is my pillow. I gotta get some sleep!"

"Well, I'm afraid I can't do that, when you were late, before he left, Captain Smith made a point of telling me to make sure you two signed back into the unit nice and proper like, in the Day Log, since you been gone most of the week, and he doesn't want to cut you *any* slack, so that's going to happen before anybody passes *'go'*, or goes to chow, the Scientific or anywhere else."

"OK," rationalized Mark, "take us to HQ, then take us to New Villa, I think that's the fastest way we can pass out and not have to wake up until Sunday."

Bouncing along in the Jeep, the Kid lets Birnbaum ride shotgun and he keels over on the gear in the back seat. There had never been a time or place on his Vietnam tour where he felt as worn down, depleted, spent, sapped, mentally pulverized and hung out to dry as he did right here and now.

"Stocker," Gelbach was shaking his arm, "we're here, dude, get up there, sign the book and I'll drive you to the Villa!"

The Kid dragged his ass into the stairwell, up the stairs, into Battalion HQ and over at the clerk's desk, he could see a figure waiting for him in front of a large book. The figure was smiling, friendly and familiar, even saying something to him that the Kid did not understand. He knew Mike Valenti, but he hadn't seen him in a while because he was company B and out in the field. But as the Kid stepped in front of the desk and Mike slowly opened the Day Log to the appropriate page and turned it around for the Kid and held out the pen for him to sign in. *Then he morphed into St. Peter at the Pearly Gates!* Kid could now only assume he was being asked to sign off on the Book of Life, the record of his life now that it was over and complete. When he looked down at the pages of the book, with their rows of names recorded, the comings and goings of soldiers, he was sure he was right!

The Kid balked, took a step back and gasped at the perceived reality of it all.

"Stocker, you fucking drama queen," Valenti exclaimed, what the fuck? Just sign the book!" he laughed, amused and sure the Kid was clowning around.

Shocked at the thought of facing the end, the Kid looked around for a way out. Then he spied Lt. William Culp, the 10th Battalion's Printing officer who happened to be the Officer of the Day, the only officer on duty when the unit was in repose. Culp was appearing to be amused as well, thinking it was just some more of the Kid's endless shtick until the Kid took a couple of steps toward him.

"Lt. Culp! Sir! I need to talk to you, Sir, right now, *in private!*"

"What, Stocker? You can tell me here."

"No Sir, I can't," the Kid gestured at Valenti, "we need to talk in private, please, it's important."

"Well, OK, I suppose we could go into the colonel's office here, since nobody's here."

They opened the door and entered Colonel Willie O's empty office. Closing the door behind the Kid, Culp walked across the room and turning, leaned back against the colonel's desk and crossed his arms and said, "OK, Stocker, what is it?"

For a moment, the Kid stared at the blond and crew cut spectacle wearing lieutenant from Atlanta. He was immediately relieved, knowing out of all the officers in the unit, Culp was most sympathetic to the men of the tribe. As printing officer, he had direct daily contact with the majority of the pot smokers in the unit and frequently joked about it.

"Uh Sir, I'm not dead, am I?"

"Say what?" Culp's head reactively snapped to one side as he fielded the question with a query back to insure he had heard it right.

"I'm not dead, Sir, tell me that's not like the Book of Life out there and I'm signing out. Am I?"

Culp smiled, looked at the floor and sympathetically back to the Kid. It looked like he was trying to figure out if the Kid was playing him or if he was really freaking out over *God knew exactly what?*

"Uh, No. Your are certainly not dead, Stocker, although there are a few officers here who might think that was not such a bad solution… you're very much alive, I assure you. Sgt. Valenti is not CQ at the pearly gates today." He smirked at the whole preposterous situation. "Uh. What the fuck happened out there, anyway?"

"Long story short bottom line, Mark and I have been up for almost 48 hours and didn't sleep well before that for two nights because of mortars and stuff, and last night, we almost friendly fire shot a bunch of our own men! Long story shortened to the bottom line; I gotta hit the rack, Sir, especially since I'm not dead."

"All right, then, let's go sign the book," Culp pushed off the desk and went to the door and held it open, waiting for the Kid to exit the office and closed it behind them. As they walked over to Valenti's desk, Culp intoned low from behind, "Don't worry, Stocker, while you were away, things have cooled down. You're not walking into a hornet's nest."

A wave of relief poured over him. Valenti smiled back as the Kid signed the book, right below Mark, who had done his while they were in the Colonel's office.

"Ready?" Glebach asked as the Kid laid down the pen.

"More than." the Kid glanced at his Seiko; it was 1800 hours. *Talk about a fucked up internal clock! I think mine is going to blow a mainspring right before it melts like a Salvador Dali.*

455

The Kid never remembered the jeep ride back to the New Villa. He also never remembered going inside, stowing his gear, undressing or going to bed. Nor did he ever recall any dreams from the 16 continuous hours he was asleep.

Chapter 65

They were four deep on the rail. Every single man in the unit who was a member of the Tribe, or accepted by the Tribe, was there that night. On a normal evening, after chow and showers, there might have been between 5 & 10 men smoking at any one time; *tonight there were more than 40! This is not to mention the comings and goings of troops, which put the pre movie smoker total easily into the fifties. It was shoulder to shoulder, hard to move around and the crowd was Mardi gras festive.*

The occasion was created by the movie HELP! And what a glorious night it was. After waiting for almost two weeks from the time they heard they were going to get it, it was finally here! The Beatles! It was the movie everybody actually wanted to hear every bit as much as see. Since members of the Tribe *were tres familiar with pot's ability to enhance music, you can bet your ass there was a whole lot of "enhancin'" going on. If somebody in any major city in America saw this much smoke rolling off the balcony of a high rise, they'd call the fucking fire department! That's what I'll say in the book.*

The start time for the movie was set for 2000 hours but the party had begun the second everybody got back to the New Villa and had only since gained momentum. Standing on the rail, straight out from his window, the Kid was virtually in the middle of it. Tall John and Ken were on his right. Boyett, along with the rest of the band; Richie, Benny, George and Don were hugging the rail to his left, with JC Compton, Wimbish and Ramjet standing right behind him. Delirious with anticipation, each of them had their own joint and they were being smoked like victory cigars.

There were pipes, bongs, huge spliffs made out of shoebox tissue paper and filter tip joints galore on fire from one end of the Embassy to the other! The smoke cloud being generated was a near solid gray curtain, rising on the dawn of a new age. You could feel the confidence of the Tribe that this thing was so big on so many levels, that there wasn't anybody going to fuck with it.

That night was a *'pounder'. That is to say, without a doubt, the Tribe smoked a pound of weed. In all likelihood, that much was smoked before the movie. But, when it was all said and done, it had to be a lot closer to two pounds that went up in smoke off the embassy balcony that evening. But, it wasn't 'just' the volume that made it special. It was ultra top shelf, a variety collected on numerous forays into the populace by many GIs, seeking quality flower tops. Vietnamese green, Cambodian black and Thai blond were all glowing with red hot embers. The cache was the marijuana equal of many a fine wine cellar, one that in 1969, would have been impossible to assemble in the United States. Just like that lieutenant from New York said, if you rolled it up and sold pinners in Time Square, it was a million-dollar smoke out!*

March 14th was a Friday night, meaning there was limited duty the next day so everybody's plan was to party their fucking asses off beyond infinity. Those of the Tribe who had gotten guard duty managed to swap times with a bunch of the hard swilling country western fans, who distained the Beatles, so that in two showings, everybody who wanted to see it could; some before guard duty, some right after.

And some of us will get to see it twice!

How perplexing the whole situation must have been to the 20 or so Lifers and Alkies who gathered to peer down from the Roof Club rail, in sheer wonder, at the Tribe having the time of their lives not 6 feet below them! Was it truly possible that such a massive and flagrant violation of Army regulations, *by a majority of the unit…* could take place so openly and there was nothing anybody could do about it? Didn't the captain call the pot smokers out in a company formation, just 3 weeks ago, saying he was going to put an end to it… *and this is what happens?*

Apparently.

If there had been any officers there that night, it would have been interesting to see if the smoke out would have materialized on the scale that it did. But the fact that no officers had come over to see the movie, or even dared to seek an invitation, was taken by all as a sign that Willie O. had given teeth to their deal for peaceful co-existence, *so long as the smokers excelled at their jobs.* It was like the Tribe was enjoying what could only be described as *defacto decriminalization* of pot within the unit.

Finally RV Smith hollered down, "*Why is it* you guys smoke that fucking shit anyway?"

The Kid quickly responded, "Stand right there for another five minutes, RV, and you'll find out!"

The grand realization that they were all being engulfed by the pungent cloud of weed smoke came to the Lifers as a group, and the sudden jerk with which the entire gang simultaneously disappeared, made the Tribe roar with laugher so loud and hard, it's a wonder a couple of them didn't fall in the swamp!

Between the Lifers above and the Tribe below, If the VC had shot an RPG round into that side of the New Villa right before that instant, they would have taken out over half of the 10th PSYOP Battalion!

That thought crossed the Kid's mind as he watched the Vietnamese who lived in the neighborhoods below gather to look up and observe them. They had to be wondering *what the occasion was.* Certainly March 14th, did not come up as a holiday on anybody's calendar, foreign or domestic.

The Vietnamese didn't speak Beatles, they only spoke "House of the Rising Sun."

"This is going to be so bitchin'"" exclaimed Benny Vargas, "My God! HELP! I've already seen it four times and I can't wait to see it again! *'Help me Help meeeeee oooah!'* he vocalized the end of the title song.

In addition to the smoke, the Tribe was not being shy that night about the consumption of alcohol, so when the time came for them to stream off the balcony and surge up to the Roof Club, they were a loose and borderline surly lot.

The Lifers knew how the Tribe was feeling about this movie and discretion had prevailed. They left the front 4 rows of chairs all empty and the Tribe acknowledged them for it as they settled in, with their drinks and ash trays. Then the lights were killed and amid a caterwaul of hooting and howling, the film began to roll.

"HELP I need somebody, HELP not just anybody, HELP you know I need somebody NOWWWWWWW..."

And they were off! The screen lit up and the title song rolled forth out of the projector system speakers: *"When I was young, much younger than today, I never needed anybody's help in any way. But now these days I'm older and I'm not so self-assured, I need your help in any way... Help me if you can I'm feeling down... and I do appreciate you being round."* The Kid knew the lyrics to almost every Beatles song by heart.

As the plot opens and the bad guys are after Ringo's ring and finger, the flight into escapism was launched. The Kid had landed in a butterfly chair and he just leaned back and let the music wash over him. As the song came forth, he reflected his life on them, much like a person might do with Tarot cards being laid down for a reading. *'The Night Before' drove him to recalling how it was with Flo before he left, "We said our good byes the night before... Love was in your eyes, the night before... last night is the night I will remember you by...when I think of things you said, it make me want to cry... Treat me like you did the night before"....* 'You've Got to Hide Your Love Away', was another Flo song, "*...here I stand head in hand, turn my face to the wall, if she's gone I can't go on, feeling 2 feet small".* When they sang, *'I Need You,'* it was the same thing. Flo. But, when they got to *'Another Girl,'* he suddenly had his though process derailed to Donna Nadeau... "*For I have got another girl, another girl who will love me till the end...through thick and thin she will always be my friend..."*

'You're Going to Lose That Girl,' was a quandary. He had given up Donna for Flo and now had lost Flo but Donna was gone and if he tried to win her back she likely wouldn't give him 10 seconds worth of time again in her life. Truly, he had lost that girl *and that girl.*

But when they finally got to *'I've Just Seen a Face'*, the Kid was transported back to the theatre that night in Nashville, at the premier of Leroy Van Dyke's movie, *'The Auctioneer'* and Flo's face, that he just saw so briefly, when the exit crowds crushed them together, him on one side of the velvet rope, her on the other. She was a living picture of perfection in a yellow dress that hugged her form, in the mold that always made him melt; that dark haired Natalie Wood quality face to die for and the words leaped from his mouth in the scant second that he stood in front of her, said more as a statement than a question... *'I'll see you later'.* "*I've just seen a face I can't forget the time or place where we just met she's just the girl for me and I want all the world to see we met... ooo ooo ooo we met... falling yes I am falling, Yes I am falling in love with her..."* The Kid didn't normally cry at movies, but he was considering it now.

Tonight the geckos running all over the screen did not distract. The cat calls from the Lifers, at the points of the show they thought demanded ridicule, did not distract. The heat, bugs and sweat did not distract and when the Boys were cavorting in the Alps and the long distance swimmer emerges out of the ice hole and asks direction to the White Cliffs of Dover and the Boys point, all the Kid wanted on earth was to jump into that water and swim away!

When the movie finally came to an end, the Lifers got up to get more drinks and retire while the entire Tribe euphorically paraded back downstairs to the Embassy and fired up all over again. The energy was undiminished. And once the first wave of guards who were just relieved from duty got their buzzes on, the projector was cranked up and the whole show performed over again.

460

About a dozen of the hard core were going for a triple dip but the Kid, like the majority, was toasted way beyond the darkest setting to crispy critter and joined the wave of attrition opting for bed!

He dropped off totally satisfied, the lyrics of 'I've Just Seen a Face,' echoing in his head, I can't forget the time or place, but I'll dream of her tonight...

Chapter 66

The very next week, the Lifers got their movie equivalent of *HELP!* Riding to their rescue was a Hollywood hero of the First magnitude, especially in the macho war making department. It was none other than John Wayne in *"The Green Berets."*

A very hot movie back in the States, *The Green Berets* had come out after most of the soldiers present arrived in Asia. And now, to actually see the Green Berets while in Vietnam was going to be the equivalent of holy communion for those who worship at the alter of the Duke!

Patterned after how the Tribe had gone all out to make the Beatles movie an occasion, the Lifer Alkies pulled out all the stops for the Duke. Deals were made to change guard duty times with all who requested. The whole process was so civil that the Lifers couldn't believe the Tribe members weren't holding them up for more ransom in the swaps. But the truth was, the Tribe already had what it wanted most; *peaceful co-existence.* It was easy to show gratitude in the appropriate place.

If it hadn't been a Wednesday, they'd have started drinking at noon. As it was, they all made up for lost time as soon as they were back from Chow. Observing this behavior, the Tribe noticed the time for the movie was fast approaching and they were too sauced to set up the chairs.

Sensing the moment, Tearman, Barry Fisher, Terry Stage, Little, Ramjet, Willert and the Kid began arranging the furniture, much as the Lifers had done while they were all getting stoned for HELP! A few of them noticed what the Tribesmen were doing and there was a smattering of applause and low whistles of appreciation. After all, we were only in different sub-cultures, not different armies and it behooved the Tribe to find a way to get along.

In the few minutes remaining before the film, while everybody was going for a fresh drink and hitting the can and selecting their seats, a dozen or more officers arrived, "Don't anybody holler tin hut, now," Lt. Harry Regan smirked as he *emerged from the stairwell by the bar and as quickly added a* "at ease!"

The group contained a number of Company B officers, who had found a way to get in from the field to see it. Among them was Lt. Sauer, from Go Cong.

"Oh, hey, Lt. Sauer," the Kid happens to be standing nearby when he came u[p the stairs, "I see you found a way to make it in for John Wayne! Let me buy you a beer!"

"Stocker! How the hell are you?" he extended his right to shake the Kid's hand, "Thanks, I'll take you up on that!"

The Kid obtained the necessary beers and handed one to Sauer. "Too bad that Stansel & Simko could come in for *HELP!*"

"Yeah, RHIP, *Rank has its privileges*, you know," he smiled.

"So did you find out where you're going next after Go Cong?"

"Not yet, the colonel is still doing some planning and didn't have my assignment totally fleshed out as of today. But I don't care, I could stand a couple of days R&R in Saigon, but it's still 3 or 4 weeks off."

"How ironic you should be here, Sir," the Kid's comment kind of caught the Lt. off guard, "I was thinking about Go Cong the other day, like today, I mean."

"Oh, yeah?"

"Well, Sir," the Kid indicated the Lt. should step over out of the traffic pattern so they could talk, "Since the day we had lunch with you all out there, I've had this thought stuck in my head, about what you said, that PSOYPS was working itself out of a job in Go Cong… and this one line has sort of been writing itself in the back of my head, over and over sort of a *'news flash: PSYOPS figures fastest way out of Vietnam… replace every American with a Vietnamese and we all go home!'*"

"Oh? Really? Wow, funny YOU should mention it. I did think about that very thing after you guys left. *What a logical a thing to do.* That was my thought and then I forgot about it. And now you say we are a one liner, huh?"

"Well, Sir, it'll take at least a couple of paragraphs to set the one line up."

"This is pretty funny. We rate a couple paragraphs? I can't wait to tell the guys!" Sauer gestured with a beer can salute that the conversation was at an end and he needed to move on because the good seats were going fast. *But he was shaking his head like the old 'I don't believe it.'*

463

Once the movie gets rolling, it rapidly becomes apparent that the plot of the whole film is that the reporter, played by David Jansen, the Fugitve, is skeptical about the rational for war behind the country's involvement in Vietnam and since he's never been to Vietnam, he's going to go and have a catharsis and end up being for it.

The theme song, *"The ballad of the Green Beret,"* by Staff Sergeant Barry Sadler, had been popular in February of 1966 when the Kid had become a DJ on KOLR, in Sterling, Colorado. He must have played it over the air at least a hundred times. *"Fighting soldiers from the sky..."* They didn't let Barry sing it for the movie, however.

Needless to say, as nice as the Tribe was to let the Lifers have the good seats and help them out with guard duty swaps, they were relentless with their kibitzing of the movie. And there was so much ammunition! I mean, George Takai, *Mr Sulu from Star Trek,* was the head ARVN! But, both sub-cultures got to share one big laugh, not that it was a laugh in any movie theater on Earth, other than this one. It was when the old Montagnard tribesman described the leaflets falling down from the sky, the whole unit howled, high fived, stomped their feet and laughed their asses off! *PSYOPS has been recognized by Hollywood!*

When the movie ended and the Lifers were milling about, trying to figure out if they were gong to show the stupid thing a second time, B Company First Sergeant John T. Johnson, who was perched on a stool, motioned for the Kid to come speak to him.

"Yes, Sergeant, What is it?" the Kid was surprised he had anything to say to him, since he wasn't in B Company any more.

"We've got a convoy going out tomorrow, up to Vinh Long, and I need another volunteer to ride shotgun, and occurs to me what I need is a hand who has some combat experience, do you want to go?"

"No."

"No?" Johnson appeared to be a little perplexed, like it was a simple request and no, was not the answer he expected. "Why not? Are you chicken?"

The Kid could hardily believe he'd heard the word. "Chicken? *Chicken?* You think you can get me to go on a convoy by *calling me chicken?* That's a laugh! Two things, Sarge; first, your opening statement to get me to go cited my combat experience so obviously, we *all* know you know I'm not chicken. Second, for the *chicken* gambit to work, It would be necessary for me to actually care and I don't give a rat's ass if you think I'm chicken or not. Hey, Sarge, why don't YOU go…?" the Kid turned the tables and a surprised Sgt. Johnson hesitated the slightest bit, allowing the Kid to jump right in with a smile, *"what's the matter, Chicken?"*

Chapter 67

It's quiet. Yeah, too quiet, the Kid whispered, performing a mock radio show to an audience of himself, since nobody else was present in the sand bag lined guard station on top of the Villa Cruz. It was the Kid's preferred post when pulling New Villa guard duty, as he had now for some time. *Why do you think that is, Kid? Well, Kid, it gets like that when they turn off the printing presses and the generators! Kid, you're not laughing... Don't you get it? Of course I get It, Kid; they've only been off for 15 seconds! That strange feeling you are experiencing right now is your ass no longer vibrating!*

What he also felt was just a touch of breeze and it was surly welcome in the humid darkness that engulfed everything. There was no such thing as a cool night in Vietnam but any breeze was appreciated. Plus, it might help him achieve his immediate goal. The only definitions that were not silhouettes, came from some light emanating out of the Villa Cruz's front gate and two lights, one at either end of the bridge that crossed the canal, a long block to his right, vibrating on the ripples of the moving water, defining its banks.

His M-16 was propped up against the sandbags on his right side and his flak jacket was resting to his left with his steel pot sitting on top of it. The brown sandbags were two rows deep and made a platform the guard could lean on and look up and down the street or straight down on the front gate of the Battalion's printing plant and officer's billet. The bags would have stopped a bullet but not an RPG. Leaning forward while sitting on the edge of the guard chair, he used it as a work table to fashion a paper airplane.

It all started so innocently, from one sheet of paper left for some reason in the guard post, one paper airplane made and thrown out from the guard post, floating on the breeze, heading for the opposite bank of the canal, it might make it, it's got a chance... gonna be close... didn't make it! And thus began the quest to make it across the canal that had the Kid pick up beau coup sheets of trashed paper as he passed through the press room on his way to the top guard post. Tonight, he'd have enough stock to make an airplane that could cross the great canal! Even if he had to try a hundred times!

For his purpose, being at the Villa Cruz was like being stuck in Scrooge McDuck's money bin. Only the currency was paper and not coins. With all it took to run the 10th PSYOP battalion's massive printing operations, with 3 gigantic presses cranking out a million leaflets every couple of days, the Villa Cruz was *swimming* in paper. There was freaking wasted paper everywhere. It was an endless supply.

The Kid's design had been going through a metamorphous. From his boyhood standard of the shorter bodied broad wing approach with the weight in the wings, he had gone narrow with legal size sheets. Flipping the folds over made the wings smooth across the top and he folded back the nose to create the forward weight. Now he could futz with back ends and get some lift like ailerons. He checked the levelness of the folds. *This baby is going to make it! Not too much lift, don't want it to stall out, just the slightest bit to keep it going. And now ladies and gentlemen, it appears Lucky Lindy is about ready to attempt his cross canal flight, non stop, 50 yards, hopefully, from the top of Villa Cruz, to the scuzzy neighborhood over there… God speed, Lucky…we got a little breeze, it's a good launch… picking up speed, good glide path, catching a little wind, going… going… going… annnnnnnnnddddd he can barely fucking see it… Ker splash! Lindy is down! Send in the Medivac!* The Kid quickly slings another prepared paper craft after it! *Don't worry Lucky Lindy, we got you covered… Oh no! The medivac goes DOWN like a fucking rock! Oh crap! Barely cleared the road… and we don't' have another medivac! No so lucky tonight, Lindy… how long can you tread water? OK, Fans.* The Kid picked up another sheet and began folding anew. *Whose next? We need somebody with a kamikaze frame of mind, somebody who knows how to swim!*

"And here's just the man!" The Kid continued to fold his next plane as Ron Edwards walked into the area from the post directly behind him.

"The man for what?" Edwards was smoking a cigarette.

"To fly all the way across the canal without taking a swim!" said the Kid.

"I could go for a swim," said Ron as he approached and looked over the Bastian, "Hell, if we were a couple of feet closer to the edge, we could high dive off of here, *ala* Acapulco!"

The Kid finished a plane and with very little fanfare, threw it and was watching when Ron said, "Hey, I want to make one!' And soon, they were both making and throwing airplane after airplane.

After about 5 minutes, it struck Ron, "Uh, I'd better get back to me post."

"Good. I've got work to do!" said the Kid, reaching for another piece of paper.

About 30 planes later, the sky was finally beginning to lighten and it was near 0545 hours, approaching the time for his guard shift to end. One of his planes had not yet completed a successful cross canal flight. Leaning over the sandbags looking down, the Kid chanced to see Don Hartmann, the drummer for the band and a printer, come out of the gate, and stretch out with both arms over his head. Obviously glad his shift was over, he lit up a cigarette and exhaled a big puff of smoke.

Then the Kid had a prankish idea. Lifting his M-16, he chambered a round. The metallic sound carried crisply on the morning air and when Don heard it, knowing what it was, he instantly flattened himself on the ground. The drummer realized there was no threat when he heard the Kid attempting to conceal laughing from above and turning over to look up, he flipped him the bird.

Chapter 68

"The colonel wants to see you in his office," Wimbish spoke the words in an even tone as he stood next to the Kid's desk in the corner of the graphics room.

Generally, one would think when somebody walked up to your desk and spoke those words, you might feel trepidations, but the Kid didn't feel anything untoward in Lou's tone of voice.

"OK," he said, rising to his feet and picking up a legal pad and a ballpoint in the process. As he walked to the door, the Chief, Boyett, Weston, and Edwards all looked up from their work at him with that *'you know what's up?'* expression, but the Kid didn't know what was up. *Hopefully not the jig…*

Placing the pad in his left hand and the pen in his pocket, the Kid knocked on the colonel's door and was greeted with an immediate "Enter!" Through the door, the Kid takes his first sample of the flavor of the meeting. *He's smiling!* "Specialist Stocker reporting, Sir!" *snappy salute and a smile back at you.*

The battalion commander returned the salute from the sitting position and immediately rose to come around his desk, "At ease, Specialist Stocker, why don't we sit down over here at the coffee table, there are a couple of things I like to discuss with you."

A couple? At the table? "Yes Sir," the Kid sat down in the chair because he knew the colonel preferred the small brown leather couch he'd found for the purpose of having a place in his office less formal than his desk for discussions. Upon sitting, the Kid was all ears.

"So, Specialist Stocker, would you like a coke? That's all I've got in my fridge today, I could have Wimbish bring us in a couple."

"Yes, Sir, thank you, Sir!"

Willie O. got up and walked to the door and leaned out while holding on to the frame, "Specialist Wimbish, 2 cokes, please," was all he said before returning to his seat. "So how excited are you about your turn as editor?"

"Very much, Sir, to say the least! I've got a really good idea for the April cover story."

"Excellent!"

Wimbish entered with the cokes; smiles all around, again confirming that no part of this meeting was going to involve the Kid's ass getting chewed for anything. The cokes were in the can, nicely chilled but no ice in the glass, not that the Kid was going to complain. Here he was, invited to the commander's office and served drinks.

I wonder what the hell is going on here. I wonder if this is going to involve marijuana. Like he's going to order me to get everybody to stop. I think he smokes but I'll never ask. I doubt he could ever tell me, although I think the way he treats it, he has some experience. He is so unusual in his approach to a lot of things. Maybe he'll ask us to stop. If he does, the least we'll do is get a lot sneakier! I'm so short, I can't let anything fuck me up now. I just want to get out of here with no more trouble.

After Wimbish had left the room and he had taken a drink, Willie O. sat his can down and looked the Kid in the eye. "I'm curious, Stocker, did you ever try or *want to try to* get a story into *"Stars and Stripes?"* He inquired about the Kid's history with the Serviceman's newspaper that was published weekly and distributed in overseas theaters of operations.

"No Sir, I haven't. In DINFOS, they did have a section where they talked about it and how to do it, the AP style guide format they want stories in and what kind of stories they like. But no, I've never invested any time or energy in getting something in. I've hardly ever given it much thought, really." *Light bulb!* The Kid brightened his smile and held his right index finger in the air as he *got the clue,* "But now that you bring it up, Sir, *why not?"*

"All right Stocker! Why was I sure that would be your attitude," he said more as a statement than a rhetorical question. "You know, I've been reading the Stars and Stripes for quite a while. In fact, some buddies and I have a little contest going where we try to get stories about our units into the paper and whoever has the most since we last saw each other has to buy the beer. We haven't had one in from the 10th yet, Stocker, so I'm counting on you. I want you to do a story for the *Stars and Stripes.*"

"Uh, Sir," the Kid kind of squinted at him, "I kinda get the feeling that you have something specific in mind here today?"

"Yes, Stocker, I do." and he placed his elbows on his knees folded his fingers together and got to the point. "Lt. Sauers, when he was in last week, said to me before he left, he was concerned about your *'attitude'*. He said

470

that you told him you wanted to make his team's Go Cong pull out a 'one liner' in Battalion Happenings and he was hurt. First, you left him out of the 9th Division article and he feels they've accomplished great things in Go Cong deserve a little bit more recognition than you relegating it to an afterthought on the back page and I agreed with him. He told me the slightly sarcastic joke you made down there, about *if we replace every American with a Vietnamese everywhere we could all go home.* But when he told it to me, my immediate thought was, *why the hell not? That's a hell of a good idea!" That's the story I want for Stars and Stripes!*

What gives? Am I on the carpet or not?

"Sir, you gotta believe me; I never dissed Lt. Sauers or the team! When I was talking one liner, I was talking about that actual *'one line: if we replaced every American in Vietnam with a Vietnamese to do their job, we could all go home!* I wanted to write it somewhere and I didn't think we have a lot of room for more 9th Division stuff after last issue so I was trying to shoe horn it in."

"Well, Stocker, after we kicked it around some more, we realized we *both* liked it! *Replace all Vietnamese with Americans and we can all go home."* A whole new take on our mission in Vietnam that is about something other than body count! Replace and rotate, something like that… *I love it!* And Lt. Sauers is right. His team does deserve a lot more recognition than a one liner!"

"Yes, Sir." *The Kid was next door to dumbfounded. His one time off handed flippant try for a laugh was taking on a life of its own and the degree to which it was happening startled him.*

"When I first made the decision to move Team 10-E-4 out of Go Cong, my motivation was the need for more manpower and resources to use in a district where things weren't going as well. I never for a second thought of it the way Sauer said you did, when you were being your obviously normal sarcastic self. In fact, I like it so much, this is what we're going to do.

"I know what *Stars and Stripes* likes. Instead just pulling the team out and reassigning them in the middle of the night, I'm going to make it some kind of official. When we hand over their duties to the ARVN PSYWAR bloc, it will be in an *official ceremony*. If it's one thing the boys at Stars and Stripes love, it's a story about a ceremony. Never seen it say no to a ceremony story and this will be the first one they've ever seen for this! So, Lt. Sauer will get more recognition than he ever thought possible! Plus, think what it will do for ARVN pride and confidence! I'm inviting the Go Cong Province Chief, the Province Deputy Senior Advisor and a bunch of other brass to attend this *momentous and significant* event! That should give you some suitable material to frame your *one liner.*"

Quite possibly for the third time, the Kids mouth was again hanging wide open over something that happened in Colonel Lawton's office! His little scrap of satire was now going to be a full blown *Stars and Stripes* article!

"We're setting it up for Saturday, April 5th. We'll fly down on Air America. I'm having a plaques and certificates made up to give them. You'll shoot some pictures, and *I know* you'll write me one hell of a story! PSYOPS has been doing a tremendous job and damn it, *IT* deserves recognition! The men of the 10th have been doing a tremendous job and they deserve some recognition. They'll really like seeing the unit in *Stars and Stripes!* And the angle is fresh! Why shouldn't that be the goal of every American unit? And of course, lunch will be served!"

Well, no pressure here all the sudden. "Wow! Jeeze! Sir! That's amazing! Yes Sir, this is exciting!"

"Uh, this obviously wasn't your idea for the April front page, was it?"

"Oh, no," the Kid quickly responded, "it wasn't but if you want it on the front page, Sir… "

"What have you got?" Willie had just about finished his coke.

"For the front page, Sir, I'm thinking about that operation Lt. Broyles and Specialist Butler are on right now, at Nui Coto 'mountain', *so to speak,* up on the Cambodian boarder. From what I've heard, it's like a gigantic pile of rocks that's been a regular VC stronghold for years. Sergeant Sweet's up there with them for a story and photos. We've reserved two pages for him and I'm betting there's at least one really good shot they'll bring back that's cover worthy. We hear they're getting some Hoi Chanhs, so that's gotta be the hottest thing going in the whole Battalion right now."

"Great choice!" he said and added with a noticeable drop of his gaze, "I've been following it. The situation's not the same, but it definitely reminds me a little of Pork Chop Hill. Mostly because it happened about this time of year." He looked back up at the Kid with a small smile and changed the subject. "So you never even tried to get an article into *Stars and Stripes?* Why not? It would look nice on your resume."

"Well, yes, I guess, Sir, but not half the *'nice'* the Radio Saigon extension would have been. I never really saw the value in *Stars and Stripes,* probably because I think of myself as a broadcaster first and a journalist second. That and if I'd gotten the AFN gig, I'd have flown the jet home last week!"

472

Big pause. "Yet, here you are. Preparing to write an article for me to put in *Stars and Stripes.* The one lesson all soldiers learn in war, sooner or later or one way or another, is that *we must all do what we must do!* I know you'll do the unit proud, Stocker." Another big pause. "Despite you're bent for controversy." *Big smile.* With that, Willie O. rose to his feet, indicating the interview was over. "I'll keep you posted on the travel plans," he was clearly waiting for the Kid to rise and salute, which swiftly he did.

Taking his salute down, the Kid said, "Thank you, Sir, for the vote of confidence," and he paused, "actually, Sir, thank you for *all* the votes of confidence. I won't let you down!"

"Believe me, *I know.*" The colonel said, imparting a very positive vibe.

The Kid closed the door behind him. He squeezed the hell out of the Buffalo nickel all the way back down the hallway, ignoring all of the geckos and was all but mobbed when he walked back to the graphics room.

"What gives?" asked the Chief.

"He wants me to write a story for *Stars and Stripes!*" the kid began to relate as he stopped at Boyett's centrally located desk and lit a cigarette. "And get this! He wants me to write it on the very subject I've been joking about, the *'replace every American with a Vietnamese to do his job and we can go home!' Shtick.*

"Really? *No shit?*" Edwards questioned, "We all thought he was finally going to pull the plug on the Embassy… either that or ask you for a joint!"

"Not a word about pot was spoken. I sure as hell will never bring it up!" said the Kid. "Yeah, it was Sauers, when I told him he was going to be a line item in *Battalion Happenings,* he felt slighted! *Who'd guess?* So, dig this! Willie agrees with him, says he should have a ceremony and get his story in *Stars and Stripes!* He's putting together a fucking *official ceremony,* believe it or not, and he's getting a fucking plaque made to give them! And he's calling in a bunch of the bureaucracy like the province chief and the head of POLWAR and says he's going to have them attend so it can be a story about an *'official ceremony!'*

"We're going to fly down on Air America a week from Saturday!"

"Wouldn't it be fun to be a colonel and make people do crap like that?" mused Gelbach.

"So. You've gone from a line item in *Happenings,* to one column of editorial satire to what now, for layout purposes? Inquired the Chief, seated at his desk.

"He wants pictures and now there's a ceremony to write about so it's looking a lot like a full page!" the Kid walked over in his direction.

"Well," Regan theatrically huffed, "I'm still sitting in the chair, but I sure don't feel like the editor any more now that we've got March printed. He calls you in to talk. Your joke story grows to a page and goes *Stars and Stripes?* Stick the fork in me anywhere, *I'm done. You're the Chief now.*"

Standing there in a shock of surprise, the Kid hadn't expected the Chief to pass the mantle until he actually left, but here it was, in front of the whole staff. "Uh, no... no, you're the Chief, *I'm the Kid,* can't have more than one knick name... that's the rules! You'll always be the Chief, even if I'm going to be Editor this issue, to me, you'll always be the Chief!" he shook Everett's hand, "and I envy your incredible shortness!"

"You're right! God, there were times when I thought it would never end!" the Chief opined, "I'm so happy I just might come out on the balcony and smoke some of that wacky weed with you criminals tonight!"

To which everybody laughed their asses off because, Everett *E. Regan never ever smoked pot. That the Kid knew of.*

Chapter 69

"Hey Mona... heeeeyyyy Mona...." "Hooo Mona... hoooooooo Mona!"
Richie sang and the band and the audience moaned the reprise back as
the beat, words and rhythm exerted their infectious grip on the crowd. The
consensus was that Mona was their single best song and the dance floor
always loaded up when they played it.

The Kid sat with Willert, Edwards and Ramjet, nursing a beer, at a
table near the back of the dance room. Of course the place was packed. The
Band's fame was spreading and GIs were actually coming to Ben Xe Moi
to find the Hollywood and hear them.

In fact, the Kid had even pulled off his first "booking' as the band's
manager. A top sergeant from an engineering compound about a half a mile
north up the road had asked if the band could come up there a play a set.
Sure, for $100, said the Kid and the Sarge said OK without batting an eye!

Ozelle had been in the Hollywood that day and when he heard about
it, he insisted on attending just to see what the hell was going on. The
engineering sergeant left and returned with two jeeps for transportation of
band and instruments. When the 10th Nervous Breakdown finished their set,
they Zipped over and set up, but only had time to play for about 30 minutes
before Ozelle made them break down to make curfew. But the Kid collected
the $100 MPC. Since it was the first time, the Kid did not keep his $2
commission due from each band member when he distributed the funds.
There was now talk of this revenue stream being pursued on a far more
active basis.

Tonight, however, there were bigger, more urgent fish to fry. Although
he had no idea about it, Ken had been working on it for more than a week.
It had to do with a ploy the men of the unit figured out that enabled them
to spend an entire night with a woman rather than just do *short time.* One
made an arrangement with Mama San that before the Hollywood closed
for the night and everybody left for curfew, a couple of GIs would ease
upstairs with girls and stay over. Their buddies would cover for them and
that way, you had a really grand experience instead of being pressured by

the prostitute to hurry up and get your rocks off as quickly as possible. Oh, it cost a little more, but it was an investment in a tantalizing bit of escapism at an *E ticket* level. It insured a truly Horney GI he could do it at least a couple of times, if not three, while locked in the building until sunup. It was daring but, in all appearances, relatively low in risk.

Ken didn't say anything about it until he had it arranged and then sprang it on the Kid: *tonight's the night!* It cost them $10 each. Although they couldn't, for some reason, pick the girl they wanted to spend the night with, Ken had been guaranteed by Mama San her choices for them would not disappoint.

Lately, the Kid had been taking care of the urge at the Scientific, since there weren't any quicker, more reasonably priced or more convenient options in Can Tho. But there came a time when the pretend blow jobs left the Kid wanting something more, like the feel of a real vagina surrounding his 21 year old cock, for example. In fact, he hadn't been laid since R&R and the situation was *getting out of hand,* so to speak.

Once they got the high sign from Mama San that they were on for sure, they bolted and rushed back over to the New Villa where they could grab their toothbrushes, a pack of filter tipped joints and one other thing they both deemed totally necessary; his .38 pistol. Of course, it couldn't *look* like a rush trip, as if they were planning on going somewhere, it had to be cool, not chomping at the bit.

"Be careful not to make eye contact with RV," joked the Kid, "for some reason, he can ferret shit like this out!"

They enter the New Villa and casually stroll through the orderly room to the stairs and up the four flights to their room on the 3rd floor. Along the way, they make it a point to say hi to as many people as they can, their intent being to register their presence in the halls of the Villa before their *di di mau.*

Once in their room, the Kid makes sure nobody sees him strap the .38 shoulder holster on under his fatigues. To leave with an M-16 would be a total red flag; anybody who saw them would know immediately something was up. But there was no way in hell the Kid was spending the night outside the wire without a weapon. Grabbing some extra cigarettes and their toothbrushes, they knew in the morning, it being Saturday, they'd have to wait for after chow, to safely reappear in the unit, like they were returning from Eakin.

As they walk across the dusty street that separates the Hollywood from the MP station, the Kid notices the MP sentry watching them. *I wonder if that guy is capable of keeping it straight in his head whose come and who's gone and whose not gone and stayed to cum. Why is he watching? Why should he even care? Oh yeah, he's a sentry!*

Back at the Hollywood, they found the crowd just starting to break up. It was now less than an hour to curfew on a Friday night and the band was cooking hot but some soldiers didn't want to get caught in the lurch.

Edwards and Ramjet had saved their seats. Once in his, the Kid now had a reason to pay closer attention to the women of the Hollywood. *One of them soon will be mine!* He knew his chances of the getting the one girl he really wanted, the one that didn't dress western style, were slim to none but it didn't matter, the mission tonight was to get laid, re-laid *and par-laid.*

"You guys all set?" Ramjet asked with a smile, got your *rubbers?*"

"Yeah," replied Willert, "we're ready."

"Way past ready," added the Kid. "I'm a little worried about RV, he's kind of made it his business to keep track of me for some reason, can't imagine."

"Don't worry about RV," Edwards lit up a Winston, "first we'll breathe out rat's revenge and then tell him you're looking for him and he'll think he's hiding from you!"

The group surveyed the crowd to see if there were any NOCOMs present that might be a problem if they noticed the pair moving toward the upstairs rooms at closing time. *Didn't seem to be.*

"Mama San is giving us the nod," Ken bumped the Kid's leg, "come on, and let's go!"

"Have a good one," smiled Edwards, "and if it's good have two! We've got you covered!"

"No sweat, GIs," Ramjet ventured a positive note, "nobody's been caught yet! Oh, wait, that's like talking about a no-hitter!'

"Ramjet! Why would you say that?" the Kid superstitiously reacted.

"If you're worried, I'll take you place."

Not a chance.

They exited the dance room and followed after Mama San, who walked around the far end of the bar to a staircase located just behind it. Neither Ken nor the Kid had previously taken advantage of the short time opportunities at the Hollywood, so they didn't know the drill. The stairs were slightly steep and long because of the high ceiling of the building's first floor. When they got to the landing at the top, they stood beneath a single light bulb and Mama San established eye contact with both of them.

"I get you girls numba one! For sure! $10 MPC you pay each. You want beer, pho? You pay extra, everything extra," she squinted, hardening her face into the business woman wolf that she was.

There was a moment of pondering if the room service option would be available later so Ken hedged. "Well, I'd go for two beers and a bowl of pho would be nice, *bon U?*" Ken asked, *how much?*

"You pay $5 MPC," the shrewish matron extended her hand, palm up.

"Toy Sem sem," the Kid concluded as he went for his wallet.

Each of them extracted the proper amount and handed it over. As soon as the bills were safely stuffed into the folds of her many colored blouse, she knocked on the door. It immediately opened, tended by a young girl, about 10 years old, and they were admitted into a hallway that had a half dozen doors strung down the right hand side. The ceiling on the second floor was high and also only lit by a single naked bulb. The doors were old and wooden, with the window vents flipped open up top. The white pajama clad scrap of a girl with tightly pulled back hair closed the door immediately behind them and resumed her post in a nearby chair. She and Mama San exchanged fond smiles.

"One room you," Mama San opened the first door and pointed to Ken and continuing down the hall, opened the second door, "one room you," she pointed at the Kid. "Girls come with beer and pho soon!" and as soon as she turned, the door keeper was up and on the knob, pulling it open so Mama San didn't miss a step and the pint sized dynamo was gone.

The Kid peered into his room and turned on the lite switch next to the door. The single bare bulb showed not much in the way of furnishings *but the one item we need is here.* He walked over the brass antique double bed and sat on the mattress. *Bouncy but firm enough.* It had four pillows and was covered with a quilt. Even with the ceiling fan humming away, nobody was going to need a quilt in this room tonight. There were no windows but the ceilings were vented a foot down the walls. He turned on the lamp that sat on the night stand next to the bed and turned off the overhead. Another night stand across the room held a pitcher of water sitting inside a bowl on top of a towel and a chamber pot peeked out from underneath. A rickety table with one wooden ladder back chair, painted black, completed the decor. There were no rugs on the floor.

Ken appeared at the Kid's door, "Hey, shall we eat in one of our rooms, drink a beer and smoke a joint before we retire to the fucking?"

"Why not? I suppose one is as good as another," agreed the Kid.

"Well, I think my table is a little bigger," said Ken, "why don't we go in there to eat the pho. You might want to bring that chair. We can make the girls sit on the bed while we eat."

Sounded like a plan so the Kid did exactly that. Once the furniture was moved, they sat down at the table and Ken broke out his pack of joints and they each lit one up. There was an ash tray in the room because who doesn't smoke after they have sex?

"Am I ever looking forward to this," Ken blew out a deep puff, "I'm so Horney the crack of Dawn was starting to *look good!* I just hope they are a little cute!"

"I'm not so horney that I'd fuck the last woman on earth, but her friend, maybe," laughed the Kid. "Shit, I sure as hell hope I don't have to make that choice."

"That's great the Imrem and Compton are back from the hospital!" said Ken, homing in on some positive news. "Still, that was a serious wake up call."

"Well, we better hope to fucking high heaven nothing happens tonight because I've only got 5 bullets!"

"Amen that, brother!" Ken took another big hit. "We're taking a little bit of a chance, but I think it's going to be worth it."

"Better be. I'm down to 53 days and this would be one hell of a bad time to fuck up and get killed over something like this. At least I wouldn't have to explain it."

Half an hour later, about the time the duo was beginning to wonder where the promised *babes* were, the door echoed from what sounded like kicking. The child harem keeper *opened sesame* and into the hallway walked two women, each carrying a bowl of pho in one hand, two beer bottles in the other with a purse tucked up under one arm.

Both had short cut hair, about 3 inches off their collars, clearly *coiffured* into shape. They wore western style blouses and short skirts that hit easily six inches above the knees. Immediately upon seeing the men in the same room, they had a quick private chat and one of them peeled off to the Kid's room and came back with the pho and beers but not her purse. When she set the groceries on the table, she turned and smiled broadly at the Kid while the other girl went directly over to Ken and put her arm around his neck and kissed him on the cheek.

Hmmm. Seems to me like the choice of girls has already been made by the girls.

Being Friday, Headquarters had knocked off early, barely two hours after lunch. Kid had been stoned all afternoon and even though he'd had a couple of beers, he wasn't drunk enough that just any girl would look good to him. *She's pretty enough.* Then he suddenly realized while this was not the one girl he really wanted… *it was the girl who really wanted him.*

A slow smile spread across his face as he recalled the incident a couple of weeks earlier, when she had sat down next to him in the club. He had snapped a picture of her with his Pentax to try out a flash unit Birnbaum loaned him and she must have taken it as a sign he liked her because she came on to him extremely hard, to get him hard and to go upstairs for *short time.* She had been visibly unhappy when he declined her generous fondling.

"*Chow, Co dep,*" he said to her.

"*Chow, Ong,*" she dipped her eyes but brought them right back up. The unshaded light bulb hanging from the ceiling sparkled in their darkness.

"Here, Mama San send for you," Ken's girl dug into her purse and pulled out some utensils and a beer opener, "eat now!" she handed each man an Asian shaped white porcelain spoon and a pair of chop stix and placed the opener next to the *Beir 33's.* The men proceeded to dive into the *pho. It was delicious.*

While the Kid was eating, every time he looked at his date, she was looking back at him. "I am Quan," she finally said at one point, "call you, Cut?"

"*Cut? OK Toi Cut*" the Kid pronounced it back the way she said it. *She knows my freaking name!*

"Cut," she repeated it back with a flip of hair. "*Cut*"

Once the pho was finished, they both lit up after dinner cigarettes but didn't smoke them half way down before they both knew it was time. "Welp," the Kid opened his second beer to leave Ken the church key and stood up, snuffing his out in the ashtray and grabbing the back of his chair and both beer bottles, "to the business at hand! Or in this case, to the business at *pants!*" Ken knowingly grinned back and as Quan, the Kid and the chair sashayed out the door, he closed it behind them.

Upon entering their room, the Kid parked the bottles and chair as Quan closed the door. She stood, looking at the Kid, who came over to her to check and see if the door had a lock. *It does not. That bothers me more than*

480

a little bit. He moved the chair into a position where he could see if it would do for a jam. *Weak at best.*

She was standing by the bed, with a sly smile on her well proportioned oval face and the Kid had to admit, she was definitely far prettier than he would have settled for. Her eyes were slightly wider apart than most Vietnamese girls. Other than that, everything about her had his interest and he wondered seriously why he hadn't screwed her the other day. Walking over to her, he remained silent and she placed a hand on his chest and then, with a smile, began to unbutton his fatigue shirt. When she knocked it off his shoulders and it dropped directly on to the floor, the .38 snub nose immediately caught her eye. *Back up a step.*

The Kid smiled assuredly, as he took the shoulder holster off and hung it on the bed post. His belt next attracted her attention. She pulled it loose, and in a jiffy, unbuttoned and unzipped his pants, causing them to drop on the floor. Sheer anticipation had already presented the Kid with a fairly solid erection and it was barely concealed by his shorts. Quan's eyes went right to it and she moved her hand to pull back the elastic waist band. Peering down, looking right at it, with it's one eye peering straight up back up at her, she breathed out, the words, *"Choi duc oi!"*, and let the elastic snap back, concealing a giggle with a hand swiftly placed over her mouth.

'I'll bet you say that to all the soldiers," the Kid quipped, while simultaneously realizing she would likely not get that joke.

Looking down, the Kid could see his combat boots hugging his ankles above his pants. Sitting on the bed, he untied them, pulled his feet out, peeled off his socks, stuffed them into the boots and nudged the whole pile, pants around boots, back underneath. Leaning back on the bed, propped up by his arms, he smiled at Quan, attired in nothing but his green boxers, round gold glasses and his lucky beaver nickel.

Standing in front of him with her leg defiantly spread, Quan began removing her clothes. It was not a striptease. The process was quick and methodical as she unbuttoned her blouse and tossed at the chair, missing. She thrust out her left hip as she stood there in her short brown skirt and white bra while his eyes traveled up and down her body. After a moment, she reached back and unhooked her bra and dropped it on the floor. The Kid noticed it was padded and her nude breasts small but he didn't care. She unzipped the skirt and let it fall to the floor, leaving her in nothing but a pair of pink bikini panties. With her thumbs, she slid them down to her knees and let them drop softly to the floor.

Stepping over to where the Kid sat, she pushed him in the chest, making him lay down on his back. Then she tugged at his boxers and he pushed them past his hips so she could remove them. As she pulled, the elastic snagged his boner and brought it forward before it snapped back, making them both laugh. Tossing his shorts on top of her bra, she bent forward and took his penis in her hands and lifted it up off his belly. After looking at it for a couple of seconds, she kissed the tip very gently and then suddenly jammed her mouth down on it and started sucking with a vengeance!

Didn't see that coming! The Kid almost lost it and after a couple of hearty sucks, lifted up her head and said, *"Quan! Bou coup di di mau fast! Slow down!"*

With a slightly puzzled look that initially questioned how he could not like what she was doing, she realized what he was saying and backed off.

I thought all the girls wanted a little foreplay. Guess I'm wrong.

The Kid moved to the middle of the bed and waited, propped up on one elbow, for Quan to join him, which she promptly did. Pushing him flat on his back, she swung a leg over and immediately mounted him. Poised high on her knees, with her right hand, she lifted his throbbing dick up from his belly and began to rub the tip into her surprisingly wet pussy until she felt the head engage her opening. That instant, she dropped down and his dick was all the way inside her very hot and moist vagina. Thus impaled, she leaned forward and kissed him so hard he feared she might suck his tonsils out! Then she said, *"Bou coup long time I wait to fuck you, GI Cut!"*

Yes, I can see that. So now let's fuck for bou coup long time Co dep!

Engulfed to the hilt, she began to move upon him, rocking back and forth, going more for the clit rub than the in and out strokes. He looked up at her and found her eyes trained right on him! The Kid grabbed her tight ass with both hands, got into the rhythm of her rocking motion and was just beginning to revel in the joy of complete penetration when the epiphany came upon him: *Oh shit! I forgot the condom! It's too close to going home to risk getting VD. Fuck. Too late now! There is no point in even giving it a second thought; the deed is done. It's bareback all the way tonight!*

From the way she had taken him like a cat in heat, it was no surprise that she came first. *Talk about aggressive! Wow! She fucking wanted it!* Indicating he desired to change positions, Quan got off and centered herself in the middle of the bed. Climbing in between her legs, the Kid sunk it home as she lifted her pelvis up to meet him. *Now for a little of the old in and out.* With her hands tightly holding his cheeks in a death grip, she answered every thrust and the old brass bed was squeaking and rocking so much the Kid could only hope it wouldn't come unhinged! The best part, he knew, was not having to last before the first load left the chamber because tonight, *it was only the beginning.*

The room didn't have any windows. When they both broke into full body sweats, the ceiling fan's evaporative effects finally kicked in a little but it was still hot, hard work, creating sexual friction between their private parts. The Kid slowed the pace as he worked toward getting his second nut off and let his mind induce the fantasy that it was Flo on the other side of his tightly closed eyes. That it was she he was in. He yearned for how it was that afternoon back in the Traveler's Motel, *almost a year ago. Hey! My year is almost up!* He opened his eyes and saw that Quan was now the one with eyes closed. She moved to wrap her legs around his body and straining against him, gave in to another rather apparent orgasm. He joined her in it, spasmodically delivering in the neighborhood of 5 to 10 million sperm cells very deep into her nether regions, along with the tensions that are know to follow sperm, where ever they go.

Rolling off, he lay on his back and looked up at the ceiling fan while he let out a big sigh. Reaching his arm under the bed for his clothes, he fishes out his pants and retrieves his lighter and gets the filter tipped joints from out of his fatigue shirt and lights up. Realizing he needed the ashtray, he rose and walked nude across the room, got it and his last beer 33, already opened, and brought them back to the bed putting them on the night stand next to his glasses. He offers Quan a puff.

She looks at him cockeyed and asks, "Kai ye?" *what's that?*

"Cong sa," he replied, *gesturing for her to take it.*

"Cam bao ya!" Never. she shook her head, "numba ten!"

Cam bao ya. The Kid couldn't hear that phrase and not think of *Wally and the Beaver and the girl next door.* And he couldn't think of them without a visit from *Captain Robinson.* He took in a deep inhale and held it, hoping the sexual release, the pot and the beer could turn out to be the magic combination that would permit him to completely relax.

He sank into the bed and after a few hits, almost had it made when he remembered where he was! *Outside the wire in a whorehouse, breaking curfew and taking a chance that no combination of VC will show up requiring more than five bullets to dispatch and that nobody of authority will discover his ruse and bust him lower than dirt. What would PM Smith give to know where I am right now? What time is it? The Seiko says 2200 hours. It's going to be another 11 hours before we can get out of this place without being noticed. Shit, I hope we can get some more room service!*

Where am I going to get a glass of water for tonight? I wonder how Ken's doing? He sat up and snuffed out the joint. Ah ha! I hear squeaking springs in the next room!

Quan lay on the top of the quilt, on her right side with her head propped up on one elbow, looking at him. Rolling over, she rose up from the beds opposite side and padded over to the night stand with the pitcher of water and the bowl. She lifted the pitcher out, set the bowl on the floor, removed a wash cloth that had been under the pitcher, and poured out some water. Squatting Asian style, she cleansed herself of their mutual bodily fluids, then took a piss in the chamber pot and dabbed it dry on the wash cloth.

That reminds me to give Mr. Johnson a bath. Hmmm. I wonder if that water's potable. What a great start! Now, once more in the middle of the night, when we wake up for whatever reason, and again with the morning wood. That will certainly be getting my $10 worth!

They hadn't bothered to turn the bed down before they went for it and as she did, he was glad there were now dry sheets and no wet spot. *At least to begin.*

Pulling his toothbrush and Colgate from his cargo pants pocket, the Kid inquired through sign language and his fading Vietnamese, if he could use the water in the pitcher to brush his teeth. *"Nouc OK?"* He said while pantomiming brushing and pointing at the pitcher. Quan nodded in the affirmative so he proceeded with his night time ritual.

First, since there was no drinking glass in the room, he rinsed out the empty beer bottle before carefully filling it half way up. Brushing vigorously while he walked around the room, still naked, checking things out; he discovered there wasn't squat in the room to check out. *Except him.* Quan eyed him with a pleasant, if not devilish smile. He spat into the bowl where she had bathed her beaver, took another swig out of the bottle and spat it out too. The water tasted OK but he still wasn't sure if it was truly potable or not so he refrained from swallowing. It would be interesting to see if he could make it through the night without taking a drink.

The Kid pulled out the chamber pot and took a piss, holding it up by one handle so as not to splash. He then gave his unit a wipe down with the only wash cloth in the room and dried it on the towel. Walking back over to the bed, he sat on the edge and yawned big. Quan was starting to fade with eyes fluttering mostly closed and he didn't doubt she would soon be asleep.

There was no radio to listen to AFVN or a record player or tape for music, so all the Kid could do was smoke a KOOL and listen to the sounds

484

that came to him through the walls. *The streets of Ben Xe Moi seemed relatively quiet, but Ken is still having at it next door! Listen to that bed rattle and squeak!*

Not long after the squeaking next door stopped, the KOOL was extinguished and the Kid made sure where his glasses were before turning out the lamp. Laying on his back he stretched out to full length and inhaled the odors of the room deeply into the lungs of his fatigued body. *Too hot. Always too hot.* He let his mind wander over vast territories as he attempted to stumble upon sleep. Random thoughts jumped from scenes and memories of *Nashville to Boulder to California to the place where they shot Wally and the Beaver and the Girl Next Door. From the first time he smoked dope to the night he first met Flo and as rapidly back to the day he met Donna Nadeau, the real reason he went to Nashville in the first place. Where he met Flo. And ended up here, in Mama San's Hollywood whorehouse and dance emporium, with Quan, whose apparently been after my ass for a couple of weeks! Got to admit, I liked it. For being in Vietnam, it is one of the good nights.*

The air was hot and the irritating little squeak the fan made with every revolution, was just loud enough for the Kid to notice it didn't revolve very fast. There was nothing he could do about the squeak because he certainly wasn't going to turn it off. *It is like noticing a clock ticking, sometimes it seems to get louder and louder and then, you don't hear it at all because you finally fall asleep. Let it hypnotize me and let me get some sleep. How did I ever last in the oven? Poor Gaugle. How could anybody live in that room for a year? No wonder Boujold wanted to go to the field. Darkness at last settled upon the Kid.*

Chapter 70

It was a dead sleep, not that one uses the word 'dead' frivolously in Vietnam, but the Kid was stone cold deep in sleep at the very least. His sub conscious was not projecting and he was immersed in no dream. He'd been asleep like that for a good three hours when the disturbance began.

At first, it did seem like a dream. But reality rushed into his head so mercurially fast, he became instantly wide awake, because the situation that confronted the Kid was far worse than any nightmare he could have conjured up!

"SOLDIERS! IN THE BUILDING!"

Doors banged, many boots tattooed the floor of Mama San's bar. Frantic voices exchanged shouts of authority, none understandable to the Kid in actual words, but unmistakable in tone and volume.

Oh my dying ass! Soldiers could mean VC, ARVNs, MPs, or even White Mice! None good, two eternally bad!

The sound of boots pounded up the staircase, banging ensued on the door accompanied by more shouting, all unmistakable harbingers of worse things to come! Feeling for his .38, the Kid takes it out of the holster. *Maybe I should get dressed first? I wonder if the little girl is there on duty to let them in or if they're going to break the door down. Who the fuck are they? They don't sound like American MPs... is that good or bad? Should I turn on the light?*

Feeling in the dark, the Kid finds his glasses and secures them on his face; *no time to get dressed, no place to hide! Getting under the bed won't work.* That would have put him at a huge disadvantage if he had to react. So the Kid was paralyzed into doing the only thing he could do. Sitting on the edge of the bed with his left leg up and his right foot on the floor, facing the door, he pulled a pillow over his lap to cover his nakedness and the .38 in his right hand, and held it pointed directly at whoever might enter.

By this time, Quan had come out of her slumbers and was sitting up, inquiring in Vietnamese what the hell was going on, to which the Kid could

486

not understand or reply. They both heard the hallway door come open and an all male voices argument between unseen parties ensue right outside their room; in *Vietnamese.* Quickly, Quan was on her feet and crossed to the nightstand and grabbed the towel and wrapped it around herself. There was just enough light in the room from the ventilation openings at the top of the door and walls into the hall, that he could read the tension on her face as she stood by the bed.

They didn't bother to knock, somebody turned the handle and pushed the door, easily knocking away the barrier chair. A hand came in and hit the overhead lite switch before the door opened all the way, revealing a steel helmeted ARVN soldier peering in to see who occupied the room with two more soldiers crowding him close from behind. His eyes met the Kid's but no sooner did that happened when Quan ran at the door, screaming words in torrents!

The expression on the soldier's face was a combination of confusion and fear! He stopped dead in his tracks as the fury of Quan broke upon him like a wave on a shore! Whatever it was she was saying to him, she had his attention, and an expression of surprise grew on his face, displayed through the bulging whites of his eyes! She took a step back from the door, all the while continuing to deliver her tirade. Now she was pointing at the wall, then at the Kid who sat still as a statue on the bed, pillow across his lap, sweat running down his back and his finger on the trigger, then back to the trooper, pointing her finger like a pistol.

Much to his total surprise, not to mention considerable relief, the ARVN stepped back and Quan quickly shut the door in his face!

I hadn't move a muscle. I didn't say a word! Quan somehow turned them away, single handedly! Shit! I wonder if they're hassling Ken! I thought I heard a door open and close! But I don't hear any altercation!

Indeed, the only audio report was of boots descending the stairway! The Kid frantically sought out his boxers and quickly pulled them on. Striding to the door, he opened it and went to Ken's room, where the door was closed. "Ken!" he knocked twice.

"Curt!" came the tense response and the Kid entered and hit the light switch, seeing Ken and his girl were both still under the covers. "Talk about fucking scary! *Christ all mighty!* I heard Quan shouting, then one of them opened our door, hit the light, then turned it off that quick and closed it. What the fuck was that all about?

By this time, Quan had followed him into the room and stood there, still clad in the towel. They both looked at her, since she'd done all the talking!

"ARVN soldiers *sem sem* MPs", she explained, "they look for ARVN do what you do, stay with us all night off limits. When they find, they make pay *bou coup or take in! I tell, you no ARVN and you have gun!* I say you have gun, too!" she pointed at Ken. "*Mai* too much trouble, they *di di mau!*" she said, smiling broadly.

"Wow, Quan," the Kid moved to show his gratitude by placing a hand upon her shoulder and looking her in the eyes, "is there any way we can thank you enough for what you did for us!"

Lifting his hand off her shoulder and taking it between both of hers, she smiled as she pulled him gently toward the door, "I know a way," she intoned.

Back in the room, the Kid happily was paying her price, marveling at how it all worked out as she rode him again from the top. She's been after him for a month and his plan had been to wake up at some point during the night for this very purpose! *And we didn't get killed or busted. Somehow, it all works out. Yes, this is a very good night for Vietnam; very good indeed. That's what I'll say in the book.*

Chapter 71

Exactly a month ago to the day, on March 5th, was the first time the Kid had ever been in Go Cong Province. Today, April 5th, he was willing to bet, would be the last. *Or would it?* This time, he was 30 days shorter and arriving in style! It wasn't often one got to fly in the company of the Commander, to do something specifically at the CO's bidding, but that's what was happening today.

The Kid had gotten up early to have a big breakfast at Eakin and he wanted to be in the office when the colonel showed up, ready to go. But Willie O. beat him in!

The Kid would be taking his own story photos today so no Ling Fook nor Birnbaum, but joining them, he found out, were Captain Rostyslaw Smyk, CO of Company B and Sergeant Major Russel Kelley, the top enlisted man in the unit. The Kid could understand why Smyk was there; it was his company! But the Sergeant Major's attendance had been a surprise. He'd never gotten a good read on the new Top Shirt and hadn't had a chance to talk with him for more than 5 or ten minutes the short time he'd been in the unit. The Kid couldn't figure out who was avoiding whom. It was Kelley who caddied the box containing all the plaques and certificated the colonel had concocted to give out as awards at the impending 'ceremony'.

Moyssiadis drove them to Can Tho Field.

The PSYOPs contingent was met in the terminal building by the two more traveling companions, introduce to the Kid by the colonel as Robert Bruce Stirling, Assistant Province Advisor of PSYOP activities for Go Cong and Navy Lieutenant Commander John W. Nyquist, Assistant Chief for Programs, Administration and Naval Liaison of IV Corps Tactical Zone. *What ever the hell kind of a mouthful titles are those?*

"Colonel Lawton," RB Stirling smiled, pointing with his aviator special sunglasses, held by the earpiece, out to the flight line, "Our chariot has arrived!" There sat an Air America PC-6 Turbo STOL aircraft, *waiting for us.* "The pilot's in taking a piss, should be out any second. Anybody else?" Robert Bruce Stirling, pointed around at everybody like taking a head count.

The Kid did not have to take a piss. *Let's see: me, the colonel, 'Smyk', 'Irish', the 'Bruce', Sailor Boy and the pilot: I guess that plane holds at least seven. When the colonel says he's putting something together, he doesn't fuck around. I find it interesting, Spec 4 me, being the lowest ranking mutha on this junket, that Sergeant Major Kelly is carrying the box! Maybe that is why Willie brought him!*

There was no mistaking the Air America pilot as he stepped out of the latrine. He was entirely typical of the breed; middle aged, *they liked men with experience,* short graying hair, grey slacks, and white shirt with epilates and aviator sunglasses, *just like Stirling's,* hanging from the pocket. Confidence oozed from every pore. *We're in the hands of a pro. Don't bother asking his name. Don't put him in the story.*

It was a little after 0800 hours when the STOL craft lifted off the Can Tho Airfield runway, after a take off roll of possibly less than 100 feet! *Amazing!* Rising up over the Delta, the PC-6 gained altitude and airspeed for the run over to Go Cong. *This is much more fun than the Caribou!*

The Kid was seated behind Willie O., who sat behind the pilot, next to the *Bruce,* who sat behind the *Sailor,* who was riding in the co-pilot's seat. Smyk sat to the Kid's right and the Sergeant Major ended up all the way in the back. The engine was noisy enough that conversation would not easily take place between the Kid and his Lt. Seat mate. The Kid had interviewed Smyk for the paper the previous month when he'd taken over as B Company Commander, so they had some favorable interaction.

The Kid snapped a pic of the colonel's and the pilot's profiles.

It was a cloudless morning in the Delta, a beautiful day for a flight. The bright blue canopy of sky highlighted the dry season's promise of no rain on their parade today and the turbo whirred right along. The Kid took a picture out the window of what he believed had to be Vinh Long by the river, before remembering he wasn't shooting color. *Wasted a frame, that'll be worthless in black and white!*

20 minutes later, they were approaching the Go Cong Airfield. Anyway, that's what the Kid thought until the pilot informed his passengers that the Go Cong Airfield had not been operational since Tet and we'd be landing on a road next to it.

The pilot made one pass over to visually check it out. Since there was no tower there to aid him, this was the least he could do. Circling back, the white haired airman dressed in the egg shell Air America uniform shirt, dropped the PC-6 on the road and rolled to a stop in less than the distance of a football field. Waiting for the party were Lt. Sauers and Sp 5 Andy Simko, who stood next to their ¾ ton truck, big enough for all to make it into town with one trip. The PC-6 rolled to a stop about 50 yards short of their parking place.

Once the STOL craft's engine shut down, the passengers deplaned and the Kid stood on the road and stretched while SM Kelley unloaded the prize box. Sauers walked briskly up to the group and saluted smartly as he greeted Willie O. and the rest of the dignitaries, "Welcome to Go Cong, Sirs," he took the salute down and presented another one to Navy Lt. Commander Nyquist, who returned it smartly, and then returned salutes to *'Irish'* and the Kid. The SM had to juggle the box to do it. "We've got plenty of room for everybody in the truck, we wouldn't want to leave anybody here, except for you, Sir, of course," he indicated the pilot, "and you can see, your security squad is just arriving." The Lt. pointed at a group of a half dozen ARVNs headed in their direction on bicycles. All sported M-16's except one of them, who had a PRC-25 radio strapped to his back. The Kid lifted his Pentax and snapped a picture as he pedaled by.

Even with Go Cong as pacified as it supposedly was and even though an ARVN security detail was there, the Air America pilot had not planned on leaving his aircraft unwatched and had brought his own lunch. *It was SOP.*

With the group moving toward the truck, Sauer walked with the Kid, "So, Stocker, glad you could make it, although you could have probably written your one liner in a couple of seconds, mailed it in and stayed home."

"Excuse me, Sir?" the Kid responded.

"Yeah! You made me mad when you said our operation was a *'one liner'*! Well, we are your one liner, *never more!*" the Lt. expressed himself with dramatic flair so the Kid played it.

Ah, the Green Beret comment. "Sir, I *would* have given you at least a paragraph. But hey, Sir, I never said your operation was a one liner and *never* was I going to be anything but positive about you and the team! Seriously, Sir, the 'one liner' thing, I was talking about is my hook, you know, how *simple is it to see the Army should be duplicating what happened here… everywhere?* Look! We're having a freaking ceremony and you aren't happy? This is going in Stars and Stripes," This is all only happening because you cried about not getting enough press, Sir… in *this man's Army,* isn't doing a good job reward enough?" the Kid good naturedly blustered back. *"And"* the Kid turned his head back, "you tried to bust me on *attitude* to the colonel, "the Kid turned his head and as much said it to Willie O, who was walking almost right behind them.

"Glad to see you two are *getting along,*" Lawton said as Sauer turned around to see where the Kid was looking.

To say the three shared a laugh would be an understatement.

"Now that Specialist Stocker is here to do a story on your Team and its achievements…for *Stars and Stripes,* Lieutenant, you'll have to treat him right because nobody else is going to make you a Star!"

"Yes Sir, *thank you,* Sir!" Sauers almost did a mandarin bow, "we're here to commemorate a milestone! I like it more all the time!"

"Well, as you have been telling me, Sir," the Kid cut in, "there's no guarantee on a *Stars and Stripes'* story getting printed or when, but I can tell you now it's going to be a whole page in the April Dimension, *for sure!* However I doubt this is going to make the papers back home because there isn't any body count," the Kid added and then stopped in his tracks, *"Wait a minute…* when you stop and think about it, what we do here in PSYOPS is get *LIVE body count!*

Lawton was already stopped in his tracks. *"I LIKE that!* Almost as much as I like *Vietnamizing* the dam war so we can all go home!" Then to Sauer, "Huh? See why I kept him around?"

Arriving at the truck, Simko is there with the passenger side door opened and Robert Bruce Stirling slides in first to let Willie O. ride shotgun. Before the colonel climbed in, he surveyed the passengers climbing into the open back; Navy Lt. Commander Nyquist was among them. Being a real gentleman, he offered Willie O. shotgun. Of course, the commander declined. Then he looked directly at the Kid and as soon as the Kid's face lit up he said, "No, Stocker, *you can't have it!"* Everybody laughed while he climbed into the cab and shut the door.

Good one, Sir. The Kid tried hard not to overact his *chagrin.*

The drive into town was a couple of minutes. Upon arrival at PSYOPS Hq, everybody pretty much hustled inside because that's where the cold drinks were waiting.

"We were able to secure some extra ice for today," Sauers informed the Colonel, as everybody took off their hats and mopped up sweat. "And of course, Ma has whipped up some of her specialties for our dignitaries, Sir!"

"I've heard amazing things about her cooking and I'm really looking forward to it," Willie O. was clearly having a grand time.

"And poor old Stocker here, if I recall," Sauer pointed in the Kid's direction, "was experiencing a little *lower tract distress* the last time you had lunch with us. I hope that's all past."

"Yes Sir, that was a month ago, been back and gone twice since, but better today, Sir, and *shorter,* too, I might add!"

492

Waiting for the group in town had been the Go Cong Province Chief, ARVN Colonel Nguyen Tat Thinh and Ti Ui Ngoc, the Chui Hoi Chief along with Province Deputy Senior Advisor, Lieutenant Colonel John D. Howard.

The Kid remembered both ARVNs from his earlier visit but the Colonel had done well to pull the Deputy Senior Advisor out for his little dog and pony shindig. *Titles and ceremony, that's what Stars and Stripes wants,* the Kid knew the colonel had it figured out. What the Kid couldn't figure out was Willie O.'s driving desire to have this particular story in *Stars and Stripes* and not Nui Coto, *for one good example. I'll have to ask him.*

The drinks were waiting on one of the tables that had been pulled out of the way, from where it usually stood, in the middle of the far half of the room. Its absence created an open area where the plan was obviously for the colonel to present the awards from there.

SM Kelley was taking the award plaque and certificates out of the box and placing them on the desk situated by the wall, to be handy for the Colonel. Since Willie O. had concocted, designed and ordered the awards and commendations, he totally knew which was which.

Once the colonel had his drink, he took the *Bruce* aside and was discussing something with him about who was going to say what and when, while the Kid sipped his coke standing next to Lt. Sauers and Capt. Smyk.

"Ma is pissed at you, Stocker," Sauers said, clearly for amusement, "for making her work overtime. She might poison you."

Captain Smyk's lit up, "Actually, *Captain Smith* sent me down here to do exactly that."

"*Which* Captain Smith?"

"Take your pick!" Smyk chuckled.

Simko and Stansell, the two enlisted men of team 10-E-4, emerged from the kitchen where they'd been hanging out with and helping Ma. Both honorary members of the tribe when in from the field, they each gave the Kid a nod of the head as they assumed their positions because it appeared Willie O. was getting ready to do the deed. One could tell by the way he looked out over the crowd, noting one by one, the people in the room who were picking up on his serious demeanor.

The Kid would have to take both notes and pictures today, so he was mentally preparing as *the Bruce* and Lieutenant Colonel Howard took up positions on either side of Willie O. The Vietnamese half of the daily double was also gathering, mostly from the kitchen, all smiles and mini bowings to the dignitaries, *in anticipation of the ceremony where they were the rising stars.*

Calling the small room to virtual attention by gently clearing his throat, Colonel Lawton began, "Thank you all for attending today, I am Lieutenant Colonel Lawton, Commanding Officer of the 10th PSYOP Battalion. We are here today in recognition of some great human efforts that have today made possible our marvelous event. For the very first time, the 10th PSYOP Battalion is officially turning over control of all PSYOP activities *in an entire province,* Go Cong Province, to our Vietnamese counterparts at the Vietnamese Information Service *(VIS)*

"But first, none of this would be possible and we wouldn't be here today without the dedicated hard work and sacrifice of Battalion Field Team HE 10-E-4. Lieutenant Sauers, Sergeant Stansell, and Specialist Simko, please step forward."

The three comply with crisp but less than West Point precision to end up blocking the Kid from getting a good shot of the proceedings as Willie O. prepared to bestow his honors.

"For each of you, a Letter of Commendation will be placed in your permanent files, and this is a copy of it. It cites the fact that before your team arrived, the Hoi Chan rate in Go Cong province for the first six months of 1968, was 220 Returnees. After your team arrived, over the last 6 months of the year, the Hoi Chanhs numbered 1,174 that is an increase of 433%! That number is a record in the Battalion and surpasses all other provinces in the IV Corps Tactical Zone. Congratulations on an incredible job well done!"

The gallery applauded politely as Willie O. shook all their hands and when that was completed, the three saluted. The colonel returned it, and they withdrew, in far more orderly manner than they had approached.

It had happened so fast and the Kid was so busy transcribing what the colonel was saying, the Kid had failed to reposition for a picture! *Damn I'll get a picture of the team later...he's moving right along!*

As soon as the three had resumed their positions standing in the small crowd, Willie O. gestured to *the Bruce* to step forward to stand by his side and when he did, he put his right hand on his shoulder.

"Please let me introduce Robert Bruce Stirling, Go Cong Province Assistant Advisor for all PSYOPS activities, whose brilliant coordination of efforts between the American and Vietnamese counterparts has a lot to do with why we are here today." Willie O. stepped to the side, giving the *Bruce* the stage. But before he started speaking, the *Bruce* gestured for ARVN Go Cong Province Chief, Colonel Nguyen Tat Thinh, to join him up front and once there, he began.

"This rather informal presentation called today, with the help of the 10th PSYOP Battalion, is to show our appreciation for cooperation with the Vietnamese Information Service, the Chieu Hoi Office the ARVN PSYWAR Bloc. And in particular, their cooperation with Field Team 10-E-4." The *Bruce* had gestured to each of the groups and individuals as he mentioned them.

"Lt. Sauers and his team," he continued, "have managed to work themselves out of a job because of the cooperation that reflects the attitude of the people. I have nothing but the highest regard for the team and its efforts in Go Cong Province.

"The function of PSYOPS, from this point forward in Go Cong Province, will be in the hands of the VIS and the ARVN PSYWAR Bloc. In commemoration of this changing of the guard, Mr. Hai Thanh Liem, VIS Chief of Go Cong, please step forward! Colonel Lawton has something special for you!"

The colonel had placed the Certificate of Commendation for the VIS Chief in a leather-bound folder to best exhibit the work of the graphics department. They had truly spiffed it up with fancy fonts and unit logos. As Liem approached, the colonel opened it up to show the Letter on one side and the list of the Province's PSYOPS achievements opposite, to the gathering. Sensing the moment, the Kid moved into position.

"Mr. Liem," the colonel presented it to him, "please accept this plaque with this Certificate of Commendation to mark this event, the first of its kind for the 10th PSYOP Battalion, and I hope, the harbinger of events to come in the future!"

The Kid lifted the Pentax to his eye in anticipation of the moment that Mr. Liem would take the award from the Colonel. The Bruce had stepped aside to give Willie the stage for the presentation so when the Kid snapped off the shot, he had Willie and Liem centered, smiling at each other making the exchange and Lt Colonel Howard beaming at them from behind. Only the left ear of ARVN Colonel Thinh made the shot.

Leather cased Letters of Appreciation were then awarded to ARVN Captain Phan Van Triem, Chief of Sector S-5 and ARVN 1st Lt. Pham Thanh Ngoc, the Province Chieu Hoi Chief before Lt. Sauers was called upon for a final remark.

"Thank you all for your support," the Kid sensed the Lt. was going to make it brief, "although we will miss the all the friends we have made here in Go Cong Province, *and Ma's cooking,* we are more than happy to move on to another province where the need is greater!"

Cut and wrap and on to lunch. It wasn't even 1100 hours.

Ma's cuisine was presented buffet style and there was plenty of it. Somebody must have robbed a PX over in Dong Tam because there was a plethora of American food along side the Vietnamese. Hamburgers on French bread, slices of Spam, fried to a nice golden brown, tomatoes and cucumbers in vinegar and rice wine, slices of pineapple and Pho in bowls with all the side garnishes and plenty of nouc maum. *Didn't see any snake or dog.* There was lots of Coke and ice, but no booze was being served today.

At one point, when the Navy Lt. Commander Nyquist was off filling his plate with seconds, the Kid slipped into his vacated seat on the sofa that fronted the coffee table where Willie O. was dining. "Well, Sir, all I really have left is to make a tour of the room and check the spelling on everybody's names and titles, of course... I think it went pretty smooth!"

"Yes! I think it did, too! Did you get some good shots?" He put down his burger and used his napkin.

"Yep. Except I missed the one where you gave the Letters to the team; when they lined up, they kind of screened me out. But I think we've got a shot of them somebody took when they were out in the field on an operation. But I'll get a back up shot before we leave. I got what I think is going to be a pretty good shot of you giving the plaque to Mr Liem. Since it's still at least 3 weeks before we'll be ready to print the April DIMENSION, I'm going to do the Stars and Stripes story as soon as we get back, while it's still all fresh."

"Excellent. Once you've got it, I can't wait to see it and we'll get Wimbish to ship it off. I've got all the addresses and information we need to get it sent back in my office."

"One more thing, Sir, do you really think this story has a better shot of making Stars and Stripes than the Nui Coto operation? Seems to me that has a lot of the elements that make for a good war story and a good PSYOPS story. Leaflets, loudspeakers and aerial broadcasts... 3 kinds of PSYOPS and Sweet is bound to have plenty of really great pictures." The Kid watched him as he considered how to phrase his answer.

"Are you just trying to get out of writing this story, Specialist?" he gave the Kid a sly look.

"No Sir, not at all. I love to write. I want to write this story, but this seems so tame compared to Nui Coto."

"You keep pushing this Nui Coto thing but ask yourself this, Specialist Stocker; how many hills have been 'taken' in this war and how many more will be? How many stories have been written about them? *Any hills you can think of in the last war?* There have been lots and lots of stories about taking hills! Gregory Peck took Hamburger Hill for God's sake! While I have yet to see a story about somebody working themselves out of a job in a war zone! And it was your quip that started it all, about *we do this everywhere and we can all go home?* I secretly laughed my ass off while Sauers told me about it, *because it struck me, why the hell not?* When you stop and think about it, what else can this man's Army do? We aren't going to nuke'em. Can't kill them all one by one. Impossible and in the long run America hasn't got enough sons or the tolerance for bloodletting to win a war of attrition. And I think you hit the nail on the head out on the runway, with your live body count idea because this is also story about how PSYOPS is saving lives. *On both sides.* The more VC we get to Chu Hoi, the more of *their lives* and *our soldier's lives* we save. The more we get the Vietnamese to own the war, and take over, *the sooner we're gone.* It's as simple as that."

Silence. The Kid did find the simplicity of the colonel's big picture stunning. All from his one liner? Really?

"Although the whole thing will most likely end up like Korea," Willie O. added, "lord only knows how long we're going to keep a token force of troops there to show our resolve."

Nyquist had filled his plate but upon his return, saw that the colonel was jawing the Kid so he meandered elsewhere.

"I requested PYSOPS, Stocker, because it appeared obvious to me that to have any hope of success in this war, as clichéd as it has become, we must win the *hearts and minds* of the Vietnamese people. But once I got here, I began sensing another PSYOPS mission, that of convincing the South Vietnamese military and government establishments to take responsibility for the eventual outcome of the war. And now, this *work ourselves out of a job* thing, I think it has the potential to address both of those necessities and thus, we can get everybody pointed in a *right direction!*"

"I might need to lob you a couple of 'softball ' questions for some suitable quotes for the Stars and Stripes article when we get back to Can Tho."

"Specialist Stocker, were in a war here, I expect you better make them *hardball* questions!"

Chapter 72

It was like he was commanding his own unit. Men with guns and bullets, a truck, all the accoutrements of war, not to mention five band members dressed like they escaped from Soho London haberdashery, toting three guitars and a drum set. The truck was rolling slowly down Highway 4, between Can Tho Field and Bin Thuy Airbase, looking for a little stretch of paddies where they could pull off and stage their publicity shoot for the band.

It was all part of the Kid's plan to 'discover' them upon his return to the World. The band would be in the paddies and the soldiers would have them covered, pointing their rifles at imaginary *(we can only hope)* foes. while the *10th Nervous PSYOPS Breakdown* performs for a phantom audience. He tallied them up; in addition to the 5 band members and himself, Ramjet, Tearman, Stage, Edwards and Willert.to act in the thing, while Birnbaum, Mike Imrem, Gellbach, and Ling Fook were along to shoot the whole thing. *All told, we've got 16 people motivated to do this, counting Moyisiadis driving. Shoot! This is a squad maneuver!*

The Kid lifted his camera and got a great shot of Ramjet, riding along in his jungle hat, his shades making him inscrutable. It was amazing how many guys had wanted to be in on this. When the idea of the publicity shoot first emerged, the Kid imagined the band all wearing their steel pots, *because he had never completely given up on the idea of that being the band's name,* for the triple intender it created. But the guys talked it out and they preferred the "HELP" look, a parody of the movie. *After all, who needs more help than a band stuck in the middle of a rice paddy in the Mekong Delta in April of 1969?* Most of the participants doing the soldier portion of the photo shoot also opted for more stylish jungle hats rather than the steel pot, but there were a couple guys who were wearing them, *hopefully not just for their protection.*

Anything to do with the band was high on the list of activities guys would most likely love to spend their time doing. The band had become the beacon light of coolness, entertainment and sanity in the unit. Everybody was sure the Kid could work his magic and make them famous, as soon as he returned to the World and in particular, *Nashville. They are that good! Hence, the picture portfolio is an absolutely necessary.*

They needed an open space, where they could pull the duce and a half off the road and have quick access to the paddies where they'd stage the publicity pictures for a genuinely Vietnam inspired and bred band. It would be an easy thing and not muddy at all, since it was nearing the end of the dry season, the paddies were in the neighborhood of bone dry. Main thing was, the gang didn't want to hang out in the middle of nowhere too long. Granted, the rifles they were using for props were loaded, but to draw any shooting today was the last thing on anybody's mind.

The Kid, on the other hand, had lots and lots of stuff on his mind. Foremost was the *Stars and Stripes* article from yesterday's ceremony down in Go Cong. It was difficult to concentrate on other stuff, like this, with that story writing itself in his head. Second was the promotion boards coming up in about a week. He was up for E-5, one of 10 men going for three slots. It was his intention to test well and get the promotion and raise that came with it. It wasn't the twenty question test that made the task daunting, it was that Capt PM Smith was the promotion board head. Third was his orders; they would be in any day now and hopefully, *with them will come a drop, which will be welcomed even if it is just one lousy stinking day! As it stands, I got 46 days and a wake up. In 46 days, I hope to God to be out of PSYOPS forever! Please make my assignment somewhere in or at least close to California, or Tennessee. That would be bearable. Anywhere else will be sheer torture for the last year before I get out.* Forth on his mind centered on his cock; was *that actually a little 'burn' I felt this morning when I pissed? Try not to think about it.*

At last, Moyssidais spots a suitable pull off and brings the big truck to a stop.

Dropping down to the ground, the Kid held on to his Pentax so it wouldn't flop up and hit him in the mouth. Then he took Tearman's M-14 so he could more easily climb down and right away, the same favor for Ramjet.

As the party tumbled out into the dry paddy and scuffed thru the scrub rice stocks left from the last harvest, the Kid searched with his mind's eye, for the proper setting. He pictured the band standing near a dyke *so you know it's a paddy,* like they were bravely ready to play, *never mind the Mekong Delta environment!* The Soldier Boys covered their every contingent for trouble so the band could just worry about the music. *Glen Campbell only wishes he could sing Galveston right fucking here!*

When they first staged the scene, the concept was working well for everybody except Richie, the vocalist who was the only band member without a prop. The grim, slightly perplexed and unhappy look on his face was not what the camera needed to see. Tom, Benny and George all had their guitars and Don, not his whole freaking drum set, but enough to make it look like he was ready to wail!

The Kid immediately saw that Richie was right; he needed something, "Too bad we didn't take the time to go over to Mama San's and grab the tambourine, but shit, here we are, we gotta make the best of it, I don't think we can get the truck for another run and all these guys together like this again very easy. Maybe kneel down like you're taking cover or try standing there with your chest puffed out, looking brave as hell?"

"What do you think?" Richie turned to the Kid, puffing the billowy sleeves of his white Taj the Taylor shirt, "maybe point at them like a used car salesman," both arms outstretched, palms up, "or maybe, I've got it," sweeping arm motion, *"a game show host!"*

Birnbaum and Ling Fook were shooting in color, so the Kid was viewing their material with the probability of it filling the bill. His pics would just be personal, not anything to use. Other people alternately posed as soldiers and took their own shots of this very strange event. People were snapping away like crazy! *Here's what I did in the war, kids! All of these pictures will be worth plenty if the band is ever famous!*

A number of poses were suggested by all involved personages; Boyett had an idea, "Let's try to look like we're just *passing through,* kind of laid back, but Delta blues on a whole other level. *'Delta',* get it? At least it'll be different from looking like we're trying to play."

So did Benny and George. "How about dueling guitars," said Benny.

"How about Shiva guitars!" suggested George?

And Don tried his drums both kneeling and standing, playing and posing, while Richie tried positioning himself from one end of the band to the other, easily working up a sweat in the 100 plus degree weather.

When it was all over and the tribe was heading back to the truck, the Kid felt the urge to take a leak so he stopped and let the group get ahead, turned around and hauled it out. As the urine began to flow from his dick he knew, with painful certainty, where he'd be Monday morning; *Fucking A! Sick call!*

500

Chapter 73

The Clinic at Eakin Compound was set out of the way of the largest flow of traffic, which was to and from the mess hall. It was off to the side, near the wall, where it even had a small shaded area with benches for the waiting patients.

The physician who handled the patients with the Kid's particular symptoms, was named *Johnston, or Johanson, Johnsen or Johnson; he'll always be the Johnson doctor to me. Doc Johnson, that's what I'll call him in the book.*

There weren't that many GIs on sick call that day, about a dozen, but while they were all patiently waiting on the benches to be called, a GI came up and proclaimed, "I'll be going to the head of the line, fellas, take a look at my eyes!" and at that, he walked from bench to bench, bending slightly to display for all to see, the yellowest whites of anybody's eyes the Kid had ever seen! Traffic light yellow, glowing out so dominate, you really couldn't even notice what color his eyes really were. "All right! This is my ticket home and *out of the Army!*"

The blond-haired chisel jawed Spec 5 was ecstatic, hardly what one would expect from a person who'd just discovered he had a major, possibly life-long, debilitating disease.

The GI next to the Kid leaned over and whispered, *"I'd rather still be in the fucking Army than have hepatitis for the rest of my life!"*

On that one, the Kid had to agree, despite his own aching desire to be out of the Army.

It wasn't long before the Kid found himself sitting across the desk from *Doc Johnson.* "Sooooo," the physician drew it out while finishing a note in a chart, "what seems to be the problem, Specialist? I mean tell me as if I didn't already know."

"Uh, well sir," the Kid stammered, "I seem to have a burning sensation when I piss and there's a little bit of a clear looking discharge."

Finishing his note, he put the pen down and without looking up at the Kid, rose from his chair and went over to a counter where there was a box of rubber gloves. Pulling on a pair with a snap on the cuff of each glove, he turned and faced the Kid with a cotton cue tip in hand. "Well, drop your drawers, I'm 99% sure this is a typical case of *gonorrhea,* of the brand we have going around here right now, but we need to take a look and get a sample to be sure you don't have something else along with it."

How encouraging; I might have a couple of different ones. DAMN! That fucking hurt! The Kid was surprised at how much it did hurt when Dr. J jammed the cotton tipped stick up his pee hole and he began paying some of the pain penalty for his sexual transgression.

As Doc Johnson harvested his sample, the luck that the Kid thought he'd accumulated at the Hollywood, when the soldiers turned out not to be MPs or VC, was evaporated. The beaver nickel let him down, or he overused it too much on the soldiers so that he was screwed right here and now.

The Kid had VD.

"Now what we're going to do," Doc Johnson went over to a table where there was a microscope set up, smeared and slid a glass slide under it, "is take a quick look at this see if we might confirm that it is only the clap or if I think I need to send it to the lab for more testing. If it is just the clap, *and I've seen a lot of it lately,* I'll give you a shot of penicillin and some more pills for you to take over the next ten days, with no alcohol, *Soldier,* and that should take care of it. Yes, yes," he dialed the focus on the scope, "looks like the local clap all right, no surprise. It's at the applause stage but still short of a standing ovation."

The Kid forced a laugh at his joke and with a totally serious expression on his face, *Dr. J* continued, "You should be more careful in the future, Soldier. This is not the kind of thing you can just catch over and over and take antibiotics to get rid of it. They lose their effectiveness, a little each time, when you must use them. Lucky for you its not *syphilis,* the disease and cure are both far more painful than what you're getting."

While dropping his short and bending over the exam couch in preparation to receive the needle, the Kid inquired of his diagnosis, "How long until I'm not contagious any more, Doc?"

"Give yourself 21 days, just to be on the safe side. And don't go thinking that now you've got it and you're on the medicine, that you can go do some more whore fucking without protection, soldier, or you'll be giving it to other guys." He jolted the air bubbles to the top of the elevated hypo chamber with the flick of an index finger and gently depressed the plunger until a couple drops squirted out the tip to confirm it was expelled. "You look smart enough to figure that one out." That said, he sank the shank in the Kid's left flank.

Frickin' ouch! Well, that wasn't even close to half as bad as that gamiglobian shot in Sadec... but I'd trade five of those not to have the clap. What a total fuck up. I fucking fucked up. The rubber was there in the room! You had it on you, you fool! So what she jumped your bones! This is my Karma for pushing my luck in Saigon and Kuala Lumpur. Not a subject that is ever going to appear in a letter home. To anybody.

"Thank you, *Dr. Johnson,* "I think it's safe to say, I've learned my lesson on this one. *With a real big slice of humble pie served up on the side.*

Chapter 74

The Kid stared at the blank sheet of paper in the typewriter on his desk and it stared back at him. Occasionally his eyes lifted up from the paper's blankness to the drawing taped on the wall directly behind his Smith Corona. It was a color sketch of a girl that the Kid had stumbled across in the clip art catalogue files of the graphics department. It looked so much like Flo that the Kid had pulled it out and taped it up there. *If you knew her, you would agree she might have posed for it.*

It was time to write the Stars and Stripes article. He had composed it in his head many times over, as was his method, to mentally write it and then set it to paper. By the same token, when he glanced up at the drawing, another composition took place in his head, a letter he would never put to paper or send. *Dear Flo, Last week I caught the clap but don't worry, I'll be all cured in 21 days and I've still got 45 left, so when I get back, I'll be good to go! Hello Mrs. Stuckey, I see you're still reading Flo's mail. Now don't go pull a throat muscle doing the I told you so's... but this doesn't mean I don't still love your daughter and who among us is perfect? ISYL.*

To say the discovery of his diseased state had thrown him off his game would have been an understatement, but he was slowly coming to terms with the consequences of his recklessness. The Kid had been fairly amused with the rumor he'd heard back in the beginning of his tour, that LBJ's youngest daughter's husband, Patrick Nugent, had caught the clap on his Vietnam tour with the Air Force. But now, it was no longer a laughing matter.

Oh, well, some guys get the Purple Heart but what do I get? The purple dick. Unlike a Combat Infantry Badge, for the purple dick, it doesn't matter what your MOS is. An officer could have a major purple dick. Enough self-pity. Write the damn story. You have no choice.

10th PSYOP Battalion FIELD TEAM TERMINATES MISSION

By Specialist 4 Curtis L. Stocker

504

The 10th Psychological Operations Battalion Field Team HE 10-E-4, (audio-visual) has worked itself out of a job in the coastal province of Go Cong. Their mission was terminated in ceremonies April 5 that turned control of all provincial PSYOPS activities over to Vietnamese agencies.

This rather unique ceremony was held in honor of 10th PSYOP Battalion personnel First Lieutenant Lawerance B. Sauers, Specialist 4 Andrew P. Simko and Sergeant Jere R. Stansell who, along with their Vietnamese counterparts, achieved what can only be called a significant milestone in this struggle for freedom.

"This is the first time we can remove one of our teams because all of the agencies have done such an outstanding job," praised Lieutenant Colonel Willie O. Lawton, Commanding Officer of the 10th PSYOP Battalion. "But in particular, we are extremely proud of Team 10-E 4. Prior to their arrival on May 25th, the Hoi Chanh numbers for the province for the first six months of the year were only 220 returnees. Then, when you look at the number of Hoi Chanhs for the next six months of 1968, it is 1,174! That is a record breaking increase of 433%! These results could not have been achieved without close cooperation between our Battalion and the Vietnamese Information Service. It is the VIS's demonstrated ability to perform in a leadership capacity that has made it possible for them to assume control of all PSYOP activities in Go Cong Province here today," Colonel Lawton said.

In attendance at the ceremony was Robert Bruce Stirling, Assistant Province Advisor of PSYOPS Activities. He cited the mutual cooperation between the US military and the many Vietnamese agencies that made the event possible.

"Today's presentations," Stirling said, "are to show our appreciation for cooperation with the Vietnamese Information Service, (VIS), the Cheiu Hoi Office and the ARVN PSYWAR Bloc and in particular, their cooperation with Field Team 10-E-4. Lt. Sauers and his team have managed to work themselves out of a job because that cooperation reflects the attitude of the people. I have nothing but the highest regard for the team and its efforts in Go Cong Province."

Colonel Lawton put the day's achievements into perspective. "The significance of today's event points to a path that could be taken by virtually all-American units. When we succeed in training our Vietnamese counterparts to do our jobs, it hastens the day when conduct of the war becomes the sole responsibility of the Vietnamese, thus allowing Americans to go home!"

"The role of PSYOPS in today's events is noteworthy," Lieutenant Colonel Lawton proudly declared. "PSYOPS saves lives on both sides of the conflict. What we generate is a live body count, plain and simple. In fact, progress in this area is two-fold because whenever we can convince an enemy to become a Hoi Chanh, we save not only his life, but all the lives on our side he would have taken."

Also present at the ceremony were Navy Lieutenant Commander John W. Nyquist, Assistant Chief for Administrative Programs and Naval Liaison of IV Corps, 10th PSYOP Battalion Company B Commander, Captain Rostyslaw Smyk and 10th PSYOP Battalion Sergeant Major Russell Kelly.

Fini

The Kid pulled the sheet from the typewriter and read it over. It was kind of a hybrid first draft, very close to a finished piece. He didn't think it was going to need much tweaking, but Willie O. wanted to see it as soon as it was written, so off to the colonel's office he went.

Walking up to Lou Wimbish's desk, he inquired if the colonel was available.

"Pretty much always…for you!" Wimbish smirked, "I'll go see if he can see you now. Back in a few seconds, Lou waved the Kid toward Willie O's office.

A rap upon the door, "Enter!" came the reply.

"Sir, Specialist Stocker Reports!" the Kid saluted.

"At ease, Specialist," he replied as he returned it and motioned for the Kid to meet him at the couch.

"Ah, so here it is!" Willie O. took the two pages from the Kid.

"I think I got all the pertinent points covered," he prefaced as the Colonel looked it over, "I encapsulated the *replace all Americans with Vietnamese* concept in a quote you pretty much kind of said, that is to say, Sir, if you read the story out loud, you will be making the quotes accurate!"

"I see what you mean, but let me just read through it once," Willie O's concentration went to the paper, his lips moving slightly as he read. "Is this the part right here? He began reading it aloud: *'Colonel Lawton put the* day's achievements into perspective, *"The significance of today's event is that it points to a path that could be taken by virtually all American units. When we succeed in training our Vietnamese counterparts to do our jobs, it hastens the day when conduct of the war becomes the sole responsibility of the Vietnamese, thus allowing Americans to go home!"* Is that it? I like it."

"Yes, Sir, and the next paragraph, too, about PSYOPS."

He read the rest of it out loud. "There you go, Stocker, I read it, so I said it! That's exactly how I wanted it put! I mean, that's *exactly how I put it,*" he said with his magnificent grin. "Nice work!"

"I also plan on submitting two pictures, Sir, one of you giving out the award to the Vietnamese and I've found a picture of the team in the field on a MEDCAP, from a couple months back. It shows all three of them nicely."

"Excellent. Get all of that together, do make a couple carbon copies, and as soon as the pictures are printed, we'll get Lou to bundle it up and send it all off, maybe even this afternoon?"

"Let's go with first thing in the morning, Sir, the prints are in the soup right now."

The colonel rose, so did the Kid, preparing for the salute exchange but the colonel had one more question. "So Stocker. Are you ready for the promotion boards on Thursday?"

"I think so, Sir, it's been a little busy here lately, but I made some time to study."

"That's good, I'd like to see you get it. I think you deserve it. Dismissed, Soldier," he said with a smile. Their salutes rose simultaneously.

"Thank you, Sir!" The Kid did a fairly snappy 180 degree turn and let himself out, pulling the door closed.

It's a good thing to make the commander smile! The Kid thought, as he headed back to Graphics, his problem with the clap temporarily forgotten.

"Hey, Curt!" the Kid heard the unmistakable voice of Wimbish calling to him, "dude, *come here,* I've got something I'm sure you'll want to see, *ASAP!*"

Making a U turn, the Kid strolled to a stop in front of Wimbish's desk. "What?" *Wimbish is grinning, it's going to be good!*

He held a handful of papers to his chest and he looked for all the world like the cat that just did eat the Tweety. 'Your orders are in."

"NO!"

"Yes! Want to know where you're going back in the States? Want to know your exact DEROS?"

The Kid's mouth was gaping open in shock; he was about to find out not only the day he would climb on the jet to go home, but where the Army, in all it's wisdom, had decided to send him upon his return.

"Fucking YES! Give!" As soon as Lou held them out the slightest inch, the Kid snatched them from his hand and with a fresh case of the jitters, began trying to sort through the Army-esee typewriter mumbo jumbo for the pertinent information.

Special Orders Number 79. 31 March 1969. EXTRACT

Stocker, Curtis L. RA 12966317, Assigned to: USARV Rtne Det APO 96375 for fus asg to RO USA Hospital, Ft. Carson, Colo.

"Colorado," he slowly mouthed, ironically stunned. *He was going home to Colorado!* The Kid had never considered the possibility. He wanted so badly to be near Nashville or Flo that was the only mantra in his head when he thought about his military future had been Tennessee or California. Now the Army was sending him home.

DEROS: 19 May 1969. May 19th? I just got a one-day drop! "Wow!" he said, holding the orders in his now slightly shaky hands, sort of crumpled together with the story of how the Vietnamese can take over the war, "I'm down to 44 days and if I go up to Group a week before, I'm down to 37 days here in Can Tho! Dare I call myself fucking SHORT? *I say hell yeah in 5 days I'll be under 40!"*

Chapter 75

They were the center of attention. Fresh back from Nui Coto, up on the Cambodian border, John Butler and Jim Sweet were adjusting their consciousness on some very appropriate sweet Cambodian bud as they related their tales. *And there were plenty of tales and bud!*

"There weren't any ARVN regulars there," Butler explained the make up of the military contingent between hits, "it was 2 battalions of Ruf Pufs working with, we never knew for sure, must have been at least a platoon of Green Berets advisors or an A team, whatever the fuck they call themselves this week, but they were every fucking where, could have been two A teams! But I didn't know it wasn't against the law to put so many Ruf Puffs together in the same place, let alone let them do an assault!"

The operation had gone on for a full month, having commenced on March 5th with a sweep of the area hamlets that surround the mountain, in preparation for the assault.

"At one point," Sweet began, "they landed a loudspeaker team on top of the hill, protected by a mobile strike force, and for three days, they broadcast the appeal for some trapped VC to rally before they were killed."

Loud speaker team on top… it could have been me!

"Glad I got to advise them over the radio and wasn't up on top myself, *THAT's* for damn fucking sure," exclaimed Butler.

"Good strategic thinking!" endorsed the Kid.

The pair related on all the bitchin' PSYOPS tools they got to see in field action. In addition to loudspeaker teams, the operation featured an aerial element in two phases. The first was the C-47 equipped with loudspeakers, knick named "Gabby", that flew circles around the mountain blaring propaganda, that of wifely appeals and babies crying ilk.

"The fucking thing succeeded in keeping us awake, too. "lamented Sweet.

The second audio PSYOPS at work was the quick reaction appeal. This happened when a recent rallier to the government consented to make an appeal to his comrades over a PRC-25 radio that was relayed to the C-47 and literally broadcast live as it flew circles around the mountain!

"One night, after a heavy B-52 bombing attack, the VC lit up the mountain with cooking fires, like saying to us, 'we're still here, mutha fuckahs… come and get us! Talk about *'reverse PSYOPS'*! "Basketball sized cahonies those boys have, for sure GI!" Butler marveled at the tenacity of the foe.

All the while they talked and smoked on the rail, various GI's, including the Kid, of course, were busy making paper airplanes and seeing if they could fly them on to the roofs of the Vietnamese houses just across the swamp pond. A couple of the Kids' planes now resided on the top of their dwellings. Others were caught by the rowdy group of boys who had made a contest of catching them before they hit the ground. At least those planes that did swim with the snakes in the pond.

Sweet's film was in the dark room, and everybody was anxious to see the negative proof positive sheets as soon as they were available, especially the Kid, who wanted to find his cover shot for the April issue.

"Bummer you guys missed the *HELP* movie!" Edwards chortled, "You should have seen this fucking place!" he gestured with his arms, "from one end to the other, 3-4 deep! *It was a fucking forest fire!* "

"Did anyone take a picture?" Butler asked with expectation on his face.

"None of us, but they threatened to," shot in Tall John, "they always threaten it. That's their main argument against us, that they are going to take pictures from somewhere out there, and whoever is in the picture will be charged. Imagine for a second, if they DID have a picture of what went on here that night, and they could prove everybody in the picture was smoking weed, what I think they'd do is suppress it!"

"I don't think a picture from any distance will do them any good legally unless they have the identifiable object that's in the picture," speculated the Kid, "if that had even a remote chance of working, they'd have tried it by now."

"So what did you guys do, live on MREs for a month?" Barry Fischer asked.

"Pretty much," said Butler, "I'll fucking tell you it was a treat to eat in the mess hall tonight!"

"Though I'd never hear anybody say that", laughed Willert.

Chapter 76

Early in April, the offices of Battalion HQ received two uninvited visitors;

One the ultimate in instilling fear and the other one, a cute little bundle of purring fur. The Bat and the Cat both arrived unannounced.

The bat came first. It infiltrated through some unknown hole in a window screen, ceiling or some other such avenue. It's presence became know one afternoon when it flew a sortie from one end of the battalion front area to the other, sending GIs and civilian workers diving under desks and rolling up papers and looking for objects with which they could defend themselves! At the end of its run, it cut a left into the room occupied by S-2, where it hung upside down up in the very corner of the 10 foot high ceiling, aerial evil concentrated in a very small but foreboding black package.

From then on, everybody feared it because after all, bats are known to carry rabies. But nobody had the balls to go after it, because, well, *after all, bats are known to carry rabies.*

The little vampire came to prefer mainly haunting S-2 and S-3, two connected rooms of the floor plan and usually it was in one or the other, hanging upside down, plotting its next terror run. A week passed and still, nobody had mustered the guts to approach it or attempt a capture, fearing a counterattack would send the hypothetical Bat catcher off to the medics for ultra painful rabies shots.

That was the situation in Battalion HQ when the cat arrived. It literally came to them out of the blue! It happened one afternoon when the Kid and Tom were taking a smoke break on the roof porch of the HQ building. It was a quite little spot, about ten feet by ten feet, accessed by a stairway out of the back of the graphics room, which at one point, the men figured, had been the kitchen of the building. The remains of a clothesline arrangement showed the landing had all the trappings of a haunt for the hired help, a place they could go to escape work by pretending to be working. There was a convenient place to sit on the edge of the rainwater collection system that gathered the flow coming off the peak of the building and channeled it into the cistern.

They first took notice of the small grey and tiger stripped feline when it meowed at them, its head appearing over the peak of the rooftop. It hesitated not one whit as it walked right down to the pair and got friendly, purring like a Mercedes and doing a little dance. The Kid held out his index finger and it slicked back with either side of its chin. Judging from its diminutive size, he figured it couldn't have been more than 6 months old.

"Look at this! Where do you think it came from?" the Kid wondered.

"Hell if I know," Tom answered the rhetorical question, "doubt that it's been living up here... could have jumped over from there," he gestured at the next door structure, the roof of which was within five feet of the Battalion HQ building.

Scooping it up and holding it over his head, the Kid attempted to determine its sex, "I think it's a girl," he announced, pretty sure by what he saw or more likely, didn't see between her little legs. "I wonder of it belongs to anybody?"

Traversing back down the stairs and into the graphics room, the Kid held up their prize, "Hey, guys!" he called out to the other DIMENSION staffers, holding up his prize, "look what we found! I think it's a girl!"

"Or more accurately," Tom corrected, "look what found us!"

The Kid sat her on Tom's graphics light table and stuck out his finger for her to rub her chin against again, which she immediately did.

"What are you going to call her? "Dunnacek inquired.

"Oh, I don't know..." the Kid pondered, "something suitable for a unit mascot, like, say... *Psuyzie Psyops? And Suyzie spelled with a 'P'?*

It stuck immediately. Psuyzie sat on the table, the center of attention, looking around at her new owners and all present, cat and soldiers alike, felt the bond immediately form.

"Let's get something to bring some milk back from lunch at Eakin," Bob Weston began planning for her care and maintenance, "and some food, too, I wonder what she eats?"

"Anything, if she's hungry," Ron Edwards guessed, "we better fatten her up pronto if she's going to have a fighting chance in this place; she's barely half the size of an average local rat!"

The Kid had seen a large number of dogs while in-country, but he hadn't seen many cats. Dogs, of course, were a staple on the Vietnamese menu and he'd heard they'd eat a cat, too, but this one was so skinning, it wouldn't have made an appetizer, let alone a meal.

It was Gelbach who went to the $64,000 question, "do you really think they'll let us keep her?"

"Let's go find out!" was the Kid's instant response.

"Newsflash!" Gelbach held up his hands in mock headline presentation, "Stocker opens Graphics Cat House!"

The whole graphic crew paraded out from their back office, with the Kid carrying their new prize held up in front of them as they entered the front of HQ, "Look what WE got!" the he held the kitten high over his head for all to see. "It came in over the roof!"

"OOOO's AAAHHHH's and COOL!" were the overwhelming responses to the brand new pet; it had taken Psyuzie less than a heartbeat to win over the entire unit!

From that point on, she had the run of the place. It wasn't long before she had half a dozen soldiers feeding her and making places for her to sleep, but mainly, she inhabited a space in the Graphics room, where her true new owner worked.

That is, until she discovered the Bat.

It took less than a week for her notice the aerial rodent. It caught her eye on one of its strafing runs and from that second forward, she tracked whenever it flew. She'd run around the room beneath it, looking for an opportunity, bounding off chairs, jumping up on desks with her tiny jaws snapping in anticipation. Simply put, the *Bat drove her nuts!*

Her obsession gave the Kid pause to consider that she might be older than her size indicated. Her hunting style showed development, such as in the way she set up and attempted to conceal her observation post over the Bat's location. No telling how old she was but clearly, she fed herself partially by hunting before throwing in with the 10th. She was small, but the Bat was smaller and it was crystal clear, Pysuzie would like nothing better than to get her claws on *das fliedermaus!*

It was a Thursday night and the Kid, Boyett, and a few other GIs were working a graveyard shift so they could have Friday off. As it neared midnight, the Bat was getting restless, knowing it was night outside and time to fly, but it was trapped inside, illuminated by the fluorescent lights of the offices and everybody was beginning to wonder how long a bat could live in a building without going out for a nightly meal or at least, a snack.

The Kid happened to be in S-2 at about 2300 hours, when the Bat kicked up and began circling the room. As it flapped around the area, for once, it's built in radar betrayed it and the Bat collided with the swirling blade of a ceiling fan! Whenever the Bat flew, the Kid paid attention if he was in the room so he was watching when it happened. Just like the Bat was a pitched ball and the fan blade was a baseball *bat*, it hit the Bat square and line drive drove into the nearest wall. No sooner did the stunned blood sucker slide down the wall and hit the floor than Psyuzie pounced on it like a lioness on a gazelle!

Acting like a soul possessed, Psyuzie secured the bat in her mouth and emitted a low growl while looking around for a place to take her long coveted meal. She was a cat on a mission! Thinking that it would not be good for Psyuzie to eat a bat that could have rabies, the Kid attempted to grab her, but she was too fast.

An hour later, she emerged, looking satisfied as any cat who finally got to eat the canary, and began licking herself in cleanup mode.

If a cat eats a bat that has rabies, will it get rabies? The Kid wasn't the only person in the 10th to ponder that! Nobody seemed to know the answer. But the general consensus was, the Bat was certainly healthy looking while it lived for almost half a month in the HQ, so it likely did not have rabies. Nobody knew where there was a vet to ask.

But the very next day, Psyuzie was passed out cold on her Graphic sleeping pad and the boys couldn't rouse her! Knowing there was no Vet, it appeared there was nothing they could do to save her and sadly, began waiting for her to die.

On the second day of being essentially comatose, during which the whole unit thought for sure she was a goner, Pysuzie snapped out of it and woke up like nothing ever happened. Relief was building wide because she was the cutest thing in the entire 10th PSYOP battalion.

Pysuzie was the Heroine of the office for single handedly taking out the Bat. If only her tiny little chest were big enough for a medal! That's what I'll say in the book.

Chapter 77

The promotion board interviews were conducted in the Roof Club. All the chairs and tables were pulled toward the movie screen, creating an open area in the back half, toward the bar and the stair well. An elongated table and 3 chairs had been placed, smack dab in the middle, facing west. About 10 feet back from the table, a lone Army issue straight back wooden chair awaited the candidate.

When the candidate emerged from the stair well, he could see the chair, but not the men at the table. The candidate was to march to the chair, stop, do a right face, present a salute and report to the ranking officer of the inquisitors, in the most military manner he could freaking muster.

There were 10 candidates for the three E-5 promotional slots. The group agreed to draw numbers in order of appearance and the Kid was 8th. The Tribal candidates waited to be called, mostly hanging out on the Embassy balcony in clean uniforms, hair cut, shaved up faces and boots spit shined screaming eagle style, literally the works. There was a lot of nervous smoking going on, *of tobacco,* as they awaited their chance to get a little more rank and a raise in pay. They quizzed each other while marking time.

"What is the next rank up from Major General?" Ron Edwards flipped out the question.

"Lieutenant General," shot back Bill Sutton, who had come in from his packing up duties in Go Cong to take his turn with the Board.

"That's right, but go fucking figure," exclaimed Ron, "a major way outranks a lieutenant so why doesn't a major general outrank a lieutenant general?

"I don't think that's an actual question they will ask today," Ramjet interjected. He wasn't there to do the boards, just there to kibitz the candidates. "You need stuff more like what is S-4?"

"Supply," answered the Kid, then responding to the right to ask the next question, "What is the function of S-1?"

"Admin," Gerald Efird had the answer ready. It was a good thing because Efird was first up. There was no real advantage of going early or late, the questions were the same for everybody and there was a study guide. It was just a matter of what one could recall on the spot and how a candidate acted under the artificial pressure the inquisitors were there to supply.

The Kid separated himself from the group that was gathered right outside of his, Willert's and Ramjet's room and went down to the corner, lit a KOOL and began to compose himself for the little exam. When he became an E-4, out in the field with Wilson, there hadn't been any promotion board BS. There was a slot, and he was the only one there so he got to fill it.

It was 1300 hours. The board interviews were planned for the first part of the afternoon with the results being available and orders being cut for the promotions at the end of the day. Nice as it would be to get a promotion to E-5, the only thing the Kid really cared about was that in just two days, he'd be under 30! Home was so close he could taste it, so he had taken preparations for the exam as a sweet diversion.

The Kid's advantage against the field lay in the fact that it was an oral exam. *My strong suit.* His distinct disadvantage on the other hand, lay in the fact that the makeup of the board, of two enlisted men and one officer, was entirely comprised by individuals with whom he had histories.

One of them was First Sergeant John T. Johnson. The Kid thought back to that night after the first showing of *HELP,* when Sergeant Johnson had tried to cajole him to volunteer to ride shotgun on a convoy up to Vinh Long by calling him *chicken.* Since that night, the Sarge and the Kid maintained what could only be described as cordial friendliness when they encountered each other. One time the Kid could have sworn that he heard Sergeant Johnson softly clucking like a chicken, when he walked through the orderly room, real low, kind of like a poultry version of the rat's revenge. The Kid turned around really fast to look, Johnson was sitting at his desk, looking down at a sheet of paper, trying like hell not to crack a full smile. *That was pretty amusing. He could go either way, but Johnson is a fair man and I think he respected my right not to volunteer.*

The second EM on the board was Sergeant Major Russell B. Kelley. Thinking back to the Go Cong ceremony trip, the Kid wondered if maybe, he should have volunteered to carry the box of stuff. *Sergeant Major Kelley never said a single word or made any body language attempts not to carry the box of plaques and letters, but if the Kid had known then what he knew now, he damn well would have carried that box! Considering that whole trip was happening for Willie O's story, rather he saw the Kid as a journalist or the colonel's lap dog didn't much matter. Since then, they had been a lot friendlier and hey, we'll always have Go Cong. No problems here.*

Now, the Officer in Charge. Big large problem. This is PM's solid gold chance to fuck me over. He's going to be loaded for bear. How can he not be holding a grudge about the marijuana thing? I'm blatantly breaking the law, but I could have busted him? He is still trying to figure that one out! Can't imagine he's going to let go of that bone. After all, under any other circumstances, like, if he had seed one, his shot would be Stocker in the corner stockade.

Efird was back and Edwards went up; and on it went, with military precision. He lit up another KOOL and reflected on how he really felt about his whole military experience. *It's all nothing but a big fucking game. Here's the promotion board questions you gotta memorize, here's the spit shine and polish hoops you gotta jump through, here's the ass you gotta kiss. You know that PM has a serious case of the ass over his not getting kissed. This whole thing is so fucking far outside the rules of his game, it's gotta be blowing his mind! He has to make a move.*

Looking back down the balcony to its one entrance, the Kid marveled at what took place there. It could only have been an accident of fate that the Embassy's layout had, indeed, made possible the establishment of their almost other worldly pot subculture. Here, they smoked with impunity. Was it Bonnie, Clyde or Jesse James who said, *'you gotta be honest to live outside the law?'* Everybody knew it but nobody could or would do anything about it although most of the lifers still felt strongly that somebody should. None more so, than PM himself.

If the whole fucking country was stoned, on both sides, the war would be over! I wonder if I could get Willie interested in a story about that?

Then the Kid had a seizure of the infamous pot paranoia; *Saaaayyyy, I wonder if the Army let happen what is going on here so they could study us? And the Colonel is in on it and that's why we keep skating? Naw. Not a chance.*

"Stocker!" Edward's voice brought him back to reality, "you're up!" he gestured like a matre d', showing him the way to his table.

I'm up? Seemed quick. He flicked the KOOL off the rail, sailing it far into the swamp.

One last swig of water and he was off, striding to the stairwell and up the stairs, *not too fast, don't want to be even the slightest bit winded.* At the top of the stairs, the Kid composed himself and strided in even steps to the chair on his left. Executed a right face, he reported with a salute to the ranking man, "Sir, Specialist 4th class Stocker reports!" holding the salute until PM had returned it.

"At ease, Specialist," PM released him, "please be seated."

The Kid complied, sitting ramrod straight but making sure his back was not touching the chair, with his hands resting on his thighs. He smiled a small but confident grin and could see, upon a quick eye contact survey, that both Johnson and Kelley were giving off far more favorable vibes than PM, whose mouth turned down ever so slightly and he was squinting noticeably.

Who is the cat and who is the mouse?

"For the record, would you state your name, rank and serial number," PM opened.

"Yes, Sir, Curtis L. Stocker, Specialist 4th Class, RA 126 66 317."

"Well, he got that part right," Sergeant Johnson grinned, "welcome, specialist Stocker, to your promotion board interview. So far today, the candidates have been very sharp, and we anticipate no less from you. Now, first question, when field stripping the M-16 A1, what is the first step?"

"First Sergeant, the first step when field stripping the M-16 is to check and clear the chamber."

"Correct, Specialist." Johnson was not surprised.

"Specialist Stocker," Kelley began, "please recite your chain of command from your company up through Battalion."

"Sergeant Major Kelley, my chain of command is as follows: First sergeant Ozelle Jones, Company Commander Captain Powell M. Smith," the Kid nodded at the captain, acknowledging his presence, "and the Battalion commander, Ltc. Willie O. Lawton. For work purposes, as the editor of DIMENSION, this month, I am my department head, and I report to Information Officer First Lieutenant Daniel Chiles and, of course, LTC Lawton."

'Very good, specialist," Kelley nodded as he wrote something down on his score sheet.

"Specialist Stocker," PM got ready with his first question, "Who is currently the commander of the American Forces in Vietnam?"

"Sir, the current commander of American forces in Vietnam is General Creighton Abrams."

"Correct."

And so it went for 18 more questions, some by the sergeants and a couple more by PM; what's the purpose of this… who's in charge of that… where can I get one of those…, the answers to which the Kid had down cold. Then came the tricky part.

"Specialist Stocker," began SM Kelley. "…when calling in an artillery strike, which map coordinates do you communicate and in what order do you communicate them?" a slight smile crossed his lips as he spoke the two words, *'map coordinates,'* while posing the question.

Almost immediately, the Kid recalled a conversation they had both been involved in, on the Go Cong trip, a week and a half earlier. The discussion had been about field operations and the Kid had mentioned that his experience included receiving artillery support during a fire fight, but knew if his life depended on it, he was incapable of calling in the coordinates for a strike because he didn't know one from the other. SM Kelley had been listening in and *this was the question they ask you that they know you don't know the answer to and the point is to see how quickly you admit you don't know! He telegraphed it to me!*

"Sergeant Major," the Kid replied with a smile, after a very brief pause, "I do not know the answer to that question."

"Somehow, I didn't expect that you would," Kelley showed a full-on grin and was chuckling with Johnson and acting for all the world like the interview was concluded, but Captain Smith, the Kid noticed, was glaring at them. In the millisecond that the sergeants took to notice the captain apparently was not through, all eyes turned to the Kid.

"Specialist Stocker, I have one more question," PM displayed a particular vein of slyness, tilting his head to one side and cocking an eyebrow as he posed it, "if you were a non commissioned officer, and you saw a soldier smoking marijuana, what would you do?"

The Kid was visibly taken back. This is not a question from the prep sheet! This was the smoking gun kill question of all questions! It was in the first seconds of silence that he realized what was happening. PM began exhibiting a detectable smirk. The Kid looked over to the sergeants, where he gleaned a small element of surprise from their facial expressions.

There were a couple of points the Kid immediately took into consideration, the first of which was, can anything I say here today be used against me? Did they ask everybody this question? Edwards would have told me in a NY second if they had asked HIM this question! Is this a simple assault on my integrity or a fishing expedition? PM knows how I feel; does he want to be able to accuse me of lying to the Board? That bastard thinks he has me! And maybe he does. The amazing thing is, I don't give a shit! I don't fucking care if I'm ever promoted in this man's Army because all I want is out. I will not sacrifice my integrity.

Looking PM as straight in the eye as humanly possible, these are the words that came out of the Kid's mouth: "Sir, if he wasn't on duty, I wouldn't do anything."

That was the honest fucking truth. Every man in the room knew it. The sergeants were visibly surprised by it all as the Kid and clearly, unsure where it was all going or to what it was leading. PM must have been gauging if the answer given was enough to suit his purpose. He seemed unsure of what to do; like go deeper and ask me why I wouldn't cite the guy? What? Tension became electric before he pulled the plug.

"Thank you, Specialist Stocker, that concludes the interview, you are dismissed." PM said with a measure of what could only be identified as satisfaction. Laying down his pen, he prepared to return the Kid's salute.

The Kid rose and delivered the salute and once PM returned it, he took his down and began the right face to march out of the room when he stopped, pivoted back and said, "Sir, one thing I would like to add, I'd much prefer my friends to be stoned on pot rather than drunk on their asses. Thank you."

He had addressed an officer after dismissal and had actually stated that he preferred his comrades at arms to be lawbreakers! Talk about a big military *no no*. Not waiting to see if he'd be cited or receive a reply, the Kid swiftly executed a snappy right face and made his exit.

"Fucking A!" he declared, bounding back onto the balcony, pointing at the other candidates, "did PM ask any of you guys what you'd do if you were a NCO and caught a GI smoking pot?"

"No," said Stanton.

"No," said Efird.

"No!" Edwards immediately responded, *"He asked you that?"*

"Yes! Fucking yes, right at the end, the last thing!"

"Wow!" exclaimed Efird, "that's gotta hurt! What did you say?"

"Well, needless to say I was a little more than shocked and I said, *if the GI wasn't on duty, I wouldn't do anything!"*

"And what did he say back?" Ramjet quickly glanced up and added, "We better keep our voices down, they might be trying to listen!"

"Nothing. He said *thank you, the interview is over!*"

"Did either Johnson or Kelley say anything?" Edwards asked.

"No! Not a word!" the Kid said, "I gotta say that the two of them looked sort of surprised by the whole deal, too. PM just wrote something down on his paper and dismissed me.

"That does not bode well," Ramjet shook his head," I wonder what's going to happen? Shit, that could totally kill your chances for E-5."

"No shit, Sherlock!"

Talk about unsettling! With the interviews completed, the candidates jumped in the waiting duce and returned to Battalion HQ. Sitting in the graphics room with Boyett, Weston, Wilson, Imrem, Edwards, Dunnachek, Gelbach and the Chief, the Kid could do nothing but wait. The rest of the candidates, who were in from the field or did not have headquarters workstations, waited up in the foyer in front of Wimbish's desk. The results of the promotion board were to be available that afternoon and promotion orders would be cut dated today.

Turns out the wait was not very long. At a half hour, Edwards went up front and discovered the results of the Boards were in and Wimbish was preparing the promotion orders for the colonel's signatures *and* he'd gotten a look at them.

"Sutton made it, Efird made it, *Ralph* made it... I didn't make it and Curt, you didn't make it. In spite of the fact that... get this... you were the first candidate in the unit to get a max score on a promotion board, making you the top scorer of all 10. PM is not promoting you based on the way you answered that one question about pot!

The news was the equivalent of a military slap in the face. Everybody stared at the Kid, who was seated at his desk, to see what his reaction was going to be.

Reaching for his pack of KOOLS, he lit up, "Shit," *exhale,* "why I am not surprised?"

Seriously not surprised. After all, the Kid knew deep down there was no way in the whole fucking Milky Way Galaxy that PM would have let an opportunity like this slip away. From the second PM played the pot card, the Kid saw the Music Man sized ass bite parade coming down Broadway. It was the lever on PM's trapdoor where he'd finally have the pleasure of hanging the Kid and watching him twist, slowly in the wind, for all of the marijuana bullshit. It might not be the same as busting him a grade or putting him in the Long Binh Jail, but keeping the Kid from advancing a grade and not getting a raise was clearly a PM victory!

Or anyway, it would have been if the Kid actually gave a shit. He was two wake ups away from being under 30 days. It truly mattered not to him what rank he was when he got on that plane... Seriously not surprised, not at all.

However. The ensuing events that transpired between then and chow, surprised the freaking fuck out of everybody!

In less than 30 minutes, Wimbish came busting into the graphics room, his eyes saucer wide with amazement, talking to the room but directly looking at the Kid. "You guys will not believe what just happened! Willie refused to sign the promotion board orders, came out of his office, said *get Captain Smith up here to my office pronto!* So PM comes up, goes into the colonel's office…and I couldn't tell what he said, but… *I actually heard Willie raising his voice!* PM is in there for less than 3 minutes, comes out totally red faced, steaming and smoking and grinding his teeth, doesn't even stop, walks by my desk as he snarls out some words I couldn't understand and storms down the steps! Seconds later, the colonel is standing at my desk, drops the orders on it and says, 'rewrite these and promote the top three scorers. *'Captain Smith cannot alter the promotion board standards by asking just one soldier a single question and disqualifying him based solely upon the answer, he said, 'You just can't do it. I won't allow it!'* So… Stocker, you were at the top of the list… you got one of the three promotions! You're an E-5, Dude!"

The Kid sat there at his desk, dumbfounded, wallowing in that shithouse you fall into where you come out smelling like a rose! In the last hour, he had gone from *not promoted* to promoted, all in a turn of events that was sure to cause major talk in the unit, on all levels and in all groups. Obviously, the Kid knew the colonel was in his camp, but this act was in itself, just plain amazing. *Strength to the Kid, strength to the Tribe!* It happened so fast, the Kid had not yet even begun to formulate a response to PM's maneuver. Then the perfect response was custom crafted for him and delivered with the power of Thor's hammer! By the only man in the unit had the ability to do things like that. And the best part… *the Kid didn't even have to ask!*

"Oh," Wimbish added, almost as an afterthought, "Willie wants to see you in his office. Now."

The Kid knocked.

"Enter."

Opening the door, he stepped through, closed it, turned and reported. Willie looked irritated as he returned the salute with a punctuating snap and said, "I can't believe Captain Smith did that! If he had told the sergeants what he had planned, they could have saved him a lot of embarrassment. Not to mention, Specialist Stocker, for this act of prejudice, aimed specifically and only at you, you could put his tit in the legal ringer...*again!* It is a clear act of conduct unbecoming an officer! By what regulation is he altering the promotion board protocol and applying an arbitrary value to one question he asked *only* you? *Unbelievable!!*" He paused.

The Kid remained silent.

"To attempt bending a promotions board interview into an investigative tool, designed to make you incriminate yourself or lie, either way he rationally has a predetermined reason for not promoting you. That was his plan, so you are the wronged party, Specialist."

"Yes Sir," the Kid can only listen.

The slight smile crosses his lips, "But somehow, I get the feeling that you're not going to want me to pursue this any farther... am I right?"

"Yes Sir."

"Good decision. All things considered." He put a hand to his chin, like he was the one doing the considering, "how many days have you got left?"

"31 and a wake up, Sir."

Willie stood and circled around his desk to stand in front of the Kid. "Congratulations on your promotion, by the way, *Specialist 5,*" he extended his hand to the Kid for a ceremonial shake, broad smiles exchanged. "But, in these last days, I strongly suggest you tread lightly, lay low and keep out of his way."

"Yes Sir," salute, "I'll do my best, Sir."

And I meant it.

Chapter 78

It was a festive mood that permeated the Embassy that evening after chow. Over a half dozen men were smoking and making paper airplanes in the perpetual contest to have your plane make it to the roofs of the houses just on the other side of the swamp. The craze had taken on a life of its own. GIs trying to come up with new designs that would set the record for the longest trajectory. The evening breeze over the swamp aided greatly in the duration of the flights.

At first, when the paper airplane fad got off the ground, so to speak, the Vietnamese living in the houses below found it amusing and indeed, the kids like to chase down the planes and catch the ones they could still in the air. It was after all, a source of paper for them. Now, as the fad wore on, not so may watched and not so many kids chased after them.

"So, *Specialist 5* Stocker," Little began, "there is no denying that Willie likes you. *Everybody* knows that. But god damn, man, I mean, shit; he makes a company commander change a promotion board decision? What the fuck? Are you *blowing him?*"

Everybody laughed, even the Kid, and when it subsided, he said, "Apparently I don't have to! But maybe that's a tactic that PM ought to consider!" Big laugh.

"OK," Tearman just arrived, "I know you've probably told it a dozen times, but since I just got off duty, will you tell me now or do you want me to wait till another five guys want to hear it too?"

"No," the Kid passed Tall John a joint, "I'll tell, wasn't a very long meeting. I walked in, Willie was flat pissed, told me what a fuck up PM was, congratulated me on the promotion and said he figured I wasn't going to try and fuck with him legally, *although I could.* I said no, he said that's good and suggested for the remainder of my tour, I *lay low!*"

Fucking amazing was the general take.

"PM must be talking to himself!" Ron chortled, "But really, what do you think it is? I mean shit, Curt, we want to know. What made Willie O decide to become your personal fucking guardian angel?"

The Kid seriously considered it. "Well, here's what I speculate; he came into the unit, right when Lt. Wilson was court martialing me for eating in the mess hall, he saw the injustice of that whole thing. Then, when my extension for Armed Forces Radio was turned down, reasons given by Group of no opening and no need for my MOS, he saw those reasons were both lies in the face of the audition letter from AFN requesting my services. I think he saw Group was clearly punishing me over winning the court martial. He's a fair man. I'd be willing to bet that Willie has been screwed over in his military career, didn't like it and personally decided I didn't deserve *to be* screwed! Anyway, that's about the only way I can figure it out.

"And you never talked about marijuana, he never asks you what all this marijuana shit about? Not even in light of what Smith's question was? No orders or suggestions to stop smoking it?" Willert quizzed.

"Nope. Ken, don't you remember at our meeting, how quickly Willie moved away from the marijuana part of what happened and into the legal part of what PM did and shouldn't have done or what we could or should do to him? If he's not bringing it up, I'm sure not!"

"So, he's your friend... I sure as hell feel like he's *everybody's* fucking friend here on the balcony," declared Little. "The colonel being a brother, I'd lay odds he's had a toke or two in his life. Had to have encountered some homies with some weed at some point in his travels."

"I'm never going to ask," the Kid said.

Just then, the alert went up from Barry Fischer, the Embassy sentry on duty. *"Why hello, First Sergeant JONES!"* he loudly announced the approach of the first shirt, "and what brings you down here tonight?"

Ozelle stops and stands in front of Barry and looks down the balcony to see half a dozen lit joints arc like tracers into the swamp. Shaking his head, he turns and continues walking. "I'm here to bust Stocker..." he announces.

Say what?

The Tribe parts, leaving the Kid standing at the rail, ready to launch his latest paper airplane design.

'If you want to hang on to your brand new stripe, *Specialist 5 Stocker...*" Ozelle pointedly cited his ultra recent promotion, "I strongly suggest you hang on to that airplane. I am here to bust you, all of you, but you, *in particular,* Stocker, about that very thing," he pointed at the plane. "I just had a visit from a committee of civilians who live down there," he gestured with a sweep of his left hand to a group of a dozen Vietnamese, gathered at the corner of the little store and the swamp. "They are plain tired and insulted by the way you men are littering their neighborhood with all of these fucking paper airplanes! They just came over here to request that it stop. Do you read me? All of this has to stop…AND IT WILL STOP… *right fucking now!*"

Whoa! The Kid wasn't the only one standing there with a paper airplane in his hand. Sheepishly, they all looked to their planes and then down at the neighborhood action committee, looking up at them. The Kid began to comprehend the number of white paper planes that lay littered around the swamp and realized; the craze had gone into overkill *squared.*

Holding up the plane in his hand, for the Vietnamese to see, he ripped it in half and wadded it up and stuffed it in his pocket. Sensing a moment, everybody else who held a plane, did the same thing. The civilians nodded and waved their approval as a group and dispersed.

And thus, the great paper airplane air force of the New Villa aerodrome was permanently grounded.

"This is all your fault, Stocker," Ozelle came up to get in his face, "pissin' off the neighborhood like that, you should be ashamed of yourself. I heard how you started this whole fucking craze on guard duty over at the Villa Cruz. And there will be no more making and flying paper airplanes all night long over there, *either.* You're suppose to be paying attention to fucking guard duty." He waited a couple of seconds for a reply the Kid chose not to make. "Do I make myself perfectly clear, Specialist *"5" (he loudly emphasized the 5)* Stocker?"

"Yes First Sergeant!" the Kid loudly replied.

"You gonna go running to the colonel and ask him to still let you fly?"

"Don't think so, First Sergeant!"

"I don't care how you got that stripe," Ozelle wasn't done yet, "but sure as he gave that to you, *I can take it away!*"

"Yes, First Sergeant."

"You may be short, but that don't excuse you from obeying all the rules and you can bet your ass, Stocker, there are more than a couple of people looking for you to fuck up!" The first shirt broke his eye contact with the Kid and turned and walk off the balcony.

"Wow!" Ramjet was open mouthed, "I guess he told you!"

"There you go," Tall John put his fists on his hips, "proof positive that Curt Stocker is not bullet proof! Good thing for you paper airplanin' is not a court martial able offense!"

The Kid had only to think for a nano second; "I didn't think eating in the mess hall was, either. Wouldn't hurt to pull out the old UCMJ and check it, maybe under *policing the area* or is *littering* a court martial offense?"

While everybody chuckled about the frivolity of such an undertaking, all the humor was suddenly sucked out of the hot damp delta air by an explosion that sent a shockwave through the building and a wave smoke and burning diesel fumes barreling down the alleyway from the Ben Xi moi street!

"WHAT THE FUCK WAS THAT! There was a universal look of complete surprise spread across all their faces. They all rushed to the corner of the balcony to see if they could determine what had just happened!

From out of his room, which was on the alley side of the balcony, Billy Smith was already at the rail, taking a look out toward the street. "Holy fuck! They blew up one of our trucks!"

Sure enough, directly at the end of the alley was the twisted smoking pile of hot burning metal and rubber that up until seconds ago, had been one of the battalion's duce and a halfs. People on the street could be seen running around it, jumping up and down, determining civilian collateral damage to people and structures caused by the attack on the Americans. The MPs appeared from out of their compound, some sporting M-16's, obviously still not sure of exactly how it happened. No telling what damage and injuries resulted from the truck becoming shrapnel. It burned orange, hot and black, sending a heavy diesel fueled cloud rolling up into Can Tho's evening sky. It was far from dark and the smoke would be seen for miles.

The sobering though ran through all of their minds; over a dozen men had all just ridden back from Eakin Compound on that truck. From the way it went up, it was likely a grenade in the gas tank that set it off. The VC would take a hand grenade, wrap the handle to the body of the grenade with electrical tape, then pull the pin and drop it into the gas tank of a vehicle. Then, as soon as the electrical tape is dissolved and loosened by the gasoline, the handle flips up, activing the grenade, blowing up the fuel tank and causing one hell of an explosion. The VC use the tape so they can be a long ways off when it blows. Also, they want it to be full of GIs when the explosion happens! And they had come within 20 minutes of blowing up a load of the battalion's finest.

Perhaps they used a couple too many wraps of tape in their delay timing, because nobody was killed. But they sure did kill the hell out of our truck. And even though nobody died or got wounded tonight, just knowing that a bunch of us almost did get killed was enough to universally raise our stress

527

and anxiety to absurd levels. Even without the pyrotechnics, we knew that the enemy was out there, every day, trying to kill us just like that.

That night, the Kid got as drunk as he ever got in the 'Nam. It was more to blot out the fact there were still hundreds of ways a short timer could die, even in town… than it was to celebrate his promotion.

Chapter 79

Due to its nature, membership in the Tribe was exclusive to enlisted men; no officers allowed for obvious reasons.

There was one officer in the unit, however, that the Tribe universally loved. It was First Lieutenant William Culp, from Atlanta, Georgia, who was the 10th Battalion's Printing Officer.

As the Officer In Charge (OIC) of printing, Lt. Culp had a working relationship with most of the Tribe, who were printers. After all, due to the fact that a majority of the 10th PSYOP mission was dependent on the printing operation, the unit had three shifts manning the three monster presses 24/7. The safe conduct passes, the B-52 leaflets, the Chu Hoi stuff and the vast array of propaganda materials all of it had to be generated by the Good, the Bad and the Ugly, as the Volkswagen sized presses were christened.

The presses were also the same ones that printed DIMENSION, so by default, the Kid, even though he wasn't a pressman, also had a plenty of reasons to interact with the blond, bespectacled lieutenant. Indeed, he was eternally grateful that Lt. Culp had been the CQ on duty the day he and Birnbaum returned from the 9th Division assignment, and he'd experienced his sleep deprived freak out.

Upon Culp's arrival in the unit, the previous printing OIC had been newly felled with a case of hepatitis so even though he had no previous printing experience, he was thrown into the slot. "The Finiest Little Printing Shop This Side of the Pacfic," fell to him by default and with it, his inevitable relationship to the Tribe.

At first, in an effort to learn the business of printing, Culp had made the mistake of being too much 'hands on' for the boys and his constant presence in the press room was annoying. Once those boundaries were settled, the EM and the OIC forged a tight bond that blossomed into a broad friendships.

Then came the day, or actually, it was on a night shift, that Lt. Culp casually mentioned to some Tribe members that he wouldn't be opposed to trying the infamous *Con Sa* himself. The revelation was a total surprise, but the men sensed he was legit and not attempting to set any kind of a trap, so the plan was born.

Lt. Culp's birthday was in April. The head Vietnamese guard at Villa Cruz lived just one block behind the printing plant. Thanh was approached and asked, if we could hold a birthday party for Lt. Culp at his house. Not only did he say yes, but for a small fee, his family would cater the event!

It would be a high security private affair, with invitations carefully issued, due to the risk all would be taking. The band was going to attend, sans instruments, as Richie, Benny, George and Don, were printers. Boyett was the only band non-printer. Willert, Ramjet, Sweet, Edwards, JC Compton, Birnbaum and the Kid rounded out the guest list.

The plan was set for a Sunday, not his birthday, but the day it could be pulled off. The dinner party was to commence at approximately 1700 hours. The attendees were to ride over to the Villa Cruz on the guard duty truck, pick up Culp, who had no idea, and go out the back way over to Thanh's. Then after the party, they'd return to Villa Cruz in time to ride the guard truck back to the New Villa at the 2200 hours guard change.

Who would notice? So they were taking a ¾ ton truck to do the guards as opposed to a jeep... there were 10 of them instead of 4 and they were leaving an hour early. Some of the printers attending were already at the Villa Cruz waiting.

If anybody had the timidity to figure it out, it was RV, so extra care was taken not to give him or his associates even a hint of what was transpiring.

Moyssiadis had the ¾ ton in position as the guards and party goers casually filed down and loaded up for the ride over. Nobody of import was paying any attention to what was going on Sunday afternoon. Everybody on guard duty had the trust of the NCOs that they'd be at their appointed spot and nobody else had a spot to be.

Upon arrival at the Villa Cruz, the Tribe waited down by the presses while JC went upstairs and found Culp in the Officer's day room and asked him to come down and take a look at one of the presses for some confabulated reason.

When Culp came down the stairs, clad in a white T-shirt, he was surprised to see printers there who were not scheduled to work.

"Lt. Culp," Benny stepped forward, "in honor of your birthday, we have arranged a dinner party! Thanh's family is hosting it and we are walking over to his house right now!

"We suggest you tell your cohorts that some of us are taking you to the USO for a birthday celebration, the Kid suggested, "and then we can *move out smartly!*"

The Lieutenant's expression was a mixture of surprise and anticipation. Bounding up the stairs, he was back in a flash, dressed in his uniform and ready to roll. As the group was filing out the back gate, Culp leans over and asks the Kid, "Did you guys bring some?"

The Kid just smiled and said nothing. As a broad smile spread across his face, Culp clearly got the message; oh yes.

Thanh's whole family was there to greet the party of the party. His house was quite spacious and they had set up a table (or tables) running down the center of their living room, ready to seat 15 people. It was covered with a red and white checkered table cloth and was set with plates, serving utensils, and nouc mam bowls, chop stix, forks and tiny white porcelain bowls with condiments.

As the Tribe filed in and selected their seats, Lt. Culp was placed to the right of Thanh, who was invited to sit at the head of the table. Once everybody was seated, his wife, cousin and daughters began serving everybody Carling Black Label Beers.

When everybody had a drink, Willert rose and proposed a toast: "We are gathered here today to wish a happy birthday to our OIC and friend, Lt. William Culp! "Happy birthday, Sir! And may you enjoy many more of them in the future, under better circumstances that we are experiencing here tonight!"

"Hear hear!" the Tribe resounded and everybody drank.

"Thank you!" Lt. Culp beamed, "actually, I am finding these circumstances to be just fine! In fact, I can't thank you all enough for this and the way you go above and beyond what you need to do to insure our success as a unit. And, uh, I don't think I need to say it, but every single one of you fuckers would be in the stockade if you weren't so damned proficient at your jobs! And speaking of marijuana… *where is it?*"

In an instant, Willert slapped a carton of KOOLs on the table, "Here you go!"

The look on Culp's face was priceless. "You mean it comes in cartons?"

"It does when we trade tobacco for it!" Ken said as he emptied the packs out on the table and passed them up and down to the partiers.

As the Kid watched Culp pick up a pack, examine it and begin to break the seal, he realized this was the first officer they'd ever trusted with their

531

slickest trick. Every one of them had at least one carton of joints in their locker and if the lieutenant was doing this as a 'mole', they were at this point, all fucked to the Nth degree! But he had to know that was not the case.

Culp tore the foil and opened a pack. Tapping one of the joint cigarettes out, he held it up and examined it, looking at the unfiltered end to see what he could see. "Interesting!" Then he placed it between his lips and fired off his Zippo. Taking a couple of smaller puffs to get it going, he finally takes a big drag, inhales and immediately coughs it all out, much to the amusement of the Tribe.

"Smaller hits to begin with, Sir," Birnbaum coached as he opened another pack and took one out. "See, like this," he struck his own Zippo, took a smooth hit, held it for a couple of seconds and exhaled.

"OK,' Culp took another hit, smaller, and held it.

"Well, I hope to hell you do better your first time out than I did," spoke up JC Compton, "this is your first time, right?" he inquired.

Holding his third hit, Culp made his eyes go wide at the question before exhaling, "Yes, it is."

"Yeah! Piped up Willert, "it took us a *fucking week* to get JC high!"

By now, half of the 10 packs were opened and up and down the table, everybody was lighting up their own joint. Soon, the room was filled with Con Sa smoke and the Kid took a look at Thanh's family, to see what they were making out of the strange party the had consented to host. They are smiling and giggling so much at the antics of the Americans, the Kid thinks they're already on a contact high but... *they can't all be stoned on contact highs yet because we just lit up.*

A cloud of smoke bellowed up from the elongated table and the only thing that was missing from the party of some music. Nobody in the Tribe had been smart enough to plan ahead for that one and Thanh's family didn't have a record player.

What they did have was a menu planned for us that was spectacular! Culp was also a favorite person of Thanh's and he pulled out all of the stops and all the Tribe did was give him $30 MPC to work with.

It didn't take long at all before Culp announced to the Tribe, "Hey, boys, I think I'm feeling it! Which is strange because now, I'm not feeling my lips!"

Big laughs!

"One of the things I noticed, when I started smoking," contributed the Kid, "was that when I spoke, my words would leave my mouth but not make any sound until they were like about 2 feet in front of me!"

"That's exactly what I'm experiencing!" Lt. Culp exclaimed, pointing to a spot two feet out from his mouth.

"Even though we didn't bring any music, Lieutenant," Birnbaum began, "when you get back to Villa Cruz after the party, put on some records and you will be amazed at how pot enhances tunes. Play something you really like and your mind will be blown away!"

"All right! I will," Culp enthused.

The subject of "shortness" came up.

"So, Stocker," Culp inquired, "what are you down to?"

"28 days, Sir!" marveled the Kid, "am I the shortest fucker here? I can't fucking believe I'm finally under a month."

"Yeah. You need to get out of here. Captain Smith would give anything to get at a piece of you… your scalp or your balls, it would be a tough choice."

"No doubt. He still pretty smoked about the promotion board?"

"Understatement!" Culp exclaimed, "He got so drunk that night and got into such a fucking rage at you. You should have heard the things he called you and what he said he'd do to you, if he ever got the chance. He said some pretty dicey things about the colonel, too. Good thing the colonel didn't hear any of it. I will say one thing, Stocker, if your body turns up missing, PM is the first person the CID should investigate!

Roaring laugh.

"All right, let's say you survive PM and get to DEROS," Culp continued, "Stocker, what's the first thing you are going to do when you get back to the world?"

The Kid took a hit and blew it out. "Fuck if I know. I guess I'll go see Flo and find out if any part of that is still viable, but shit, I don't know. I'd love to find a way to just get out of the Army, *even if I had to claim I was a homo…* '

Big laugh.

"You know," began Richie, "I've been hearing some stuff about an underground anti-war newspapers that the GIs are putting out. At Ft. Lewis in Tacoma, it's called Counterpoint, and at Fort Hood, they got one named the Fatigue Press. They're really going after how bad the war is and the brass and shit," blinding flash of realization, "... *why don't we publish an underground paper?*"

"Hey!" Ron almost jumps out of his chair, "why don't we? We got all the stuff!"

The immediate reaction from the diners was *hell yeah!*

But Culp suddenly became noticeably unnerved. "Uh, that's probably something you can do in the States, but I think it might be a problem here in the war zone," he cautiously began, "if you produced anything that was out and out anti war, the brass could say you were giving 'aid and comfort to the enemy'. I don't think you want to take that one on... even with the colonel on your side," he pointedly aimed the last line at the Kid.

Everybody looked to the Kid. "Well, I gotta go with the Lt. on this one. I don't think publishing an anti-war underground paper would aid my efforts to maintain a low profile for my last 28 days! I don't know what I'm going to do when I get back home, but you can bet your asses that I'm going to do everything I can to oppose this war in every way possible!"

"That's really picking up steam all over!" Richie said, "There's those 27 men they are trying for munity at the Presidio in San Francisco, and there's that guy who's trying to start an Army union!"

The food hit the table and conversation was reduced to a minimum as the soldiers stuffed their faces. It was quite easy to see that Lt. Culp was in the initial throws of munchies madness, enhanced taste buds and all!

For the rest of the evening, the Tribe smoked and drank and ate to their heart's content. They reveled in their friendship with the Lt., knowing what a special night it was that they could take him and get him stoned to the max!

The Kid had brought his Pentax and began snapping some shots of the event. He got one of Lt. Culp taking a hit; it didn't take him long to adapt to the style of smoking the joints.

There was a shot of the KOOL packs laying around the table and he took one of an ash tray filled with filter tipped roaches. When he did, the Kid noticed something about them; the paper was showing the black resin. *Opium! This particular batch of pot had been dusted with opium! No doubt about it.* But, he chose not to say anything about it because he didn't want to complicate the situation. Besides, there wasn't enough opium in them to addict anybody. When he made his realization, the Kid noticed Edwards taking a seriously appraising look at the joint he was smoking and he snapped a picture.

The Kid made a note to check his own cache when they got back to the New Villa and would throw out any other OJ defiled pot but he could find but he didn't see any sense in throwing the damper on this party over that.

It was a hot evening and a bunch of the tribe took off their fatigue shirts and partied in their T's, and nobody was offended when JC took off his shirt and sat at the table bare chested.

As time approached to wrap it up, thank you's were extended to Thanh and his family for their hospitality. Now all they had to do was walk back to the Villa Cruz, wait for the guard truck and return to the New Villa and cherish their little secret birthday party where they got a lieutenant stoned to the max. It would all be smooth if PM wasn't standing at the back door.

And he wasn't.

Chapter 80

There was one other officer that members of the Tribe smoked pot with in Vietnam. It happened around the corner from the Hollywood Bar, back off the Ben Xmoi Street, at Mama San's place. Her name wasn't really Mama San, but that's how the Kid and the Tribe knew her.

She wasn't a mama san in the sense she hired out girls, she was a mother and had a daughter that lived with her. She was always home and offered her humble abode as a place the boys could relax. In return, they treated her like a queen. Who befriended her first or how they came to hang out at her shack was kind of vague but beginning some time in March, the Kid and various members of the Tribe spent many a pleasant afternoon drinking tea, eating biscuits and smoking pot and conversing in her living room.

Mama San's house was one of those hovels that spread out behind the commercial buildings that lined Ben Xmoi's main drag. It wasn't much more than a living room dominated in one corner by her glass encased Buddhist shrine which sat atop a cabinet behind a brass incense burner. There was a low couch with a thick foam pad pushed against the wall that also served as her bed and another one across the room for her daughter, Ki, who was in her mid 20's. It was hard to tell how old the slim, diminutive Mama San was; she could have been 40 or 55 but she always had a smile on her pleasant face. There was no *Mr. Mama San.* Whether she had a job and worked or how she supported herself was a mystery but she was always home when the boys dropped by and made tea and serve it with homemade biscuits. They always left a hefty gratuity, but it wasn't like her place was a cafe.

There was a hole in the thatch of her ceiling in the kitchen, just off her tin roofed single room that bordered the sidewalk which ran behind the Hollywood building.

One day, the Kid asked Sweet to take his picture with his head sticking up through her kitchen roof, showing just the top of his head with sunglasses, like Kilroy, flashing a peace sign. Mama San thought that was so funny, she asked Sweet to take a picture of her sticking her head out of the hole with the Kid.

One day, when the Kid, Sweet, and Benjamin went to visit Mama San, they found her already in the company of an Air Force captain, who was sitting on her couch bed smoking a hand rolled joint and drinking a cup of tea. He was dressed in tiger fatigues, slight of build, with redish blond hair that was receding quite quickly for his apparent age.

"Call me *Max*," he said as they all shook hands. Turns out *Max* flew a Spooky out of Bien Thuey airbase and was very near the end of his tour. He had a burnt out look and vibe that certainly indicated he'd been at it for a while.

Before they whipped out their own pot, the boys took a hit of the joint he was smoking and figured since *Max* supplied it, he wasn't a plant or a threat. When they started talking, they discovered he was of the anti war persuasion.

"While we're in the air, waiting for orders to fly fire support for whoever calls for it, we fly around looking for targets of opportunity in free fire zones. We mostly attack boats moving at night along rivers. Last week, I was watching through a Starlite sniper scope when we found a boat. If they're traveling under cover of darkness, that makes them guilty. The guns opened up, I could see the bodies being riddled and falling in the river out of the boat, which we shot straight to hell! Some of them looked small enough to be kids, not that any of'em are too big. I'm down to 21 days and I can't wait to be out of this fucking war and the Air Force! I am so going to be against this war when I get home."

Amen, brother.

"I'm down to 27," the Kid took the opportunity to flaunt his own low number. "In one week, I'll be in the *teens!* Wow, we're just six days off of flying home on the same plane!"

"How did you find this place," Sweet asked the one thing the three of them were wondering.

"Somebody in the Hollywood, that I asked if they knew a safe place to smoke," he made the hand gesture, with pinched fingers as in smoking a doobie, "and they gave me directions here," *Max* said.

That made them wonder who it was that violated their security and gave an officer the location of their private smoking lounge. Still, *Max* was a nice enough guy that nobody made an issue out of his presence.

"Flying around and shooting up the whole fucking jungle is pretty impersonal. I've always been glad I don't have to see the faces or the bodies of the people I've killed. And only God knows how many that is. Most of what we do is at night," he took another hit.

The Kid noticed that he could see Max in the mirror of Mama San's cabinet and decided to snap his picture without point the camera directly at him. "Earlier in my tour," he addressed Max, "I was attached to the ARVN infantry and saw some of the faces. Not of people I killed, *I don't think I've killed anybody,* but just people who got killed. It's something I could have lived without. I've seen what Spooky can do to the ground. We had Spooky flying circles and hosing the ground down around us, while we set up a perimeter one night when we were still engaged and it was getting dark! *Was that you? Thank you, if it was.* That was pretty nice. And flying around at a cool 3,000 feet of altitude must be a nice benefit?"

"Oh that part is nice. Only we don't shoot from 3,000, more like 1,000. And all the return fire is pretty much small arms at best, no anti aircraft ground to air stuff, thank God. Sometimes, it's pretty spooky... *in the Spooky,* watching the tracers go by and feeling the occasional hit! You think they'd be a little busy running and hiding, but no. They're getting right after it!"

"No shit!" the Kid added, "I saw them going after jets in an air strike once! The jet's would come over and drop their ordinance as they high tailed it out, the VC were up out of their holes and shooting at them!"

"Say, *Max,*" Sweet began, with no military courtesies, such as calling him 'sir' or captain, "I'm curious, about how many of the officers out there at Bien Thuy do you know that smoke pot?"

He thought for a few seconds, screwing his face up into a wad as he indexed his mind, "Well, that's hard to say. Personally, I know less than a half dozen, since most of us spend our time trying to conceal it. I estimate, it is at least somewhere in the neighborhood of about 10, 20 percent."

"It's gotta be close to 50% in our unit for EM,' the Kid speculated. "I imagine you all have a lot more to lose if you get caught."

"You got that right. It would get me grounded, for sure, and busted in a very unpleasant manner. That's why I come up to town; I never smoke on the base. Most of the time, I just get a cyclo and ride around while *I do a doobie...doobie do.*"

Mama San rose to tend the whistling tea pot, pouring the boiling water into the small white spouted ceramic server and bringing it to steep in from of the newly arrived soldiers. They soon each poured a cup and lit up their own joints and offered a filter tipped KOOL to Max, who was surprised to see that joints came with filters. With this much pot around, there was no real reason not to share.

"After we get done here, I need to hit the pharmacy," lamented the Kid, "I got guard duty tonight, last shift and I'm out of *Obisitol, and I know I'll never make it without it.*"

Sweet smiled; he was still in B Company and thus, when in from the field, immune from guard duty. Between that and all the goods he had on Wilson, who was still his nominal OIC in the field, Jim had it pretty good. *Sweet probably could have gotten out of the Nui Coto operation if he'd so chosen, but he had been hot for the story.*

"We're printing the April issue Thursday night," the Kid said to Sweet, "that picture of the Nui Coto with the clouds rising up above it is going to be a bitchin' cover!"

"Well, Wilson's sending me back out Thursday morning so you'll have to ship me one. You do know he's out of here in two weeks… *the fucker is shorter that you!* So I gotta go out there and take care of business until they decide on his replacement."

"I was thinking," said *Max,* in a comment not related to Sweet and the Kid's conversation, "when we were out flying around the other night, when I get back, I should tell the Air Force I am now a conscientious objector!"

"Uh, isn't that a little bit late? I mean, why wait until you get back?' asked an incredulous Benjamin.

Max scoffed like it was all so obvious, "Well, if I told them now, it takes a lot longer than 21 days for the paperwork to go through and all it that would happen is my life would become pure living hell. So if I wait until I get back, I still got a little over a year left and I won't mind them fucking with me state sides. It's not like they can send me out to get killed, you know?"

"See, Stocker," Sweet turned to the Kid, "there's a wise man. You should take a page out of Max's book here, and stop fucking with the brass, play it safe a little bit."

"Hey; they're fucking with me. *Same as it ever was.*"

"All I know for sure, today," declared Max, "is when I get home, I'm not just forgetting about it!"

"Well, that's probably a good plan, because I can see right now a lot of this is going to be hard to forget, *even if we try,*" replied the Kid.

Chapter 81

It began when, upon arriving at the pharmacy, the Kid discovered they were all sold out of Obisitol. *Rats! "You have sem sem Obisitol?"*

The young man with the bushy black hair behind the counter, who didn't look old enough to have graduated from any accredited pharmacy school, looked at the Kid and nodded his head in a positive manner. Then he made a running in place kind of motion, swinging his arms, before turning and picking a small white box off the shelf behind him and laying it on the counter in front of the Kid. "500 pi," he stated the price.

The Kid, deducing from the clerk's pantomime, that product would supply him with the necessary extra energy, pulled out his wallet and paid the man. He hadn't been sleeping very well lately and he feared if he went on the last guard shift without support, at 2 am, he could easily nod off. It would not do to have the likes of PM Smith discover him asleep on guard duty. *And I wonder if PM had something to do with me getting the late shift; so he can check to see if I'm flying paper airplanes at a time when I think nobody is looking! Talk about getting hit with the book! PM would rightfully flatten him with it, should he ever be so lucky as to catch the Kid so compromised, like say, asleep with a plane in his hand.*

The shorter he got, the more life was like a daze to the Kid. He watched the movie, smoked a couple of joints, wrote some letters and went to bed. He was lying there, awake, when the CQ came to get him.

"Yo, Stocker, fall out, you got 10 minutes to get ready for the truck to Villa Cruz," *Al* summoned him for duty.

Checking his Seiko, he found it to be 0145 hours. Not bothering to brush his teeth, the Kid hustled to pull on his fatigues, rounded up his canteen and M-16 with a couple of clips, grabbed his steel pot and stumbled down the stairs to the orderly room. Feeling in his pants pocket, he had a pack of KOOLS and the bottle of pills that he would need for the artificial energy that he was counting on getting him through the night.

The sounds of the Good, the Bad and the Ugly cranking out leaflets emanated from behind the wrought iron gate of the Villa Cruz as the guard truck unloaded it's cargo. It would wait for them to relieve their counterparts so they could be returned to the New Villa, where their bunks awaited.

The nightshift printers paid little attention to the guards as they filed through to their posts. The Kid was taking his normal favorite, top side front, while Ron Edwards would have top side back.

George McCaulley was more than happy to see the Kid emerge from the building to relieve him.

"Bout time," he yawned as the Kid cached his M-16 and stood back from the front of the sandbags to light a cigarette.

The Kid exhaled, "What do you mean, 'bout time? We're *right on time*. Well, I guess this counts as my wake up, so I've only got 26 more days to go!"

"Well, have a good one, you short bastard," said George as he gathered his equipment and hatted out.

The Kid stepped to the front of the sandbags and looked down. He watched the truck depart with the just relieved guards and sat down in the folding chair. Reaching into his pocket, he pulled out the bottle of pills and examined it. Like nearly all of the pharmaceuticals, it was a French product and he could not read the directions but saw the numeral "1" by *instructiones* and assumed that would be a good dosage with which to begin. Opening the bottle, he took out a pill, unscrewed the top to his canteen and washed it down.

When he finished his cigarette, he stood up and gazed up and down the canal. *Nope, don't see any VC.* With a yawn, he settled back to wait for the speed to kick in. He didn't have long to wait. But instead of feeling the boost, he was startled beyond reason as he felt his body and mind begin to noticeably slide downhill, sinking into shut down and it didn't take him but a mini second to realize *he'd been sold a downer and not an upper!*

Oh my God! It was like a dark tide rolling in and the Kid panicked with the realization of how precarious his situation had just become. His first reaction was to consider sticking his finger down his throat to vomit it out. But, it must have already dissolved and gone into his bloodstream, so that would likely not work. He was on the verge of hyperventilating when Ron Edwards emerged from his position at the rear post.

"So, no flying tonight. What a bummer!" Ron lamented but the Kid did not respond. *"Curt? Are you OK?"*

"No. I'm not OK…"

"What's wrong?" Ron voiced concern.

"I think these uppers I bought are downers! I took one about 20 minutes ago and I feel like I'm going to pass out!"

"Shit! Fuck! I came over here to borrow one of those from you!" Ron stared at the Kid and between them passed the realization that if they'd both taken one, they might have both ended up getting busted for sleeping on guard duty; one of the Army's most unforgivable sins!

"Dam!" the Kid swore, "I'll bet PM is going to be checking tonight to see if he can catch me flying airplanes… and if he finds me asleep… *my ass is grass!"*

"Well, uh," Ron fumbled for an answer, "the best I can do is come and check on you about every 15 minutes. I'll listen for anybody coming up the stairs so I can make sure you're OK! I better get back to my post."

"Thanks, Ron."

Taking a deep breath, the Kid marshalled his mental forces. Lighting up another cigarette, he began to march in place, figuring if he kept moving it would help his fading alertness.

What have I done? I'm fucked! I can't believe I've fuck up like this when I'm so short! That pharmacist must have thought that I was too hyped up and wanted to come down. Or he's a VC and knew I was going on guard duty and his plan is to put us to sleep so they can attack! Oh no! Now I'm getting whacky paranoid!

I have to fight against it! I have to make a conscious fucking effort to stay awake! I'm short. So short. I have to think about how in just 26 days I'll be back in the States. It's so close, hard to believe, but this could be the longest night of my life. No. That would be out there in Binh Trung on the NITECAP. That was an operation… this is just fucking guard duty! The chances of being attacked tonight are microscopic. Less than the chance I'll pass out! I can't fucking pass out! OMMMMMMMMM stay awake stay awake… OOOOOOOMMMMMMMMMMM stay awake stay awake!

After what seemed an expansive amount of time, the Kid heard a voice from behind, "Curt… are you OK? Still awake I see, or you're asleep on your feet?"

"Thanks Ron," the Kid turned to look at him and then to his Seiko; *0300 hours, only 15 minutes had passed.* "thanks for having my back. Literally!"

"You got it! I'll be back."

Three more hours to go. Shit. Time is traveling at the speed of a turtle, a microcosm of my whole Vietnam tour. I can see the finish line and I'm sprinting toward it but it feels like I'm running through water, across flypaper, being held back by a headwind...stuck in perpetual slow motion! Got to think about Flo. I can't believe I'm actually going to see her in 26 days. Wow. Scott is going to be here in 56 days!

The reality of that thought blew the Kid away. He was counting down to go home and his brother was now counting down to come over! The Army had it down exactly. Since as brothers, only one of them could be in the war zone at a time, they had Scott pegged to go almost exactly 30 days after the Kid came home. He had just completed his training to become a medic at Ft. Lewis, Washington. Since the Kid had so graciously loaned his older brother his VW, the arrangement had been made for Scott to drive down the coast and meet him in Oakland. From there, they would drive to LA, where Scott would catch a plane to Denver to see the parents. His new bride, Nancy, was on an overseas semester in Costa Rica for her Spanish major and he likely did not have the funds to go see her. Meanwhile, the Kid would beat a path straight to Vista and Flo.

When we see each other, we'll fall into each other's arms and be instantly back together and maybe even engaged again. But is that what I want? Is that what she wants? She's still the one I want, that's for sure. Gotta keep walking, walking around in little circles. Gotta keep the feet moving, gotta keep the eyes open. OOOOOMMMMMM. Walk walk walk. Boy, making paper airplanes would keep me awake! No. That will not do. Trouble there. I'm sure the officers do not have to give up their paper airplanes first... Ha ha. I crack myself up. Anything to stay awake.

He marched in his little tight circle, around the guard chair, smoking cigarettes and slapping himself in the face with a wet hand, all in an epic effort to stay awake. Every second time around, he would stop and look up and down the canal; yep...no VC yet.

Without fail, Ron would pop in every fifteen minutes and make sure he hadn't bitten the bullet and succumbed to the siren's song of slumber. Amid his chain smoking of KOOLs, he would try to sing every Beatles song on Sgt. Pepper's Lonely Hearts Club Band, in order, without stopping. He almost welcomed his visit from Wally and the Beaver and the Girl Next Door, right before the upper half body of Captain Robinson paid his usual call on his psyche. Yes, it's always hard to sleep with a view of the Captain's entrails randomly popping into your brain. Sadly, Captain, you have been keeping me awake for months, but I thank you tonight, this one time!

There was enough death and destruction to review from his tour that it could take him the rest of the night; the tall VC with his brains blown out and his two riddled companions, the ARVN who got his junk blown off in front of him, all the dead and wounded he had seen and helped to load on choppers. Then there was the reprise of Captain Robinson's guts dragging across the ground when they hustled to load his stretcher. I will never forget Captain Robinson. When I got home, I will not forget. I will not forget Wally and the Beaver and the Girl Next Door.

When his Seiko showed 0500 hours, the all night DJ in him triggered the pretend radio show. In his brain, he was back in Nashville at WKDA doing his show. What the hell? I used to stay awake all night for a living! The Kid early on had come up with a final hour gimmick. He named it the HAPPY SUN UP HOUR and his schtick had been to come off as ridiculously energetic! Like a ninja preparing for the fight, he would center himself, shuck off the all night late night lethargy, up the energy level and kick radio ass until Doc Holliday relieved him at 6. He pulled out all his drop in voices, sound effects and gag bits and got the other DJs to record some at his request. When they saw what he was doing with them, they were only too happy to oblige.

DJ Dan and Bill Langford had done the most. Bill went new school with rockets and DJ Dan went old school with Gabby Hayes.

"Look! Up in the Sky! Is that a tactical Polaris? No It is but the Sun and the Happy Sun UP Hour… coming right at YOU!"(missile launch background into next song)

"Yo, Buckaroos! Rise and shine… It's the Happy Sun Up Hour! It's time to ride the range and milk the cows! Yeeehhaaaa!" (sound of stampede runs into next song) and only up tempo music!

The Kid relived his favorite Good Guy radio moment, the night when Bill Langford got stoned on pot for the first time, right there in the WKDA control booth, on the 12th floor of the Stahlman Building, at 2:00 am on a Saturday night/Sunday morning. Langford was a local just graduated from high school kid who lucked out in getting a part time position while he was still a student. That nighty he was working Jonny Wailin's 8 to 12 shift and stuck around when the Kid relieved him. The 18 year old was the only other staffer near the Kids age so the two had quickly become best friends. Bill had thought about trying pot even before the Kid arrived in the Music City. So with Earl, the white haired night watchman and elevator operator on call to alert them to anybody's approach, they smoked a joint right there in the 'WKDA control room and got just totally wiped out. The Kid, of course, continued to do his show and Bill just sat there, marveling at the feeling of getting off for the first time. Then it happened; from the WKDA studio's 12th floor perch, they had a perfect view of a warehouse fire that had erupted a few blocks to the north, up by the river and was getting bigger by the minute! Being stoned, the gargantuan fire was spectacular, and they could actually see firemen on the tops of ladders, silhouetted by the blaze, spraying hoses into the blaze! Of course, the Kid began talking about it on the air and they contemplated calling the station's newsman, Gary Nolan, but decided since he had a police scanner, if he hadn't gotten up and gone already, he didn't care. The Kid gets a phone call; it's Bill calling from a phone in the FM control room, in the character of an old black man. Instinctively, the Kid interviewed him and played it straight! "I'm just an ole homeless man, who swore he's smell smoke' Bill launched into his bit... 'I tole 'em I smell it and I sez, where there's smoke, they's fire! I TOLE 'em...but 'who believes an old black man...nobody... and now look at it. I'd tell 'em sumthin' different now... where's there's fire, there's smoke...' Bill was hilarious and the Kid went with it, then treated the ensuing characters like real people as well. The fire burned all night and after the old man, Bill did a fireman and a policeman. Fireman Al and Officer Frank. The Kid got a little worried when Bill came off as public servants but all he was saying was 'the fire is hot (about 12 ways) 'and stay out of the area'. "Yes, everybody take Officer Frank's advice... but you don't have to be close to see it, I'm a half mile away and I see it! The most amazing thing was, that the next day, nobody ever said a word about any of it!

At last, the eastern horizon lightened over his shoulder, as his post faced west, and relief came rumbling down the road in the form of the truck, arriving to take them back to the New Villa; his watch at last coming to an end. Ron came and collected him. Captain Powell had not popped up to check on him, not that he knew at any rate.

And even though there was no attack or even any real fear of one, it would stand forever as the scariest tours of guard duty he would ever pull!

Chapter 82

Eakin Compound's mess hall seated about 200 soldiers at any one time. It was by no means the largest nor smallest of the Army's mess halls and when you were seated at a table out in the sea of GIs, it could have been any mess hall on any army post in the world.

Compared to what the soldiers had access to in the field, the Eakin Compound mess was *haute cusine.* The Kid had always told all those who pined and whined to go to the field, if they enjoyed any kind of regular diet, *stay in town! Be happy with the roast beef, fried chicken, meatloaf and shit on a shingle! Rat, snake and dog awaiting you GI!*

They occupied a four top table in the very middle of the hall, with JC Compton at the Kid's left, Ken Willert to his right and Ron Edwards directly across. They were consuming their dinner at a leisurely pace, in preparation of working all night. For the 2 printers, their graveyard shift didn't officially began until midnight but they were going in early with the Kid and Edwards, to help prepare for DIMENSION's April press run. This was the only issue that would see the Kid's name listed as Editor & Chief. When the next one printed in May, he'd be on the jet home and Ken Bradley would be editor. Working until about midnight earned him the whole day off Friday and when he woke up, he'd be down to 23 days!,

The menu that night featured Salisbury steak and mashed potatoes with brown gravy, a green thing that might have been spinach or the Mekong Delta equivalent of collard greens, some mixed fruit, French bread, corn and apple cobbler for dessert.

"All he said was, they're not going to print it and when they sent it back, they didn't say *why,* but *DID* say, *don't resubmit it.*" Kid was recounting the crux of the meeting he'd had earlier that afternoon with Colonel Lawton, informing him that Stars and Stripes would not be printing the *'Go Cong replace every American with a Vietnamese and we go home'* story. "And when he told me, over the years, he's seen a few of stories about his units' rejected for one reason or another, but to get *no reason* and instructions not to resubmit it was, for lack of a better word, 'strange.' So I don't know what the fuck the deal is. The colonel thought it was a great piece, I thought it was a *pretty good* piece. I hope Lt. Sauers is not too pissed, after we hyped him all up and everything. At least the story will still be in DIMENSION, he'll have that to send home."

"Bummer," commented Willert, "so no by line in *Stars and Stripes* for Stocker."

"Like I give a shit if I ever have an article in that fucking rag! I'm so short I'm almost a midget!" exclaimed the Kid. "This is my *last issue* of DIMENSION, I'll have some stories in the next one, but this is my last fucking issue!"

"Settle down," JC scoffed, 'jeeze it's not like everybody at this table doesn't know you're short for Christ sake!"

Between bites, the Kid looked at his Seiko; *1830 hours.* The plan was for the staff to assemble not later than 1900 hours at the Villa Cruz with all the parts and the issue should be rolling off the presses by midnight. Then the newspaper staff would sit around and drink beer and shoot the shit until the 2 am guard duty shuttle, ride back and hit the rack. *Followed by a day off!*

Everybody was almost done eating but JC was first of the group to finish and when he did, he reached into his pocket and pulled out a pack of Marlboros. Drawing one from the pack and placing it between his lips, he produced a Zippo and lit up. Taking in a deep draw, he exhaled a rolling cloud of smoke, primarily in the direction of the Kid.

To say that JC's breath knocked him over, would be the understatement of the war, for the smoky reality that engulfed the Kid was... *JC had mistakenly lit up a joint!*

Holy fucking bat shit! I can't believe it! How do I tell him? Oh Jesus! What if a NCO smells it and grabs him?

Almost instantly, the Kid rises, struck too dumb to speak, picks up his tray and heads rapidly for the exit. Being as short as he is, all he wants to do is put space between himself and that burning liability. Scraping his tray, he shoves it through the window, tosses his silverware in the tub and hustles out the door!

He stood there outside the mess hall, still shaking at the seriousness of JC's mistake, wondering why he'd been so terrified he hadn't been able to warn his companions? *I wonder how long it's going to take them to figure it out!*

The Kid did not have to wait long for the answer to that question when, just seconds behind him, Edwards emerged from the mess hall.

"Can you believe that?" Ron is exasperated. "As soon as you got up with that *I seen a ghost* look, I caught a whiff! Jeeezus!"

Then right on his heels, Ken comes out. "God damn! I about shit my pants!" he swears.

"Did you say anything to him?" the Kid asked Ken.

"No! When I realized what he did I was out the door... *just like you guys!*"

The three of them stood there, stunned by what was going on just inside the mess hall door, totally perplexed of what they should or could do when JC himself emerged from the mess hall and stood there in front of them, his face breaking into realization with a wide, speechless and silly looking grin.

"JC..." said the Kid, looking down at his hand to see if, by some dumb stoned chance, he still held the offending contraband.

"When the three of you lit out of there the way you did, I sat there for a couple of seconds wondering *what the fuck,* then... I realized what I'd done! God! Guys, I'm so sorry! I should have my head examined."

"Yes!" the three of them chorused before breaking into nervous laughter!

"What did you do with it?" the Kid finally asked.

"I buried it in the mashed potatoes! It's in the garbage by now."

"Gee. *I've* always been afraid of doing that very thing myself with one of those packs of cigarette joints," confessed Willert, lighting up a real cigarette, "*but actually doing it in the middle of the mess hall?* That'll be my 'going to school naked nightmare' for the rest of my life! What are you, JC? Too high? Did we finally get you *TOO FUCKING HIGH* for your own good?"

After a pregnant pause, "Could be."

"Do you think anybody else noticed?" Edwards wondered.

"I don't think so." JC looked over his shoulder, checking his back trail, "nobody seems to be coming after me, but why don't we go anyway?"

"Good idea," the consensus was immediate, and the group moved for the parking lot and the waiting duce-and-a-half.

They walked in silence for a few seconds before JC defended his mistake, "You know, there must have been at least another 50 guys smoking in there, so how's anybody going to react to somebody jumping up and

548

saying; *'that smell is POT! Or, I smell something weird? Somewhere near? Bad/ good?* I mean really, guys?"*

"Point made," Ken could see his argument, "and it is true nobody appears to have noticed but us, or all the guys who *do* smoke pot are back there laughing their asses off about the dumb ass who lit up in the mess hall!"

"I just don't carry any joints in my pocket on a work day," Ron sensibly said.

"Well, yeah," JC stopped, "but this was my day off! I'm still off, but I want to help you guys print the paper, that's the only reason I'm going in."

"Hey, JC, no harm no foul," the Kid declared his Tribal mistake forgotten as they arrived at the truck, which had another dozen men already on board, waiting to fill and it looked like their group of 5 would be enough mass to roll the duce-and-a-half.

While riding anywhere in the truck, it was now nigh impossible not to think of the former truck that was blown to smithereens, a scant week previous. In addition to the guard tower that overlooked the Eakin Compound parking area, the colonel had since designated that a guard must remain with each truck during every meal since we apparently couldn't rely on the ARVN sentries.

Willert and JC were going to Villa Cruz but the Kid and Ron got dropped off at Battalion HQ, where they collected the box of page layouts, along with Boyett and Dunatchik. Tom had been processing some new negatives that were going to be added to the paper tonight. One was a pic of Pysuzie Psyop laying across a typewriter, in celebration of her killing the bat.

Tim Dunatchik, the designated unit newspaper lithographer, would be making all the negatives tonight. He was still grumping because Captain PM Smith had caught on to his private, personal joke on the Army and made him stop it. Tim had an arched curving shoulder patch made and sewn on his uniform that said: *"COMBAT LITHOGRAPHER"*. He wore it for almost a week, in the position where a troop could wear the patch *'Combat Photographer'*, before PM spotted it and called Tim for being out of uniform. That patch was unauthorized; *there is no such thing as a combat lithographer,* he screamed and made him immediately rip it off.

Tim loved that patch. And it wasn't really a lie when you stop and think about it; the front was everywhere in the Vietnamese war. Tim likely rode in the truck that night before it blew up or could have been mortared while shooting a negative. He could have easily been on the street when Imrem, Gyurisek, Johnson and JC got terror bombed. That doesn't count?

549

Back in the graphics room, the DIMENSION crew checked the page proofs one more time as they counted them into the travel box. The Kid was the editor for this issue, clear enough, but in all matters of production, pertaining to negatives or the making of plates or any part of the printing process, he would quickly defer to the units crack printing staff. Everybody knew more about printing than the Kid who, after all, was barely a journalist, let alone a neophyte editor.

Right inside the Villa Cruz gate, Lt. Culp was waiting for the Kid. "All right, Stocker, *Mistah Editah!* I see we are ready for Volume two, issue one!" He loudly made himself heard over the presses. Being the unit printing officer, he took special interest in the newspaper. "We should have this puppy flying off the presses by midnight, for sure GI!" He slapped him on the back quite hard. "They've got the camera already for you."

The first step in the printing process was to shoot negatives of the proof pages in preparation for burning the plates that would be attached to the presses, which made the actual impressions. There were special lighted worktables in a room closed off behind the presses where this activity took place. It was nice to get someplace in the building away from the noise of the presses.

The Kid began preparing the page pairs. The 16 pages were printed by eight plates, two pages to a plate, printing both sides on four sheets of 8.5" X 17" & folded. He pondered the finished product of his choices for the issue as he went through the exercise.

Pages one and 16: the front and back covers, with Sweet's picture of Nui Coto, resplendent in all of its gnarly character, full front. *Best possible choice for this issue.* Back cover; artwork and text to celebrate the anniversary of DIMENSION, written by the Kid, dictionary style, laid out in the shape of a cake with one candle on top.

Pages two and 15: the second page was always reserved for the Command Message from Colonel Lawton. This month, it was a tribute to the Battalion newspaper on the occasion of its anniversary. The bottom half of page two was a story, the first in a planned series, about leaflets and leaflet development. The first subject was *1-144-69,* a quick reaction leaflet, popular among field teams in the Delta. It was a unique 'do it yourself' fill in the blanks format, designed to grow every time a VC from that unit was killed in action. It was body count specific. The artwork of the leaflet depicted a freshly killed VC sprawled on the ground in front of a row of tombstones. Each tombstone was inscribed with the date of an action at which that particular VC unit had lost a comrade to the ARVNs. Then, if the

VC had any ID on him, his name would be listed with the day he died. Each time a unit engaged the VC and had a kill, they could just add on the new dead guy to the list, print a couple hundred on their hand cranked portable presses and have Air America do a pinpoint leaflet drop in the area where that enemy unit was operating. Page 15 was reserved for the paper masthead and *Battalion Happenings,* which cited arrivals, departures, promotions and who went on R&R. Between when the Kid had written it and now, Psyuzie killed the bat, so the Kid had inserted a pic of her sleeping on his typewriter, with congrats on nailing the bat. The issue also chronicled who in the unit had been promoted in April; of course, it made no reference to the drama that surrounded it.

Pages three and 14: page 3 was an article by the Chief, headlined *"Our 13ᵗʰ Try"*. Since this was the first issue of volume II, it was a history of the evolution of the battalion newspaper. Everett's article didn't mention Tom Roberts, the DINFOS grad who was a journalism major from Lehigh University. The way the Kid got it, the only day he'd been with Roberts, in the opium den in Sadec, Tom was the catalyst that launched it. He got no credit because he was busted for sending anti-war articles to the Lehigh college student newspaper and was exiled to the field right before the first issue. Officially, the Kid was the paper's 3rd editor, but he was technically the 4ᵗʰ. Page 14 held Mark Birnbaum's Camera Angles column and the Focal Point Picture of the month, taken in April by Richard Rock.

Pages four and 13: Four was a farewell tribute to the Chief, written by Sweet. It had a lot of the same basic information in it as the Chief's own article on the paper's first year but mostly it was about Everett. The Kid had antagonized over so much space being dedicated to the paper blowing it's own horn, but Everett leaving, the paper being a year old and Willie O choosing to praise it in his command column were just a stack of unavoidable coincidences. Page 13 was the full-page story of how the new platemaker was built by Willert, Specialist 4 Terry Stickrod and Lt. Culp; primarily the humorous side of it.

Pages five and 12: Five was a full page, by Captain Grimes, about the PSYOPS Development Section of the 10ᵗʰ Battalion. Page 12 held a full-page story, by the Chief, about Fitzhugh Turner, the civilian coordinator of CORDS (Civil Operations & Revolutionary Development Support) completing a two-year tour.

Pages six and 11: Six was the full-page story about the Go Cong Team working themselves out of a job and terminating their mission. The Kid did not put his by line on this article, as he was editor, he chose to have no personal by lines in the issue. He couldn't help but wonder, as he stared at it, why the fricking Stars and Stripes would not print that article? Was it not war like enough? The slant too benign? It didn't make any sense. How is Americans working themselves out of jobs not a good goal? Page 11 was part of a double truck; one of two in the issue. It was a farewell to the large number of 10th-ers going home, who had arrived by ship with the Packet and would be rotating out May 1.

Pages seven and 10: Seven held a humorous photo montage that the Kid though would be amusing. The trend to grow moustaches in the 10th was so universal, that the Kid set up a page entitled: "Your Son's Moustache, Father", and around it were thumbnail pics of 20 soldiers of the 10th who had 'staches. The trick was who could recognize their son: the photographs were from below the eyes to the chin, so you could only see the hair on the lips. Sweet currently did not have a moustache, so the Kid drew a handlebar on him with washable marker. He also added a pic of Psyuzie, since her whiskers were very stach-like! Page 10 was the opening half of the Packet Packs It story.

Pages eight and Nine: The center fold two-page spread was entirely dedicated to the pictures and story by Sweet, of Specialist 5 John Butler's adventure up on the Cambodian border at Nui Coto: The Peak in Dispute. It was a first-class piece of field work.

Once he had it already to go, the Kid signaled to Tim and the pair moved the galleys over to the camera to shoot the negs. As the negatives came out of development and were dried, Ron, Boyett, Tim and the Kid sat down at the art table, with bottles of opaque and tiny brushes to repair any pin holes or irregularities that could be covered to get as clean a plate impression as possible. When the opaque dried, the Kid would take the negative over to Ken, who commenced shooting the plates. By 2200 hours, the plates were all ready to go, installed on the press and ready for the check run.

Printing was a water mystery to the Kid; how the paper went through to be printed on both sides, collated, cut and folded into finished newspapers was baffling. So many belts, drives, pulleys, ink wells, paper guides; the Volkswagen sized Good, Bad and Ugly were state of the art presses for what was available anywhere in the world at the time.

When the first registration copies came off, Culp took one and placed another in the Kid's hands, who held it in such a way that it was a treasure and he feared to smear any wet ink. Culp on the other hand, rifled through his, stared for more than a couple seconds at some of the pages, threw it into the trash and rushed off to do some adjustments.

Soon the presses were tuned and percolating right along and by midnight, the 500-copy press run was complete; cut, folded and stacked.

"Well, there's your issue, *Mr. Editor...*" Boyett watched the Kid reading it for the 4th time, "I'd call you Chief, but Reagan will always be the Chief. That Nui Coto cover looks pretty bitchin!"

"Yeah! Turned out all right! We'll have to send Sweet at least a dozen copies."

The workday complete, the DIMENSION staff broke out the two six packs of Ba Mui Ba they'd brought for the wrap celebration.

While lighting up with tobacco, the Kid turned to JC, "So Joe, you want to smoke one here now or would you prefer to wait and smoke it in the mess hall?

Chapter 83

His eyes opened but he continued to lay motionless in his top bunk. Finally, curiosity won and pulling his wrist up even with his face, he read the dial of his Seiko; 1100 hours. They had gotten back from Villa Cruz at about 0215 hours and he had tumbled directly into bed, so he slept for about eight and a half hours.

What a luxury, having a day off! Only 23 more fucking days to go. On Tuesday, I'll be under 20!

The Kid stretched and let out a long, deep breath; the possibility of more sleep was remote, as the heat of the day was gaining on even the shady side of the building. He had lots to do, including get a haircut and writing a ton of letters, preparing his friends and relatives for his return. One of those letters would be a very important one to Flo.

Swinging around, he slid out of the rack and landed on his bare feet. Checking the other bunks in the room, he found them empty. No surprise on Ramjet; he was at work on his print shift. But Ken, on the other hand, was nowhere to be seen. He had stayed to finish his shift last night but should have been home and in the rack by 0830 hours. *Could be anywhere.* Stepping out on the balcony, he glanced to the right and the left; nobody around and it appeared that the Kid was alone on the third floor.

Clad only in his green boxers, the Kid trundled barefooted down to the latrine and took a piss. Returning to his room, he put on his glasses, picked up a pack of cigarettes, went to take one out but decided instead, *it's a perfect day to wake and bake!* Opening his locker, he took a pack of joints out of the converted carton of KOOLS, tore it open and selected one, returning the pack to the carton.

Picking up his Zippo, he stepped to the balcony rail and lit it up. Inhaling deeply, he held it for a few seconds and then let it slowly out. *It was some fine tasting weed.* With the second hit the feeling of calm was rising up, tinting his world in a glow of satisfaction and anticipation; *three weeks and two days, I'll be going home!* He marveled at his acute shortness.

The Kid's eye had been attracted to a pair of teenage girls who were walking down the path on the far side of the swamp. Scratching his nuts, he was relieved that his bout with the clap had been successfully concluded. No more whores for him, but today might not be a bad day to hit the scientific for a little steam and cream. Lunch at the USO and maybe go swimming at Eakin. He took a third hit and still had it in his lungs when he heard the man before he saw him.

"All right, Stocker! Drop that marijuana cigarette on the floor in front of you and come to attention! *RIGHT NOW!*"

Say what? The Kid's head snapped to the left and there on the balcony, in the place where the embassy guard usually stood duty, was Captain Powell M. Smith, his company commander, bristling with the flavor of adrenalin that comes from a hunter about to bag his quarry! *And the Kid was still holding the 3rd hit!*

"I said, *RIGHT NOW,* Specialist Stocker, that is a *DIRECT ORDER:* as your commanding officer, I am telling you to drop that marijuana cigarette on the floor and come to attention! You will not throw that *MARIJUANA* cigarette off the balcony, *THAT IS ANOTHER DIRECT ORDER!*" he firmly and unconditionally commanded.

Rats! As the joint smoldered between his fingers, the Kid was shocked out of his sleep grogginess by the scope of his own carelessness! Suddenly wide awake he quickly appraised the situation. PM was breathing hard, obviously delighted by his luck at catching the Kid red handed. But, he now stood rooted in the place where he'd originally confronted him, making the separation between them about 20 feet. The space gave the Kid more than enough time to still jettison the evidence so he did not totally panic.

Exhaling, "Oh! Captain Smith! *How are you, Sir!*" he greeted him, calmly to the point of sarcasm. "Nice day, isn't it?"

"God damn it, Stocker, *I gave you an order!*" he exasperated, "I will NOT have you disrespecting me on any level! *Obey my order at once!*"

The Kid did not immediately move to comply as he weighed his options.

"Once again, Stocker," it came through gritted teeth, "I am giving you a direct order; drop that marijuana cigarette on the floor and come to attention! *NOW!*"

The Kid stared at him for two more seconds, "You see, Sir, therein lies the confusion; *what* marijuana cigarette are you talking about?"

PM's jaw dropped, the Kid took another hit and the captain's face Doppler shifted red a dozen livid shades. He took a deep breath, "The one in your hand, Stocker. Your games are over. I was right above you in the club, listening, waiting for you to get up on your day off. And I was hoping against hope that not being on duty, you'd light up one of your *marijuana* cigarettes. When I heard someone come out, I heard a Zippo, smelled the marijuana, came right down here and found *only you!*" PM paused, to let the Kid know he'd been snared by an extremely well laid trap!

"How do you know what marijuana smells like? Your nose is a scientific instrument? *All you Smiths and your noses!*"

"Now, soon to be *less than Specialist 5* Stocker, cut the fucking crap! I am giving you a direct *AND LAWFUL* order: drop that marijuana cigarette on the floor in front of you and come to attention! *Right NOW!*" He yelled *'now'* and now himself waited, having clearly placed the ball in the Kid's court. In the captain's world and by his reckoning, the only sane option the Kid had was to drop the joint and come to attention.

But an anaconda's jaw couldn't have come any further unhinged than PM's, when the Kid replied to his statement, *with the slightest accent of Inspector Clouseau,* "Ahhh…yes, but I must again ask…*what marijuana cigar-ette are you talking a-boot?*" and took another hit knowing, however this ended, PM would never hold the joint he held in his hand. *It was destine to sleep with the snakes in the swamp. After all, that's what made the embassy an embassy.*

Smith came unglued! "Listen to me! *Your fucking joy ride is over,* Stocker!" Then, enraged as he was, he tried to maintain control by taking it down a few levels, from frothing mad to militarily correct. Speaking in a calculated tone, he laid down the law. "Right now, I'm not sure how many charges I'm going to file against you under the UCMJ. There's disobeying two lawful orders from a superior, gross disrespect to an officer, and possession of marijuana…" he smugly ticked them off. "And there won't be any article 15, I guarantee you that! You've pushed this whole thing way too far!"

There was a pause in his tirade as he waited to see what effect his scathing legal declarations had on the Kid's demeanor.

"Really, Sir? A laundry list of charges? Well, I've never heard *that* before," the Kid smiled at him. "While I must commend you on your master plan here today, Sir; all very clever and well executed, I feel obligated to point out the one item lacking for *absolute perfection.*"

The look on the Captain's face was pure *what could you possibly mean?*

"The one thing you're missing that you *really need...* and apparently forgot to bring along, Sir, is a *witness!*"

The correctness of the Kid's observation struck the captain like a Louisville slugger on a hanging curve ball. "Oh no! You're not getting out of this that easy, Stocker!"

"Ah, *but I am.* Based on what has transpired between you and me in the past, Sir, you need a third party to collaborate anything you *claim* happens between us because, Sir, your credibility alone, when it involves me, ain't worth a bucket of warm spit! This whole conversation between you and me on this balcony, Sir, *without a witness,* is just a discussion between two men. That's it! Plain and simple. *You and me; that's all it'll ever be… and why?* Let's look at your track record. You call me out and name me *ringleader* in front of a *company formation* with no evidence? You don't have any witnesses for my crime, but *I've* got a whole fucking company full of witnesses for *your crime.* The fact that there *ARE* a full company of witnesses *WAS* your crime against me! You read a list of 10 names and don't have anything but *gossip* on any one of them? Didn't you ever watch even one episode of *Perry Mason* in your whole life? And that crap last week. Making up your very own *private question* for me on the promotion board exam. Seriously, Sir, when it comes to me, you have clearly zero'd in on me, stretched the rules already and have zero credibility. I respect your right to try and somehow bust me; fair is fair. But, you can't fault me for making you play by *your* rules, that being the UCMJ. *Hardball war zone tour,* Sir. And here you are, by your own admission, laying in wait for me, on the hope of observing me in some malfeasance. You are persecuting me because of bad decisions you made involving me that came back to bite you on the ass. *Twice.* And now that I'm about to go home, this will totally look like you're making stuff up to get even, unless you had a *witness…* and of course, some *evidence* wouldn't hurt, either." The Kid brazenly took another hit.

As PM searches for his response, the Kid casually slipped in the nail. "Don't you think Colonel Lawton might feel you could make better use of your time, other than continuing to chase me? Sans evidence and witnesses, you think he'll really want to hear it?"

Steam out the ears. Literally, I swear.

"That's another thing! *You hiding* behind the colonel's skirt! You're not going to get away with this, Stocker! I am going to find a way to bring you to account for everything that's happened with marijuana in this unit!"

"*Everything, Sir? Wow!* You know, you insult everybody in the unit to infer that none of them are educated enough to make their own decisions and you further display your ignorance by believing that none of them smoked pot before they got here *and I* got them all to start. *Seriously, Sir.* I appreciate your admiration for my persuasive abilities, but I don't control these men. *And I'm pretty sure Colonel Lawton does not wear a skirt.*

He was too pissed to respond.

"Your mistake, Sir, was canceling the marijuana training in February and not allowing a forum to take place. That could have promoted a healthy exchange of dialogue between the two sides. A little humorous banter would have gone a long ways to defusing the situation. *But no.* So I wanted to debate; I was on the fucking debate team for four years… *it's what I do!* Does the fact that I do research make me a ringleader? You guys cancelled training and ran and hid! *What leadership.* I'll still debate you tomorrow or any day before I go, Sir, formal or otherwise, if you really want to address the marijuana issue in the unit, that is… *if you're not too… chicken?"*

"You can't talk to me like that! God dammit, I am your commanding officer!"

"I think I just did talk to you like that, Sir. *Man to man. Don't you remember, that's all this is!* But, Sir, any time you want to, you always have the option to call me to attention… *you being a captain and all*…and I will come to attention, according to Army regs, which state, quite clearly, that I must get rid of the cigarette…*Sir.*"

In other words, the Kid was telling PM again, in no uncertain terms, there was no way, in Hell or on God's Green Earth, that he would ever possess the joint in his hand.

"But why do you feel you have to create all this friction by so blatantly flaunt the rules? I know you have your convictions and opinions and you are extremely honest about them, *to a fault.* But, Stocker, are they worth going to jail for?"

"Who's going to jail, Sir?"

"Why do you have to smoke that stuff? Why don't you just drink like the rest of us?" Smith questioned.

"I can't believe you said that! *Well,* Sir, for openers, I think it's better than drinking because you don't get hung over, you maintain your equilibrium and aren't falling down stumbling stupid and puking while you're high, you don't slobber on yourself or slur your words and you can remember what happened the next day. Plus, if you have to react, *you can!"*

"If you men continue to smoke pot here on the balcony, we're going to take photographs of you and charge everybody in the photograph!"

"With what? The crime of being on the balcony or maybe, *posing?*" The Kid shook his head and held up the joint, "you're going to take a picture of this from across the street and tell a judge, from that photo, you can certify the physical contents? Beyond a reasonable doubt? How could you even prove what cigarette was in the picture? Let alone that it was marijuana. Really, Sir. Go ahead and take all the pictures you want. It's your willingness to go around the rules of evidence or not knowing what evidence is, that keeps getting you into trouble. I could have had your career, *twice now,* and let you go. Sir, the first time, all ten of us could have had your slanderous ass up on charges and *we let you go.* You know that, right?"

Now the piss off quotient was elephant sized! The Kid surmised PM was using every bit of his will power to keep from running down there and just plain beating the crap out of him!

"Someday they are going to have a blood test or urine test to prove if you are smoking pot, just like alcohol!"

"*Right.* And I'm short 23 day; don't think they'll have either one ready by then. I get out in 17 months; think they'll have it before then?"

"*God!* I have had enough of your *SHIT!* Specialist Stocker... *TEN HUT!*"

At that command, the Kid first looked the captain in the eye, turned to make sure he was flicking the joint into the middle of the tallest, most snake infested weeds he could find, sent it sailing and then snapped to attention, hands at his side, head back and chin sarcastically in. He had not been able to click the heels of his bare feet.

It was another time, if looks could kill, that the Kid would have been drilled dead through the pupils of a Smith. With daggers flowing from his eyes, PM turned and walked off.

Five seconds later, the Kid hollered after him, *"Sir? Am I dismissed?*

Hearing no response, the Kid rushed immediately to the stairwell to confirm he was gone. Then it was off to his locker to remove the carton of joints and take it down to the latrine cache. Frantically, he check to make sure he hadn't missed anything that could get him into trouble in a shakedown for he surely expected the Captain to quickly return... *with a witness...* and do exactly that!

But he didn't return.

The Kid did not leave for lunch at the USO. He did not go swimming or to chow at Eakin. He stayed and waited for each Tribe member to arrive and

559

alerted them to secure their lockers for the pending danger. They trickled in and by the time everybody was back after chow at the evening curfew, everybody was ready.

In light of the fact that PM and the officers had not yet struck, the Tribe gathered to strategize their defense.

After hearing the story of the confrontation, a group of about a dozen was gathered in the Kid, Ken and Ramjet's room. Nobody was toking out on the balcony and the members were growing nervous, talking amongst themselves about bad possibilities, when Little offered an interesting observation.

"You know, my desk is right next to Ozelle's at the front door and nobody comes and goes without the two of us knowing it," the slim and shirtless curly headed A company clerk was leaning against the Kid's locker and held a pack of cigarettes in one hand. "We were both working at our desks when PM came in, at about 1000 hours. All he said was 'hello' and breezed on through. We both looked at each other and wonder what the hell he's doing here at this time of day, but didn't much care what it was. So, he's somewhere in the building for about an hour. We were still working when he rushes out at about 1115, looking super pissed… *and now I know why,* without so much as a *howdy de do, goodbye, or have a nice day!* Now, if he was ever going to come right back up there and jump in your shit, don't you think he would have just grabbed Ozelle…*Ozelle's not your friend,* and did it right then? After what you said happened, my bet is, if he didn't tell Ozelle, if he didn't say something then, he ain't tellin' *nobody, ever!* I mean, what's he going to say; *'hey ya'll, let me tell you how I was embarrassed by the Kid. Again.'* Words I don't think he wants to come out of his mouth because how would he explain it to all his officer buddies?

Nobody was really buying it; they couldn't imagine the Kid could piss the captain off so bad and he wouldn't do anything.

"We cleaned out our lockers and everybody's room is ready, right?" Little continued with his analysis, "Now, we know they know about the 'stach over the toilet because they busted it before. But they don't know about the joints in the cartons. However, because ya'll went and put your cartons up there, if they find them, they'll think we had to have a reason to put them there. Use your heads, people, the safest place for them is back in our lockers, like they are just cigarettes and nothing to worry about."

"The reason I took mine down there," the Kid spoke up, "was because I was smoking one when he caught me… and I'm not sure if he picked up I was smoking a filter tip, but if he did, he might figure it out."

"Hmmm," Little rubbed his chin, "I'd be willing to bet there was way too much going on his head for him to take in and register on that kind of detail. And consider, since they busted our stash last February, did we change it? No. Have they ever been back to bust it again? *Strangely*, no. So, gents," Little pulled the seal off the pack of Marlboros in hand, took one out and said, "All this talk about getting busted and shakedowns makes my head spin, I need a toke. Anybody joining me?" he tossed the pack back into the room as he walked out onto the balcony and lit up. The whole room followed.

Speculation continued to run wild as they smoked but to one thing they all did agree; the brass had an MO of running shakedowns early on weekend mornings, when everybody was present and sleeping in. It was Friday night, they wouldn't have long to wait to find out.

Chapter 84

April 28, 1969

Dear Larry,

Happy Late April Fool's Day! I'm down to 20 days! Tomorrow I will be in the TEENS!!!! WAAAAAAAAHHHHH! WOOOOHOOOO!!!

Dude! Other than the time I got left alone at the front in September, this last Friday I got the biggest scare of my whole freaking tour! (so far) And it didn't involve dodging real bullets! It was actually scarier than some of the times I did get shot at and it could have been another court martial, not the kind I want to try and beat. Dig this; I had a day off so when I got up, I went to do a # on the balcony. I was the only one there so the usual security was not in place. Turns out my CO was in observation above my position & flanked me, with the # on fire, demanded I give it to him! Long story short, I asked him if he was calling me to attention and he said yes, so that meant I had to throw the # away in the swamp! Boy was he pissed. Said I disobeyed his order... I said who witnessed that? Don't have time or space and the censors do read our mail to tell you the whole story here, but wait till I tell you how it came down! Clue: (Gary Cooper movie, Sun directly overhead?). There is a chance it's not over yet but my plan is to keep the Schnozola well laundered for the time I have left in this stinking hole. I leave here for Saigon in 2 fucking weeks from today!

If things go right and my luck doesn't finally run out, I'll be back in the States on May 18, because of the International date line, I get back the day I leave! Scott is bringing my bug to Oakland and I'm driving straight down to see Flo and then, whatever is the deal with her, I'll be heading for Boulder no later than May 23. Maybe I'll be there sooner if she sends me packing. So I'll see you before I go to Nashville, one way or the other. And now that I'm going to be at Ft. Carson for 15 months, we'll get to see each other plenty!

What an experience this has been. Now that I'm here, when I get back and talk to war hawks, I'll have a special ration of shit for them about what

562

this war really means to both Americans and the Vietnamese. I now know what it's like to be in an army of occupation. If we have been fighting for freedom all this time, why do I feel so much like a Red Coat? We are in a war of attrition and there is no way America can ever put up enough blood to win.

You are wise to avoid this experience at all costs. Is Bob Duncan still planning on becoming an Air Force pilot? I'll have to have a talk with that boy when I get back...

See you real soon!

Curt

As he finished Larry's letter and looked up, the Kid found someone standing quietly at his table, in the roof Club, where he was writing home. It was none other than Stoney, returned from the field. The man who was afraid the war would pass him by.

He was attired in garb that immediately identified him as a *boonie* trooper; fatigues topped by a jungle hat that was flat brimmed all the way around, sort of an Aussie style, and a red kerchief wrapped around his neck with an Army issue .45 hanging from a pistol bet on his right hip.

"I see the Kid is still in control," a large grin occupied his freckled Irish face, "I was hoping I'd get in to see you before you left."

"Stoney!" the Kid stood and extended his hand, "great to see you! How's my favorite field rat?"

"Doing good, mostly," Stoney left his hat on while he talked, "well, good and bad, but not too bad, all in all."

"You ended up in Bac Lieu, right? So how is it going down there?" the Kid sensed a story.

"The good news is, I'm going to get a Purple Heart!" big grin, "the bad news is, I got wounded," and as he said it, he pulled down the red bandanna tied around his neck. "And the not too bad is I just got nicked here in the neck, just above my adams' apple," he pointed, "grazed me, so it could have been a hell of a lot worse!

It reminded the Kid a lot of Tom Robert's scar on the arm; about a half an inch in a straight horizontal line. And like Tom's wound, a very small piece had nicked him going sideways and consequently did not actually penetrate with any depth.

563

"It would have really fucked me up if it had hit my adam's apple," Stoney grimaced. "Or if it hit six inches up and six back, it would have gone in my temple; the thing might have killed me. They lobbed some mortars in, around midnight, and running from my cot to the bunker, I caught this on the way! Talk about seeing God!" he pulled the bandanna back up. "You remember how hot I was to go out there?"

"Yes."

"Well, those days are fucking over! The night I got this, they killed 4 of our ARVNs and wounded another 3; I was just lucky as hell, that's all. And with the other action I've seen, you were right, Stocker; a man can get killed out there pretty fucking easy! I know there's no way I can come back in before I DEROS, because I *begged* to go out, but you can bet your ass I don't volunteer for *nothing! You were right, Kid, don't fucking volunteer for nothing!"*

Amen Brother.

"Funny you should say, however," the Kid smiled back, "just the other day, I was thinking about my fun filled days in the field when I didn't have to sweat things like the company commander…" He gave Stoney a *Cliff's Notes* version of the *PM High Noon Standoff.* "Yep, for a minute there, I was the one wishing for some of that low profile *anywhere but here* field time! But the shakedown hasn't come yet, so we're thinking PM was too embarrassed to tell anybody how he could catch me with a smoking joint but not take me down. Be careful while you're here."

"Wow. You are one lucky son of a bitch, Stocker."

Don't I know it! Beaver nickel. "Well, hey, I got a couple more letters I gotta get out to people to let them know when I'm coming, so let me do this and we can smoke in the Embassy here in a bit. I want to hear all your war stories, Stoney! You got your wish! You're a combat vet!"

"Yeah! I made it! See you down there!"

April 28, 1969

Dearest Flo,

Hope this finds you with things going well and graduation is happening! Hard to believe, but in 22 days, it will be a year since we were together. That means, of course, in 20 days, I will be home!

564

Right now, my date for departure is May 18. Scott is meeting me with the bug in Oakland and then, we are driving to LA, where he'll catch a plane and I'll drive on to Vista.

Babe, I know things will not be the same between us. We are no longer engaged, but all I do know is, for this entire year, all I have wanted is to see you and be with you! No telling at this point how we will feel when we are once again in the same room but we have to find out! After all, I said I'll see you Later!

I got my orders 3 weeks ago. I wanted California (or Tennessee) but does the Army give me that? No way San Jose! They have never given me anything I wanted, so why should they start now? I have been assigned to Ft. Carson, in Colorado Springs. That's about 75 miles from Boulder. Sure as hell could have been worse! If I would have asked for Ft. Carson, maybe then I'd have gotten Tennessee or California. More likely it would have been Cleveland or Newark or some other such backwater hole, so I can take Ft. Carson. Supposedly, I am assigned to the post hospital closed circuit radio station, so I might finally get to work in radio. Not holding my breath.

Things here have been a cross between too boring and so exciting that there isn't room in this letter to write the exciting part…(Hi Mrs. Stuckey, how are you?) Not that I have been getting shot at or anything, but I did have what can only be described as a VERY VERY VERY close call!

The VC did blow up our chow truck 2 weeks ago, with a grenade in the gas tank, but nobody was in it at the time. 20 minutes earlier, it would have gotten like at least 20 of us.

The enclosed issue of DIMENSION is the one I got to edit! Here, all I wanted was to be a program director by 21 but what happens? Editor by 21. Dam Army! I hope I can find a part time radio job in Colorado Springs. I know the closed-circuit station won't be real radio. The Army has no idea of how to use a real radio station.

Did John and Lo have their baby yet? Is he doing OK here? You don't have to write me here anymore; I probably wouldn't get it before I left anyway. Just curious. You can tell me in person in 19 days!.

If your graduation is happening around when I get back, maybe I can come to it? That is, if it's not before I have to go to Boulder and Nashville. I know your Mom hates me and she might not want me there, so I could just hide out in the back of the room or something.

Do tell your Dad Hi for me. He doesn't read these, right?

Anyway, it looks real good now that I'm going to make it home. Hope I didn't jinx myself with that line, but Floretta K. Stuckey, I cannot wait to see you!

I'll See You SOONER (than Later)

XXXXXXXOOOOOXXXXXXX&X !!!

Curt

Chapter 85

Mail call had gotten kind of slow for the Kid, as he neared the end of his tour. Of course, Flo's letters did not arrive anywhere near as often. Every couple of weeks he might get one but the 'every day' routine ended with their engagement. The need for care packages was never as crucial in Can Tho, as it had been out in the field, so he'd stopped asking for them.

The Kid's fan mail from Nashville had almost dried up completely. That likely had to do with some DJ turnover and the new on-air talent did not know the Kid or talk about him being in the war. One fan, however, was loyal to the end. It was Pat Bowen, the self-appointed *(and Kid endorsed)* President of his nearly mythical Fan Club. Her Letter was the only one he received on May 2nd.

April 20, 1969

Dear Kid,

Hope this finds you safe and in good spirits. By my reckoning, when you get this, you should have less than one month left to be there. Have you found out the date when you get to come home? When do you think you'll be here in the Music City? Have you found out where they are sending you when you get back? That's a lot of questions!

Things have been kind of rough down at the station. Since Smokey got killed and Dick Buckley took over as GM, things have gone downhill like I've never seen before at WKDA. The Good Guys got knocked out of #1 in the last ratings and Dave Allen resigned as PD. Jonny Wailin left, Doc Holliday left. Baby Bill Craig is still there but I don't know for how long. Your shift is on the third DJ to have it since you left so all of us are excited about you coming back. Tell me again, how much longer do you have left in the Army after you get back from Vietnam?

I know how you feel about it, but I want you to know that I pray to the Lord every night for your safety and that you'll come home in one piece. If you make it, I will thank the Lord for you, since you are too pig headed to do it yourself.

WKDA is having the Dick Clark Caravan of Stars concert again next week. I hope I can win some tickets. If not, my sis Teresa and I are going to buy some and go anyway.

It's just not the same as it used to be, I guess that is the way it is with the whole world. Anyway, let me know when you're coming to Nashville. I can't wait to see you and to know that you are finally safe for keeps!

Take care, all my prayers!

Your Friend,

Pattie B. the Ghoul

President of your Fan Club!

May 2, 1969

Dear Mom and Dad,

Here is the last issue of the paper I will ever send you from Nam. Not only that, I'm close behind it. There is even a chance I might get a drop of two or three days, because other guys are, but the way the Army works, it really doesn't make much sense to plan on anything. We'll see how the luck is. If I do, Scott will still be in Tacoma and that might present a problem with the car. We'll have to wait and see.

As you will notice, I got to be 'Editor for a Month!' That is not going to hurt the old resume in the future. I'm still a radio person and not really a journalist. I will admit, the issue could have been better, some things not in my control and some were. I'm glad this editor thing was a one-shot deal.

Getting so short I can't stand it. I leave for Saigon in 12 days and 15 days to the Jet! More stories in person!

568

Love,

Curt

PS: ARE YOU READY?

Chapter 86

This would be the last story he would ever write for DIMENSION. It was one of his *Personality Features,* the subject of which for May, was George McCauley, super clerk of S-1.

'Georgi', pronounced *'George-eye'*, as the Kid had nicknamed him, was the son of a military man, born in Atlanta. His dad had been a lieutenant colonel in the engineers, so he moved around a lot while growing up.

George had a biting sense of humor and was capable of rivaling the Kid for sarcasm. He was a *never a dull moment* kind of friend. For the March issue of DIMENSION, the Kid got him to pose as the *"April Fool"*, with a white mop on his head for hair, reclined like a bathing beauty, on the edge of the Eakin Compound swimming pool. It was printed on the backside of the real playmate countdown calendar that was part of each issue.

The interview was scheduled at 0630 hours, in George's room, because the Kid had heard about his iron clad morning routine. Hardily ever going to Eakin for breakfast, he would instead brew fresh coffee on a hotplate and have it with a *'Danish-go-round,"* a pastry delight well supplied to him by his mom. The Kid could smell the coffee and when he ceremonially knocked on the door of the second-floor balcony room, he found Georgi standing there with the coffee pot in his hand.

"Morning, Georg-i, that coffee smells great!" The Kid sat his notebook down on the card table, prepared in advance by George for both the breakfast and the interview.

"Morning Curt," he poured, "I know that the only reason you wanted to conduct the interview over breakfast was so you could get at my Danish-go-rounds!"

"Guilty. You saw right through me," admitted the Kid; the Danish-go-round was already served up, made rounder by sitting on a square white plastic plate. "It looks great!"

"You seem to be in a good mood today," George took his seat.

"*Who wouldn't*, at 11 and a wakeup! And I'm outta Can Tho exactly one week from today. It's so almost here, I can hardly fucking stand it! This story is the last thing I have to do that resembles work. So, what I'll do is work on this Danish and you tell me the Cliff Notes version of the life of Georgi!"

"Even though I was born in Atlanta, I mainly grew up in Newark," he began and he talked while the Kid ate and drank coffee with one hand and took notes with the other. "I started college as a pre-med major, but somehow, got channeled into economics and in 1967, I got my degree in that at Wooster College, in Ohio. My main interest in economics is in the advertising game. Shortly after graduation, I think it was exactly four months, I was invited to join Uncle Sam's Finest."

"Tell me one 'something' about yourself that might surprise the unit," the Kid waited for what he might hear.

"Well," Georgi look to the ceiling for a few seconds before he said, "after AIT, at Ft Jackson, I was invited by the Army to attend OCS at Ft. Benning. There I was at the bus terminal, ready to go, when I had a sudden change of heart and turned back. The next day, I knew I had made a mistake. I think I would have liked to have been an officer, to see what I could have done with it."

"OK. That is surprising!" the Kid winced, "then we couldn't have been friends."

"Why not? Aren't we all friends with Culp?" He brought up the exception to the rule.

"True enough, *Culp*, but he's the only exception."

"Not so!" Georgi gestured to hold his right index finger pointing straight up, "the colonel is your friend!"

"Not my friend like we're going out for a beer, or not like Culp, that we actually *smoked dope with him* friends," the Kid proffered a bar for the friendship to clear.

"Yeah, right. He's more like a *'because of me, you're not going to jail,'* friend. You know, my dad was a lieutenant colonel and I can tell you right now, he'd have flipped out if anybody would have run the shit on him that you did on PM! It's a good thing you're leaving. From where my desk is, I catch bits of officer conversation and a popular topic right now, pretty much among all of them at HQ, is about *Willie,* not letting them take you *down!*"

The Kid sat there for a second and then tugged on the chain around his neck that held his lucky Beaver Nickle, bringing it out from his shirt.

571

Dangling it, he said, "What can I tell you?" I didn't get shot, blown up or busted smoking pot. I won a court martial and the colonel, for whatever reason, picked me to be his project, *knock on wood*," and he did. "Like I could have picked *HIM!* I'm guilty of being one lucky son of a bitch, George. *No fucking doubt about it.* Although, while I'm not sure if *actually* coming here to Nam was lucky, I have been uber fucking lucky here. And even though I didn't get Armed Forces Radio, leaving here alive in one piece is about all a person can ask for."

"I've been pretty lucky here, too," decided George, "to be in such a low danger and risk department. S-1 senior clerk is an OK job, no real problems, only it's hard to make myself get up and go to work. Hence the little ceremony that gives me something to look forward to in the morning," he took a bite of his Danish and after swallowing, continued. "Even though I haven't enjoyed this job, I try to do my best. It's not the kind of job that shows results, like working on the newspaper: you can see the issues before you. For a clerk, it's just you and that typewriter and that's not enough."

"Now Georgi," the Kid tapped the end of his pen on the table, "another thing one of your room mates, who shall remain nameless, has told me something about you that I want to *verify* before I print anything about it, and that is… that you ogle and drool on the foldouts in *GOURMET Magazine,* the way the rest of us do a *PLAYBOY* spread; care to elaborate about that?"

He chuckled, as if he wanted to ask which roommate, but instead answered, "There is no doubt I enjoy eating. It goes back to my father, who went to work for Dupont when he got out of the service. Sometimes, I would go with him on business trips, and we would always eat in the best restaurants and Dupont would pay for it! But my favorite meal is less gourmet, give me a reeeel good home made beef stew with a wine base!"

It was time to wrap it up. "So, What are your plan for when you get out of the Army?"

"Well, when I get out, I'm going to take off and travel abroad."

"Georgi…you're pretty much 'abroad' for a year right now!" the Kid quickly cut in.

"What I mean is Europe or someplace *nice*. But I would still eventually like to join one of those volunteer organizations like the Peace Corps or Vista."

'My brother was in the Peace Corps when he got drafted," said the Kid.

"There's one thing I won't have to worry about," figured Georgi.

After the interview and the danish, the Kid went to Eakin and had breakfast anyway. He might have gone back to sleep if he hadn't drank Georgi's coffee, but it smelled so dam good, he couldn't resist. It was for the better, he knew; there was much to do in preparation for his departure, *a week from today.*

After chow, he paid a visit to Taj the Tailor, the man who sold everything, offered every service and knew everything happening on the streets. The sign out in front of his store said he was a barber shop, had clothes for all occasions, could dry clean and alter any garment. If his sign said all of the things he really did, it would have been two stories tall. *Money changer. Rumor monger. Dry goods purveyor, fashion mogul, tattoo parlor, set you up with a whore, of course sell you pot. If you could name it, Taj would either have it, know where to get it or who to call about it.*

Taj was standing out in front of his store, right elbow propped atop his sign, smoking a Salem. The Kid raised his Pentax and snapped off a couple of frames by which to remember him. Taj made a point of being friends with all the GIs.

"Ah, Mister Curt pays me a visit!" he said, as the Kid took the camera down from his eye. " You are you leaving soon, right?"

"Yep, one week from today!"

"So sad to see you go," he frowned theatrically.

"That makes one of you," laughed the Kid, "but I'm here today, Taj, and I need *bou coup* stuff so I'll be your good customer one more time, *at least!*"

His face lit up, "What is it you be needing, Mr. Curt?"

"Haircut for openers," the Kid said, "and some kind of small briefcase because I'm going to be traveling light. I might buy some souvenirs for some people back in the States but let's do the haircut first."

Taj ushered him into the store. Since October, he had made a lot of purchases from the transplanted Indian merchant. His establishment was a fairly cavernous mercantile, with a two-story high ceiling that was easily 30 X 40 feet deep. The Kid perused the samples of the GI souvenir clothing one could buy, all types of jackets, some with maps of Vietnam embroidered on the back, others had artfully done tigers in various snarling poses, some hidden in bamboo. There were hats of all styles, shoes galore and many ready-made shirts but not so much in the pants department. Luckily, the Kid's dad had mailed him the requested pair of Levis that he would don in Oakland, at the first permitted instant.

The barber shop, all of one chair, was over in the far corner. Taj snapped his fingers and a man came running out from the back and stood at attention beside the chair, smiling at the kid as he approached

"Chou Om," said the Kid as he sat down.

"Chou Trung ui," the barber read his rank as sergeant.

'Bic English?" the Kid asked.

"Yes," replied the barber with a smile. His greying hair made him appear to be at least his late 50's or early 60's; all the younger men were gone to one side's army or the other. Likely he was a veteran. "What you like today?" He smiled, *his teeth were still great.*

"Just a haircut, no shave," the Kid kept the instructions simple. As the protective cover was secured around his neck with the clip, the Kid realized this would be his last Vietnamese haircut. *Soon he'd eat his last meal at Eakin, take his last swim, get his last blow job at the Scientific, pack and ship off his hold baggage and spend his last night smoking dope in the Embassy. He'd take his last flight up to Saigon, the return drive up to Long Binh and soon, he'd be seeing the guys!*

All, *save John Imbach.*

Getting ready to go home was like decompressing, coming up for air after being submerged deep in the waters of the war zone for a year, almost afraid if he came up too fast, he'd get the bends. Was he really going home? Yes. California, Boulder and Nashville... there would be homecomings in all of them! As Nguyen clipped away, he considered how events in Vietnam had affected his life. If he had gotten the AFVN assignment, he would just be arriving back in Vietnam, not going home. And he would only have 11 months left in the Army, instead of the 17 months he was facing. He would have gotten to work in radio for a year and get out six months early but it wasn't meant to be. Nor was it meant for him to die assaulting tree lines, with Lt. Wilson, or on an Armed Propaganda Team commando raid. He'd won one court martial but still didn't know if his destiny was to avoid getting busted by Captain Smith, but the more time that elapsed since their confrontation and the shorter he got, the stronger he felt.

The Kid heard Nguyen stropping the straight razor and knew he was coming to the part that both thrilled and terrified him... the part where the Vietnamese barber shaved the hair off one's ears with a straight razor. It felt incredible, but how could one not think of being cut with an implement like that? The feel of the blade going over the top of his ear and the gentle scraping sounds it made gave him goose bumps. The barber also used the straight razor to take the short hairs off the back of his neck. Cool breeze.

He was going home!

Chapter 87

It wasn't as big a party as the movie *HELP,* but the turnout was substantial because everybody in the unit had an opinion on the Kid. So the Kid's last night in Can Tho was celebrated, on May 14th, by those who happily toasted with him his good fortune to be the shortest man in Can Tho and those who flat wanted him gone; *good riddance!*

Their room had been turned into a munchies buffet and all the men had contributed from their care packages goodies to make it festive. Needless to say, the unit weed cache would need replenishing in the morning. It was also in the back of their minds that if ever there was to be an assault on the sanctity of the Embassy, to catch everybody in some kind of dragnet, *it would be tonight.* But if it happened, the resulting mayhem and confusion was guaranteed to be unmeasurable.

The Embassy guards were on red alert.

He knew, as he circulated among the partiers that the overwhelming majority, he would never see or hear from them again. It had been the same for each of the levels of the Army through which he had traversed. Men he'd bunked with for two months at basic training and with whom he had endured the traditional hardships; he'd never see any of them again. The men who had been his classmates at DINFOS; already he knew he'd never see any of the ones who hadn't come to Vietnam. Of the ones who would theoretically join him for the flight home, no telling who after that, would remain in touch over the years.

Still, in the year he'd been in PSYOPS and for the time he'd been in Can Tho, following his court martial, he had made a raft of what he would consider lifelong friends. *Surely, some of us will stay in touch!*

Around 2200 hours, after the movie was over, which the Tribe did not attend, the Kid went up to the Roof Club to say goodbye to some of the lifers. One of the first men he saw bellied up to the bar ordering a beer was B Company First Sgt. Johnson. Sneaking up behind him, he got six inches off from his left ear *and clucked softly; bwaaaak buc buc buc.*

Johnson spun around,"*Ho!* Stocker! My favorite miscreant! It's going to be dull around here without you to stir the pot… so to speak!" They both laughed. "And I just want to say, *I know you're not chicken…* suicidally radical maybe… bat shit crazy is a strong possibility, *but not chicken!*"

"Why thank you, Sergeant. I enjoyed having you as a member of the promotion board! That will be one fun memory!" *Bwaakkkk Bwaaakkkk!*

"Yeah, really. That was not a *white feather* day! Of all the promotions boards I was ever on, I'll have to say, that one was …*different!* I'd tell you good luck and keep your nose clean, but I know you don't need any more luck and I also know your nose will always be an issue in your future. How much time do you have left when you get back?"

"16 months, First Sergeant."

"Then I *will* wish you good luck. I can foresee a real hard 16 months back in the States for you because you are truly a person who doesn't know when to quit!"

'I will take that as a compliment, First Sergeant! And good luck to you!" They firmly shook hands.

After having a fresh brew stuck in his paw by Barry Fischer, the Kid spied RV Smith, *Al* and *Frank* jawing at one of the tables over by the movie projector stand. As soon as one of them spotted him headed their way, all three turned to his approach.

"Gentlemen," he smile that smile only a short timer can accurately affect. "How are you all doing on this *fine* night?"

"Hey, Stocker," the trio mumbles, expecting him to deliver his standard ration of bullshit.

"RV, got a minute?" the Kid motioned that he wanted a word over by the rail.

"Sure, why not?" RV grinned uneasily as he rose with his beer in hand, looking to Al and Frank with an expression that clearly said; *I hope you got my back!*

When they got to the rail and stood directly above the Embassy, looking west, they both lit up cigarettes and took a puff.

"So you're out of here tomorrow," RV exhaled, "I'm down to 30 myself!"

"Yeah. I know how good that feels. And it only gets better; I mean, if you wanted, you could call yourself 29 and a wake up right now!" *The Kid took a puff and exhaled.* "RV, I just wanted to say, you've been a worthy foil and opponent. No hard feelings about you being the man who spotted the fact that I never got duty. *It was good while it lasted.* And about the *STRATEGO* game incident, the reason why I wanted to talk to you is to let you know, the Rats Revenge is over."

The look on RV face was all perplexed. *"It's over?* What do you mean it's over? What the fuck is 'over'?"

"Well, it's like this, RV. My father is the inventor of the Rats Revenge. What it consists of is the victim fearing *whatever* the act of revenge could possibly be for a long, extended period of time. All of the thoughts you had of when it might happen and how bad it might be…all the time you spent on guard, not knowing what I might DO, when I might strike; that in itself… *IS the Rats Revenge!* And it's over so you can stop worrying about it!"

RV didn't know what to say until he sought clarification. "So, what you're telling me is there is no Rats Revenge?"

"No. What I'm telling you, RV, is that the Rats Revenge consists of you *thinking* something bad is going to happen when nothing ever does. *THAT* is the Rats Revenge. Perhaps I should draw you a picture? The Rats Revenge is something *YOU* do to yourself. Kind of like the way you have sex."

There was a pause of consideration before he said, " Stocker, I won't fucking miss you or your bullshit."

"Nor I yours, RV. Have a good life." They shook hands.

The next lifer of import that caught the Kid's eye was First Sergeant Ozelle Jones. He was sitting with Sergeants Pepper and Zazulak.

"Sergeants!" the Kid greeted them as he approached their table, "If any of you ever get to Nashville, I'm sure you won't look me up!"

The three of them snickered.

"Sgt. Jones," the Kid addressed him using his best *'Eddie Hascall' impersonation,* "I know you and I did not always see eye to eye, but I want to tell you that I appreciate the opportunity to serve under such a *hard working and eminently qualified* professional military man, such as yourself…"

He got a laugh out of all three.

"Stocker…" Ozelle shook his head and rolled his eyes to the other two NCOs before he said, "You know, I don't care what all of the others say, I personally will miss your special brand of *B-U-L-L-S-H-I-T,*" he spelled out each letter, *slowly,* as he extended his hand, "because it is grade A! You're one of a fucking kind, Stocker…*thank God!*"

578

The Kid shook his hand and then paused, as if in thought," *Hmmm,* I don't get it. RV just told me he wouldn't miss me or my bullshit… and here, from you, I get a vote of confidence and it's the *same BS!* Go figure."

"Well, I guess there's no accounting for taste. *Have a nice flight,*" Ozelle gave him a send-off.

"Sgt. Z, it's been a pleasure serving with the tallest NCO I've ever met," and to the diminutive Sgt Pepper, "Sergeant P, love your album but *hate your radio show;* see ya in the funny papers!" they both smiled but said nothing in reply.

Back on the balcony, Edwards handed the Kid a joint. "Here ya go, short timer, I'm down to 60 tonight myself; two more months!"

"When I was at 60 days, I thought it would take forever, but standing here tonight, I am amazed at how fast it goes by. I am blown away with the fact that tomorrow, I am fucking out of here *forever!* And almost out of PSYOPS and almost on the jet!"

"You are one fucking lucky dog, Stocker." *General consensus.*

As men came and went saying their goodbyes, the Kid finished packing and when he was done, he viewed his traveling luggage. He had compressed the scant amount of clothing he was taking into the black valise. Most of it his uniforms and clothing he had shipped home via hold baggage, along with his tape recorder and some other odds and ends. All of his papers; consisting of his orders, notebooks and a complete set of DIMENSIONs, he had fit into a cheap black brief case. Next to them sat a pair of class A dress shoes and a pair of flip flops. *Traveling light and fast!*

"Let's go over to Boyett's room and listen to Big Pink again," the Kid suggested.

Tom was more than happy to oblige. After that, they put on Sergeant Pepper's Lonely Hearts Club Band. That shot the Kid right back to Tra Vinh and all the time he'd spent with Wen and her family, listening to *Pepper* and eating home fried potato chips.

The Kid recalled saying his goodbyes to Boujold and before that, Paul Hoch, and before that Paul Heineman in Tra Vinh. Now it's MY turn! It gave him a shiver!

"What are you doing for pot?" Birnbaum inquired as they smoked later, near the midnight hour.

"Well," the Kid paused, "I think I'm taking one pack of joints with me for Saigon, that should hold me for the 3 days I'll be there. But, when I go

up to Long Binh, *I'm going up clean!* Smoked my brains out here, am going to be very careful on the way out. Not a time to get busted!"

"No shit! I remember Boujold almost went down the night before!"

"Yeah. What a scare that was!" the Kid couldn't help but to recall it. "Yes, I'm going to miss having the best pot in the world, all that I want to smoke when I want to smoke it at $5.00 a pound. There ain't none of THAT in the States! Shit, when I started smoking pot in Boulder, in 1966, I paid $5.00 for a *matchbox!* Once again I say, the only redeeming feature of Vietnam, *is the pot!*"

Long after the festivities ended, well after midnight, when everybody had retired, the kid couldn't sleep and sat on the bench outside of his window, smoking one last Embassy joint. Off in the distance, his focus was on the one red light atop the tower at Binh Thuy Airbase. It had an almost hypnotic effect on him and he had spent many an hour staring at it, wishing this very moment was at hand. He had taken care of all the necessities, like selling his .38 and getting rid of the three 50 caliber rounds he'd kept from Tra Vinh as a souvenir. Those would never get through inspection to board the plane.

It was looking more and more like he was destined to live through the Vietnam experience. He recalled the medivac that came in to dust off wounded soldiers on one of their earlier operations with the ARVN 14th Regiment. The pilot had requested special security efforts because he was down to 10 days. Now the Kid was at 6 days; less than a week. How ironic would it be to get picked off this balcony by a sniper tonight? Considering how close he had come to being picked off the balcony by PM Smith, he had to admit, anything was possible. He took solace in the fact that nobody had ever been shot by a sniper at the New Villa. Lucky this place will never be named after me!

He finished the joint and flipped the roach into the swamp. Standing, he stretched and turned to enter his room. After tonight; my room no more. He wondered who was going to get his bunk? The competition was intense and a decision wasn't made yet. It wouldn't be RV Smith because he only had a month left. The Kid didn't care! He had no vote because he wouldn't have to put up with whoever it was.

He was going home!

Chapter 88

The Kid was so amped, he couldn't sit still. Pacing the graphics room, he hot boxed a KOOL while dropping ashes all over the floor.

"When is the flight?" Tom Boyett looked up from his work on the May DIMENSION.

"1000 hours," the Kid face was plastered with an irremovable goofy grin, "one fucking hour!"

Just then, Wimbish popped through the door, "Hey, Curt, the colonel will see you now."

"Thanks!" he followed Lou up the corridor to the front of Battalion HQ, slapping over what could well be his last three inter-building lizard pilots along the way. As Lou passed the colonel's door he signaled to the Kid that Willie O. was waiting for him.

Knock on the door.

"Enter!"

Goes in, closes door, turns, salutes and reports; "Sir, Specialist Stocker reporting!"

"At ease, Specialist Stocker," Willie gave him one of his patented grins with the salute, "your day has come at last!"

"Yes Sir! It has!"

"Let's sit at the coffee table, I believe you've got a couple of minutes to spare," he led the way and took his customary seat and the Kid sat down on the edge of the couch. "I'll bet you thought this day would never get here…"

"Well, Sir, yes and no. Always hoped it would, knew if I made it, it eventually would and figured if I didn't make it, I wouldn't know the difference!"

"That's one way of looking at it."

"I just want to say, Sir, thank you for the opportunities you gave me here."

"You're welcome, Stocker," he paused and looked the Kid over, "I wish I could say that all the officers in the unit enjoyed working with you as much as I did." *And he laughed.*

"Thank you, sir. I just wish they would have printed that story in *Stars and Stripes.* Did you ever find out what the problem was with it?" the Kid had continued to wonder about it.

"No. Not a word. Still the single strangest thing that ever happened with anything any of my units ever submitted over the years...I still don't get it. It's such a good idea, replacing Americans with Vietnamese, you'd think they'd be all over it! Oh well," Willie O. said, "you did a good job on it and it looks great in the April DIMENSION. So, you're going to Ft. Carson, Colorado?"

"Yes Sir."

"I've never been to Colorado. Like to go some day."

"Yes Sir, it's beautiful. Of course, I wanted Tennessee to be close to my radio job, or California, to be close to my now ex fiancée. But Colorado, can't think of another place in the world I'd rather be in the Army... if I still have to be in."

The colonel gave the Kid a sideways glance, "yes, the Army is just not right for some people. I got a feeling you're certainly one of them. We all know you made some waves here, Specialist, but somehow, you managed to keep your canoe from tipping over!"

"Yes, Sir, it wasn't easy. And, Sir, I want to thank you because I know my canoe would have been riding a torpedo straight to the bottom without your support and understanding."

"You're welcome, Stocker. I sensed when I first heard about your court martial that it was a put-up job. And it's a shame Group didn't let you extend for the Armed Forces Radio gig. You might have a whole different opinion of the Army if you had gotten that instead of taking it in the shorts in those two circumstances, the one unfortunately connected to the other. I want you to know I appreciate the work you did for me." He rose, extending his hand, the Kid rose and took it. "Good luck, Specialist!" they shook, "and bon voyage!"

The Kid saluted! "Yes, Sir, thank you, Sir!"

Willie O. returned it, "Dissmissed!"

Outside the colonel's door, the Kid checked the Seiko; 15 minutes until he would leave for the airport. He savored the moment.

Wimbish approached him. "Moyssiadis is driving you, Curt, and he's ready when you are. Who's riding along?"

"Boyett, and Edwards."

"Oh, hey, you might not have heard yet, but Colonel Lawton is bringing Sweet in from the field. He picked him to take your slot and he's supposed to be up from

Tra Vinh today, but it's not looking like he'll make it before you leave."

"Bummer!"

"Why don't you come over to my desk and sign out now?" Wimbish suggested.

"OK!"

As the Kid picked up the pen to sign out of the unit's Day Log for the last time, he flashed back on the day he and Birnbaum had returned from Dong Tam. *"Gee. I'm glad I'm not dead!"*

"All right," Lou smiled, looking at his signature, "you're no longer a member of the unit! You are freaking *out of here*, Kid!" Lou extended his hand, "It's been real, I hope we get to see each other again, some time, anyway."

"Yes, that would be great! It's been fun, Lou! I hope your extension goes good!"

"Thank you."

Moyssaidis appeared at the stairway door to the Kid's left. "Stocker! Let's hit it!"

It took his breath away! "All right! Let me get my stuff!" and he ran back to the graphics room, where his luggage was waiting, along with Boyett and Edwards. He petted little Pysuie Psyop one more time, "Good bye little cat... lay off the bats and watch out for the rats, OK?"

The Kid put the Pentax around his neck, placed his steel pot on his head and slung his M-16 over his right shoulder while Ron grabbed his valise and Tom picked up his briefcase. When they emerged from the back, the personnel of Headquarters was lined up like a gauntlet and clapping mixed with cat calls greeted the Kid as he walked through the office for the last time, giddy with the significance of the situation, shaking hands and exchanging toothy grins.

"Gary, I'll see you in Boulder!" he shook hands with Gary Reed.

He gave one last salute to the colonel, who stood at his door and when got to the stairs, waved a last farewell to all. PM Smith was nowhere to be seen.

Once the jeep was rolling, the Kid pulled out a joint and lit up. Tom and Ron took exception to the no smoking on duty rule and got into the hit rotation.

"We must stay in touch," he turned and hollered to Tom as he passed him the number, "we gotta get the *10th Nervous Breakdown* a recording contract!"

"Sure," Tom laughed, "I'm counting on it!" *Sarcasm.*

"No. Really. We're going to do it! Might not be next week or next month, but hopefully, within the next year. I still think, because of the Vietnam connection and all, that *STEEL POT* would be a great name for the band!"

"Curt, if you get us a recording contract, we will seriously consider that as the group name," Tom made the slightest concession to the possibility of a future adjustment.

They pulled into Can Tho field about 20 minutes before the Kid's flight. Moyssaidis stayed with the jeep and the Kid proceeded to check in and confirmed he was on the manifest. Then the three of them walked over to the terminal windows and looked out on to the flight line. A Caribou was set up to load passengers for the 1000 to Saigon.

"Look!" the Kid pointed, "my first *'Freedom Bird!'*"

"Look!" Ron pointed at a helicopter that had just landed over to the right of the Tower, "here comes Sweet!"

Indeed, running toward the terminal, as fast as he could, lugging a duffle bag and his M-16, his steel pot bouncing on his head, was Jim Sweet; *he'd made it in!* The trio stepped out the door as he approached.

Stopping in front of them, Sweet dropped his duff, puffing, and setting his rifle on top of it, he gave the Kid a bear hug. "This is fucking great! I was hoping I'd get to say goodbye to you!"

"Well, you're doing more than that! I hear you're replacing me! And if you're slick, you'll get my bunk, too!" grinned the Kid.

"Jesus would THAT be super! Anything but the oven! Sweet stepped back, "Look at you, all fuckin' ready to go!"

"Yep. Lucky to be alive and on my way!'

Just then, the call came; "All personnel on the manifest for the 1000 hours to Saigon, the aircraft is now boarding, please ensure all weapons are cleared."

The Kid stepped back inside the door, and picking up his M-16, stuffed the business end into the barrel by the door, jacked the slide bar back it and pulled the trigger; *click, all clear.* He re-slang it, picked up his two pieces of luggage and with a deep breath, emerged to board his flight. *"This is it!"* the Kid wanted to jump up and down, maybe click his heels together or possibly, just wet his pant! "Men, it's been real!"

"*Unreal* would be more accurate," Ron laughed, "Goodbye, Curt!"

"I might come up and see you in Colorado while you're there," Tom said, "Me and Robin are talking about moving up there; I've about had enough of Oklahoma!"

"Well, my parents are listed in the Boulder telephone book, under Dwain; there's only 2 Stockers, so you'll be able to get ahold of me!" The Kid dropped his bags and the pair exchanged a back slapping hug,"hang in there, Tom!"

"It was quite a ride, *Kid...*" said Sweet, "good luck! Not that you need it!" they shook.

"See ya in the States!" the Kid picked up his stuff and walked, with a bounce in his step, to his flight. He found it was fully packed and he stood at the back of the loading line. He didn't care; he was going home. Still, it went fairly fast and at 1005 hours, the Caribou was lined up for takeoff. The Kid was one step over the 'giddy' line when the wheels lifted up off the corrugated metal runway. *Don't cry!* As the high winged aircraft began to rise up over the city, he could easily pick out the New Villa before they turned to head north. Hey! *You can see the embassy!*

Memories went back to the flight from Saigon down to Can Tho, when he was first in country. Looking down then, at the paddies, canals and tree lines, he could only fearfully wonder what terrors awaited him. Those then unknown terrors were now his emotional baggage. From his small window, as they approached the Mekong River, he picked out what he was fairly certain must be Vinh Long. There was Highway 4 running from it to the north; the same road he, Wilson and Boujold had driven down from Sadec. And there was Highway 4 going to the southeast, the one they did not take to try and reach Tra Vinh before returning to Sadec and waiting for a chopper. He was amazed when flying over My Tho, that he could now actually identify the 9th Division's massive compound. Within my site must

585

be the place where Imbach was killed. Dave must be down there getting ready to leave, too! He eyed Highway 4 coming out of Dong Tam, trying to place the location of Bien Trung, scene of the NITECAP. I'm lucky to be alive. His hand went to the Beaver Nickle. The flight was short and soon they were settling down on the Ton San Nhut runway. Step one complete!

A jeep was waiting for him at the terminal; Wimbish had made sure of that. Arriving at Group HQ, he began the necessary steps to process out of PSYOPS. He turned in his M-16 to the armory, along with his steel pot. Once the Kid had secured his belongings in the Quonset hut barracks, he made plans to pay a call on *Alan P.* None of his other PYSOP comrades were yet in from the other up-country battalions.

Walking out of the gate of the compound, the Kid hailed a taxi. Between the Kid's fading knowledge of Vietnamese and the driver's limited English, he was delivered up to the AFN Vietnam Network compound in just 15 minutes; it wasn't even noon. Entering the building, the Kid went to the information desk and asked for *Alan P; yes, he is at work.*

Five minutes later, he appeared in the lobby. "Kid! I was thinking it was about time for you to be going home... because I'm so fucking close!

"*Alan,* my man! Yeah I'm down to 4 and a wake up!"

'Wow, that's great! 34 and a wake up for me! So, let's go back to my desk."

They strolled through the facility to the area where *Alan P.* had his work space. It was in a large room, with the entrance to the control booth located on the far side. He pulled up a chair next to the desk and the Kid sat down. "Where is your assignment back in the States?"

"Ft. Carson, Colorado. There's a post hospital there that supposedly has a closed-circuit radio station. Is Scott Manning here? I want to kick his ass!"

Alan P. looked at the Kid and shook his head, "No, he doesn't come in until later, you obviously know when his show is on."

"You mean *MY* show?" the Kid quickly countered.

"Uh, yes...*Sergeant Pepper.* You can't blame him for doing it. I mean after all, you didn't get the transfer, so why shouldn't somebody do it? Hell, Stocker, it was a great idea...and to tell you the truth, I'd have done it, if I though I never had to see you again!"

"Sadly, Alan, I know you are right." The Kid chagrined, "but what pisses me off, is that when I came in for R&R and Shamus wrote me that letter stating that I had passed the audition and that they wanted me, I was positive it was a done deal. But you know what I group said? *'No opening in my MOS.'* It was a total fucking lie!"

"Why did they say that?"

"Had to be the 4ᵗʰ Group was getting even with me for beating that court martial. It just happened to be the third one in a row they lost. I can't think of any other reason. Just this morning, my colonel down in Can Tho as much as told me that's what happened. He said the two events were related. If I had gotten that, I'd be coming to work in this building tonight and I'd be less than 11 months from ETS!"

"And instead, you are 4 days away from going home and never having to worry about the 'Nam again. Where is the downside to that, Stocker?"

The Kid though about Alan's point for a few seconds. "Yeah. You're right. I was just convinced that if I got to do this, I could use it as a springboard to a lot of bigger stuff."

"Hey, want a Coke? We've got a ton of ice!" *Alan P.* offered.

"Sure."

While Alan P. was off getting the Cokes, the Kid walked over to the control room and looked in at who was currently on the air. It was somebody he didn't know but it looked like he was having a great time. *The Kid had an envy attack.* The Army had so screwed him with its' *contract* for Armed Forces Radio, which in reality, was totally worthless. Since DINFOS, he had never even so much as gotten to sniff a control room. That fact did much to stoke the slow burning fire that was building in his gut. PSYOPS had been a beat down, never mind the fact that Lt. Wilson almost got him killed more times than he could count.

Alan P. returned with the soft drinks and glasses filled with ice. "You want to party tonight? We could go see Li. Surely you remember her?"

The Kid had to laugh, "Yes, I'll never forget her, but no, I don't think so. *Unfortunately,* I had a bout with the clap last month and now that I'm cured, I won't be taking any kind of a chance before I leave. The rest of the *PSYOPS Warriors* are supposed to be checking in today or tomorrow at the latest, and we're all riding up to Long Binh together. So I'm going to hang out and see them. As a matter of fact, I'm going back now to see if Davies, Erio and Viator have made it in yet."

'Why don't you all come visit tomorrow, if they make it in, or at least before you all head up to Long Binh."

"OK. *And thanks,* for trying to help me stay in this God forsaken hole for another 11 months!"

'Don't mention it!"

Chapter 89

Outside the studios, the Kid took off his wire rims and put his prescription shades on while he pondered what to do for the rest of the day. It was nearing lunch time at the 4th PSYOP Group mess hall. *First, smoke a joint! But where was a safe place to do that? Then he remembered what Captain Max, the Spooky Pilot had said; 'sometime I just ride around in a cycolo and smoke.' There's one now!*

It was actually a pedicab, where the driver powers the carriage from behind on a bicyle like apparatus. The Kid stuck up his arm and waved at the driver. The man on the bicycle seat smiled broadly as he dropped out of traffic and brought his rig to the curb to let the Kid board.

"Ton Son Nhut!" the Kid instructed with a wave, knowing that command would breach the language barrier. The airport was certainly far enough off that he'd have time to indulge in a leisurely smoke. The driver, whom the Kid reckoned, could have been anywhere in age from the later 40's to the 50's, nodded his understanding. He wore a pith helmet and sunglasses, was sans facial hair, clad in a sweat stained light green button up shirt and tan shorts. Standing up with flip flops on the pedals and leaning over the handlebars, he got the pedicab moving and once in motion, sat back down on the seat to continue the locomotion.

When they were well out into the Saigon traffic, the Kid took out the pack of KOOL joints and lit one up. *Great idea, thought the Kid of Max's suggestion of a safe place to smoke! Walking around would be OK, too, but this, moving through traffic, smoking a cigarette joint; much more pleasant and nobody could possibly know!*

Since the Captain PM Smith incident on the balcony, there was something about the third hit that made the Kid hear voices and today, strangely enough, it happened again. Only this time, it was not an angry triad but a friendly request for information from the most unlikely source!

"Pardon me, please, Sir, but could I ask you a question?" It was the driver, leaning down to speak into the Kid's right ear in perfect English.

The Kid just about spit the joint out! Turning around, he looked at the man, who was smiling, friendly like, as he continued to pedal. The Kid was blown away! "Your English is perfect! Yes, you can ask me a question!"

"All Vietnamese are very curious; why do you American GIs smoke *Con Sa* and not opium? The French were here for years and nearly all of them smoked opium. This is the opium capital of the world! But you American GIs ignore it and smoke this *marijuana.* It was nothing but a worthless weed in our yards until you Americans arrived. Not even good enough to make rope."

"Sure, I'll answer your question!" the Kid turned to sit sideways in the carriage so he could converse, realizing he could employ the full spectrum of his vocabulary. "Ironically enough, when I first went to Sadec, I did happen to visit to an opium den by accident and smoked opium all one afternoon. And I purchased a little for later. I never had it before. But, after using it just a couple of times, I could see how addictive it was, and I threw it into the river! After all ,heroin is nothing but refined opium and in all its forms, opium is physically addictive. This, on the other hand," the Kid held up the joint, "is not like that. It is not as strong and it does not create a physical dependence like opium or even tobacco. If I can't find any marijuana, that's not a big deal. You can easily live without it. The feeling of not having tobacco, once you begin to smoke it, is far worse. I really like the pleasant feeling it gives you. Have you ever tried it?"

"No."

"God! I can't get over how perfect your English is!"

"Yes, and my French is perfect. And if Germany ever invades Vietnam, my German will be perfect... as was my father's Japanese." *The man was at minimum, tri-lingual! It made the Kid feel a touch inferior.*

"What is your name?"

"Thanh."

"Thanh, my name is Curt, very pleased to meet you," the Kid extended his hand to shake and the driver lifted his right hand from the handlebar long enough to do exactly that. *Very strong grip.*

"I am still blown away with how good your English is!"

"Why are you so surprised? Is it that Americans think Vietnamese are not smart enough to learn English? *Americans* are sadly unaware that one of the main Viet Cong sources of information is American soldiers talking in taxi cabs, dismissing the Vietnamese drivers in general, as too ignorant to understand."

Wow. This guy is saying he could be a Viet Cong spy! "I would think, with your expertise in languages, that you could obtain a much better job than driving a pedicab. For one thing, you could be an interpreter!"

"True. But I have no desire or need to work for either the Americans or the ARVNs. I own this pedicab so I am my own boss. I make money with my pedicab and my perspiration. I do not have the expense of gas and oil that a taxi driver does. I go home at night."

"Are you married?

"Yes," Thanh nodded to the affirmative, "I have two sons and two daughters. My daughters are older; 21 and 19. The sons are younger; 12 and 10. My sincere hope is that this war ends before the Army can take either of them."

Interesting; there is a seven year break between the boys and the girls, like he was away someplace, like in the army maybe fighting with the Viet Minh at Dien Bien Phu for seven years?

"Are you a veteran?"

"No."

"Why didn't they ever get you?" wondered the Kid, taking a hit.

There was a pause in the conversation, as if Thanh was weighing his answer before he said, "*My health;* it was not meant to be!"

OK. Fair enough. The Kid could sense it would not do to pursue that line of questioning, although Thanh was certainly healthy enough, at this stage of his life, to keep pedaling that cab and converse without becoming winded! They drove leisurely up one street and down the other. The Kid didn't care. *As long as he doesn't turn into an alley where his VC cronies are waiting to machine gun me dead 4 days before I fly home!*

He bought a coke from a street stand while they waited for the traffic at one intersection. *What a way to tour Saigon!*

The Kid had another question for him; "Thanh, who do you think will win this war?"

"Who can say? America has so much money and weapons that Thieu has the most powerful friend he could have. However, Vietnam has a long history of not being conquered by foreigners. The Chinese for a thousand years could not conquer Vietnam...the Japanese failed, the French failed... my sincere belief is that our problems can only be truly solved by Vietnamese. No foreign power will ever prevail."

Interesting; he started out neutral but ended up with the foreigner (Americans this time) cannot and will not win. "Time will tell," said the Kid, "I'm going home on Sunday, so I will not be here for the victory or the defeat!"

Finally the Kid asked Thanh to drop him at 4th PSYOP Group, which ironically, he knew the location of, without directions… leading the Kid to even stronger suspect that he might have spent the afternoon with a Viet Cong agent! He had been very careful not to speak of military matters, not that he knew anything of use to the VC. The fact that Americans did not like opium was obviously no secret.

Once back inside the PSYOPS compound, the Kid had way missed lunch, but decided he wasn't that hungry. He checked to see if his DINFOS classmates had arrived yet. Nope. He could either go find some local lunch or he could take a nap in the air conditioned Quonset hut. *The air conditioned nap won.*

At 1800 hours, the Kid was awaken by somebody shaking the bottom of his single bunk, "Yo! Lazy ass Kid!" it was Tom Davies, "are you going to sleep through DEROS?"

"Tom!" He sat bolt upright! "Hey! We're going fucking home! Can you believe it?

"Yes, I'm a Believer! *Monkee Song!* "Curt! How have you been? No more court martials or anything, I take it?"

"Closer than you can believe."

"Close for you or a normal person?"

"For me." Cliff notes version of PM.

"I'm glad I don't live like you. Let's go eat!"

Chapter 90

May 17, 1969

Dear Dave and Pasty,

This is the last letter I'll ever write you from Vietnam. Yes, Dave, I'm almost done with the time in my life I have to spend up front, next to the cannons. Literally. This is coming to you from Scenic Saigon, the Pearl of the Orient and so is the Kid, coming to you from Saigon.

In fact, in less than an hour, "we five", me and my four buddies are being driven to Long Binh to get on our magic carpet ride, May 18! My brother is meeting me in Oakland and I'm going see Flo in Vista first, then Boulder and then and THEN... the KID will be appearing BACK in the MUSIC CITY!!! I think it should be there by about May 30th and for sure by June 1. And I have some really great souvineers for ya'll!

Almost all my luck must have gone to making it to the plane because I had some bad luck yesterday. We were coming out of the mess hall at lunch and I was changing from my round gold wire glasses to my prescription shades and I dropped my wire rim glasses on a tile floor and they BROKE! No way I can get them fixed before I get back! Bummer city! Now all I have is my ugly army specs.

I hear there's some interesting happenings at the station, from Patti B. and that my 3rd replacement has now been installed. I still won't be able to come back to work for another 16 months, I wonder how many they will be up to by then? Anyway, I want to be Jonny Wailin's replacement! Langford can have midnight to 6! I was hoping you'd still be the PD when I got back.

Well, as you know, I never got to be Sgt. Pepper and I went over to AFN to kick the guy's ass who stole my idea, but he was out and I'm not missing my plane to stick around for that!

Ready for the understatement of the decade? This has changed me. Can't wait to SEE YA'LL!

Take care,

Curt

PS. Who would expect the Army to station the KID FROM COLORADO in COLORADO? I'm as shocked as you are.

The Kid finished the letter, put it in an envelope, addressed it and went up to the orderly room. The CQ took it and flipped into the outbound basket. "Usually its *Nick Surovy* who drives the Long Binh run," he said, "you guys all ready? He's bringing the truck around right now. Taking you guys up and bringing the next set of 71R20's back, *poor fucking fools,* to replace you. And it starts all over; they'll be a bunch of whinie bastards just like you guys, *'going oh jeeze… why didn't I get Armed Forces radio?' And they'll put in for a bunch of transfers…"*

Pete Erio, George Titley and Al Viator, all materialized through the day on the 16th and by Saturday, May 17th, just after lunch at 1300 hours, all was in readiness for departure. All weapons and gear had been checked in and paperwork completed and so it was, the DINFOS classmates were all signed out of the 4th PSYOP Group for the final time. The agreement was universal; they had been *screwed royal* by the assignment because PSYOPS was not what anybody had taken the extra year to do. Still, they were all in one piece and tres happy they had not ended up in the Infantry, like Waterhouse and Imbach.

The duce-and-a half came slowly around from the motor pool at the back of the compound and pulled up right in front of the Headquarters sign where the five waited in the shade. "You guys are my load, right?" Nick stated the obvious, "let's *load it and road it!"*

It was a Chinese fire drill in reverse; within a minute, they were aboard and slapping flat fives as the truck rolled out the Group Headquarters Gate, destination Bien Hoa!

Things had changed in the year since they had arrived in-country. No longer did the soldiers of the United States Army travel in *Class A* uniforms; fatigues were now the uniform of attire for both for arrival and departure. Plus, the atmosphere on the road between Saigon and Bien Hoa must have cooled noticeably in the 14 months since the Tet Offensive, as the Kid noted that there apparently was not one weapon present on board the truck, *unless Nick had a .45 in the glove compartment.*

593

The group would, however, be on high alert for any passing Honda that might be a threat to lob them a grenade. *Nobody wanted to go down this late in the game.*

As the truck reached the edge of the city proper and was headed for the open road, all had removed their baseball caps in anticipation of not having them blow off. The Kid sat back against the passenger's side of the truck, prescription shades in place to fend off the near high noon sun. Before the truck began to open up, the Kid signaled the group to put their heads together.

"OK, men," the Kid pulled out the remaining pack of KOOL joints he still possessed and held them in front of the group, "Gentlemen, *I propose a toast*...so to speak. This looks like a good time... I'm smoking my last joint in Vietnam right now and you all can too, because I am throwing the rest of these away and going in *squeaky clean*! I ain't taking NO chances! This is my last joint in Vietnam!"

After everybody took one, the Kid pitched the rest of the pack out the back of the truck. Tom shared his Zippo with George and with his held between his lips, the Kid brought up the Pentax strapped around his neck and snapped a pic of Pete and Al lighting up. Once everybody had fire, they held them up like bumping glasses for what could only be described as an ultra appropriate *'Fare-well-and-good-bye-for- ever- Pfucking-PSYOPS-and-Vietnam'* toast!

It will remain forever one of the most euphoric joints the Kid would ever smoke, primarily because it was the LAST one in 'Nam! The sweetness was infinitely compounded by the fact that their destination was the freaking airport to go home! Flying down the road, each was left to his own private thoughts as it was difficult to converse over the noise of the truck and traffic. The Kid remembered how excited Imbach was to be going down to Dong Tam on a chopper a year ago and wondered if Dave Waterhouse was coming back in by chopper today.

To say the men had a healthy buzz on when they rolled through the rough looking streets of Bien Hoa would be like saying Paul Revere only hollered out a couple of times on his way to Concord.

The entry gate of the Long Binh complex was an extremely welcome sight, but nothing compared to what they saw one minute later, when they arrived at their actual destination. It was such an impactful thing of beauty that the Kid lifted up the Pentax, standing in the back of the truck, and recorded it for posterity! From the fact they all had on sunglasses, the Kid didn't know if anybody else had shed a tear of joy.

He jumped down in front of the sign, configured like a white entry arch leading into an open sided corrugated tin roofed building. It read: GOING HOME? REPORT HERE - U S A- BOUND. He turned and took the bags being handed down by Tom and when Tom climbed down, they hugged each other.

Almost like magic, a jeep pulled up and out stepped Waterhouse! And while he was pulling out his gear, a ¾ ton arrived containing Pete Cuzzo, Ken Smith and Paul Irish! It was stunning how closely all of them had arrived, one year later, to all be on the same flight home.

"Kid!' Waterhouse hugged him, "here we fucking ARE!"

Then, Cuzzo standing there addressed the Kid, before he even said 'hello', hands on hips, like a headmaster taking a student to task; "Well, Kid, did you succeed? In your quest to be stoned or asleep for the entire year?

Slilghtest pause… Deadpan delivery "Yes." *HUGE laugh,* and as soon as it subsided the slightest bit, he matter of factly threw in, "oh…wait…I had to stop a couple of hours for my court martial." *Bigger laugh, because they knew he wasn't kidding.*

"Shit yeah!" Ken Smith gave the Kid a back slap, "we couldn't believe it when we heard that story!"

"Gentlemen!" Waterhouse snapped the group back, "later tonight, all of us, a moment for John…"

Nobody is laughing now.

"And let's make it soft drinks, *everybody,* he would appreciate if we didn't toast him with booze," Dave plainly stated.

"Hey, guys!" Ken Smith gestures toward the arch, reasserting the pep, "are we fucking *USA Bound* or what? But we still go through the motions, we still gotta get in line, we're still all in the Army here…wake up people! Let's all step this way!" and acting like an usher, he lead the way under the arch and off they went, DINFOS classmates reunited on their out processing Odessey!

Orders and luggage in hand, they passed through a fairly rapid moving line where a glance at their paperwork cleared them to go stand in another line, where they were to set down their bags and wait. Just when they were getting antsy, because the new line wasn't moving anywhere, they discovered the new line wasn't a line at all, but a row. There were actually four rows that set up a pre-boarding *open* ranks spacing to facilitate an inspection of everybody's luggage.

"All right, men, listen up!" a rather rotund Italian looking sergeant at the head of the shed hollered in a deep voice, "According to Army regulations and Federal Aviation Regulations, there are certain items you may not possess, bring on board an aircraft or attempt to possess or carry across international borders. Right now, under this roof, is the only place you will receive amnesty for items you should not have in your possession including a number of items that are absolutely unsafe to fly with. DO YOU UNDERSTAND: if you have any firearms, ammunition, grenades of any kind, mines, flares, detonator caps, plastic explosives, marijuana or any other drugs or contraband…*give it up now!* Take it right out and set in front of your bag. If you don't and I look in your bag and *FIND IT*… your ass is mine and you DO NOT, and I repeat, *DO NOT,* get on that jet! The inspection begins NOW!"

That sent a stir through the crowd. No problem for the DINFOS boys; they all had been smart enough to make sure this choke point was not going to create any issues. But all around them, pistols and ammo and bayonets and packages of god knows what were coming out and ending up on the floor beyond where men were standing.

The teams of sergeants began their chore, one looking over the troop, one sorting through the baggage and another collecting the jettisoned contraband into a duffle bag.

"I wonder what they do with all of that stuff?" Viator observed the activity that was about a dozen soldiers down the line from reaching them.

"It will all be available later tonight on the black market, don't you know it for a fact," Cuzzo stated the obvious.

"I would bet you all of these sergeants extended for this position and that all of them also own at least 3 or 4 bars and/or whorehouses, in addition," Erio speculated.

"Hey, wait a minute…" Davies pointed, "that sergeant just kicked that guy out of line for his haircut!"

"Ow! Imagine that; missed your flight because your haircut was not up to snuff and you get mortared that night and killed! *Knock on wood,*" the Kid said *and did* simultaneously, rapping his knuckles on the 4X4 support upright of the building.

"Gruesome thought." Ken Smith winced. "God. *Poor Imbach,*" he spoke the name of the missing classmate.

A soldier from up the line stepped back to them, "don't worry guys, there's a barber shop 3rd row of building's over, so if you just got in from the bush and need a haircut, you can get one; I used to work next door to it."

596

"For your whole tour?" Smith wanted to know.

"Yep. That and extended here 2 months to get a 6 month drop. ETS the second I get home, makes my enlistment 18 months…*what a deal that was!*"

You didn't need any mime translator to know this guy was elated. Would the Kid trade with Monty Hall *for his deal right now? Yes.*

The fashion sergeant had no problem with the Kid's personal grooming; his razor shaved ears and neck were a 100 % pass. The custom's sergeant pawed and poked through his stuff, but all the pot the Kid had on him was some place the sergeant couldn't look; in his blood. And urine. And hair. And thank God they did not have a test for any of that in the year of our Lord, 1969.

After completing the final shakedown, the sergeants herded the happy herd over to the line where each soldier turned over his approved luggage to be loaded on a certain flight. His turn! Keeping only his shaving kit and the Pentax, the Kid's hands trembled as he exchanged his bag and brief case for the rectangular piece of paper that read: AIRLINE PASSENGER TICKET, BAGGAGE CHECK –and- MAC BOARDING PASS!

The Kid's throat went dry. He found a place to sit down on the ground, with his back up against one of the building support 4X4's. Thrilled beyond expectation, he admired it for a few seconds before taking the lens cap off his Pentax and after dialing in a shutter speed and checking the light with the lens meter, while holding the paper in his left hand, he focused and clicked. Boarding Number 139. My ticket home!

Chapter 91

Once everybody had gotten their boarding passes and bunk assignments for the night, the group dispersed into a flurry of different activities; chow, showers, letter writing, grabbing some last minute trinkets and drinking.

When time crept on to the point it was becoming next to impossible to assemble all 10 of them, the three roommates gathered for a specific moment. All or one of the three had been with John from the time he arrived at DINFOS to the end. Dave, Ken, John and Curt; roomies through journalism school and on to broadcast school. That had taken a little over five months, from November 1967 to April of 1968, with Curt and John going to POS training and Dave going on with John, to the 9th Division.

Each of them had gotten a Coca Cola and they picked a table in the club away from the action and sat down.

Ken Smith hadn't heard the details of John's unfortunate final day so Waterhouse related them.

"Geeze, Imbach," Ken assimilated the scenario that lead to his death. "Baby Huey volunteered to take the point position for a rifle squad, in order to write a story about the experience? See, too much listening to Sp. 4 Knight in Journalism class! He's the one who suggested that kind of thing was good copy, always wanted to write combat stories. That's the Ernie Pyle syndrome. But God! John went and did it and ended up being the story instead, in the hometown news release of his death! Poor John, poor John's family."

"To John," Ken lifted his Coke, "we will never forget you." They drank.

Waterhouse raised his Coke, "If somebody would have told this class, you are going to lose a single man, John would have volunteered to be that man to take it for all of us. Thank god we only lost one." They drank.

The kid lifted his Coke, "When – if/ when I write my Vietnam novel, it will be dedicated it to John," they drank.

"How's that going, by the way," Waterhouse turned to the Kid, anticipating a typical bullshit answer, since 'the book' was a long-time running Kid narrative.

"Well, I think it's safe to say, I've almost completed the research," the Kid quickly quipped.

"Careful with the SAFE word! It's not safe to say!" Ken immediately knocked on the wooden table, "I'll think 'safe' when the plane lands in Oakland, is what I think I'll think!"

"Still working on a working title. I've got a couple in a nautical vein," the Kid mused, "I was thinking, something like instead of "Two Years Before the Mast' make it ' One Year Before the Bong!' or 'Munity on the Balcony...'"

"Or if you chose a world war one theme, you could go with 'All Stoned on the Western Front...'" Waterhouse responds, or 'Charge of the Lit Brigade'!"

"How about, ' 30 Seconds Over TuDo Street?" Ken got in the mix, "kind of a world war II thing."

"'Not bad," the Kid had to admit, "I'm stealing all of these, you know, fair warning, this was A MEETING about my book title. In the back of my mind, I've always been partial to... 'Catch 69?'"

"That would leave little doubt as to where the Kid's head was at when he wrote it!" Waterhouse laughed, "more the front of your face than your brain!"

The reminiscing continued and a couple of the other classmates spotted them at the table and came over. More toasts of sadness for John and then the prevailing attitude became toasts to going home! *John would have wanted it that way.*

Around 2230 hours, the Kid, Waterhouse, Viator and Davies headed out from the club for the barracks with the intent of hitting the sack. They walked at a mildly intoxicated pace through the darkness that was created by the post blackout policy, designed to make it more difficult for the VC to lob in mortars. The night air was hot, but as far as Vietnam went, tolerable. All up and down barracks row, the only light was off the glowing tips of GIs' cigarettes. They were congregated outside the doors to their quarters, quietly talking and laughing, clearly too excited to go to sleep.

When they arrived at their barracks, they discovered there was a major gabfest in progress. There must have been from 20 to 30 GIs, between two barracks that faced each other across the path, sitting and standing around, awash in the sublime nectar of *last night.* The four all stopped to listen. GIs were speaking up from various locations within the group, in an open give and take.

"America needs to be out of this fucking war," a voice emphatically *stated.*

"America needs to stop pussy footing around and win this war!" a response came, like a real forum, a town hall meeting of GIs who had just, (well, almost) completed their tours in the war zone. *Who could better know?*

"If we stop now, everybody who has died here will have died in vane!" a voice implored.

"If we stop now, we stop having more people die in vane," came the *counter claim, "because more dying does not change anything, if the people have already died in fucking vane!"*

"I can't wait to eat that steak in the Returnee's Steakhouse!" a voice ignored the politics.

"If people ask you, I mean, when people ask you, how will you define your year here?' another voice posed a question, possibly meant for the person sitting next to him in the dark, but it was out there for the group to contemplate.

Interesting, thought the Kid. Being an old debater, he stayed to listen as his companions continued on into the barracks.

"I was here defending America..." one declared.

"I was here trying to keep my ass alive so I could be here tonight!" one was more emphatically realistic.

"None of this 'my country right or wrong'...it IS wrong for us to be here and the sooner we realize that and get the hell out, the better!" another was resolute!

"OK, everybody who got ripped off exchanging currency on Tu Do street raise your hand..." politics be damned by another!

The Kid was actually standing there, trying to think of some ultra witty throw down one liner with which to slay the crowd when it came to him... *in a FLASH!*

...because it WAS a flash, a brilliant ball of luminance to the point of blinding, accompanied by NO NOISE. *The pure white flash rose up from right in their midst... cloaked in complete and total silence!*

YOU NEVER HEAR THE ONE THAT GETS YOU! was the Kid's instant thought followed by a straining to hear… anything at all! And consequently, since he heard not a single sound, he made the only logical assumption:

I AM DEAD! They got me on my final night!

Instantly, the Kid's hands shoot up to his chest, where he feels frantically, trying to locate where the schrapnel went through! Where he should start bleeding! Feeling feeling…

"What the fuck?"

"Yeah! What the FUCK was that?"

"Jesus FFFing Christ! Who the fuck did that?"

Now laughter, at first slow, then building in nervousness, a lone voice, emanating from the center of the group, claims credit, *"I did…"* a soldier holds up a flash camera; he had set off a flash bulb in the center of the group! Some practical joke! He was the only one laughing and he pissed off a lot of people!

"Why you SOB!' was the judgment leveled by the group and the culprit, whose identity and rank were obscured by the dark, was shoved around and roughly pummeled!

The Kid, on the other hand, *fresh back from the dead* and feeling relieved just to be alive, went happily to his bunk.

WOW! What a feeling THAT was! That time in the orderly room, with Sergeant Vallenti, I only thought I might be dead. Tonight, I was sure I was dead… for a fact! I didn't hear the one that didn't get me but thought because I didn't hear it, it got me. Get it? I thought I GOT 'got', it but I didn't get got at all! Amazing!

Chapter 92

The flight was scheduled for 1600 hours. It had been agony, hanging out in Long Binh, having to eat two more mess hall meals, with all other movement restricted because everybody was manifested.

The busses moved the troops from the holding area out to the flight line beginning a little before 1430 hours so by 1530 hours, the men had been in position, slow baking under the high canopied roof of the airfield for about an hour. But nobody was complaining. GIs no longer had canteens, so nobody had anything to drink. But nobody was complaining. There weren't any benches to sit on. But nobody was complaining. They had to remain in their approximate boarding order, so no walking around talking to people. *A little complaining on that one.*

At least they were in the shade and the ultra high ceiling let a nice breeze blow through and it was turning from the dry to the wet season; a breeze always helped.

The DINFOS boys had been split up by their boarding numbers but the Kid and Al Viator had 138 and 139, so they remained together.

"Remember how it was, when we got here?" Al harkened back to the beginning, "how all those guys were partying down here, when we got off and they were getting on?"

"Yes."

"It just doesn't seem like we're partying as hard as they were," he gazed around as he spoke. "I don't see ANY cigars, and I think it looks a lot more like you're going to a party if you're dressed in class 'A's.'"

The Kid had been daydreaming, but snapped out of his daze and took a look. "Maybe when the plane gets here; everybody's kind of fried right now. I know I could use an energy boost. But when that jet pulls up, we'll all be riding the adrenalin monkey and you know this place will go fucking bananas! Gotta be here any minute."

Murmurs moves through the throng; *It's landing!*

"It's landing, Al! Did you hear that? Somebody says they can see it landing," not that the Kid and Al could, from where they stood, four rows deep in the queue, but it was great news to them.

The Kid took the lens cap off his Pentax. For today, he had loaded color slide film and he truly wanted a shot of the Jet that would carry him home! The engine noise was increasing as it approached the loading area and there! Appearing to their left was the nose of the Jet! A cheer literally exploded from the chests of the waiting men and as it was pulling across in front of them. Amid the delirious celebration of the GIs surrounding him, when it became framed right in the middle of the building, the Kid took his shot. *Flying Tiger Line. He was going home on a Flying Tiger!*

The white and red trimmed jet turned it's blue tail to the gallery and the ramps were run out and the doors popped. The charter civilian jet crews did not like to spend any amount of time on the ground.

Off came the *'longest time left* soldiers in country, marching quickly down the ramp, in the direction they have been pointed, past the *shortest* damn soldiers in all of Vietnam. The looks on the newbies' faces had to be time travel images of what theirs' had been last year. Off comes the duffle bags brought to the war, tossed on to the waiting duce and a half, while the duce and a half with the *shortee's* baggage circled, waiting for the all empty to go in for the *fill.*

There were no trucks out for refueling. The Kid had heard the flight plan was one stop in Japan to fill up for the non-stop to Oakland. They would be in Yakuska, Japan for about an hour.

The fresh blood was half unloaded when the command came for the line to prepare for boarding. The newbies looked on with anguish as the rowdy, boisterous GIs moved up on the opposite side of the rope, boarding passes in hand, chomping at the bit to occupy their jet home! Finally, the cannon fodder parade was over and the green light given to load for departure.

When the GIs handed over their boarding passes to the loadmaster, from that point, it was a sprint to the stairs of the DC 8 because there was no assigned seating. The Kid and Al ran like children just turned loose in Disneyland; this was the 'E ticket' of E tickets: the best ride in the park! No, make that the best ride on the whole fucking planet!

The pair ended up on the rear loading ramp and as the Kid's right foot hit the step and he picked his left foot up off the soil of Vietnam, it was like magnetic boots had been removed from his feet; he bounded up the stairs and entered the aircraft. There were two empty seats three rows from the back on the left.

"Al! right here!" the Kid signaled, and the pair landed in them, next to a black GI with a shaved bald head, who had taken the window. Talk about showing teeth; that soldier had them on display, as did every soldier on the whole plane!

Of course, the flight attendants were smiling; how could they not? How much better was this compared to the departure scene they had all been forced to play for all those guys who just got off? What a mood swing!

"Men! How are you doing today! As if I need to ask!" their seat mate welcomed them to the row, they exchanged flat fives. "My name is Charles, pleased to meet you, Stocker and Viator," he read their name tags.

"More than pleased and honored to meet and ride with you today," the Kid now shook Charles' hand and tossed his shaving kit under the seat in front of him.

The intercom came to life. "Good afternoon, Gentlemen, this is the Captain speaking, the sooner you all get settled and buckled into your seats, the sooner we can get this bird in the air, and I know that's what we all want...so please extend the utmost cooperation with the flight crew and we will be getting you all right out of here...at jet speed!"

He didn't have to tell us twice! All the seats filled, the flight attendants closed the doors and moved into position for the pre-flight briefing '...This is a seat belt... in the event of a water landing... Mae West bla bla bla.' The luggage truck was pulling away. The ground crew was moving into position, pulling out the blocks from the landing gear.

"Al! This is all happening so fast!" exclaimed the Kid, who was flat tingly all over! It was beyond losing his cherry in high school! Way past the first time he ever rode the BIG roller coaster... far more significant than the night of his debute as a Good Guy on WKDA, the number one radio station in Nashville, as a 19-year old kid!

The engines began to fire up. It was a rush-rush job that the flight attendants did...the wheels lurched into motion...each taking a section and insuring everybody's seatbelts were fastened, seatbacks forward, tray tables up and carry-on bullshit stored; all done before jumping into their own jump seats, just as the massive jet pivots into take off position. The crew clearly wanted off the ground nearly as much as their GI cargo! The head attendant makes the call to the Captain and his response is immediate.

"Prepare for take-off!"

The engines begin to throttle up, the Captain holds the aircraft back with the breaks for a five second count, building some thrust before beginning the roll, which comes with a sudden jerk as he releases the brakes while making the engines crescendo toward full thrust!

The Kid and Al could only look at each other with wide opened mouthed grins of *Christmas morning* wrapped up with *graduation day* and *'I'm really getting laid by a Playboy center fold tonight'* quality. The wheels of the giant intercontinental jet liner telegraphed the feel of the runway to the feet and seats of the GIs. Along with the vibrations, they felt the pushback of the added G's, pressing them into the seats, the revelation of increasing momentum; the building of unstoppable force unleashed by the screaming turbines of the 4 Pratt and Whitneys, *faster and faster.*

The Kid and Al looked toward the window but didn't care that it was blocked by the head of their traveling companion, who was glued to it. They both sensed that the moment they were waiting for would be in the feeling, the one point in time that they had counted their days down to…that instant to be locked forever in their memory would be the very point they left Vietnam, that first clear feeling of the wheels no longer touching earth and *here it comes!*

A smoothness denoted the break but it was the sudden lift that triggered the cabin to erupt in a thunderous roar, resplendent with displays of emotion that nobody on the plane remembers through the slobbery hugging and tears of sheer joy and relief! It was an aircraft upon which every passenger was emotionally overwhelmed. They were lucky ones who had lived through the war. Some passengers unbuckled to stand up and look for comrades they were not sitting with, waving the Churchill victory sign and clinched fists.

Al and Curt hugged and laughed as they felt the landing gear retract into the plane and the thing really started gaining elevation.

"Let me see!" the Kid unbuckled and leaned over Al and tapped Charles on the shoulder and he leaned back.

There below, the Kid watched the landscape detail shrinking and growing smaller for a few seconds, before it became uncomfortable to stretch across two men. "Wow!" and then, in the *'Kronauer' style, 'GOOOOOD BYEEEEE VIETNAM!'" He heard a smattering of gawfaws and a 'good one…" as he buckled back up.*

Al gave him an appraising look, "*Great one liner,* but not title material; you don't want to be saying goodbye at the very front of the book!"

After about 30 seconds of total abandon mayhem and *whoo hooing* their asses off, the Captain dinged in on the intercom; "Uh, gentlemen, if you would all resume your seats, I have not turned off the seat belt light so you may not jump up and down, even in place… you don't want to make this aircraft hard to handle. *This is the Captain, please comply immediately.'*

The buzz became more of a collective sigh when the jet reached an altitude at which everybody was quite sure we were out of any kind of missile range.

"We made it!" a jubilant Viator screamed out.

The relief was universal from one end of that aluminum tube to the other! There was no alcohol on the flight but the attendants begin getting soft drinks out to the thirsty mob. Nobody needed booze or a joint, LSD, a mushroom, peyote or laughing gas to be high in that moment.

"So what's your plan when we get to Oakland?" the Kid asked Al.

"Well…I'm going to catch a flight straight to Boston. I gotta see the parents before I try to connect with any of my friends. What about you?"

"If it all goes according to plan, my brother is meeting me in Oakland with my car. I'm taking him to LA and I'm going on to Vista, to see Flo."

"What do you think is going to happen?"

"Don't know. Haven't a clue."

On the way to Japan, the Kid managed to change seats with some GIs to visit with the classmates. Davies was off to Kate… Waterhouse was off to Tina… Cuzzo was off to play the field, with his newly minted Vietnam combat vet status sure to impress. The Kid had a great time, laughing with Ken Smith, going over all of the *'Smiths'* he'd encountered, telling the stories that went with each one.

In what seemed like no time at all, but was close to 4 hours, the Captain dinged the cabin to prepare for landing at Yakuska, the huge American air and naval base. It was just like Hawaii, dark with nothing to see; get out and stretch your legs in the terminal. We were on the ground for barely an hour, exactly as long as it took to pick up a new flight crew and ready that bird for the trans oceanic hop.

Have you ever been to Japan? Yes. Have a good time? Yes. What did you do? I left to go home.

The takeoff from Japan was a fraction of the rush it was from Vietnam, but a rousing cheer once again shook the cabin! Next stop Oakland, California, USA!

As their 'Freedom Bird' arrived at cruising altitude, the Kid asked one of the flight attendants for a blanket and a pillow and promptly conked out.

606

Riding the Tiger in his sleep, headed due west, he was too unconscious to dream. Or was it because he was actually living his dream, he was incapable of dreaming any other dream? It didn't matter; the Kid was going home.

Chapter 93

Pulling the bathroom door shut, He locked the bolt and sat his shaving kit down on the small counter to the left of the minuscule beige sink.

Turning around, he lifted the commode lid, dropped his pants and boxers, sat down and immediately took a huge dump. *Yep. Things are going to be different on this flight.*

As the stink of digested Army mess hall food permeated the miniscule jet airliner bathroom, the Kid looked at his face in the mirror, two feet away.

How did I come to be here? By being lucky as Hell! It wasn't fucking easy but here I am! I made it! What is it that makes me such a lucky son of a bitch? Why is that? Then, his small run of bad luck reared its ugly head; he was wearing plastic army glasses because he had dropped and broken a lens of his round gold wire *John Lennon* glasses! He was going to have his reunion with Flo in these ugly frames instead of with his new persona! *Rats. I wonder how she's going to like the moustache?*

Sitting there on the commode, he recalled the night he got mortared in the latrine at Dong Tam. Waterhouse was getting tons of mileage off that story! One version now had toilet paper trailing stuck to his foot!

Finishing his business, the Kid hiked up his pants and washed his hands and face. Drying off, he pulled out his toothbrush and the tube of Colgate from the kit. All it had in it was toothpaste. If the Army has a system where they send word on ahead and run up the red flag; 'check certain guys who might be likely to try something...real close and maybe look in places like the toothpaste...' if that ever happened, they were going to find toothpaste. He hadn't brushed his teeth since yesterday morning and it felt great. While wiping off his mouth, the Kid glanced at his Seiko; it was 0100 hours, in the time zone were his watch had been set. What time zone they were actually in was a fluid question, on a jet doing over 500 mph in the middle of the Pacific, in the vicinity of the international date line...what difference did it really make? The Kid was going home!

Exiting the micro latrine, he offered a smile to two flight attendants, who were sharing a snack, in the slow time, while standing up. Beyond the lit galley and bathroom area at the rear of the plane, the cavernous tube was in near total darkness, as suited the tired and predominantly sleeping troops. He had only 3 rows to go forward to reach his aisle seat. There weren't more than a half dozen personal reading lights over seats in use, all the way up to the crew service area in the front.

Charles and Al were long gone to sleep, as had been the Kid, prior to having to visit the head. Reclining his seat as far as possible, he leaned back in pure relaxation. The Kid pulled out a KOOL and lit up. Yes, indeed, the physical need for nicotine was far greater than the need for marijuana. There wouldn't be any pot in his life for an unknown number of day but it mattered not. He thought about how easy it would have been to bring a couple of cartons of joints home; who would look in unopened packs in cartons? He easily could have made enough money to pay cash for a new car! He might well have done it if he hadn't have become such a visible proponent of the lifestyle choice. Even a 1% chance of getting caught in the exit process was 100% way too much.

Blowing out white smoke, the Kid mused over the fact that he had just lived through an incredible social experiment. The pot subculture that exists alongside the alcohol culture in Vietnam is nothing short of amazing. It is a closed society wherein the two sides are locked up together and must meet and interact, where the efficiencies of each can be compared to the other over the same types of tasks. The properties of each could be studied. The pot smokers so kicked the alkie's asses in every department! Alcohol so totally incapacitates you while pot does not. It is so clear, when you see the effects side by side. Pot is much more like smoking cigarettes than drinking.

I do not understand how there is a prohibition on pot in America without a constitutional amendment? I am going to look into this and find out how it happened. How can something so obviously less harmful than alcohol can be treated like that? It is not as bad as cigarettes because you smoke a whole lot less! I am ready to argue pro legalization with anybody. I'm betting the reason Larry couldn't find me a study for my training class ambush is there aren't any. Now I can find out for myself. Imagine if all that happened was that they made up a bunch of shit about how bad marijuana is and none of it is true? What if there was NO research at all to back it up? That can't be legal.

Have I got stories for Larry! I went to Vietnam, became a combat vet and beat a court martial! For eating in the mess hall, for God's sake! Good thing I have the paperwork to prove that really happened.

He had fought the Viet Cong and his own damn army and had come out on top! He had lived long enough to turn 21. Sitting in the seat, hurdling *toward the homeland of the country that had sent him to war, the Kid realized he had learned a few things in Vietnam through lessons that could never be forgotten. He was a veteran of many actions; he had not run, except when tactically necessary. In addition to his debate mentality, combat had given him a certain steely nerve and entitlement he could have never earned any other way. That had a lot to do with his ability to talk down Captain PM Smith; what was Smith going to do, shoot him? Beating the court martial had shown him that indeed, he did not have to take the Army's bullshit. And he wouldn't! Let the Army take some of mine!*

The Kid had arrived at some conclusions. War is not good. Wars are not fought in the interest of the people. Wars are fought in the interests of politicians. They might espouse a noble cause as being worth killing for or more likely, dying for, but what munitions manufacturer pays that's politician's mortgage? And from how far away does he watch? How right was Ike about that 'military industrial lobby' bullshit?

Vietnam is a civil war. In a civil war, the armies of both sides ravage the population. Regardless of which side the people choose or how often they are convinced to switch sides to secure some level of safety, they are going to be ravaged either way and both ways in the ebb and flow of war, always and for forever!

The war has changed me. The Kid is no more. The Kid was all about fun; I can never be The Kid on the radio again because fun is no longer on the front burner. I can't go home and act like life is all just swell and let the war become a far-off memory. 'You'll forget about it and get on with your life,' they say. 'They were only Vietnamese,' the gunner said, of the men we almost shot. Thank all the Gods and Spirits I did not have to shoot our own men, even if they weren't Americans... Hostile fire, friendly fire, American, Vietnamese...dead is dead either way.

Thank God I didn't have to kill anybody. Then he remembered the one time he fired his weapon in combat to suppress the sniper on the road to Cang Long; *at least I don't know that I killed anybody.*

Americans should not be required to die to demonstrate South Vietnamese resolve. If the war is to be won, they must win it. No foreign power has any chance of winning by dying longer and in greater numbers than the Vietnamese people. Only Vietnamese can sort it out and I get a real strong feeling, the end won't end like Korea.

What about this war is worth dying for? Are we fighting for the right of Vietnamese to live free under a Thieu dictatorship? Are we fighting so they can have a free country wide election? Wait a minute... that was what the Vietnamese fought for and won against the French! That's the election America stopped from happening! America blew it when we didn't let that election happen in 1956. Ike really fucked up there; he should never have listened to John Foster Dulles. Ho Chi Minh would have been the democratically elected leader and back then he LOVED America! He plagiarized our Declaration of Independence for Vietnam's! There would have been no war. Thank you, France, for painting him with your communist brush because you were such a bunch of sore losers! This is all France's fault! The Catholic French Vietnamese were like an aristocracy lording over the Vietnamese Buddhists!

The Kid remembered the ex-VC Captain of the APT, who had fought at Dien Bien Phu and whose only reason for switching sides was to get somebody to recognize his ancestral deed! He died for his ancestral deed; not for either side. It mattered not which side he was fighting on the day he got killed. He's dead. Both sides told him they were for his better interests but he's dead. Did both sides lie to this man? How many times is the only real question.

The Kid questioned his own moral resolve. Why couldn't I do anything to save Wally and the Beaver and the Girl Next Door? Now that Beaver; there was a ten-year-old MAN.'Cam Bao ya!' He took on a whole company and came within a hair's breath of killing Tu Ta and me! That boy gave his life trying to save his brother and his sister. They had to be related; why else would a lone boy attack more than 50 armed men? He wouldn't switch sides to save his life. Why should I have cared if Herschel and Minnesota and Tu Ta called me a liar? I should have done it. I should have reported it. They shot those 3 kids who were prisoners of war. 'Don't have the spare men to watch them, Tu Ta says, we need some body count, Tu Ta says, so that was all OK with them. It was a clear violation of the Geneve Convention. That is my biggest shortcoming in the war. I should have fought through all the crap that would have come with reporting it. I will have to make up for that my whole life.

He thought of Imbach volunteering to walk point to write that story. No story, in and of itself, is worth dying for. But Imbach's point was, hundreds of GIs had to risk death performing that function every day and he was going to write about it and how dangerous it was. And he was as right as he is dead. Birnbaum and I could have been killed getting that NITECAP story. What benefit would that have been to anybody? Was John's or any GI's death necessary to keep the VC from invading America? No. That was never Charlie's plan. The VC will never invade America and by the same token, they will never stop fighting to kick us out. All the John Imbach's in the world dying will not change that!

611

Who is going to stop the dying in Vietnam? It matters not who is in the White House; I went under Johnson and spent 4 months under Nixon. No difference. Surprisingly, there hasn't a word about the 'secret plan' to end the war. Where's your secret plan... Dick? America needs a third party that actually is based on doing what's right for the people. How sweet would THAT be? I'll have to look into that Libertarian thing I've been hearing about when I get back.

The Kid took the picture of Flo from his breast pocket and gazed upon it in the light coming off the galley. He was on his way to her; but was there going to be any 'there' there? Only time would tell. The whole Flo romance had been defined by his being snared by the Army and getting sent to Vietnam. It was like being trapped in a bad time travel plot; he had spent such a little amount of time with her. Now he had to see if there was some way they could capture more time. Or if... it was just too late. Life without Flo was a definite possibility. That fact made him think of Donna Nadeau, the original reason he had dropped out of school, went to Nashville and got drafted. Was she the real lynchpin of his love life; or was he yet to meet his true soul mate? She would at least be aware he'd made it back, because their families were friends. Donna might be in Nashville but why even try to see her? He wasn't going to be spending any real time around Nashville for a year and a half. The biggest obstacle he still faced was the 16 months of Army life after his 30-day leave.

From his innate nature, the Kid knew he'd have a really rough time keeping his mouth shut. That had never been his style at any point in his life! And now, when it came to the Vietnam War, he had earned the credentials that made it so that nobody could tell him SHIT!

When I get back, whatever else I do, however else I live the rest of my life, I will work to end this war. I will work to help shorten it in any possible way... to keep others from having to die... not for freedom. We have that and it isn't the VC hiding in the middle of the jungle who is going to take it away. It is politicians lying us into this war for reasons that do not serve the interest of the American people, that takes freedom away.

Fuck it ALL! If it's one thing I can do, it's give a speech. I got plenty to say about this war. I fought for freedom. Now I am going to exercise my right to free speech, and nobody is going to stop me! Hey! I signed up for Armed Forces Radio and they made me a journalist. Well, maybe I can start one of those anti-war underground GI newspapers! Only it won't be 'underground,' it'll be aboveground!

Snuffing out the KOOL in the arm rest ash tray, the Kid rearranged his pillow and blanket to settle in for a nice long high-altitude snooze. He closed his eyes, lulled by the steady purr of the jet engines. But instead of a dream about Flo, what did he in his mind's eye?

Oh. Hello, Captain Robinson...I somehow knew you'd be riding home with me.

###

Me and Mama San, enjoy a moment of hilarity, peeking through the hole
in her kitchen roof! (Photo by James Sweet)

Mama San. She made her place was our private club, just across the street from the New villa.

My boarding pass home!

The signpost up ahead said FREEDOM!

MACOI-A

26 December 1968

SUBJECT: Audition of SP4 Curtis Stocker

TO: Personnel Division
    4th PSYOPS GP
    Saigon

FROM: NCOIC
      AFVN Radio Network

This is to certify that SP4 Curtis Stocker RA 12966317 was auditioned
in the studios of the American Forces Vietnam Network in Saigon this 15th
day of December 1968. SP4 Stocker was found to be qualified and desirable
for use in the AFVN Network.

In the event that 1049 action is completed by you and processed by
USARV and MACV, the American Forces Vietnam Network would be able to utilize
his talent either at the key station or one of the other radio-tv detachments
in the republic.

Clem J. Shamus
SFC U.S. Army
NCOIC, Radio Branch

1 INCL

The letter Sgt Shamus wrote to 4th PSYP Group, in December, in support
of securing my transfer, after not hearing about the request,
which had been submitted in late September.

617

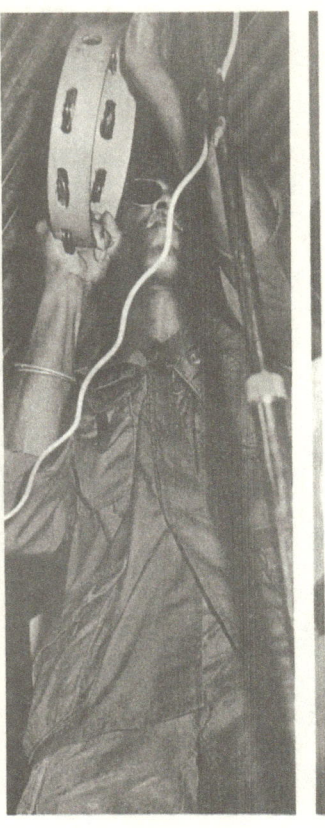

SOUND OF 10th Nervous PSYOPS Breakdown

Lead Guitar; Tom Boyett

Singer; Richie Wells

The walls resound with music when the "10th Nervous Breakdown" practice. As their music echoes through-out the New Villa, the rooms of bunks and lockers fade away and are replaced by images of dark crowded night-clubs shot with sudden bolts of strobe lights or the amorphous blobs of undulating shape and color of psych-edelic light shows.

The bands first performance was impromtu. At the 10th PSYOP's New Year's Eve party, the hired Viet-namese band took a break The 10th's musicians stepped into the Viet's place and began to play. Their music became better and better as they discovered what

their instruments could do. They slowly formed into a unit, as the cohesiveness of the music took its effect.

After the party, the group arranged for rental of in-struments and electronic equipment. It was then that the hall's of New Villa began to come alive with nightly rehearsals. They would meet in Richie Well's room on the third floor. When all of the equipment was as-sembled there was just enough room for the players. This rehearsal room adds to their creativity. Don Hartmann is probably one of the few drummers who can play perched half off and on a bunk.

Their music is a variety of songs from the rock groups

Photos are from a pool made available to me for the story, by at least a half a dozen guys... from which I selected the best available shot of each band member.

618

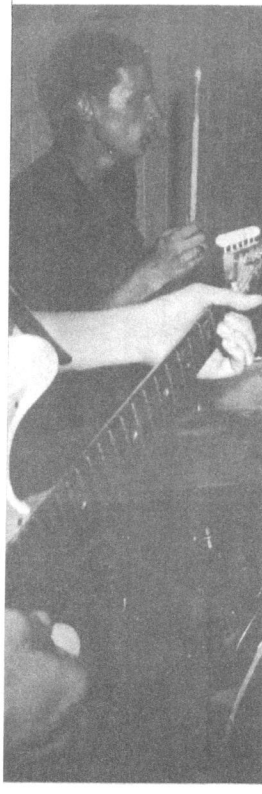 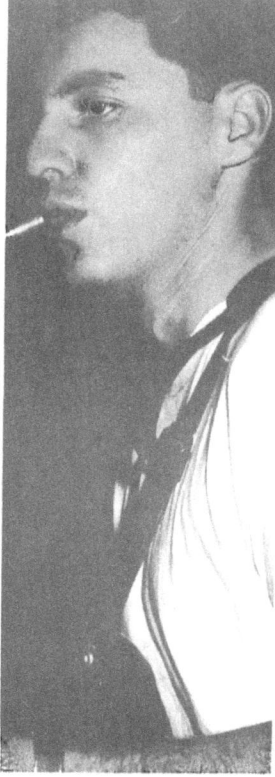 

Drummer; Don Hartmann   *Rhythm Guitar; Ben Vargas*   *Bass Guitar; George Carillo*

of today. It doesn't lend itself to exact classification, but the group's own interpretations give a unity to all that they play. Lead guitarist Tom Boyett is responsible for this. As the "Nervous Breakdown" play, he appears almost isolated from the group, but his innovations are what give their music much of its newness and unity. Boyett has a rapport with music and he quietly leads the band down new paths.

The band performs frequently at the USO and on weekends at the Hollywood Bar in Can Tho. To watch a performance is to see modern America in Vietnam.

As the tambourine beats against his arm, singer Richie Wells cries out, "Born to be wild." Echoing his cry, Ben Vargas, rhythm guitar, and George Carillo, bass guitar, shout back, "Born to be wild." The music acts as a magnet on the audience. Feet move under tables and soldier's shoulders begin to slowly move with the beat. The faces change too and the expressions are those of minds coming to rest. "This is how life was and how it will be again." Richie calls out, "Have mercy baby..." And now not only the guitarists but the entire audience answers, "Have mercy, have mercy on me."

The "10th Nervous Breakdown" plays on...

News from B company

Two major operational changes were made within B Company this month. First Lieutenant Richard Ballard's 10-E-3 Team is now located at Dong Tam with the 2nd Brigade, 9th U.S. Division.

First Lieutenant Henry Vales is the new Team Leader of 10-E-1 in Vi Thanh.

B Company received 10 new enlisted men this month. They are: Specialists Four Raymond Johnson, Peter Hahn, Richard Hamilton, Royal Springs, Richard Rios and Richard Olson; Specialist 5 Michael Davis and Privates First Class Joseph Gibbs, Robert Kinser and Donald Workman.

In Dong Tam Staff Sergeant Paul L. Johnson of Team 10-B-3. was lightly wounded early this month while on an I CAP mission. His team was walking along a trail when a mine was tripped. Sergeant Johnson spent a few days

A mortar put this hole in the MSQ 85 van of Lieutenant Herschell Wilson during an operation in Vinh Binh province. No one was injured.

in the hospital, but is now released and performing his regular duties.

In Go Cong, success rewarded the efforts of Detachment 10-E-4 when they conducted operations in Hoa Loc District. In two days

Sergeant Lex Koestner distributes during a field team operation.

82 Viet Cong turned themselves in to the GVN's Chieu Hoi program.

The team, composed of First Lieutenant Lawrence B. Sauers and Specialist 4 Andrew P. Simko worked with the S-5 PSYWAR team in Trai Ca Hamlet.

Field team begins PSYOP pacification

GO CONG - "We're going to a movie tonight."

So said Lieutenant Lawrence B. Sauers, Detachment 10-E-4 team leader here, to Specialist 4 Andrew P. Simko at the commencement of a Psychological Warfare Pacification Operation in Tan Thanh Village extending from November 7th through the 9th.

After setting up their projector in a crowd-filled market place, the Sector PSYWAR team and PSYOP personnel showed their "Thursday Night at the Movies" starring Miss Phung Dung, a renowned Vietnamese actress-singer and native of Tan Thanh.

"The theme of these movies is to depict the struggle of the Vietnamese over the French Imperialists and show how many of these same patriots were later delivered

into the ranks of the VC. These men are no longer fighting for liberation of the South, but are battling as puppets of the North. It is meant to be an enlightening film series which attempts to convert the people and gain their active support for the Government of Vietnam," stated Lieutenant Sauers.

The operation continued the following day with "a walk in the sun" from the PSYOP base camp at Ap Cho to the treeline perimeter of Tan Thanh Beach. Pasting posters, distributing leaflets, radiocasting, conducting a MEDCAP, suggesting the destruction of malaria-infected water ponds to the villagers, and visiting homes of widows whose husbands had been killed by Viet Cong - these occupied the time of the PSYOP team during that day.

With bullhorns slung over the shoulders of selected members, the PSYOP-PSYWAR team walked along the rice paddy trails of Giong Ba Lay on November 9th.

A Christmas card capturing the spirit of the season, whether East or West, is being designed by Specialist 4 Deldon Caldwell for IV Corps.

Page from November DIMENSION: Photo of the damage to the MSQ-85, from what Lt. Wilson did, to test out his wacky "Claymore Mine Defense" (which was, 'a truck decked out with claymores could blow them off and drive through any ambush!') He was wrong... then he falsified the report, claiming the damage was from a mortar attack, and also made Sgt. Jim Sweet submit a false report as well..

Lt. Colonel Lawton

Militarily and intellectually capable

"The emphasis will be placed on you. You are highly trained and skilled for your work in psychological operations. We must combine our efforts so that we can continue to progress here in Vietnam, toward the accomplishment of the PSYOP mission."

These words were the enlisted men's introduction to the new Battalion Commander of the 10th Battalion, Lieutenant Colonel Willie O. Lawton.

At the Battalion's change of command ceremony, Group Executive Officer, Lieutenant Colonel Albert A. Rosner, offered the following description of Colonel Lawton, "You are receiving a new commander, an officer who has the necessary military and intellectual capabilities to direct and control the actions of a psychological operations unit."

The intellectual and military capabilities and experience are indeed possessions of Colonel Lawton's His military career includes tours in both Germany and Korea. During the Korean conflict .he .took part in the well-known battle of "Pork Chop Hill."

He lists his types of assignments as varied, for they have included operational training, instruction of ROTC at Lincoln University, in Jefferson City, Mo., intelligence work, as well as command assignments.

Colonel Lawton's last duty station before coming to Can Tho and the 10th, was with the 82nd Airborne Division. He has worked on both battalion and brigade levels of that unit.

He looks upon the 82nd Airborne as a "special" type of unit. "It was a unit which required a continual state of readiness. We were always prepared to deploy at any time and to anywhere in the world and to fight upon arrival. This meant that every trooper had to be at the peak of physical fitness and alertness.

"This assignment with the 82nd offered me a wonderful opportunity to associate with some of the finest troopers in the world," he says.

Although his ROTC work at Lincoln University might have been new to him, the university was not, for it was there he received his bachelor of science degree. Colonel Lawton also holds a master of science degree and has done specialized work in education and psychology at the University of Missouri.

He is the recipient of the Bronze Star with "V" device, and the Army Commendation Medal with oak leaf cluster, the Purple Heart with oak leaf cluster, the Combat Infantryman's badge and is a master parachutist.

Colonel Lawton feels there are too often misconceptions about the role of psychological operations. "People think in terms of leaflets and loud-speakers and ignore the fact that we basically deal with people. We must first know our target group, its behavioral patterns, ethnic groups, and attitudes. All these facets together make up the target audience, and without that knowledge, our psychological efforts will fail."

Colonel Lawton is married and has four children, a boy, 11, and three girls, 16, 13 and 6 years old.

Page from November DIMENSION: Personality profile of
Lieutenant Colonel Willie O. Lawton. Story
and photos by Everet Reagan.

Ernie Diorto, Pete Johnson and the Kid,
in Mi's kitchen in Tra Vinh.
Photo by Paul Hoch.

Lt. Wilson, as we waited for an
Air America Plane, from which
the Kid will make a leaflet drop.
When I took this picture, I said, "...
Just in case you are famous some day!"

Our interpreter: Corporal Ba.

Lt. Herschel Wilson, dressed in the
uniform on the Armed Propaganda Team..

Lt. William Culp's birthday party, where his printing crew took him and got him stoned out of his mind at a Vietnamese family's home. Lt. Culp far left, Sgt. Sweet far right.

Stoney fresh back from the Field!

Culp party: from L to R: Ken Willert, Mark Birnbaum, Ron Edwards.

Benny Vargas. Note the joint packages disguised as KOOLs!

The Tra Vinh Mess Hall I was ordered not to eat in... thus the scene of my "insubordination" for breakfast, lunch and dinner! Back in the days of the French, this was the kitchen and servant's quarters for the compound.

The Binh Trung Village defensive position, which struck me as a kind of "Peter Pan-Lost Boy'" sort of fort.

Mark Birnbaum and a Regional Force member, with the flag left by the VC during the Nite Cap, 300 meters from our position.

The VC flag, before we took it down.

My Freedom Bird home! Bien Hoa Air Base, May 18, 1969.